Airport Planning & Design

S. K. KHANNA
Ph.D. (Engg.), FIE, FNAE, FNASc
Transportation Engg. Consultant
(Formerly Chairman, All India Council for Technical Education,
Vice-Chairman, University Grants Commission and
Professor & Head, Deptt. of Civil Engineering
University of Roorkee, Roorkee)

M. G. ARORA
Ph.D., (Engg.), FIE, MASCE
Calgary (Alberta), Canada
(Formerly, Professor of Civil Engineering,
University of Roorkee, Roorkee)

NEM CHAND & BROS; ROORKEE (U.P.)

First Edition 1969
Sixth Edition 2009
Reprinted 2012
Reprints 2017
Reprinted, ***2019***

ISBN 81-85240-68-X

Published by
Nem Chand & Bros., Civil Lines, Roorkee 247667, India
e-mail: ncb rke@rediffmail.com
Photo set and Printed at the
Roorkee Press, Mahavir Marg, Roorkee 247 667

PREFACE

TO SIXTH EDITION

The book has been revised in general and updated. Chapter 1 and 2 have been revised. Chapter 1 has been revised keeping in view the formation of a single agency i.e. Airports Authority of India (AAI) in place of National Airports Authority (NAA) and International Airports Authority of India (IAAI). The AAI was formed with a view to accelerate the integrated development, expansion and modernisation of the operational, terminal and cargo facilities at the airports in the country conforming to internationational standards. It manages the 5 international airports, 87 domestic airports and 28 civil air terminals at defence airfield with a total of 120 in the country. It also controls the entire Indian air-space extending even the territorial limits of the country. The Mission of AAI is "Progress through excellence and customer satisfaction with world class airport and air traffic services fostering economic development". Chapter 2 has been revised with the latest statistics including forecasting of traffic and projected fleet of Indian Airlines, Air India and Vayudoot. The details of the Heavy Weight Deflectometer (HWD) which is an important equipment for structural evaluation of airfield pavements have been included in Chapter 9.

PREFACE

In revising this book, authors have freely consulted the literature published by Airports Authority of India (AAI), International Civil Aviation Organisation (ICAO), Federal Aviation Agency (FAA), Indian Roads Congress (IRC), Reports of the Planning Commission, Government of India. Some papers included in the Proceedings of National Seminar organised by CRRI and Army HQ in New Delhi in February 1990 on Airfield Pavements including the guidelines prepared by Ministry of Environment and Forests, Government of India have also been Consulted. The help derived from these sources is gratefully acknowledged here

We hope that the book in the present form would be more useful to the engineering students and the professionals engaged in planning, design, operation and Control of airports.

August 2009

S. K. KHANNA
M. G. ARORA

PREFACE

TO FIRST EDITION

Various educational institutions have now included the teaching of the subject of airport planning and design in their undergraduate curricula. This book is an up-to-date and complete text for the students and the field engineers. In preparing this book authors have freely consulted the literature publised by *International Civil Aviation Organization, Federal Aviation Agency, Journals of ASCE-Air Transport Division and US Corps of Engineers and Navy Department*. The help derived from these sources is gratefully acknowedged here.

Authors have been teaching this subject to the undergraduate and postgraduate students at the University of Roorkee for several years. This book is thus based on their understanding of the need of the students. It is hoped that the book would be welcome as a useful contribution to the developing concept of aviation in our country.

September, 1969 S. K. KHANNA
Roorkee M. G. ARORA

CONTENTS

1

AIR TRANSPORT

1.1 GENERAL

Transportation is an important factor for the social and economic development of any region or country. It is very difficult to imagine society without any mode of transportation. The economic development of the nation links its direct benefits with the efficient system of transportation. The basic function that the transport system performs is by carrying passengers and goods, from one place to another. No region or country can develop if it lacks the transport facilities. In respect to the transportation of goods, it is essential that they cost the minimum and are available when and where wanted. The low cost of production, the time and place of utility are greatly influenced by a transport network. If for the process of manufacturing, it is required to bring the raw materials from far off distances to the factory site, with inefficient or inadequate transport system, the cost of production would be obviously high. The same concept would apply if the finished product needs a long time and distance to reach marketing centres. Thus in total economic process, the transport need is deeply concerned. The various economic benefits from the transportation system are listed below·

1. Utilization of resources
2. Regional specialization
3. Savings in travel time

Other benefits are like social, cultural and political.

One of the greatest inventions, in the present mankind has been of the *wheel.* Early man's main occupation was the procurement of food, shelter and then clothing. With advent of civilization, man felt more and more the need of movement of individual and the group. Such need or urge gave rise to the development of transport modes. The movement of people and goods has been a major activity of the human race and the propulsive means used, mainly animals on land and sails at sea, remained virtually unchanged until the 19th century. Egyptians were the first who developed the first real ship. *Watt's* development of the steam engine in the *seventeenth century* gave rise to many efforts for developing steam propelled vehicles. A French man, *Nicholas Joseph Cugnot* invented in 1770, the first self propelled vehicle. Comparatively, the air transport follows its origin to the *nineteenth century.* The discovery and application of steam and electricity and of the internal combustion engine in the 20th century revolutionised travel and transport and introduced the present era of mass travel and airfreight. The advent of long range aeroplane after world war II and particularly of jet aircraft which opened the whole world to the immense benefits of air travel, airfreighting of light goods which in only 25 years have almost totally replaced surface means for all but for short distances. As far as India is concerned, supplementing road and rail transport by developing air transport has been and will continue to be necessary because of the geographical distance. Further, air transport will increasingly become an essential instrument of the socio-economic development of the country alongwith that of telecommunications.

1.2 DIFFERENT MODES OF TRANSPORTATION

Land, water and air have been used by the mankind for developing the transport modes like roadway, railway, water way and airway. In India railways were assigned priority of developments in the past, chiefly because, it was one mode which helped mass transportation of goods and passengers.

Railways and roadways in India and abroad are in competition today for providing better transport facilities. Waterways and air transportation are used for long distance travels and the first mode is mainly for inter-continental movements.

In India, the road transport system has become stagnant, and is unable to play its full part in the promotion and growth of tourism. The railway system, though fairly extensive, is good only in parts. In any case, in a large country such as India and the short time available at the average tourist, rail travel is too slow to satisfy the needs of international tourist. Therefore, it is essential, that the growth of civil aviation is properly planned, monitored and co-ordinated to ensure that it covers all aspects of civil aviation, which has not always been the case in the past. Also, in view of the inadequacy and antiquity of the existing ground infrastructure, the development of civil aviation must be on modern lines so that India gradually comes abreast of the more developed countries in providing the facilities where there are serious deficiencies today.

The air transportation possesses a few distinct advantages as compared to other modes of transport. These are listed below :

1. *Rapidity :* Air transport maintains the highest speed. Designs have been finalised for supersonic jets which travel faster than sound.

2. *Continuous journey :* Air transport mode is continuous over land and water without loss of the time unlike other modes of transport.

3. *Accessibility :* Air transport has the unique ability to open up any region that is inaccessible by other means of transportation.

The air transport has few limitations as indicated below :

1. *Operating expenses :* The operating expenses are generally very high including the cost of air vehicles, traffic control system etc. Thus the freight charges are comparatively high. This mode of transport accomodates very few travellers and small cargo which have to bear high expenses for the unit weight.

2. *Capacity :* Weight carrying capacity of aircrafts is the lowest amongst other carriers of transport. Heavy articles of low grades cannot be carried.

3. *Weather conditions :* The weather conditions greatly affect the operation of air transport. Foggy days are absolutely not convenient for the landing and take off operations of aircraft.

4. *Flight rules :* The air transport is more beneficial for the international travel, as such certain laws in respect to the international aviation have to be observed. *International Civil Aviation Organization* (ICAO) is one body which develops standards and laws for international flights. More details about ICAO is given in article 1.8

1.3 HISTORY OF AIR TRANSPORT

Reger Bacon was the first man who studied the flight of birds and made a prophecy in 1266 that the source of energy for flight can be derived from fire. It can well be imagined that the human beings must be dreaming of flights like birds from the very beginning. The experiments started with flights in balloons. The first flight was made on December 17, 1903 by a bicycle repairman, *Orville Wright*, in a power driven aircraft which was heavier than air. He propelled himself through the air, a distance of 35 m (120 ft) near Kitty Hawk, North Carolina, U.S.A.

During the world war 1914-18, *Zeppelin* aeroplanes were freely used by Germans for the passenger transport. In U.S.A, long distance air mail service was first introduced in May, 1918 between Washington and New York.

The first international air service started in 1918 between *Toulouse* and *Barcelona* in *France*. *London - Paris* service commenced in 1919. In 1927, *Lindburg* made first solo flight between *New York* to *Paris*.

First jet flight was made on August 27, 1939 in Germany. The jet aircraft was manufactured by Heinkel Aircraft Company in Germany.

1.4 STRUCTURE AND ORGANISATION OF AIR TRANSPORT

Civil aviation is a major international industry that carries more than half a billion passengers each year in aircraft that fly for an aggregate of approximately 8000 million km. Since aviation is largely international, problems are created that individual nations cannot solve unilaterally, consequently from the earliest days of civil aviation there has been an attempt to find international solutions through the creation of international bodies. Typically, civil aviation requires the building of airports to accepted international standards, the establishment of standard navigational aids, the setting up of a world wide weather reporting system, and the standardization of operational practices to minimize the possibility of error or misunderstanding.

The first attempt to reach an international consensus was unsuccessful in 1910, wherein representatives of 19 European nations met to develop an international agreement. Another attempt was made to internationalize civil aviation standards after World War I, when the Versailles Peace Conference set up the International Conference for Air Navigation (ICAN). Although this organisation lasted from 1919 until World War II, its effectiveness was extremely limited because of the regionality of air transport even up to the early 1940's.

World War II provided a huge impetus to civil aviation. A generation of peacetime development had been crammed into the period of the European war from 1930 to 1945. In early 1944, the United States sought out its allies and a number of neutral nations, 55 in all, to discuss post war civil aviation. The result of these exploratory discussion was the Chicago Convention on Civil Aviation in November 1944, attended by 52 countries.

The Chicago Convention established 96 articles, which outlined the privileges of contracting stages, provided for the establishment of international practices, and recommended that air transport be facilitated by the reduction of formalities of customs and immigration. After rctification by the legislatures of 26 national states, the International Civil Aviation Organization (ICAO) came into existence on April 4, 1947. By 1975 the original 26 retifying states had grown to 131 member states. The modus operandi of ICAO is stated in Article 1.8.

There are a number of industrial organisation active in the area of air transport, both at the international and national levels. The most important of the international organizations are as follows :

(i) International Airport Transport Association (IATA). An organization with more than 100 scheduled international carrier members. Its role is to foster the interests of civil aviation, to provide a forum for industry views and to establish industry practices.

(ii) International Civil Airports Association (ICAA). An association of civil airport authorities established to serve as a forum and focus for the views and interests of civil airport operators.

(iii) Institute of Air Transport (IAT). An association of individuals and organizations with interest in civil aviation.

In the United States, the more important domestic organizations with views and policies affecting the civil aviation industry are the Air Line Pilots Association, the Aircraft Owners and Pilots Association, the Air Transport Association of America, the National Association of State Aviation Officials, the Airport Operators Council International and the American Association of Airport Executives.

1.5 DIRECTORATE OF CIVIL AVIATION

Though the Directorate of Civil Aviation was set up in 1927, the civil aviation department really took shape only in the year 1945 with the establishment of the post of Director General of Civil Aviation (DGCA).

The functions of the DGCA were as under :

(i) Regulatory functions such as airworthiness of aircraft, licensing of personnel, investigation of incidents/accidents, bilateral matters, approval of tarrifs/schedules etc.

(ii) Administering the domestic airports other than the four international airports which were run by IAAI.

(iii) Providing navigation/communication facilities and air traffic services.

With the establishment of the National Airports Authority (NAA) effective from 1st June, 1986 functions (ii) and (iii) above hitherto under DGCA have been performed by NAA up to 31 March 1995.

1.6 NATIONAL AIRPORTS AUTHORITY

The National Airports Authority (NAA) was established to carve out the DGCA on June 1, 1986 through an act of parliament. It was managed by a board consisting of Chairman four full-time members and eight part-time members. The NAA managed all domestic civil airports and civil enclaves to a total of 116. It spreads it wings from Porbandar in the west of Tezu in the north east from the snow clad peaks of Leh in the north to the sun-kissed beaches of Trivandrum in the South. While the airlines fly the aircraft from one airport to another, the NAA provided all the essential facilities to make these flights possible by managing, the runways, the technical buildings, air traffic control services, radio navigation and security etc. and ensured the safety of all operations.

1.6.1 Major Responsibilities of NAA

The major responsibilities of NAA was to manage the air routes and air space in the country for domestic airports, aeronautical communications, navigational and radar services at domestic and international airports, visual aid and ground safety service at domestic airports, airport environment, civil aviation training centres and organisation of search & rescue throughout the Indian air space for which India is responsible.

1.6.2 Objective of NAA

The objective of NAA was for the maintenance of efficient air traffic services at domestic and international airports to ensure the highest standard of air traffic control system using modern communication systems, radars, navigational and landing aids, maintenance of international standards in air traffic control, aeronautical communications and ground safety operations. Maintenance and upkeep of domestic airports and civil air terminal at airports controlled by IAF and Indian navy and ensure quick and efficient passenger handling activities at domestic airports.

1.6.3 Achievements of NAA

The achievements of NAA were :

(i) Construction of commissioning of new airports at Shimla, Agatti, Calicut and Pondicherry.

(ii) Construction/extension of terminal building/commissionning of new civil air terminal at Jammu, Leh, Gorakhpur, Ranchi, Trichy, Lucknow, Trivandrum and Varanasi.

(iii) Commissioning of airports for Vayudoot operations at Ziro, Along, Daparijo, Kamalpur, Malda Thanjavur, Sholapur, Jagdalpur, Kolhapur, Ballurghat, Kailashshar, Passighat, Neyveli, Shimla, Bilaspur, Rojouri and Desa.

(iv) Extension / strengthening of runways/pavements at Imphal, Dimapur Bhubaneswar, Coimbatore Cuddhapah, Khajuraho, Aizawal, Ahmedabad, Jodhpur, Jabalpur, Keshod, Mangalore. Porbandar, Varanasi, Amritsar, Jorhat, Patna, Ludhiana and Tirupati.

(v) Consultancy Services rendered to State Governments/ Private Organisations, at Amravati; Neyveli, Kolhapur Sholapur Hubli, Latur, Sagar and Kangra.

(vi) Flight Calibration/Consultancy Services to foreign countries such as Angola, Bhutan, Bangladesh, Laos, Nepal, Vietnam and Maldives.

(vii) Installation of Doppler Very High Frequency Omni Range (DVOR) at Bombay and Madras.

(viii) Installation of Very High Frequency Omni Range, (VOR) at Gulbarga, Rajkot, Udaipur, Sikanderabad, Dibrugarh and Jammu.

(ix) Commissioning of Instrument Landing System at Imphal, Patna, Jaipur, Bhopal, Lucknow, Jammu, Amritsar, Varanasi, Dibrugarh, Agartala, Guwahati, Calcutta and Ahmedabad. Communication facilities for air ground communication on Single Side Band (SSB) mode provided at 28 airports. Automatic Message Switching System commissioned at Delhi, Bombay and Hyderabad airports, flight calibration for two Dornier (DO—228) aircraft Fitted with Automatic Flight

Inspection System (FIS) have been procured for calibration of Radio Navigational Aids.

(x) Installation of Airport Surveillanced Radar at Bombay.

(xi) Night Landing Facilities at Ranchi, Vadodara, Rajkot Bhopal, Agartala, Udaipur, Hyderabad, Indore, Calicut and Khajuraho.

(xii) Installation of Solar Powered Obstruction Lights at Udaipur and Khajuraho.

(xiii) Introduction of 52 High Capacity Modern Crash Fire Tenders at major airports.

1.6.4. The Role of NAA at International Airports

In addition to 88 domestic airports, the National Airports Authority provided all technical services and exercises air space control to Mumbai, Calcutta, Chennai and Delhi airports which was being managed by International Airports Authority of India (IAAI) by providing Air Traffic Control Service, Communication, Navigation and Radar facilities, Instrument Landing System (ILS), Very High Frequency Range (VOR) and Distance Measuring Equipment (DME), Airport Surveillance Radar (ASR), Air Route Surveillance Radar (ARSR), Precision Approach Radar (PAR) and Inter-communication services co-ordinating operation by various airlines.

In the 4th year of its monumental existence, the NAA continued to match the high standards of performance, it has set for itself since its inception. The air traveller could reach the remotest corner of the country through operators inducted into these interactable regions by the dedicated personnel of the Authority. Next only to the VSA, our country could boast of a vast network of well-managed and adequately equipped aerodromes and the country proud and inspires the NAA to forge ahead to meet the Civil Aviation challenges of the 21st century.

Civil Aviation in the country does not merely depend upon the acquisition of new state-of-the-art aircraft by the national operators. The NAA worked silently day and night to make the flights possible, in the first place, and safe and comfortable in the greatest measure. Faster and more sophisticated aircrafts cannot appear on the aviation scene before the required facilities were provided by the NAA. The NAA was, indeed, the 'mainstay of civil aviation' in the country and a proud of its vital contribution to the national endeavour to hasten the process of social and economic development of the country.

1.6.5 Development of Model Airports

In India, most of the airports were constructed during World War-II and transferred to the Civil Aviation Department after the war. From time to time, these airports have been expanded and modified according to operational requirements, but still much more has to be achieved. With the ever increasing demand for air travel, it has become necessary to introduce a degree of standardisation in the facilities provided at the terminal building and also the technical infrastructure in terms of runways and navigational aids. Therefore, as a first step it has been decided to develop 12 airports in the country as model airports which will have such standardised facilities. The airports selected cover all the five regions in the Civil Aviation Sector. The selected airports are as follows :

(i) Bombay Region : Nagpur, Vadodara and Indore

(ii) Calcutta Region : Bhubaneswar and Patna

(iii) Delhi Region : Jaipur and Lucknow

(iv) Madras Region : Coimbatore, Hyderabad and Calicut

(v) North Eastern Region : Guwahati and Imphal

The development projects at model airports include extension of runways and associated infrastructure, provision of additional navigational aids, communication and safety services, construction of new terminal buildings and expansion/modification of the existing terminal buildings.

The terminal buildings at model airports will have spacious concourses, adequate seating capacity, air conditioned departure lounges, restaurants, coffee counters, telecom bureaus, travel counters, toilets for the handicapped, viewing galleries for the public and reserved lounges, among other facilities. The total capital outlay for developing the model airports is of the order of nearly 300 crores. The construction projects will have a time-frame ranging from two to three years from the date of the award of work.

1.7.8. INTERNATIONAL AIRPORTS AUTHORITY OF INDIA (IAAI)

With the introduction of jet aircraft, and a gradual increase in the size of the aircraft, passenger air traffic increased considerably resulting in serious congestions and delays at the airports. To review this situation and to recommend measures which could enable civil aviation in India to keep abreast of world wide developments, the Government appointed a Committee under the Chairmanship of Mr. J.R.D. Tata in July, 1967. Based on this Committee's recommendations, the International Airports Authority of India (IAAI) was set up in April, 1972 to plan, develop, construct and maintain the four international airports in India, viz., Bombay, Calcutta, Delhi and Madras.

1.7.1 Role of IAAI

The International Airports Authority of India took several new initiatives to provide passenger facilities dealing with increased problem of environmental control and maximum security in and around the airport terminal buildings and for operational, preparedness at the Indira Gandhi International Airport.

In an effort to provide advance information regarding incoming and outgoing flights, the IAAI management at the airport contemplated to instal an automatic answering machine so that people can get advance information about the arrival and departure of flights without coming to the airport. In addition, a remote control noise emitting device for effective dealing with the bird menace in and around the airport was also planned.

Most of the flights were coming during night, the IAAI tried to reduce the air traffic congestion. To effectively deal with the bird menace at the international airport, the Authority had deployed sharp shooters along the main run-way. In 1989, no bird hit incident took place inside the airport. IAAI planned to instal a remote control noise emitting device to create sounds at particular heights to scare away the birds.

The IAAI was planning to increase the number of counters in the international terminal building. In addition to the construction of four new bays for the new air buses, the

Authority was planning to add 10 more bays to provide parking facilities. Regarding the tightening of security in and around the airport, the IAAI has already launched various schemes like fencing, laying new roads for patrolling to check infiltration, construction of watch towers for stricter surveillance, night vision binoculars and close circuit TV.

According to IAAI sources, the secondary run-way was being extended to ensure adequate landing facilities for the domestic as well as international aircrafts. IAAI also proposed to recarpet the main run-way at a cost of Rs. 2.5 crore.

Some of the projects which the IAAI had completed since its inception were Phases I and II of the international terminal building at Bombay, the new domestic terminal building at Madras and the Indira Gandhi International Airport at Delhi. The activities of IAAI have been somewhat handicapped due to :

(i) Inadequacy of funds provided in the Five-Year Plans.

(ii) Lack of integrated development of the aviation industry. While the national airlines, viz., Air India, Indian Airlines and foreign airlines operating to India geared themselves to the traffic growth and expanded, IAAI could not keep in step with this expansion, mainly because of lack of funds.

(iii) Increased requirements of infrastructural facilities during the concentrated peak hour traffic due to bunching of flights and under-utilisation of these facilities at other hours of the day. The magnitude of this imbalance at the international airports in India is abnormally high due to its geographical position and night curfews at airports in the East and the West.

1.8 AIRPORTS AUTHORITY OF INDIA

1.8.1 Introduction

The Airports Authority of India (AAI) was formed on 1st April, 1995 by merging the International Airports Authority of India (IAAI) and the National Airports Authority (NAA) with a view to accelerate the integrated development, expansion and modernisation of the operational, terminal and cargo facilities at the airports in the country conforming to international standards. The Airports Authority of India manages 5 International Airports, 87 Domestic Airports and 28 Civil Air Terminals at Defence Airfields with a total of 120, in the country. Figure 1.1 shows the location of airports in India maintained by AAI. It controls and manages the entire Indian airspace extending even beyond the territorial limits of the country.

The mission of AAI is "Progress through excellence and customer satisfaction with world class airport and air traffic services fostering economic develoment".

Table 1.1 Shows the details of traffic handled by AAI during 1995-96.

Table 1.1 Details of Traffic Handled by AAI during 1995-96

Particulars	Units	International	Domestic	Total
Aircraft Movements	Nos	92516	314727	407243
Passengers Handled	In 000	11450	25564	37014
Cargo	M. Tons	436738	212631	649369
Mail Handled	M. Tons	5358	25527	30885

Source : First Annual Report for 1995-96 of AAI, New Delhi.

Airports in remote areas like North East Region, Lakshadweep, Jammu & Kashmir and Andaman & Nicobar Islands have been given due emphasis for expansion.

1.8.2 Facilities at Airports

During the year, the following Communication, Navigation and Surveillance System (CNS) facilities were installed :

* Instrument Landing System (ILS) at Bangalore, Bhubaneshwar, Mumbai and Thiruvananthapuram.
* Doppler Very High Frequeney Omni Range (DVOR) at Agartala, Jorhat, Belgaum, Calicut, Bhavnagar, Tirupati and Rajkot.

- Distance Measuring Equipment [DME (HP)] at Coimbatore, Raipur, Jaipur, Bhopal, Jorhat, Patna, Jammu, Varanasi, Udaipur, Jodhpur, Bagdogra, Indore, Cochin, Calicut, Chiluk, Sikandrabad, Tirupati, Rajkot, Khajuraho, Agartala and Mohanbari.

(i) Passenger facilities at International airports

- STD/ISD/PCO facility at all the international airports has been augmented for passenger facilitation.
- Entertainment Television provided at airports complemented with Cable/Star TV Network.
- Soft drink vending machines installed in security hold of domestic terminals.
- All black and white x-ray machines are being replaced by colour machines for security check. The first phase of replacement with 30 machines have been completed.
- Multi-channel voice recorders have been introduced for recording sensitive conversation to prevent bomb threats and improved security and for investigation of emergency events.

(ii) Cargo facilities

- In order to facilitate exports of fruits and vegetables, a walk-in-type cold room has been installed at Calcutta airport.
- Airline oriented functions such as palletisation/depalletisation have been commenced for Air France and Cargolux at Chennai airport.

1.8.3 Future air navigation system

India was one of the few countries which recognised the need for introduction of satellite aided systems in the Civil Aviation and endorsed it in 1991 in International Civil Aviation Organisation (ICAO), Montreal, Airports Authority of India has commenced the task and Satellite Aided Communication, Navigation and Surveillance and Air Traffic Management will be inducted in the country in a phased manner. The target date as laid down by ICAO is 2005.

The Authority has drawn up ambitious long-term plans to meet challenges posed by ever increasing air traffic and sophisticated growth of aircraft technology year after year. A smooth transition to the 21st century has been envisaged and the Authority is actively engaged in the pursuit. Some of the major plans are :

Coverage of the Indian land mass through Satellite Communication VHF Data Links and Monopulse Secondary Surveillance Radars with Mode 'S' Capability.

* Establishment of Global Navigation Satellite System (GNSS) alongwith ground segment comprising of Wide Area Augmentation System (WAAS).
* Provision of Automatic Dependant Surveillance System.

1.8.4 Training

The Civil Aviation Training College (CATC). Allahabad and the Institute of Aviation Management (IAM), New Delhi offers excellent training facilities to Controllers, Technical Officers, engineers and other executives. They have been recognised for TRAINAIR Programmes under ICAO.

1.8.5. Environmental issues

Airport development is land intensive in nature calling for environment protection. A process has been evolved by which the environment is protected while developing new airports. In that endeavour, it has been ensured that the guidelines issued by the Ministry of Environment are followed.

1.9 INTERNATIONAL CIVIL AVIATION ORGANISATION (ICAO)

The nations of the world have established the International Civil Aviation Organisation (ICAO) to serve as the medium through which the necessary international understanding and agreement between nations in all the technical and economic and legal fields so that the air can be the high road to carry man and his goods anywhere and everywhere without fetter and without halt. ICAO's membership comprises 151 sovereign states. With the signing of a treaty in December 1944, ICAO was created as an Inter Governmental Organisation and in 1947 became a specialised agency in relationship with the United Nations Its headquarter is in Montreal and it has regional offices in Bangkok, Cairo, Dakar, Lima, Mexico City, Paris and Nairobi.

ICAO provides the machinery for the achievement of international co-operation in the air. Successful results depend on the willingness of the nations of the world to make concessions to work together to reach agreement. The success which international civil aviation has achieved in the past three decades is abundant proof that nations can work together effectively to achieve good results.

ICAO provides the international link between civil and military flying activities. Specific recommendations and guidance, issued by ICAO cover the following :

(i) Co-ordination between military authorities and air traffic services.

(ii) Co-ordination of activities potentially dangerous to civil aircraft.

(iii) Strayed or unidentified aircraft, and

(iv) Interception of civil aircraft.

ICAO works in close co-operation with other members of the United Nations family such as the World Meteorological Organisation (WMO), the International Telecommunications Union (ITU) and the Universal Postal Union, (UPU) the World Health Organisation (WHO) and the Intergovernmental Mantime Consultative Organisation (IMCO). Non-governmental organisations which also participate in ICAO's work include the international Air Transport Association (IATA), the International Federation Airline Pilot Association (IFAPA) and the International Council of Aircraft Owner and Pilot Association (ICAOPA).

The ICAO regions are :

European-Mediterranean	EUM
Middle East	MID
Africa/Indian Ocean	AFI
South East Asia	SEA
Pacific	PAC
South American	SAM
Carbbean	CAR
North America	NAM
North Atlantic	NAT

To assist in administrative support and technical advise, seven regional offices as given below provide secretarial services for these regions.

Bangkok	SEA and PAC
Mexico City	CAR and NAM
Cairo	MID
Dakar	AFI (WEST)
Lima	SAM
Paris	EUM
Nairobi	AFI (EAST)

ICAO also provides assistance to developing countries by the provision of international experts, instructors, training, equipment and fellowships or training abroad. This assistance covers ground services, flight safety, air law and regulations and the organisation and administration of civil aviation.

1.9.1 Structure of ICAO

(a) The Assembly

The assembly is the sovereign body of ICAO & meets every 3 years at a place and time convened by the Council. All contracting states may be represented and decisions are taken by a majority of votes cast. The financial arrangements of ICAO are determined and a triennial budget voted. The work of the Council is reviewed and directions and recommendations given for future action.

(b) The Council

The council is the permanent governing body and composed of 33 members elected by the Assembly. The Council elect its own President.

The Council is responsible to the Assemble for taking whatever steps are necessary to maintain the safety and regularity of international air transport and to encourage and regulate the growth of air services throughout the world. One of its major duties is to adopt international standards and recommended practices and to incorporate them as Annexes to the Convention.

The Council controls and co-ordinates the work of six additional representative bodies. These are : The Air Navigation Commission, The Air Transport Committee,

Committee for Joint Support of Air Navigation Services, Legal Committee, Finance Committee and the ICAO Secretariat.

The ICAO Secretariate is headed by a Secretary General and is divided into five divisions. These divisions are : Air Navigation Bureau, Air Transport Bureau, Technical Assistance Bureau, Legal Bureau and Bureau of Administration and Services. In addition to the regular staff, the services of experts are obtained from time to time by loan from member states.

PROBLEMS

1. Explain the comparison of air transport with other modes of Transportation.
2. Discuss in brief the historical development of air transport.
3. Explain in brief the structure and organization of air transport.
4. Discuss the functions of Directorate of Civil Aviation.
5. Discuss the role of International Airport Authority of India for functioning of airports in India.
6. Discuss the role, responsibilities, and achievements of National Airports Authority of India (NAA).
7. Explain the role of International Civil Aviation organisation (ICAO) for proper functioning of airports and aircrafts for better air transportation.
8. Discuss the Structure of ICAO.

2

GROWTH OF AIR TRANSPORT

2.1 GENERAL

Year 1911 is recorded as beginning of air flight in India by *Henri Piquet*, a Frenchman. The flight was planned from *Allahabad* to *Naini* junction which is a distance of 7 km (4.5 miles). Same year, *Sir George Loyd* undertook the organization of air flying between *Bombay* and *Karachi*. Air service between these cities were considered as purely temporary and was taken as a government venture.

In 1927, British government established *Civil Aviation Department* and this organization helped in building up of a few aerodromes and bringing up of some flying clubs. A regular weekly service commenced between Karachi and Delhi in 1929 under *Imperial Airways Service*. In 1939 *Tata Airways Limited* started internal air services between Allahabad, Calcutta and Colombo. Later, *Indian Trans-Continental Airways Limited* was formed for the foreign flights in 1933.

The second world war helped this country for having large number of technical personnel.

Air Transport Licencing Board came into being in 1946, Tata Airlines changed its name as *Air India Limited* in July

1946. There were about eleven operating units by 1947. The night services commenced in 1949. For external air services, the Government of India entered an agreement in November 1947, with a new formed organization, named as *Air India International Limited* It inaugurated its first international service to London on June 8, 1948 via Cairo and Geneva with a fleet of three *constellation-749* aircraft. The initial frequency of one flight a week was gradually stepped up to seven *Super-Constellation* services a week with alternate stops at Paris, Prague, Duesseldorf, Zurich, Geneva, Rome, Cairo, Beirut and Damascus.

The Government of India appointed an Air Transport Committee in 1950 keeping in view the critical situation in which India's air transport industry was placed. The above committee once again recommended restricting the number of scheduled airlines to four However, the government decided complete nationalisation and in March 1953, the Parliament passed the Air Corporations Act, under which Air India International and Indian Airlines were formed as Public Sector Corporations from Ist August, 1953. Air India to operate long range international services and Indian Airlines to operate all domestic and short range regional routes to adjacent countries viz. Pakistan, Bangla Desh, Sri Lanka and Nepal.

In April 1960, Air India celebrated entry into the jet age by starting *Boeing 707* services to London and later in May to New York—thus becoming the first Asian carrier to operate over the Atlantic.

In July 1967, the Government of India set up the *International Airport Committee* under the Chairmansnip of *Mr. J. R. D. Tata* to advise the Government regarding the improvements which are required in the existing international airports in India in view of the continuous growth of air traffic and the likely introduction of very large subsonic and supersonic aircrafts in near future. The interim report of the committee was submitted to the Government in April, 1968.

On January 2, 1971, Indian Airlines inaugurated the daily Boeing 737 service on the Bombay-Calcutta and Delhi-Bombay sectors. The country for domestic flights is divided into four flight information regions with centres at Delhi, Bombay, Madras and Calcutta.

Directorate of Civil Aviation set up in 1927 really took shape only in the year 1945 with the establishment of the post of Director General of Civil Aviation (DGCA).

International Airport Authority of India (IAAI) was set up in April 1972 for the operation, management, planning and development of the four international airports. National Airport Authority of India (NAA) was established in June; 1980 to manage all domestic civil airports and civil enclavery. These two Airport Authorities have been merged into the Airports Authority of India Act. 1994, new organisation called the Airports Authority of India (AAI) established on April 1 ; 1995.

2.2 NATIONAL AIRLINES

The civil aviation transportation system in India is based on domestic services being provided primarily by Indian Airlines (IA), with Vayudoot providing some short haul services. Air India (AI) operates international services while Indian Airlines operate to some neighbouring countries. In addition, foreign carriers also operate international flights connecting India directly with about 37 countries. The main function of Pawan Hans formed in 1985, is to provide helicopter services to oil Industry.

The National Airports Authority (NAA) manages 86 airports and the civilian enclaves at 26 defence airports and provides the air traffic services throughout the country. The International Airports Authority of India (IAAI) operates the four major metropolitan airports, namely Bombay, Delhi, Calcutta and Madras. The regulatory and licensing functions, bilateral issues, approval of tariffs/schedules, etc. are entrusted to the Director General of Civil Aviation (DGCA).

2.2.1 Indian Airlines & Air India

The formation of Indian Airlines and Air India by nationalization of private airlines was done in August 1953. Since then, the civil aviation industry has registered a tremendous growth, with substantial backing from public expenditures, as shown in Table 2.1.

Since 1953, the growth of the two National Airlines has been as under :

	1953/54*	1993/94
(i) Air India		
Available Tonne Kilometers (ATKMS—Millions)	18.375	1999.093
Revenue Tonne Kilometers (RTKMS—Millions)	11.657	1103.067
(ii) Indian Airlines		
ATKMS - Millions	74.957	965.707
RTKMS - Millions	51.052	684.233

*Indicates the data for 8 months (August 1953 to March 1954).

Table 2.1 Public Plan Expenditures on Civil Aviation

Source : Five year plan documents.

Plan	Period	Amount Rs. (crores)	Aviation as % of Transport sector	
First	1951—56	23	53	
Second	1956—61	49	4.5	Although
Third	1961 – 66	49	2.5	expenditure for
Fourth	1969—74	177	7 0	1985—90 is over
Fifth	1974—79	294	5.2	Rs. 2000 crores.
Sixth	1980—85	931	6.6	Hence, percentage
Seventh	1985—90	758*	3.3	share of plan
Eight	1992—97	**		expenditure might be higher.

* Outlay, ** Figure not available.

Table 2.2 shows the details of the specification of aircrafts operated under Indian Airlines. Table 2.3 shows the aircraft wise fleet of Indian Airlines during 1992-93. The fleet strength during 1992-93 of Air India is given in Table 2.4. As per the recommendations of Planning Group on Civil Aviation (PGCA) set up by Government of India, the details of the requirement of aircrafts till 2000—2001 AD is also given in Table 2.3

Emperor Ashoka, Air India's first Boeing 747 (Jumbojet) was introduced in April 1971. The Jumbo is two and a half times the size of Boeing 707. Aircraft manufacturing companies have been established in Kanpur and Bangalore. The particulars and characteristics of few aeroplanes manufactured in India and abroad are given in the Appendix at the end of the chapter. The diagrams are given in Figures 2.1 to 2.7.

Table 2.2 Details of the Specification of Aircrafts Operated Under Indian Airlines

Aircraft Name	A300 B2	A300 B4	Boeing (B – 737)	H - 748
Manufacturer	Airbus Industries France		Boing Company USA	HAL, Kanpur
Number of Aircrafts in Fleet	8	2	25	7
Max. Number of Passengers Accomodated	271	271	126	44
Year of Induction	1976	1976	1970	1967
Engine	Turbofan CF6—50C Turbofan CF6—50C—2		Turbo Fan JT8D – 17 JT8D – 17A	Turbo Prop Dart 532—2
Engine Manufacturer	General Electric USA		Pratt & Whitney USA	Rolls Royce UK
Engine Power	50C=51000 LB Thrust 50C—2,52500 LB Thrust		14500 LB Thrust 16000 LB Thrust	1910 SHP
Average Fuel Consumption Per Engine	50C—3710 LTR/HR 50C—2=3800 LTR/HR		1800 LTS/HR	450 LTS/HR
Number of Engines Per Aircraft		2	2	2
Maximum Cruising Speed	0.78 MOK		0.74 MOK	260 KNUT
Maximum Pay Load (Fuel & Oil Tanks Fuel	22400 KG.	28,900 KG	800 KG. 1500 KG.	2.7 Tons 3.7 Tons
Maximum Fuel	34000 KG	47500 KG.	16000 KG	4.1 Ton
Maximum Loading	130 Tons	134 Tons	46.7 Ton	18.2 T

Table 2.3 Fleet of Indian Airlines

Sl. No.		As on 1-3-85	Fleet Position & Requirements 1992-93	2000-2001
1.	A-300 B 2/B4	10	10	38*
	A-320	—	25	80**
	B-737/200	25	18	75***
	Turbo Prop a/c	19		—
2.	Revenue Passenger Km (in millions)	7360.1	11237.4	32,000
3.	No. of passengers (in millions)	5.25	7.3	40

*300 + Seater aircraft, **150 + Seater aircraft and ***100 + Seater aircraft

Table 2.4 Fleet Strength of Air India During 1992—93

Aircraft Type	No. of Aircrafts
A—747/400	0
A—310 G	8
AB—300	3
B—747/237	9
B—747/300	2
Total	22

Figure 2.1 HAL HOP—27 Krishak

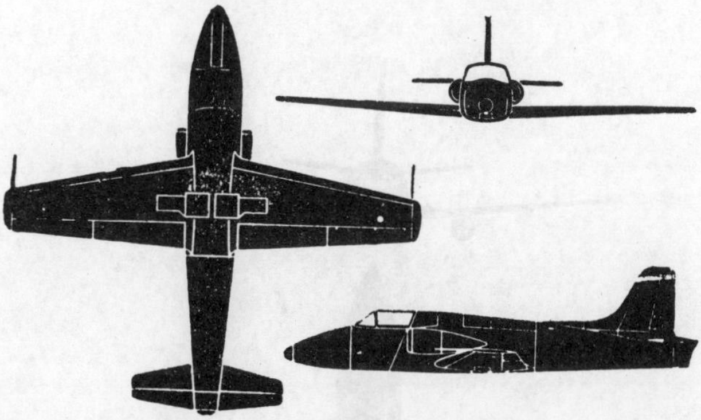

Figure 2.2 HAL HJT—16 Kiran

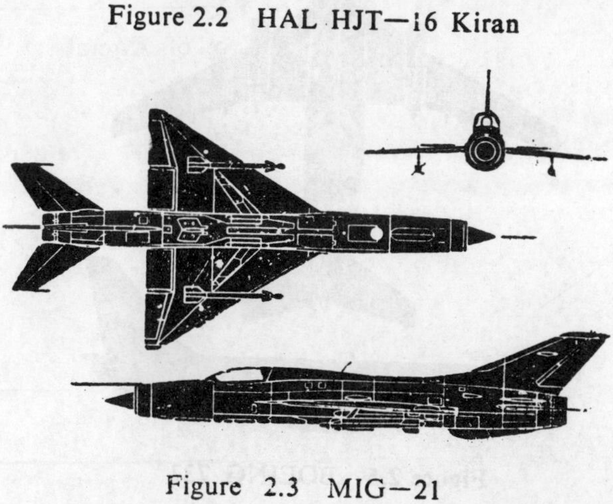

Figure 2.3 MIG—21

Figure 2.4 FOKKER F-37 Friendship

Figure 2.5 BOEING 737

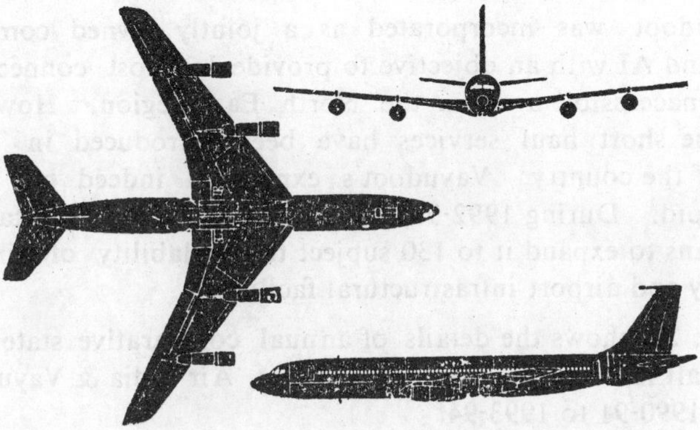

Figure 2.6 BOIENG 707-320 B

Figure 2.7 BOEING 747 (Jumbo jet)

2.2.2 Vayudoot

Vayudoot was incorporated as a jointly owned company of IA and AI with an objective to provide low cost connections to the inaccessible areas in the North East region. However, overtime short haul services have been introduced in other parts of the country. Vayudoot's expansion indeed has been very rapid. During 1992-93, Vayudoot operates to 97 stations and plans to expand it to 130 subject to availability of aircraft capacity and airport infrastructural facilities.

Table 2.5 shows the details of annual comparative statement of aircraft movements of Indian Airlines, Air India & Vayudoot during 1990-91 to 1993-94.

Table 2.5 Comparative Statement of Aircraft Movements of IA, AI & Vayudoot for 1991-92 to 1993-94

Airline		Aircraft Movements			
		Domestic	International	Total	% Growth
Indian	1991-92	80733	5185	85918	
Airlines	1992-93	70368	4795	75163	−12.5
	1993-94	71395	5948	77343	2.9
	1991-92	4864	12296	17160	–
Air India	1992-93	4885	12542	17427	—1.6
	1993-94	4864	12872	17736	—1.8
	1991-92	16945	–	16945	–
Vayudoot	1992-93	10784	—	10784	—36.4
	(Upto Oct. '93)				
	1993-94	—	Not Available	–	

Source :—Air Transport Statistics for 1993-94, Directorate General of Civil Aviation, New Delhi, Dec. 1995.

2.2.3 Pawan Hans

Pawan Hans was formed in 1985 with 51 percent equity participation of the Government of India and 49 percent of Oil and Natural Gas Commission (ONGC). Its primary goal is to reduce the foreign chartering of helicopters for use by the oil industry. It presently has a fleet of 41 helicopters. Out of the above, few helicopters are leased out for civilian use. They provide services in regions where road transportation is extremely difficult and time consuming. Due to the very high cost of operation of the helicopters, their utilisation for regular short haul air services must be avoided where alternate means of transport, either by road or by fixed wing aircraft is possible. The helicopters are suitable for special uses e.g. to the oil industry, electrification projects air ambulance and emergency services, etc. Considerably attention is required to be paid to the creation of capacity and its utilisation by coordinating the growth of Pawan Hans to its special markets.

Pawan Hans is dependent entirely on the defence service for its requirements of pilots, engineers and technicians. There is a need for training the entire technical staff of Pawan Hans by setting up a helicopter training institute or organising special courses at the Indira Gandhi Rashtriya Uran Akademi. Coordination is also required in developing infrastructural requirements, especially in areas where no navigational aids are available. The construction of helipads require comparatively small resources of land, expense and time as against providing facilities for fixed wing aircraft, but the provision of radio aids at remote, all-weather stations is an important factor. Both of these, infrastructural needs will have to be met by the Airports Authority of India in consultation with Pawan Hans.

2.2.4 Air Taxi Policy

The Government of India announced an air taxi policy in 1985 to allow resident and non-resident Indians to start air taxi services within India. However, no air taxi company recommended that the air taxis would support tourist movement and that the aircraft be used as air taxis ought to have a maximum capacity of 10 seats. Some of the policy related issues which require examination are :

(i) identification of the markets and tourist centres to be served.

(ii) the investments required for acquiring equipment, manpower and airport facilities,

(iii) whether 10-seater aircraft are the most economic and relevant to the market needs.

(iv) the extent to which funds will be diverted from the development of existing services and facilities, and

(v) the impact on foreign exchange flow.

2.2.5 Helicopter Corporation of India (HCI)

The Government of India, had announced the formation of HCI, as an autonomous corporation in the aviation sector. Because of its high cost, the requirement of helicopters purely for civil transport needs is very minimal except in rare cases where the nature of the terrain or other special reasons do not permit the use of other modes of transport. Because of the prohibitive cost of transport by helicopters, its use is extremely limited even in highly developed countries.

2.2.6 Total Investment on Fleet Acquisition

The total investment up to the year 2000 according to PGCA recommendations required for the purchase of aircraft by the three national carriers is given in Table 2.6.

Table 2.6 Total Investment Required by 2000 for Purchase of Aircraft

Type of National Carriers	Amount (Rs. in crores, 1985-86 prices)		
	1986-90 1	1996-2000 2	1986-2000 Total (1+2)
Air India	1746.00	2385.00	6073.00
Indian Airlines	1768 00	4848.00	8998.00
Vayudoot	100.02	148 93	341 50
Total	3614 02	7381.93	15,412 50

2.3 GROWTH OF INTERNATIONAL TRAFFIC & AIR INDIA'S PERFORMANCE

The average annual rate of growth of international passenger traffic to and from India from 1974 to 1984 has been 16.0%. As against this; the growth rate achieved by Air India during the same period was 13.2%. Air India's share of the Indian originating market is currently 35.9%. During the period in which Air India achieved the growth rate of 13.2% in passenger traffic and 12.4% in the total RTKMS performed, the capacity measured in terms of ATKMS performed, increased by 11.3% which indicates that Air-India's utilization of the capacity has been quite satisfactory.

Air India's route coverage has been extensive and it has utilized its compact fleet efficiently. However, in the last few years. the spectular growth of some of the Asian carriers has resulted in some erosion of Air India's share of the originating market.

In recent years, the India/Gulf route has been dominant contributing as much as 31% of the total traffic to and from India.

For international traffic to and from India, the Planning Group (set up by Planning Commission in 1985 under Sri J.R.D. Tata) examined the various scenerio available and arrived at a likely growth in passenger traffic at an average annual growth rate of 6%. The number of passengers based on these growth rates are given in Table 2.7

Table 2.7 Number of Passengers Based on Estimated Growth Rate

Year	1986	1990	1995	2000
No. of Passengers (Thousands)	4,509	5.897	7.896	10,576

The average annual growth rate of 6% is for the total traffic including tourist and non-tourist traffic. If further emphasis is placed on the development of tourist infrastructure, then tourist traffic could grow at a significantly higher rate say 10%. Comparison of tourist traffic at 6% and 10% growth rate are given in Table 2.8.

Table 2.8 Comparative Statement of Growth Rate per Year

Growth Rate per year	Year (Figures in thousands)		
	1985—86*	1995—96+	2000—2001+
6%	876	2273	1982
10%	876	2273	3328

*Actuals, +Estimated

As far as international cargo traffic is concerned, growth rate based on Air India's carriage alone as projected is given in Table 2.9.

Table 2.9 Air India' International Cargo Traffic

Year	1986–90	1990–2000	Overall
(Average annual growth rate %)	6.2	5.9	6.1

2.3.1 International Air Services

In comparison to international standards, Air India is small airline. It cannot compete with major airlines with larger fleets and extensive network of destination. AI must build up its niche in the market by distinguishing itself as a high quality airline. It should concentrate on the routes to the Middle East and South East Asia as the main markets to provide it with sustained profitability.

Considering the net profitability of the last ten years, AI has been consistently and substantially profitable only on its services to the Middle East. On the sectors to Europe, USA, South East and Far East Asia, Australia, etc. the airline lost money. AI's fleet planning and aircraft selection required more rigorous operations and financial analysis than has been done in the past. The induction of additional capacity will reduce the average age of the fleet permitting it to operate non-stop services to many destinations as do the competing airlines operating from India.

2.3.2 International Air Cargo

International air cargo consists of high-value, low-volume items. Even though in terms of tonnage, it formed a minimal portion on the total trade. In 1985-86, it accounted for nearly 30 percent by value, of India's total exports and about 13 percent of the imports. The handling of air cargo is constrained by :

(i) cumbersome procedures and methods of clearance and ground handling,

(ii) imbalance of trade. and

(iii) insufficient export cargo uplift capability of the airlines. The tonnage of air cargo to be handled is expected to rise nearly four-fold by 2000 AD The opportunity of reaping substantial benefits exist by speeding up all aspects of cargo handling.

Air India can gain appreciably by improving its cargo handling capability. Improvement of the quality of ground handling is required to reduce the total transportation time of cargo. Introduction of the 'one-window' concept for clearing paperwork, 'round-the-clock' acceptance and checking of cargo at major airports, better consignment tracking and retrieval systems. quicker uplift of the export and import cargo, faster security checks of the export cargo. provision of consolidation facilities and training of staff would reduce the throughput time.

Development of some airports as hubs for handling international transhipment cargo needs examination. Handling services provided at such airports would result in a remunerative service A uniform practice of allowing transhipment of international import cargo. by IA from the gateway airports to final destinations at inland airports need to be evolved in consultation with the Customs Department.

2.4 GROWTH OF DOMESTIC TRAFFIC

During the period 1984-85 to 1993-94 domestic air traffic (passenger, cargo and mail) has increased from 668.580 million RTKMS to 1757 3 million RTKMS representing an annual average growth rate of approximately. Table 2.10 shows the details of annual comparative statement of total traffic on schedule services of national carriers (i.e by IA, AI. & Vayudoot).

The domestic air passenger traffic has trebled between 1974-75 and 1984-85 in terms of number of passengers and in terms of Route Passenger Kilometres (RPKMS) In 1984-85 Indian Airlines carried 0.08 million passenger and Vayudoot 0.16 million passengers. Passengers traffic accounts for as much as 81% of the total RTKMS performed on the domestic sector. During 1993-94 the national carriers on domestic schedule

Table 2.10 Annual Comparative Statement of Total Traffic on Scheduled Services of National Carriers

Operations	Year			Percentage Variation	
	*1993-94	1992-93	1991-92	1993-94 over 1992-93	1992-93 over 1991-92
1, Passenger Carried (000)	9832	10212	11153	- 3.7	—8 4
2. Passenger Kms. Performed (Millions	15235	1:687	16141	—2.9	—2.8
3. Available Seat Kms. (Millions)	24010	22880	24124	—4.9	—5.2
4. Passenger Load Factor (%) (2/3)	63 5	68.6	66.9	—7.5	2 5
5. Freight Carried ('000 Tons)	143 5	139.1	158.2	3 2	—12 1
6. Mail Carried ('000 Tons)	19.6	17 8	17.7	10.1	0.9
7. Ton Kms. Performed (Millions)					
(i) Passenger	1335.7	1369 8	1118.5	—2.5	22.5
(ii) Freight	421.9	380.6	384.5	10.9	—1.0
(iii) Mail	29.7	26 5	25.9	12.1	2.3
(iv) Total (i)+(ii)+(iii)	1787.3	1776.9	1528.9	0.6	16 2
Total Available Tons. Kms	2964.3	2853.5	3047.2	3.9	— 6.4
Weight Load Factor (%)	60 3	62.3	50.2	—3.2	24.1

Source :—ICAO ATR Forms A-1 furnished by Indian Airlines, Air India & Vayudoot

*Does not include Vayudoot Figures

services carries 9.8 millions passengers and 2964.8 million available ton km (AT KMS)

Air traffic in India has grown at a faster rate in terms of total revenue passenger kilometres, air traffic still accounts for only about 1.5% of the total traffic (by Air, Rail and Govenment run Road Transport). Comparing this with U.S, the air travel accounts for nearly 85% of the passenger kilometers of the total traffic (airline, rail, road and roadcoach traffic).

Cargo traffic of Indian Airlines has grown at an annual average rate of 19% during 10 years span from 1974-75 to 1984-85.

Indian Airlines has a route network covering 73 stations including 9 international stations. Over the last years, Indian Airlines has shown a shift towards operating a higher percentage of direct flights as opposed to hopping flights.

Table 2.11 shows the annual traffic and operating statistics on scheduled domestic services of Indian Airlines during the last ten years 1984-85 to 1993-94. Table 2.12 shows the annual total domestic passenger traffic carried by IA, AI & vayudoot during last ten years.

The Planning Group of Civil Aviation (PGCA) accepted the traffic forecast arrived at an average annual growth rate over the actual traffic in 1985-86 of 11.5% for passenger traffic and 11.2% for cargo traffic which results in the following projection in the period upto 2000 A.D. as per the details given in Table 2.13.

2.5 FLEET REQUIREMENT

Based on the traffic projections, the fleet requirements have been estimated for Indian Airlines, Air India and Vayudoot and are shown in Tables 2.14, 2.15 and 2.16 respectively.

Currently, IA also operates some B 737's and A 300 B on lease. The number of leased aircrafts varies from time to time. IA has ordered 19 A 320's for delivery in 1989-90 with options on another 12. In the period beyond 1995-96, IA is likely to have 4 or 5 types of aircraft in service.

AI will require 45 aircrafts including replacement of 10 existing aircrafts. Currently, AI leases frieghter aircraft. It will require two B747—300's Combi's in the near future.

Table 2.11 Annual Traffic and Operating Statistics on Scheduled Domestic Services of Indian Airlines During Last Ten Years

Month	A/C Flown Hours (No).	A/C Flown Kms. (000)	Passengers Carried	Passengers Kms. Performed (000)	Available Seat Kms.	Pax. Load Factor (%)	Cargo Carried (Ton) Freight	Cargo Carried (Ton) Mail	Cargo Carried (Ton) Total	Ton Kms. Performed (000) Pax	Ton Kms. Performed (000) Freight	Ton Kms. Performed (000) Mail	Ton Kms. Performed (000) Total	Available Ton Kms. (000)	Weight Load Factor (%)
1	2	3	4	5	6	7	8	9	10	11	12	13	14	15	16
1984-85	106935	52500	7008123	6131243	8172305	75.0	95938	18197	115135	495330	95002	17114	607446	879005	69.1
1985-86	117718	58486	8616568	6834798	9097424	75.1	97080	18055	115135	556832	97720	18149	672701	960359	70.0
1986-87	125117	63110	9176006	7463330	9994443	74.7	90129	17555	107684	613801	90992	17512	722305	1031490	70.0
1987-88	127012	65827	9934958	8251515	10412679	79.2	103177	16175	119352	673081	105390	17770	796241	1081114	73.7
1988-89	114859	63077	9541788	8243895	10103320	81.6	105634	16776	122410	670816	107579	18257	796652	1032950	77.1
1989-90	109570	61164	9390656	8271810	10650345	77.7	96602	16200	112802	674069	98663	16984	789716	1074493	73.5
1990-91	88798	48705	7471120	6800737	8588895	79.9	82277	14941	97218	561585	87965	16055	665605	872784	76.3
1991-92	106929	57457	8311844	7498354	10107965	74.2	77968	15687	93655	613021	82938	16769	712728	1010819	70.5
1992-93	94622	50060	7268443	6623188	8889576	74.5	67734	16436	84170	539648	71284	17754	628686	881983	71.3
1993-94	96280	52855	7229810	6475 19	9447538	68.5	65475	18185	83660	530100	67264	20003	617367	947842	65.1

Source :—ICAO ATR Form A-1 furnished by Indian Airlines

Table 2.12 Annual - Total Domestic Passenger Traffic Carried by IA, AI & Vayudoot During Last Ten Years

(Passengers in Millions)

Year	IAC	AI	Vayudoot	Total
1984-85	8.10	0.20	0.20	8.50
1985-86	8.60	0.20	0.20	9.00
1986-87	9.40	0.20	0.30	9.90
1987-88	9.90	0.30	0.40	10.60
1988-89	9.54	0.30	0.45	10.29
1989-90	9.39	0.38	0.14	9.91
1990-91	7.47	0.39	0.44	8.30
1991-92	8.31	0.30	0.30	8.91
1992-93	7.27	0.31	0.21	7.79
1993-94	7.23	0.28	N.A.	*7.51

Source :—ICAO, Form A-1 furnished by respective Airlines
*Exclusive of Vayudoot Figures

Table 2.13 Forecasting of Traffic

Year	1985-86	1990-91	1995-96+	2000-01+
RPKMS (Million)	7,336	12,643	19,540	37,548
No. of Passengers (thousands)	9,130	15.803	24,423	46,935
Cargo (Tonnes)	1,11,214	1,89,098	2,89,139	5,46,682

+estimated

Table 2.14 Projected Fleet of Indian Airlines

Yerr end	A 300	A 320	B 737	T Prop
1985-86	10	—	25	15
1990-91	10	36	20	15
	300+Seats	150+Seats	100+Seats	
1994-95*	20	42	42	
2000-01*	38	80	75	

(Source : PGCA, 1986), *Projected

Table 2.15 Projected Fleet Size of Air India

Year end	B 747	A 300	A 310	New	B 747 F	A 310 C
1985—86	10	3	5			
	400 + Seats	300 + Seats	200 + Seats	240/280 Seats		
1990—91	11	3	12	—		—
1995—96*	11	—	12	9	5	—
2000—01*	16	—	12	12	3	3

(Source : PGCA, 19·6), *Projected

Table 2 16 Projected Fleet Size of Vayudoot

Year end	Do 228	T' Prop	New T' Prop
1985 86	10	4	—
1990—91	11	—	12
	20 + Seats	—	40 + Seats
1995—96*	18	—	20
2000—01*	29	—	33

(Soucrce : PGCA, (986), *Projected

2.6 TECHNOLOGICAL DEVELOPMENTS

There are several major technological developments which are likely to occur in the field of flight equipment and its operational envirorment in the next few years, and it is important that these are kept in view in planning the future growth of civil aviation.

In the field of flight equipment, fuel efficient propulsion systems like still higher bypass ratio jet engines will be followed by the geared or ungeared ducted or unducted fans offering fuel burns improvements of 25% and upwards.

Light weight composite materials will come increasingly into use, enabling valuable savings in weight combined with structural stren th and freedom from corrosion.

The considerable improvement already achieved in cockpit instrumentation and automated flight management in the latest type of aircraft will no doubt be further advanced with increasing use of digital technology and computer software concepts. Along with this, improved communication and navigation systems, of fly by wire flight control system with side stick and use of computers with artificial intelligence will provide notable improvements in pilot work load, reliability and safety of operation. These advanced systems will have their impact on functional requirements of crew and their training.

It is envisaged that the existing operational restrictions on twin engined aircraft will be progressively relaxed with further improvements in power plant and system reliability.

The growth in air traffic density and technological advances in airborne equipment will require commensurate advances in flight environment. Airport capacity limitations will have to be tackled with computer based communications, navigation, surveillance and traffic handling systems so as to achieve optimum airport usage.

Major changes in the area of navigation will result from the implementation of microwave and satelite based navigation systems. Two such systems which are likely to be introduced before 2000 A.D. are the Global Positioning Systems (GPS) and the Microwave Landing Systems (MLS), Combined use of both these systems may eliminate the present 'Positioning Determination Systems' (PDS).

Developments in the navigational field by introducing the concept of managed air space will be a significant departure from the existing traffic monitoring system. This will require a combination of both dependent and independent surveillance of inflight aircraft. This will also provide improved air safety while holding the load on the ATC systems within reasonable limits.

Besides flight equipment and ground navigational communication aids, technological changes likely in the terminal area will be the growing use of automatic ticketing, machine readable tickets, computarized photo identifications of passengers for immigration control etc. These improvements would be needed in order to facilitate a higher and faster throughput of passengers through the terminal area. Baggage sorting machines will become increasingly common which, besides providing faster handling of baggage will also ensure automatic system for baggage accounting and security.

It is also reasonable to expect aircraft with increased size and carrying capacities to the extent of 1.5 times the present 747s being marketed in the near future. Along with the increased size, there is a likelihood of introduction of new and larger supersonic aircraft by the turn of the century, to cater to specialised segments of traffic. It is therefore necessary for advance preparations to study and adopt the above development.

These technological developments are bound to have a major impact on the civil aviation infrastructural facilities to be provided by the year 2000 However, many of these developments and take appropriate action well in advance, particularly in the field of navigation/approach aids, communication and search and rescue

Application of these technological improvements will greatly enhance the efficiency of the civil aviation sector and what is even more important, its safety standards especially to Indian conditions.

Airports Authority of India (AAI) takes care of the comforts of the increasing number of passengers in Indian airpors but also has adopted new and never technologies for ensuring safety in the air.

2.7 INFRASTRUCTURAL DEVELOPMENT

The development of airports, navigation and communication facilities has not been commensurate with the growth of air traffic and the introduction of new aircraft by the airlines because of the lack of timely and coordinated planning between the airlines and the airport authorities. The gestation period for airport development has been insufficient as rapid demands are made for new or upgraded facilities to handle air services. While flights can easily be suspended if the traffic potential on a route is not upto expectation, infrastructural facilities could result in wasted resources if they remain unutilised.

The development of navigational and communication infrastructure throughout the Indian controlled airspace should be accorded a high priority to match capacity and safety levels required by growing traffic. These ought to be economically justified. One of the most important issues of infrastructural development, from financial and policy considerations, is the provision of a second airport to serve Bombay. With the continuance of the present pattern of operations, the airport will soon be saturated despite the maximum expansion of its facilities. Thus, there is a need to plan short term action to enhance its capacity keeping the long term imperatives in mind. The short term plan for Bombay requires.

(i) Measures to maximise the annual throughput of the airport.

(ii) Control of peak demand by limiting the number of operating slots. The allocation of slots can be implemented through different methods e.g. through mutual accommodation between airlines, offer of incentives such as differential landing charges for peak and non peak hours, auctioning of operating slots and if all else fails, by regulatory action.

(iii) Encouraging airlines to operate point to point services which by-pass Bombay to reduce the use of Bombay as a transfer or transit airport. This policy may require upgrading and opening up selected domestic airports

A matter of concern is the peaking of traffic at the large airports. At Bombay and Delhi, nearly 50 percent of the traffic is handled in six hours of the morning. In the case of domestic flights, nearly 35 percent of the total daily passengers are handled in an hour and a half The unbalanced utilisation of facilities adversely affects the quality of handling and maintenance services. Effective intervention at different levels is necessary to correct the above state of utilization.

With the state-of-art communication, navigation, surveillance facilities and air traffic services, the AAI is managing nearly 3 million sq. NM of airspace of which two-third are occanic airspace. About 800 Air Traffic Controllers are engaged day and night to ensure safety in the air. Satellite based systems (CNS/ATM) are being introduced to enhance safety measures, the AAD has also augmented the infrastructural facilities at the gateway airports and domestic airports to meet the rapid growth in the cargo traffic.

2.8 INSTITUTIONAL DEVELOPMENT FOR PLANNING

The PGCA has recommended that the planning departments in all organisation ought to be strengthened, since at present, these are extremely deficient or non-existent. Concurrently, there is scope for a greater degree of coordination and cooperation between the organisations requiring knowledge of the systems being integrated This suggests efficient central direction which should be undertaken by the creating of a special planning cell under the charge of a Technical Advisor (Planning) in the Ministry of Civil Aviation.

A review of planning Practices in aviation highlights the following areas which need strengthening :

(i) The economic and physical data base used for planning do not have a common data base framework which is useable by all the organisations in the sector.

(ii) Each organisation normally undertakes its planning exercise independent of detailed input from other organisations at project formulation and preparation stage. By the time other organisations are involved, it is sometimes too late to incorporate any significant changes required by the users.

(iii) Most of the infrastructure planning is capacity related. Planning techniques make limited use of economic and cost benefit analysis. It is at the project stage that a review of the financial viability is done, rather than examining economic viability at a national or regional level.

(iv) Costs of serving passengers and cargo are not indicated in any of the industry reports.

2.9 MANPOWER DEVELOPMENT

Civil Aviation is dependent upon manpower with skills in many diverse fields to manage, operate, coordinate and maintain the complex network of services provided by a variety of organisations using capital intensive high technology equipment. At present, the organisations have a high manpower figure relative to the quantum of service provided by them. The major reasons for the situation are low productivity norms, overstaffing, undertaking certain services in house which may be done by contract, insufficient automation and insufficient training.

Supplementing the functioning of the aviation organisations are the regulatory agencies at the airports, e.g. Customs, Immigration and Security control. In their case, beside the reasons already mentioned the regulations to be implemented and the practices followed also necessitate large manpower strengths. There is scope for improvement in the working of all the organisations.

The manpower development programme ultimately leads to the need to :

(i) Review the training syllabi for technical staff, ATC controllers, operating and maintenance personnel of communication and navigational equipment.

(ii) Upgrade the courses at the existing training institutes, namely, the Civil Aviation Training Centre and the Indira Gandhi Rashtriya Uran Akademi,

(iii) Identify the change required in certification procedures for technical personnel,

(iv) Identify functions which can be contracted to outside agencies, and

(v) Encourage technical and engineering institutes to include in their syllabi specialised courses related to aviation technology, and start special courses if sufficient volume of trainees are identified.

2.10 REGULATORY PRACTICES

The demand for air services has outgrown the capacity generated and considerable congestion is experienced on many routes. The present rates and fares charged by domestic airlines do not always reflect the cost of services. It is suggested, therefore, to adjust the rates to encourage optimum resource allocation between civil aviation and other transport mode. An assessment of the routes which are commercially non-viable in the revised regulatory regime but have to be operated as a social service, should be made. It is recommended that the quantum of losses for these routes be fully reimbursed by the Government, but no general subsidies be allowed to airlines or the airport authorities.

The international services operate in an environment where bilateral agreements limit the traffic rights of airlines and the markets, the level of outputs and pricing freedom is limited through IATA rate-making, revenue pools, etc. Pooling removes competition and increases load factors. Though AI and IA operate in this environment, they are increasingly being forced to face up to the competition created in deregulated markets like the North Atlantic, parts of Europe and South East Asia. Some key factors in this situation are that the high IATA tariffs have encouraged low-fare scheduled and charter operations which are used frequently by price sensitive tourist traffic. In some cases, predominantly in the USA, the airlines are forbidden to enter pools or be involved in the rate-making practice of IATA.

The Director General of Civil Aviation (DGCA) administers economic regulations related to airworthiness and safety, setting standards and ensuring their implementation for maintenance, overhaul and the quality of engineering training, licensing and workload schedules of flight and cabin crew, technicians, engineers, et al, standardising and ensuring safe operation level of aircraft, the infrastructure at airports, navigational and communication aids and meteorological standards, etc. It is important in these areas to review the practices of the constituent organisations in the light of international practices.

2.11 AIRPORT AND AIRPORT FACILITIES

The facilities and services provided by India need considerable improvements to bring them up to the international standards, particularly in the air traffic services, communications and approach aids at domestic airports. The reasons are, lack of planning, time consuming procedure for improvement, lead time for indigenous development, inadequacy of reliable communication networks etc. The observations of the DGCA regarding the various airports are given in the successive paragraphs.

The AAI has undertaken large scale upgradation of various facilities at the airports are the airside and landside. More and more passenger amenities are added to meet the increasing traffic. It has identified 12 important domestic airports which are developed as model airports to meet the challenges of passengers comfort and safety.

2.11.1 Bombay (Mumbai) Airport

(a) International Passenger Traffic

The Phase-I of the international terminal complex with the passenger handling capacity of 2.5 million passengers per annum was commissioned in 198 . Phase-II having the same capacity but with certain improvements in facilities had commissioned in 1986. The international passenger traffic to and from Bombay is likely to be increased from 3 85 million in 1984-85 to 8 30 millions in 1994-95 and 11.10 million in 2000 AD Based on the above data, it was found necessary to immediate sanction of Phase-III of the international terminal complex. Measures like modernization of air traffic control system, improvement of taxiway/runway complex and spreading of flights throughout the day-night could delay the saturation being reached before 2000 A.D.

(b) Domestic Passenger Traffic

The domestic passenger traffic to and from Bombay is estimated to increase from 3.74 million passengers in 1984-85 to 9 70 million passengers in 1994-95 and 14.00 million passengers in 2000 A D. Therefore, it is clear that even with the planned extension of domestic terminal and other improvements, Bombay airport reached saturation point in respect of domestic traffic.

(c) Cargo Traffic

The international cargo traffic to and from Bombay is estimated to increase from 1.23 lakh tons in 1984-85 to 7.30 lakh tons in 2000 A.D.

The domestic cargo traffic to and from Bombay is estimated to grow from 0.39 lakh tons in 1984-85 to 1 32 lakh tons in 1994-95 and 2.54 lakh tons in 2000 A D.

Bombay airport reached the saturation point in 1990 because of non availability of land left for expanding the cargo handling capacity.

(d) Runways, Taxiways, Apron and Other Facilities

In order to ensure full utilisation of runway 27, diversion of Kurla-Andheri road needs to be undertaken at the earliest. The existing VASIS will have to be replaced by PAPI. The taxiways will have to be provided with centreline lighting. Therefore early planning, acquisition of land and other activities for the new airport for Bombay is necessary. The studies carried out so far indicate that the site at Mandava-Rewas is the best suited for development of new airport which is approximately 90 km from Fort area. The cost of development of this site alone estimated as 4000 crores. The new airport should have 2 parallel runways, 4000 metres long. Development of new airport needs to be undertaken in a phased manner considering cost involved in this project. The existing airport can be utilised for domestic traffic and the international operation could be shifted to the new airport. Air taxi services may be required between the two airports for transfer of passengers from one airport to the other.

2.11.2 Indira Gandhi International Airport at Delhi

(a) International Passenger Traffic

The international passenger traffic to and from Delhi is estimated to increase from 2.19 million, passengers in 1984-85 to 4.73 million passengers in 1994-95 and 6.34 million passengers in 2000 A D The new international terminal building commissioned in the year 1986 had the capacity to handle 3.33 million passengers to meet the requirements for the year 1990. With the second module, the international terminal complex will meet the requirements up to the year 2000.

(b) Domestic Passenger Traffic

The domestic passenger traffic to and from Delhi is estimated to increase from 2.70 million passengers in 1984-85 to 7.00 million passengers in 1994-95 and 10.80 million passengers 2000 A.D. The planned first module for domestic traffic will have capacity to handle 4.5 million passengers. Further, there should be need to start work on the second domestic module by after 1990 itself and the requirement for the third module will rise by 1997 to meet the estimated traffic growth.

(c) Cargo Traffic

The international cargo traffic to and from Delhi is estimated to increase from 0.71 lakh tons in 1984-85 to 2.52 lakh tons in 1994-95 and 4 44 lakh tons in 2000 A.D. Considering the projected growth rate of cargo, the need of second cargo terminal of similar capacity felt which would meet the requirements up to the year 2000.

(d) Runways, Taxiways and other Facilities

The present runway is likely to meet the requirement for the aircraft movement up to the year 2000, if the traffic is properly spaced by arranging and optimising the utilisation through proper scheduling. However, it would be a prudent plan to provide for the parallel runway by the year 2000. The taxiways will have to be provided with centre-line lighting. The existing VASIS will have to be replaced by PAPI.

2.11.3 Calcutta Airport

(a) International Passenger Traffic

International passenger traffic to and from Calcutta is estimated to increase from 0.38 million in 1984-85 to 1.00 million passengers in 1994-95 and 1.46 million passengers in 2000 A D.

With the commissioning of first module of domestic terminal, the domestic traffic is handled from the new terminal and the present terminal building is used exclusively for international traffic. It is possible to handle 1.85 million passengers and with some additions its capacity could be increased to 2.2 millions. The international terminal building will thus be able to cater for the international passenger traffic requirements up to the year 2000.

(b) Domestic Passenger Traffic

The domestic passenger traffic to and from Calcutta airport is estimated to increase from 1.47 million passengers in 1984-85 to

4.29 million passengers in 1994-95 and 6.17 million passenger in 2000 A D.

The first module of the terminal after commissioning meet the requirements of 1995 for domestic passenger traffic. The domestic terminal after commissioning will be able to meet the requirements up to 2000.

(c) Cargo Traffic

The international cargo traffic is estimated to increase from 0.08 lakh tons in 1984-85 to 0.17 lakh tons in 2000 A.D.

With the existing provision for expansion of cargo complex, it will be possible to meet the requirements for international cargo. It will be possible to expand this to meet the requirements up to 2000 if the area left for airline services could be made partially available for airlines cargo.

(d) Runway, Taxiways and other Facilities

The present main runway will meet the requirements up to the year 2000. Removal of obstruction in the approach area and resisting of ILS commensurate with the shifted threshold will be necessary. The secondary runway will need extension so that it can handle airbus type of aircraft. The shifting of the Masjid. which is causing operation/security hazard, is considered necessary. The existing VASIS will have to be replaced by PAPI The taxiways will have to be provided with centre-line lighting

2.11.4 Madras (Chennai) Airport

(a) International Passenger Traffic

The international passenger traffic to and from Madras airport is expected to increase from 0.34 million passenger in 1884-85 to 0.98 million passenger in 1994-95 and 1.51 million passengers in 2000 A D.

A need was felt in 1990 for commencing the construction of the new international terminal at Madras airport to meet the traffic requirements of 1993. There may be need for major additions/alterations in future which, will cater for the need of Madras airport up to 2000. With no space available for constructing another terminal, Madras airport will be saturated by 2000. However, if Meenambakam village is acquired, additional terminal could be made in that space which may meet the requirements beyond 2000 A.D.

(b) Domestic Passenger Traffic

The domestic passenger traffic to and from Madras airport is estimated to increase from 1.17 million passenger in 1984-85 to 4.6 million passengers in 2000 A.D. The second terminal of same capacity needed to meet the current needs. With additions and alterations, it may be possible to use these terminals to meet the requirements upto the year 2000 A.D.

(c) International Cargo Traffic

The international cargo traffic is expected to increase from 0.2 lakh tons in 1984-85 to 0.76 lakh tons in 2000 A.D. With the modifications in hand, it is expected that the present cargo hangars will meet the requirements very soon.

(d) Runways, Taxiways and other Facilities

IAAI is planning to increase the present main runway from 10050 ft. (3015 m) to 1200 ft. (3600 m) and the secondary runway from 6200 ft. (1800 m) to 7200 ft. (2160 m). The existing VASIS should be replaced by PAPI. The taxiways should be provided with centre-line lighting.

The details of the international passenger traffic, domestic passenger traffic, and international cargo traffic to and from Bombay, Delhi, Calcutta and Madras airports are given in Tables 2.16 to 2.18 respectively.

The details of the investment required for airport and airport facilities are given in Appendix A 2.2.

2.11.5 Financial Implications

For the above projected requirements, IAAI had provided Rs. 131.00 crores for the period 1986-90 and Rs. 1083.20 crores for the period 1995-2000, at the price level of 1986. The details of development plans of the four international airports are given in Table 2.19.

Details of the proposed development programmes up to the year 2000 on the airports for international operations and domestic operations are given in Tables 2.20 and 2.21 respectively. Table 2.22 shows estimated phasing of projects and expenditure for Bombay airport.

Table 2.23 shows the details of operating statistics for Indian Agriculture operators during 1993-94. Table 2.24 shows the details of non-scheduled operations by Pawan Hans Limited during 1993-94. Table 2.25 shows the traffic carried by non-scheduled operators excluding Pawan Hans Limited during 1993-94. Table 2.26 shows the fleet details of non-scheduled operators including agriculture operators.

Table 2.16 Details of International Passenger Traffic to and from Mumbai, Delhi, Calcutta and Chennai Airports

Year	Passenger Traffic (Millions)			
	Mumbai	I.G.I. Airport at Delhi	Calcutta	Chennai
1984—85	3.85	2.19	0.38	0.34
1989—90	5.90	3.23	0.61	0.61
1994—95+	8.30	4.73	1.00	0.88
2000 AD+	11.10	6.34	1.46	1.58

+Estimated

Table 2.17 Details of Domestic Passenger Traffic to and from Mumbai, Delhi, Calcutta and Chennai Airport

Year	Passenger Traffic (Millions)			
	Mumbai	I.G.I. Airport at Delhi	Netaji Subhash Chandra Bose Airport Calcutta	Chennai (Madras)
1984—85	3.74	2.70	1.47	1.1
1989—90	6.30	4.50	2.60	1.97
1994—95+	9.70	7.00	4.20	3.03
2000 AD+	14.00	10.80	6.17	4.66

+Estimated

Table 2.18 Details of International Cargo Traffic to and from Mumbai, Delhi, Calcutta and Chennai Airports

Year	Cargo Traffic (Lakh tons)			
	Mumbai	I.G.I. Delhi	N.S.C. Bose Airport Calcutta	Chennai
1984—85	1.23	0.71	0.08	0.20
1989—90	2.17	1.43	0.10	0.32
1994—95+	4.01	2.52	0.13	0.51
2000 AD+	7.30	4.44	0.17	0.76

+Estimated

Table 2.19 Details of Development Plans of the Four International Airports

(Rs. in crores)

Name of Project/Work	Estimated Cost	Provision in 7th Five Year Plan	Schedule for Completion		8th Five Year Plan	9th Five Year Plan
			Start	Completion		
1	2	3	4	5	6	7
(A) NEW TERMINAL PROJECTS						
Mumbai						
1. New International Terminal Complex Phase-III at Mumbai Airport	39.02	40.00	April 86	March 90		
2. Expansion of Domestic Terminal Complex at Mumbai Airport	9.70	10.00	Sept. 86	Sept. 88		
3. Tunnel joining Terminal I & II at Mumbai Airport	9.70	9.00	Jan. 86	March 88		

Table 2.19 (Cont:) Details of Development Plans of the Four International Airports

1	2	3	4	5	6	7
Delhi						
1. International Terminal complex Phase-II at IGI Airport	80.00	30.00	Jan. 88		50.00	
2. Domestic Terminal Complex at IGI Airport	80.00	4.00	Jan. 90		76.00	
3. Domestic Terminal Complex Phase-II at IGI Airport	80.00					80.00
Calcutta						
1. Domestic Terminal Complex at Calcutta Airport	19.51	20.00	Jan. 86	March 90		
2. Domestic Terminal Complex Phase-II at Calcutta Airport	19.51				20.00	
Chennai						
1. New International Terminal Complex at Chennai Airport	9.84	8.00	March 86	April 89		

Table 2.19 (Cont.) Details of Development Plans of the Four International Airport

1	2	3	4	5	6	7
(B) CARGO WORKS						
1. Construction of Foreign airlines Cargo Complex at Mumbai Airport	2.13	1.12	Sept. 87		1.01	
2. Expansion of Import/Export Cargo Complex at Mumbai Airport	0.30	0.30	April 85	March 87		
3. International Cargo Terminal Building at I.G.I. Delhi Airport	3.00	0.25	April 89			
4. Cargo Complex Expansion at Chennai Airport	1.25	1.25	April 87	Sept. 89		
(C) RUNWAYS & TAXIWAYS						
1. Extension of Runway 14-32 on 32 end by 150 m at Mumbai Airport	1.40	1.00	April 87	Sept. 89		
2. Parallel Taxi Track for Runway 09-27 at Mumbai Airport	1.80	1 80	April 87	Sept. 89		

Table 2.19 (Cont.) Details of Development Plans of the Four International Airports

1	2	3	4	5	6	7
3. Strengthening of Secondary Runway at N.S.C. Bose Airport	0.90	0.90	Work already completed			
4. Strengthening of 12/30 Runway including 7.5 m Wide Shoulders at Chennai Airport	3.00	3.00	Work completed			
5. Extension of Secondary Runway at Calcutta Airport	1.5				1.5	
6. Extension of Secondary Runway at Chennai Airport by 150 m	0.35	0.35	April 87	Jan. 88		
7. Extension of Secondary Runway at Chennai by Additional 150 m	0.50				0.50	
8. Extension of Main Runway at Chennai Airport	2.00				2 00	

Table 2.19 (Cont.) Details of Development Plans of the Four International Airports

1	2	3	4	5	6	7
(D) New Airport for Bombay— Acquisition of Land and Development					500.00	1000.00
(E) Providing Centre Line Taxi Lights on all Taxi Tracks						
I.G.I. Delhi Airport	2.5				2.5	
Mumbai Airport	1.5					1.5
N.S.C. Bose Airport Calcutta	1.0					1.0
Chennai Airport	0.7					0.7
TOTAL COST :	371 11	131.00			653.5	1083 2

Note : All estimated costs are approximate and are at price level of 1986.

Table 2.20 Proposed Development Programme upto Year 2000 on the Airports for International Operations

Sl. No.	Name of Station	Technical Complex	Development of Pavements	Development of Terminal Complex	Baggage Handling System	Improvement of Access System	Augmentation of Water and Power Supply
1.	Amritsar	—	4.50	1.50	0.50	0.35	0.25
2.	Ahmedabad	—	5.50	1 75	0.35	0.25	0.35
3.	Nagpur	—	4.75	4.50	0.40	0.25	0.25
4.	Hyderabad	—	2.50	6 50	0.45	0.35	0.25
5.	Trivandrum	—	3.25	0.50	0.15	0.15	0.20
6.	Trichy	—	4.50	3.50	0.30	0.20	0.35
7.	Patna	—	2 75	1.85	0.25	0.30	0.25
8.	Varanasi	—	4.50	2 50	0.25	0.15	0.25
9.	Goa	—	3.15	2.50	0.35	0.30	0.25
10.	Bangalore	—	1.50	1.75	0.25	0.35	0.15
11.	Chennai	15	—	—	—	—	—
12.	Mumbai	15	—	—	—	—	—
	TOTAL :	30	36.90	26 85	3.25	2.65	2.55

Grand Total : 105.00 Crores + 40 Crores on Land Acquisition wherever required (Tentative)

Provision of Passenger Amenities like PA System, CCTV System, Operational—Flight Information System at all Airports ... ... Rs. 5 Crores

Provision of Operational Vehicles for all Airports ... Rs. 10 Crorse

Table 2.21 Proposed Development Programme upto Year 2000 on the Airports for Domestic Operations

(Rs. in crore)

S. No.	Name of Station	Development of Pavement	Development of Terminal Complex	Baggage Handling System	Improvement of Access System	Implementation of Water & Power Supply
1.	Srinagar	1.5	3.5	0.50	0.55	0.35
2.	Jammu	2.5	2.75	0.50	0.35	0.25
3.	Chandigarh	2.75	2.25	0.45	0.45	0.35
4.	Jaipur	5.50	4.50	0.55	0.50	0.35
5.	Jodhpur	0.75	2.25	0.35	0.45	0.25
6.	Udaipur	2.75	2.50	0.40	0.40	0.30
7.	Lucknow	5.25	3.50	0.45	0.35	0.30
8.	Bhopal	2.50	1.75	0.35	0.45	0.30
9.	Khajuraho	3.25	1.75	0.35	0.40	0.25
10.	Agra	1.25	2.50	0.25	0.45	0.20
11.	Kanpur (Chakeri)	3.50	2.75	0.45	0.35	0.25
12.	Guwahati	1.75	3.50	0.50	0.45	0.30
13.	Agartala	2.50	2.55	0.45	0.35	0.25
14.	Silchar	3.50	3.50	3.35	0.55	0.25
15.	Bhubaneshwar	3:75	2.50	0.45	0.50	0.35
16.	Bagdogra	3.50	3.75	0.55	0.50	0.35
17.	North Lakhimpur	3.75	2.15	0.45	0.55	0.25
18.	Porbandar	4.25	2.53	0.55	0.55	0.35
19.	Keshod	3.75	2.25	0.35	0.45	0.35
20.	Belgaum	3.75	2.25	0.45	0.50	0.30
21.	Nasik	3.00	2.25	0.45	0.35	0.25
22.	Pune	2.50	3.75	0.45	0.60	0.45
23.	Jamnagar	3.75	2.75	0.45	0.45	0.35
24.	Coimbatore	6.50	3.75	0.55	0.65	0.25
25.	Cochin	5.50	2.75	0.45	0.65	0.35
26.	Bangalore	8.85	3.75	0.45	0.65	0.45
27.	Tirupati	4.75	2.75	0.45	0.50	0.30
28.	Vijayawada	4.50	2.75	0.45	0.55	0.45
	Total	101.00	79.45	12.30	13.50	8.75
	Grand Total .	215.00 Crores				

Note : These are the tentative cost estimates worked out on the basis of 1986-87 cost index.

For Vayudoot operation about 25 crores will be needed for development of airports.

Table 2.22 Estimating Phasing of Projects Expenditure For Bombay Airport

Existing Facilities			Facilities Proposed	1986–1990 Cost in Lakhs	1990–1995 Cost in Lakhs
Communication,	Navigational	Radar facilities			
VHF-9	NDB	ATIS	UHF/Microwave Link Between		
ER VHF-3	VOR/DME	VOLMET	1. Airport and City P & T	20	
HFR 1-12	VDF, ARSR	FC 10, FC 12	2. Airport Remote Rxs and Transmitting station	40	
	ASR/PAR, SSR	FC 13, W/T-5	3. Automatic Trunk Switching for DSC	3	
	ILS/DME	RTT-2, LTT-2	4. Dedicated Satellite Earth Station	90	
		SATELLITE	5. SSB Mode on FC-10, FC-12, FC-13	24	
		TELE-TYPE-5	6. Cat. II ILS with DME – 2 Nos. (09 and 14 Runways)	296	33
		SATELLITE	7. TVO (Holding, Approach, entry TMA)-7 Nos	350	
		TELEPHONEY-2	8. SSR (Mode-S) - 2 Nos.	940	470
			9. 40 NM Radar	320	150
			10. ASDE	400	200
			11. FDPS	150	75
			12. RDPS	150	75
			13. OIDS	40	20
			14. VCCESS with EPAX	50	25
			15. Speed Recorders (38 Chnls) 2 Nos.	48	
			16. Enroute HFRT, SSB Mode on RDARA	8	

Table 2.23 Operating Statistics for Indian Agriculture Operators During 1993-94

Operator	Aircraft Type	No	Hours Flown (No.)	Agricultural Area Covered	Revenue Earned (Rs.)
Agricultural Aviation	BELL 47G-5	2	735	82,395	5,292,353
U.B. Air	BEL 47G-5	2	21	3,334	4,34,000
Maneckji Aviation	BELL 47G-5	1	No	Operation	
Agro Avn. Division	Basant	3	No	Operation	
Vayudoot	Beaver Chetak				
Air Works India			No	Operation	
M.S. Bharat Air	BELL 47G-5	2	No	Operation	
P.L. Finance			No	Operation	
Pushpaka Aviation			No	Operation	
Punjab Co-Operative Ltd.			No	Operation	
Total			756	85,729	5,726,353

Source (i) Monthly Agriculture Operators Statistics furnished by Operators
(ii) Air Transport Statistics for 1993-94. DGCA, New Delhi, Dec 1995

Table 2.24 Monthly Non - Scheduled Operations by Pawan Hans Ltd. During 1993-94

(Revenue in Lakh Rs.)

Month	No. of Aircraft as on		Hours Flown	Revenue Earned
	1st April	31st March		
1990-91	13	21	14,007	4,920
1991-92	16	18	17,194	6,098
1992-93	17	19	16,296	8,449
1993-94	17	18	18,276	9,273
April	17		1,488	743
May	22		1,605	795
June	19		1,387	729
July	20		1,483	759
August	18		1,490	763
September	20		1,465	758
October	20		1,578	799
November	20		1,529	777
December	20		1,611	809
January	20		1,579	798
February	20		1,520	764
March	18		1,541	779

Source (i) Monthly Return on Non-Scheduled Traffic/Revenue furnished by Pawan Hans

(ii) Air Transport Statistics for 1993-94, DGCA, New Delhi, December 1995.

Table 2.25 Traffic Carried by Non-Scheduled Operators Excluding Pawan Hans Ltd During 1993-94

Sl. No.	Operator	Flown Hours	Flown Kms	Passengers
1.	Air Survey Co. of India	426	106,762	0
2.	Kudremukh Iron Ore Co. Ltd.	252	39,024	540
3.	Air Works	......No	Operations......	
4.	Aviation Co-op Society Ltd.	......No	Operations......	
5.	Aparna Aviation	...... No	Operations.. —	
6.	Bharat Air	......No	Operations......	
7.	Cama Aviation	...... No	Operations......	
8.	Delhi Gulf Airways Services	.. No	Operations......	
9.	Raymond Woolen Mills Ltd.	..... No	Operations	
	Total	678	145,786	540

Source (i) Monthly Traffic Returns furnished by Non-Scheduled Operators.

(ii) Air Transport statistics for 1993-94, DGCA New Delhi December 1995.

Table 2.26 Fleet of Non-Scheduled Operators Including Agriculture Operators

(As on 31st March '94)

Sl. No.	Name of the Operator	No. of A/C	Type of Aircraft
1.	Agricultural Aviation	1	Bell 47/G-2
2.	Ahmedabad Aviation Academy	1	Cessna-152
3.	Air India Charters	n.a.	
4.	Aparna Aviation	1	Maula-5
5.	Air Survey Co. of .ndia	1	Cessna 320-A
6.	Air Works India Engg.	1	DC-3
		1	Cessna-172
7.	Aviator's Coop. Society	1	Bonanza A-35
8.	Bharat Air	2 (H)	Bell 47G-5
9.	Birmi Flying Academy	1	Piper Seneca 2
10.	Delhi Gulf Airways	1 (H)	Ecuriel AS-350 B
		1 (H)	Alouette III
11.	Hindustan Inst. of Engg. Tech.	1	Cessna 172 L
12.	Indamer	1	Beechcraft King Air C-90
13.	Indira Gandhi Rashtriya Udan Academy	7	Trinidad TB 20
		2	King Air
		1	Robinson
14.	Indian Airlines	n.a.	
15.	J K Industries	1	DC-3
16.	Kudremukh Ore & Iron Co.	1 (H)	Chetak
			Aloutte III
17.	Mesco Airline	2 (H)	Hiller UH 12 E
18.	Mithila Motors	1	Cessna 180
19.	Pawan Hans	24	Daufin(19),Mi-8(3) R-44(1),Bell 206(1)
20.	Raymonds Woollen Mills	1	DC-3
21.	Udan Research & Flying Instt.	1	Cessna 152
		2	Cessna 172
22.	U.B Air	1 (H)	Bell 47 G-5
23.	Vayudoot	n a.	
		(H)	Helicopter

Source (i) AT-I Section DGCA
(ii) Air Transport Statistics for 1993-94 DGCA New Delhi, December 1995.

PROBLEMS

1. Discuss in brief the growth of National Airlines in India.
2. Explain in brief the aspects involved in the Indian Airlines forecasts and requirement for 2000-2001 A.D.
3. Discuss the growth of International Traffic and Air India's performance with respect to international air services and air cargo facilities.
4. Explain in brief the growth of domestic air traffic in India.
5. Compare the fleet requirement in respect of Indian Airlines, Air India and Vayudoot.
6. Discuss in detail the following with respect to the growth of civil aviation in India :
   - (i) Technological development
   - (ii) Infrastructural development
   - (iii) Institutional development for planning
   - (iv) Manpower development.
7. Compare the facilities, services provided and future requirement of different airports with respect to :
   - (i) International passenger traffic
   - (ii) Domestic passenger traffic
   - (iii) Cargo traffic
   - (iv) Runways, taxiways, apron and other facilities at airports.

A2.1 PARTICULARS AND CHARACTERISTICS OF SOME AIRCRAFTS IN INDIA AND ABROAD

HALHT—2. It is the first Indian powered aircraft of indigenous design. It currently serves with the Indian Air Force, Naval Aviation and Indian Civil Aviation. The first prototype of the HT-2 was flown on August 13, 1951. An entirely redesigned second prototype flew on February 19, 1952. By mid of 1961, about 160 such planes were manufactured. Twelve of these were supplied to the Ghana Air Force and one as a gift to the Indonesian Airforce. Four more of these were built in 1963, followed by six in 1964. The HT-2 equips several of the seven Indian Air Force auxillary quadrons and is of all metal construction with full night and blind flying equipment. It has the following characteristics :

H.P. = 155, Four-cylinder air-cooled engine, Cruising speed 185 kph (115 mph), Initial climb 250 m/min (800 ft./min), Empty weight 715 kg (1540 lbs), Maximum loaded weight 1020 kg (2240 lbs) Wing span 10.5 m (35 ft), Length 7.40 m (24 ft. 3.5 in), Height 2.67 m (8 ft 11 in).

HAL HUL—26 Pushpak. It flew for the first time on September 28, 1958. It is in production since 1969 and about 100 have been delivered by the beginning of 1965. The Pushpak is of the conventional onstruction. The wings have metal spars and ribs. The fuselage is a welded steel tube structure, the whole being covered by fabric. Most of these aircrafts have been placed in service with Indian Flying Clubs. It has the following characteristics :

H.P. = 95, Four-cylinder air-cooled engine, Cruising speed 112 kph (70 mph), Initial climb 150 m/min (500 ft/min), Empty weight 395 kg (870 lbs), Maximum loaded weight 615 kg (135· lbs), Wing span 10.8 m (36 ft), Length 6.3 m (21ft), Height 2.75 m (2 ft. 1 in).

HAL HAOP—27 Krishak. It was flown for the first time in November, 1959. Employing essentially the same wing as of the Pushpak. The Krishak is readily adaptable for the agricultural spraying and dusting, and air ambulance roles. It has the following characteristics.

H.P. = 225, Six-cylinder air-cooled engine, Cruising speed 211 kph (132 mph). Empty weight 895 kg (1970 lbs), Loaded weight 1270 kg (2800 lbs). Wing span 11.25 m (37 ft 6 in), Length 5.92 m (19 ft 9 5 in). Height 3.22 m (10 ft 9.5 in).

HAL HF—24 Marut MK—1. It is the first Indian jet combat aircraft of indigenous design and was first flown on June 17, 1961. It is a multi-purpose fighter and can carry 1820 kg (4000 lbs) offensive load externally. It has the following characteristics :

Maximum speed 1130 kph (750 mph) at sea level, Empty weight 6150 kg 13,520 lbs). Loaded weight 8820 kg (19,450 lbs), Wing span 8.85 m (29 ft 6.3 in), Length 15.47 m (51 ft 7.3 in), Height 3.92 m (13 ft 1.5 in).

HAL HJT—16 Kiran The Kiran was designed to succeed vampire trainer and was first flown on September 4, 1369. It is provided with turbo jet engine. It has the following characteristics :

Cruising speed 775 kph (485 mph). Initial climb 1432 m/min (4774 ft/min), Time to fly 9000 m (30,000 ft) is 10 min, Loaded weight 3400 kg (7496 lbs), Wing span 10 5 m (35 ft), Length 10.42 m (34 ft 9.3 in). Height 3.55 m (11 ft 10.75 in).

MMPL—II Kanpur II. The Kanpur four seat light cabin monoplane was designed primarily for air observation post duties by Air-Marshal Harjinder Singh and two proto types have been built at the Indian Air Force's Maintenance Command Development Centre at Kanpur where aircraft are manufactured for IAF service. The first prototype having a horse power of 180, was flown in 1960 and this was followed in October 1961 by MMPL-II Kanpur II with a 250 H.P. The fuselage accommodates a Pilot and three passengers or one casualty stretcher and a medical attendent.

AVRO—748. It is manufactured in HAL Kanpur and is used in Indian Air Force. It has payload of 5600 kg (12,400 lbs) and cruising speed of the order of 400 kph (250 mph).

HF—24. It is manufactured in Kanpur. It is the first supersonic aircraft manufactured in India for military use. It has a speed of about 1150 kph (720 mph).

GANTS. These are also for Indian Air Force and are manufactured at Bangalore. It has a maximum speed of about 1300 kph (800 mph). It is considered to be one of the most efficient intercepter in Indian army. It proved very effective in Pakistan aggression in 1965.

MIG—21. A single seat, day point defence intercepter served with the Soviet Air Force and the air arms of most of Russian satellites. It has been delivered to Cuba, Egypt, Finland, Indonesia, Iraq and Yugoslavia. It is manufactured under licence in India. It is at present, the most versatile fighter bombar that the Indian Air Force possesses. At the time of Pakistan aggression, there was only one squadron of the Migs and hence it could not be tested in the combat Indian skies. It has the following characteristics :

Maximum horse power 12.500, Maximum speed 2110 kph (1320 mph), Combat radius 600 kph (375 miles), Maximum weight 9300 kg (20,00 lbs), Wing span 7.5 m (25 ft), Length 14 m (47 ft).

BOEING 707—320. The model 707 is the first U.S. Jet transport and it flew for the first time on July 15, 1954. The model 707-320 was the first true international version of the basic model 707 design, and while it retained the fuselage cross-section of earlier version. overall length was increased by 2.4 m (8ft) and wing span increased by 3.6 m (12 ft). The first 707-320 flew on January 11, 1959. It was introduced in service on August 26, 1959 in U.S.A. Operators include Air France, Air India, American Airlines, etc. It has the following characteristics :

Turbo jet engine, Maximum speed over 960 kph (600 mph), Empty weight 62,500 kg (137,530 lbs), Maximum loaded weight 150,000 kg (328,000 lbs), Passengers upto 189, Range over 9600 kms (6000 miles). Wing span 43.7 m (145 ft 9 in), Length 45.6 m (152 ft 11 in), Height 12 75 m (42 ft 6 in).

BOEING 707—420. It provides accommodation for 110 to 189 passengers and first flew on May 20, 1959, entering service in March 1960, becoming the first U.S. turbo fan powered airliner to operate over commercial routes. It has the following characteristics :

Maximum speed over 960 kph (600 mph), Empty weight 60000 kg (132,000 lbs), Maximum weight 142,000 kg (312,000 lbs), Height 12.75 m (42 ft 6 in), Wing span 43.7 m (142 ft. 5 in), Length 45.6 m (152 ft 11 in).

Boeing 727. It is designed for short to medium haul transport and was flown for the first time on February 9, 1963. U,S. airline inaugurated its service on February 6, 1964. It is known for its rapidity. It has the following characteristics.

Maximum speed over 960 kph (600 mph), Empty weight 36,700 kg (80,602 lbs), Maximum loaded weight 73,000 kg (161,000 lbs), Passengers upto 131. Range over 4800 km (3000 mile), Wing span 32.4 m (108 ft), Length 39.95 m (138 ft 2 in) Height 10.2 m (34 ft).

Douglas DC—3. The prototype DC-3 flew for the first time in U.S.A. in December 22, 1935. In its initial form it was powered by 1000 H.P. In its present form, it has the following characteristics :

H P. =1200, Maximum speed 345 kph (215 mph). Empty weight 8100 kg (17,720 lbs). Loaded weight 12.200 kg (26,900 lbs), Wing span 28.5 m (95 ft). Height 5.10 m (16 ft 11.5 in), Length 19.35 m (64 ft 6 in).

Douglas DC—4. The DC-4 was originally designed in cooperation with five U.S. airlines, the prototype flying in June, 1938, More than 260 DC-4s are in commercial service is being registered in the U.S.A. Out of which 58 are active. It has the following characteristics :

Maximum speed 448 kph at 5070 m (280 mph at 16,900 ft), Initial climb 264 m/min (880 ft/min), Range 2688 km (1680 miles). Empty weight 18,560 kg (40,806 lbs), Loaded weight 33.200 kg (73,000 lbs), Wing span 32.25 m (117 ft 6 in), Length 28 17 m (93 ft 11 in), Height 8 25 m (27 ft 6.25 in).

Caravalle. The Caravalle, which is manufactured in France first flew on May 7, 1955, There are several modifications of the basic caravalle series. The characteristics given below refer to Caravalle VI-R :

Maximum cruising speed =840 kph at 7500 m (525 mph at 25,000 ft), Empty weight 26,000 kg (57,484 lbs), Maximum weight 50,000 kg (110,230 lbs), Wing span 33.75 m (112 ft 6 in), Length 31.5 m (105 ft), Height 8.57 m (28 ft 7 in)

Fokker F-27 Friendship. It is manufactured in Netherlands and it first flew on November 24, 1955. It has following characteristics :

Normal cruising speed 472 kph at 6000 m (295 mph at 20,000 ft), Empty weight 10.500 kg (23.096 lbs). Maximum loaded weight 19.000 kg (42 000 lbs), Wing span 18 55 m (95 ft 2 in) Length 22.72 m (75 ft 9 in), Height 8.25 m (27 ft 6 in).

Boeing 737-200. It was first flown on August 8, 1967 First delivery was made to United Airlines in December 29, 1967. It has the following characteristics :

Maximum cruising speed 810 kph (506 mph) at 780 m (2600 ft), Range with maximum pay load of 31321 lbs is 3328 kms (2080 mile), passengers capacity is 113 and 6 abreast sitting Wing span 27.9 m (93 ft), length 30 m (100 ft) height 11.1 m (37 ft).

Boeing 747. It is also known as *Jumbo jet*. This U.S. Jet transport flew for the first time in December 1968. The special features of this transport carrier are the higher gross weight, increased passengers capacity longer wing span, longer length and greater height. It is shown in Figure 2 7. It has the following characteristics :

Maximum speed over 960 kph (600 mph). Gross weight 310.000 kg (680,000 lbs) Passenger upto, 490, Range over 9600 km (6000 miles), Wing span 53 7 m (165 ft 8 in), Length 68.17 m (227 ft 3 in), Height 16 m (63 ft 5 in).

Emperor Ashoka. Air India's first Boeing-747 touched down at Santa Cruz airport at 8.23 AM on April 18, 1971. The 747-B is a 352,280 kg (775,0(00 lbs) gross weight passenger plane that is able to carry 347 passenger load more than 10,560 km (6,600 miles) non stop. The plane cruises at 1000 kmph (625 mph). One steps into the Spacious Age in air travel on boarding through one of its ten wide doors. There are two broad aisles in a cabin 6 m (20 ft) wide and 2.4 m (8 ft) long. In economy as well as in first class sections, the seats are extra comfortable and there is plenty of room around and above.

SST B 2707. U.S. Boeing Supersonic Transport (SST). It may travel with a speed which is nearly 3 times the speed of sound. The characteristics of this supersonic transport are as follows :

Maximum speed 2880 kph (1830 mph), Gross weight 307,000 kg (675,000 lbs), Passengers capacity upto 350, Range over 6400 kms (4000 miles), Wing span 32.2 m sweep, 53.1 m extended (107 ft sweep, 177 ft extended), Length 91.8 m (306 ft), Height 14.4 m (48 ft).

B 747-400 Aircraft "KONARK"

Air India has embarked upon a major fleet renewal and modernisation plan to prepare itself for an intensely competitive aviation market of the 21st century. As part of this plan, the first of the 4 new generation B 747-400 aircraft chirstened "Konark" joins the Air India fleet on August 14, 1993. A major objective of this plan is to bring in 5 million foreign tourists into India in the next 5 years and increase the foreign exchange earnings to Rs. 10,000 crores.

This aircraft incorporates specially designed interiors to reflect a unique Indian ambience and is fitted with state-of-the-art seats and the latest in communication and entertainment equipment. Every cabin of this aircraft has telephone facility so as to have a contact any where in the world, thus naming it to be a truely global aircraft. A special economy section has also been added for the first time to provide additional leg room for seating comfort. This new "Economy Plus" concept would provide Air-India, a major competitive advantage for long-haul economy travel.

The acquisition of this advanced technology aircraft includes the higher seating capacity (407 passengers), non stop distance of about 14000 km, high speed (1.00 kmph), lower crew & operating expenses, lesser loading and unloading time (about 7 minutes) and 25% less fuel consumption. It is powered by four engines, made by Pratt and Whitney and each is capable of providing 24640 kg] . (56000 lbs) of thrust.

A2.2 INVESTMENT FOR AIRPORT AND AIRPORT FACILITIES*

(Rs. in Crores)

Facilities Required	During 1990-95	During 1995-2000
1	2	3
I. TERMINAL COMPLEX		
Mumbai Airport		
(i) III International Module	—	—
(ii) Parallel Taxiways with high speed exit	—	—
(iii) Second Airport for Mumbai	—	—
NSC Bose Airport, Calcutta		
(i) Domestic module I	—	—
(ii) Domestic module II	19.51	—
I.G.I. Delhi Airport		
(i) Domestic Module I	—	—
(ii) Domestic Module II	80.00	—
(iii) International Module II	80.00	—
(iv) II Cargo terminal	3.00	—
Chennai Airport		
(i) New International Terminal		—
(ii) II Domestic Terminal	—	—
Domestic Airport		
(i) R/W extension at Ahmedabad, etc.	101.00	
(ii) Terminal facilities	91.75	
(iii) Cargo facilities	12.30	

*Ref : PGCA Working Group, 1986

A2.2 (Cont.) **Investment for Airport and Airport Facilities**

1	2	3
2. *NAVIGATION/APPROACH AIDS*		
(i) Installation of ILS at domestic airports and R/W 09 at Mumbai and R/W 10 at I.G.I. airport Delhi	10.36	11.84
(ii) Microwave Landing System	—	8.00
(iii) Vorsdem's, TVOR'S, DVOR's	18.21	5.39
(iv) Runway/approach lighting system VASIS/PAPI	28.30	10.80
3. *COMMUNICATION FACILITIES*		
(i) VHF coverage throughout India	0.25	—
(ii) Replacement of VHF equipment	6.34	—
(iii) HFSSB on domestic route	0.25	—
(iv) Automatic message switching system and data links	—	—
(v) Satellite Earth's Stations	3.60	9.00
(vi) VHF/Microwave links between Airport and city centres	3.40	—
(vii) MAS (WT) circuits to be upgraded to LTT circuits	1.21	—
(viii) Automatic, Trunk Switching DSC/ATS circuits	0.18	—
(ix) Voice Controlled Communication Switching System	4.55	—
(x) Electronic Intercom and Telephone Exchanges	2.20	—
(xi) Speech Recorders	3.96	—
(xii) ATIS broadcasting facility	1.00	—

A2.2 (Cont.) **Investment for Airport and Airport Facilities**

1	2	3
4. AIR TRAFFIC SERVICE		
(i) SSR coverage	61.10	—
(ii) Automation of ATC and Technical Blocks	15.00	—
(iii) Terminal area radars and air route surveillance radars	166.80	—
(iv) Digital VDF equipment	1.05	1.50
(v) Meteorological Facilities	23.81	23.13
(vi) Rescue and fire fighting equipment first aid	8.70	1.00
5. GENERAL		
(i) Modernisation of Civil Aviation Training Centre and Regional Training Centres	6 00	6.00
(ii) Computerisation of inventory control and system engineering management	—	—
(iii) Test equipment	42.00	—
(iv) Regional maintenance centre	2.40	—
Total expenditure	798.29	81.00

3

AIRCRAFT CHARACTERISTICS

3.1 GENERAL

Any machine which finds its support in the atmosphere due to reactions of the air is defined as an aircraft. It can be heavier or lighter than air and may be power or non-power driven. For example, airships are lighter than air and are power driven. Balloons are also lighter than air but are non power driven. Aeroplanes and helicopters are also heavier than air but are power driven. The land airplane is the most practical type of machine to navigate in the air and thousands of them are in daily use. They are designed to take off and land on runways with much steeper angles than the helicopters. The helicopter can rise vertically off the ground and can also hover stationary in the air. Unfortunately, such aircrafts have inferior performance as compared to the normal types of airplanes as their load capacity is extremely small and their top speed is very low. Helicopters are further discussed in Chapter 15.

Airplanes can also be designed to operate on water. Typical *floatplane* is shown in Figure 3.1. It is seen from this figure that floatplane has long pontoon floats on which it rests when it is on water. Sometimes these machines are constructed as *amphibians* which means that they have wheels as well as

Figure 3.1 Typical Floatplane

floats and, therefore, can alight on either land or water without alteration. This has been accomplished in most cases by arranging the wheels inside the floats, so that they can be drawn up inside the floats while landing on water.

3.2 RELATION BETWEEN AIRCRAFT AND AIRPORTS

Aircraft and airports are dependent on each other in providing a service for the passenger in conventional air transport system. In the past, the system evolved largely with separate planning of the airport, the route structuring and the aircraft technology. With the advancement in technology, the major factor in the growth of the mode, have been quickly utilized by the airlines in expanding their route structures. Advancement in engine and airframe technology have also been found significant in the reduction of real cost of air travel and at the same time have led to improvements in system performance. The improvement in speed, range, ticket price, comfort, and reliability led to the high growth rates. In addition, the operating costs of the aircraft have continued about 85% of the operating costs of the entire air transport system, the airports contribute 10%, and the remaining 5%, goes for navigation charges and overheads of governmental control. This has resulted in a natural tendency for the airports to accommodate any changes in aircraft design and performance that could maintain the trend to lower the aircraft direct operating cost (DOC). Figure 3.2 shows, how the runway length of a major international airport had to be progressively increased to keep ahead of aircraft field length requirements.

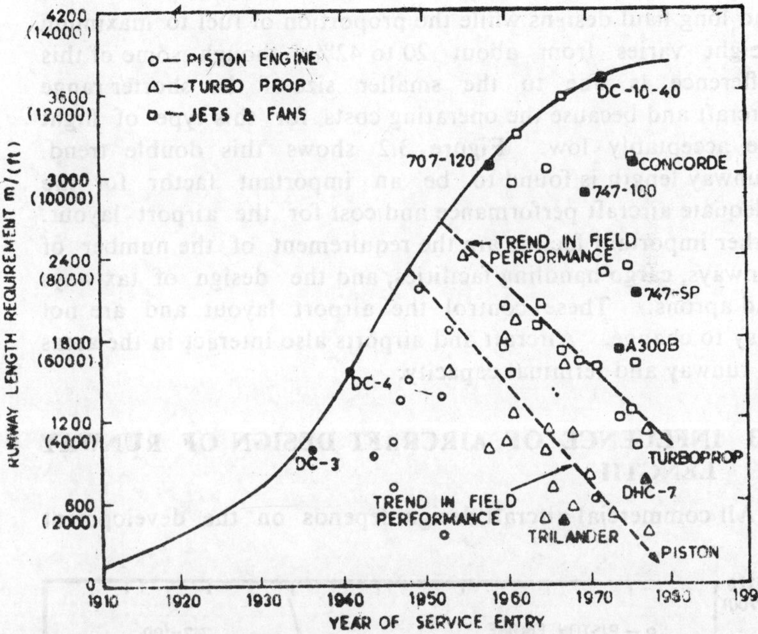

Figure 3.2 Trends in Runway Length Requirement for Different Type of Aircrafts

The trend of allowing aircraft DOC was broken by several factors because the design dominates to the air transport system. Primarily in the neighbourhood of the airport, environmental considerations are causing compromises between aircraft design and airport location. Increase in the land acquisition values and construction costs led to the rise in the total capital costs of the system. It becomes unreasonable for aircraft designers to call for increase of runway length on a massive scale. The short range aircraft needs lesser runway length than the long range type, since there is a smaller fuel requirement. In addition, advances in the technology of producing of high lift for takeoff and landing allow a further reduction in the runway requirement without too much penalty in DOC. Therefore, the pressures from the airport to reduce runway length requirements can be met out by the aircraft operator. At the same time, the growth in runway length for long range operations has leveled off as new demands for increased range no longer appear. The proportion of empty to maximum weight varies from 63 to 49%, between short and long haul designs while the proportion of fuel to maximum weight varies from about 20 to 42%, though some of this difference is due to the smaller size of the shorter range aircraft and because the operating costs for this type of flight are acceptably low. Figure 3.2 shows this double trend. Runway length is found to be an important factor for the adequate aircraft performance and cost for the airport layout. Other important factors are the requirement of the number of runways, cargo handling facilities, and the design of taxiways and aprons. These control the airport layout and are not easy to change. Aircraft and airports also interact in the areas of runway and terminal capacity.

3.3 INFLUENCE OF AIRCRAFT DESIGN OF RUNWAY LENGTH

All commercial aircraft design depends on the development

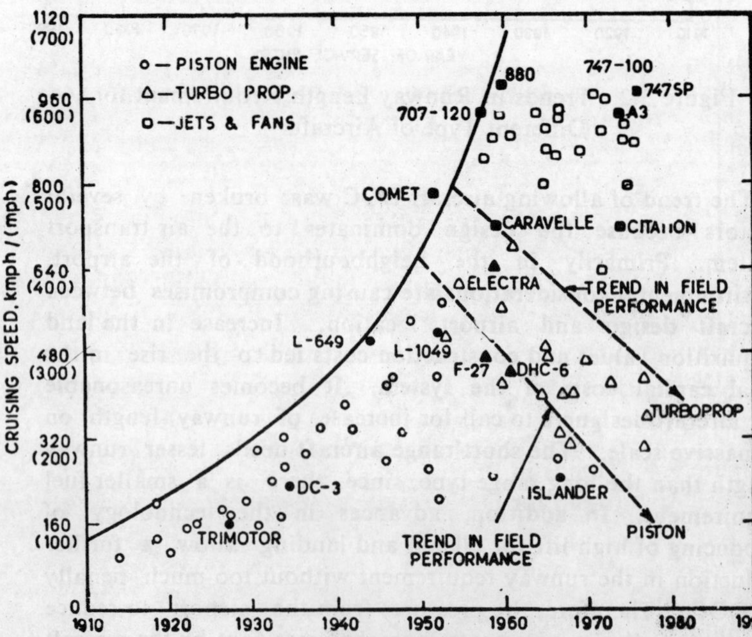

Figure 3.3 Trends in Cruising Speeds for Different Type of Aircrafts

of propulsion systems and the application of aerodynamic theory. The above advances led to the full use of propulsive improvements. In particular, speed capability has increased as shown in Figure 3.3. The combination of improvements in speed and absolute size has resulted in the upward trend in seat km (mile) per hour productivity as shown in Figure 3.4. This trend is also reflected in seat km (mile) per gallon because of advances in engine fuel efficiency with the exception of the early pure jets. All these effects combined with economics of scale led to the reduction in real costs per tonne kilometer. At the time of the design of wing of Doughlas

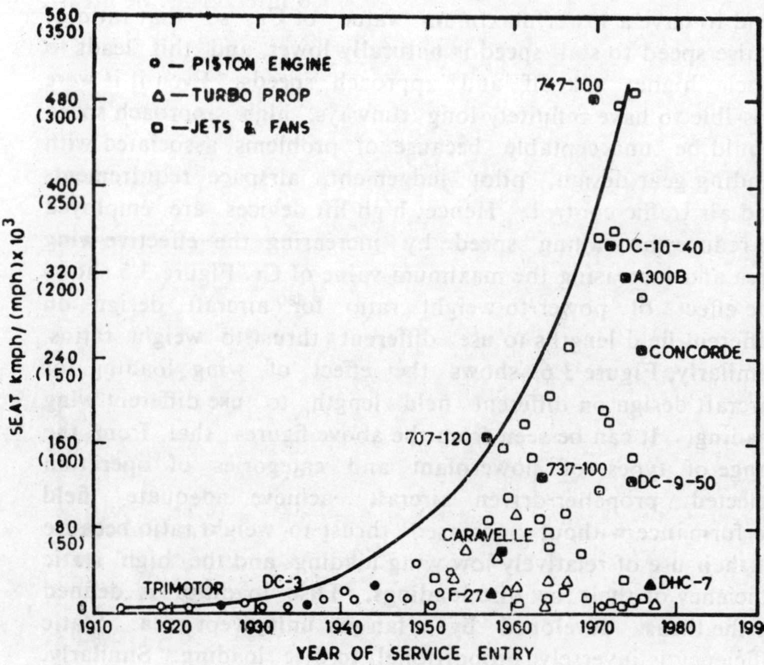

Figure 3.4 Trends in Productivity on Passenger Seat kmph (mph) for Different Type of Aircrafts

DC-3, economical cruising flight also allowed a reasonable short field length because the aircraft could sustain at a quite low speed.

$$\text{lift} = \text{weight} \backsim \rho V^2 S C_L \qquad (3.1)$$

where ρ = air density, kg/m^3

V = forward speed of the aircraft, kmph

S = area of the wing, m^2

C_L = nondimensional coefficient of lift which is approximately proportional to the angle of attack of the wing.

$$\text{or} \quad \frac{W}{S} \; (= \text{wing loading}) \sim \rho V^2 C_L \tag{3.2}$$

where W = aircraft weight

At a given value of C_L, higher speeds allow a smaller wing and lower weight and drag. Unfortunately, high speed wings tend to have a lower maximum value of C_L, so that ratio of cruise speed to stall speed is naturally lower, and this leads to much higher takeoff and approach speeds. Even if it were possible to have infinitely long runways, high approach speed would be unacceptable because of problems associated with landing gear design, pilot judgement, airspace requirements and air traffic control. Hence, high lift devices are employed to reduce the stalling speed by increasing the effective wing area and increasing the maximum value of C_L. Figure 3.5 shows the effect of power-to-weight ratio for aircraft design on different field lengths to use different thrust-to weight ratios. Similarly, Figure 3.6 shows the effect of wing loading for aircraft design on different field length to use different wing loading. It can be seen from the above figures that from the range of types of powerplant and categories of operation selected, propeller-driven aircraft achieve adequate field performance without increased thrust-to weight ratio because of their use of relatively low wing loadings and the high static efficiency of their low disc loadings. Disc loadings is defined as the thrust developed by a fan per unit swept area. Static efficiency is inversely proportional to disc loading. Similarly, the helicopter achieves vertical takeoff with the same installed power as a light conventional aircraft of the same weight. On the other hand, pure jet aircraft require much higher installed thurst if their takeoff field length is to be reduced substantially, with commensurate reduction in wing loading, or more powerful flaps if the landing field length is to be similarly reduced.

3.4 REQUIREMENTS OF AIRCRAFT TYPES

Above discussion attempts to indicate the interactions that

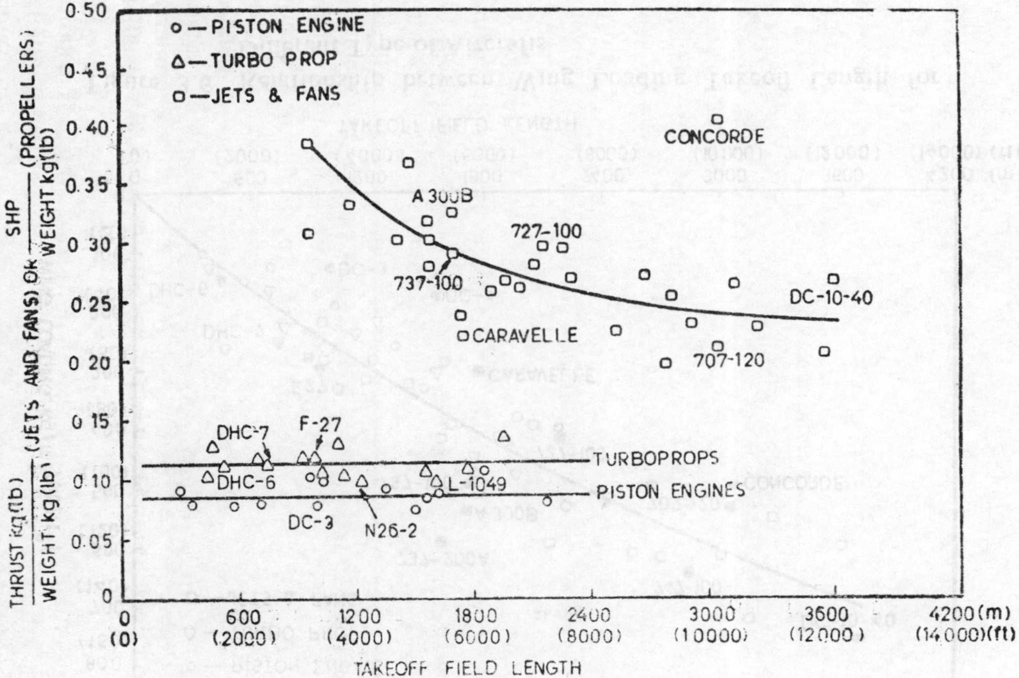

Figure 3.5 Relationship between Power to Weight Ratio and Take off Field Length for Different Type for Aircrafts

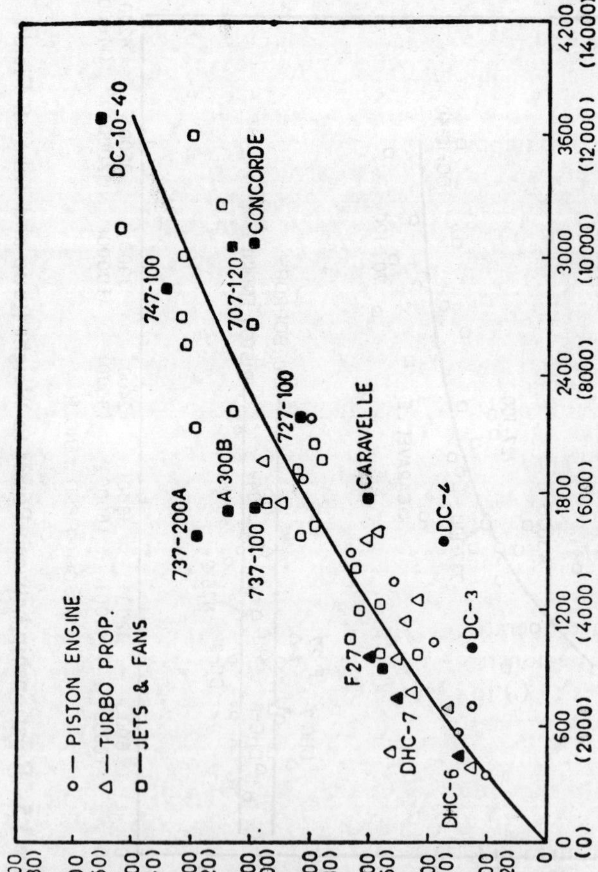

Figure 3.6 Relationship between Wing Loading Takeoff Length for Different Type of Aircrafis

take place in aircraft design between the field length and other factors. Fundamentally, there are three different types of interaction. With long range aircraft, a long takeoff run needs large fuel requirement. Medium and short range aircraft for trunk and local airline operation depends to their cruise performance with the need to use a large number of medium length fields. Aircraft for feeder and general aviation roles normally operate over short ranges where cruise speed is not essential, thus a low wing loading is permissible and can operate with short field lengths without a significant design penalty. Tables 3.1 present the characteristics of a wide range of aircraft. It is important to realize that the speeds, field lengths, weights, and maximum stage lengths given are all for quite specific conditions of operation. Cases of variation from these specific conditions have an important effect on the field length requirements and are discussed in detail in article 3.5

3.5 FIELD LENGTH REGULATIONS

Table 3.1 shows the details of the field length. The field length determined not only on the basis of the aircraft's design capability, but also by the safety regulations made by the responsible bodies. In the United States, the regulating authority is the FAA. The ICAO issues worldwide advisories that are similar in philosophy and content to the FAA regulations. Field length requirements for a given class of aircraft are based on the performance of several critical and rigidly specified operations. In essence, an aircraft type is required to demonstrate the field length required for the following cases : (i) to complete a takeoff to 10.5 m (35 ft) altitude with all engines operating, (ii) to complete a takeoff to 10.5 m (35 ft) altitude with an engine failure at a critical point, (iii) to stop after aborating a takeoff with an engine failure at the same critical point, and (iv) to stop after landing from a height of 15 m (50 ft).

The demonstrations take place under carefully controlled conditions of flying speed, aircraft weight and configuration and airfield altitude and temperature. Safety margins are then added to these demonstrated distances to allow for variation in pilot performance, aircraft performance and environmental conditions in service. The margins are typically 15% in the all-engine-operating takeoff case and 67% in the landing case,

Table 3.1a Aircraft Characteristics of Air Carriers : Powerplant, Dimensions and Number of Passengers

Aircraft Type	Powerplant	Dimensions (ft)						Number of Passengers (Max)
		Span	Length	Height	Turning Radius	Wheel Base	Track	
Intercontinental								
747-200B	4×46,950 lb	195.7	231.3	63.4	146.0	84.0	36.0	500
DC-10	3×50,000 lb	165.3	182.2	58.1	123.9	72.3	35.0	380
Concorde	4×30,850 lb	83.9	203.8	37.9	127.0	59.7	25.3	128
707-320B	4×19,000 lb	145.8	152.8	42.5	—	59.0	22.1	219
Transcontinental								
A300 B4	2×51,000 lb	147.1	175.8	54.3	111.5	61.1	31.1	345
Short haul								
737-200	2×15,500 lb	93.0	100.0	7 0	56.4	37.4	17.3	130
DC-9-50	2×16,000 lb	93.3	125.6	28.0	68.0	56.1	16.4	139
Commuters								
HS-748-2A	2×2,280 eshp	98.5	67.0	24.0	74.0	20.7	24.8	60
F27-503	2×2,140 eshp	95.2	82.3	28.6	65.9	31.6	23.7	56
DHC-7	4×1,174 eshp	93.0	80.3	26.2	62.0	27.5	23.5	54
Nord 262C	2×1,145 eshp	74.1	63.3	20.3	57.0	23.1	10.3	29

1 ft = 0.30 m and 1 lb = 0.454 kg

Table 3.1b Aircraft Characteristics of Air Carrier : Weight, Field Length, Cruise Speed and Payload

Intercontinental	Weight (lb × 1000)			FAR Field Length (ft)		Cruise Speed (knots)	Payload Range ISA, Still Air, No Reserves			
							Range at Max Payload		Max Range Payload	
	Takeoff (max)	Landing	Empty Operating	Takeoff	Landing		(nautical mi)	lb × 1000	(nautical mi)	lb × 1000
Intercontinental										
747-200B	770	564	367.4	10,500	6150	506	4330	159.1	7140	62.6
DC-10-30	555	403	267.3	10,490	5960	499	4390	104.5	6660	47.8
Concorde	400	245	174 8	10,280	8000	1176	4430	28	4480	23 5
707-320B	333 6	247	147.8	10,000	6250	478	5175	53.9	6500	33 3
Transcontinental										
A300 B4	330.7	293.2	191.3	8,740	5950	481	1820	77.6	3400	39.8
Short haul										
737-203a	115.5	103	60	6,550	4290	460	1280	35	2740	21.4
DC-9-50	120	110	65	7,880	4680	465	1275	33	2420	21.4
Commuters										
VFW-614	44	44	27.6	4,000	3600	390	850	9 04	1600	5.44
HS-748-2A	46.5	43	26	5,380	3370	242	1160	12.5	1740	9.0
F27-500	45	42	26.3	5,470	3290	248	825	13 2	2180	5.66
DUC-D7	41	39	24.4	1,800	1,900	238	637	11.1	1740	6 44
Nord 262C	23.8	23	15 9	3,510	1720	211	270	6.78	1280	4 53

1 ft = 0.30 m, 1 lb = 0.454 kg and 1 nautical mi = 12 mi = 19.2 km

Table 3.1c Characteristics of General Aviation Aircraft

Aircraft	Powerplant	Dimensions (ft)			Number of Passengers (max)	Weight (lb × 1000)			FAR Field length (ft)[a]		Cruise Speed (knots)[b]
		Span	Length	Height		Take-off (max)	Landing (max)	Empty Operating	Takeoff	Landing	
HS-125-600 ft	2×3,700 lb	47 0	50.5	17.2	14[c]	25.0	22.0	12.9	5350	2550	441
Citation	2×2 200 lb	43.8	43.5	14.4	6[c]	11.0	11.0	6 35	3275	2300	351
Twin Otte	2×715 eshp	65.0	51.7	18.6	20[c]	12.5	12.5	6.70	1200[d]	1050[d]	165
Merline 3	2×905 eshp	46.3	42.2	16.8	7[c]	12.5	11.5	6.99	3080	2860	275
MU 2K	2×724 eshp	39.2	33.3	12.9	6[c]	9.92	9.44	5.91	1700	1490	318
Cessna 421	2×375 hp	41.9	36.1	11.6	8[e]	7.45	7.45	4 43	2507	2178	235[e]
Piper PA-31 P	2×425 hp	40.8	34.6	13.1	8[e]	7 80	7.80	4.90	2200	2700	244[e]
Cessna 337	2×225 hp	38.0	29.9	9.1	6[a]	4.63	3.63	2.71	1675	1650	170[e]
Cessna 210	1×285 hp	36.9	28.3	9.7	6[a]	3.80	3.80	2.12	1900	1500	164[e]
Cessna 150	1×100 hp	02 7	23.8	8.1	2[a]	1.60	1.60	1.00	1385	1075	102[e]

1 ft = 0.3 m, 1 lb = 0.454 kg

a = refer to sea level, 59°F dry runway and zero wind for worst applicable FAR regulation

b = eost economic true air speed (TAS)

c = plus two crew but sometime may need only one

d = Short Takeoff and Landing (STOL) regulations and

e = include crew, maximum speed.

the difference is due mostly to the extra difficulty of controlling and monitoring an approach compared with the relatively fixed and known conditions on takeoff.

Field length requirements can be used for the following purposes :

(i) Checking the ability of an aircraft to take a specified payload form, or land at a specified airfield in specified environmental conditions.

(ii) Calculating the allowable maximum payload that may be moved under those specific conditions when the payload is limited by available field length.

(iii) Planning and provision of field lengths required at an airport to allow operation of a specific type from that airport to specified destinations on a specified percentage of occasions annually (determined by local environmental history), with a specified percentage of its maximum payload.

The takeoff distances required to be demonstrated for transport category aircraft are presented in Figure 3.7. The speeds to be controlled during the demonstration are described as follows :

V_1 = critical engine failure speed chosen by the aircraft manufactures > V_{me}, < speed at which brakes overload, < V_R.

V_{me} = minimum control speed i.e. speed at which engine failure can occur and still allow straight flight at this speed in fully controlled manner.

V_{LOF} = liftof speed ≥ 1.1 V_{mu} (≥ 1.05 V_{mu} with one engine out)

V_{mu} = minimum unstick speed > minimum speed that gives hazardous characteristics.

V_2 = takeoff climb speed at
10.5 m (35 ft.) ≥ 1.2 V_s, ≥ 1.1. V_{mc}.

V_s = stall speed in takeoff configuration.

V_R = speed at which nosewheel can be lifted from runway.

Within the limits of controllability, rotation speed and brake failure, the first variation V_1 can be chosen by the

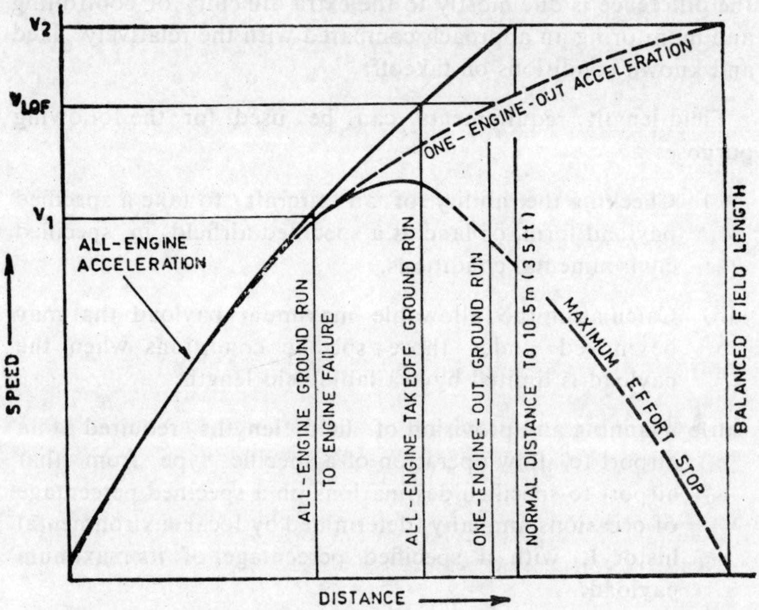

Figure 3.7 Relationship Between Speed and Take off Field Length (Distance) for Different Types of Aircraft

manufacturer. If the engine fails before this speed is reached, the pilot must abort the takeoff. If failure occurs at or above this speed the pilot must continue the takeoff despite the loss of power. When only a normal hard runway is available, the minimum engine-out runway requirement is obtained if V_1 is chosen so that the distance needed to stop is equal to the distance to reach 10.5 m. This is called the balanced field length. The field length in this case is determined as the larger of the balanced field length and 115% of the all-engine distance to a height of 10.5 m.

Turbojet engine have proved to be so reliable that engine failure on takeoff has become very uncommon. This has allowed the introduction of a second variable, namely the ability to substitute stopways and clearways for some portions of the hard runway.

A clear way is defined an area beyond the runway not less than 150 m wide, centrally located about the extended centerline of the runway, and under the control of the airport authorities. The clearway is expressed in terms of a clearway plane, extending from the end of the runway with an upward slope not exceeding 1.25% above which no object nor any portion of the terrain protrudes, except that threshold lights may protrude above the plane if their height above the end of the runway is not greater than 65 cms (26 inches) and if they are located to each side of the runway.

A clearway may not be longer than half the difference between 115% of the distance between the liftoff point and the point at which 10.5 m (35 ft) altitude is reached for an engine-out takeoff A stopway may be used as a substitute only for the part of the accelerate-stop distance that is greater than the full-strength runway requirements determined from clearway allowances. The hard runway must extend for the full length of the takeoff run, defined as the point equidistant between the point at which V_{LOF} is reached and the point at which a height of 10.5 m is attained.

Table 3 1 also shows the takeoff field lengths scheduled in the flight manual ' must be the greater of the demonstrated engine-out accelerate-stop distance. The demonstrated engine-out distance to 14 0 m (35 ft) altitude, or 115% of the demonstrated all-engine distance to 10.5 m altitude. The engine failure speed (V_1) may be chosen by the manufacturer, within the limits shown in Figure 3.7, but the same speed must be used for both the aborted and the continued takeoff.

The flexibility of choice is extended to the pilot faced with a particular runway situation, so that greater the takeoff distance available relative to the emergency stop distance available, the lower he will choose his V_1 speed. Similarly, the airport planner can take advantage of these alternatives. It is frequently advantageous to use a clearway because it saves on full-strength runway without penalizing the operation. Conversely, a high V_1 will give an even shorter full-strength runway requirement at the expense on a long stopway in the engine failure case, but the normal takeoff or landing cases then may become critical from the point of view of the length of full-strength runway.

3.6 RESTRICTIONS ON PAYLOAD - RANGE PERFORMANCE

The field length shown in Table 3.1 refers to maximum

takeoff weight at sea level and 59°F (ISA). Equation 3.1 indicates that lift is proportional to air density. Since, air density falls with increase of either altitude or temperature, either the takeoff and landing speeds must rise which requires a greater field length, or the lift, hence the weight, must fall. Table 3.2 refers to transport category operations, but the effects on general aviation are equally substantial. The situation is complicated by the effect on engine performance, which tends to produce a greater deterioration in the takeoff case unless the engine is flat rated, (i.e., its output at high air densities is deliberately limited to avoid overloading its components). It frequently happens that different criteria becomes critical in defining the field length, because of the need to choose a V_1 speed. Therefore, under hot and high conditions, it becomes necessary to use longer field lengths or to reduce weight. In addition, the hot and high cases frequently make it difficult to meet the requirements for engine-out climb gradients at a given weight, even if the runway is long enough to meet the field length regulations at that weight. Therefore, the payload range can be compromised by runway length and by altitude and temperature. The allowable operating weights, hence the payload-range capability can also be affected by runway strength limitations. Figure 3.8 shows the relationship between aircraft gross weight and range and the relative effects of strength and length limitations, as well as the reduction in potential profit margin.

3.7 WEIGHT COMPONENTS

To meet runway requirements, it is not always difficult to reduce weight because aircrafts usually are flexible in the makeup of their maximum weight, as indicated by the following definitions :

(i) Empty operating weight is a constant weight for a type except payload and fuel.

(ii) Zero fuel weight is the sum of empty operating weight and the maximum payload.

(iii) Maximum takeoff weight is determined by structural limits and performance requirements and is made up of

Table 3.2 Increase in Field Length (ft × 1000) Due to Changes in Altitude and Temperature

Aircraft	Takeoff				Landing			
	Sea Level		5000 ft		Sea Level		5000 ft	
	ISA	ISA+20°C	ISA	ISA+20°C	ISA	ISA+20°C	ISA	ISA+20°C
Concorde	10.28	12.35	12.50	13.08	8.00	8.00	9.28	9.28
707-320B	10.00	11.40	12.65[a]	12.84[a]	6.25	6.25	6.94	6.94
L-1011	7.75	9.25	12.95[a]	13.30[a]	5.70	5.70	6.40	6.40
727-200	10.08	13.19	13.81[a]	14.12[a]	4.80	4.80	5.31	5.31
737-200	6.55	7.73	8.80[a]	10.20[a]	4.29	4.29	5.14	5.14
DC-9-50	7.88	9.80	10.85[a]	12.15[a]	4.68	4.68	5.30[b]	5.10[b]
HS-748-2A	5.38	5.70[a]	5.50[a]	5.90[a]	3.37	3.36[b]	4.76[b]	4.67[b]
Nord 262 C	3.51	3.68[a]	3.84[a]	3.94[a]	1.72[b]	1.72[b]	1.94[b]	1.88[b]

1 ft = 0.30 m

a = Weight limited by climb gradient requirement on takeoff.

b = Weight limited by climb gradient requirement on overshoot.

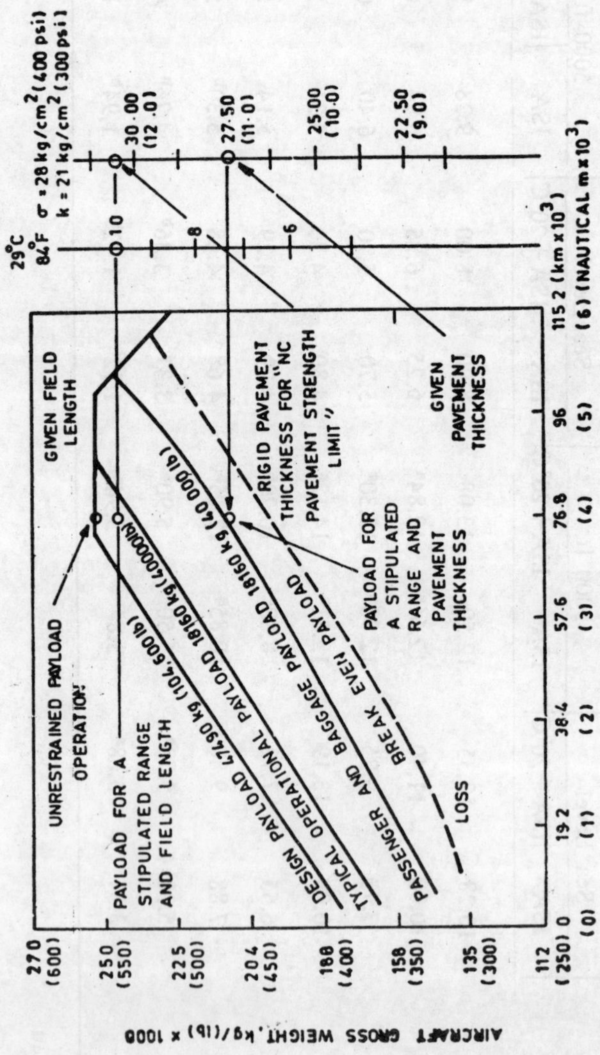

Figure 3.8 Relationship Between Aircraft Gross Weight and Range

the empty operating weight and a flexible combination of payload and fuel.

(iv) Maximum ramp weight is slightly higher than the maximum takeoff weight so that the fuel required for queueing and taxiing does not prejudice the load that can be lifted for the flight.

(v) Maximum landing weight is less than the maximum takeoff weight by an amount dependent on a reasonable mean expectancy of the weight of fuel burned during a flight. Thus the landing gear can be designed for lower landing loads without prejudice to the aircraft's lifting ability.

Table 3.1b and 3.1c show the maximum takeoff, maximum landing and empty operating weights. It can be seen that there is flexibility in both the size and the make-up of the difference between the takeoff weight and the empty operating weight.

3.8 AEROPLANE COMPONENT PARTS

The schematic diagram of an aeroplane with its various component parts is given in Figure 3.9. Its photograph is shown in Figure 3.10. The following are the essential parts of an aircraft :

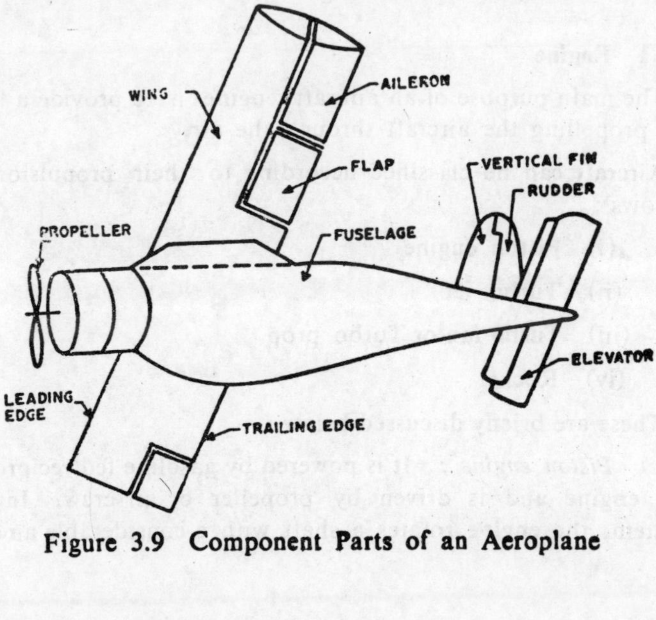

Figure 3.9 Component Parts of an Aeroplane

Figure 3.10 View of a Twin Engine Aircraft

1 Engine
2 Propeller
3 Fuselage
4 Wings
5 Three controls
6 Flaps
7 Tricycle under-carriage

3.8.1 Engine

The main purpose of an aircraft engine is to provide a force for propelling the aircraft through the air.

Aircraft can be classified according to their propulsion as follows :

(i) Piston engine
(ii) Turbo jet
(iii) Turbo fan or Turbo prop
(iv) Rocket

These are briefly discussed below :

(i) Piston engine : It is powered by gasoline fed reciprocating engine and is driven by propeller or airscrew. In this system, the engine rotates a shaft with a considerable amount

of torque. A propeller is mounted on the shaft to absorb the torque. When the rotating propeller attains its rated speed, huge masses of air hurled rearward, thereby pulling the aircraft forward and creating lift on the wings. These conventional aircraft engines are suitable to operate at low altitudes and moderate speeds. They also present cooling problem. They have been improved upon by the jet engine aircraft in which the inherent disadvantages of the conventional engine, associated with the propellers at high forward speeds and at eight altitutdes, are eliminated by merely doing away with the propellers.

(ii) Turbo jet : The principle of jet propulsion is very simple. Take a balloon and inflate it. Close the open end with a thread and leave it on a table. The balloon stays stationary. Now unite the thread. The air is forced out of the open end and the balloon starts wandering across the room vigorously first and slowly later, until it becomes flat and motionless. This is the simplest illustration of jet propulsion. The balloon forces the air in one direction through the opening. Since action and reaction are equal and opposite, the escaping air pushes the balloon in the opposite direction. Lower the velocity of the escaping air, lower is the action and hence smaller the reaction. As the air pressure inside the balloon gradually falls, the escaping air loses its speed and hence the speed of the balloon also reduces slowly until it finally becomes motionless.

The schematic diagram of jet engine aircrafts is given in Figure 3.11. To start the machine, the compressor is rotated with a motor. As the compressor gains its rated speed, it sucks in air through the air intake and compresses it in the compression chamber. The air is ignited here by a fuel like kerosine oil. The expanding gases pass through the fan like blades of the turbine. The turbine extracts that much power from the gases which is sufficient to keep the compressor rotating. The compessor rotates at the same speed as the turbine because the two are fastened solidly to one shaft. The hot gases, with the remaining energy escape through the tail pipe which becomes smaller in diameter at the exit end. The hot exhaust gases, having high velocity, give a forward thrust to the engine. It has been reported that if exhaust gases come out with a speed of 1600 kph (1000 mph), the forward thrust

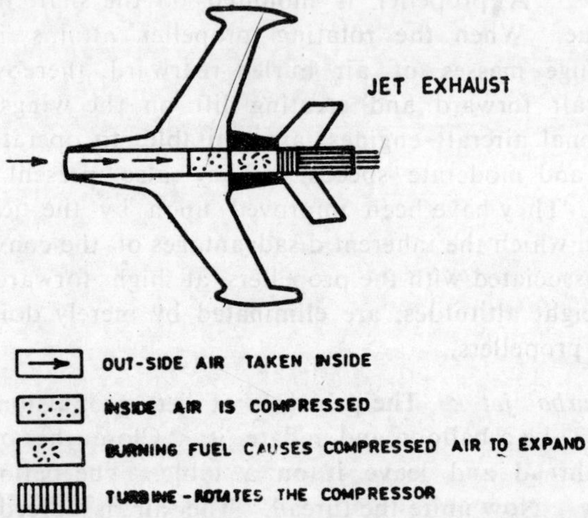

Figure 3.11 Principle of Turbo Jet Propulsion

may push the plane with the speed of about 800 kph (500 mph). The relative efficiency of the turbo jet is enhanced at high altitudes owing to the drop in the atmospheric density (which offers less resistance to the passage of aircraft) and greater temperature difference through the turbine.

(ii) Turbo prop : It is similar to the turbo jet engine except that a propeller is provided in it. Main difference is in the design of turbines. The turbine in turbo prop extracts enough power to drive both the compressor and the propeller. Only a small amount of power is left as a jet thrust. Principal advantage of the turbo prop is its high degree of performance over the general range of altitude. While the turbe jet has a considerable lower performance ratio at moderate altitudes than at high altitudes, the turbo prop performs well at both. Therefore, the curve of rate of climb for the turbo prop is much more abrupt than for the turbo jet.

(iv) Ram jet : It is an engine with no moving parts. It must be operated at comparatively high speed if it has to function at all. It cannot operate statically unless a continuous source of air is flown past the engine. Its principle of working is very simple. Air enters the air intake. By shaping the tube with a diverging-converging configuration, as shown in Figure 3.12, the air velocity is decreased in combustion chamber

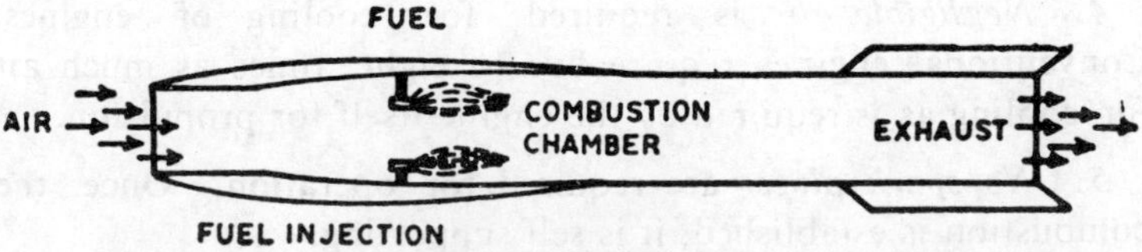

Figure 3.12 Ram Jet

with a consequent incrase in the pressure. Fuel flow and combustion are continuous. A spark plug is used for starting only. The heated air expends and rushes out of the exhaust nozzle at high velocity creating jet thrust. The advantages of ram jet are the simplicity of design and high speeds. But it requires the assistance of other types of power plants to reach the operating speed and has a very high specific fuel consumption.

(v) Rocket engine : The rocket produces its thrust in the same manner as the ram jet except for one outstanding difference. All the engines described previously have definite ceilings, depending upon when they run out of oxygen necessary to support the combustion. But for rocket engines, there is no limit on altitude since oxygen in the atmosphere is not relied upon for the combustion. The engine carries its own supply of oxygen placing it in the category of non-atmospheric engines. It may be noted that the first airplane which had flown faster than the speed of sound was powered by liquid-fuel rocket engine. But amongst all the engines described herein, the rocket engine has the highest specific fuel consumption.

Advantages of Jet Engines over Conventional Engines

The jet engines have numerous attractive features which are briefly reviewed as below :

1. *Freedom from vibrations*

2. *Simplicity of control :* The power produced is applied in the best possible way, that is, directly. No transmission or conversion mechanism is required. Thus certain energy losses are eliminated.

3. *No radiators or other cooling surfaces* are required which will add to weight and drag on the jet units.

4. *Negligible air* is required for cooling of engines. Conventional engines require five to eight times as much air for cooling as is required by the engine itself for propulsion.

5. *No spark plugs* are required for operation. Once the combustion is established, it is self supporting.

6. *No carburettors* and hence no mixture control is required.

7. *Noiseless operation :* This means less fatigue to the pilot and thus less cabin insulation to dampen the noise.

8. *Decreased fire hazards.*

9 *Lower specific weight.*

10. *Less consumption of lubricated oil*

Because of its modest output, jet engine has been universally accepted as a recognised means of aircraft propulsion and has in some cases, superceded the conventional piston engine propulsion. Table 3.3 shows the comparison of various types of aircraft propulsions.

An aeroplane can be single engined or multi-engined. If single engined, the engine is usually mounted at the nose of the fuselage. If the aircraft has two or four engines, they are usually housed in the leading edge of the wing and are equally disposed off on either side of the fuselage.

There are several reasons of using more than one engine in an aircraft. First reason is that the power of the machine and its weight carrying capacity are multiplied. Another reason is reliability. It is quite difficult to produce an engine which is so reliable that it can never break down. If a break down occurs in a motor car or a locomotive, the only effect is a loss of time. But if this happens in a single engined aircraft., it is compulsory that the machine must land. It is likely that a satisfactory landing ground may not be available within the reach. Under these conditions, it may be difficult for the pilot to avoid crash. The chances of accidents are reduced if the aircraft has two or more engines, since it will continue to fly satisfactorily even if one engine has failed. The photograph of a twin engine aircraft is shown in Figure 3.10.

3.8.2 Propeller

This is provided in the conventional piston engine

Table 3.3 Types of Aircraft Propulsion

Engine	Use	Speed limit kph	Advantages	Limitations
Piston	Long range, moderate speed, transports and bombers	250	Low fuel consumption, reliability, long service life.	Operates at relatively low altitude
	Moderate range high speed fighters	750	Versatile, reliable	Relatively high fuel consumption, medium altitude.
	Small private air pleasure aircrats	400	Low initial cost, reliable	Low altitudes' short range
Turbo prop	Intermediate and long range transports and bombers	Sub-sonic	Low fuel consumption at high powers, long range.	Speed limited by propeller efficicence,
Turbo-jet	High speed; medium range fighters	Sonic	High speed at relatively high altitude, smooth performances.	Payloads and range limited by fuel consumption
Ram Jet	Pilotless aircraft, guided missiles	1280 to 2400	Simple design, cable of great speed.	Very high fuel consumption
Rocket	Missiles, high speed interceptor aircraft	4600	Extremely high speed, can operate outside oxygen bearing atmosphere.	Extremely high fuel consumption

aircrafts as well as in turbo prop engines. When engine and propeller are in front, the machine is described as a *tractor* type. Sometimes, but not very often, the engine and airscrew are behind the wing and this is known as a *pursher* installation. The propeller usually has two or more blades which are driven round in a circular path. The blades deflect air backwards with an acceleration and thus impart forward thrust to the aeroplane.

3.8.3. Fuselage

It forms the main body of the aircraft and provides for the power plant, fuel, cockpit, passengers, cargo etc. It must be large enough to give sufficient tankage space and yet be as small as possible in order to reduce the wind resistance. It is shaped to a fine point at the rear end and yet be not too fine as it will otherwise be unable to resist the twisting stresses due to the wind. It is desirable to have it deep for strength and yet be not very deep as otherwise the side area may become very large which is undesirable for safety and efficiency.

3.8.4 Wings

The purpose of an aircraft wing is to support the machine in the air when the engine has given it the necessary forward speed. To understand the principle of lift, let us consider an inclined plane held in the wind as shown in Figure 3.13. The force P caused upon it, is indicated in magnitude and direction by the lines OR. This force we will now regard as a resultant and split into two components OM and ON. The vertical component OM, whose magnitude is equal to P Cos α, is known as the *lift* component. The horizontal component ON, whose magnitude is equal to P Sin α is known as the *drag* component. It is desirable to have the lift component greater than the *drag* component and more the difference is between the two, the more effective is the lifting ability of the plane. The value of the *lift-drift ratio* for an inclined flat plane will depend upon the angle of incidence and the *aspect ratio* of the plane. As the *angle of incidence* increases, the drag component also increases while the lift component reduces. The

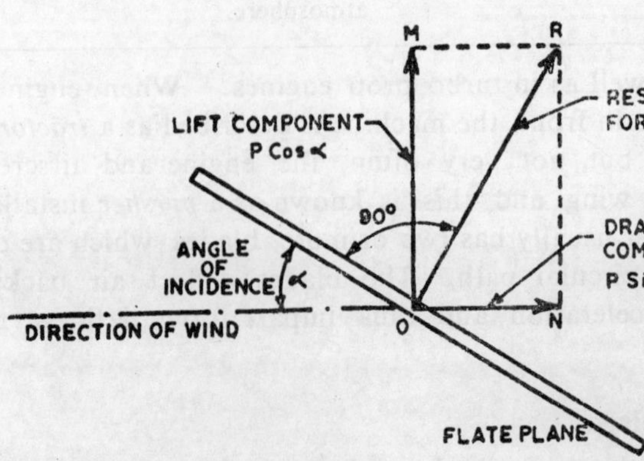

Figure 3.13 Lift and Drag Forces on Flat Plane

aspect ratio of the plane means the relation between the length and breadth of the plane, For example, a rectangular plane with a length of 6 m and a breadth of 1.2 m has an aspect ratio of five. When the aspect ratio increases above 10, it does not have much influence on the lift-drift ratio.

Aerofoil ordinarily used in aeroplanes are cambered. Both theory and practice indicate that there are marked advantages in giving a camber to the wing section. An ideal shape of the wing is shown in Figure 3.14.

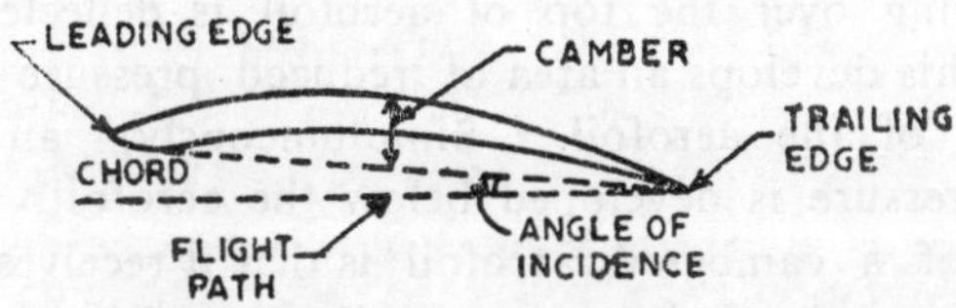

Figure 3.14 Various Parts of a Wing

Comparison of the action of air currents on flat and cambered plates is illustrated in Figure 3.15. Consider the Figure 3.15-A in which flat plane is dropped vertically. Owing to the compression below the plane and the refraction of the air above it, there is bound to be the circulation of air from below the plane to the less dense area above it. This gives rise to a vortex motion. Now consider the action on the flat plane

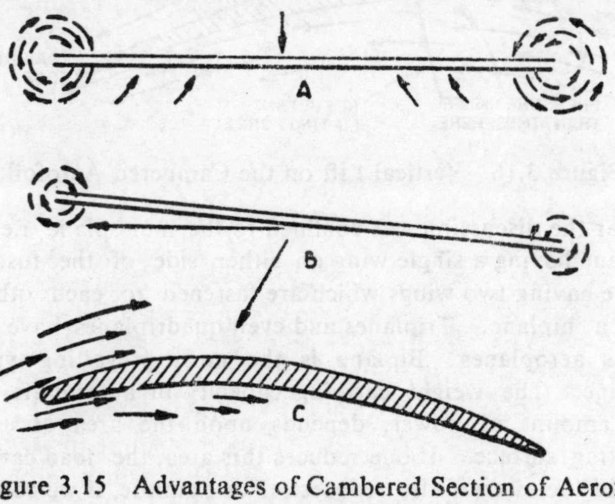

Figure 3.15 Advantages of Cambered Section of Aerofoil

moving in a horizontal direction as shown in Figure 3 15-B. Here also there is a vortex action. The leading edge does not meet the air in the most efficient manner due to considerable shock and resistance to the forward motion. To avoid the vortex action and to meet the air without shock, the aerofoil is cambered as shown in Figure 3.15-C.

Figure 3.16 explains how the vertical lift is obtained on the cambered aerofoil because of air pressure. To meet the air without shock, it is necessary that the leading edge be curved down and the aerofoil has a good streamline shape. The air stream flowing over the top of aerofoil is deflected upward sharply. This develops an area of reduced pressure above the top surface of the aerofoil. Simultaneously, an area of increased pressure is developed below the aerofoil. The real advantage of a cambered aerofoil is that it receives a current of air in an upward direction and directs it downwards, thus obtaining a lift reaction. The best design of an aerofoil is the one which gives the greatest area of negative pressure on the top and the greatest area of positive pressure at the bottom. It should be shaped such that there is no back or eddies in the streamline airflow over its surfaces.

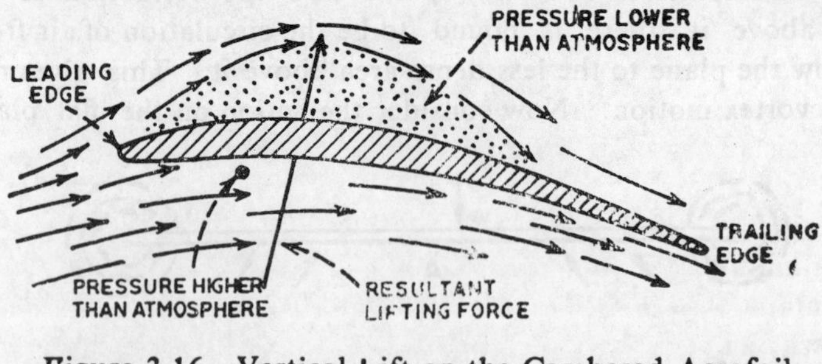

Figure 3.16 Vertical Lift on the Cambered Aerofoil

So far the discussion was confined to the monoplane i.e., an aeroplane having a single wing on either side of the fuselage. A plane having two wings which are fastened to each other is called a biplane. Triplanes and even quadriplanes have been used as aeroplanes. Biplane is the most prevailing type of aeroplane. The weight carrying capacity of an aircraft, for a given amount of power, depends upon the area of useful supporting surface. If one reduces this area, the load carrying ability of the aircraft also reduces. For example, if we consider biplane having 12 m spread and 1.8 m chord, the total area of supporting surface is equal to 43.2 sq m. If one desires to obtain the same area in monoplane, keeping the aspect ratio almost same, it would be necessary to use a single plane having 18 m spread and 2.4 m chord. The design of a wing structure of these dimensions is a complex problem. It is, therefore, sometimes necessary to use biplane arrangement. Tests have indicated that unless the vertical gap between the wings is at least twice the chord length, there will be an interference due to conflicting air currents between the two aerofoils arranged one above the other. The usual spacing in biplanes is equal to the length of the chord. Although, it is not most efficient one, but it is commonly adopted on account of the structural reasons. In this case, the efficiency of the biplane is about 80 percent of the monoplane having the same wing area and the aerofoil section. The efficiency of the biplane arrangement can be further increased by staggering the plane, i.e., setting the leading edge of one plane some distance ahead of leading edge of the other. This results in the increase of the lift coefficient as well as the lift-drift ratio. Staggering improves the efficiency of the upper plane, because it reduces greatly the disturbed area between the plane. The staggering is usually done by amount two-fifths of the chord length.

The wing structure must be torsionally stiff to resist forces which tend to twist the wing. It should also be strong enough to resist flexure or bending forces. The plane and sectional view of a wing framework are shown in Figure 3.17. The covering of the wing may consist of a light metal alloy e.g., duralumin. The numerous cross members which serve to maintain the curvature of the upper and lower covering are known as ribs. The ribs are built with two principal longitudinal members called spars. The bending forces are carried by the spars. Torsional stiffness is obtained because of box like construction formed by the skin covering, i.e., the framework of ribs and the spars. Light spanwise members or stringers between the ribs also contribute to the measure of stiffness as well as providing attachment for the skin plating.

3.8.5 Three Controls

There are three axes about which an aircraft in space may move. These axes and the possible aircraft movements are

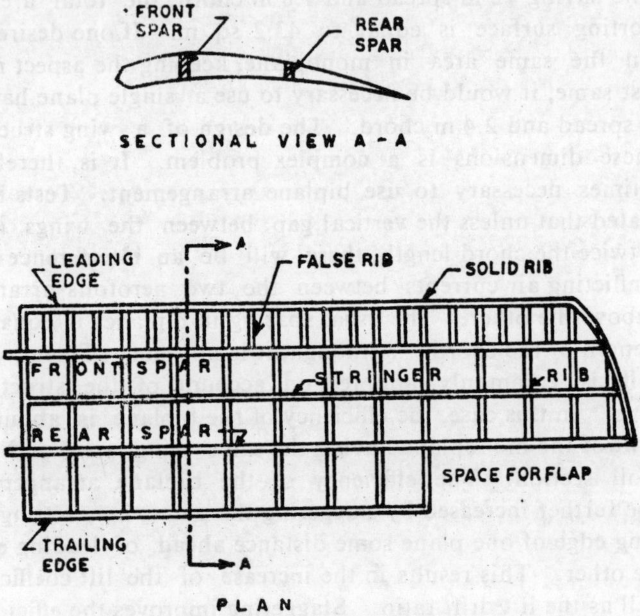

Figure 3.17 Framework of a Wing Structure

shown in Figure 3.18. The movement of aircraft about the X axis is called *lateral* or *rolling* movement. The movements about Y and Z axes are called *pitching* and *yawing* movements respectively. To control these movements, the airplane is provided with three principal controls, viz., (i) elevator

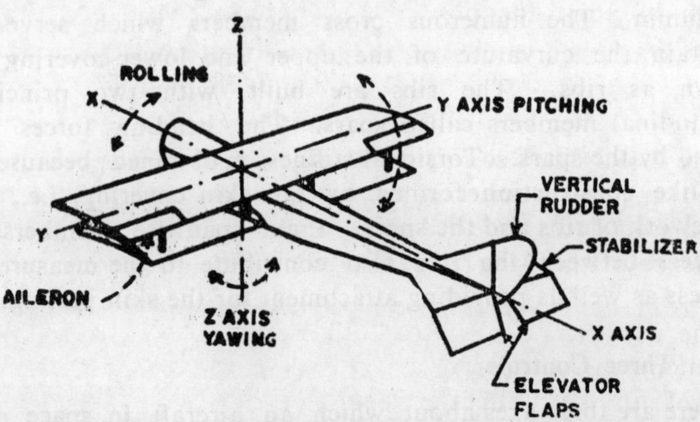

Figure 3.18 Three Axes of Movements

(ii) rudder and (iii) aileron. The first two controls which are provided at the tail end of the fuselage are also known as *empennage*. Each control can be operated by the pilot from his cabin. They are shown in Figures 3.9, 3.10 and 3.18 are explained below :

(i) Elevator : It consists of two flaps capable of moving up and down through an angle of 50° to 60°. They are hinged to a fixed horizontal surface (called a *tailplane* or *stabilizer)* placed at the extreme rear of the fuselage. It controls the *pitching* or up and down movements of the aircraft. When the elevator flap is raised, there is increased air pressure on it causing the tail to go down and the noise to point up. When the elevator is in a neutral position, the air pressures are equal at the top and bottom of the flaps and aircraft flies along the normal line of flight.

(ii) Rudder : It consists of a streamlined flap hinged to a vertical fine provided at the tail end of the fuselage. It can be moved right or left of the vertical axis through an angle of about 30°. It is utilised for the turning or *yawing* movement of the aircraft. The same action that has been explained in relation to the elevator will work in about the same way when the vertical rudder is tilted to the right or to the left. The reaction of the air against the inclined surface naturally pushes the back end of the machine in the direction on which the force is acting. In this way, it is possible to steer the aeroplane in the air, just as a boat is steered in the water. When the rudder is inclined towards the left of the vertical axis, the tail moves to the right and the nose moves to left. If the pilot disires to point the nose of the aeroplane to the right, he moves the rudder to the right of the vertical axis.

(iii) Aileron : It is a hinged flap which is fixed in the trailing edge of the wing near the wing tip, as shown in Figure 3.19. It is so rigged that when aileron in one wing is pulled up that in other is pulled down. The effect of pulling the aileron down is to increase the camber and angle of incidence of the wing. This results in an increased lift under the wing. Pulling an aileron up reduces the lift on the part of the wing which it governs. The result of doing these things simultaneously is to give a very powerful lateral or *rolling* control to the aircraft about its longitudinal axis. The function of aileron is not only to enable the pilot to balance

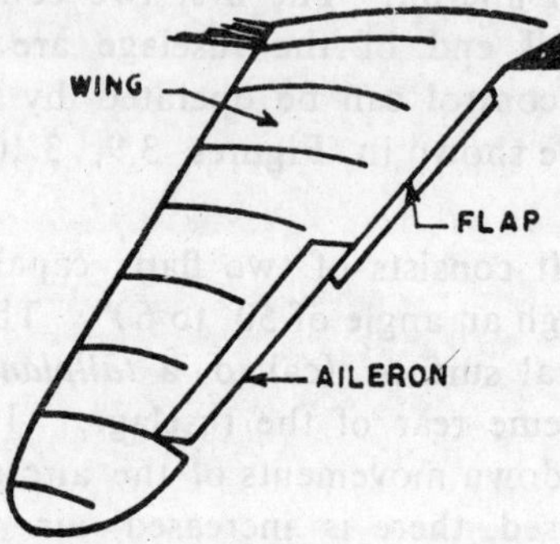

Figure 3.19 Loacations of Aileron and Flap

the aeroplane when it is tilted by a gust of wind, but also to tilt the machine purposely, when it is describing a circle and it is desired to bank the machine.

3.8.6 Flaps

These are somewhat similar to ailerons and are used for increasing the lift on aerofoils. Like the other three controls, this can also be operated by the pilot from his cabin. They are fitted only to the inner portion of the wing as shown in Figure 3.19, and are so arranged that the flaps on each side are pulled down together. Sometime these flaps are so constructed that only the under portion of the wing acts as a flap, as shown in Figure 3.20.

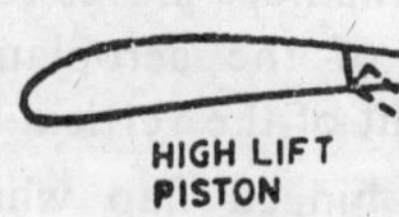

Figure 3.20 Lift Position with a Flap

3.8.7 Tricycle Under-Carriage

It is a structure to support the aircraft while it is in contact with the ground. It has two principal functions to perform as listed below :

(i) *To absorb landing shocks :* When an aircraft lands, it always touches the ground with certain vertical velocity. Thus a given amount of energy has to be dissipated during the touch down. It is one of the functions of the undercarriage to do this as smooth as possible.

(*ii*) *To enable the aircraft to manoeuvre on ground :* For this, wheels are required over which the aircraft may run and carry the entire weight of the aircraft. The major portion of the total load is carried by two main gears which are provided in the fuselage or in the wings near the junction of fuselgae and wings. Therefore, the third wheel, which is provided near the tail or the nose, carries very small portion (about 10%) of the total load.

When the third wheel is kept at the tail, it keeps the nose up and the wings are at greater angle of incidence. In the event of powerfull wind, the aircraft may lift off the ground or be pushed backwards even when the aircraft is stationary and the engine is not working. Tail wheel is, therefore, not preferred. If the third wheel is kept at the nose, it keeps the noise in the down position and the wing angle is reduced. The wing does not create any appreciable lift. It is for this reason that the nose wheel is preferred even though it is slightly inconvenient for the loading of the passengers and goods.

The various possible wheel configurations are shown in Figure 3.21. The twin and twin-twin wheel assemblies are for military aircrafts.

The main reason of using multiple wheel arrangement is to distribute the aircraft load over a large area of the pavement and thus reduce the pavement thickness.

3.9 MILITARY AND CIVIL AIRCRAFTS

There is a considerable difference between the aircrafts for military and civil purposes. The necessary characteristics of military aircrafts are weight carrying capacity, manoeuvrability, speed, climb and effective armament.

Fighter planes should be able to carry heavy weights. Even the single seater, fighter, which is not normally considered as a weight carrier, must be able to carry considerable weight of the guns and ammunition if it has to perform its functions well. In case of bomber, it is obvious that, greater the weight of bombs it carry, the better it is.

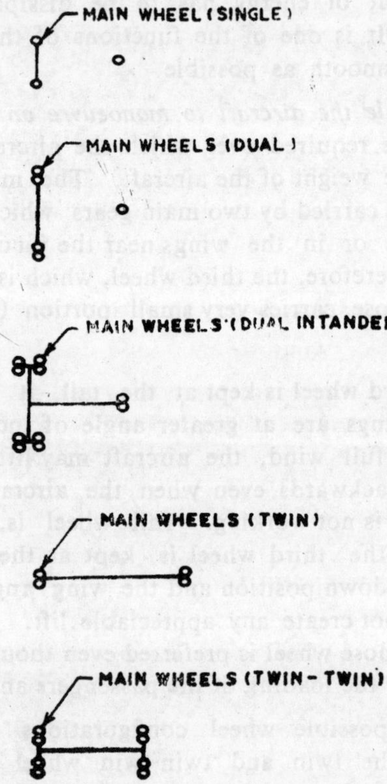

Figure 3.21 Basic Wheel Configurations

Manoeuvrability is especially important for fighting aircrafts which are consequently concerned in putting themselves quickly into the safer positions with regard to the enemy. Ability to manoeuvre rapidly makes it easier to escape if the aircraft is attacked by the enemy fighters.

As regards the speed, the fighting aircraft should be designed to maintain very high speed irrespective of the cost. The safety of a bomber depends on the speed with which it can hide itself in clouds overhead.

The fighter plane should also be able to climb rapidly with as large angle as possible. An interceptor plane cannot intercept unless it can climb rapidly.

With regard to equipment, the military aircrafts differ very much from the civilian aircrafts. Everything is arranged for greatest possible efficiency in fighting or bombing. Guns, gun positions, bomb sights must all be in special places from where the best view of the ground underneath can be obtained. In fact, the whole layout of the fighting aircraft is marked by its grin purpose.

Thus the design of military aircraft is governed entirely by its fighting efficiency, while the commerical aircraft has to be designed to pay commercially. In other words, the desirable characteristics of a commercial aeroplane are the payload capacity, speed, passengers, comfort, safety and enemy. This leads to the point that it is necessary to design commercial aircrafts for low running cost and low cost of maintenance. The speed of the aircrafts should be fast enough to attract all the available traffic. But it should not be faster than is necessary, since any increase in speed increases the operating cost considerably Passenger comfort is one of the most important things from a commercial point of view. Even if the aircraft can go fast and is reliable it may not be able to fetch enough passengers, unless it can make them comfortable This means that the cabin must provide comfortable chairs and lavatory accommodation, efficient ventilation and air conditioning, refreshments, complete meals on long runs, etc. This makes the dimensions of the fuselage of a commercial aircraft often larger than those of a military machine of similar weight. From the passenger comfort considerations, the engine noise and vibrations should also be kept out of the cabin as far as possible.

3.10 CIVIL MILITARY CO-ORDINATION

The airspace is shared by the civil and military users. The existance of restricted, prohibited and danger areas under the control of military adds the complexities of air traffic management. India has implemented Air Defence Indentification Zones (ADIZ) in the western sector requiring civil aircraft to obtain Air Defence Clearance from Flight Information Centres ten minutes before entering the Indian territory. Similar clearance is also required from ATC before take-off.

The optimum use of airspace with a maximum degree of safety, regularity and efficiency can be ensured only with appropriate civil military coordination between civil ATS units and military air traffic. Occasionally good coordination exists in ground navigation and communication facilities of both civil and military installations. However, it is felt that there should be a wider coordination on institutional basis between civil and military authorities and the need for civil aircraft to oblain air defence clearance should be dispensed with.

3.11 CLASSIFICATION OF FLYING ACTIVITY

Flying is the most flexible means of transport. Before studying the aircraft characteristics we should know the various possible kinds of flying, viz personal, non-scheduled, commerical, scheduled commercial and military. These are detailed below :

(a) Personal

1 Local
2 Cross country
3 Aircraft sales
4 Glider
5 Autogiro

(b) Non-scheduled commercial

1 Aircraft testing
2 Executive personal travel and sales representation
3 Forest patrol
4 Crop dusting
5 Aerial photography and mapping

(c) Scheduled commerical

1 Loyal schedule
  (i) On line
  (ii) Feeder
2 Intercontinental
3 Transoceanic
4 Air Cargo
  (i) Intracontinental
  (ii) Intercontinental
  (iii) Transoceanic

(d) Military operations

1 Flight training

2 Tactical

(i) Fighter

(ii) Light bombing

(iii) Heavy bombing

(iv) Patrol

(v) Medical

(vi) Transport e.g. personnel, cargo etc.

3.12 RELATION OF AIRCRAFT TO LANDING FACILITY

The planning and designing of airports necessitates a proper understanding of present day aircrafts, their various types, sizes and the probable future improvements in their design. It is, therefore, essential to know the aircraft performance characteristics which will decide the landing and ground facilities required for their handling and servicing. Because aircraft design has not yet reached a static stage, the likely improvement in their design in the near future should be anticipated while deciding the airport layout. Even though the existing pattern may enable to completely meet the future aircraft needs, but then the extension will be rossible economically keeping in view the future requirements.

3.13 AIRCRAFT CHARACTERISTICS

Aircraft characteristics are of prime importance to the airport planner and designer. The following characteristics need to be studied :

1 Type of propulsion

2 Size of aircraft

3 Minimum turning radius

4 Minimum circling radius

5 Speed of aircraft

6 Capacity of aircraft

7 Aircraft weight and wheel configuration

8 Jet blast

9 Fuel spillage

10 Noise

Major characteristics of some aircrafts are given in Table 3.4. Few of these characteristics are discussed below :

3.13.1 Types of Propulsion

The types of aircraft propulsion have been discussed in article 3.8.2. The size of aircraft, its circling radius, speed characteristics, weight carrying capacity, noise nuisance etc. depend upon the type of propulsion of the aircraft. The performance characteristics of aircrafts, which determine the basic runway length, also depend upon the type of propulsion as explained in article 6.2. That heat nuisance due to exhaust gases is a characteristic of turbo jet and turbo prop engines. How all these affect the planning and design of airports has been discussed in the following articles.

3.13.2 Size of Aircraft

The sizes of aircraft involves following important dimensions : (i) Wing span (ii) Fuselage length (iii) Height (iv) Distance between main gears, i.e. gear tread (v) Wheel base and (vi) Tail width. These are shown in Figure 3.22. The wing span decides the width of taxiway, separation clearance between two parallel trafficways, size of aprons and hangars, width of hangar gate etc. The length of aircraft decides the widening of taxiways on curves width of exit taxiway, sizes of aprons and hangars etc. The height of aircraft, also called as *empennage height*, decides the height of hangar gate and miscellaneous installations inside the hangar. The gear tread and the wheel base affect the minimum turning radius of the aircraft.

3.13.3 Minimum Turning Radius

In order to decide the radius of taxiways, the position of aircrafts in loading aprons and hangars and to establish the path of the movement of aircraft, it is very essential to study the geometry of the turning movement of aircrafts. The turning radius of an aircraft is illustrated in Figure 3.23. To determine the minimum tuning radius, a line is drawn through the axis of the nose gear when it is at its maximum angle of rotation The point, where this line intersects another line drawn through the axis of the two

Table 3.4 Characteristics of Principal Transport Aircrafts

Manufacturer	Model destination	Wing span (m)	Length (m)	Maximum height (m)	Distance between main gears (m)	Wheel base (m)	Minimum turning radius (m)	Maximum gross take off Wt. (kg)	Maximum landing weight 5 kg)	Maximum passenger capacity (No)	Type of engine	No. of engines	No. of wheels in main gear	Main gear dimensions (cm)
Douglas	DC-6	35.25	30.50	8.72	7.40	9.35	21.60	44,000	6,400	72	Piston	4	2	75
Convair	880	36.00	37.85	10.87	5.60	15.90	20.67	84,000	50,500	110	Turbo jet	4	4	53.7×113
Vickers	Viscount 802	28.10	24.55	8.02	7.15	7.45	21 00	29,300	26,600	48	Turbo prop	4	2	47.5
Bristrol	Britania 300	42.67	37.27	11.20	9.30	10.57	—	75,000	(8 ,600	133	Turbo prop	4	4	75×120
Lockhead	Eiectra	29.70	31.37	9.2	9.35	11.10	19.52	5 2,700	43,500	74	Turbo prop	4	2	39.3
Boeing	707-120	39.25	43.35	11.47	6.62	15.70	30.30	112,300	79,500	179	Turbo jet	4	4	85×140
Boeing	707-120B	39.25	43.35	11.47	6.62	15.70	30.30	116,200	84,000	179	Turbo prop	4	4	85×140
Boeing	707-320	42.72	45.87	11.60	6 62	17.70	32.70	137,000	90,000	189	Turbo jet	4	4	85×140
Boeing	707-320B	42.72	45.87	11.60	6.62	17.70	32.70	143,000	94,300	189	Turbo prop	4	4	85×140
Boeing	720	39.25	40.25	11.42	6.57	15.20	29.70	92,500	75,000	140	Turbo jet	4	4	78×125
Boeing	720B	39.25	40.85	11.42	6.57	15.20	29.70	100,000	75,000	140	Turbo prop	4	4	78×125
Boeing	727	32.57	30.22	10.12	6.05	15.85	21.05	64,500	59,500	114	Turbo jet	4	2	87.5

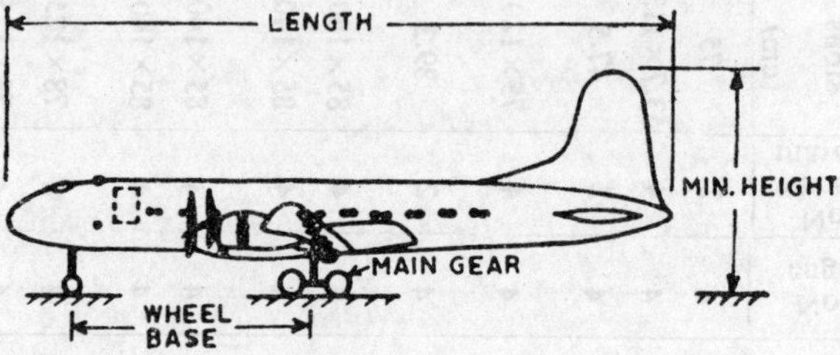

(a)

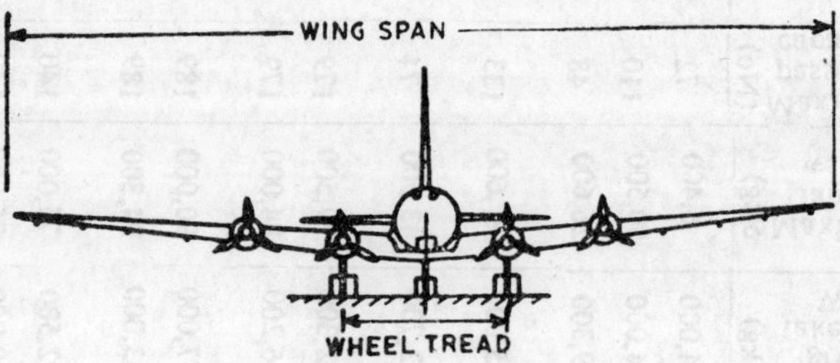

(b)

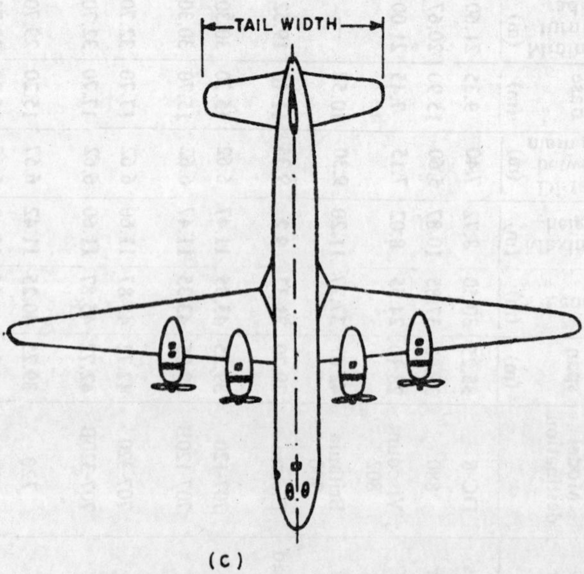

(c)

(a : Side view. b : Front view and c : Plan)

Figure 3.22 Aircraft Dimensions

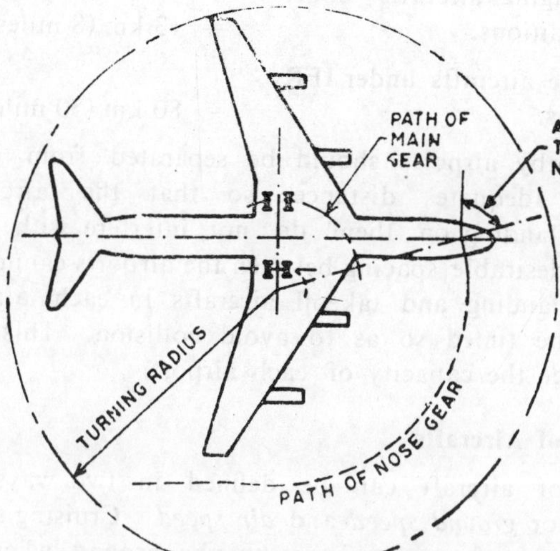

Figure 3.23 Turning Radius of Aircraft

main, gears, is called the *centre af rotation*. The distance of the farther wing tip from the centre of rotation represents the minimum turning radius. Theoretically, the maximum angle of rotation is 90°. Corresponding to this, turning radius would be absolute minimum, the condition which causes skidding of one of the main gears thereby producing excessive tire wear. To keep the tire-wear of the main gears within reasonable limits, the maximum angle of rotation of the nose gear has been limited by the manufacturers. For example, for a large turbo jet this angle is between 50° to 60°.

3.13.4 Minimum Circling Radius

There is certain minimum radius with which the aircraft can take turn in space. This radius depends upon the type of aircraft, air traffic volume and weather conditions. The radii recommended for different types of aircrafts are as follows :

(i) Small general aviation aircrafts under UFR conditions. = 1.6 km (1 mile)

(ii) Bigger aircrafts, say two piston engine under VFR conditions. = 3.2 km (2 mile)

(iii) Piston engine aircrafts under IFR conditions. = 13 km (8 miles)

(iv) Jet engine aircrafts under IFR conditions. = 80 km (50 miles)

The two nereby airports should be separated from each other by an adequate distance so that the aircrafts simultaneously landing on them do not interfere with each other. If the desirable spacing between the airports cannot be provided, the landing and takeoff aircrafts in each airport will have to be timed so as to avoid collision. This will obviously reduce the capacity of each airport.

3.13.5 Speed of Aircrafts

The speed of aircraft can be defined in two ways viz. *cruising speed* or *ground speed* and *air speed* Cruising speed is the speed of aircrafts with respect to the ground when the aircraft is flying in air at its maximum speed. Air speed is the speed of aircraft relative to the wind. Thus, if the aircraft is flying at a speed of 500 kph and there is a head wind of 50 kph, air speed will be 450 kph.

3.13.6 Aircraft Capacity

The number of passengers, baggage, cargo and fuel that can be accommodated in the aircrafts depends upon the capacity of aircraft. The capacity of aircraft using an airport have an important effect on the capacity of runway systems as well as that of the passenger processing terminal facilities.

3.13.7 Weight of Aircraft & Wheel Configuration

Weight of the aircraft directly influence the length of the runway as well as the structural requirements i.e. the thickness of the runway, taxiway, apron & hangars. It depends not only on the weight of the passenger baggage, cargo and fuel it is carrying and its structural weight, but also on the fuel which is continuously decreasing during the course of the flight. The details of the weight component is given in article 3.7. Table 3.1 b and 3.1 c shows the maximum take-off, maximum landing and empty operating weights. The various possible wheel configuration are shown in Figure 3.21. However, article 3.8.7 can be referred for more details about wheel configuration.

3.13.8. Jet Blast

At relatively high velocities, the aircrafts eject hot exhaust gases, The velocity of jet blast may be as high as 300 kmph. This high velocity causes inconvenience to the passengers travelling in the aircraft. Several types of blast f nces or jet blast deflector are available to serve as an effective measure for diverting the smoke ejected by the engine to avoid the inconvenience to the passengers. Since, the bituminous (flexible) pavements are affected by the jet blast, therefore, it is desirable to provide cement concrete pavement at least at the touch down portion to resist the effect of the blast in preference to the bituminous pavements. The effect of the jet blast should also be considered for determining the position, size and location of gates.

3.13.9 Fuel Spillage

At loading aprons and hangars, it is difficult to avoid spillage completely, but effort should be made to bring it within minimum limit. The bituminous (flexible) pavements are seriously affected by the fuel spillage and therefore, it is essential that the areas of bituminous pavements under the fueling inlets, the engines and the main landing gears are kept under constant supervision by the airport authorities.

3.13.10 Noise

Noise generated by aircraft create problems in making decisions on layout and capacity. The correct assessment of future noise patterns to minimize the effect of surrounding communities, is essential to the optimal layout of the runways. The FAA noise regulations came into force in 1969 for jet-powered aircraft with bypass ratios greater than 2. In 1973, they were modified to apply to all aircraft manufactured after that date. The regulation with respect to noise on the side line and below the approach path is indicated by the solid line in Figure 3.24, the broken line shows regulations for take off. It can be seen that the first generation jets and some of the second generation jet would not meet the regulations on approach noise, though they would have less trouble with the sideline limits. Although this tendency is

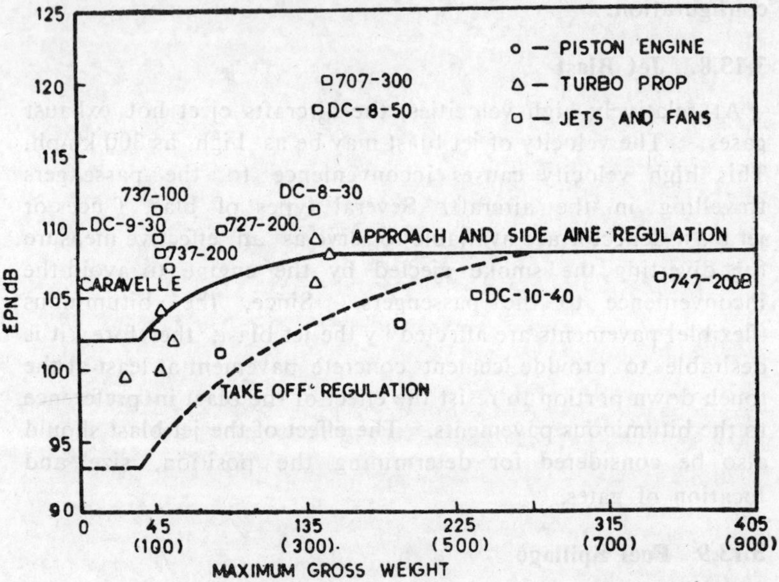

Figure 3.24 Relationship between Aircraft Noise (EPNdB) and Maximum Gross Weight for Different Types of Aircrafts

not shown, the aircraft generally meet the takeoff requirement more easily than the approach case but less easily than the sideline case. Some small allowance is given for one or more of the criteria to be exceeded, provided any such excess is completely offset in the remaining cases. The third generation jets have little difficulty meeting the current requirements. However, future legislation will ensure continuous reduction down to the level at which aerodynamic slipstream noise over the aircraft structure becomes the limiting factor at a rate commensurate with technological capability. The so-called self-noise is likely to create approximately 80 EPNdB (EPNdB) = effective perceived noise decibels).

Reduction in field length is found to be the most effective ways of minimizing the impact of aircraft noise. Although subject to the crosswind difficulties mentioned earlier and to a penalty in terms of DOC per seat km (mile) aircraft that can utilize the shorter runways do tend to increase runway occupancy rate, reduce expenditure on new runways and improve aircraft utilization at the trip ends. The combined effect of the shorter field length with the steeper approach and takeoff paths is potentially quite dramatic as shown in Table 3.5 when taken with other improvements.

Table 3.5 Effect of Field Length on Noise Footprint

Technology	Noise Footprint (km^2)	
	90 PNdB	80 PNdB
1960 Long haul STOL	180	450
1970 Short haul STOL	60	250
1970 Short haul STOL (FAR Part 36)	20	55
1970 Short haul STOL + engines silenced to 10 PNdB	5	20
Future RTOL with engines silenced to 10 PNdB	3	10
Future STOL	1	3

PNdB = perceived noise decibles

The rate of progress towards the noise levels indicated in Table 3.5 will depend to some extent on the airlines tolerance of the exchange of reduction in DOC for reduced noise, particularly for longer haul. In the long term, the main hindrance in achieving the containment of the 80 EPNdB contour within the airport boundary will be the rate at which current aircraft types are replaced.

3.14 FUTURE TRENDS IN AIRCRAFT DESIGN

This article deals with the interaction of aircraft design with the runway length. Despite the hesitant start made by Concorde, the logarithmic growth of cruise speed with time as shown in Figure 3.25 appears to be linear. However, Table 3.1 indicates that pressures for increased runway length to allow advances in cruise speed and range may have reached their peak. Over the shorter range, aircraft are already being designed to compromise their cruise performance to obtain

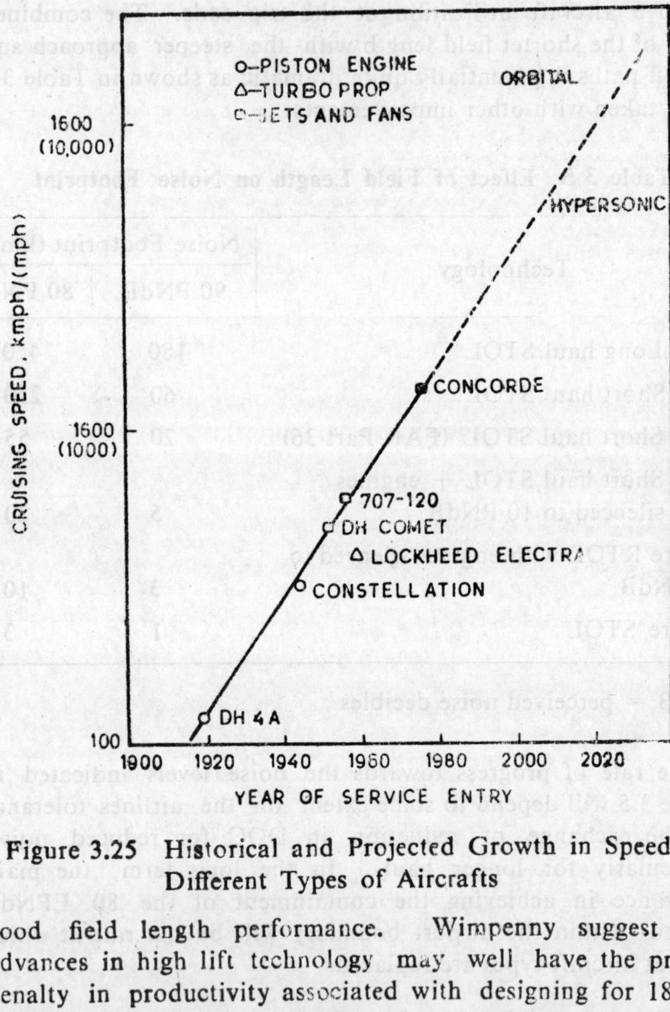

Figure 3.25 Historical and Projected Growth in Speed of Different Types of Aircrafts

good field length performance. Wimpenny suggest that advances in high lift technology may well have the present penalty in productivity associated with designing for 1800 m field length. Stampur predicts that combined advances in aerodynamics structures, propulsion systems and equipment and active control technology should produce a 20% improvement in DOC for a given aircraft size and performance in the next decade. This improvement in economy may be sufficient to allow the expenditure of some money on the evolution of shorter field length requirements, with the following multiple objectives :

(i) Serving the smaller airports that could not justify runway expenditure for low density operations.

(ii) Conversion of long runway into tandom RTOL runways allowing simultaneous takeoff and landing for short haul operations.

(iii) Reduction of noise footprint area.

(iv) Increase in runway capacity, supplementing the trend toward more frequent services with smaller aircraft.

The trend as shown in Figure 3.25 is a beginning propeller for new designs combining subsonic cruise, good fuel efficiency, quietness, and good field performance, at the expense of some reduction in passenger comfort.

The potential demand for ever larger aircraft exists on the routes that already have adequate frequency. Whether these designs are accepted into service will depend more than ever before on their ability to match the runway strength and terminal design requirements to the airports capabilities.

PROBLEMS

1. Distinguish between aircraft, aeroplanes, helicopter and amphibians.

2. Discuss in brief the relationship between aircraft and airports.

3. Explain in detail the influence of aircraft design on runway length.

4. Discuss the design requirement of present day aircraft types.

5. Discuss the importance of field length regulation. How the field length requirements are useful for different purpose for planning and operation of aircrafts ?

6. Discuss in brief the importance of restriction on pay load range performance.

7. Explain in detail the effect of weight components in the planning and design of airports. What are the different gear configurations generally used to support the aircraft weight ?

8. Draw a neat sketch of an aeroplane and explain its various component parts.

9. What are the different types of aircraft propulsion ? Discuss in brief each type.

10. Explain with neat sketch how the wings of an aircraft help it to rise in air above the ground.

11. Explain how the movement of an aircraft is controlled by the pilot.

12. Classify the flying activities according to the purpose to travel.

13. Name the different characteristics of aircrafts. How do they affect the planning and design of airports ?

14. What are the special characteristics of jet aircraft ? How do they affect the planning and design of airports ?

15. Discuss in brief the effect of noise created by aircrafts in the layout of airports. What are the noise regulations recommended by FAA ?

16. Discuss in brief the future requirements and trends in the aircraft design.

17. Write short notes on

 (i) Floatplane

 (ii) Military airports

 (iii) Coordination between civil and military airports.

 (iv) Advantages of jet engines over conventional engines.

4

AIRPORT PLANNING

4.1 GENERAL

Airport planning requires more intensive study and forethought as compared to planning of other modes of transport. This is because aviation is the most dynamic industry and its forecast is quite complex. Unlike rail, road and water transportation, air transportation has yet not reached a steady state in design. It is very difficult to predict for the airport, satisfying the present needs, whether this airport shall prove adequate for the new types of aircrafts which may emerge after 10 years. The airport design engineer, therefore is required to keep in touch with the recent trends and also with likely future projections in the aviation activities.

4.2 AIRPORT MASTER PLAN

Airport master plan refers the planner's idealized concept of the form and structure of the ultimate development of the airport. This plan is not simply the physical from of ultimate development but a description of the staging and both the financial implications and the fiscal strategies involved. Master planning can apply to the construction of new airports as well as to significant expansion of existing facilities. The objectives of the master plan according to FAA are :

(i) To provide an effective graphical presentation of the ultimate development of the airport and of the anticipated land uses adjacent to the airport.

(ii) To establish a schedule of priorities and phasing for the various improvements proposed in the plan.

(iii) To present the pertinent back-up information and data which were essential to the development of the master plan.

(iv) To describe the various concepts and alternatives which were considered in the establishment of the proposed plan.

4.2.1 FAA Recommendations

The structure of the airport master plan procedure recommended by the FAA consists of four separate phases.

Phase I : Airport Requirements

The first phase essentially is an examination of the scale and timing of new facilities with respect to the anticipated demand and the status of existing facilities in the context of anticipated environmental implications.

Phase II : Site Selection

The second phase begins, once a prima facia case for the construction of a new airport or the major expansion of existing facilities has been established. Evaluation of the available sites should include study of airspace requirements, environmental impact, development, access, availability of utilities, land costs and availability, site development costs and political implications.

Phase III : Airport Plans

The proposed facility is then represented precisely with respect to the following points :

(i) Airport Layout Plan : Indicates the configuration location and size of all physical facilities.

(ii) Land Use Plan : Details of land use within the proposed airport boundary and the land use of areas outside the boundary that are affected by the siting of the airport.

(iii) Terminal Area Plans : Show the size and location of the various buildings and activity areas within the terminal area complex.

(iv) Airport Access Plans : Show proposed routings for the various access modes to the transportation information of the region.

Phase IV : The Financial Plan

The final phase involves collection of data in the four principal areas of financial importance :

(i) Schedules of Proposed Development : Indicate the short, intermediate and long term stagings of development, timed to coincide with demand estimates.

(ii) Estimates of Development costs : Staged to conform to the scheduled development strategy.

(iii) Economic Feasibility Analysis : Examines whether the expected revenue generation will cover the anticipated costs.

(iv) Financial Feasibility Analysis : Undertaken to determine whether the scale of facility consideration can be financed within the fiscal capability of the authority involved.

4.2.2 ICAO Recommendation for Master Plan

A planner operating outside the United States probably may have to use ICAO Manual procedures or national procedures based on the ICAO manual Obstructions to Airspace.

The ICAO procedure for airport master planning is very similar to that recommended by the FAA and is summarised in Table 4.1. However, since member countries of the organization range from highly industrialized to quite under-developed nations, the procedures outlined are less specific environmental impact and the manner in which economic analysis is to be carried out.

Table 4.1 reveals heavy emphasis on physical planning. Obviously these procedures need modification in terms of existing planning and fiscal legislation for the area in which the study is conducted.

Table 4.1 Outline of ICAO Master Planning Process

Planning Step	Description
Planning method	Philosophy, planning system, planning organization, planning team, planning procedure, forecasts and systems concepts
Forecasting for planning purposes	Requirements forecasts required, accuracy, methods and principles of forecasting demand forecasts and projections
Site evaluation and selection	Land required, location of potential sites, outline plans and estimates of costs and revenues and evaluation
Airport configuration	Steps in planning configuration, runways, taxiway, holding bays and location of major facilities
Aircraft apron	Location, layout, characteristics, stands, equipment, parking areas and apron accommodations
Passenger area	Preparation of master plan, planning Principles, capacity and demand
Passenger building	Planning objectives, building characteristic and flow principles
Departure	Flow landside roads, passenger unloading positions, landside entrance, check-in concourse, check-in departures concourse, government frontier controls, airside waiting area, airside exits, aircraft-exit connections, aircraft gates, passenger gangways, apron passenger loading positions, departures baggage flow and customs baggage inspection
Arrivals	Passenger gangways, aircraft gates, pens and apron passenger vehicles, apron passenger unloading positions, airside entrance, transit passengers, transfer passengers, government frontier controls, baggage reclaim, customs inspection, arrivals concourse, landside exits, landside passenger vehicle loading position, baggage and general facilities
Cargo area	Planning principles, siting. system, traffic type, cargo building, cargo apron, roads and vehicle parking

Table 4.1 (Cont.) Outline of ICAO Master Planning Process

Planning Step	Description
Landside roads and vehicle parks Other building and facilities	Visual aids, radio navigation aids, control tower, apron control, aircrew briefing and reporting, meteorological station, communications, rescue and fire fighting, electricity generating station, maintenance, fuel depot, offices and administration buildings, medical centre, flight catering, ground vehicle fuel depot and hotels
Access	Defining access problem, planning and operating criteria, planning objectives and principles

4.3 REGIONAL PLANNING

The planning of an airport should be done considering the air traffic needs of the nation as a whole rather than an individual locality. Airport planning including the airport administration, if not done on a regional basis, would seriously impair the effective air traffic services of the country. It may further result in surplus or shortage of airport facilities on regional basis. Improper location of airports in relation to the areas served would result in unrealistic planning and undersirable air space conflicts. Airport planning on regional basis avoids the creation of separate airports by individual jurisdiction. If airports are located in close vicinity and if the locations are not properly co-ordinated, the total capacity and the efficacy of the airports will be greatly reduced. Planning on regional basis would also enable to implement *zoning laws* in the areas where new airports are needed in future.

The need for planning of airports on the basis of air traffic demand of the country as a whole is, thus, scientific. In India, Civil Aviation Organization is doing this job in collaboration with the states. The regional plan usually provides the following information :

1 Approximate locations of the airports in national map.

2 Classification of airports

3 Location of air strips

4 Routes of air travel

The following data is collected for a scientific and sound planning on regional basis.

1 Population
2 Topographical and geographical features
3 Existing airports in the vicinity
4 Air traffic characteristics

These are briefly discussed below :

4.3.1 Population

The population growth of an area to be served and the character of population based on the income groups and activities should be determined. The trend and needs of the people towards saving of travel time should also be studied.

4.3.2 Topographical and Geographical Features

Sometimes because of the topography, air service is the only accessible mode of transport. The geographical location of the area to be served is also equally important. Consider the case of two nearby cities, viz.. Bombay and Pune. Bombay has an international & domestic airport whereas Pune has only domestic airport.

4.3.3 Existing Airports in the Vicinity

Distance, population and economic character of the adjoining areas having air service should be studied. Two nearby airports should be located sufficiently apart so that the encircling radii of the two aircraft landing simultaneously do not overlap.

4.3.4 Air Traffic Characteristics

Various existing modes of transport, with their merits and demerits in the area to be served, should be carefully studied. The future expected volume of air traffic in terms of passengers, cargo, mail etc., and the number of aircraft movements required for the above should also be determined.

4.3.5 Development of New Airports

Before deciding to develop a new airport, full consideration should be given to the possibility of improvig the existing airport capacity so as to make it suitable for the increased future air traffic. Efforts should be made to accommodate new types of aircrafts likely to ply in the near future. The scientific approach for improving the existing airport, therefore, consists of the following steps :

(i) Traffic forecast

(ii) Determination of the capacity of existing airport

(iii) Improvement of airport capacity

(iv) Planning of a new airport.

Step I : The most important item in an airport planning is to estimate the future volume of air traffic. Peak hour volumes of passengers, cargo and mail are required for proper allocation of space in the terminal building and for determining the size of the building. Peak hour aircraft movements assist in the design of runways, taxiways and loading aprons.

Following data is collected for the traffic forecast :

(i) Area to be served

(ii) Origin and destination of the residents and non-residents of the area

(iii) Population growth in the area

(iv) Economic character of the area

(a) Income level per capita

(b) Types of business activities and the labour employed

(c) Trends in existing local air traffic

(d) Trends in national air traffic volume

(e) Population growth and economic standards of adjacent areas

Having collected the above data, the forecast of the traffic for some future years, say 15 years is carried out reviewing past trends of the local air traffic and future anticipated trends of the national air traffic. It may be pointed out that the process employed in making the forecast of air traffic is, however not a precise science. It requires considerable experience and judgement. The procedure of air traffic forecast is discussed in detail in article 4.8.

Step 2 : The next step is to ascertain whether the existing airport can handle the amount anticipated air traffic. Following points are considered in this respect :

(i) Suitability of approaches for the type of airports.

(ii) Capacity of runways and taxiways to handle the peak hour traffic (see chapter 7 for airport capacity).

(iii) Adequacy of terminal building of handling passengers and cargo.

(iv) Adequacy of aprons and servicing facilities.

Step 3 : If the foregoing considerations prove that the existing airport is inadequate to handle the anticipated traffic, the possible method for improving the capacity of the present airport should then be investigated. The improvement can be done in the following ways :

(i) Runway extensions, new or parallel runways and high speed exit taxiways.

(ii) Rearranging or increasing the size of terminal building and/or loading apron.

(iii) Improving the traffic control devices

Step : Inspite of all the possible ways as listed above, if it is worked out that the present airport cannot handle the air traffic, the designer thus arrives at the obvious answer, i.e. to propose a new airport.

4.4 DATA REQUIRED BEFORE SITE SELECTION

Having decided to develop a new airport, the first thought that comes to the design engineer is regarding the selection of a suitable site. Before this is done, the following information concerning the future airport are gathered :

1 Peak hourly volume of air traffic to be handled.

2 The present and future, types of aircrafts which may use the airport. Besides this their characteristics viz. size, turning radius, encircling radius, weight and wheel configurations etc. should also be studied.

3 Facilities to be provided for the passengers, baggage and cargo, for landing and take-off and servicing of aircrafts should be determined.

This decides the type of airport to be developed. Based on the classification of airport, the geometric standards of approaches, runways and taxiways are determined. Thus the planner gets an idea of the approximate land size required for developing a new airport. The limits of the maximum altitudes of the topographical and man-made features in the approach zones and turning zones can also be decided.

4.5 AIRPORT SITE SELECTION

The selection of a suitabte site for an airport depends upon the class of airport under consideration. However, if such factors as required for the selection of the largest facility are considered, the development of the airport by stages will be made easier and economical. The factors listed below are for the selection of a suitable site for a major airport installation :

1 Regional plan
2 Airport use
3 Proximity to other airports
4 Ground accessibility
5 Topography
6 Obstructions
7 Visibility
8 Wind
9 Noise nuisance
10 Grading, drainage and soil characteristics
11 Future development
12 Availability of utilities from town
13 Economic considerations

Above factors are briefly discussed as follows :

4.5.1 Regional Plan

The site selected should fit well into the regional plan, thereby forming it an integral part of the national network of airport.

4.5.2 Airport Use

The selection of site depends upon the use of an airport i.e. whether for civilian or for military operations. However, during the emergency, civilian airports are taken over by the defence. Therefore, the airport site selected should be such that it provides natural protection to the area from air raids. This consideration is of prime importance for the airfields to be located in combat zones. If the site provides thick bushes, the planes can be stored inside unnoticed. Sometimes the topography is such that the planes can be hidden by the underground installations.

4.5.3 Proximity to Other Airports

The site should be selected at a considerable distance from the existing airports so that the aircraft landing in one airport does not interfere with the movement of aircraft at other airport. The required separation between the airports mainly depends upon the volume of air traffic, the type of aircraft and the air traffic control, i e. whether the airports are equipped with instrumental landing facilities or not. The following minimum spacings have been suggested as a guide for planning :

(i) For airports serving small general aviation aircrafts under VFR conditions = 3.2 km (2 miles)

(ii) For airports serving bigger aircrafts, say two piston engine, under VFR conditions = 6.4 km (4 miles)

(iii) For airports operating piston engine aircrafts under IFR conditions = 25.6 km (16 miles)

(iv) For aircrafts operating jet engine aircrafts under IFR conditions = 160 km (100 miles)

If the suggested minimum spacing between the airports cannot be provided, then the landing and take-off of aircrafts in each airport are properly timed to avoid interference. This obviously reduces the capacity of each airport.

4.5.4 Ground Accessibility

The site should be so selected that it is readily accessible to the users. The airline passenger is more concerned with his door-to-door time rather than the actual time in air travel. The time to reach the airport is, therefore, an important consideration specially for short-haul operations. The time required to reach an airport in a passenger car, from the business or residential centres, should normally not exceed

30 minutes. The best location is a site adjacent to the main highway. This provides a quick access and minimises the cost of an entrance road. Availability of public transportation facilities, e.g., bus, taxi etc, further qualifies the suitability of the site and may also improve the business potentiality at the airport.

4.5.5 Topography

This includes natural features like ground contours, trees; streams etc. A raised ground e.g. a hill top, is usually considered to be an ideal site for an airport. The reasons are :

(i) Less obstruction in approach zones and turning zones
(ii) Natural drainage, low land may result in flooding
(iii) More uniform wind
(iv) Better visibility due to less fog

4.5.6 Obstructions

When aircraft is landing or taki.g off, it loses or gains altitude very slowly as compared to the forward speed. For this reason, long clearance areas are provided on either side of runway known as *approach areas* over which the aircraft can safely gain or lose altitude. The areas should be kept free of obstructions. The obstructions may consist of fences, trees, pole lines, building and other natural or man made objects. Sometimes the ground itself may slope upwards from the end of the runways to such an extent that it forms an obstruction to the aircraft operation. If obstruction exists around a site over which an airport is to be built, the removal is imperative at any cost. The future growth of undesirable structures is controlled by zoning laws.

4.5.7 Visibility

Poor visibility lowers the traffic capacity of the airport. The site selected should therefore be free from visibility reducing conditions, such as fog, smoke and haze. Fog generally settles in the area where wind blow is minimum, e.g. in a valley. Smoke and haze nuisance exist at sites nearer to the industrial areas. Therefore, trend of the future development of industrial area should also be studied and the site should be selected accordingly.

4.5.8 Wind

Runway is so oriented that landing and take off is done by heading into the wind. Wind. data, i.e., direction, duration and intensity of wind should be collected over a minimum period of about five years. This helps in proper orientation of runway and influences the shape of the site needed for the development of airport. The site should be located to windward direction of the city, so that a minimum smoke from the city is blown over the site.

4.5.9 Noise Nuisance

The extent of noise nuisance depends upon the climb-out path of aircraft, type of engine propulsion and the gross weight of aircraft. The problem becomes more acute with jet engine aircrafts. Therefore, the site should be so selected that the landing and take off paths of the aircrafts pass over the land which is free from residential or industrial development. Sometimes *buffer zone* may have to be provided between the take off end of a runway and a nearby residential area. If buffer zone cannot be provided, some accoustical barrier may have to be installed. *Federal Aviation Agency* (FAA) recommends that to minimise community disturbance due to noise, the area as shown in Figure 4.1 should be kept free from the residential development and places of public assembly.

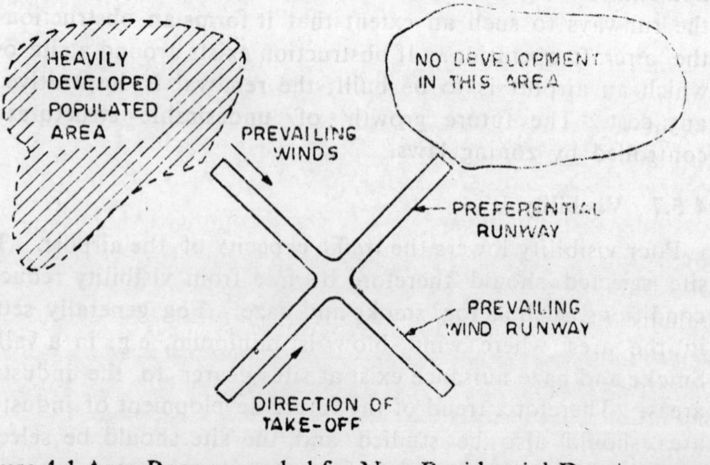

Figure 4.1 Area Recommended for Non-Residential Development

Sometimes it so happens that the area under the flight path which is oriented along the direction of prevailing winds, is highly developed with residences and industries. However, if runway is constructed at right angles to the previous direction, the area is found to be scarcely developed. If the wind intensity over the site is low for large percentage of time, it will be possible to use the latter direction of runway during the above period and consider it as the *preferential runway* for take-off. This is explained in Figure 4.2. Thus, sometimes an extra runway may have to be constructed merely to reduce the noise nuisance.

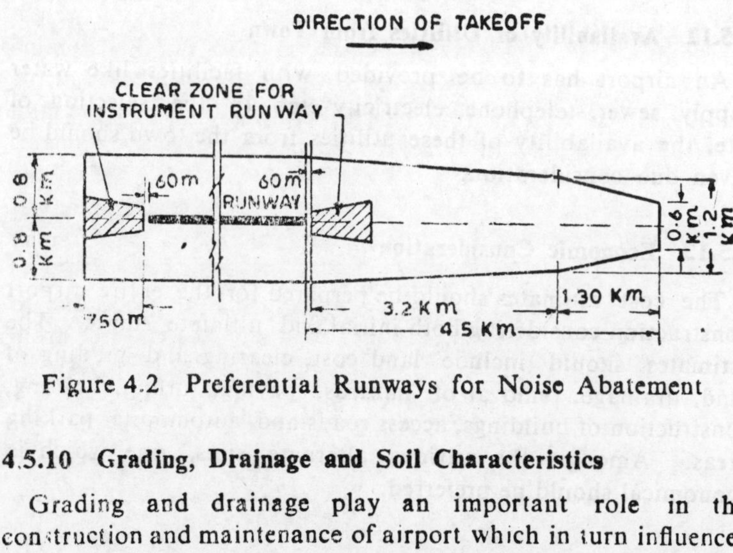

Figure 4.2 Preferential Runways for Noise Abatement

4.5.10 Grading, Drainage and Soil Characteristics

Grading and drainage play an important role in the construction and maintenance of airport which in turn influences the site selection. The original ground profile of a site together with any grading operations, determines the shape of an airport area and the general pattern of the drainge system. The possibility of floods at the valley sites should be investigated. Sites with high water tables, which may require costly subsoil drainage should be avoided. The cost of grading and drainage can often be reduced by selecting a site with favourable soil characteristics. The most desirable type of soil for airport construction is the one which contains a reasonable amount of previous material such as gravel, sand of decomposed granite combined with a suitable natural binder. The soil that becomes plastic when wet is the most undesirable type.

4.5.11 Future Development

Considering that the air traffic volume will continue to increase in future, more number of runways may have to be provided for an increased traffic. Similarly, more facilities may be required for processing of passengers, baggage and cargo and for shelter of aircraft. Additional traffic control devices may also have to be installed. Taking into consideration the anticipated future developments in the airport, larger area should be acquired initially. Zoning ordinates should be implemented to prevent the growth of undesirable structures within the area.

4.5.12 Availability of Utilities from Town

An airport has to be provided with facilities like water supply, sewer, telephone, electricity etc. In the selection of site, the availability of these utilities from the town should be given due consideration.

4.5.13 Economic Consideration

The cost estimates should be perpared for the entire airport construction considering both initial and ultimate stages. The estimates should include land cost, clearing and grading of land, drainage, removal of hazards, paving, turfing, lighting, construction of buildings, access roads and automobile parking areas. Amongst the various alternate sites, one which is economical should be preferred.

4.6 SURVEYS FOR SITE SELECTION

Keeping in view the various factors which influence the site selection, the types of surveys to be carried out at each site are summarized as follows :

1. *Traffic survey :* To determine the amount of air traffic including the anticipated traffic for future.

2. *Meteorological survey :* To determine direction, duration and intensity of wind, rainfall, fog, temperature and barometric pressure etc.

3. *Topographical survey :*

(i) To prepare contour map showing other natural features such as trees, streams etc.

(ii) To prepare a map showing such constructed objects as pole lines, building, roads etc.

These maps will be helpful in the jobs of clearing, grading and drainage.

4. *Soil survey :* To determine soil type and ground water table. This assists in the design of runway, taxiway, terminal building and the drainage system.

5. *Drainage survey :*

(i) To determine the quantity of storm water for drainage. This can be obtained from the rainfall intensity and the contour maps

(ii) To locate possible outlets for drain water in the vicinity of the site.

(iii) To study the possibility of intercepting or diverting the natural streams of nallas flowing towards the site under consideration.

6. *Material survey :* To ascertain the availability of suitable construction materials at a reasonable cost and the mode of transportation of these materials to the site.

4.7 DRAWINGS TO BE PREPARED

The surveys conducted at the various possible sites will guide in the selection of the most suitable site. The following plans are to be prepared for the finally selected site.

1 Topographical plan showing original and finally proposed contours, locations of trees, streams, buildings, roads, property lines etc. A typical topographical map is shown in Figure 4.3.

2 Obstruction map showing safe approach zones and turning zones for the aircrafts.

3 Drainage plan showing the layout of proposed buildings, runways, taxiways and the drainage network. The proposed ground contours and the cross-sections and longitudinal profiles of runways and taxiways should also be plotted. The sizes of pipes, percentage gradient and such other details of the drainage network should be clearly indicated.

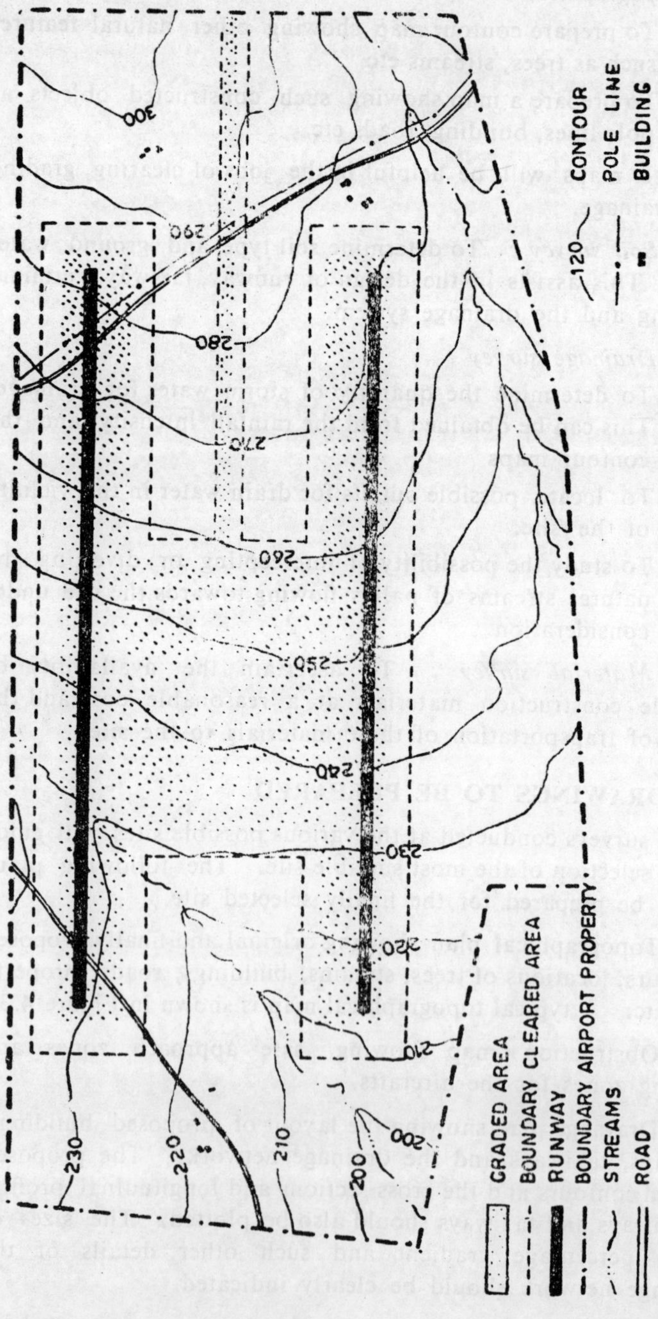

Figure 4.3 Typical Topographical Map for the Airport Layout

4 Airport master plan showing the ground contours, layout of runways, taxiways, terminal buildings, control towers, hangars, approns, access roads and parking areas etc. It provides means by which an airport may be efficiently constructed in stages to meet both the immediate and the future requirements. Preparation of a master plan may guide in the development of the airport in a logical sequence, thereby resulting in a better airport at a minimum cost. A typical layout of airport master plan is shown in Figure 4 4.

4.8 ESTIMATION OF FUTURE AIR TRAFFIC NEEDS

One of the most important tasks in planning an airport is to develop figure for the future air traffic that the airport may be required to handle. Based on the estimate, the various component parts of the airport are planned and their implementation is recommended in stages. The various data collected for air traffic forecast are enumerated in article 4.4. The principal items of air traffic, for which the future estimates are normally needed, are as follow :

(i) Annual passenger volume

(ii) Annual volume of aircrafts

(iii) Peak-day and peak-hour volume of passengers and aircrafts

(iv) Air cargo

(v) Air mail

(vi) General aviation

4.8.1 Annual Passenger Volume

Suppose that the region A has an airport since 1978. Due to increase in the air traffic, the existing facilities at the airport are to be improved. The improvement or the expansion is to be based on the future air traffic. It is now required to estimate the annual number of enplaned passengers for region A for the years 1995 and 2005. There are two possible methods for the estimation.

First method It involves the following steps :

(i) Get the data of the number of enplaned passengers for region A for the past years. Collect similar data for the nation

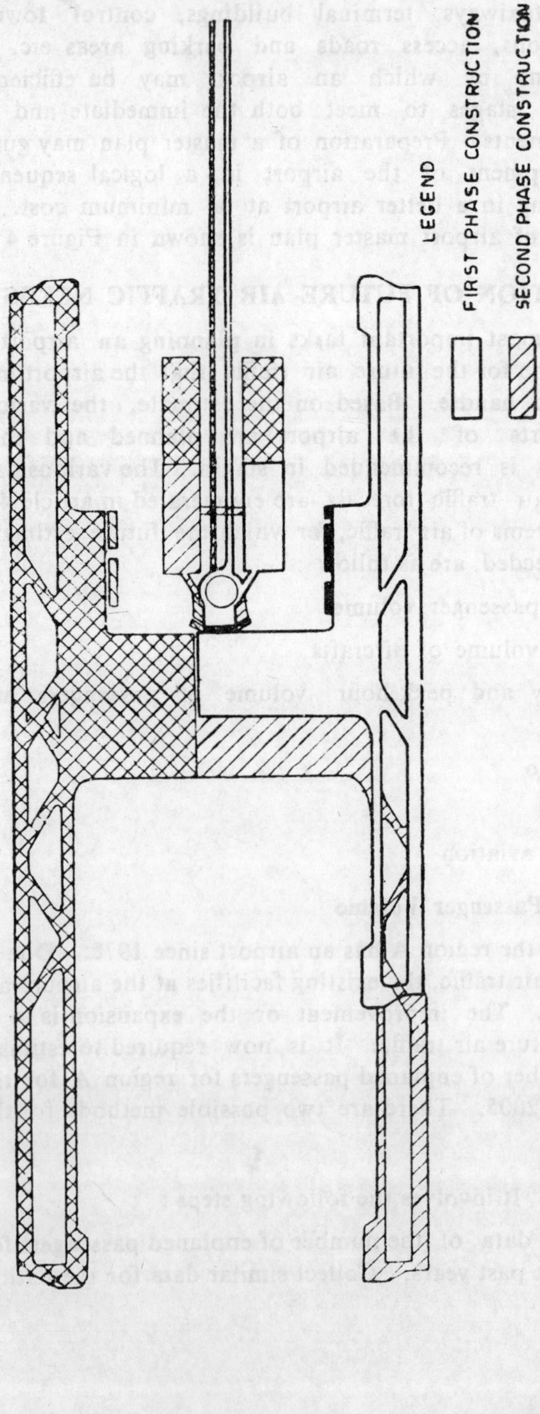

The ultimate development is indicated by cross hatching

Figure 4.4 Typical Master Plan for Airport Layout

as a whole and obtain the percentage of enplaned passengers for region A with respect to the nation.

(ii) Adjust the above percentage to suit the future potential growth of the region A.

(iii) Apply the adjusted percentage of the forecast value to the enplaned passengers for the concerned year for the nation as a whole, and thus obtain the forecast for the region A.

Table 4.2 Annual Enplaned Passengers for Nation and Region A

Year	National value, thousands	For region A, thousands	Region A with respect to nation, percentage
1978	700	22.40	3.2
1979	800	27.20	3.4
1980	950	34.20	3.6
1981	1080	42.10	3.9
1982	1230	51.70	4.2
1983	1400	57.40	4.1
1984	1590	65.25	4.1
1985	1780	72.10	4.0
1986	2000	82.00	4.1
1987	2250	96.80	4.3
1988	2508	110.50	4.4

The above technique is explained by an example using the hypothetical data for the nation and region A. The data is given in Table 4.2.

It is observed from this table, that during the last 10 years, the enplaned passengers of region A increased from 3.2 percent to 4.4 percent of the total enplaned passengers for the natio as a whole. The economy of the region A in terms of production, sales, industry etc. reveals that the above percentage may rise by slight amount in the future years. An index of 5.0 percent is, therefore, chosen for estimate of future passenger volume for region A. The choice of such an index is based more on calculated guessing with no rational basis. The above index is applied to the national forecast for the years 1995 and 2005 and the details are given in Table 4.2.1.

Table 4.2.1

Year	National forecast enplaned passengers (thousands)	Forecast Index percentage	Forecast of region A, enplaned passengers (thousands)
1995	4700	5.0	235
2005	7500	5.0	375

This method of forecast has a limitation that it does not amount for the population growth of the region A. This will not make significant difference so long as the forecast is short-term. But if it is to be projected over a longer period, it is desirable to give due consideration to the population changes as well. The forecast procedure which considers the population growth is described below :

Second method

Following are the steps : (i) From the previous records, obtain the percentage of enplaned passengers per 1000 population for the region A.

(ii) Obtain the similar indices for the nation as a whole and determine the ratio of the two indices for the past years.

(iii) Adjust this ratio to suit the future potential growth of the region A.

(iv) Multiply the adjusted ratio by the forecast national index for the future year. This yields the forecast index for the region A.

(v) Apply the forecast index of the region A to the forecast population of the region. This gives the forecast enplaned passengers for the region.

The above procedure has been illustrated by using the hypothetical data as given in Table 4.3. It is observed from this table that index for the region A has steadily decreased since the year 1978. The index of 830 is chosen to represent the local to national relationship for the years 1995 and 2005.

Table 4.3 Enplaned Passenger per Thousand Population

Year	National Value			Region A			
	Population millions	Enplaned passengers		Population thousands	Enplaned passengers		
		Number thousands	Per thousand population		Number thousands	per thousand population	Index or percentage of national value
(1)	(2)	(3)	(4)	(5)	(6)	(7)	[(7)/(4)] × 100
1978	300	700	2.33	1091	22.40	20 50	880
1979	311	800	2.57	1196	27.20	22.70	883
1980	320	950	2.96	1315	34.20	26 00	878
1981	328	1080	3.28	1470	42.10	28.70	875
1982	338	1239	3.64	1630	51.70	31.70	870
1983	348	1400	4 02	1642	57.40	34.90	868
1984	356	1590	4.47	1695	65.25	38.50	861
1985	364	1780	4.90	1720	72.10	42.00	857
1986	370	2000	5.41	1782	82.00	46 20	854
1987	377	2250	5.97	1905	96.80	50.80	851
1988	384	2508	6.53	2000	110.50	53.30	816

Thsee indices are applied to the national forecasts as per the details given in Table 4.3.1.

The values obtained by the two methods should be compared and the greater of the two should be adopted for the airport planning. Thus the forecast values of the annual enplaned passengers should be used for planning the terminal facilities of region A, as per the details given in Table 4.3.2.

Table 4.3.1

Year	National values: Population millions	National values: Enplaned passengers: Number thousand	National values: Enplaned passengers: Per thousand population	Region A: Population thousand	Region A: Enplaned passengers: Percentage of national value	Region A: Enplaned passengers: Per thousand population	Region A: Enplaned passengers: Number thousand
1995	440	4700	10.7	2700	830	89.0	240
2005	750	7500	15.0	3500	830	124.4	435

Table 4.3.2

Year	Annual enplaned passengers, thousands
1995	240
2005	435

4.8.2 Annual Volume of Aircrafts

The forecast technique for the annual volume of aircrafts is similar to the procedure for estimating the passenger volume. The steps for this forecast are given below :

(i) From the previous records, obtain the number of enplaned passengers for aircraft departure for the nation as a whole and also for the region A. Determine the ratio of the two for the past years.

(ii) Adjust this ratio to suit the potential growth of the region A in the future years.

(iii) Apply the adjusted ratio to the national forecast of the number of enplaned passengers per aircraft departure. This will yield the corresponding index for the region A.

(iv) Apply the above index to the forecast value of the number of enplaned passengers for the region A. This gives the number of departing aircrafts. Assuming that each aircraft has two movements, viz arriving and departing, the total number of aircraft movements is twice the above number.

The procedure is explained by using the hypothetical data and the details are given in Table 4.4.

Table 4.4 Enplaned Passengers per Aircraft Departure

Year	National value	Region A	Ratio of region A to nation, per cent
1978	6.18	13.90	224.5
1979	6.88	15.13	220.1
1980	7.34	16.00	217.0
1981	7.92	16.87	213.0
1982	8.43	17.65	209.0
198	9.97	20.45	205.3
1984	10.40	21.00	202.0
1985	10.83	21.60	199.0
1986	11.23	22.00	196.0
1987	11.52	22.20	192.5
1988	11.81	22.40	189.7

From Table 4.4, it is observed that the index for region A gradually reduces from 224.5 to 189.7 Considering the economic growth of the region A in future years, its indices for the year 1995 and 2005 are determined as 170 per cent. They are applied to the national forecast values, Table 4 5.

The index for region A is applied to its forecast annual enplaned passengers and the details are given in Table 4.6.

4.8.3. Peak Day and Peak Hour Volume of Passengers and Aircrafts

Peak hour volume of passengers is required to determine the

Table 4.5 Forecast of Enplaned Passengers per Aircraft Departure

Year	National forecast	Ratio percent	Region A index
1995	14.0	170	23.8
2005	17.0	170	28.9

Table 4.6 Forecast of Annual Aircraft Movements

Year	Annual enplaned passenger	Index for region A	Annual aircraft departure	Annual aircraft movements
1995	240,000	23.8	10,100	20,200
2005	435,000	8.9	15,050	30,100

extent of the facilities needed in the terminal building and for proper allocation of these facilities. Peak hour aircraft movements are required for design of runways, taxiways, and loading aprons. Although a specific hourly volume (thirtieth highest hourly volume) is used for geometric design of highways, for airports no such criterion exists. The peak hour volumes are examined for the past years and a reasonable volume is chosen for the design. To estimate the peak hourly volume, the peak month and peak day traffic are first determined. The forecast procedure is explained below :

A. For Peak Day Volume :

(i) From the past years records for region A, obtain the percentages of annual enplaned passengers the occurred during the peak months. Decide the suitable percentage or the peak month to annual number of passengers.

(ii) Apply the above percentage to the forecast annual number of passengers as determined in article 4.8.1. This will give the peak month enplaned passengers for the region A.

(iii) From the previous years records, obtain the percentages that occurred on the peak days. Decide the percentage of the peak day to peak month number of passengers. Apply this percentage to the forecast peak month enplaned passengers as obtained in step (ii). This will give the forecast peak day enplaned passengers. The above procedure is explained by using the hypothetical data given in Table 4.7.

Table 4.7 Peak Month as Percent of Annual Enplaned Passengers for Region A

Year	Highest month	Second highest month	Third highest month	Average per cent
1983	11.2	10.5	9.3	10.3
1984	11.5	10.8	9.7	10.7
1985	11.8	11.1	10.1	11.0
1986	12.1	11.5	10.3	11.3
1987	12.8	12 1	11.1	12.0
1988	13 0	12.3	11.3	12.2

It is observed from Table 4 7, that the index for region A increased from 10.3 to 12.2 during the period 1983-1988. The index for future forecast is fixed as 14 5%. The percentage is now applied to the annual enplaned passengers as follows :

Year	Region A annual enplaned passengers	Index	Region A peak month enplaned passengers
1995	240.000	14.5	34.800
2005	435.000	14 5	63.000

Next step is to obtain the percentage of peak month passengers that occurred on peak day as explained in Table 4.8.

From the Table 4.8, it is observed that the index for region A varies in an irregular pattern from 3.80 to 3.97. Taking an

Table 4.8 Peak Day Enplaned Passengers as Per cent of Peak Month for Region A

Year	Highest peak month	Highest peak day	Second highest peak day	Third highest peak day	Average
1983	157.0	4.0	3.9	3.8	3.90
1984	183 0	4.1	3.9	3.8	3.93
1985	210.0	4.0	3.9	3.7	3 87
1986	242 0	3.9	3.8	3.7	3.80
1987	288.0	4 0	3 8	3.7	3 83
1988	326.0	4.1	4.0	3.8	3.97

average value of 3.90 as the representative index for future forecast, the peak day passenger volume is obtained as follows :

Year	Peak month	Ratio per cent	Peak day
1995	34,800	3.90	1358
2005	63,000	3.90	2460

B. For Peak Hour Volume :

In order to forecast the peak hour volume of passengers, it is necessary to forecast the peak hour aircraft movements and then multiply this number by the number of enplaned passengers per aircraft departure. It is usually assumed that the number of enplaned passengers per aircraft departure equals the number of enplaned passengers per aircraft arrival. The procedure of forecast is as follows :

(i) Determine the peak day aircraft movement by a similar procedure as used for finding out the peak day passenger volume.

(ii) Determine the percentage of peak day aircraft movements that occur on peak hours. Discuss with the airport authorities, the possible scheduling of aircrafts and select suitable percentage for future estimation.

(iii) Obtain the peak hour aircraft movement from the following relationship.

Peak hour aircraft movement =

$$\frac{\text{Peak month}}{\text{Annual}} \times \frac{\text{Peak day}}{\text{Per month}} \times \frac{\text{Peak hour}}{\text{Peak day}} \times \text{Annual}$$

(iv) Multiply the fore cast peak hour aircraft movement by the forecast enplaned passengers per aircraft departure. This gives the forecast peak hour passenger volume.

Table 4.9 Peak Month Aircraft Movements as Per cent of Annual Movements

Year	Highest month	Second highest month	Third highest month	Average per cent
1983	10.8	10.6	10.5	10.63
1984	11.2	10.9	10.7	10.93
1985	11.5	11.1	10.9	11.16
1986	11.7	11.3	11.1	11.36
1987	12.1	11.6	11.5	11.73
1988	12.4	11.9	11.6	11.96

The above procedure is explained using the hypothetical data. Table 4.9 deals with the peak month aircraft movements.

The suitable percentage for the forecast may, therefore, be assumed as 13.4. Proceeding on similar lines, the suitable percentage of peak month aircraft movements that occur on peak day is determined. Suppose this percentage is 3.70. It means that 3.70 per cent of peak month aircraft movements represent the peak day movement. Next, select after the careful study of airline schedules, the peak hour aircraft movement as per cent of peak day movement. Suppose this figure is 15 percent.

Therefore, the ratio of peak hour to annual movement

$$= 0.134 \times 0.037 \times 0.15$$
$$= 0.000744$$

The peak hour aircraft movement can now be obtained as follows :

Year	Annual aircraft movement	Factor	Peak-hour aircraft movement
1995	20.200*	0.000744	15.0
2005	30,100*	0.000744	22.4

Applying the peak hour aircraft movement of the number of enplaned passengers per aircraft departure for the years 1995 and 2005, and enplaning and deplaning passenger volumes being assumed as same, the forecast total peak hour volume of passengers are obtained as follows :

Year	Peak-hour aircraft movement	Enplaned passengers per movement	Peak hour passenger volume
1995	15.0	23.8*	357.0
2005	22.4	28.9*	647.0

It may be noted that the peak hour passenger movement as obtained above does not include the traffic due to general aviation or military operation etc. The passenger volumes due to these operations should be estimated separately and added to the above values.

*See Tables 4.5 and 4.6

4.8.4 Air Cargo

The air cargo is a relatively younger industry and its past performance may not be a true representation of the future. The estimation may, however, be done as follows :

(i) Obtain the ratio of the air cargo of region A with respect to the nation as a whole.

(ii) Adjust this ratio taking into consideration the potential growth of the industries.

(iii) Apply the adjusted ratio to the national forecast values for the future years and obtain the total air cargo in tonnage for the region A.

(iv) Estimate the number of aircrafts required to carry the air cargo quantity.

4.8.5 Air Mail

The future estimation of air mail and air parcel is necessary only when their volume is so large that they require separate aeroplanes for their transport. Usually the post office department sends its own space requirement in the terminal building. Thus the airport authorities need not necessarily feel the responsibility of the forecast of this item. However, this can be done in a way similar to that for the passengers.

4.8.6 General Aviation

It includes all flights which are done through other than commercial airline. This may be divided into the following categories :

(i) Business flying, e.g. agriculture, mining, construction, manufacturing etc.

(ii) Commercial flying including aerial spray of chemicals, seeds, aerial survey, aerial advertisement etc.

(iii) Instructional flying

(iv) Pleasure flying

Evaluation of general aviation activity in terms of passengers and aircraft movements is very essential since it may sometimes exceed the commerical airline fleet. The procedure of forecast is as follows :

(a) For region A, determine the hours flown by each component of general aviation e.g., business, commercial, instructional or pleasure flying.

(b) Compare these hours with the similar values for the nation as a whole and determine the ratios Select suitable ratios for future forecast looking to the trend of the general aviation activity of the region.

(c) Multiply these ratios by the national forecast values. This gives the forecast of hours flown by each component of the general aviation.

(d) Divide the hours flown by each component of the general aviation by the appropriate factor. This yields number of aircrafts required for the above components.

(e) Multiply the number of aircrafts for each component by the number of annual movements per aircraft. This gives the total annual movements for each component of the general aviation.

PROBLEMS

1 What are the objectives of airport master plan.

2 Compare the recommendations of FAA and ICAO with reference to airport master planning.

3 Why is it necessary to plan airports on regional basis ? What information are obtained from the regional plans ? What data are to be collected for such planning ?

4 Suppose you are given an option of either improving upon the existing airport or developing a new airport to cater the increased air traffic anticipated in the near future. Explain the step by step procedure you will follow in arriving at the final conclusion.

5 Enumerate the various factors which you would keep in view while selecting a suitable site for an airport.

6 Explain the various survey to be conducted and the data to be collected for airport site selection.

7 What are the different drawings and maps that should be prepared for the finally selected site for developing an airport ?

8 Explain why the top of a hill is more suitable site for locating an airport than a valley site.

9 Discuss the effect of noise on airport planning.

10 What are the various features which are shown in the topographical map of an airport ? Sketch a typical topographical map for an airport which is planned for two parallel runways.

11 What do you understand from the master plan of an airport ? What features are shown in this ? Sketch a typical master plan of the airport which is to be developed in three stages.

5

AIRPORT OBSTRUCTIONS

5.1 ZONING LAWS

It has already been discussed in Chapter 4 that the site for airport should be so selected that it does not obstruct the safe landing and take-off of aircrafts. Steps should also be taken to curb the possibility of developing any future obstruction. Purchase of the entire flight approach areas and the turning areas to prevent the undesirable growth of structures is not always feasible economically. As such zoning ordinances regarding the permissible height of structures and the land use within the airport boundary need implementation as soon as the site is selected for the airport development. The permissible height of structures depends upon the airport and the aircraft types which would use the airport. The use of land for manufacture of certain items which may result in smoke nuisance, foul odour etc. is also controlled by the zoning laws. It should, however, be confirmed that all zoning ordinances are reasonable and the application is fair; otherwise they are likely to create resentment from the public and may result in mass disobedience. Whenever it is felt that the zoning laws are provocative, sufficient compensation should be announced in order to ascertain its effective implementation.

5.2 CLASSIFICATION OF OBSTRUCTIONS

Obstruction to safe air navigations are broadly divided into the following two categories :

1 Objects protruding above certain imaginary surfaces.

2 Objects exceeding their limiting heights above the ground surface in approach zones and turning zones.

These are discussed in subsequent paragraphs,

5.2.1 Imaginary Surfaces

The types of imaginary surfaces are :

(i) Take-off climb surface

(ii) Approach surface

(iii) Inner horizontal surface

(iv) Conical surface

(v) Transitional surface

(vi) Outer horizontal surface

The characteristics of these surfaces for different types of airports* are described below and summarized in Table 5.1 and 5.2. The perspective and schematic views of these surfaces are shown in Figures 5.1 and 5.2 respectively.

Take-off climb surface

The take-off climb area shall be established beyond the end of runway or clearway for each runway direction intended to be used for the take-off aeroplanes. At aerodromes where the proposal for runways extension exists, the requisite surface shall be determined from the proposed extended runway strip or associated clearway as applicable. They are shown by perspective view in Figure 5.3. At aerodromes, where there is only one runway, the take-off climb areas and the associated surfaces shall be prescribed as for the main runway. According to the Directorate of Air routes and Aerodromes (DARA) of the Government of India, circular No. 6 of 1978, for more sophisticated types of aircrafts expected to operate in the future, if the conditions exist that no object reaches the 2

*See article 6.4.1 for airport types

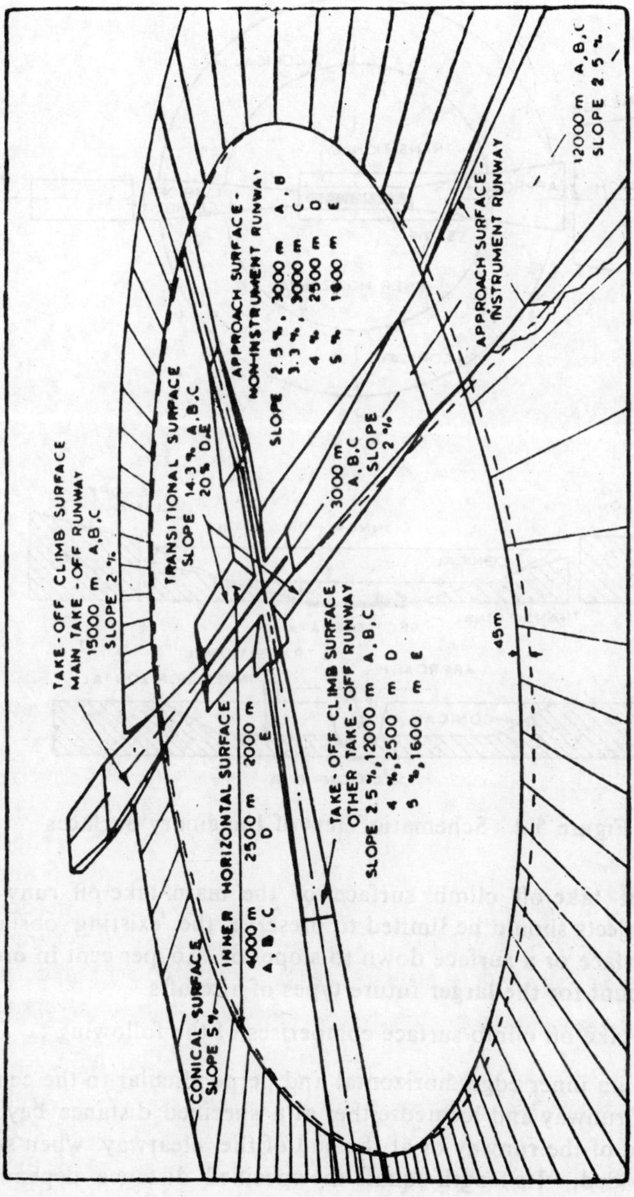

Figure 5.1 Perspective View of Imaginary surfaces

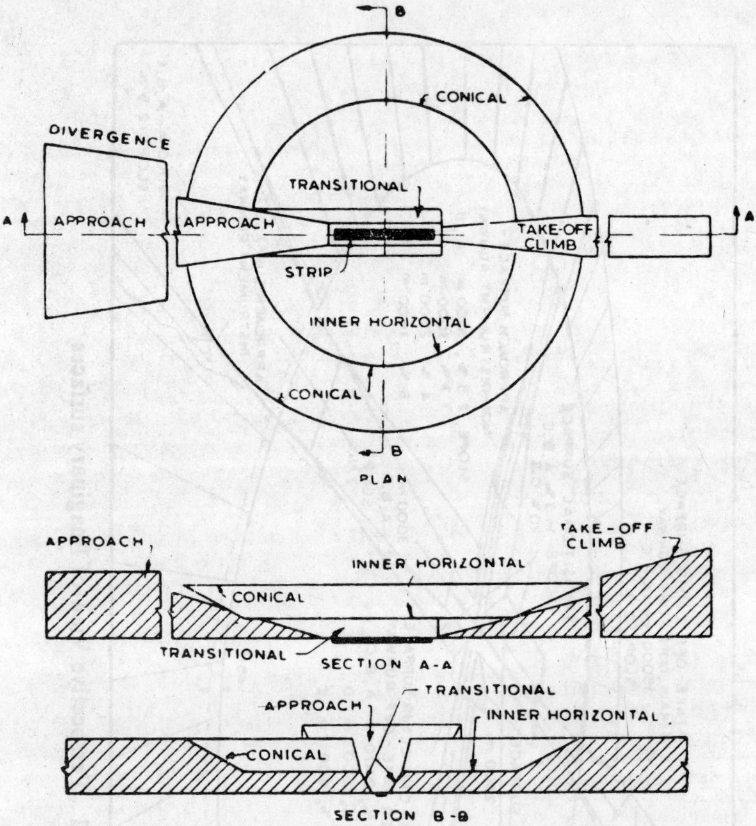

Figure 5.2 Schematic View of Imaginary Surfaces

per cent take-off climb surface of the main take-off runway, new objects should be limited to preserve the existing obstacle free surface or a surface down to slope of 1.6 per cent in order to account for the larger future types of aircrafts.

The take-off climb surface comperises of the following :

(a) an inner edge, horizontal and perpendicular to the centre line of runway and located either at a specified distance beyond the end of the runway or at the end of the clearway when such is provided. Its length equals the specified distance depending upon the type of aerodrome under consideration. The elevation of the inner edge shall be that of the highest point on the extended runway centre line between the end of the runway and

Table 5.1 Dimensions and Slopes of Take-off Climb Surface

Runway Classification / Item	Main take-off runways ABC*	Other runways ABC	Other runways D	Other runways E
Length of inner edge, m (ft)	180 (600)	180 (600)	80 (260)	60 (200)
**Distance from runway end, m (ft)	60 (200)	60 (200)	30 (100)	30 (100)
Divergence on each side, percent	12.5	12.5	10	10
Final width, m (ft)	1800 (6000)	1200 (4000)	580 (1900)	380 (1250)
Length, m (ft)	15,000 (50,000)	12,000 (40,000)	2500 (8300)	1600 (5200)
Slope, percent	2	2.5	4	5

*See article 6.4.1 for airport types

**Or end of clearway if the clearway is established

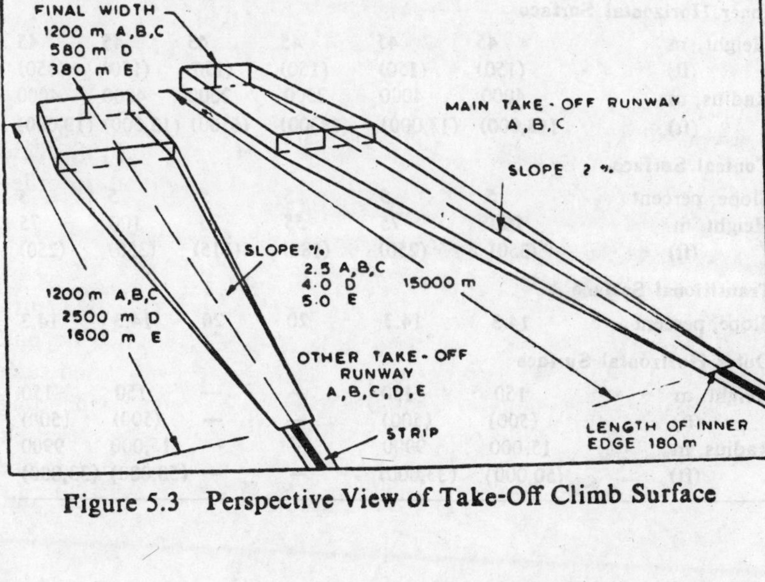

Figure 5.3 Perspective View of Take-Off Climb Surface

Table 5.2 Dimensions and Slopes of Obstacle Limitation Surface for Approach Runways

Runway Classification / Surface & Item	Non-Instrument Approach AB	Non-Instrument Approach C	Non-Instrument Approach D	Non-Instrument Approach E	Instrument Approach AB	Instrument Approach C
Approach Surfaee						
Length of inner edge, m	150	150	80	60	300	300
ft	(500)	(500)	(260)	(200)	(1000)	(1000)
Distance from threshold, m (ft)	60 (200)	60 (200)	30 (100)	30 (100)	60 (200)	60 (200)
Divergence of each line, percent	10	10	10	10	15	15
First Section						
Length, m	3000	3000	2500	1600	3000	3000
(ft)	(10,000)	(10,000)	(8300)	(5200)	(10,000)	(10,000)
Slope, percent	2.5	3.3	4	5	2	2
Second Section						
Length, m	—	—	—	—	3600	3600
(ft)					(12,000)	(12,000)
Slope, percent	—	—	—	—	2.5	2.5
Horizontal Section						
Length, m	—	—	—	—	8400	8400
(ft)					(28,000)	(28,000)
Total Length, m	3000	3000	2500	1600	15,000	15,000
(ft)	(10,000)	(10,000)	(8300)	(5200)	(50,000)	(50,000)
Inner Horizontal Surface						
Height, m	45	45	45	45	45	45
(ft)	(150)	(150)	(150)	(150)	(150)	(150)
Radius, m	4000	4000	2500	2000	4000	4000
(ft)	(13,000)	(13,000)	(8300)	(6500)	(13,000)	(13,000)
Conical Surface						
Slope, percent	5	5	5	5	5	5
Height, m	100	75	55	35	100	75
(ft)	(350)	(250)	(180)	(115)	(350)	(250)
Transitional Surface						
Slope, percent	14.3	14.3	20	20	14.3	14.3
Outer Horizontal Surface						
Height, m	150	150	—	—	150	150
(ft)	(500)	(500)	—	—	(500)	(500)
Radius, m	15,000	9900	—	—	15,000	9900
(ft)	(50,000)	(33,000)	—	—	(50,000)	(33,000)

the inner edge except that when a clearway is provided the elevation shall be equal to the highest point on the ground on the centre line of runway.

(b) two sides originating from the ends of the inner edge, diverging uniformly at a specified rate along the take-off track to a specified final width. It continues thereafter at that width for the remainder of the length of the take-off climb surface. The surface extends at a specified slope upwards and outwards which for straight take-off flight path shall be measured in vertical plane containing the centre line of runway.

(c) an outer edge horizontal and perpendicular to the specified take-off track.

Approach Surface

The approach surface shall be established from the smaller ends of runway strip for each runway direction intended to be used for the landing of aeroplanes. It comprises of the following.

(a) an inner edge of specified length, horizontal and perpendicular to the extended centre line of the runway and located at a specified distance before the threshold. An elevation of the inner edge shall be equal to that of the mid point of the threshold.

(b) two sides originating at the ends of the inner edge and diverging uniformly at a specified rate from the extended centre line of the runway. The surface extends upwards and outwards at a specified slope which shall be measured in the vertical plane containing the centre line of the runway.

(c) an outer edge which is parallel to the inner edge. The perspective views of approach surfaces for instrument and non-instrument runways are shown in Figure 5.4.

Inner Horizontal Surface (IHS)

It is the surface located in a horizontal plane above an aerodrome and its surrounding. The shape of the IHS need not necessarily be circular. The raidus or outer limits of IHS shall be measured from airport reference point (ARP) or points established for such purposes. Where the runway length is 600 m (2000 ft) or more but less than 750 m (2500 ft), the IHS

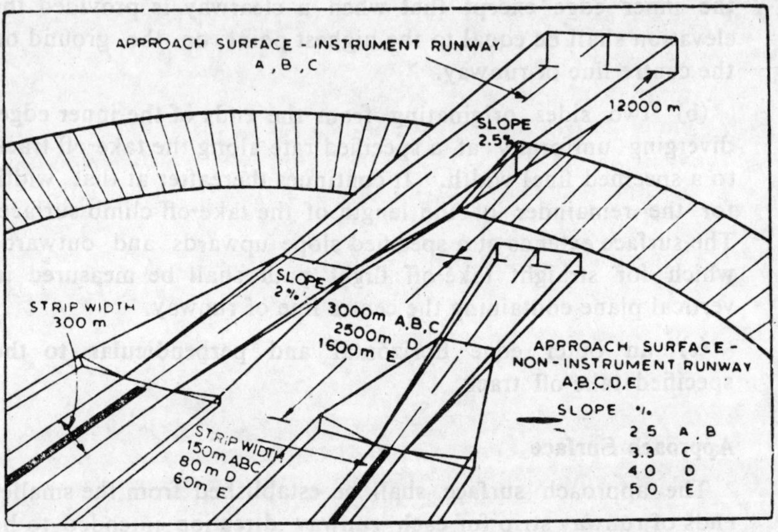

Figure 5.4 Perspective View of Approach Surface

shall be a circular surface with radius of 4000 m (13000 ft) from ARP. Where the runway' length is 900 m (3000 ft) or more but less than 1500 m (5000 ft), the inner horizontal surface shall extend to a horizontal distance of 3900 m (13,000 ft from the ARP. Where the runway length is 1500 m (5000 ft) or more, the 'HS shall be a composite pattern which consists of two circular arcs centered at the two runway ends with a radius of 4000 m (13000 ft) from ARP. Where the runway length is 5000 ft or more, the IHS shall be a composite pattern which consists of two circular arc centered at the two runway ends with a radius of 4000 m. These arcs shall be joined tangentially to form an elliptical shape. Where it is required to protect two or more widely spaced long runways an even more complex pattern involving four or more circular arcs is formed. These arc should be joined tangentially by straight lines and the IHS shall be defined by the external limits of the resulting pattern.

Conical Surface

It extends upwards and outwards from the periphery of the inner horizontal surface. The limits of the conical surface shall comprise the following :

(a) a lower edge coincident with the periphery of the inner horizontal surface.

(b) an upper edge located at a specified height above the inner horizontal surface. The slope of the conical surface shall be measured in a vertical plane perpendicular to the periphery of the inner horizontal surface.

Transitional Surface

It is a complex surface along the side of the strip and part of the side of approach surface that slopes upwards and outwards to the inner horizontal surface. This is intended to serve as the controlling obstacle limitation surface for buildings etc. The limits of a transitional surface shall comprise :

(a) a lower edge beginning at the intersection of the side of approach surface with the inner horizontal surface and extending down the side of the approach surface to the inner edge of the approach surface and from there it extends along the length of the strip parallel to the runway centre line.

(b) an upper edge located in the plane of the inner horizontal surface. The slope of the transitional surface is measured in a vertical plane at right angles to the centre line of the runway. The slope shall be 14.3 per cent (1 : 7) where the length of runway is 900 m (3000 ft) and above. For the runways of length less than 900 m, the slope shall be 20 per cent (1 : 5).

Outer Horizontal Surface (OHS)

It is not proposed to establish OHS for aerodromes with runways of length less than 900 m. It is circular in plane with centre located at ARP. Where the longest runway is more than 900 m in length but less than 1500 m, the OHS shall extend to 9900 m from the ARP. For airports where the length of the longest runway is 1500 m or more, the OHS shall extend to 15,000 m from the ARP. The height of OHS is 150 m above the ARP elevation. The constructions protruding above this surface shall not be permitted.

5.3 APPROACH ZONE

During landing, the glide path of an aircraft varies from a

steep to flat slope. But during take-off, the rate of climb of aircraft is limited by its wing loading and engine power. As such wide clearance areas, known as approach zones are required on either side of runway along the direction of landing and take-off of aircraft. Over this area, the aircraft can safely gain or loose altitude. The whole of this area has to be kept free of obstructions and as such zoning laws are implemented in this area. The plan of approach zone is the same as that of the approach surface. The only difference between the two is that while approach surface is an imaginary surface, the approach area indicates the actual ground area.

5.3.1. Clear Zone

The inner most portion of approach zone which is the most critical portion from obstruction view-point is known as *clear zone*. Its configuration and dimensions are shown in Figure 5.5.

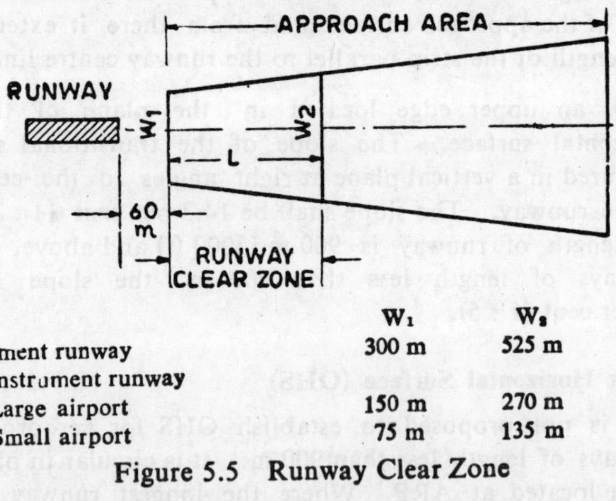

	W_1	W_2	L
Instrument runway	300 m	525 m	750 m
Non-instrument runway			
(a) Large airport	150 m	270 m	600 m
(b) Small airport	75 m	135 m	300 m

Figure 5.5 Runway Clear Zone

The purchase of land in this zone is recommended for the effective implementation of zoning laws. It is not necessary to grade this area, but all obstructions are removed. Naturally a level area is preferred, but it is not essential. Fences, ditches and other minor obstacles are permitted.

5.3.2 Highway and Railway Clearances

Roads and railways are not objectionable in clear zones

provided they comply with the clearance standards and the vehicles within this zone are always in motion. The essential clearances over a highway or a railway located any where in the approach area are shown in Figure 5.6.

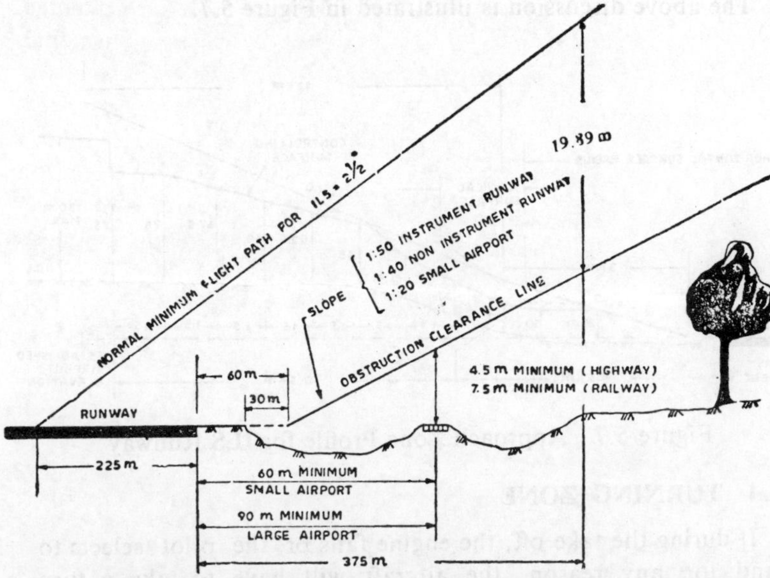

Figure 5.6 Clearances Over Highway and Railway

5 3.3. Objects Exceeding their Limiting Height above Ground

Any object exceeding certain *limiting height* above the ground shall be considered as an obstruction to the air navigation, unless it is not considered objectionable by special aeronautical studies. The discussion below pertains to the approach areas of runways equipped with instrumental landing facilities.

(i) Within 4 5 km (3 statute miles) distance from the runway end, any object shall be considered as an obstruction if its height is more than 30 m above the ground or above the level approach end of runway whichever is higher.

(ii) Any object which is located beyond a distance of 4.5 km (3 statute miles) from the runway end, shall be considered as an obstruction if its height above 30 m increases by more than 7 5 m for each additional 1.5 km (1 statute mile) distance from the runway end; or if it exceeds 75 m within 15 km (10 statute miles) distance from the runway end.

(iii) Any object which protrudes above the minimum approach flight altitude or whose height exceeds 150 m above the ground is also to be considered as an obstruction.

The above discussion is illustrated in Figure 5.7.

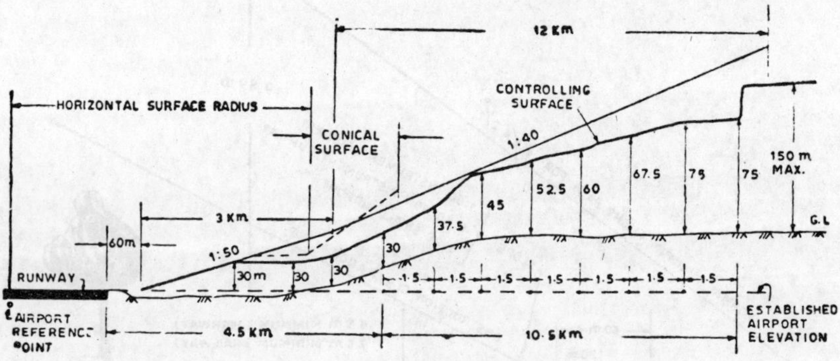

Figure 5.7 Approach Zone Profile for ILS Runway

5.4 TURNING ZONE

If during the take-off, the engine fails or the pilot selects to land for any reason, the aircraft will have to take a turn and come in line with runway before landing. The area of airport other than the approach area, which is used for turning operations of aircraft is called *turning zone*. Since in turning zone the aircraft operates at a considerably low height, it has to be ascertained that this area is also free from obstructions.

The following discussion pertains to the turning zone of instrumental runway :

(i) Any object located with a distance of 4.5 km from the runway reference point shall be considered as an obstruction, if its height is more than 51 m above the established airport elevation or above the ground whichever is higher.

(ii) Any object which is located beyond a distance of 4.5 km (3 statute miles) from the runway reference point shall be considered as obstruction if its height above 51 m increased by more than 30 m for each additional 1.5 km (one statute mile) distance from the airport reference point or if it exceeds

150 m within a distance of 15 km (10 statute miles) from the runway reference point.

The above description is illustrated in Figure 5.8.

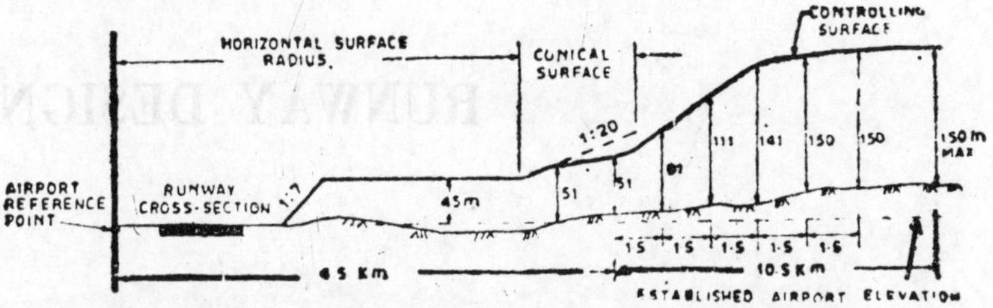

Figure 5.8 Turning Zone Profile for ILS Runway

PROBLEMS

1. What are the imaginary surfaces ? What is their significance ? Explain with the aid of neat sketches the shape of each surface for different types of airport.

2. A railway line and a highway pass through the clear zone area of an airport. Explain with sketch the clearance required over the highway and the railway line for safe landing and take - off of an aircraft.

3. Explain with neat sketches the limiting heights of objects in the approach and turning zone of an instrumental runway.

4. Write short notes on :
   (i) Zoing laws
   (ii) Clear zones
   (iii) Approach zone
   (iv) Approach surface
   (v) Take-off climb surface
   (vi) Inner and outer horizontal surfaces.

6

RUNWAY DESIGN

6.1 RUNWAY ORIENTATION

Runway is usually oriented in the direction of prevailing winds. The head wind, i.e. the direction of wind opposite to the direction of landing and take-off, provides greater lift on the wings of the aircraft when it is taking-off. As such the aircraft rises above the ground much earlier and in a shorter length of runway. During landing, the head wind provides a braking effect and the aircraft comes to a stop in a smaller length of runway. Landing and take-off operations, if done along the wind direction, would require longer runway.

6.1.1 Cross Wind Component and Wind Coverage

It is not possible to obtain the direction of wind along the direction of the centre line of runway throughout the year. On some day of the year or hour of the day, the wind may blow making certain angle with the centre line of runway. If the direction of wind is at an angle to the runway centre line, its component along the direction of runway will be $V \cos \theta$ and that normal to the runway centre line will be $V \sin \theta$ where V is the wind velocity. The normal component of the wind is called *cross wind component* and may interrupt the safe landing and take-off of the air-crafts.

The maximum permissible cross wind component depends upon the size of aircraft and the wing configuration. FAA recommends that for small air crafts, the cross wind component should not exceed 15 kmph (10 mph) and for mixed traffic it should not exceed 25 kmph (15 mph). For airports serving big aircrafts ICAO recommends that the cross wind component should not exceed 35 kmph (23 mph). The percentage of time in a year during which the cross wind component remains within the limits as specified above is called *wind coverage*. According to FAA, the runway handling mixed air traffic should be so planned that for 95 per cent of time in a year, the permissible cross wind component does not exceed 25 kmph. For busy airports, the wind coverage may be increased to as much as 98 percent to 100 percent.

6.1.2 Wind Rose

The wind data, i.e., direction, duration and intensity are graphically represented by a diagram called *wind rose*. The wind data should usually be collected for a period of at least 5 years and preferably of 10 years, so as to obtain an average data with sufficient accuracy. As far as possible, these observations should be taken at or near site selected, since the wind conditions may vary considerably with location particularly in hilly regions.

A typical wind data is given in Table 6.1. In this table, the duration of wind for any one direction covers an angle of 22.5 degrees as shown in Figure 6.1. It is assumed that the wind may come from any point within the 22.5 degree sector. It is possible the wind for a particular location have not been recorded. In such cases the data from two or more of the nearest wind recording station should be used to fix up the wind characteristics of the site. However, this can not be done if the intervening terrain is mountainous. In such cases, the observations of the wind at the actual site should be recorded for at least one year and these results should be used in the interpretation of the data of the nearby weather station as applied to site. Wind rose diagram can be plotted from the data of Table 6.1. It helps in analysing the wind data and obtaining the most suitable direction of the runway.

Table 6.1 Wind Data*

Wind direction	Duration of wind, per cent** 6.4–25 kmph	25–40 kmph	40–60 kmph	Total in each direction percent
N	7.4	2.7	0.2	10.3
NNE	5.7	2.1	0.3	8.1
NE	2.4	0.9	0.6	3.9
ENE	1.2	0.4	0.2	1.8
E	0.8	0.2	0.0	1.0
ESE	0.3	0.1	0.0	0.4
SE	4.3	2.8	0.0	7.1
SSE	5.5	3.2	0.0	8.7
S	9.7	4.6	0.0	14.3
SSW	6.3	3.2	0.5	10.0
SW	3.6	1.8	0.3	5.7
WSW	1.0	0.5	0.1	1.6
W	0.4	0.1	0.0	0.5
WNW	0.2	0.1	0.0	0.3
NW	5.3	1.9	0.0	7.2
NNW	4.0	1.3	0.3	5.6

Total per cent = 86.5

*Average of 8 years periods.

**Percentage of time during which wind intensity, is less than 6.4 kmph is 100−86.5 = 13.5 percent. This period is called calm period and does not influence the operation of landing or take-off because low wind intensity.

Wind rose diagrams can be plotted in two types as follows :

Type I : Showing direction and duration of wind

Type II : Showing direction, duration and intensity of wind

Type I Wind Rose

This type of wind rose is illustrated in Figure 6.2. The radial lines indicate the wind direction and each circle represents the duration of wind. From the Table 6.1, it is observed that the total percentage of time in a year during which the wind blows from north direction is 10.3 percent. This value is plotted along the north direction in

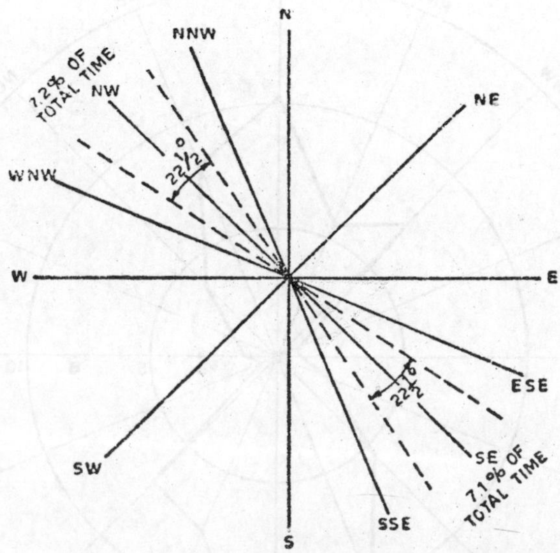

Figure 6.1 Angle Showing the Wind Coverage

Figure 6.2. Similarly other values are also plotted along the respective directions. All plotted points are then jointed by straight lines as shown in Figure 6.2. The best direction of runway is usually along the direction of the longest line on wind rose diagram. In Figure 6.2, the best orientation of runway is thus along NS direction. If deviation of wind direction upto (22.5°+11.25°) from the direction of landing and take-off is permissible, the percentage of time in a year during which the runway can safely be used for landing and take-off, will be obtained by summing the percentages of time along NNW, N, NNE, SSE, S and SSW directions. This comes to 57.0 per cent. *Calm period*, i.e., the percentage of time during which wind intensity is less than 6.4 kmph is also added to the above period. The total percentage of the time therefore comes to 57.0 + 13.5 = 70.5. This type of wind rose does not account for the effect of cross wind component.

Type II Wind Rose

This type of wind rose is illustrated in Figure 6.3. The wind data as in the previous type, i.e. of Table 6.1 is used for this case. Each circle represents the wind

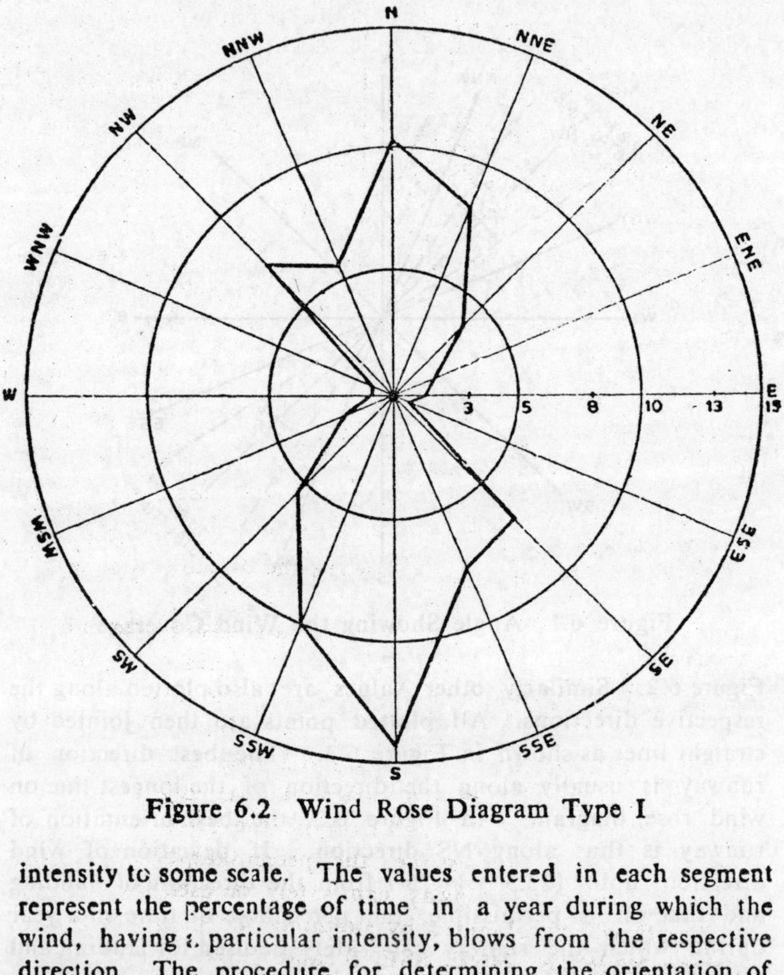

Figure 6.2 Wind Rose Diagram Type I

intensity to some scale. The values entered in each segment represent the percentage of time in a year during which the wind, having a particular intensity, blows from the respective direction. The procedure for determining the orientation of runway is described below :

(i) Draw three equi - spaced parallel lines on a transparent paper strip in such a way that the distance between the two near by parallel lines is equal to the permissible cross wind component. This distance is measured with the same scale with which the wind rose diagram is drawn. In Figure 6.3, the permissible cross wind component is 25 kmph.

(ii) Place the transparent paper strip over the wind rose diagram in such a way that the central line passes through the centre of the diagram.

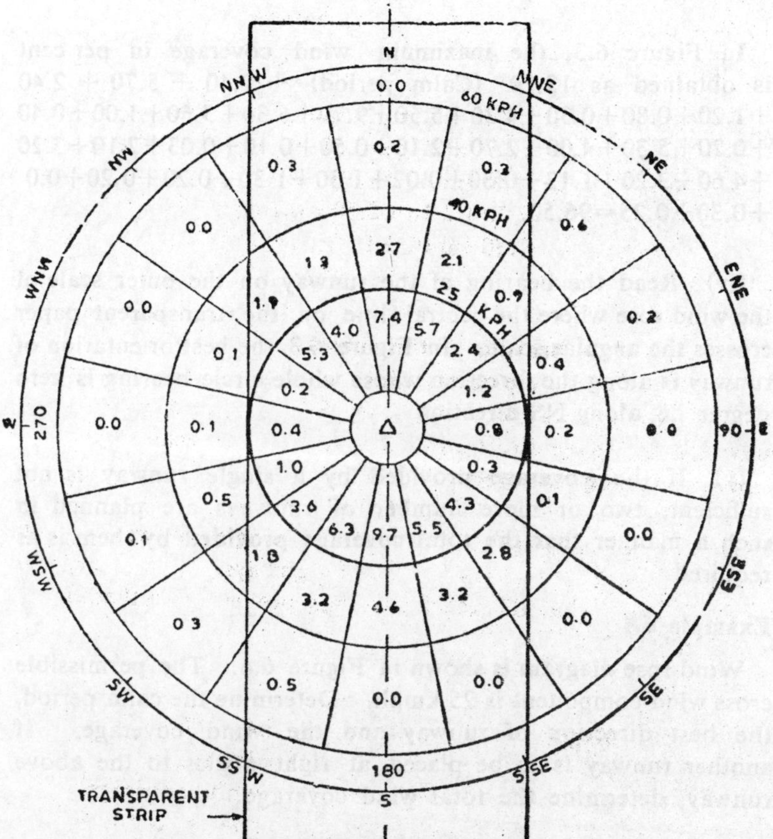

Figure 6.3 Wind Rose Diagram. Type II

(iii) With the centre of wind rose, rotate the tracing paper and place it in such a position that the sum of all the values indicating the duration of wind, within the two outer parallel lines, is the maximum. The runway should be thus oriented along the direction indicated by the central line. The wind coverage can be calculated by summing up all the percentages shown in segment. The percentage value is assumed to be equally distributed over the entire area of the segment. When of the outer parallel lines of the transparent strip crosses a segment, a fractional part of the percentage appearing in that segment within the outside lines is also counted in the summation. Fractional areas are determined by judgement to the nearest decimal place.

In Figure 6.3, the maximum wind coverage in per cent is obtained as 13.50 (Calm period) + 7.40 + 5.70 + 2.40 +1.20+0.80+0.30+4.30+5.50+9.70+6.30+3.60+1.00+0.40 +0.20+5.30+4.00+2.70+2.10+0.50+0.10+0.03+2.10+3.20 +4.60+3.20+1.13+0.30+0.02+1.50+1.30+0.20+0.20+0.0 +0.30+0.25=96.50.

(iv) Read the bearing of the runway on the outer scale of the wind rose where the central line on the transparent paper crosses the angular scale. In Figure 6.3 the best orientation of runway is along the direction whose whole circle bearing is zero degree i.e. along NS direction.

(v) If the coverage provided by a single runway is not sufficient, two or more number of runways are planned in such a manner that the total coverage provided by them is as required.

Example 6.1

Wind rose diagram is shown in Figure 6.4. The permissible cross wind component is 25 kmph. Determine the calm period, the best direction of runway and the wind coverage. If another runway is to be placed at right angles to the above runway, determine the total wind coverage.

Solution

Calm period is the percentage of time during which wind intensity is less than 6 kmph.

If is therefore, equal to 100 −(7.8 + 4.8 + 3.7 + 1.5 + 2.3 + 2.4 + 5.0 + 6.4 + 7.3 + 4.4 + 2.6 + 1.6 + 3.1+1.9+5.8 + 4.8 + 4.9 + 1.3 + 0.1 + 0.1 + 0.3+0.4 + 1.1 + 3.2+7.7 + 2.2 + 0.9 + 0.1 + 0.4 + 0.3 + 2.6 + 2.4+0.3 + 0.1+0.2 + 0.2) = 5.1 per cent.

Runway oriented along 150°−340° line (S 33° E) gives the maximum wind coverage as obtained by summing up the data within the two outer parallel lines :

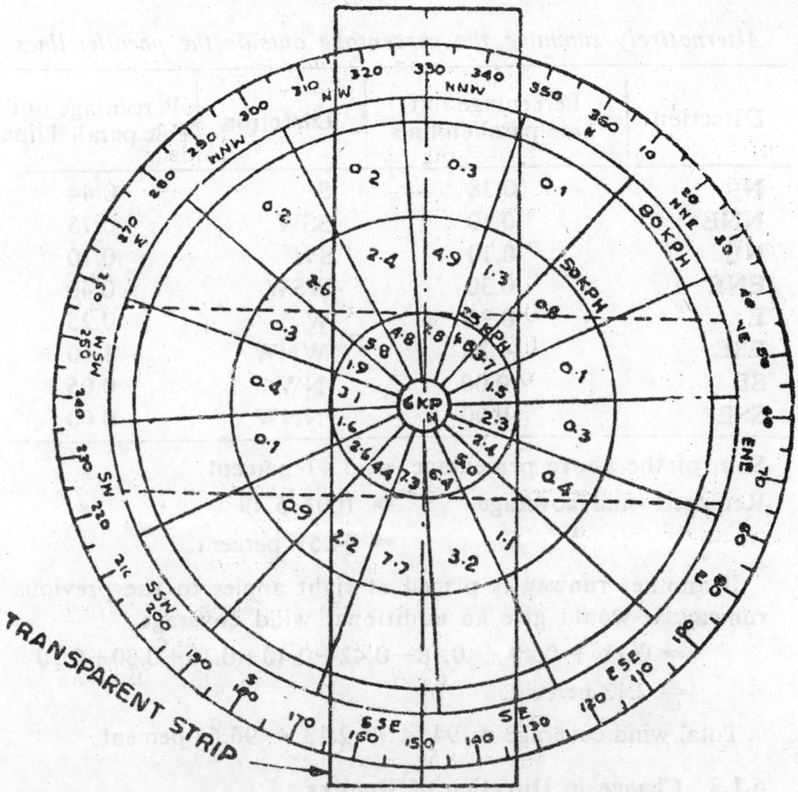

Figure 6.4 Wind Rose Diagram Type II

Direction	Percentage within outer parallel lines	Direction	Percentage within outer parallel line
N	5.67	S	6.00
NEE	3.85	SSW	2.62
NE	1.50	SW	1.60
ENE	2.50	WSW	3.10
E	2.40	W	1.95
ESE	5.80	WNW	7.10
SE	9.60	NW	7.35
SSE	15.00	NNW	13.00

Sum of the above percentages = 89.04
Add calm period = 5.10 per cent
The required wind coverage is = 89.04+5.10 = 94.14 percent

Alternatively summing the percentage outside the parallel lines

Direction	Percentage out side parallel line	Direction	Percentage out side parallel line
N	0.38	S	0.44
NNE	0.60	SSW	0.75
NE	0.10	SW	0.10
ENE	0.30	WSW	0.40
E	0.32	W	0.25
ESE	0.30	WNW	1.50
SE	0.00	NW	0.05
SSE	0.00	NNW	0.00

Sum of the above percentage = 5.49 percent

Required wind coverage = 100 − 5.49

= 94.51 percent.

If another runway is placed at right angles to the previous runway, it would give an additional wind coverage

$$= 0.21 + 0.40 + 0.10 - 0.42 + 0.40 + 0.10 + 0.30 + 0.20$$
$$= 2.13 \text{ percent.}$$

Total wind coverage = 94.51 + 2.13 = 96.64 percent.

6.1.3 Change in Direction of Runway

It may not be always possible to orient the runway exactly along the direction as determined from the wind rose. Slight adjustment in the direction may be imperative because of the following reasons :

(*i*) *Obstructions :* For layout of the runway, obstruction free approaches are more essential than the permissible cross wind component. As such, site providing fewer obstructions in the approach zones is preferred over the one which provides greater wind coverage.

(*ii*) *Excessive grading :* The runway orientation may need alternation due to the excessive grading and earth work, even if the orientation otherwise is satisfactory in respect to the safe approaches and the wind coverage.

(*iii*) *Noise nuisance :* If the runway orientation, from the above considerations, is along the direction, where highly developed residential areas and places of public assembly etc.

fal! within the take-off path, it is desirable to alter the orientation. If the wind intensity at the site is low, preferential runway from the noise abatement consideration may have to be developed. This is discussed in detail vide article 4 5.9.

6.2 BASIC RUNWAY LENGTH

It is the length of runway under the following assumed conditions at the airport :

(i) Airport altitude is at sea level
(ii) Temperature at the airport is standard (15°C)
(iii) Runway is levelled in the longitudinal direction
(iv) No wind is blowing on runway
(v) Aircraft is loaded to its full loading capacity
(vi) There is no wind blowing enroute to the destination
(vii) Enroute temperature is standard

The basic runway length is determined from the performance characteristics of the aircrafts using the airport. The following cases are usually considered :

Normal landing case

Normal take-off case

Engine failure case

For jet engine aircrafts, all the three cases, as mentioned above are considered. For piston engine aircrafts, only the first and the third cases are considered. The case which works out the longest runway length is finally adopted. All the three cases are illustrated in Figures 6.5 to 6.7.

The *landing case* requires that aircraft should come to a stop within 60 per cent of the landing distance. The runway

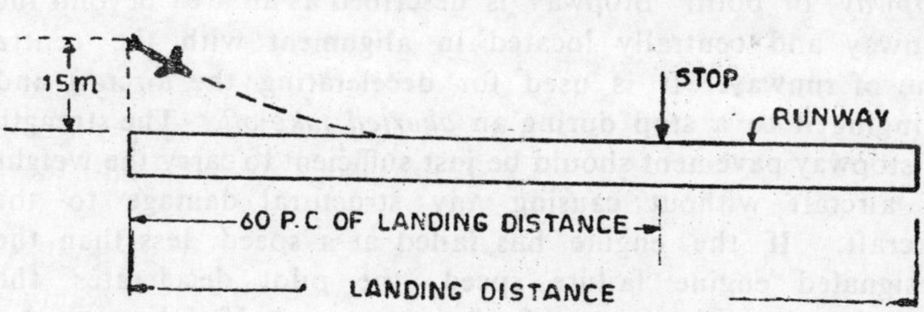

Figure 6 5 Normal Landing Case

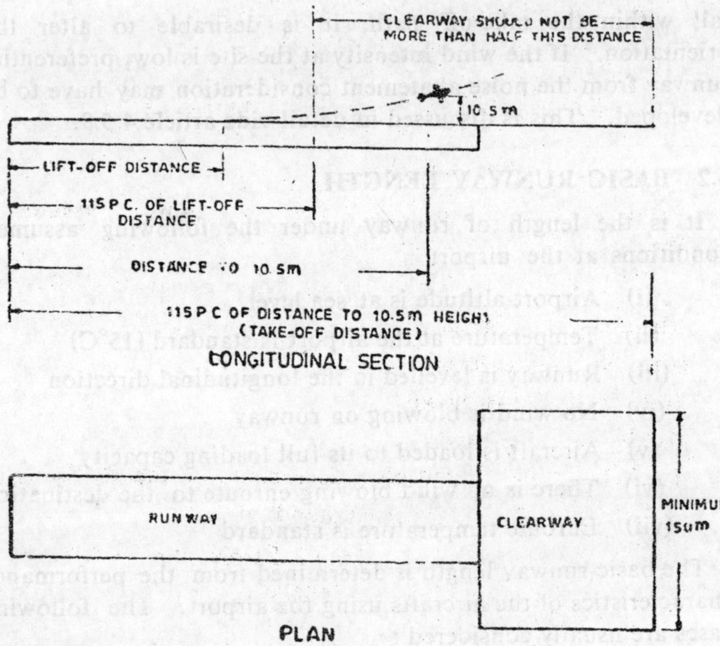

Figure 6.6 Normal Take-off Case

of full strength pavement is provided for the entire landing distance.

The *Normal take-off case* requires a *clearway* which is an area beyond the runway and is in alignment with the centre line of runway. The width of clearway is not less than 150 m (500ft) and is also kept free from obstructions. The clearway ground area or any object on it should not protrude a plane inclined upward at a slop of 1.25 percent from the runway end.

The *engine failure case* may require either a clearway, or a *stopway*, or both. Stopway is described as an area beyond the runway and centrally located in alignment with the centre line of runway. It is used for decelerating the aircraft and bringing it to a stop during an *aborted take-off*. The strength of stopway pavement should be just sufficient to carry the weight of aircraft without causing any structural damage to the aircraft. If the engine has failed at a speed, less than the designated engine failure speed, the pilot decelerates the aircraft and makes use of the stopway. If, however, the

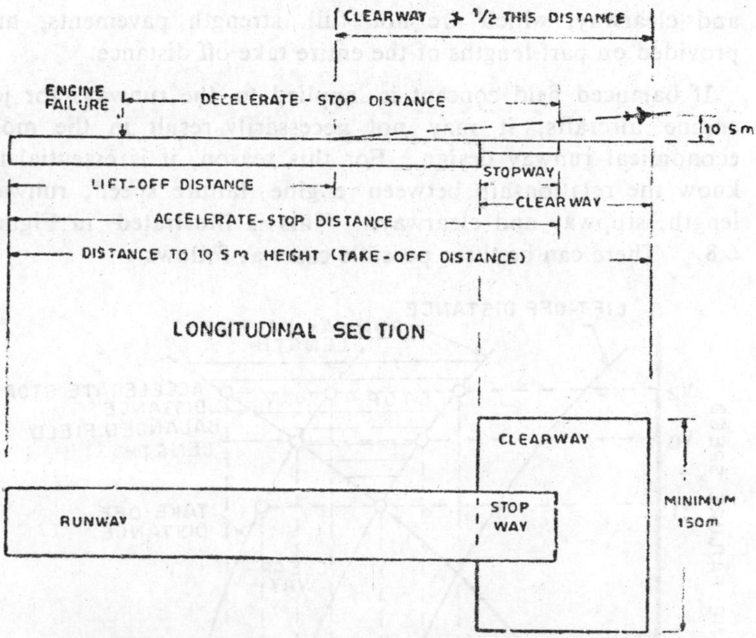

*When clearway is provided, the approach area should begin from end of clearway

**If stopway is longer than clearway, the approach area begines 60 m from end of stopway.

Figure 6.7 Engine Failure Case

engine fails at a speed higher than the designated speed, there is no other option to the pilot except to continue to take-off. The pilot may later take a turn in the turning zone and land again for a normal take-off.

For piston engine aircrafts, full strength pavement is provided for the entire take-off distance and the accelerate—stop distance. As such the designated engine failure speed for the above type of aircrafts is so chosen by the manufacturer that the distances are equal. The basic runway length thus obtained is considered to base on *Balanced Field Concept* and is called *balanced runway length*. This results in the minimum runway length for piston engine aircrafts. For jet engine aircrafts, the engine failure is not so common as it is in the case of piston engine aircrafts. Therefore, stopway and clearway, which are not full strength pavements, are provided on part lengths of the entire take-off distance.

If balanced field concept is applied to the runways for jet engine aircrafts, it may not necessarily result in the most economical runway design. For this reason, it is essential to know the relationship between engine failure speed, runway length, stopway and clearway. This is illustrated in Figure 6.8. There can be three possible cases as follows :

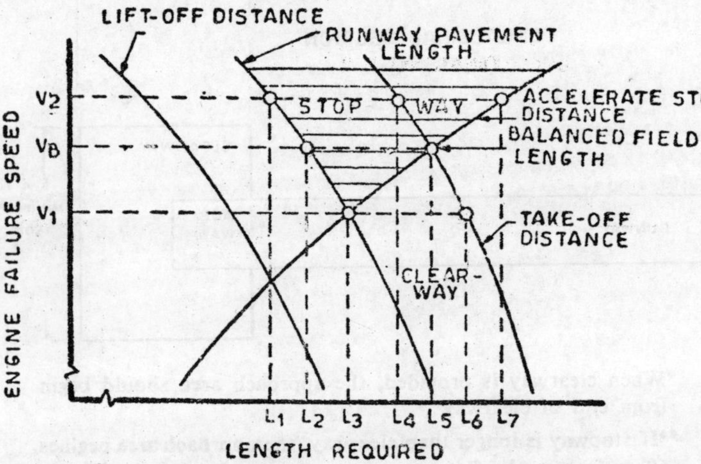

Figure 6.8 Engine Failure Case for Jet Powered Aircrafts

Engine failure speed equals V_B

i.e., speed corresponding to the balanced field concept

Engine failure speed $V_1 < V_B$

Engine failure speed $V_2 > V_B$

Case I : Engine failure speed = V_B

If the engine failure speed is considered equal to V_B, the lengths of the clearway and stopway are equal. In this case, the following lengths of runway, stopway and clearway are considered :

Runway length = L_2

Stopway length = $L_5 - L_2$

Clearway length = $L_5 - L_2$

Thus stopway and clearway lengths are equal.

Case II : Engine failure speed $V_1 < V_B$

In the engine failure speed V_1 is considered, so as to balance the accelerated stop distance with the take-off run, then the runway length required is more than the length required in the balanced field concept. Hence no stopway is required. Since stopway is also a paved area, this design may prove to be more economical than the case I

In this case, the following lengths of runway, stopway and clearway are considered :

Runway length = L_3

Stopway length = 0

Clearway length = $L_6 - L_3$

Case III : Engine failure speed $V_2 > V_B$

The another alternative is to selèct a high engine failure speed i.e. V_2 in order to reduce the take-off distance and increase in the accelerated-stop distance. In this case, the runway length is the minimum. The length of stopway is even more than clearway. This alternative may be advantageous where there are obstructions nearer to the runway ends.

In this case, the following lengths are obtained :

Runway length = L_1

Stopway length = $L_7 - L_1$

Clearway length = $L_4 - L_1$

6.3 CORRECTIONS FOR ELEVATION, TEMPERATURE AND GRADIENT

The basic runway length, as discussed above, is for mean sea level elevation having standard atmospheric conditions. Necessary corrections are, therefore, applied for any change in elevation, temperature and gradient for the actual site of construction.

(i) Correction for Elevation

As the elevation increases, the air density reduces. This in turn reduces the lift on the wings of the aircraft and the aircraft requires greater ground speed before it can rise into the air. To achieve greater speed, longer length of runway is required. ICAO recommends that the basic runway length should be increased at the rate of 7 per cent per 300 m (1000 ft) rise in elevation above the mean sea level.

(ii) Correction for Temperature

The rise in *airport reference temperature* has the same effect as that of the increase in elevation. Airport reference temperature is defined as the monthly mean of average daily temperature (T_a) for the hottest month of the year plus one third the difference of this temperature (T_a) and the monthly mean of the maximum daily temperature (T_m) for same month of the year. Thus airport reference temperature $= T_a + \frac{T_m - T_a}{3}$

ICAO recommends that the basic runway length after having been corrected for elevation, should be further increased at the rate of 1 per cent for every 1°C rise of airport reference temperature above the standard atmospheric temperature at that elevation. The temperature gradient of the standard atmosphere from the mean sea level to the altitude at which the temperature becomes −15.6°C is −0.0065°C per metre. The temperature gradient becomes zero at the elevations above the altitude at which the temperature is 15.5°C.

(iii) Check for the Total Correction for Elevation Plus Temperature

ICAO further recommends that, if the total correction for elevation plus temperature exceeds 35 percent of the basic runway length, these corrections should then be further checked up by conducting specific studies at the site by model tests.

(iv) Correction for Gradient

Steeper gradient results in greater consumption of energy and as such longer length of runway is required to attain the desired ground speed. ICAO does not recommend any specific correction for the gradient. FAA recommends that the runway length after having been corrected for elevation and temperature should be further increased at the rate of 20% for every 1 per cent of *effective gradient*.

Effective gradient is defined as the maximum difference in elevation between the highest and lowest points of runway divided by the total length of runway.

Example 6.2

The data below refers to the daily temperature for the hottest month of the year 1988 for a given airport site. Determine the airport reference temperature.

Date	Temperature, °C		Date	Temperature, °C	
	Maximum	Average		Maximum	Average
1	42.5	25.5	16	43.7	26.2
2	42.5	25.5	17	43.8	25.8
3	42.7	705.7	18	44.0	26.3
4	43.0	25.9	19	44.8	26.3
5	43.0	25.9	20	44.1	26.3
6	43.0	25.9	21	44.3	26.5
7	42.8	25.8	22	44.3	26.9
8	43.0	25.9	23	44.5	26.5
9	43.0	25.9	24	44.6	26.5
10	43.1	25.0	25	44.6	26.9
11	43 3	26.3	26	44.7	27.0
12	43.5	26.4	27	44.6	27.0
13	43.3	26.3	28	44.7	27.0
14	43.5	26.4	29	44.8	26.2
15	43.6	26 3	30	45.0	27.2

Solution

Mean of the maximum daily temperatures, T_m

$$= \frac{1311.6}{30} = 43.72°C$$

Mean of the average daily temperatures, T_a

$$= \frac{789.7}{30} = 26.32°C$$

$$\text{Airport reference temperature} = T_a + \frac{(T_m - T_a)}{3}$$

$$= 26.32 + \frac{[43.72 - 26.32]}{3}$$

$$= 26.32 + 5.80 = 32.12°C$$

Example 6.3

The monthly mean temperatures of the atmosphere, at a particular site, where an airport has to be developed, are given below. Determine the airport reference temperature. If the site is at mean sea level, determine the actual runway length. The runway is assumed to be level.

Month	Temperature °C	
	Mean value of average daily (T_a)	Mean value of Maximum daily (T_m)
January	3	5
February	15	17
March	20	23
April	25	32
May	35	47
June	40	50
July	32	37
August	30	35
September	27	31
October	22	28
November	12	18
December	6	9

Solution

The above table indicates that the hottest month of the year is the month of June.

Therefore, mean of the maximum daily temperatures,

$$T_m = 50^\circ C$$

Mean of the average daily temperatures,

$$T_a = 40^\circ C$$

$$\text{Airport reference temperature} = T_a + \frac{(T_m - T_a)}{3}$$

$$= 40 + \frac{(50-40)}{3}$$

$$= 43.33^\circ C$$

Suppose the basic runway length = L meters. Since the runway is at the mean sea level, no correction in length is required for the elevation. The correction for the temperature is necessary as the airport reference temperature is above the standard atmospheric temperature at m.s.l. (150°C). The rise of temperature = $43.33^\circ - 15^\circ = 28.33^\circ C$.

The correction is applied at the rate of 1 percent per 1°C rise of temperature.

$$\therefore \text{ the required correction} = \frac{L}{100} \times 28.33$$

$$= 0.2833 \text{ L meters}$$

The corrected length = L + 0.2833 L = 1.2833 L metre

No correction is required for gradient since, the runway is assumed as level in length direction. Therefore the actual length of runway to be provided = 1.2833 L metres.

Example 6.4

The following data refers to the proposed longitudinal section of runway.

End to End of Runway		*Gradient*
0.0 to 5.0 Chains	... ...	+ 1.0%
5.0 to 15.0 Chains	... ...	− 1.0%
15.0 to 30.0 Chains	... ...	+ 0 8%
30.0 to 40.0 Chains	... ...	+ 0.2%

If one metric chain is of 24m length. determine the effective gradient of runway.

Solution

Chainage→	0	5	15	30	40
Elevation→	100.0	101.0	99.0	101.4	101.8

Maximum difference in elevation = 101.8 − 99.0

= 2.8 m

Total runway length = 40 × 20 = 800 m

$$\text{Therefore, effective gradient of runway} = \frac{2.8}{800} \times 100 \text{ percent}$$

$$= 0.35 \text{ percent}$$

Example 6.5

The length of runway under standard conditions is 1620 m. The airport site has an elevation of 270 m. Its reference temperature is 32 94°C. If the runway is to be constructed with an effective gradient of 0.20 percent, determine the corrected runway length.

Solution

(*i*) *Correction for elevation :*

$$= \frac{7}{100} \times 1620 \times \frac{270}{300}$$

$$= 102 \text{ m}$$

Corrected length $= 1620+102=1722$ m

(*ii*) *Determination of standard atmospheric temperature at the given elevation :*

$$= 15° - 0.0065 \times 270 = 13.18°\text{C}$$

(*iii*) *Correction for temperature :*

Rise of temperature $= 32.90° - 13.18°\text{C} = 19.72°\text{C}$

$$\text{Correction} = \frac{1722}{100} \times 19.72 = 340 \text{ m}$$

Corrected length $= 1722 + 340 = 2062$ m

(*iv*) *Check for the total correction for elevation plus temperature :*

Total correction in percentage

$$= \frac{2060 - 1620}{1620} \times 100$$

$$= 27.20 \text{ percent}$$

According to ICAO, this should not exceed 35 percent.

(*v*) *Correction for gradient :*

$$= \frac{20}{100} \times 2062 \times 0.20 = 82.48 \text{ m}$$

Corrected length $= 2062 + 82.48 = 2144.48$ m

Rounding the above value to the nearest 10 m, the corrected runway length is 2150 m.

Example 6 6

The length of a runway under standard conditions is 2100 m. The airport is to be provided at elevation of 410 m above the mean sea level. The airport reference temperature is 32°C. The construction plan provides the following data :

End to end of runway (m)	Grade (per cent)
0 to 320	+ 1.00
300 to 900	− 0 50
900 to 1500	+ 0.50
1500 to 1800	+ 1.00
1800 to 2100	− 0.50
2100 to 2700	− 0.40
2700 to 3000	− 0.10

Determine the length of runway. Apply corrections for elevation and temperature as per ICAO and for gradient as per FAA specifications.

Solution

(i) Correction for elevation :

$$= \frac{7}{100} \times 2100 \times \frac{410}{300} = 201 \text{ m}$$

Corrected length $= 2100 + 201 = 2301$ m

(ii) Determination of standard atmospheric temperature at the given elevation :

$$= 15 - 0.00065 \times 410 = 12.34°\text{C}$$

(iii) Correction for temperature :

Rise of temperature = 32° − 12.34° = 19.66°C

$$\text{Correction} = \frac{2301}{100} \times 19.66 = 454 \text{ m.}$$

Corrected length $= 2301 + 454$ m $= 2755$ m.

(iv) Check for the total correction for elevation plus temperature :

Total correction in percentage

$$= \frac{2755 - 2100}{2100} \times 100 = 31.2 \text{ percent}$$

According to ICAO the total correction for (i) and (iii) should not exceed 35 percent.

(v) Correction for gradient :

The elevation of different points as per proposed grading plan will be as follows :

Chainage (100) m	0	3	9	15	18	21	27	30
Elevation (m)	100	103	100	103	106	104.5	102.1	101.8

The length obtained after applying corrections for elevation and temperature $= 2755$ m

The maximum difference of elevation

$$= 106 - 100 = 6 \text{ m}$$

Therefore, the effective gradient

$$= \frac{6}{2755} \times 100 = 0.218 \text{ per cent}$$

Correction for gradient

$$= \frac{20}{100} \times 2755 \times 0.218$$

$$= 120.5 \text{ m}$$

Corrected length $= 2755 + 120.5 = 2875.5$ m

The revised effective gradient

$$= 0.218 \times \frac{2755}{2875.5}$$

$$= 0.208 \text{ per cent}$$

Therefore, the revised gradient correction

$$= \frac{120.5}{0.218} \times 0.208$$

$$= 115 \text{ m}$$

The revised corrected length

$$= 2755 + 115 = 2870 \text{ m}$$

The design runway length

$$= 2870 \text{ m}$$

Example 6.7

The runway length required for landing at sea level in standard atmospheric conditions is 3000m. Runway length required for take-off at a level site at sea level in standard atmospheric conditions is 2500 m. Aerodrome reference temperature is 25°C and that of the standard atmosphere at aerodrome elevation of 150 m is 14.025°C. If the effective runway gradient is 0.5 percent, determine the runway length to be provided.

Solution

(a) Corrections to runway take-off length

(i) Correction for elevation

$$= \frac{7}{100} \times 2500 \times \frac{150}{300}$$

$$= 87 \text{ m}$$

Corrected length = 2500 + 87 = 2587 m

(ii) Correction for temperature

Rise of temperature = 24 − 14.025 = 9.975°C

$$\text{Correction} = \frac{2587}{100} \times 9.975°\text{C}$$

$$= 258 \text{ m}$$

Corrected temperature = 2587 + 258

= 2845 m

(iii) Check for total correction for elevation plus temperature

$$\text{Total correction in percent} = \frac{2845-2500}{2500} \times 100$$

$$= 13.8 \text{ percent}$$

According to ICAO the total correction for (i) and (ii) should not exceed 35 percent.

(iv) Correction for gradient

$$= \frac{20}{100} \times 2845 \times 0.5$$

$$= 284 \text{ m}$$

Corrected length = 2845 + 284 = 3130 m (say)

(b) Correction to runway landing length

(i) Correction for elevation

$$= \frac{7}{100} \times 3000 \times \frac{150}{300}$$

$$= 105 \text{ m}$$

Corrected runway landing length = 3000 + 105 = 3105 m

No corrections are needed to landing length for temperature and gradient.

(c) Actual runway length to be provided would be greater of (a) and (b) above = 3130 m

6.4 AIRPORT CLASSIFICATION

The geometric standards of an airport depend upon the performance characteristics of the aircrafts that will use the airport, the weather conditions and the services rendered by the airport, i.e., weather international or for domestic use. The airport classification helps in the design of airport and to establish the uniformity in the design standards. It also assists the pilots in identifying the size and the services which the airport can provide. The airports have been classified by various agencies viz. International Civil Aviation Organisation (ICAO), Federal Aviation Agency (FAA), United States Airforce etc.

6.4.1 International Civil Aviation Organisation (ICAO) Classification

The ICAO classifies the airports in two ways. In the first method, the classification is based on the basic runway length of the airport. It also describes various other geometric standards of the airport. The classification has been done by using code letters viz. A to E in which the A type of airport has the longest runway length and E type has the shortest length. This is shown in Table 6.2. In the second method, classification is based on the equivalent single wheel load (ESWL) and the tire pressure of the aircraft which will use the airport. The classification has been done by using the numerical numbers viz. 1 to 7 as shown in Table 6 3.

(i) Maximum effective grade : 1.0 per cent for A, B, C and 2.0 per cent for D and E types.

(ii) Maximum transverse grade : 1.5 per cent for A, B, C and 2 per cent for D and E types.

(iii) Rate of change of longitudinal grade : For 30 m (100 ft) length of vertical curve; 0.1 per cent for A and B, 0.2 per cent for C and 0.4 per cent for D and E types.

Table 6.2 Summary of Runway Geometric (ICAO)

Airport types	Basic runway length				Runway pavement width		Maximum longitudinal grade
	Maximum		Minimum				
	m	ft	m	ft	m	ft	%
A			2100	7000	45	150	1.5
B	2099	6999	1500	5000	45	150	1.5
C	1490	4999	900	3000	30	100	1.5
D	899	2999	750	2500	22.5	75	2.0
E	749	2499	600	2000	18	60	2.0

(iv) Safety area	Minimum width of 150 m (500 ft) for A, B, C and 78 m (260 ft) for D and E types. It extends at least 60 m beyond runway end on either side.

Table 6.3 ICAO Classification of Airports Based on Aircraft Wheel Load Characteristics

Code	Single isolated wheel load		Tire pressure	
	kg	lbs	kg/cm²	lbs/in² (p.s.i.)
1	45,000	100,000	8.5	120
2	34,000	75,000	7.0	110
3	27,000	60,000	7.0	100
4	20,000	45,000	7.0	100
5	13,000	30,000	6.0	85
6	7,000	15,000	5.0	70
7	2,000	5,000	2.5	35

6.5 RUNWAY GEOMETRIC DESIGN

ICAO gives various geometric standards for the airport design. Most of its member nations provide international air service. In order to have uniformity in the landing facilities at the airports located in different countries, it is desirable to follow the common design standards as recommended by ICAO. The following items are considered in the geometric design of runways :

(i) Runway length
(ii) Runway width
(iii) Width and length of safety area
(iv) Transverse gradient
(v) Longitudinal and effective gradient
(vi) Rate of change of longitudinal gradient
(vii) Sight distance

6.5.1 Runway Length

The basic runway lengths as recommended by ICAO for different types of airports are given in Table 6.2. To obtain the actual length of runway, corrections for elevation, temperature and gradient are applied to the basic runway length as explained in article 6.3.

6.5.2 Runway Width

ICAO recommends the pavement width varying from 45 m (150 ft) to 18 m (60 ft) for different types of airports. The typical transverse distribution of traffic on a runway is shown in Figure 6.9. The figure indicates that the aircraft traffic is more concentrated in the central 24 m (80 ft) width of the runway pavement. Another consideration in determining the runway width is that the outermost machine of large jet aircraft using the airport should not extend off the pavement on to the shoulders. This is because the shoulder is usually of loose soil or established soil etc. which is likely to get into the engine and damage it, The outer engines of a large jet transport are about 13.5 m (45 feet) from the longitudinal axis of the aircraft. As such a pavement width of 45 m will provide adequate protection to the engine from the shoulder material during normal operations.

6.5.3 Width and Length of Safety Area

Safety area consists of the runway, which is a paved area

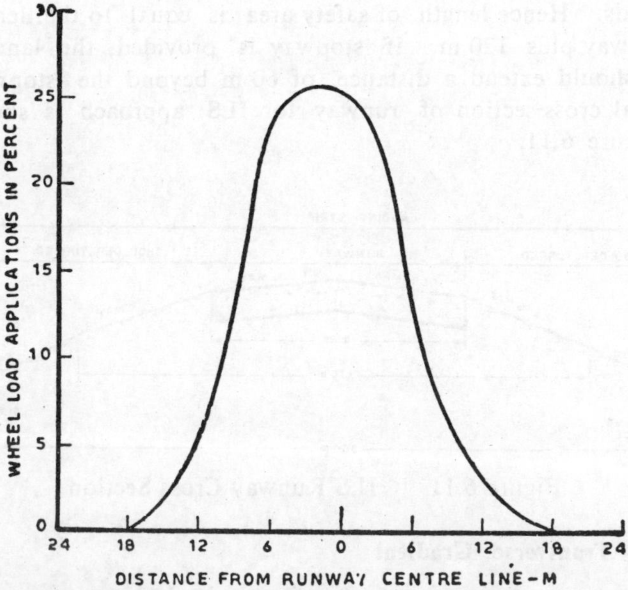

Figure 6.9 Transverse Distribution of Traffic on Runway

plus the shoulder on either side of runway plus the area that is cleared, graded and drained as shown in Figure 6.10

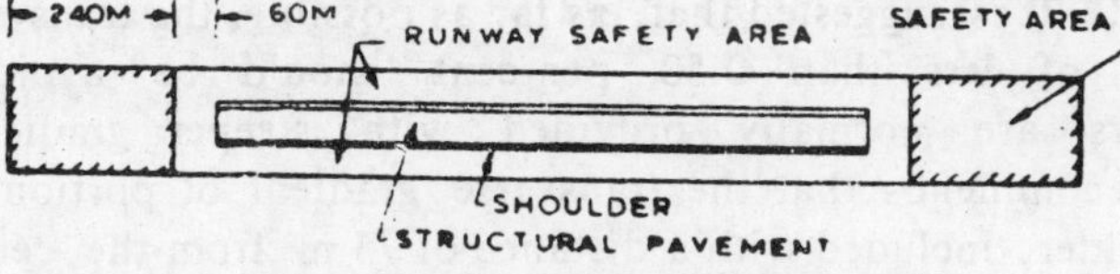

Figure 6.10 Runway Elements

The shoulders are usually unpaved as they are used during emergency i.e., when there is some abnormality in the aircraft operations. They may at the most be prepared of stabilised soil or be turfed. Another advantage of providing shoulders on either side of runway is that they impart a sense of openness to the pilot and improve his psychology during landing and take-off ICAO recommends that for non-instrumental runway, the width of safety area should be at least 150 m for A, B, C and 78 m for D and E types and for instrumental runway, it should be minimum 300 m. In length direction, the landing strip extends 600 m beyond the runway at both the ends. Hence length of safety area is equal to the length of runway plus 120 m. If stopway is provided, the landing strip should extend a distance of 60 m beyond the stopway. Typical cross-section of runway for ILS approach is shown in Figure 6.11.

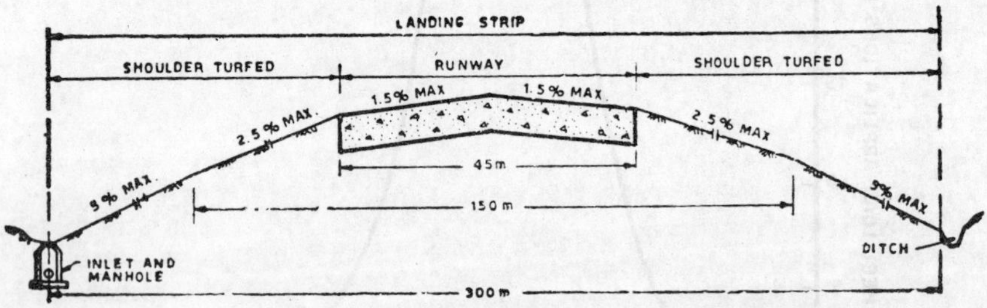

Figure 6.11 ILS Runway Cross Section

6.5.4 Transverse Gradient

Transverse gradient is essential for quick drainage of surface water. If surface water is allowed to pond on the runway, the aircraft can meet severe hazards. ICAO recommends that the transverse gradient of runway pavement should not exceed 1.50 per cent for A, B. C and 2 per cent for D and E types. It does not specify the minimum limit of the transverse gradient. It is suggested that, as far as possible, the transverse gradient of less than 0.50 per cent should be avoided. Shoulders are normally provided with steeper gradients, ICAO recommends that the transverse gradient of portion of the shoulder, included with a distance of 75 m from the centre line of runway, should be adequate to prevent ponding, but should not exceed 2.50 per cent. Transverse gradient of the remaining portion of the shoulder should not exceed 5 per cent. These recommendations are shown in Figure 6.11 for ILS runway.

6.5.5 Longitudinal and Effective Gradient

The longitudinal gradient of runway increases the required runway length. ICAO gives the following recommendations for the maximum longitudinal gradient and the maximum effective gradient.

For longitudinal gradient :

A, B and C types of airports = 1.50 per cent
D and E types of airports = 2.00 per cent

For effective gradient :

A, B and C types of airports = 1.00 per cent
D and E types of airports = 2.00 per cent

6.5.6 Rate of Change of Longitudinal Gradient

The abrupt change of longitudinal gradient restricts the height distance and may also cause premature lift-off of the aircraft during the taking-off operation. The letter drawback is observed more in the case of jet and supersonic aircrafts which have high lift off speeds. The premature lift off of aircraft will affect ths performance of aircraft during its take-off and can also develop structural defects in the aircraft. Too many changes in the gradients over a small length of runway can also restrict the sight distance and increase the runway length. This not only the changes in grade, but also the distance between such changes, are to be kept within the tolerable limits.

The changes in gradients should be smoothened by vertical curves. ICAO recommends that the rate of change of gradient should be limited to a maximum of 0.10 per cent per 30 m length of vertical curve for A and B types, 0.2 per cent for C type and 0.4 per cent for D and E types of airports. Vertical curves are generally not necessary if the change in slope is not more than 0.4 per cent. Distance between two successive points of grade intersections should not be less than the absolute numerical value of the change in slop multiplied by 300 m for A and B, 150 m for C type and 49.5 m for D and E types of runways. The recommendations of FAA are shown in Figure 6.12.

6.5.7 Sight Distance

The longitudinal gradient recommended for runway are quite gentle. As such there is hardly any sight restriction due to the longitudinal profile of runway. However, where two runways or a runway and taxiway intersect each other, there are chances of collision of aircraft, if sufficient sight distances

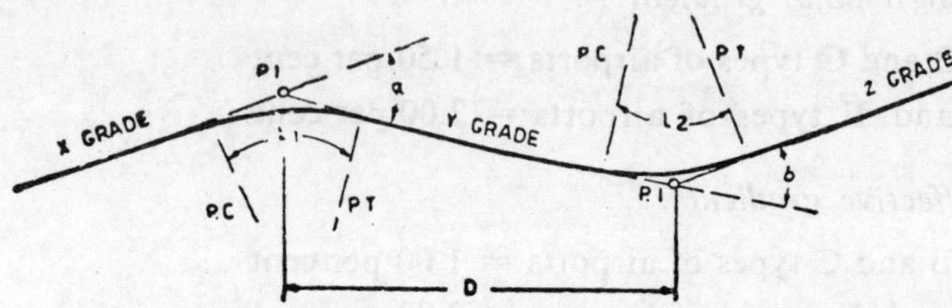

Description	Small airport	Large airport
1 Maximum grade change such as (a) or (b) should not exceed	2 per cent	1.5 per cent
2 Length of vertical curve (L_1 or L_2) for each one percent grade change	90 m	300 m
3 Distance between points of intersection of grade lines (D)	75 (a+b) m	300 (a+b) m

Figure 6.12 FAA Recommendations for Longitudinal Grade Changes in Runways

are not available. ICAO recommends that for A, B and C types of aircrafts, any two points 3 m above the surface of runway should be mutually visible from a distance equal to half the runway length. For D and E types of runway there should be unobstructed line of sight from any point 3 m above runway and to all other point 2.1 m above runway within a distance of at least one half the length of runway.

Example 6.8

In the grading operations for runway, it is proposed to have a rising gradient of 0.5 percent meeting a falling gradient of 0.7 percent. There is again an up grade of 0.40 percent. Determine the lengths of vertical curves and the distance between the grade changes of runway. Assume that the runway is required to handle jet aircraft.

Solution

Refer Figure 6.12

Here, $a = x - y = 0.5 - (-0.7) = 1.2$ percent

$$b = y - z = -(0.7 - 0.4) = 1.1 \text{ percent}$$

Therefore, $L = 300 \times 1.2 = 360$ m

$L_2 = 300 \times 1.1 = 330$ m

$D = 300 (1.2 + 1.1) = 690$ m

Example 6.9

The runway gradation map indicates that there is a rising gradient of 1.0 percent meeting a falling gradient of 0.70 percent. There is again an up grade of 0.70 percent. Design the runway profile as per FAA specifications.

Solution

Refer Figure 6.12

Here, $a = x - y = 1.0 - (-0.70) = 1.70$ percent

$b = y - z = -(0.70 + 0.70) = 1.40$ percent

Since a is greater than 1.5 percent limit for large airports, the design is to be carried out for small airports.

Therefore, $L_1 = 90 \times 1.70 = 153$ m

$L_2 = 90 \times 1.40 = 126$ m

$D = 75\,(a+b) = 75\,(1.70+1.40) = 232$ m

PROBLEMS

1 What is a wind rose diagram ? What is its utility ? What are its types ? Explain each type.

2 Explain the procedure of orienting the runway.

3 What do you understand by the term basic runway length ? Explain the procedure of determining the actual runway length required at a particular site.

4 Explain how the basic runway length is determined on the basis of the performence characteristics of jet and conventional engine aircrafts.

5 Explain the necessity of airport classification. Give different systems of classification of airports.

6 Summarize briefly the various runway geometrics as recommended by ICAO.

7 Table below gives the average wind data of the airport site when the wind intensity is above 6 kmph. Draw a suitable wind rose diagram. Determine the best orientation of runway. If the maximum deviation of wind from the direction of landing and take-off is permitted upto 33.75°, determine the percentage of time in a year during which the runway can be used for flights.

Wind direction	Percentage of time	Wind direction	Percentage of time
N	6.6	S	7.7
NNE	10.3	SSW	14.3
NE	8.1	SW	10.6
ENE	3.9	WSW	5.7
E	1.8	W	3.9
ESE	0.9	WNW	0.5
SE	0.4	NW	0.3
SSE	4.1	NNW	4.2

8 The following is the average wind data for 10 years. An airport is to be designed for a single runway. Determine the maximum wind coverage and the best direction of

Direction	Percent time with wind velocity in kmph		
	6 4−25	25−50	50−75
N	1.30	1.30	0.10
NNE	5 50	5.00	0.10
NE	8.00	7.60	0.20
EEN	3.10	2.20	0.10
E	0.60	0 50	0.00
EES	1.70	0.80	0.10
SE	3.90	2.00	0.20
SSE	1.50	0.50	0.10
S	1.60	1.20	0.00
SSW	5.20	4.10	0.10
SW	5.20	4.50	0.10
WWS	7.60	6.50	0.20
W	2 60	1.60	0.10
WWN	2.50	0.60	0.00
NW	2.50	1.50	0.10
NNW	1.50	1.50	0.00

runway. The permissible cross wind component may be assumed as suitable for mixed category of aircrafts.

9 The average wind data collected at a particular site is given below. An airport is to be designed for two runways. Determine calm period, the best orientation of runways and the total wind coverage. Permissible cross wind component is 25 kmph.

Direction	Percentage of time with wind velocity in kmph		
	6.4 − 25	25 − 50	50 − 75
N	4.5	1.3	0.1
NNE	3.3	0.8	0.0
NE	1.8	0.1	0.0
ENE	2.7	0.3	0.0
E	2.0	0.4	0.0
ESE	5.3	0.1	0.0
SE	6.3	3.2	0.1
SSE	7.4	7.7	0.3
S	4.6	2.2	0.1
SSW	2.4	0.9	0.0
SW	1.1	0.1	0.0
WSW	3.6	0.4	0.0
W	1.8	0.3	0.0
WNW	5.9	2.6	0.2
NW	5.8	2.4	0.2
NNW	6.8	4.9	0.3

10 Draw a neat cross-section of runway for an international airport having instrumental landing facilities. Show therein the various runway geometrics.

11 The data given below refers to the direction, duration and intensity of wind at a particular site over a period of 8 years. Draw the two types of wind rose diagrams. Determine the calm period and the orientation of runway from each type. Determine the percentage of time in a year during which this runway can be used with satisfactory wind conditions. Make suitable assumptions if required.

Direction	Percentage of time with velocity in kmph			
	6.4–25	25–35	35–55	55–80
N	7.8	2.7	1.6	0.2
NNE	5.1	2.1	0.8	0.1
NE	2.4	0.9	0.6	0.0
ENE	1.2	0.4	0.2	0.0
E	0.8	0.2	0.9	0.0
ESE	0.3	0.1	0 0	0.0
SE	2.3	1 8	0.9	0.1
SSE	4.5	3.0	1.0	0.2
S	6.7	5.6	2.9	0.1
SSW	4.8	2.7	1.3	0.1
SW	1.6	0.8	0.3	0 0
WSW	2.2	0.6	0.1	0.0
W	0.4	0.1	0.0	0.0
WNW	0.2	0.1	0.0	0.0
NW	2.3	1.8	0.9	0.2
NNW	4.0	3.2	1.3	0.1

12 The length of a runway under standard conditions is 1500 m. The airport is to be provided at an elevation of 110 m above the mean sea-level. The airport reference temperature is 22°C. The construction plan includes the following data.

End to end of runway m	Grade (percent)
0 to 300	+ 1.00
300 to 900	– 0.20
900 to 1500	+ 0.50
1500 to 1800	+ 1.00
1800 to 2100	– 0.30

Determine the actual length of runwy to be provided. Apply corrections for elevation and temperature as per ICAO and for gradient as per FAA specifications.

13 The following is the average of wind data for 10 years. An airport is to be designed for two runways. Determine the best runway orientations and calculate the total wind coverage.

Direction	Percentage of time with wind velocity in kmph		
	6.4–25	25–50	50–75
N	0.3	1.3	0.1
NNE	2.0	4.0	0.1
NE	5.0	7.6	0.2
EEN	2.1	1.2	0.1
E	0.6	0.5	0.0
EES	2.7	0.8	0.1
SE	3.9	3.0	0.2
SSE	2.9	2.5	0.1
S	1.6	1.2	0.0
SSW	2.0	2.0	0.1
SW	3.2	2.5	0.1
WWS	5.6	4.5	0.2
W	2.6	1.6	0.1
WWN	2.5	1.6	0.0
NW	3.5	2.5	0.1
NNW	1.5	0.5	0.0

14 The proposed longitudinal section along the centre line of a runway is as follows :

Station to station			Gradient in percent
0.00	to	8.00	+ 1.25
8.00	to	15.00	− 1.00
15.00	to	30.00	+ 0.50
30.00	to	45.00	+ 0.20
45.00	to	60.00	− 0.40

If stations are located at a regular interval of 30 m, determine the effective gradient of the runway.

15 The monthly mean temperatures of the atmosphere at a particular site where an airport has to be developed are given below. Determine the airport reference temperature. If the site is at mean sea-level how much correction is required on the basic runway length. Assume the runway effective gradient as 1 percent.

Month	Temperature, C	
	Mean value of average daily	Mean value of maximum daily
January	3.0	5.5
February	15.5	17.0
March	20.0	23.4
April	25.6	32.3
May	35.7	47.4
June	40.4	50.6
July	32.6	37.7
August	30.5	35.5
September	27.4	31.5
October	22.8	28.3
November	12.9	18.0
December	6.7	12.3

16 The length of a runway at sea-level, standard atmospheric conditions and zero gradient is 1500 m. The airport site has an elevation of 900 m, and the reference temperature as 20°C. If the proposed runway grading permits an effective gradient of 0.20 percent, determine the actual runway length required at the site.

17 The runway gradation plan indicates that there is a rising gradient of 1.4 percent meeting a falling gradient of 0.5 percent. There is again an up grade of 0.5 percent. Design the longitudinal profile of runway.

18 Write short notes on.

Cross wind component, Wind coverage, Runway orientation, Wind rose. Calm period, Basic runway length, Stopway, Clearway, Balanced field concept, Airport reference temperature, Standard atmosphere, Airport classification, Landing strip, Runway sight distance.

7

AIRPORT CAPACITY AND CONFIGURATION

7.1 AIRPORT CAPACITY

The number of aircraft movements which an airport can process within a specifined period of time, with an average dealy to the departing aircraft within the acceptable time limit is defined as *airport capacity*. Each aircraft makes two movement, viz, landing and takesoff.

Let us consider a single runway with adequate exit taxiways. Assume that only one aircraft is permitted to occupy the runway at one time. The capacity of this airport will depend upon the runway occupany time of an aircraft. The runway will be operated as its capacity when the time interval between two successive operations just equals the runway occupancy time of the aircraft. But in practice, there are variations in arrival or departure intervals as well as in runway occupancy times, thereby causing certain dealy to the aircrafts. The *practical operating* capacity is thus, considerably less than the *ideal capacity*, depending upon the amount of acceptable dealy to the departing aircraft.

As the total number of aircraft movements per hour (runway capacity) increases, the average dealy to the departing aircraft also increases. Thus, in defining a practical operating capacity, an average delay to the departing aircraft should be specified. In order that the capacities of various airports configuration may be easily compared, the Airbourne Instruments Laboratory, U.S.A. has fixed an average delay period of 6 minutes.

The following factors affect the airport operating capacity :

(i) Runway configurations and the connected taxiways

(ii) Aircraft characteristics and their arrival to departure ratio

(iii) Weather conditions

(iv) Terrain and man-made obstructions

(v) Loading apron space

(vi) Navigational aids

(vii) Aircraft processing technique

7.1.1. Runway Configurations and the Connected Taxiways

The runway configuration affects the capacity as explained in article 7.6. The appurtenant taxiways are important to clear the landing aircraft from the runways as soon as possible.

7.1.2. Aircraft Characteristics and their Arrival to Departure Ratio

Smaller and slower aircrafts occupy the runway for less time and can be spaced closer than bigger and faster aircrafts. Therefore, the capacity of airport serving smaller aircrafts is generally higher than the one serving bigger and faster aircrafts. Thus, for a given delay to the departing aircrafts, the airport capacity increases when the large turbo jet aircrafts are removed.

Landing operation is generally given priority over the taking off operation. As such, the ratio of arriving and departing aircrafts also influences the airport capacity.

7.1.3. Weather Conditions

Airport capacity during IFR conditions is usually less than during VFR conditions. The reason is that during clear weather conditions (VFR), the aircrafts on final approach to runway can be spaced closer during the poor visibility conditions.

7.1.4 Obstructions in Airport Vicinity

Terrain or man-made obstructions in the vicinity of the airport restrict the number of inbound and outbound air routes from the airport.

7.1.5 Loading Apron Space

If sufficient space is not available for loading, unloading and parking aircrafts, it may result in delay in the terminal area or even the reduction in the number of aircraft operations. Thus the airport capacity may be reduced.

7.1.6 Navigational Aids

This is particularly important in poor visibility conditions. For example, an airport having ILS facility to two runways or one runway in both directions will have greater capacity than an airport equipped with one ILS approach. Radar and surveillance radar can process the aircrafts more rapidly.

7.1.7 Aircraft Processing Technique

If the controller is provided with the computer facility, he may be able to process the aircrafts rapidly, thereby reducing the delays.

7.2 RUNWAY CAPACITY

7.2.1 General

"Runway capacity" is defined as the ability of a runway system to accommodate aircraft landings and take-offs. It is expressed in operations per unit time, i.e. operations per hour or operations per year. The ultimate or saturation capacity of a runway is the maximum number of aircraft that can be handled during a given period under conditions of continuous demand. Mathematical models or equations are available for the computation of saturation capacity, at least for reasonably simple systems for the assumed back log of aircraft waiting to be served.

Saturation capacity, is a useful design tool for the comparison of alternative systems. It does not reflect the actual operating characteristics of a runway system under conditions of applied demand. For a practical performance measure, examination of statistics of demand and delay is necessary.

The FAA employs the concept of practical capacity, that corresponds to a "reasonable" or tolerable" delay. Figure 7.1 illustrates, the average aircraft delay lengthens as the volume of air traffic using a runway system increases. A runway may be able to accommodate a number of operations per hour that is larger than its practical hourly capacity (PHC) during extremely busy period, but during these periods unusually long delays will occur. Practical hourly capacities can be exceeded by as much as 25% during saturated periods, but from an operational viewpoint, such delays are considered unacceptable. A more comrlete definition of practical capacity is recommended in which the "reasonably acceptable" delay level depends on the aircraft mix for precise estimates of capacity.

7.2.2 Factors Affecting Runway Capacity

The factors influencing the capacity of a runway system can be grouped into four classes as follows :

(i) Air traffic control
(ii) Characteristics of demand
(iii) Environmental factors
(iv) Layout and design of the runway system

7.2.2.1 Air traffic control : FAA specifies minimum vertical, horizontal and lateral separations for aircraft in the interests of air safety. In the vicinity of an airport, the minimum allowable horizontal separation is typically 3.6 to 8 nautical km depending on the aircraft size, availability of radar and the sequencing of operations. Since two airplanes are not allowed on the runway at the same time, the runway occupancy time may also influence the capacity. Figure 7.2 shows a time-distance diagram for two approaching aircraft maintaining the 4.8 nautical km separation. The solid line on the left represents the first arrival. The second arrival (the soild line on the right) is shown at a point 4.8 nautical km away when

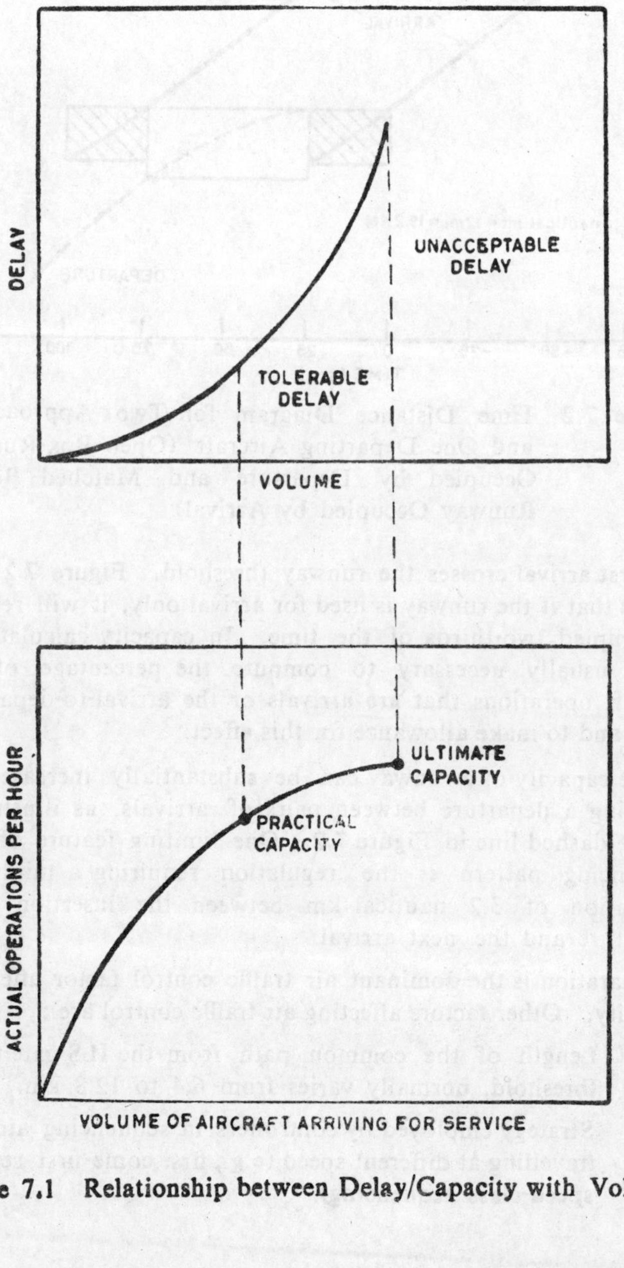

Figure 7.1 Relationship between Delay/Capacity with Volume

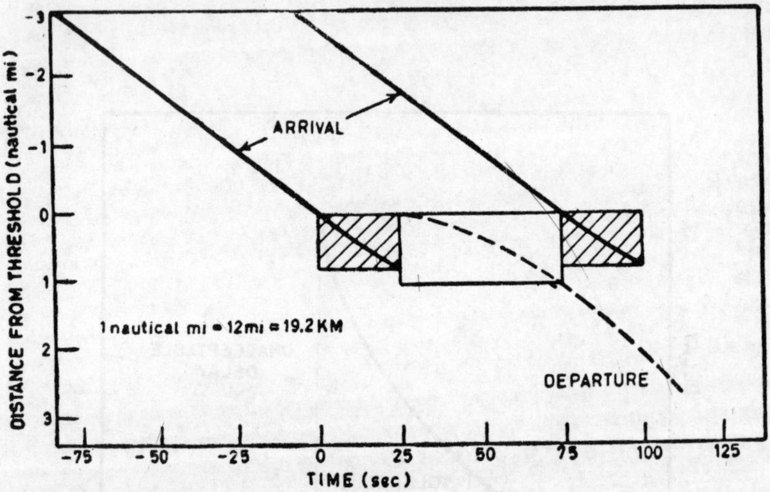

Figure 7.2 Time Distance Diagram for Two Approaching and One Departing Aircraft (Open Box-Runway Occupied by Departure and Matched Boxes-Runway Occupied by Arrival)

the first arrival crosses the runway threshold. Figure 7.2 also shows that if the runway is used for arrival only, it will remain unoccupied two-thirds of the time. In capacity calculations, it is usually necessary to compute the percentage of all aircraft operations that are arrivals or the arrival-to-departure ratio and to make allowance for this effect.

The capacity of a runway can be substantially increased by inserting a departure between pairs of arrivals, as illustrated by the dashed line in Figure 7.2. One limiting feature of this sequencing pattern is the regulation requiring a minimum separation of 3.2 nautical km. between the insertion of a departure and the next arrival.

Separation is the dominant air traffic control factor affecting capacity. Other factors affecting air traffic control are :

(i) Length of the common path from the ILS gate to be threshold, normally varies from 6.4 to 12.8 km.

(ii) Strategy employed by controllers in sequencing aircraft travelling at different speed (e.g., first come-first served, speed-class sequencing).

(iii) Allowable probability of violation of the separation rule recognizes, that, it is not possible to maintain the allowable separation with perfect precision at all times.

(iv) The sophistication of the air traffic control system, affects the precision of the aircraft delivery to the ILS gate and the ability to monitor aircraft speed and detect aircraft positions and movements.

7.2.2.2 Characteristics of demand : The FAA has introduced air traffic control rules to increase the separation between small aircraft following a heavy jet to 8 nautical km. This regulation decreases the capacity of runways that serve significant number of heavy jets and small aircrafts. Separation longer than the minimum allowed by air traffic rules must be tolerated to accommodate a mixture of slow and fast aircraft. A margin of safety must be allowed because of variations in approach speeds to ensure that the minimum separation is not violated at any point along the approach path. Touchdown speed, braking capability and ground manoeuvrability affect the runway occupancy time for landing, which, in turn, determines the time that a departing aircraft can be released.

Percentage of all aircraft arrival operations is another characteristic of demand that can significantly affect the capacity of a runway. A runway used exclusively for arrivals have a capacity different from one used for departure or mixed operations.

7.2.2.3 Environmental factors : Environmental factors influencing runway capacity are visibility, runway surface conditions, winds and noise abatement requirements. Under poor visibility conditions, pilots and air traffic controllers become more cautious. A runway or runway system may be closed to traffic when visibility is extremely limited. Similarly, wet or slippery runway surface conditions may cause longer deceleration distances and greater runway occupancy times. Heavy snow and ice accumulations warrant the closing of a runway. The wind speed component perpendicular to the aircraft path should not exceed 15 knots and the component in the direction of the aircraft's movements must not exceed 5 knots for safety reasons. Crosswinds and tail winds occasionally impose restrictions on the use of one or more runways and calculations of runway capacity should include appropriate allowances for such restrictions. Noise abatement regulations affect the capacity of runway system by limiting or restricting the use of one or more runway during certain hours of the day.

7.2.2.4 Layout and design of runway system : The airport planner considers improvements in the layout and design of the runway and taxiway system when large increase in airport capacity are needed to serve future demand. The principal factors are as follows :

(i) Number, spacing, length and orientation of runways.

(ii) Number, locations and design of exit taxiways.

(iii) Design of ramp entrances.

7.2.3 Methods for Practical Capacity Determination

A simple runway system can be described by analytical models or formulas of gueueing theory. In 1948, Bowen and Pearcey made an empirical study of aircraft arriving at the Kingsford-Smith Airport in Sydney and found that arrivals could be satisfactorily described by the Poisson probability distribution. Since flights on civil airlines are scheduled and aircraft arrivals are regular, the difference between and the expected and actual times of arrival was large and found to be more random than regular.

A runway serving landings can be described only as a single channel queueing system with first come-first served services. The "service time" is defined as the 'length of time, the most recent arrival blocks the runway from receiving any subsequent arrival'. It depends on the runway occupancy time, or more commonly, the minimum separation necessitated by air traffic rules.

Assuming Poisson arrivals and constant service times, Bowen and Pearcy derived an equation for average (steady state) landing delay :

$$W = \frac{\rho}{2\mu(1-\rho)} \tag{7.1}$$

where ρ = the load factor = $\lambda\mu$

λ = arrival rate (aircraft/unit time)

μ = service rate (aircraft/unit time) = 1/b

b = mean service time

It a more general form, this equation is known as the Pollaczek-Khinchin formula :

$$W = \frac{\rho\,(1+C_b^2)}{2\mu\,(1-\rho)} \qquad (7.2)$$

where C_b = coefficient of variation of service time = σ_b/b

σ_b = standard deviation of service time

These equations can also be applied to runways serving departure only. A more complicated formula has been developed to calculate the average delay to departure in mixed operations.

The above equations have two major shortcomings :

(i) They account only for the effects of a few factors known to influence the ranway capacity and delays.

(ii) They give 'steady state' solutions.

7.2.3.1 Capacities for long range planning purposes : The FAA has published approximate runway capacities for long range planning purposes. Both practical hourly capacity (PHC) and practical annual capacity (PAC) for a variety of runway configurations are given in Table 7.1. In addition, the table accounts for differences due to weather (VFR and IFR conditions) and aircraft mix. When the cloud ceiling is less than 300 m (1000 ft) and/or the visibility is less than 4.8 km (3 miles), IFR conditions exist. Runway capacity is normally less under IFR conditions in comparison to VFR conditions.

Aircraft mixes (Table 7.2) relate to the four numbers shown for each configuration given in Table 7.1.

Determination of airport capacities generally categorised for different aircrafts as follows :

Type A : Four-engine jet and larger.

Type B : Two-and three-engine jet, four-engine piston and turboprop.

Type C : executive jet and transport-type twin-engine piston.

Type D : light twin-engine piston and single-engine piston. and E

Table 7.1 Airport Capacities for Long Range Planning Purposes

Runway Configuration		Mix	PHO		
Description and Layout			PAC	IFR	VFR
	(1499.7 may be read as 1499.9 m)				
Single runway (arrivals = departures)		1	215,000	53	99
		2	195,000	52	76
		3	180,000	44	54
		4	170,000	42	45
Close parallels (IFR dependent)	 LESS THAN 1050 m	1	385,000	64	198
		2	330,000	63	152
		3	295,000	55	108
		4	280,000	54	90
Independent IFR approach departure parallels	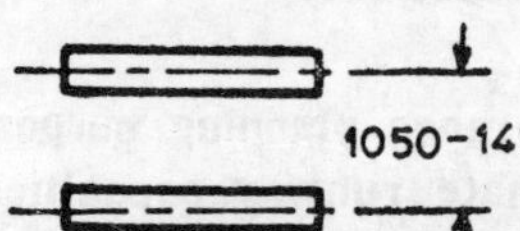 1050–1499.7 m	1	425,000	79	198
		2	390,000	79	152
		3	355,000	79	108
		4	330,000	74	90
Independent IFR arrivals and departures	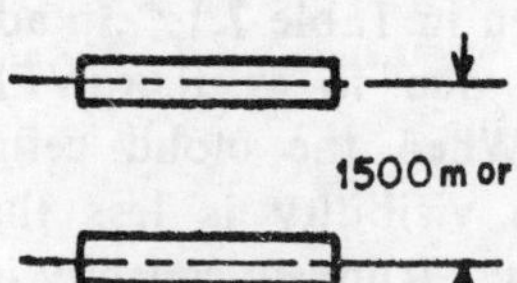 1500 m or MORE	1	430,000	106	198
		2	390,000	104	152
		3	360,000	88	108
		4	340,000	84	90
Independent parallels plus two close parallels	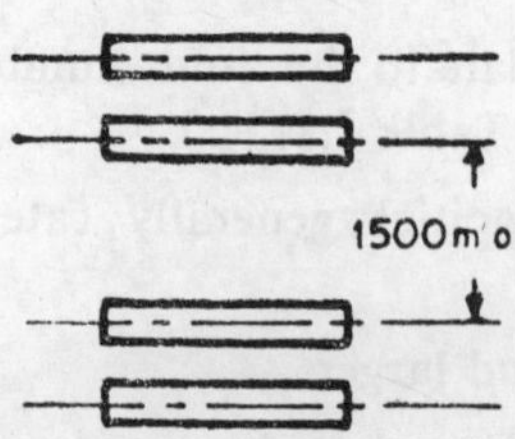 1500 m or MORE	1	770,000	128	396
		2	660,000	126	304
		3	590,000	110	216
		4	560,000	108	180
Open V, dependent, operations away from intersection	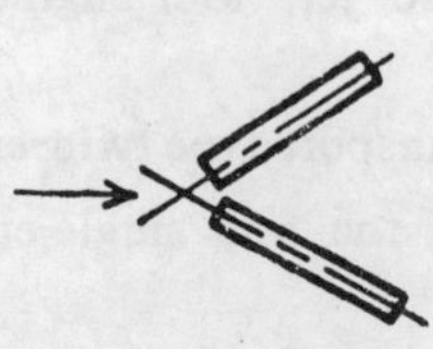	1	420,000	70	195
		2	335,000	70	136
		3	300,000	63	94
		4	295,000	60	84

Table 7.1 (Cont.)

<table>
<tr><th colspan="2">Runway Configuration</th><th rowspan="2">Mix</th><th colspan="3">PHC</th></tr>
<tr><th colspan="2">Description and Layout</th><th>PAC</th><th>IFR</th><th>VFR</th></tr>
<tr><td rowspan="4">Open V, dependent, operations towards intersection</td><td rowspan="4">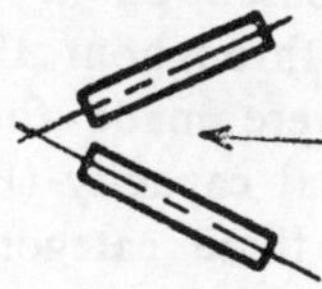</td><td>1</td><td>235,000</td><td>57</td><td>180</td></tr>
<tr><td>2</td><td>220,000</td><td>56</td><td>86</td></tr>
<tr><td>3</td><td>215,000</td><td>50</td><td>66</td></tr>
<tr><td>4</td><td>200,000</td><td>50</td><td>53</td></tr>
<tr><td rowspan="4">Two intersection at near threshold</td><td rowspan="4">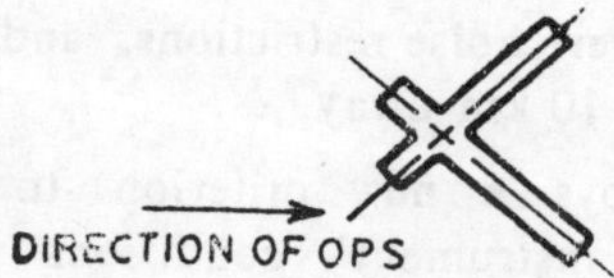</td><td>1</td><td>375,000</td><td>71</td><td>175</td></tr>
<tr><td>2</td><td>310,000</td><td>70</td><td>125</td></tr>
<tr><td>3</td><td>275,000</td><td>63</td><td>83</td></tr>
<tr><td>4</td><td>255,000</td><td>60</td><td>69</td></tr>
<tr><td rowspan="4">Two intersecting in middle</td><td rowspan="4">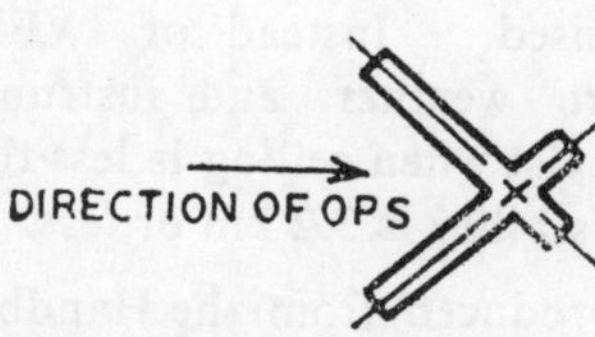</td><td>1</td><td>220,000</td><td>61</td><td>99</td></tr>
<tr><td>2</td><td>195,000</td><td>60</td><td>76</td></tr>
<tr><td>3</td><td>195,000</td><td>53</td><td>58</td></tr>
<tr><td>4</td><td>190,000</td><td>47</td><td>52</td></tr>
<tr><td rowspan="4">'Z' configuration and parallel with both intersecting</td><td rowspan="4">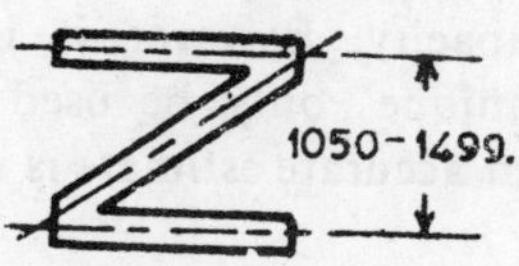</td><td>1</td><td>465,000</td><td>87</td><td>217</td></tr>
<tr><td>2</td><td>430,000</td><td>87</td><td>167</td></tr>
<tr><td>3</td><td>390,000</td><td>87</td><td>118</td></tr>
<tr><td>4</td><td>365,000</td><td>81</td><td>99</td></tr>
</table>

Source : Airport Capacity used in Long Range Planning by FAA

Table 7.2

Number	% A	% B	% C	% (D+ E)
1	0	0	0 (9-11)	90
2	0	30 (27-33)	30	40
3	20 (18-22)	40	20	20
4	60 (54-66)	20	20	0

7.2.3.2 Approaches for determining practical hourly capacities. The Airport Capacity Handbook has been used widely by airport planners in the estimation of runway capacities and delays. The techniques presented, employs a graphical approach, and are based on a large number of airport traffic surveys connected throughout the United States. With the handbook, estimates were made for practical hourly capacity (PHC), practical annual capacity (PAC), and annual delay (AD). It also defines three categories of airspace : highly 'Restricted', 'Normal', and Unrestricted'. With normal airspace, aircraft can be fanned out over three basic direction, there are no severe noise restrictions, and the closest busy airport is more than 10 km away.

The Handbook employs a new criterion to distinguish between 'visual' and 'instrument' conditions to account realistically for weather conditions at air barrier airports. The terms VAW and IAW are used. Instead of VFR and IFR referring to visual airport weather and instrument airport weather, IAW conditions exist when ceiling is less than or equal to 210 m (700 ft) and/or visibility is 3.2 km or less.

Figures 7.3 to 7.6, reproduced from the Handbook, can be used to determine capacities for single runways under VAW and IAW conditions. The figures provide approximate and accurate estimation of capacity, however it is recommended that the 'approximate technique' only be used if the necessary information to determine an accurate estimate is not available.

Example 7.1

Determine the PHC of a single runway used for arrivals and departures for the following conditions :

(i) Aircraft mix : (A=30%), (B=40%) & (C+D+E=30%)

(ii) Radar control and ILS approach used. Assume that computer-aided sequencing of arrivals and departures is not available.

(iii) The ratio of arrivals to departures = 0.30

(iv) Runway rating (RR) = 50 sec. VFR. [Runway rating is defined as 'the average runway occupancy time for a given population of landing aircraft on given runway'

(v) Airspace is 'normal'

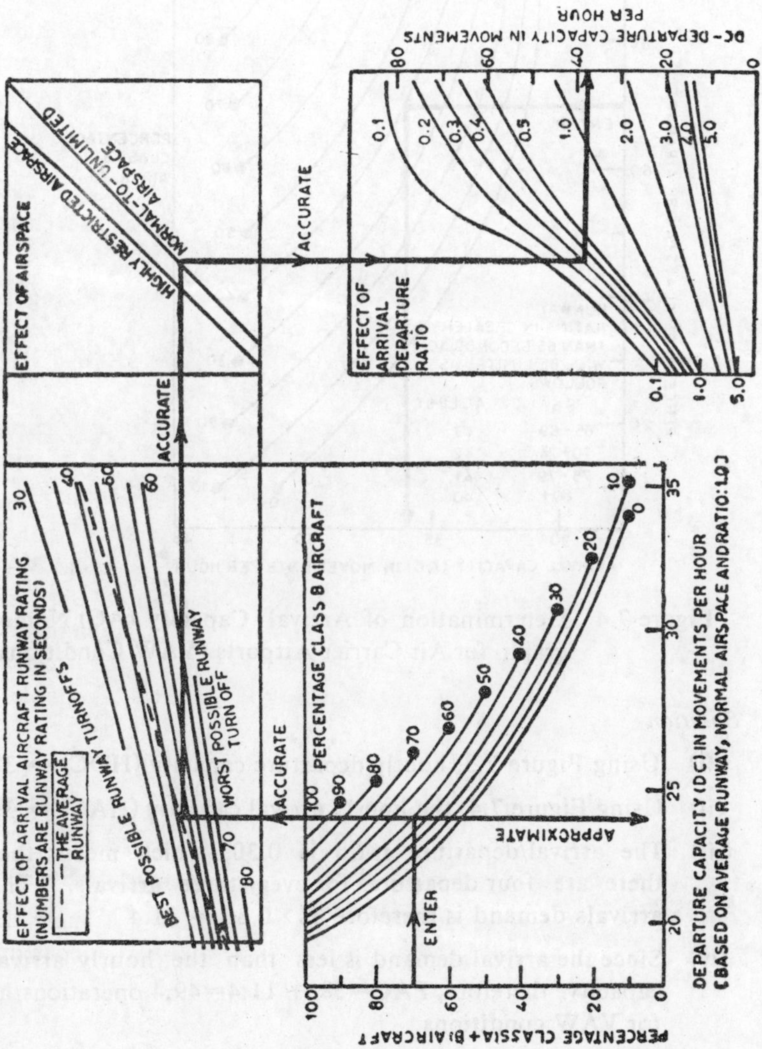

Figure 7 3 Determination of Departure Capacity (Dc) Nomograph for Air Carrier Airports (Single Runway, Mixed Operations and VAW Conditions)

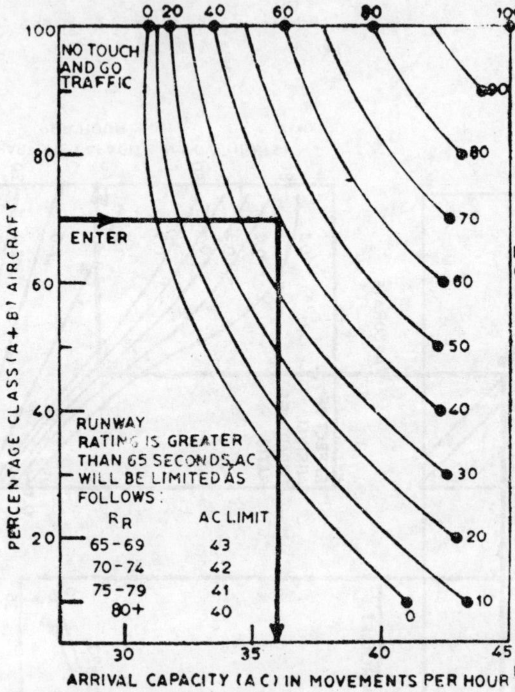

Figure 7.4 Determination of Arrival Capacity (AC) Nomograph for Air Carrier Airports (VAW Conditions)

Solution

(i) Using Figure 7.3, hourly departure capacity (HDC) = 38

(ii) Using Figure 7.4, the hourly arrival capacity (HAC) = 36

(iii) The arrival/departure ratio is 0.30, which means that there are four departures for every three arrivals. The arrivals demand is therefore $38 \times 0.30 = 11.4$

(iv) Since the arrival demand is less than the hourly arrival capacity, therefore, PAC=38 + 11.4=49.4 operations/hr for VAW conditions

(v) Using Figure 7.5, the hourly departure capacity (HDC) under IAW conditions is HDC = 34

(vi) Using Figure 7.6 the hourly arrival capacity (HAC) under IAW conditions is HDC = 35.5

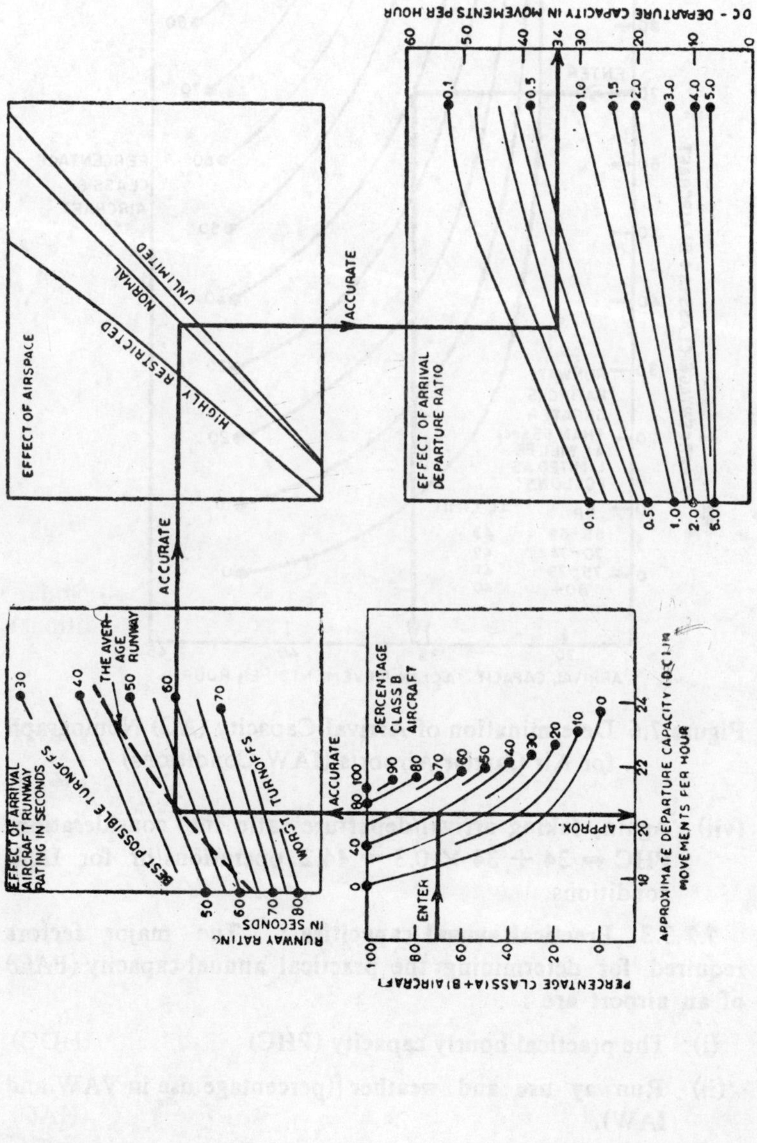

Figure 7.5 Determination of Departure Capacity (DC) Nomograph for Air Carrier Airports (Single Runway, Mixed Operation and IAW Conditions)

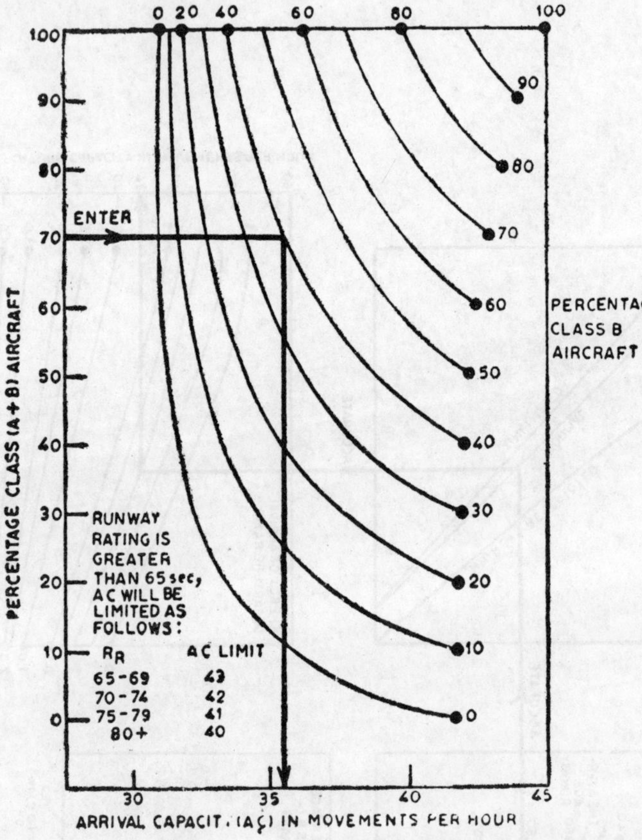

Figure 7.6 Determination of Arrival Capacity (AC) Nomograph for Air Carrier Airports (IAW Conditions)

(vii) Again, taking arrival/departure ratio into consideration, PHC = 34 + 34 × 0.3 = 44.2 operations/hr for IAW conditions.

7.2.3.3 Practical annual capacities : The major factors required for determining the practical annual capacity (PAC) of an airport are :

(i) The practical hourly capacity (PHC)

(ii) Runway use and weather [(percentage use in VAW and IAW).

(iii) Amount of allowable delay.

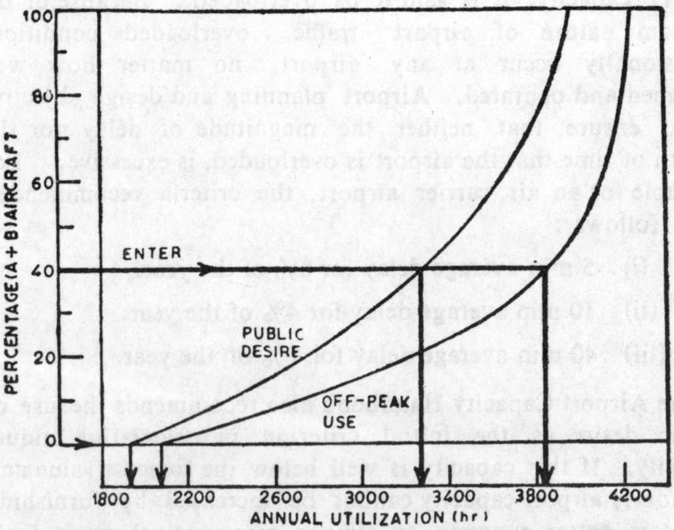

Figure 7.7 Effect of Off Peak Usage with Annual Utilization of Airports

(vi) Extent to which off-peak periods are utilized.

At first stage, it appears that PAC should be the product of PHC × 365 × 24. However this product, implies that the airport will operate continuously at the practical hourly capacity level, yields a PAC value that would have little practical meaning to the airport owner. It fails to account for the effects of runway use and weather, the need to avoid intolerable delays and daily seasonal variations in demand.

Crosswinds and other weather conditions affect the runway use throughout the year. This normally involved estimating the percentage of the average year that each runway combination will be used under VAW and IAW conditions and the hourly capacity for each such combination. Since these estimates are a function of the directional distribution and magnitude of winds, it is generally necessary to construct a wind rose diagram.

Allowance must be made for the effects of delays that may occur in addition to the 1 to 4 min average delays assumed for the determination of practical hourly capacity. When an airport is operating at a rate in excess of its practical hourly capacity, it is said to be 'overloaded'. Because of the random nature of airpart traffic, overloaded conditions occasionally occur at any airport, no matter how well designed and operated. Airport planning and design objective is to ensure that neither the magnitude of delay nor the length of time that the airport is overloaded, is excessive. For example for an air carrier airport, the criteria recommended is as follows :

(i) 5 min average delay for 8% of the year.

(ii) 10 min average delay for 4% of the year.

(iii) 40 min average delay for 1% of the year.

The Airport Capacity Handbook also recommends the use of public desire as the initial criterion in calculating annual capacity. If this capacity is well below the forecast value and the hourly airport capacity cannot be increased by furnishing more or better runways or similar measures, there is little choice to use off-peak criterion in spite of its disadvantages to the public and airport operator. Figure 7.7 shows the effect of off-peak usage on annual utilization. Annual utilization varies depending on the percentage of A and B aircraft in the population and whether off-peak use is allowed. At air carrier airports, some overloading in the peak hours must be expected. For such airports, a graphical procedure employing successive approximation is recommended to allow for the effects of overloading.

Example 7.2

Determine the practical annual capacity (PAC) of a single general aviation runway using the following data :

(i) Hourly capacities :

(a) VAW with no touch and go conditions = 70

(b) VAW with touch and go conditions = 120

(c) IAW conditions = 15

(ii) Average touch-and-go-traffic

(iii) Aircraft mix : C, (10%) and D + E (90%)

(iv) Nonradar control and VOR approach.

(v) Weather consists of VAW conditions 90% of the year, 4% of which will have crosswinds greater than 15 knots, and IAW conditions 10% of the year.

Solution

(i) Determine the maximum capacity under IAW conditions. Experience indicates that airport demand is curtailed in IAW conditions, depending on the percentage of large aircraft in the mix and the type of available IAW control and approach facilities.

Using Figure 7.8 for % (A+B) = 0

IAW demand factor = 7%

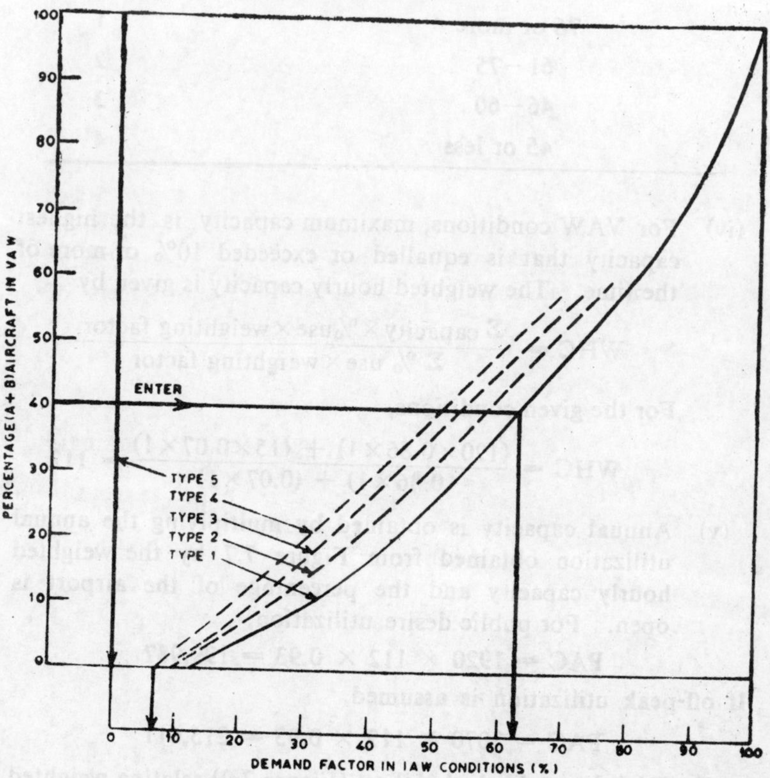

Figure 7.8 Effect of Instrument Air Weather (IAW) Conditions on Traffic Demand

(ii) The maximum capacity in IAW conditions is found as follows :

I_{max} = (VAW capacity without touch and go) × (IAW demand factor)

$I_{max} = 70 \times 0.07 = 4.9$, say 5

(iii) Since delay to operation rises very rapidly with increasing operating rate, the Handbook recommends (Table 7.3) that greater weight be given to lower capacities when evaluating airport capacity.

Table 7.3

Percentage of Maximum Capacity	Weight
76 or more	1
61–75	2
46–60	3
45 or less	4

(iv) For VAW conditions, maximum capacity is the highest capacity that is equalled or exceeded 10% or more of the time. The weighted hourly capacity is given by

$$WHC = \frac{\Sigma \text{ capacity} \times \% \text{use} \times \text{weighting factor}}{\Sigma \text{ \% use} \times \text{weighting factor}}$$

For the given conditions,

$$WHC = \frac{(120 \times 0.86 \times 1) + (15 \times 0.07 \times 1)}{0.86 \times 1) + (0.07 \times 1)} = 112$$

(v) Annual capacity is obtained by multiplying the annual utilization obtained from Figure 7.7 by the weighted hourly capacity and the percentage of the airport is open. For public desire utilization,

$$PAC = 1920 \times 112 \times 0.93 = 199{,}987$$

If off-peak utilization is assumed,

$$PAC = 2070 \times 112 \times 0.93 = 215{,}611$$

The FAA has published a chart (Figure 7.9) relating weighted hourly capacity to practical annual capacity. The use of a weighted hourly capacity accounts for the rapid increase in

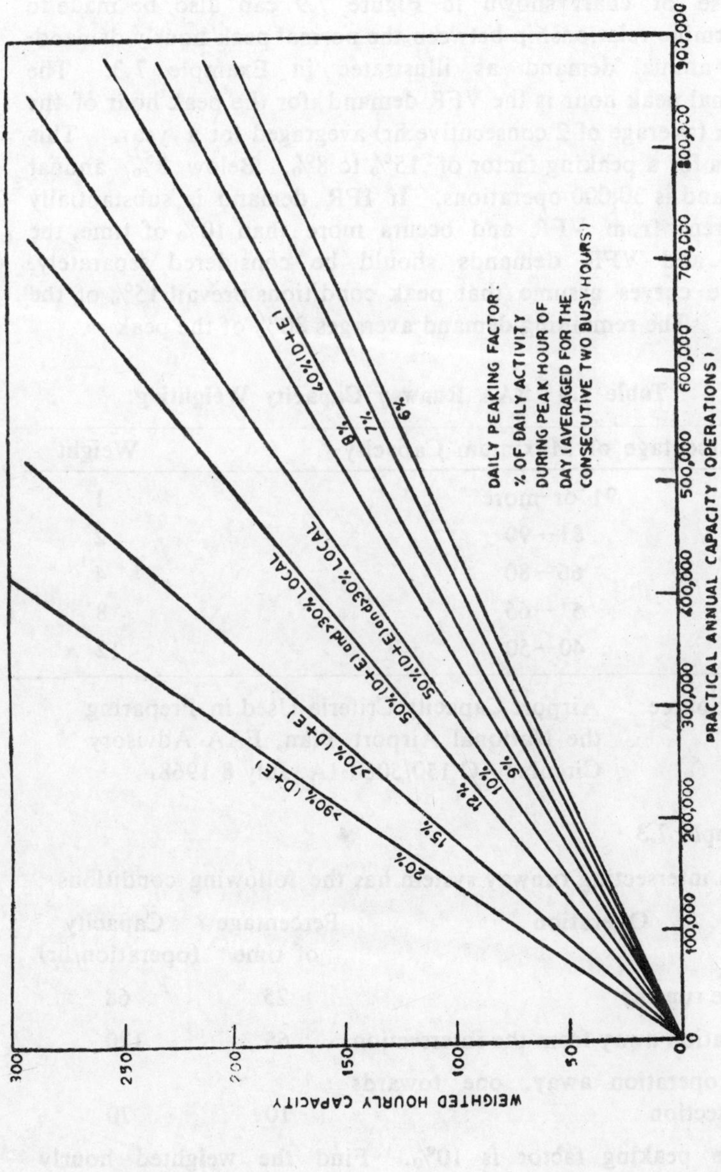

Figure 7.9 Relationship Between Weighted Hourly Capacity and Practical Annual Capacity

delays to operations with increases in the operating rate. The FAA recommends that the weights given in Table 7.4 can be used in computing weighted hourly capacity.

Use of chart shown in Figure 7.9 can also be made to determine relationship between the normal peak hourly demand- and annual demand as illustrated in Example 7.3. The normal peak hour is the VFR demand for the peak hour of the work (average of 2 consecutive hr) avegraged for a year. This holds for a peaking factor of 15% to 8%. Below 8%. annual demand is 30,000 operations. If IFR demand is substantially different from VFR and occurs more than 10% of time, the IFR and VFR demands should be considered separately. These curves assume that peak conditions prevail 15% of the time. The remaining demand averages 80% of the peak.

Table 7.4 FAA Runway Capacity Weighting

Percentage of Maximum Capacity	Weight
91 or more	1
81—90	2
66—80	4
5'—65	8
40—50	12

Source : Airport Capacity Criteria Used in Preparing the National Airport Plan, FAA Advisory Circular AC 150/5060-1A, July 8 1968.

Example 7.3

An intersecting runway system has the following conditions :

Operation	Percentage of time	Capacity (operation/hr)
Single runway	25	68
Operation away from the intersection	65	120
One operation away. one towards intersection	10	70

The peaking factor is 10%. Find the weighted hourly capacity and practical annual capacity.

Solution

(i) The weighted hourly capacity is

$$WHC = \frac{(0.25\times 10\times 68)+(0.65\times 1\times 120)+(0.10\times 8\times 70)}{(0.25\times 10) + (0.65\times 1) + (0.10\times 10)}$$

$= 73$ operations/hr

(ii) Using Figure 7.9. Practical annual capacity (PAC) $= 300{,}000$

7.3 GATE CAPACITY

The term 'gate' is defined by an aircraft parking space, adjacent to a terminal building and used by a single aircraft for the loading and unloading of passengers, baggage and mail. Gate capacity defined the ability of a specified number of gates to accommodate aircraft loading and unloading operations under conditions of continuous demand. It is the inverse of the weighted average gate occupancy time for all the aircraft served.

Gate occupancy time depends on the following factors :

(i) The type of aircraft

(ii) Whether the flight is an originating, turn around, or through flight.

(iii) The number of deplaning and enplaning passengers.

(iv) The amount of baggage and mail.

(v) The efficiency of apron personnel.

(vi) Whether each gate is available to all users or is allocated for exclusive use of one airline or class of aircraft.

Example 7.4 shows the procedure to find out gate capacity when each gate is available to all users, while Example 7.5 explains the procedure to find out the gate capacity with the exclusive use of different classes of aircraft.

Example 7.4

Determine the capacity of 12 gates that serve three classes of aircraft using the following aircraft mix and average gate occupancy time :

Aircraft Class	Mix (%)	Average Occupancy Time (min)
1	15	25
2	35	45
3	50	60

Solution

(i) Assume that each gate is available for all aircrafts. The gate capacity for a single gate is given by

$$C_{SG} = \frac{1}{\text{weighted service time}} = \frac{1}{(0.15\times 25)+(0.35\times 45)+(0.5\times 60)}$$

$= 0\ 0215$ aircraft/min/gate

If G = the total number of gates, the capacity for all gate is $C = G$. $C_{SG} = 10\times 0.0215 = 0.215$ aircraft/min = 13 aircraft/hr.

Example 7.5

Find the capacity of the 12 gates for exclusive use of the three classes of aircraft using the following data :

Aircraft Class	Gate Group	Number of Gates	Mix (%)	Mean Service Time (min)
1	A	2	15	25
2	B	4	35	45
3	C	6	50	60

Solution

(i) If the effect of mix is ignored, the capacity of group A would be the inverse of the service time : $C_A = 1/T_A = 2\ 5$ aircraft/hr. Similarly, $C_B = 1.33$ and $C_C = 1.0$, (ii) One might (incorrectly) conclude that the total capacity of these gates is the sum of the capacities of the three groups or $(2\times 2.5) + (4\times 1.33) + (6 \times 1.0) = 16.32$ aircraft/hr. When mix is taken into consideration, an overall demand of 13 aircraft/hr would result in excessive demand for grate groups B and C :

Gate Group	Demand (aircraft/hr)	Capacity (aircraft/hr)
A	0.15 × 16.32 = 2.5	2.5 × 2 = 5.0
B	0.35 × 16 32 = 5.8	1.71 × 4 = 6.84
C	0.50 × 16.32 = 8.16	1 × 6 = 6.0

(iii) The capacity of the gate system is

$$C = \min_{\text{all } i} \left[\frac{G_i}{T_i M_i} \right]$$

where G_i = the number of gates that can accommodate aircraft of class i

T_i = mean gate occupancy time of aircraft of class i

M_i = fraction of aircraft class i demanding service

(iv) For the given example

$$C_1 = \frac{2}{25 \times 0.15} = 0.53 \text{ aircraft/min} = 32 \text{ aircraft/hr}$$

Similarly, $C_2 = 15.2$ and $C_3 = 12$ aircraft/hr.

Therefore, the capacity of the gate is 12 aircraft/hr.

7.4 TAXIWAY CAPACITY

Studies based on empirical results show that the capacity of a taxiway system generally far exceeds the capacities of either the runways or the gates. There is one notable exception, namely, taxiway that cross an active runway. For such a situation, the taxiway capacity depends on the runway operations rate, the aircraft mix, and the location of the taxiway relative to the departure end of the runway.

7.5 AIRPORT CONFIGURATION

As already stated, a major determinant of airport capacity is the overall layout and design of the system. Airport configuration is the most important factor and defined as the general arrangement of the various parts or components of the airport system, are discussed in detail in Chapter 11.

7.6 RUNWAY CONFIGURATIONS

The capacity of an airport depends upon its runway

configuration. The pattern of runway to be finally adopted at the site depends upon the volume of air traffic to be handled, direction, duration and intensity of wind, availability of suitable approaches etc. The following are the basic pattern of runway :

(i) Single runway

(ii) Parallel runways

(iii) Intersecting runways

(iv) Non-intersecting runways

These are shown in Figure 7.10. The actual runway pattern may consist of a combination of two or more number of basic patterns stated above.

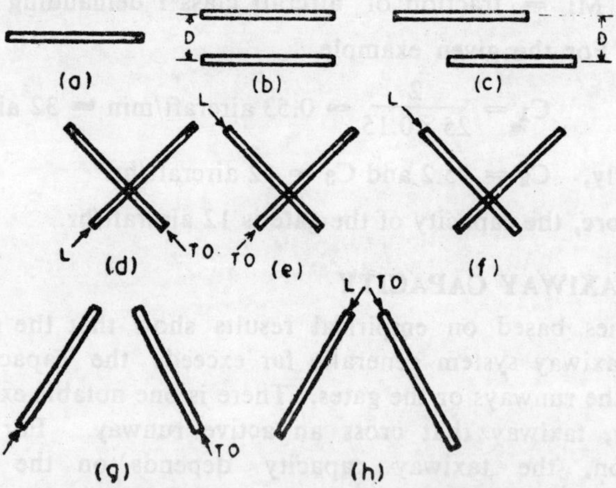

L = Landing T.O. = Taking-off.

Figure 7.10 Runway Basic Pattern

7.6.1 Single Runway

This is the simplest pattern of runway. It must usually be adopted when the wind blows in one direction for most of the time in a year and the air traffic requirement does not exceed the capacity of such pattern. In VFR conditions, single runway can provide maximum of 45 to 60 operation per hour. In IFR conditions, its capacity reduces to 20 to 40 operations per hour.

7.6.2 Parallel Runway

The capacity of this pattern depends upon the lateral spacing between the two runways, the weather conditions and the navigational aids available at the airport.

Very little information is available regarding the spacing of parallel runways which will permit simultaneous landing under IFR conditions. FAA has recommended that until more reliable information is available, a minimum spacing of 1500 m (5000 ft) may be considered for planning purposes. When the lateral spacing is in order of 900 m (3000 ft), landing and take-off but not simultaneous landing can be done on the two runways independently. This pattern can permit a maximum of 100 operations per hour under VFR conditions. Under IFR conditions, the capacity of this system may be about 80 operations per hour provided surveillance radar (see chapter 13) is available and the aircrafts are fed from two independent stocks.

If runways are located as close as 210 m (700 ft), the capacity under VFR conditions will be approximately 75 to 95 operations per hour and will be about 40 to 45 operations per hour under IFR conditions. Simultaneous landing will be possible only under VFR conditions.

If parallel runways are staggered and the terminal area is located in between two runways, the taxiway distances to and from terminal area are reduced. The capacity of this system is almost the same as that of the parallel system which is not staggered.

The present trend for large airports is towards parallel staggered runway which are located about 1500 m (5000 ft) apart so that they are capable of being used simultaneously. This layout offers the added advantage of nearly an unlimited scope for the expansion of the terminal complex located in the space between the two runways. The International Airport Committee has recommended the construction of the second parallel runway about 2250 m (7500 ft) apart from the existing runway for Indira Gandhi Airport (See article 11.8). It is expected that this runway system will meet the requirements of Delhi air traffic until or beyond the turn of the century. Calcutta airport also has two parallel runways, but they are only 210 m (700 ft.) apart and hence can be used simultaneously only when the weather is clear. The second runway of Calcutta airport may, therefore, be treated largely as a stand by for use when the main runway is under repair or temporarily, out of commission. In Calcutta, Bombay and Madras, where there is effectively only one runway, the saturation may reach before the end of this century when the need for the second airport will inevitably arise.

7.6.3 Intersecting Runways

This pattern of runways is usually adopted when wind in a particular direction does not provide the required coverage. Whether both the runways can be used for simultaneous landing and take-off, depends upon the cross wind component on each runway. When the wind conditions are favourable for use of both the runways, the capacity depends upon the direction of landing and take off, the lateral separation of the glide paths of the aircrafts and the intersection point of runways. The capacity will be maximum when the intersection point is near the runway ends and decreases as it approaches towards the centre of the runways. If separation between the glide paths of two aircrafts near the runway centres reduces to 3 km (2 miles) which is less than the desirable, the capacity of the system reduces from 35 operations per hour for pattern shown in Figure 7.10 d to 60 and 55 operations per hour for the patterns shown in Figure 7.10 e and 7.13 f, respectively.

7.6.4 Non-intersecting Runways

The capacity of this system again depends upon the wind conditions and visibility. For the system shown in Figure 7.10 h, where the flight paths are divergent, the capacity may be of the order of 80 to 110 operations per hour. If the flight paths intersect as shown in Figure 7.10 g, the capacity reduces to 66 to 80 operations per hour.

7.7 RUNWAY INTERSECTION DESIGN

The two factors which need special care in the design of runway intersection are the adequate drainage facilities and the smooth runway profiles. The aircraft should not bump when it passes over the intersection area. The following criteria should generally be satisfied :

1. For vertical curves along the edges of the paved portion of a runway, the rate of change of gradient should not exceed 0.5 percent per 30 m (100 ft) of horizontal distance. No vertical curve may be necessary if the grade change is 0.5 percent or below. If for example, the grade change is 1 percent, the length of vertical curves required will be 60 m.

2. For vertical curves along the edges of landing strip, the rate of change of gradient should be limited to a maximum of 1.5 percent per 30 m of horizontal distance.

3. On no portion of the intersection area, the slope should be less than 0.5 percent as it will otherwise obstruct the quick drainage of surface water.

4. The water should be drained away from the pavement towards the shoulders.

5. It is preferable to continue the centre line of each runway over the intersection area without any break. If this practice obstructs the quick drainage of the surface water from the intersection area, the changes in the gradients over the intersection area may be imperative. The grade change will be designed as outlined in 1 above.

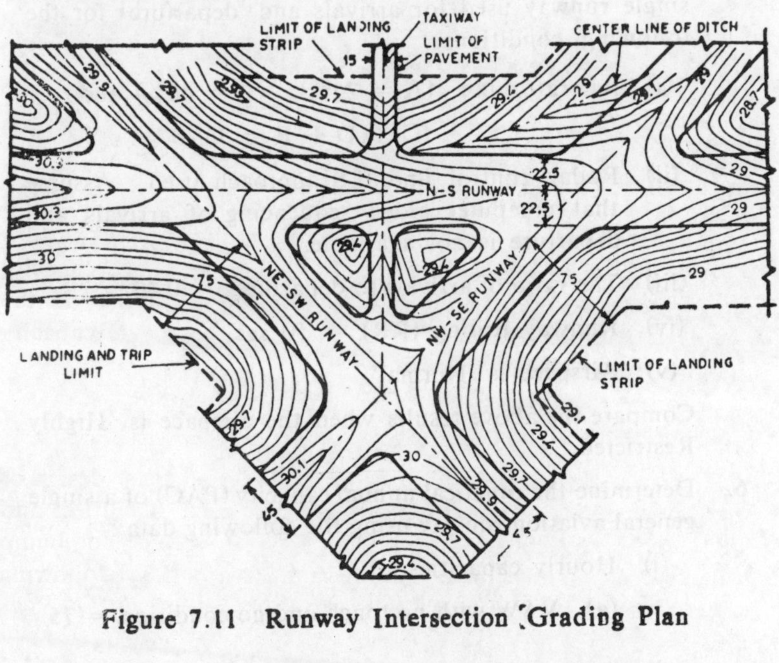

Figure 7.11 Runway Intersection Grading Plan

An example of typical intersection details is given in Figure 7.11. The figure indicates the warping of the grade required for smooth transition and quick drainage.

PROBLEMS

1. What do you understand by the term airport capacity? What are the factors which affect the airport capacity?
2. What do you understand by the term runway capacity? What are the factors affecting runway capacity?
3. Discuss in brief the factors affecting the air traffic control, characteristics of aircraft arrival demand, environment and layout and design of runway system.
4. What are the different methods for determination of practical capacity? Explain the difference between the practical hourly capacity and practical annual capacity methods.
5. Determine the practical hourly capacity (PHC) of a single runway used for arrivals and departures for the following conditions.

   (i) Aircraft mix: (A = 25%). (B = 40%) and (C + D + E = 35%)

   (ii) Radar control and ILS approach used. Assume that computer aided sequencing of arrivals and departure is not available.

   (iii) The ratio of arrivals to departures = 0.40

   (iv) Runway Rating (RR) = 50 sec.

   (v) Airspace is 'Normal'

   Compare the above results when the airspace is 'Highly Restricted.'
6. Determine the practical annual capacity (PAC) of a single general aviation runway using the following data:

   (i) Hourly capacities:

   (a) VAW with no touch and go condition = 75

(b) VAW with touch and go conditions = 115

(c) IAW conditions = 23

(ii) Average touch and go traffic

(iii) Aircraft mix ; C (15%) and D + E (85%)

(iv) Non radar control and VOR approach.

(v) Weather consists of VAW conditions 85% of the year, 5% of which will have cross winds greater than 20 knots and IAW conditions 15% of the year.

7. Define the term gate capacity. Explain the factors on which the gate occupancy time depends.

8. Find the weighted hourly capacity (WHC) and passenger annual capacity (PAC) for an intersecting runway for the following conditions.

Operations	Percentage of time	Capacity (operation/hr)
(i) Single runway	20	0
(ii) Operation away from the intersection.	65	115
(iii) One operation away and one towards intersection.	15	78

9. Determine the capacity of 15 gates that serve three classes of aircraft using the following aircraft mix and average grate accupancy time.

Aircraft class	Mix (%)	Average Occupancy time (min)
1	15	25
2	30	40
3	55	65

10. Find the capacity of 15 gates for exclusive use of the three classes of aircrafts using the following data.

Aircraft class	Gate group	Number of Gates	Mix (%)	Mean service time (min)
1	A	3	15	25
2	B	5	30	40
3	C	7	55	65

11. What are the basic patterns of runway configuration ? Discuss each pattern. What pattern has been recommended for international airports in India ?

12. Explain how the airport configuration is related to airport layout and for determining airport capacity.

13. Discuss the principles of design of runway intersection area. Draw a typical sketch showing the gradation of the intersection area.

8

TAXIWAY DESIGN

8.1 FACTORS CONTROLLING TAXIWAY LAYOUT

The main function of taxiway is to provide access to the aircrafts from the runways to the loading apron or service hangar and back. The following considerations decide the layout of taxiway.

(i) Taxiways should be so arranged that the aircrafts which have just landed and are taxiing towards the apron, do not interfere with the aircrafts taxiing for take-off.

(ii) At busy airports, taxiways should be located at various points along the runway so that the landing aircraft leaves the runway as early as possible and keeps it clear for use by other aircrafts. Such taxiways are called *exit taxiways*.

(iii) The route for taxiway should be so selected that it provides the shortest practicable distance from the apron to the runway end.

(iv) As far as possible the intersection of taxiway and runway should be avoided.

(v) Exit taxiways should be designed for high turn off speeds. This will reduce the runway occupancy time of aircraft and thus increase the airport capacity.

8.2 GEOMETRIC DESIGN STANDARDS

The speed of an aircraft on taxiway is much lower than its speed on a runway during the landing or take-off. Thus the design standards for a taxiway are not as rigid as they are for runway and can be listed as :

(i) Length of taxiway
(ii) Width of taxiway
(iii) Width of safety area
(iv) Longitudinal gradient
(v) Transverse gradient
(vi) Rate of change of longitudinal gradient
(vii) Sight distance
(viii) Turning radius

The detailed standards for different types of airports are given in Table 8.1.

Table 8.1 Taxiway Geometrics* (ICAO)

Classification by ICAO	Taxiway width m	Taxiway width ft	Maximum Longitudinal gradient, percent	Minimum Transverse gradient,	Maximum rate of change of longitudinal gradient per 30 m (100 ft), per cent	Safety area width
A	22.5	75	1.5	1.5	1.0	Turfed or paved shoulders are not mandatory but are suggested if need exists.
B	22.5	75	1.5	1.5	1.0	
C	15.0	50	3.0	1.5	1.0	
D	9.9	33	3.0	2.0	1.2	
E	7.5	25	3.0	2.0	1.2	

*Transverse slope and width are not specified.

8.2.1 Length of Taxiway

It should be as short as practicable. This will save the fuel consumption. No specifications are recommended by any organisation for limiting the length of taxiway.

8.2.2 Width of Taxiway

It is observed that the width of a taxiway is much lower than the runway width. This may be because, when aircrafts run on a taxiway they are not air borne. The speed of the aircraft on a taxiway is also lower than the speed that the aircraft may maintain on a runway. The pilot can, therefore, comfortably manoeuvre the aircraft over a smaller width of taxiway than on a runway.

8.2.3 Width of Safety Area

This area includes taxiway pavement shoulders on either side that may be partially paved plus the area that is graded and drained. This may extend upto a point where it intersects a parallel runway, taxiway or an apron. Before the advent of jet aircrafts, the shoulders were of natural ground protected with low growing vegetation. Where the soil or the climate conditions do not permit to maintain the plantation, the stabilised granular materials were used. This treatment was considered adequate to prevent the erosion of shoulder material due to high speed of the propellers. While the arrival of jet aircrafts, the erosion problem of shoulder material due to high speed jet exhaust has become more complex. When jet aircraft of transport category occupies even the central position on a taxiway pavement, it is observed that the outboard engines of the aircraft project the pavement on to the shoulders. It is felt that certain width, say 7.5 m (25 ft), of shoulders, adjacent to the pavement edge, should be paved with light strength material. This is shown in Figure 8.1. The surface must be impervious, smooth and should not disintegrate due to the hot blast of the jet engines. Bitumen treated shoulders are normally used. The shoulder must be thick enough to support the airport petrol vehicles and the sweeping equipment.

8.2.4 Longitudinal Gradient

If the gradient is steep, there will be greater fuel consumption. ICAO recommends that the longitudinal gradient should not exceed 1.5 per cent for A and B types and 3 per cent for other types of airports.

8.2.5. Transverse Gradient

This is essential for quick drainage of surface water. ICAO recommends that for taxiway pavement, like runway, the transverse gradient should not exceed a value of 1.5 per cent

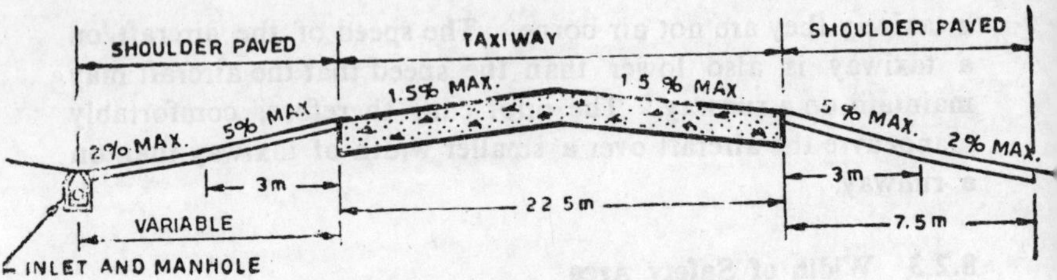

Figure 8.1 Taxiway Cross Section

for A, B, and C types and 2 per cent for D and E types of airports. Minimum value of gradient is not specified. As in the case of runways, a minimum transverse gradient of 0.50 per cent is suggested. ICAO does not specify any value for the transverse slope of taxiway shoulders. FAA recommends, that it should be 5 per cent for the first 3 m and 2 percent thereafter, for all types of airports

8.2.6 Rate of Change of Longitudinal Gradient

This directly affects the available sight distance on the pavement. ICAO recommends that rate of change of slope in longitudinal direction should not exceed 1 percent per 30 m length of vertical curve for A, B and C types and 1.2 per cent for D and E types of airports.

8.2.7 Sight Distance

Since the speed of aircraft on taxiway is lower than on runway, smaller value of sight distance will be sufficient on taxiway. ICAO recommends that the surface of a taxiway must be visible from 3 m (10 ft) height for a distance of 300 m (1000 ft) for A, B and C types and distance of 250 m (830 ft) be visible from 2.1 m (7 ft) height for D and E types of airports.

8.2.8 Turning Radius

Whenever there is a change in the direction of a taxiway, a horizontal curve is provided. The curve is so designed that the aircraft can negotiate it without significantly reducing the speed. Circular curve of large radius is suitable for this purpose. The radius can be obtained from the following formula :

$$R = \frac{V^2}{125\, f} \qquad (8.1)$$

Here R is the radius in metre, V is the speed in kmph, and f is the coefficient of friction between the tire and pavement surface. The value of f may be assumed as 0.13.

For airports serving large subsonic jet transports, minimum value of radius of curvature is 120 m (400 ft) whatever be the speed. For supersonic transports, a minimum radius of 180 m (600 ft) is suggested. Figure 8.2 illustrates, how the aircraft goes off the pavement when a supersonic transport with wheel base of 31.2 m (104 ft) manoeuvres a curve of 60 m (200 ft) radius. According to *Horonjeff** the radius of the taxiway should be so provided that the distance of the oleo strut of the nearby main gear is not less than 6 m (20 ft) from the pavement edge. The relationship between the radius of taxiway, wheel base of aircraft and the specified distance of the main gear from the edge of the pavement is given by the following

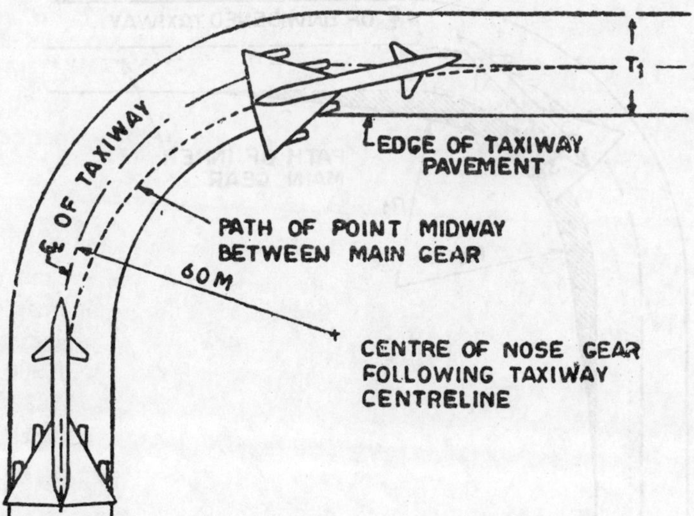

Figure 8.2 Supersonic Transport Aircrafts on a Taxiway Curve

*Professor of Transportation Engineering, University of California, U.S.A.

equation as suggested by Horonjeff.

$$R = \frac{0.388\ W^2}{T/2 - S} \tag{8.2}$$

where, R = radius of taxiway in metre

W = wheel base of aircraft in metre

T = width of taxiway pavement in metre and

S = distance between midway point of the main gears and the edge of the taxiway pavement in metre

Thus if the pilot maintains the nose gear on the centre line of the taxiway having the radius as obtained from the above expression, the oleo strut of the main gear of the aircraft would not come closer than 6 m from the pavement edge.

If the existing airport has to be upgraded to accommodate supersonic transport, it may not be always feasible to increase the radius of taxiway pavements. An alternative to this is to widen the pavement. Widening is done by providing a compound curve of radii R_1 and R_2 as shown in Figure 8.3

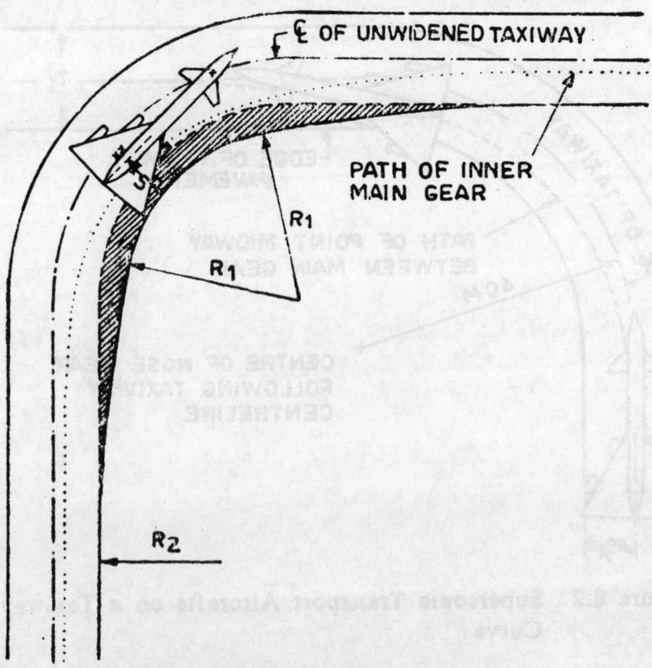

Figure 8.3 Taxiway Widening

The values of R_1 and R_2 are determined from the following equation :

$$R_2 = R - \left(\frac{0.388W^2}{R} + S\right) \tag{8.3}$$

If the expression $\left(\frac{0.388W^2}{R} + S\right)$ is less than T/2, no widening required. If it is greater than T/2, the radius R_1 should be

$$R_1 = \frac{D_r^2+(T/2)^2 + 0.30\,R - R_2^2 - RT}{2\,(R-R_2)} \tag{8.4}$$

where, R = radius of centre line of taxiway in metre

W = wheel base of aircraft in metre

S = distance between a midway point of the main gears and edge of taxiway pavement in metre

T = width of taxiway pavement in metre

$D_r = 3W - 0.4\,R$

If D_r is less than W, then use W instead of D_r.

Example 8.1

A taxiway is to be designed for operating Boeing 707–320 which has the following characteristics. Determine the turning radius of the taxiway.

Wheel base	17.70 m
Tread of main loading gear	6.62 m
Turning speed	40 kmph
Coefficient of friction between tire and pavement surface	0.13

Solution

(i) Turning radius $R = \frac{V^2}{125f}$

$$= \frac{(40)^2}{125 \times 0.13} = 98.5 \text{ m}$$

(ii) From Horonjeff's equation, $R = \frac{0.388\ W^2}{(T/2 - S)}$

Here $W = 17.70$ m

$T = 22.5$ m

$$S = 6 + \frac{6.62}{2} = 9.31 \text{ m}$$

Substituting in the above equation,

Turning radius, $$R = \frac{0.388 \times (17.70)^2}{11.25 - 9.31} = 62.9 \text{ m}$$

(iii) The absolute minimum turning radius for subsonic aircrafts regardless of any speed = 120 m.

Selecting the maximum value amongst the three cases discussed above, the turning radius to be actually provided = 120 m.

8.3 EXIT TAXIWAYS

8.3.1 Location of Exit Taxiways

This depends upon several factors. The important ones are as follows :

(i) Number of exit taxiways
(ii) Exit speed
(iii) Type of aircrafts
(iv) Weather conditions
(v) Topographical features
(vi) Pilot variability

The above factors are briefly discussed below :

(i) Number of exit taxiways : The number of exit taxiways to be provided decides their location. If there are only two exit taxiways, they would naturally be provided at the runway ends. If there are more number of exit taxiways, they are distributed along the runway length.

(ii) Exit speed : The maximum speed with which an aircraft can turn and enter the exit taxiway is limited for each aircraft. The aircraft requires certain length of runway to reduce its speed from the landing speed to the turn off speed. The latter thus affects the location of taxiways.

(iii) Type of aircrafts : Different type of aircrafts land at different speed, Therefore, the distance required by different aircrafts, to reduce their speed to the exit speed value, varies with the type of the aircraft. This in turn affects the location of exit taxiways.

(iv) Weather conditions : Wind, temperature, fog etc. affect the landing speed of aircraft. This also affects the distance required by the aircraft to slow down to the exit speed.

(v) Topographical features : The high altitude or deep valley reduce the visibility which may affect the landing speed. Obstructions in approach and turning zones may also influence the landing speed and hence affect the location of exit taxiways.

(vi) Pilot variability : The rules for landing of transport category aircrafts are quite precise. Even then some variability amongst different pilots does occur, especially in the distance from runway threshold to the touch down point and in the application of brakes on the runway. The pilot variability should necessarily be considered in locating exit taxiway.

8.3.2 Optimum Location of Exit Taxiways

The locations of exit taxiways should be such that the landing aircraft clears off the runway as early as possible. The acceptance rate of runway, with a system of exit taxiways, should be as nearly equal to the arrival rate of aircrafts as possible. Relationship between acceptance rate and the arrival rate of aircrafts is shown in Figure 8.4. Upto certain arrival rate runway is capable of accepting all the arriving aircrafts. As the arrival rate further increases, the airport cannot accept

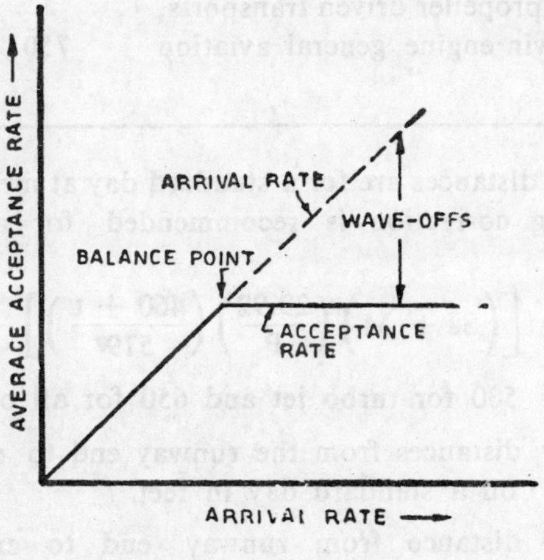

Figure 8.4 Arrival Rate and Average Acceptance Rate

all the arrival and the acceptance rate begins to deviate from the arrival rate. The point beyond which the acceptance rate deviates from the ideal relationship of equal arrival and acceptance rate is called the *balance point* and it represents the situation when runway is loaded to its full capacity. Such a situation is called *runway saturation.* At lower arrival rates, the runway is able to accept all the aircrafts. At higher arrival rates, the runway cannot accept all the aircrafts and few of them are *waved off.* For a given set of conditions, the exit taxiways should be so located that they yield the highest possible rate of acceptance. Such a location of exit taxiway is defined as the *optimum location.*

In order to develop design criteria for the aircraft engineers, the model analysis was carried out by Horonjeff using a wide range of aircraft types for an exit speed of 95 kmph (60 mph). As a result of this study, the following locations are recommended for the exit taxiway by FAA.

Aircraft type	Distance from runway threshold m	ft
Large turbo jet transports	1800	6000
Four-engine propeller driven transports, turbo prop and twin engine turbo jet.	1200	4000
Twin-engine propeller driven transports, and large twin-engine general aviation aircrafts.	750	2500

The above distances are for a standard day at mean sea level, the following correction is recommended for altitude and temperature.

$$S_e = \left[\left(S_o + M\right)\left(\frac{29.92}{P}\right)\left(\frac{460 + t}{519}\right)\right] - M \quad (8\ 5)$$

Where M = 500 for turbo jet and 650 for all other aircrafs

S_o = distances from the runway end to exit taxiway on a standard day in feet.

S_e = distance from runway end to exit taxiway, corrected for altitude and temperature in feet.

t = average temperature of the hottest month at the site in °F.

P = standard air pressure at the site in inches of mercury.

The correction suggested above is based on zero wind at the site. It is assumed that the aircraft would not miss the exit due to the wind. However, if the wind velocity is too high, its effect should also be considered. As a rough guide, it may be assumed that a head wind of 16 kmph (10 mph) may cause approximately 13.5 percent reduction in the distance to exit speed.

8.3.3 Design of Exit Taxiway Connecting Runway and Parallel Taxiway

The following principles govern the design of taxiway.

(i) The most significant factor effecting the turning radius is the exit speed of aircraft.

(ii) Slightly widened entrance of 30 m gradually tapering to the normal width of taxiway is preferred. The widened entrance gives to the pilot more latitude in using the exit taxiway.

(iii) Total angle of turn of 30° to 45° can be negotiated satisfactorily. The smaller angle seems to be preferable because the length of curved path is reduced.

(iv) For smooth and comfortable turn, the turning radius should be determined from the Equation 8.1.

(v) A high turn-off speeds of 65 to 95 kmph (40 to 60 mph), a compound curve is necessary to minimise the tire wear on the nose gear. Therefore, the main curve radius R_2 should be preceeded by a larger radius curve R_1 as shown in Figure 8.5. Aircraft path approximates a spiral. But still a compound curve is preferred as it is relatively easier to establish it in the field and its shape is similar to that of a spiral.

The following radius were found experimentally suitable.

Speed		Radius	
kmph	mph	m	ft
65	40	517	1724
80	50	731	2436
95	60	941	3138

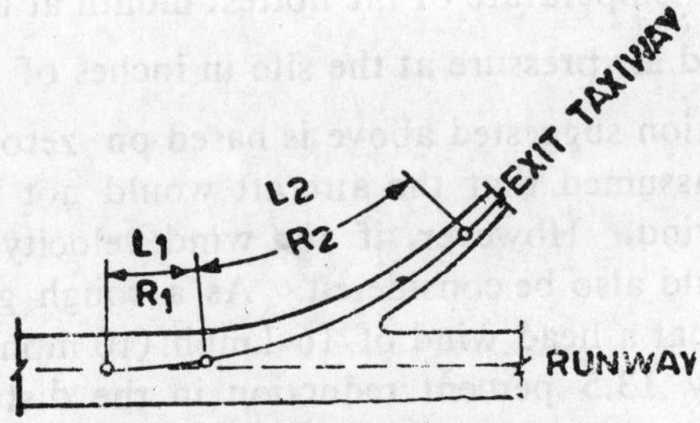

R_1 = radius of entrance curve
L_1 = length of entrance curve
R_2 = radius of central curve
L_2 = length of central curve

Figure 8.5 Radius of Curvature for Exit Taxiway

(vi) The length of larger radius curve can be roughly obtained from the following relation :

$$L_1 = \frac{(0.28\ V)^3}{CR_2} = \frac{V^3}{45.5 \times C \times R_2} \qquad (8.6)$$

The value of C is 0.39.

(vii) Sufficient distance must be provided to comfortably decelerate an aircraft after it leaves the runway. This distance may be based on an average deceleration rate of 1 m/sec² (3.3 ft/sec²). The stopping distance may be obtained from the following equation :

$$S.D. = \frac{(0.28\ V^2)}{2d} = \frac{V^2}{25\ 5d} \qquad (8.7)$$

where d is the deceleration in m/sec.² The stopping distance should be measured from the edge of the runway pavement along the exit taxiway.

Example 8.2

Design an exit taxiway joining a runway and a parallel main taxiway. The total angle of turn is 30 degrees and the turn off speed is 80 kmph. Draw a neat sketch and show therein all the design elements.

Solution

The various design elements are shown in Figure 8.6.

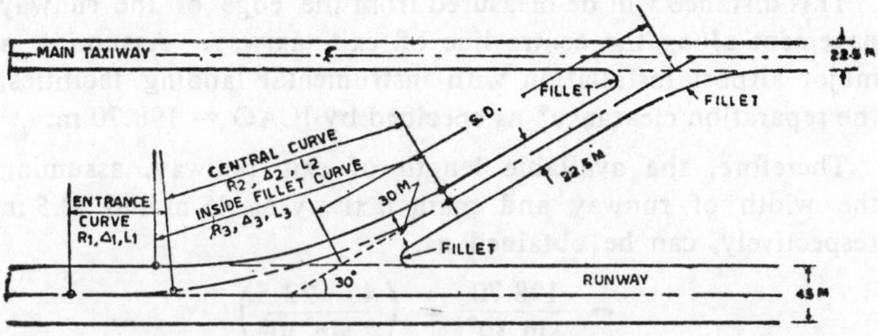

Figure 8.6 Plan of 80 kmph 30° Exit Taxiway

The radius of the central curve

$$R_2 = \frac{V^2}{125\ f} = \frac{(80)^2}{125 \times 0.13} = 391\ \text{m}$$

The radius of the entrance curve R_1 is obtained from the following table :

Speed (kmph)	65	80	95
Radius (R_1), m	517	731	941

Therefore, provide $R_1 = 731$ m

Length of the entrance curve is given by

$$L_1 = \frac{V_1^3}{45.5\ CR_2} = \frac{(80)^3}{45.5 \times 0.39 \times 391} = 73.5\ \text{m}$$

Deflection angle of the entrance curve

$$\Delta_1 = \frac{180\ L_1}{\pi \, . \, R_1} = \frac{180 \times 73.5}{3.14 \times 731} = 5.75^\circ = 5^\circ\ 45'$$

Deflection angle of the central curve

$$\Delta_2 = 30^\circ - 5^\circ\ 45' = 24^\circ\ 15'$$

Length of the central curve

$$L_2 = \frac{\pi\ R_2\ \Delta_2}{180} = \frac{3.14 \times 391 \times 24.25}{180} = 165.5\ \text{m}$$

Stoping distance

$$S.D. = \frac{V^2}{25.50\ d}$$

Assuming the deceleration rate as 1 m/sec²

$$S.D. = \frac{(80)^2}{25.50 \times 1} = 251.0\ \text{m}$$

This distance will be measured from the edge of the runway pavement along the centre line of exit taxiway. Assuming a major airport installation with instrumental landing facilities, the separation clearance* as specified by ICAO = 198.70 m.

Therefore, the available length of exit taxiway, assuming the width of runway and main taxiway as 45 m and 22.5 m respectively, can be obtained as,

$$= \frac{198.70}{\sin 30^\circ} = \left(\frac{45+22.5}{2 \sin 30^\circ}\right)$$

$$= 397.40 - 67.5 = 329.9 \text{ m}.$$

It should now be checked that this distance is at least equal to the stopping distance as calculated above. Sometimes the separation clearance distance may have to be increased to accommodate the stopping distance within the length of the exit taxiway.

Fillet's radii** 22.5 m and 60 m are provided for 30° and 150° changes in the directions respectively.

8.4 FILLETS

These are provided at the junction or intersection of two or more number of traffic ways e.g. runways, taxiways or aprons. If adequate fillets are not provided, one of the main gears of an aircraft, generally the one having large wheel base, is likely to go off the pavement on to the shoulder. As a guide, ICAO recommends that the radius of the fillet should not be less than the width of taxiway. The recommendations of FAA for fillet radii for small and large airports are as follows.

Angle of Intersection	Radii of fillets			
	Small airport serving general aviation aircrafts		Large airport serving transport category aircrafts	
	(m)	(ft)	(m)	(ft)
0 – 45°	7.5	25	22.5	75
45° – 135°	15.0	50	30.0	100
More than 135°	60.0	200	60.0	200

The above radii are also illustrated in Figures 8.7 and 8.8.

*See article 8.5 **See article 8.4

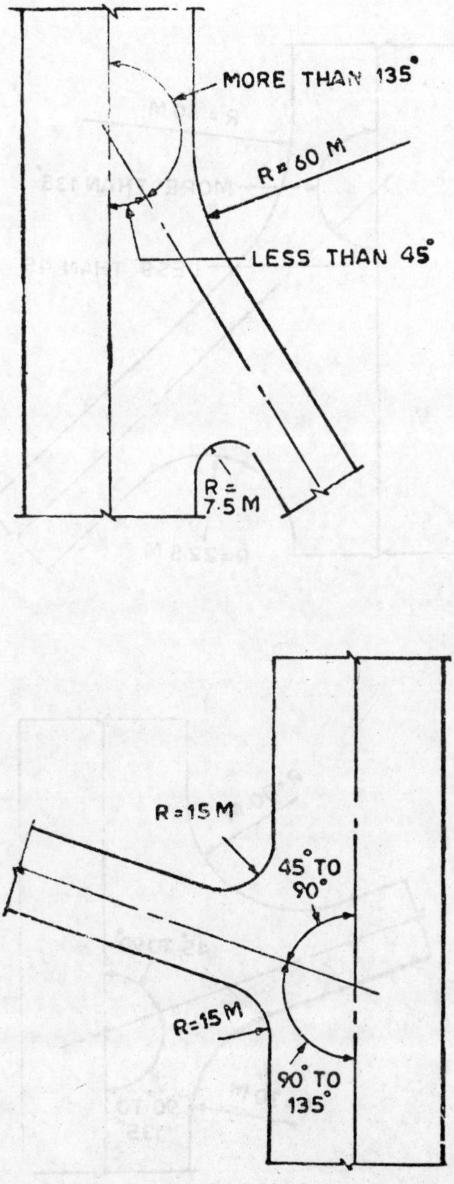

Figure 8.7 Typical Runway and Taxiway Fillets for Small Airports

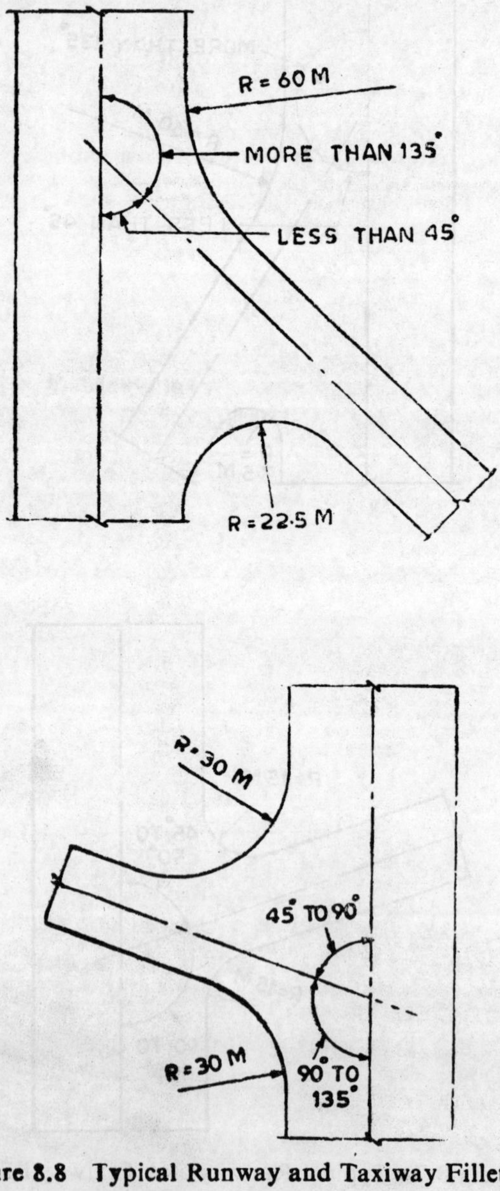

Figure 8.8 Typical Runway and Taxiway Fillets for Large Airports

At all the airports, the fillet radii for exit taxiway, intended primarily to increase the acceptance rate of runway, should be designed according to the exit taxiway design criteria. It may be noted that the correct requirement of fillet area can actually be determined by the model testing.

8.5 SEPARATION CLEARANCE

From the view point of safety, the two parallel trafficways should be separated by an adequate distance from each other as shown in Figure 8.9. The separation distance depends upon the type of airport, the wing span of aircraft and the navigational aids available at the airport. The trafficways should also be separated sufficiently from the adjacent obstructions. e.g., a building. The recommendations of ICAO for the required separation clearances are given in Table 8.2. These clearance values are based on the judgement as well as the accident reports.

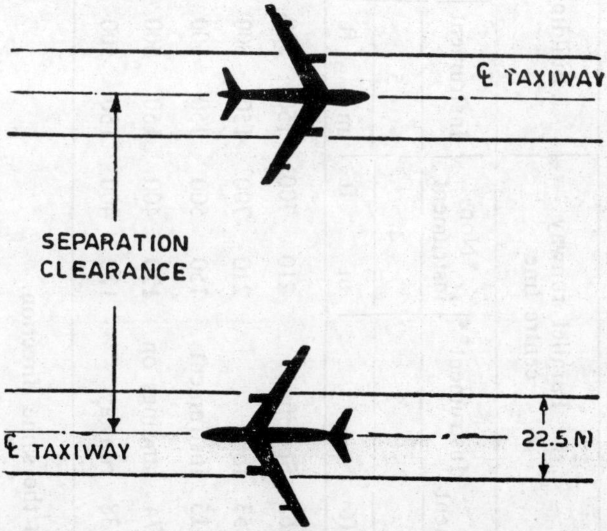

Figure 8.9 Separation Clearance for Parallel Taxiways

Sometimes large clearances, than those recommended by ICAO, may be required in order to accommodate exit taxiways and other constructions in between the trafficways.

8.6 HOLDING APRON

These are also known as *run-up* or *warm-up* paids. These are

Table 8.2 Separation Clearance Standards

Classification of ICAO	Distance from runway centre line to :											Distance from taxiway centre to :				
	Parallel taxiway centre line				Parallel runway centre line			Building line				Parallel taxiway centre line		Edge of aircraft parking area	Line of fixed obstruction	
	Instrument		Non-instrument		Instrument**	*Non-instrument		Instrument		Non instrument						
	1		2		3	4		5		6		7		8	9	
	m	ft	m	ft		m	ft	m	ft	m	ft	m	ft		m	ft
A	184	613	109	363	Specified	210	700	150	500	75	250	84	280	Same	49	163
B	184	613	106	353	for	210	700	150	500	75	250	74	245	as	41.4	138
C	169	563	95	315	instrument	150	500	150	500	75	250	57	190	Column	33	110
D	—	—	52	174	landings on	120	400	150	500	75	250	37	123	9	23.1	77
E	—	—	41.4	138	runway	120	400	150	500	75	250	30	100		19.8	66

*For operation in the same direction.

**FAA recommends this as 1290 m (4300 ft) for simultaneous landing and 1050 m (3500 ft) for independent operation, one for arrival and other for departure.

located, where the aircrafts wait for their turn to take-off, and where they are finally checked before the take-off. Holding aprons are usually provided near the runway ends and are made sufficiently large so that, if one aircraft is unable to take-off because of some defect in the machinery, another aircraft can bypass it for the take-off. If such an arrangement is provided, the aircrafts desiring to take-off would remain in a queue in the taxiway connecting the runway end since it would be difficult for the crippled aircraft to reverse and return to the terminal area. The size of holding apron depends upon the peak hour aircraft movements, the airoraft size and its ground manoeuvring characteristics. Holding apron may not be required if the volume of traffic is small. The size of holding apron should be sufficient to accommodate two to four aircrafts and to allow one additional aircraft to bypass without any difficulty. The clearance between the wing tips of the parked aircraft should not be less than 7.5 m (25 ft). The configuration of holding apron for two aircrafts as suggested by FAA is given in Figure 8.10. As far as possible, the entry into the runway should be made with an angle less than 90° as otherwise the pilot would not be able to turn the aircrafts rapidly from the taxiway. The angled entrance into the runway, as shown in Figure 8.10, permits an aircraft to enter the runway without requiring to stop. This reduces the runway occupancy

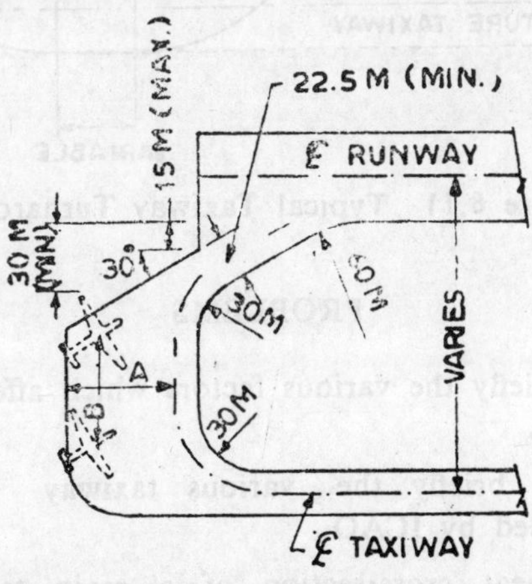

Dimension of A and B vary with the type of aircrafts.

Figure 8.10 Holding Apron Configuration

time of the aircraft which in turn increases the capacity of the airport. The precise configuration of holding apron can be decided from the model study.

8.7 TURNAROUND OR BYPASS TAXIWAY

Many airports in the initial stages have low airport traffic and are constructed without a parallel taxiway. As the traffic increases, the need of a parallel taxiway may be felt although it may not always be feasible to provide it from economic considerations. As a substitute for parallel taxiway, sometimes a turnaround or bypass taxiway is constructed which also serves the purpose of a holding apron. In such cases, the runway is also used as a taxiway. The arrangement is shown in Figure 8.11.

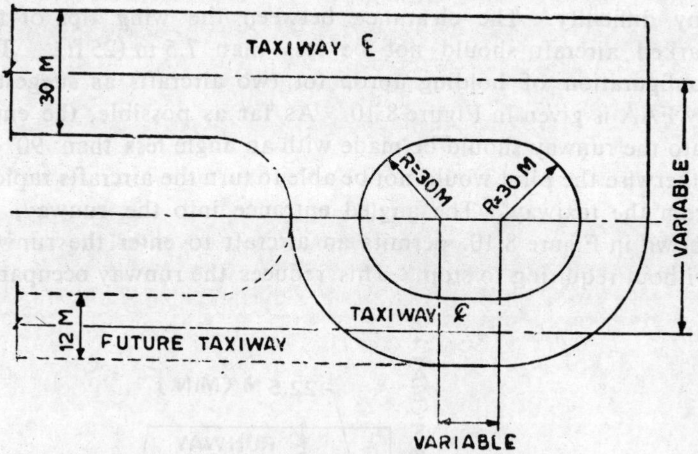

Figure 8.11 Typical Taxiway Turnaround

PROBLEMS

1 Explain briefly the various factors which affect the layout of taxiway.

2 Summarize briefly the various taxiway geometrics as recommended by ICAO.

3 Draw a neat cross-section of a main taxiway for an international airport. Show the various taxiway geometrics in the diagram.

4 Explain the various factors which affect the locations of exit taxiway. What do you understand by optimum location of exit taxiway ?

5 Give the principles of design of an exit taxiway connecting the runway and a parallel taxiway. Draw a neat sketch of the exit taxiway and show therein the various elements which are are to be designed.

6 Write short notes on :

1. Turning radius of taxiway,
2. Fillets,
3. Separation clearance,
4. Holding aprons,
5. Turnaround or By-pass taxiway.

7 Determine the radius of a taxiway for a supersonic transport whose wheel base is 35 m and the tread of main landing gear is 7.2 m. The design turning speed is 60 kmph. Assume any other data, if required.

8 Design an exit taxiway which joins a runway and a main parallel taxiway. The total angle of turning is 40° The aircraft can enter the taxiway with a maximum turn off speed of 65 kmph. Draw a neat sketch and indicate all the design elements.

9

STRUCTURAL DESIGN OF AIRPORT PAVEMENTS

9.1 INTRODUCTION

The pavement in general are classified as *flexible* and *rigid* according to their structural action. The black top pavement including gravel and water bound macadam follow the flexible group and the cement concrete pavement is the popular example of rigid group. The term flexible is associated with those pavements which reflect the deformations of subgrade and of subsequent layers on to the surface and the rigid characteristics are associated with bending strength or *beam action*. Flexible pavement do possess some flexural strength which is however negligible when compared with rigid pavements. In general, rigid pavements are capable of developing flexural strength of about 50 kg/cm^2.

As can be realised, the main function of a pavement is to carry heavy loads of aircraft and transmit the stresses over larger area of the underlying subgrade soil, thereby causing deformations within the elastic range.

Number of design methods are employed for both groups i.e. flexible and rigid pavements. In flexible group, methods based on tests like *California Bearing Ratio (CBR)*, plate bearing etc. are in use. In this group, the design methods are largely *empirical.* However method based on *Burmister's* approach is considered as semi-empirical. In rigid pavements, method based on *Westergaard* analysis seems to be widely accepted. This method is considered as rational, since it is based on the analytical treatment. Here also the plate bearing test is employed in measuring *subgrade* reaction *modulus* or moduls of subgrade reaction i.e. *K* value.

9.2 VARIOUS DESIGN FACTORS

The following design factors are considered in thickness determination :

1 Design wheel load

2 Strength characteristics of materials used in layers

3 Subgrade supporting capacity

Besides the above main factors, considerations are given to the repetitions of wheel loads, fatigue resistance, impact, volume change due to the frost-thawing and wetting-drying etc.

1 Design Wheel Load : Airport pavements are designed for the wheel configurations as shown in Figure 3.21. In general, aircrafts are supported by a nose gear and two main landing gears located in the wing area on each side. Modern aircrafts are fitted with *tricycle* assembly. Each landing gear consists of one, two or four wheels. One wheel is referred as single-wheel arrangement, two wheels as a dual-wheel assembly and four wheels as dual-in-tandem assembly. Treatment exists which converts multiple-wheel loading into equivalent single wheel load.

Characteristics of civil and military aircrafts used in India are summarized in Table 9.1. Table 9.2 shows the details of ACN and maximum seat capacity of some of the aircrafts.

2 Strength Characteristics of Materials : The strength Characteristics of different pavement layers are evaluated in different manners as per each design method. Largely; CBR or plate bearing test are carried out for flexible material. For rigid material like cement concrete mix, the flexural strength, elastic modulus and Poisson's ratio are obtained as strength parameters.

Table 9.1 Characteristics of Civil and

Nomenclature	Max. all up wt. (10^3 kg)	ESWL (10^3 kg)	Under Carriage Type	Under Carriage Track (m)	Under Carriage Base (m)	Wheel Type	Wheel Track (m)
(1)	(2)	(3)	(4)	(5)	(6)	(7)	(8)
Civil Aircrafts							
A-300 Air Bus	137.25	26.60	T	10.67	—	—	9.75
Boeing 707	141.00	23.40	TT	0.86	1.42	TC	6.73
Boeing 720	106.59	19.60	TT	0.81	1.24	TC	6.68
Boeing 727	76.60	25.00	T	0.86	—	TC	5.72
Boeing 737	49.00	15.40	T	0.76	—	TC	5.23
Boeing 747	353.30	27.40	TT	1.12	1.47	TC	11.02
Concorde	174.64	31.70	TT	0.68	1.67	TC	7.0
Convair	114.50	23.73	TT	0.61	1.18	TC	6.07
Caravelle	56.00	13.00	TT	0.46	1.07	TC	5.21
DC 7	64.84	20.70	T	0.76	—	TC	10.57
DC 8	158.76	27.20	TT	0.81	1.40	TC	6.35
Dakota	14.10	6.90	S	—	—	TW	5.64
Fawker Friend	19.73	7.66	T	0.45	—	TC	7.20
H.S. 748	20.20	8.32	T	0.48	—	TC	7.54
Ilyushin-62	160.00	25.30	TT	0.80	1.66	TC	6.8
Tristar	186.43	24.12	TT	1.32	1.78	TC	10.97
Trident	68.04	21.71	T	0.95	—	TC	5.82
Viscount	32.87	12.40	T	0.48	—	TC	7.26
VC-10	152.00	25.68	TT	0.86	1.55	TC	6.53

Military Aircrafts used in India

Arrangement		Dimension			Tyre pressure kg/cm²	LCN (LCG)
Base (m)	Load on Noise%	Wing span (m)	Length (m)	Height (m)		
(9)	(10)	(11)	(12)	(13)	(14)	(15)
15.11	—	45.68	49.06	16.61	10.0	66 (III)
17.98	7.3	43.51	46.61	12.85	11.6	62 (III)
15.44	4.6	39.88	41.68	12.66	9.7	51 (III)
19.28	7.0	32.90	46.68	10.36	9.2	61 (III)
11.38	10	28.30	30.48	11.28	2.8	40 (IV)
25.50	4.8	59.60	70.51	19.33	12.6	74 (III)
18.20	6.0	25.5	6[illegible].1	11.45	12.7	85 (II)
17.42	3.8	36.58	42.44	12.04	12.6	66 (III)
14.80	7.0	34.3	36.24	9.01	12.5	39 (IV)
12.04	11.0	38.36	34.21	9.37	8.6	51 (III)
23.62	6.7	45.24	57.13	12.93	13.5	76 (II)
11.18	—	28.96	19.63	5.16	3.4	14 (VI)
8.75	5-11.5	29.01	23.52	9.12	3.4	10 (V)
6.30	8.13	30.02	20.42	7.57	5.0	18 (V)
24.58	10.0	43.30	53.12	12.35	11.4	64 (III)
21.34	5-11.5	47.34	54.15	17.02	12.1	66 (III)
15.34	5-11	29.87	39.42	8.61	11.6	59 (III)
8.86	7.5	28.65	26.21	8.53	8.8	32 (IV)
21.98	3.5-9	44.55	52.32	12.04	9.9	65 (III)

TABLE 9.1

(1)	(2)	(3)	(4)	(5)	(6)	(7)	(8)
Military Aircraft							
AN-12	61.00	18.00	TT	—	—	TC	5.1
Auster	1.00	467	S	—	—	TW	2.03
Canberra	25.50	11.45	S	—	—	TC	4.8
Caribou	13.00	58.50	T	—	—	TC	7.0
Constellation	61.50	13.65	T	—	—	TC	8.52
Devon	4.00	1.20	S	—	—	TC	4.17
Gnat	4.31	1.92	S	—	—	TC	1.55
Hunter	9.80	4.26	S	—	—	TC	4.50
HF-24	10.65	49.30	S	—	—	TC	2.80
Harvard	2.34	10.6	S	—	—	TC	2.59
HT-2	1.00	.467	S	—	—	TC	2.95
Ilyushin-14	17.25	7.80	T	—	—	TC	7.7
Kiran	3.54	1 612	S	—	—	TC	2.42
Krishak	1.29	.580	S	—	—	TW	2.09
MIG-21	9.66	4.34	S	—	—	TC	2.79
Otter	5.25	2.34	S	—	—	TC	3.81
Packet-C 119	33.70	25.15	T	—	—	TC	9.05
SU-22	14.33	64.50	S	—	—	TC	3.83
Sea Hawk	6.20	27.80	S	—	—	TC	2.59
TU-124	38.00	11400	TT	—	—	TC	9.05
Vampire	62.00	2529	S	—	—	TC	3.43
Military Helicopters							
Alouette	2.10	945	S	—	—	TC	2.5
Bell	1.30	583	OS	—	—	TC	—
Cheetah	2.00	900	S	—	—	B	0.38
MI-4	7.60	3420	S	—	—	TC	3.82
MI-8	12 00	5400	S	—	—	TC	4.5

OS = On skids ; B = Bicycle ; S = Single ; T = Twin ;

Contd.

(9)	(10)	(11)	(12)	(13)	(14)	(15)
—	—	37.99	33.11	10.53	5.00	35 (VI)
9.45	—	11.10	7.24	2.54	1.20	1 (VII)
—	—	20.00	20.30	4.75	10.1	36 (IV)
7.77	—	29.20	22.09	9.65	2.82	9 (VII)
—	—	37.50	34.6	7.55	8.42	38 (IV)
3.96	30	17.37	11.96	4.06	3.2	3 (VII)
2.59	10	7.32	11.53	5.20	10	6 (VII)
4.80	11	10 26	14 90	4.06	13.4	14 (IV)
—	—	9.0	15.7	3.60	8.0	13 (VI)
7.93	—	12.81	8 54	2.75	2.2	3 (VII)
—	—	10.68	7.62	2.74	2.22	1 (VII)
5.37	—	31.7	21.31	7.80	5.50	18 (V)
—	—	10.7	10.60	3.63	6.50	7 (VII)
6.3	—	11.4	8.40	3.3	2.86	2 (VI)
4.71	—	7.15	14.50	4.125	8.50	12 (VI)
4.50	9.16	19.81	5.77	5.66	2.20	4 (VII)
—	—	33.30	26.2	7.98	4.50	29 (V)
5.31	—	9.3	18.78	9.99	13.00	23 (V)
3.95	10	11.89	12 28	5.11	13 30	10 (VII)
10.45	—	25.55	30 57	8 08	5.50	22 (V)
3.81	12	11.58	10.49	2.01	5.90	6 (VII)
3.4	—	11.02	12.89	2.77	4.50	4 (VII)
—	—	11.30	13.12	2 84	—	2 (VII)
3.29	—	11.02	12.92	3.09	4.50	4 (VII)
3 79	—	21.00	25.01	4.18	4.50	7 (VII)
4.26	—	21.288	25.33	5.65	5.50	10 (VII)

TC = Tricycle ; TT = Twin Tandem ; TW = Tail wheel

Table 9.2 Aircrafts Characteristics

AIRCRAFT TYPE / CODE		ACN				MAX SEATS
		RIGID		FLEX		
		B	C	B	C	
A-300-600	D	55	64	56	68	375
A-300-600R	D	58	68	58	71	375
A-300-B4200	D	55	64	56	68	345
A-310-200	D	44	52	44	54	280
A-310-300	D	54	63	53	64	280
A-320-200	C	22	26	21	26	179
B 737-300	C	39	41	33	37	149
B 737-400	C	43	45	37	41	168
B 737-500	C	38	40	33	37	132
B 747-200	E	56	67	58	71	550
B 747-300	E	55	66	58	71	660
B 747-400	E	63	75	64	79	660
B 747-SP	E	44	53	45	54	440
B 757-200	D	36	42	35	43	239
B 767-200	D	51	62	53	65	290
B 767-300	D	45	53	46	58	290
BA-146-100	C	18	21	20	22	94
BA-146-200	C	22	25	25	26	112
BA 146-300	C	22	25	26	27	128
DC-10-10	D	54	64	58	69	380
DC-10-30	D	55	67	61	74	380
DO-228-200	E	4	4	38	46	—
FOKKER-100	C	29	31	27	30	107
FOKKER-F28	C	18	19	17	19	85
IL-62	D	50	60	54	64	174
IL-76-T	D	38	38	40	45	—
IL-86	D	31	38	36	43	300
L-1011-100/200*	D	55	66	61	73	400
L-100-HERCULES	D	33	36	31	33	97
L1011-500	D	59	72	65	79	333
MD-11	D	66	79	70	85	405
TU-154-B2	D	25	32	24	30	180

Source : AAI, New Delhi

3 *Subgrade Supporting Capacity :* The supporting capacity of the subgrade is considered significant in flexible pavements. In case of rigid pavements, this value seems to influence the thickness requirement negligibly.

The climatic changes in respect of hourly and seasonal variations greatly affect the overall load carrying capacity of rigid pavements. The rise and fall in atmospheric temperatures develop the temperature gradient in cement concrete slabs which in turn cause (i) expansion and contraction of the slabs (ii) warping of the slabs (iii) develop subgrade restraint. All this phenomena induce stress conditions which are either of additive form with load stress or otherwise.

9 3 DESIGN METHODS FOR FLEXIBLE PAVEMENTS

Following methods are considered for designing the pavement thickness :

(i) CBR method
(ii) McLeod method
(iii) Burmister method
(iv) Analytical method
(v) Computer aided design (CAD) application

The above design method are discussed in the following portion.

9 3.1. CBR Method

In 1928, *California Division of Highways*, developed CBR method. Subsequently, *Corps of Engineers, USA* adopted this method during world war II for designing the military airport pavements. CBR test procedure in use has been described in *Highway Material Testing by S. K Khanna, C.E.G. Justo.* Based on the field investigations carried out by California Division of Highways, an empirical relationship was developed as shown in Figure 9.1.

The curve A and B were satisfactory for highway loadings and since the aircraft loads were much higher than highway loadings, the Corps of Engineers used the design chart as given in Figure 9.2 using shear stress computations. The procedure of developing this chart is not included here.

To obtain the *equivalent single wheel load* of dual wheel assembly, Figure 9.3 is used. The use of this figure is illustrated in Example 9.1.

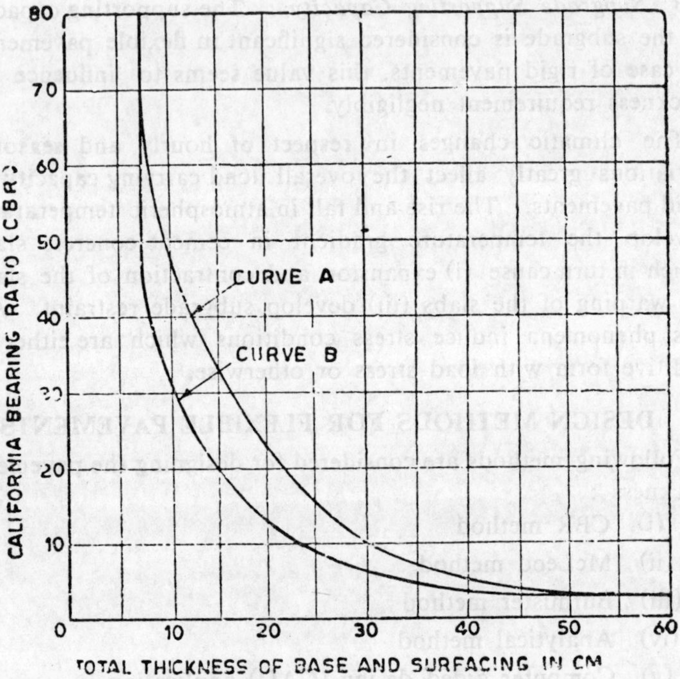

Figure 9.1 Total Thickness of Base and Surfacing from CBR Method.

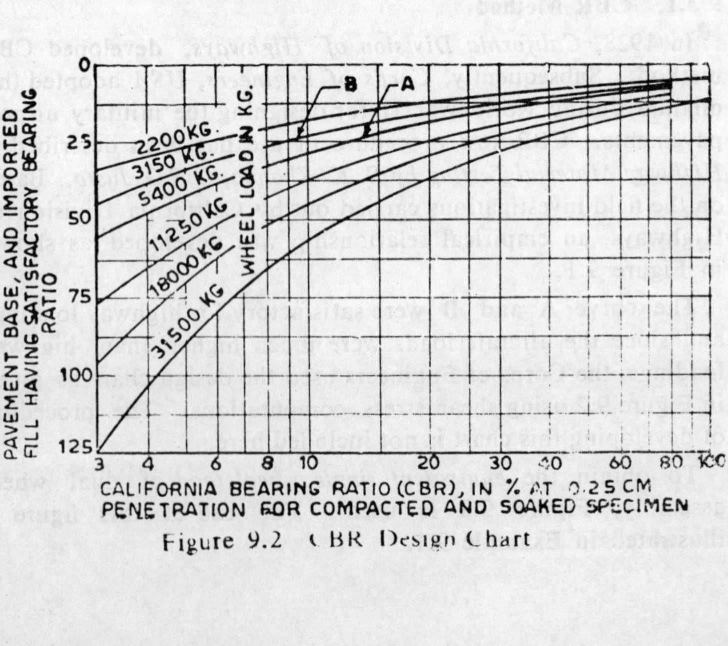

Figure 9.2 CBR Design Chart

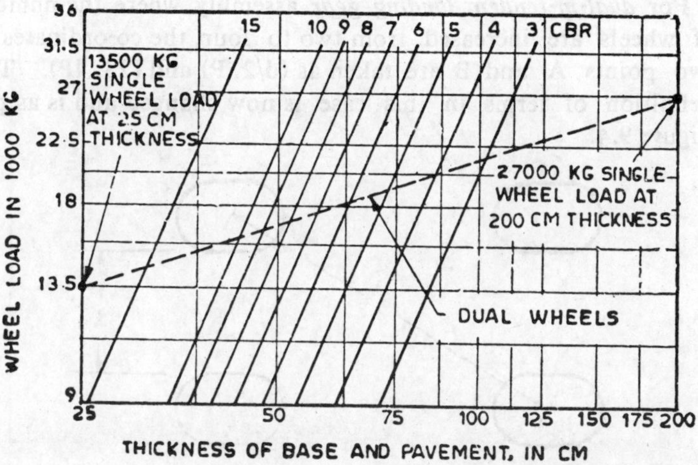

Figure 9.3 Computation of Equivalent Single Wheel Load

Example 9.1

Compute the equivalent single wheel load for a dual wheel assembly of gross wheel load of 27,000 kg where value of d = 50 cm and S = 100 cm. Here d is clear distance between the tires and S is the centre to centre distance between lines.

Solution :

Two points are plotted on Figure 9.3 with co-ordinates as (d/2, P) and (2S, 2P). The numerical values of these co-ordinates are (25 cm, 13500 kg) and (100 cm, 27000 kg). The dotted line is thus passed through these two points. Now based on the CBR value of the subgrade, the values of equivalent single wheel load can be obtained as under :

CBR of subgrade, per cent	Equivalent single wheel load kg
4	20,250
6	18,000
8	16,875
10	16,150

For *dual-in-tendem landing gear* assembly where the number of wheels are increased from two to four, the co-ordinates of two points A and B are taken as (d/2, P) and (2S, 4P). The definition of terms in this case is now changed and is as per Figure 9.4.

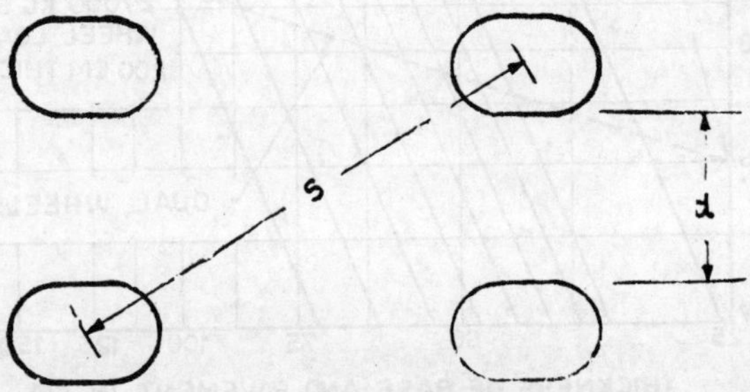

Figure 9.4 Dual-in-tandem Landing Gear Assembly

Number of design charts are developed by Corps of Engineers for different group wheel loadings and tire pressures. One typical design chart is given in Figure 9.5. The Corps of Engineers anticipate about 5000 coverages in the life of pavement and for coverages more than 5000, it is recommended to increase the thickness as under :

Coverages	Per cent increase in design thickness
10,000	7
15,000	11
20,000	14

The use of design chart is illustrated in Example 9.2.

Example 9.2

Design a runway pavement section for design gross weight of 67500 kg. Tests were conducted on pavement materials and CBR values so obtained are as under :

Compacted subgrade soil	4 per cent
Ungraded gravel	17 per cent
Graded gravel	40 per cent

The runway pavement is expected to sustain 15,000 load coverages.

Solution

Using the design chart as in Figure 9.5, the total pavement thickness over subgrade having CBR of 4 per cent is obtained as 87.5 cm. It means that 87.5 cm of pavement material is required to cover the compacted soil subgrade of 4 per cent. CBR strength which shall not develop failure deformations of the system under the gross weight of 67,500 kg.

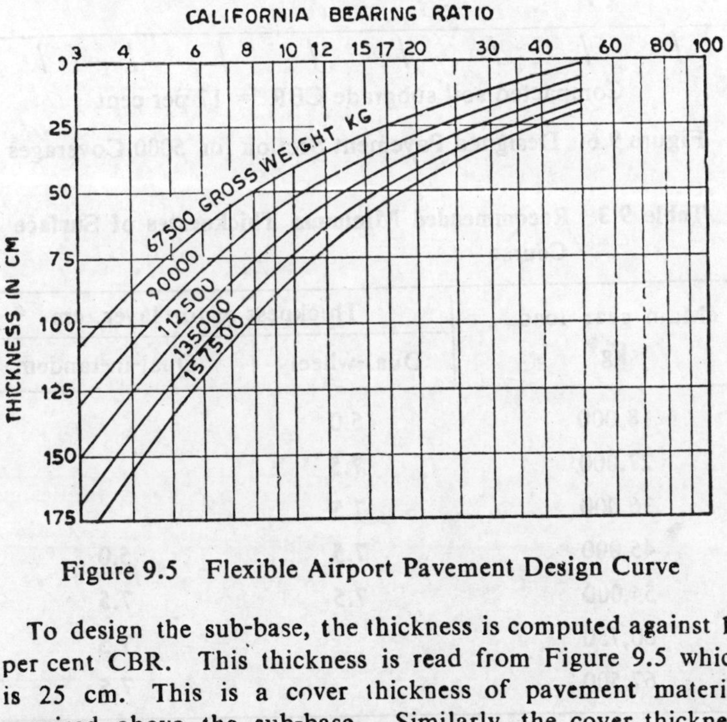

Figure 9.5 Flexible Airport Pavement Design Curve

To design the sub-base, the thickness is computed against 17 per cent CBR. This thickness is read from Figure 9.5 which is 25 cm. This is a cover thickness of pavement material required above the sub-base. Similarly, the cover thickness required above the graded gravel base course is 6 cm. Depending upon the main gear loads, Corps of Engineers have recommended the minimum thickness of the surface course of bituminous concrete which are given in Table 9.3.

Keeping in view the above recommendations, the minimum thickness of top cover is 7.5 cm for dual-in-tandem axle arrangements. The designed pavement section for 5000 coverages is, shown in Figure 9.6.

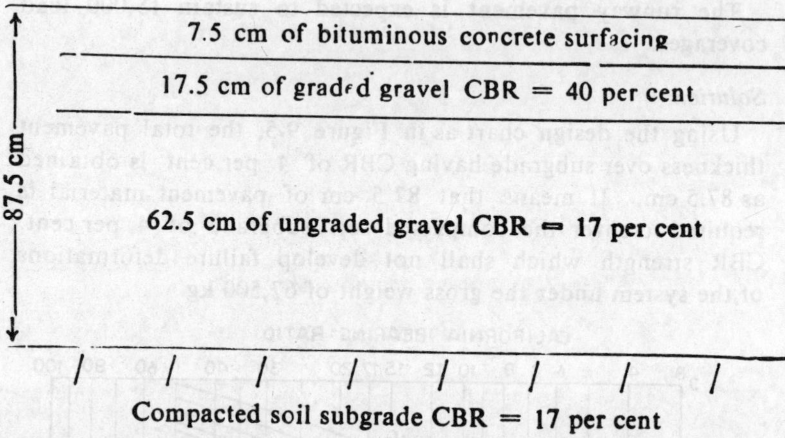

Figure 9.6 Designed Pavement Section for 5000 Coverages

Table 9.3 Recommended Minimum Thicknesses of Surface Course

Main gear load kg	Thickness of top layer, cm	
	Dual-wheel	Dual-in-tandem
18,000	5.0	
27,000	7.5	
36,000	7.5	
45,000	7.5	5.0
54,000	7.5	7.5
60,750		7.5
67.500		7.5

These thicknesses of base and sub-base need to be increased by 11 per cent for 15,000 Coverages. The design section is shown in Figure 9.7.

9.3.2 McLeod method

Norman W. McLeod through *Canadian Department of Transport* conducted extensive plate bearing tests on airfield

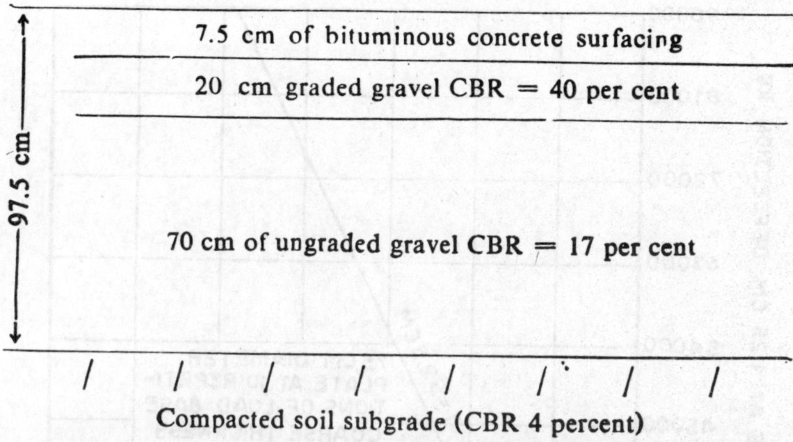

Figure 9.7 Designed Pavement Section for 15,000 Coverages

and highway pavements and developed a design method. The repetitive plate load test procedure was employed using various sizes of plate diametres. The plot as shown in Figure 9.8 was developed. From the load tests, an empirical design equation was recommended which is as under :

$$T = K \log \frac{P}{S} \tag{9.1}$$

where
T = thickness of gravel materials
P = gross wheel load
S = subgrade support
K = base course constant

Figure 9.9 shows the relationship between plate diameter and K values. To obtain the equivalent single wheel load, the procedure outlined in article 9.3.1 is used. McLeod method is illustrated by Example 9.3

Example 9.3

Design a runway pavement section for a wheel load of 27,000 kg with a tire pressure of 11 kg/cm^2. For this purpose, the plate bearing test with 75 cm diameter was carried out on soil subrade and the plate yielded a pressure of 2 kg/cm^2 at 0.5 cm deflection, after ten load repetitions.

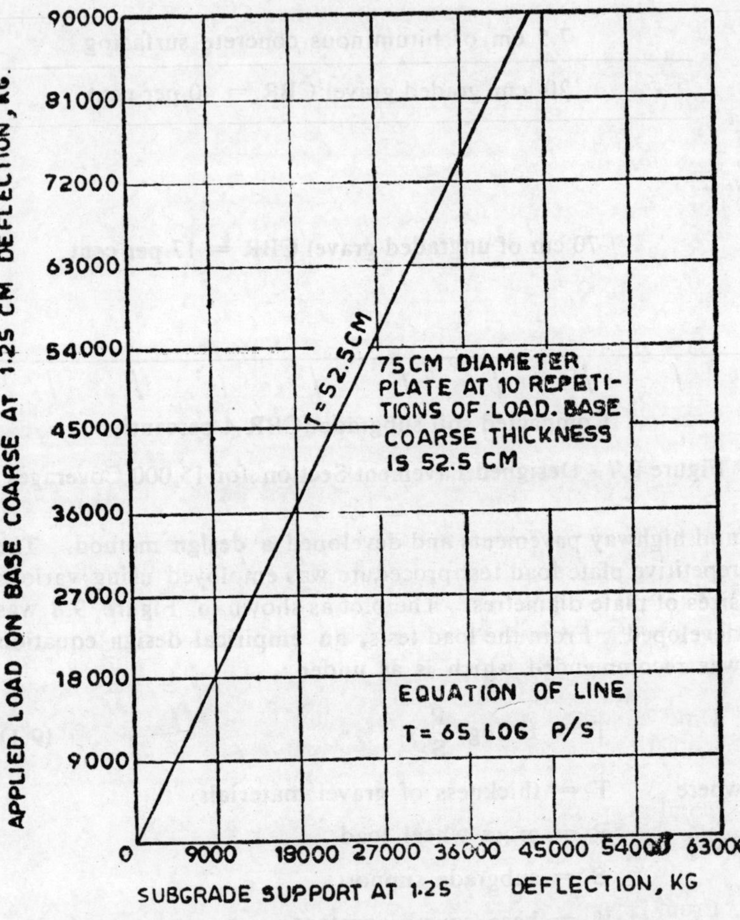

Figure 9.8 Deflection Versus Subgrade Support

Solution

The radius of contact, a is

$$\sqrt{\frac{27000}{11\,\pi}} = 28.5 \text{ cm}$$

The perimeter over area ratio is

$$\frac{P}{A} = \frac{4}{d} = \frac{4}{57.0} = 0.07$$

Using Figure 9.10 the ratio of unit subgrade support on 57 cm diameter plate at 12.5 cm deflection to unit support

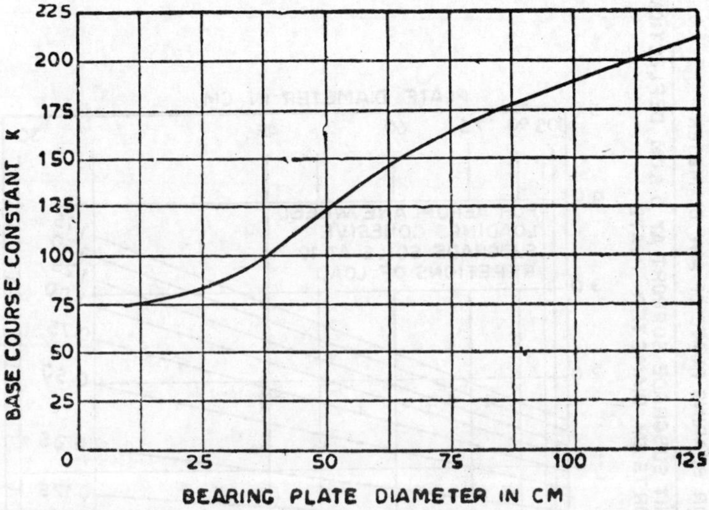

Figure 9.9 Influence of Bearing Plate Diameter on Base Course Constant (K)

on a 75 cm diameter at 0.5 cm deflection = 2.15

Unit support = 2 kg/cm²

Unit subgrade support on 57 cm diameter plate at 1.25 cm deflection = 2.15 × 2 = 4.30 kg/cm²

$$\text{Total support, } S = \frac{4.3 \times \pi \times (57)^2}{4}$$

$$= 11500 \text{ kg}$$

From Figure 9.9, the base course constant for 57 cm diamster is read out as 138.

$$\text{Therefore,} \quad T = 138 \log_{10} \frac{27000}{11500}$$

$$= 48.5 \text{ cm}$$

9.3.3 Burmister Method

Donald M Burmister, Professor Emeritus of Columbia University U.S.A. has developed the design method which is adopted by *US Navy department*. The method is known as *Navy method.* It is based on the principles of theory of elasticity and is an improvement over the single layer concept

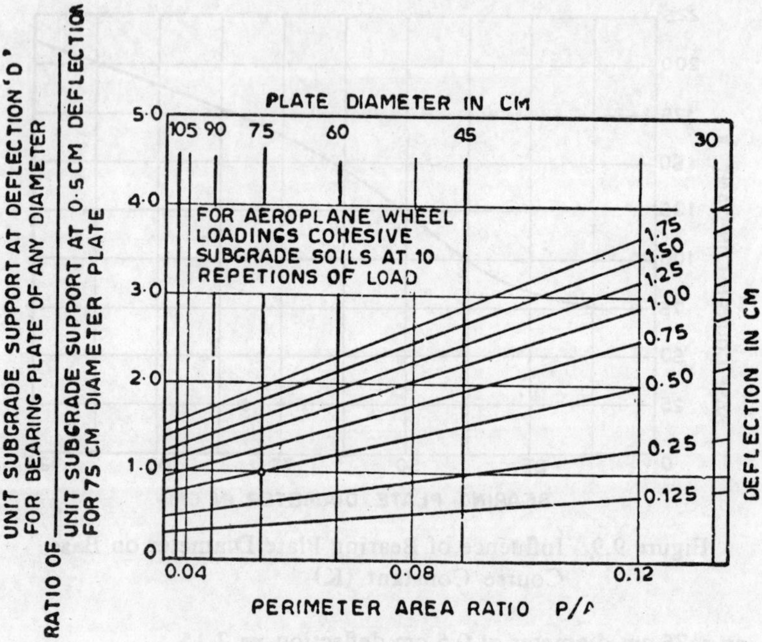

Figure 9.10 Ratio of Subgrade Support at Deflection D for Bearing Plate of any Diameter to Subgrade Support at 0.5 cm Deflection on 75 cm Diameter Plate versus Perimeter Area Ratio.

of *Boussinesq*. The effectiveness of the reinforcing action of the pavement layer is logically utilized in Burmister's approach. The deflection factor F_2 is introduced by Burmister which is dependent on

elastic modulus of pavement (E_p) / elastic modulus of subgrade (E_s) and

radius of contact area (a) / pavement thickness (h)

The comparison of Burmister two layered system and Boussinesq single system is illustrated in Figure 9.11. It is observed from this figure that the vertical stress i.e. subgrade pressure of 5 kg/cm² is reduced to 2 kg/cm² (viz. from 70 to 30 percent) by introducing a pavement layer of h = a with elastic modulus 10 times higher than subgrade soil. The Burmister's method thus utilizes reinforcing action of the pavement layer.

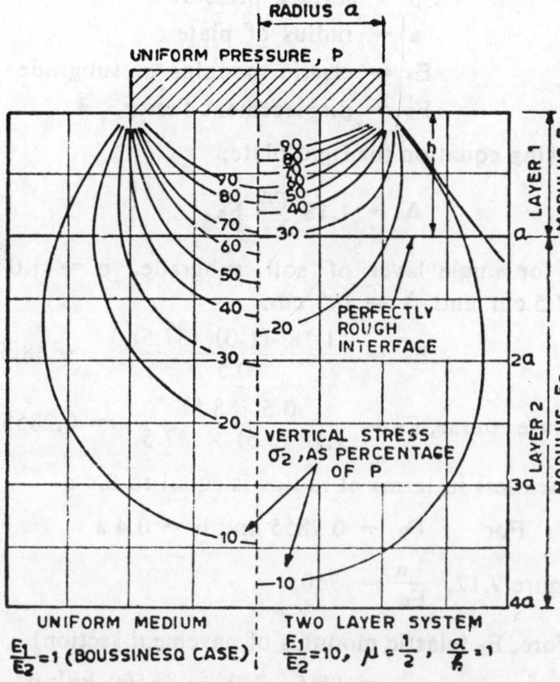

Figure 9.11 Vertical Stress Distribution

Example 9.4

Design the pavement section using Burmister's approach of two layered system. The plate bearing tests were conducted with 75 cm diameter plate on soil subgrade and 15 cm thick base course. The pressures recorded at 0.5 cm deflection for both the layers were 1.0 kg/cm² and 3.5 kg/cm² respectively. It is required to design the pavement section for 25000 kg wheel load with tire pressure of 10.5 kg/cm².

Solution :

Burmister gives following sets of design equations

For rigid plate, $\Delta = 1.18 \dfrac{pa}{E_s} F_2$ (9.2)

For flexible plate, $\Delta = 1.5 \dfrac{pa}{E_s} F_2$ (9.3)

where Δ = limiting deflection

p = surface pressure
a = radius of plate
E_s = elastic modulus of subgrade
F_2 = displacement factor.

Now using equation for rigid plate,

$$\Delta = 1.18 \frac{pa}{E_s} F_2$$

$F_2 = 1$ for single layer of soil subgrade, $p = 1.0$ kg/cm²
$a = 37.5$ cm and $\Delta = 0.5$ cm.

$$E_s = \frac{1.18\ (1.0)\ (37.5)}{0.5} = 88.5 \text{ kg/cm}^2$$

For the base course, $F_2 = \dfrac{0.5\ (88.5)}{1.18\ (3.5) \times 37.5} = 0.2855$

The thickness in terms of radius is equal to 0.4 a

For $F_2 = 0.2855$ and $h = 0.4$ a

using Figure 9.12, $\dfrac{E_p}{E_s} = 750$

Therefore, E_p (elastic modulus of pavement section)

$$= 88.5 \times 750 = 66500 \text{ kg/cm}^2$$

Now, for the wheel load to be considered in design

$$A = \frac{25000}{10.5} = 2380 \text{ cm}^2$$

$$a = \sqrt{\frac{2380}{3.1416}} = 28.2 \text{ cm}$$

Using equation for flexible plate,

$$\Delta = 1.5 \frac{pa}{E_s} F_2$$

$$F_2 = \frac{0.5\ (88.5)}{1.5\ (10.5)\ (28.2)} = 0.1$$

Using Figure 9.12 for $E_p/E_s = 750$ and $F_2 = 0.1$, the depth in terms of radius i.e. h in terms of a is read as 1.25 a.

Therefore design thickness,

$$h = 1.25 \times 28.2 = 35.2 \text{ cm}$$

In the design procedure, U.S. Navy method recommends to build nine trial pavement sections, three on each location i.e.

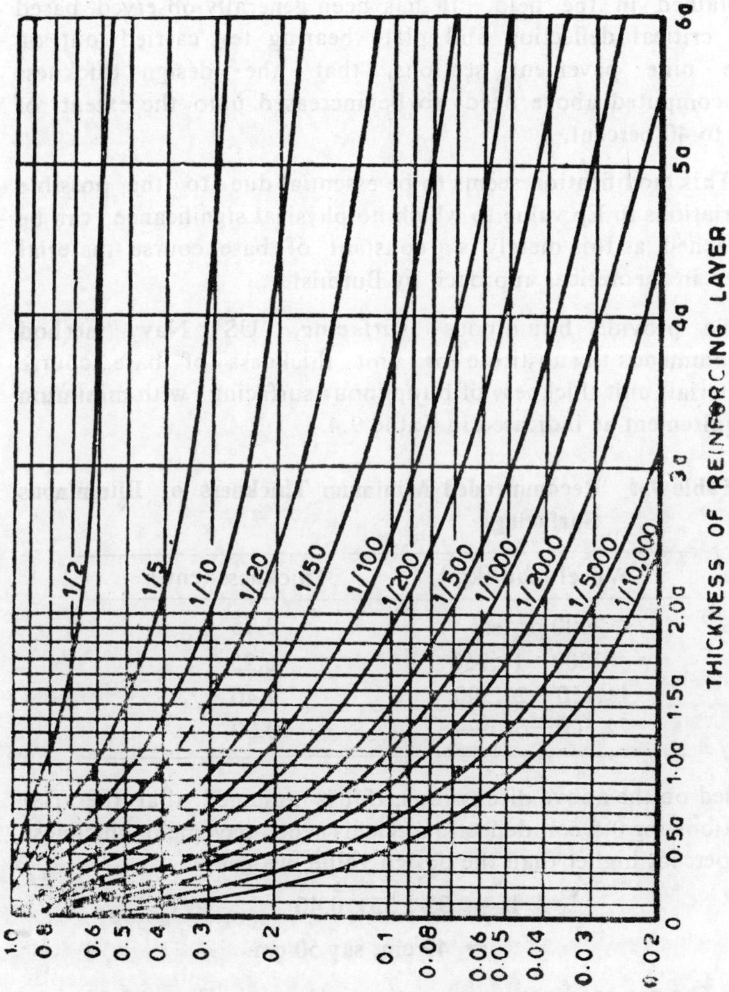

Figure 9.12 Burmister's Displacement Factors

on level, cut and fill with thickness as per (i) design (ii) 50 percent greater than the design and (iii) 33 per cent smaller than the design. The subgrade soil and base course material are compacted at the density levels that are expected to be obtained in the field. It has been generally observed, based on critical deflection and plate bearing test carried out on the nine pavement sections, that the design thickness as computed above needs to be increased upto the extent of 30 to 40 percent.

This modification seems to be essential due to the possible variations in Ep value to which no physical significance can be attached, as this merely is a constant of base course material used in theoretical approach by Burmister.

To provide bituminous surfacing, US Navy method recommends to substitute for unit thickness of base course material, unit thickness of bituminous surfacing with minimum requirement as indicated in Table 9.4.

Table 9.4 Recommended Minimum Thickness of Bituminous Surfacing

Wheel load (kg)	Thickness (cm.)
7000 or less	3.75
7000—11,250	6.25
11,250—22,500	7.40
22,500—or more	10.00

Based on the above discussions, if it is assumed that the trial sections for 0.5 cm deflection yields the pavement thickness 40 percent higher than the design value, we get

$$h = 35+35\times0.40$$

$$= 49 \text{ cm, say } 50 \text{ cm.}$$

The designed pavement section is shown in Figure 9.13.

9.3.4 Analytical Design Methods

Empirical and semi-empirical design methods for airfield pavements are applicable satisfactorily so long as the materials and conditions of loading, for which they were developed, do

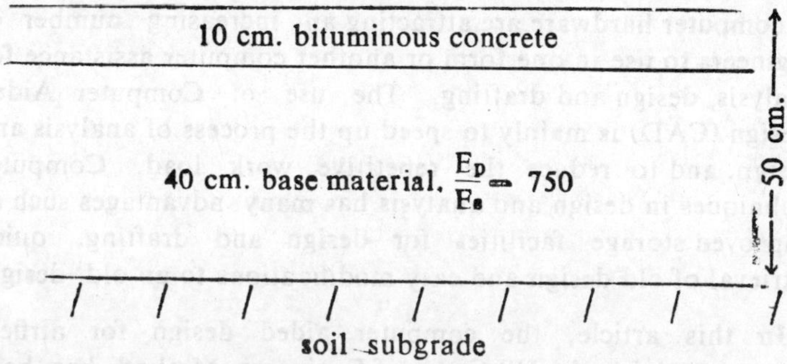

Figure 9.13 Designed Pavement Section Based on US Navy Method

not change. However, aircraft loadings have tended to increase quite drastically in recent years. The extension of semi-empirical design methods into regions of new loading and new materials can be achieved only by carrying out expensive and time-consuming full-scale pavement experiments. Analytical design methods do not suffer from these drawbacks:

Analytical design methods for airfield pavement are related to design of structures since the composition and thickness of the layers are so selected that the stresses, strains and deformations produced by design traffic loading do not exceed the capabilities of any of the materials in the pavement. The proportions of the pavement structure are adjusted until an acceptable design results in which all the critical factors are within permissible limits. The essential features of an analytical approach for structural design of airfield pavement include the following :

(i) selection of suitable design model.

(ii) solutions to the equations for the stresses, strains and deformations.

(iii) criteria for design and performance in terms of stress-strain and deformation, and

(iv) the presentation of the design system in a form that is convenient for use by the airfield pavement engineers.

9.3.5 Computer Aided Design Application

9.3.5.1 General : In developing countries, decreased cost of computer hardware are attracting an increasing number of engineers to use in one form or another computer assistance for analysis, design and drafting. The use of Computer Aided Design (CAD) is mainly to speed up the process of analysis and design, and to reduce the repetitive work load. Computer techniques in design and analysis has many advantages such as improved storage facilities for design and drafting, quick retrieval of old design and easy modifications to an old design.

In this article, the computer aided design for airfield pavements using the US Corps of Engineers Method has been discussed. For illustrating the procedure, the gear configuration of different type of aircrafts have been taken and the gear configurations of different aircrafts in operation have been considered and use of required input and output files are also given. Using the graphics program, the curves for different type of aircrafts were developed.

For illustrating the procedure, the gear configuration of B 737-200 aircraft has been taken and the required input and output files are also given. The design curves for the equivalent single wheel load (ESWL) versus design thickness were developed for C5A B 747-B wheel configurations and obtained by computer graphics and the end results are presented in this article.

9.3.5.2 Theory and design : The equivalent Single Wheel Load adopted for the design assumes that the load on a single tyre causes an equal magnitude of a preselected parameter (stress, strain, deflection or distress) at a given location within a specific pavement system to that resulting from a multiple-wheel system at the same location within the pavement structure. Depending upon the procedure selected, either the tyre pressure or contact area of the ESWL may be kept equal to that of one tyre of the multiple-wheel gear assembly. However, in the present program the equal deflection criteria for determination of ESWL was chosen.

9.3.5.3 Design of airfield pavements : The airfield pavements are designed considering the applied load (P), tyre pressure (p), geometric section of pavement and number of load repetitions required to the pavement during the design life of the pavement.

(a) Corps of Engineers method :

Based on the extensive research and performanee carried out by Brown and Rice, the following equation was developed :

T = Alpha* (Sqrt (A)* (0.0481 − 1.1562*x − 0.6414* x^2 − 0.473*x^3))

Where, T = flexible pavement thickness in mm (i.e. equivalent granular material).

Alpha = the load repetition factor (see Fig. 9.14)

A = the contact area of one tyre in Sq. mm.

x = A log 10 (CBR/p)

p = the tyre pressure at depth 'Z' used in calculating the ESWL.

(b) Procedure

The procedure involved for computer aided design of flexible airfield pavements consists of the following steps :

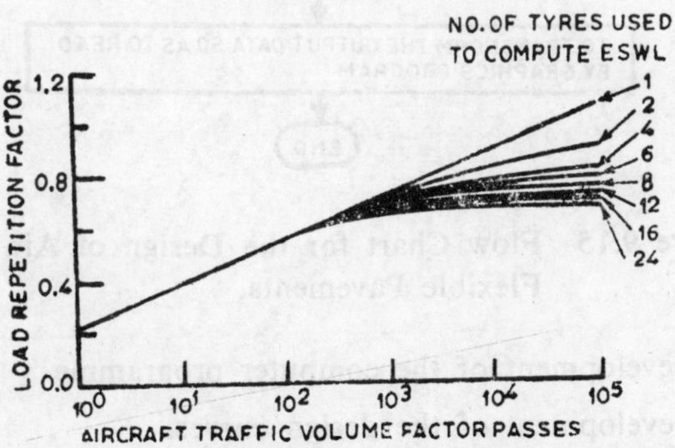

Figure 9.14 Design Thickness Repetitions Relationship Suggested by Corps of Engineers (From Brown and Rice)

(i) Development of flow charts for the necessary sequential operation in the design of airfield flexible pavements; (Figs. 9.15 and 9.16)

(ii) Creation of data file for single layer deflection factor (Fig. 9.17).

(iii) Preparation of input data file for the particular gear configuration (Fig. 9.18).

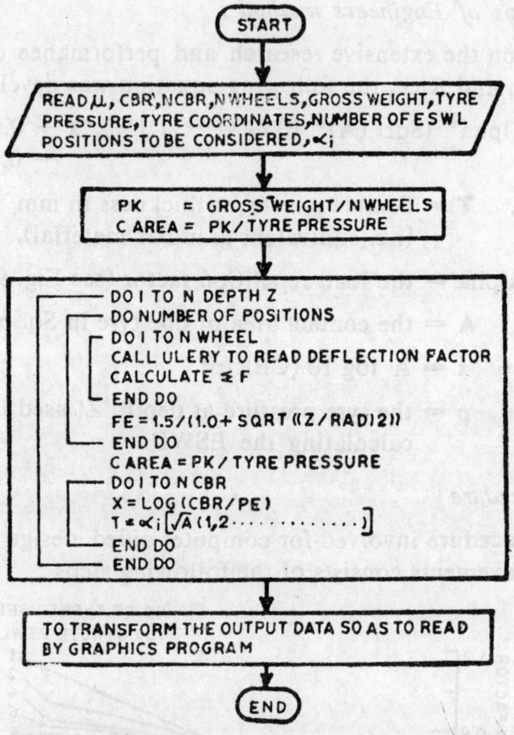

Figure 9.15 Flow Chart for the Design of Air Field Flexible Pavements.

(iv) Development of the computer programme.

(v) Development of the design curves.

(c) Flow charts

The flow chart describing the sequence of commands to be executed in the design calculations of thickness of granular material is given in Figs. 9.15 and 9.16.

(d) Deflection factor & data file

The data file consisting of deflection factors from Figs. 9.17 was created as a matrix to feed in to variable F (i j). This data file will supply the required Fij values after interpolation for the given depth-radii and offset radii ratios by the Subroutine Ulery.

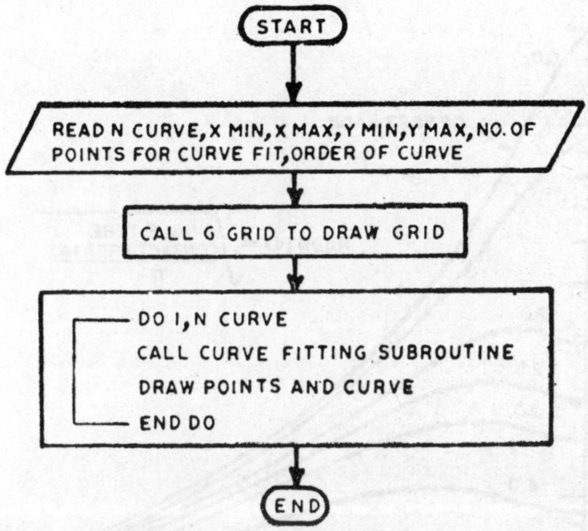

Figure 9.16 Flow Chart used for Developing Design Curves

(e) *Presentation of results*

(i) The program ESWL is found to be versatile and can be time saver by avoiding laborious man calculations and trials for the design of an airfield pavement. This can be applied universally for any given wheel configuration, tyre pressure and wheel load.

(ii) The package for the design of pavement can be easily extended and modified for auto production of design curves using graphics.

(iii) Sample design curves developed using CAD are given in Figs. 9.19 and 9.20. The design curves given in Fig. 9.20 corresponds to the wheel configuration as given in Fig. 9.18. A value of 0.45 is taken as the Poisson's ratio and can be altered where actual data is available.

(iv) The deflection factors were presently obtained by interpolating linearly with permissible error and can also be tried by fitting a polynomial curve.

(v) The end results produced by the software compared with those of manual design values for accuracy and found to be within the error limit.

(vi) With minor modifications, the package can be made interactive and useful. This can be executed on any type

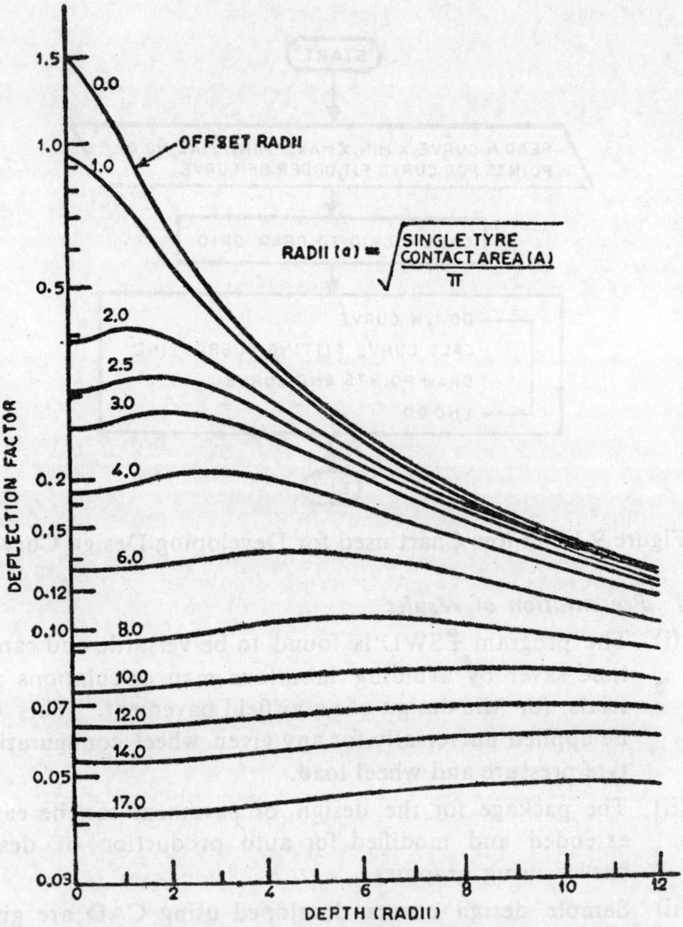

Figure 9.17 One Layer Deflection Factor Curves.

of PC by engineers who are not conversant with the computer programming.

9.4 DESIGN METHOD FOR AIR FIELD RIGID PAVEMENTS

The method for rigid pavement design is based on the use of influence charts developed by late *Dr. G. Gerald Pickett*, Professor at University of Wisconsin through *Portland Cement Association (PCA)* using the basic equations of Late *Dr. H.M.*

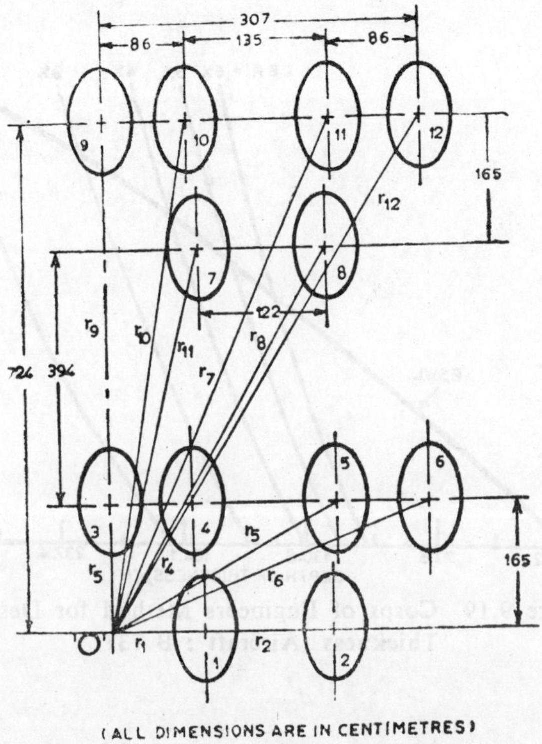

Figure 9.18 Gear Configuration for CSA

Westergaard, former Dean of the Graduate School of Engineering, Harvard University.

Westergaard assumed the rigid pavement slab to be thin elastic plate resting on subgrade which is considered as a dense liquid. This accounts for the equation p = k. Δ where k is defined as subgrade reaction modulus and p the vertical reaction proportional to the amount of deflection. Other assumptions of theory of elasticity are also observed by Westergaard in his analysis. For airports, Westergaard developed equations for stresses and deflections for interior and edge locations. The developed forms of the design equations are not included here as they are too cumbersome for the design use.

As stated above, Pickett developed the influence charts which save the time and effort in making the design calculations.

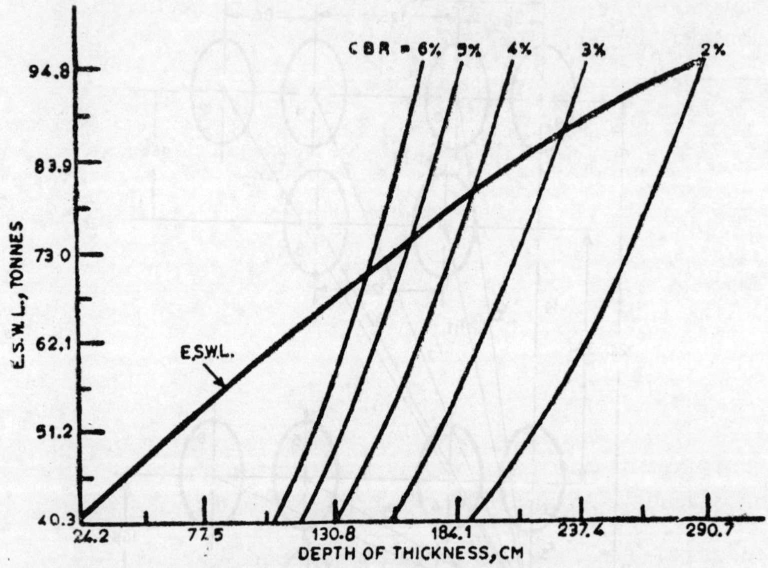

Figure 9.19 Corps of Engineers Method for Design of Thickness (Aircraft : B 737)

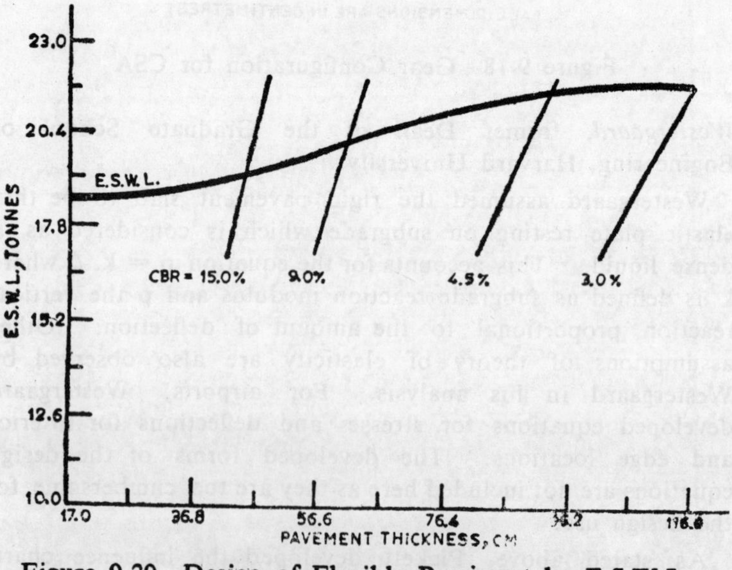

Figure 9.20 Design of Flexible Pavement by E.S.W.L. Deflection Concept for C5A Gear Configuration.

To obtain the allowable stress, it is recommended by PCA to consider the factors of safety as under :

Location	Safety factor
Apron, taxiway, runway end	1.7—2.0
Runway (central portion)	1.25—1.5

These safety factors are related to the fatigue strength of concrete.

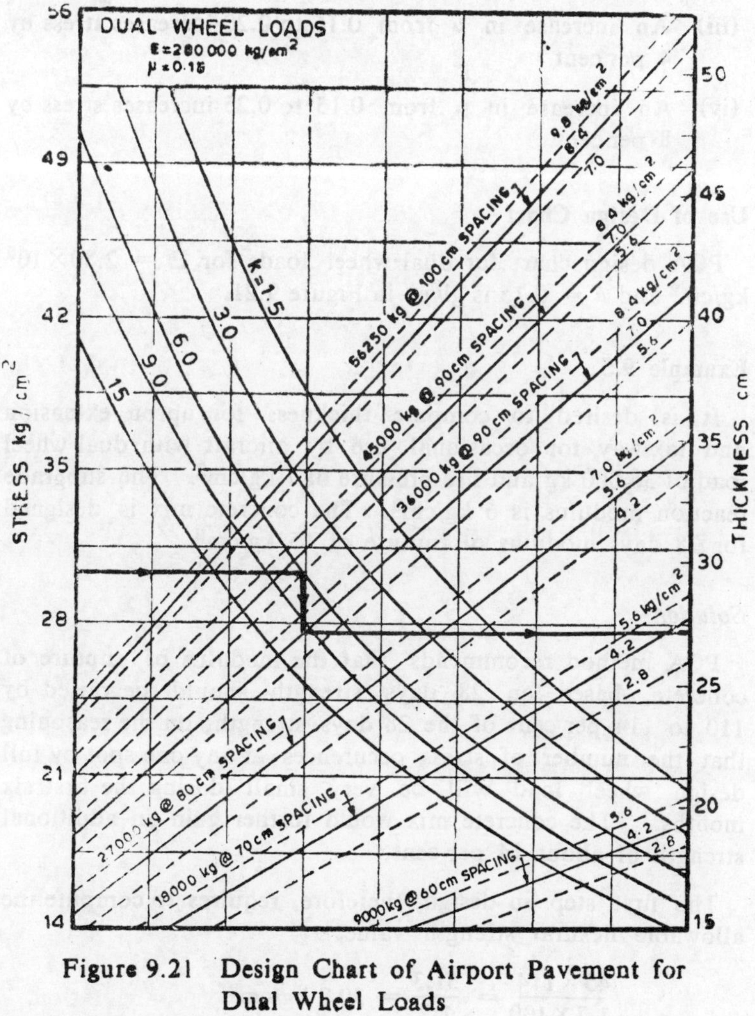

Figure 9.21 Design Chart of Airport Pavement for Dual Wheel Loads

The design charts as reported by PCA, are based on E and μ values of 2.80×10^5 kg/cm^2 and 0.15 respectively. It has been indicated by PCA that the variations in E and μ values have little effect upon the stress as detailed below :

(i) A reduction in E from 2.8×10^5 to 2.1×10^5 kg/cm^2 decreases stress by 5 per cent.

(ii) An increase in E from 2.8×10^5 to 3.5×10^5 kg/cm^2 increases stress by 4 per cent.

(iii) An increase in μ from 0.15 to 0.20 increases stress by 4 per cent.

(iv) An increase in μ from 0.15 to 0.25 increases stress by 8 per cent.

Use of Design Chart

PCA design chart for dual-wheel loads for $E = 2.80 \times 10^5$ kg/cm^2 and $\mu = 0.15$ is given in Figure 9.21.

Example 9.5

It is desired to compute thickness for apron extension and taxiway for occasional use by aircraft with dual-wheel load of 36,000 kg and tire pressure of 7 kg/cm^2. The subgrade reaction modulus is 6 kg/cm^3. The concrete mix is designed for 28 days modulus of rupture of 45 kg/cm^2.

Solution :

PCA method recommends that the modulus of rupture of concrete, based on 28 days strength should be raised by 110 to 114 per cent of the 28 days strength, on the reasoning that the number of stress occurences at any one spot by full design wheel load will be very small during the first six months. The concrete mix would further gain an additional strength of about 14 per cent.

The first step in design, therefore, requires to compute the allowable flexural strength value,

$$\frac{45 \times 114}{1.7 \times 100} = \frac{51.3}{1.7} = 30.2 \text{ kg/cm}^2.$$

Factor of safety of 1.7 is taken at the locations are used occasionally by the aircrafts. In the event of unlimited occurrence, the highest value of 2.0 would be used.

Now stress value of 30.2 kg/cm^2 is spotted on Figure 9.21 and the designated curve for k = 6 kg/cm^3 is approached horizontally The dotted line is further progressed vertically downward to meet diagonal line of 3,600 kg (dual) for 7 kg/cm^2 tire pressure This plot now is extended to the right hand scale of pavement thickness, which reads 27.0 cm. The design pavement thickness, is therefore 27.0 cm.

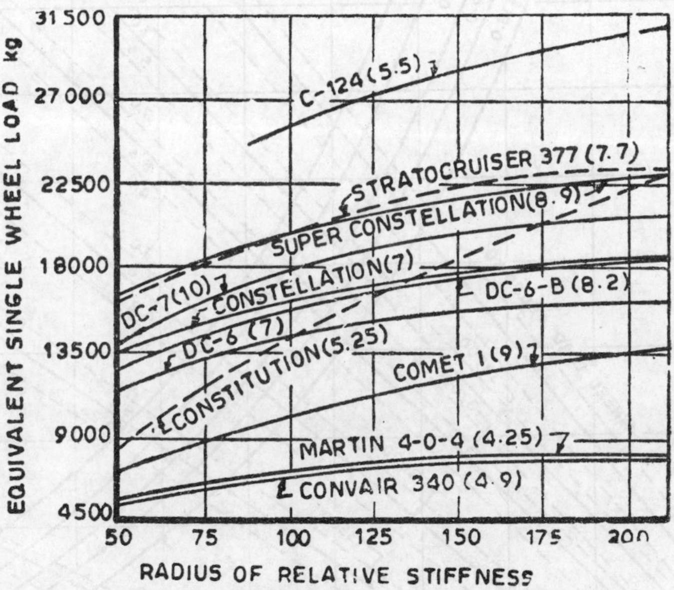

Figure 9.22 Equivalent Single Wheel Loads for Dual and Dual Tandem Landing Gears

Figure 9.22 is a special chart provided by PCA to obtain the equivalent single-wheel load (ESWL) for several aircrafts. The process thus simplifies to make use of only one chart prepared for single wheel load as given in Figure 9.23.

For example, for 25 cm pavement and k = 3 kg/cm^3, E = 2.8×10^5 kg/cm^2, μ = 0.15, the value of l = 120 cm. The Constellation (7 aircraft works out to be equivalent to a single-wheel load of 16,500 kg with tire pressure of 7 kg/cm^2.

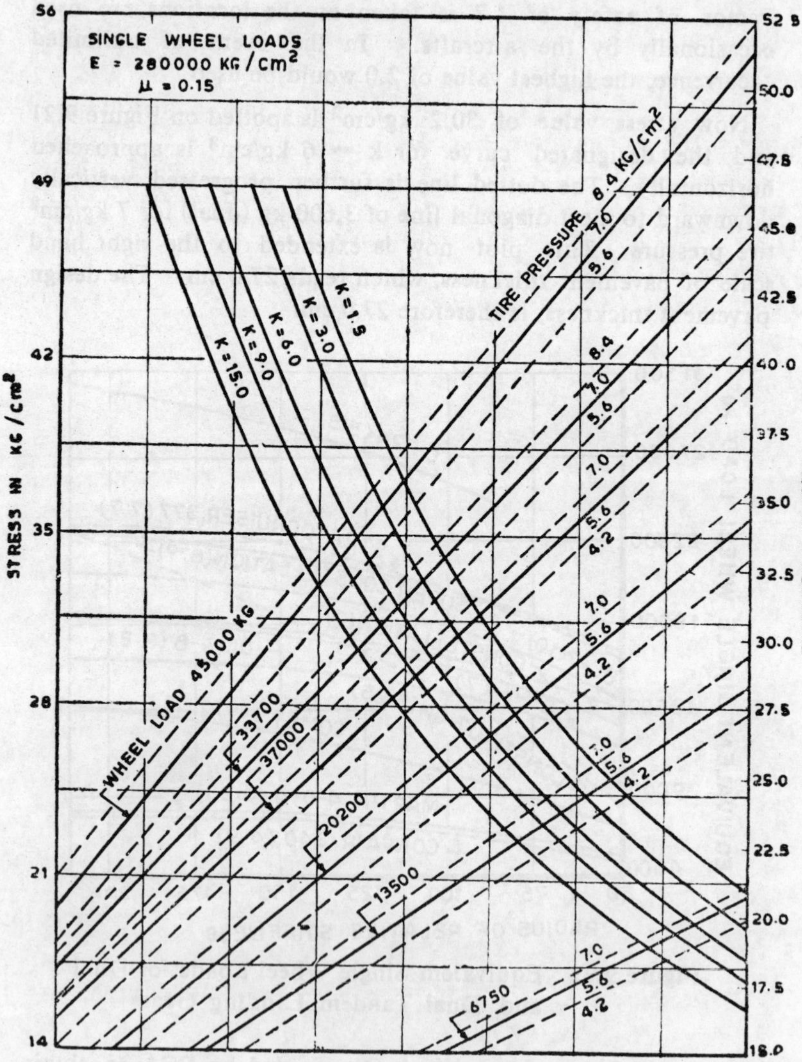

Figure 9.23 Design Chart of Airport Pavement for Single Wheel Loads

The design procedure becomes simpler now. This however, involves trials in selecting assumed thickness to obtain ESWL. In case computed value of thickness does not work out to be the same as per Figure 9.23. the calculations would be then revised.

One typical *Influence Chart* as prepared by Pickett and Ray and reported *Transaction ASCE-1951 vol. 116* is reproduced here vide Figure 9.24.

Example 9.6

Compute the stress in the interior region of 40 cm cement concrete pavement with placement of dual-tandem landing gear configuration and keeping centre of one wheel matching with interior point of slab. Total load of gear assembly is 65,000 kg with spacing of the tire imprints as drawn on Figure 9.24. The tire pressure is 11.5 kg/cm². Value of $k = 3$ kg/cm³ and $\mu = 0.15$ are assumed

Solution

$$\text{Load on each tire} = \frac{\text{Total load}}{4}$$

$$= \frac{65500}{4} = 16375 \text{ kg}$$

$$\text{Contact area} = \frac{16375}{11.5} = 1423 \text{ cm}^2$$

The imprint of an area is assumed to be a rectangle with semi-circular ends. Total length of imprint is L and width is 0.6 L. The radius of semi-circular portion is 0.3 L.

$$L = \sqrt{\frac{1423}{0.5227}} = 52.2 \text{ cm}$$

$$0.6\,L = 0.6 \times 52.2 = 31.32 \text{ cm}$$

In Figure 9.24, the scale is laid down in terms of radius of relative stiffness (l) which is defined by Westergaard as :

$$l = \sqrt[4]{\frac{Eh^3}{12\,(1-\mu)^2 k}}$$

$$= \sqrt[4]{\frac{3 \times 10^5 \times (40)^3}{12\,[1-(0.15)]^2 \times 3}}$$

The tire imprints are now drawn on the tracking in the manner shown in Figure 9.24 using the following relationship :

$$\frac{\text{Tracing L}}{\text{Actual L}} = \frac{l \text{ on chart}}{l \text{ of pavement}}$$

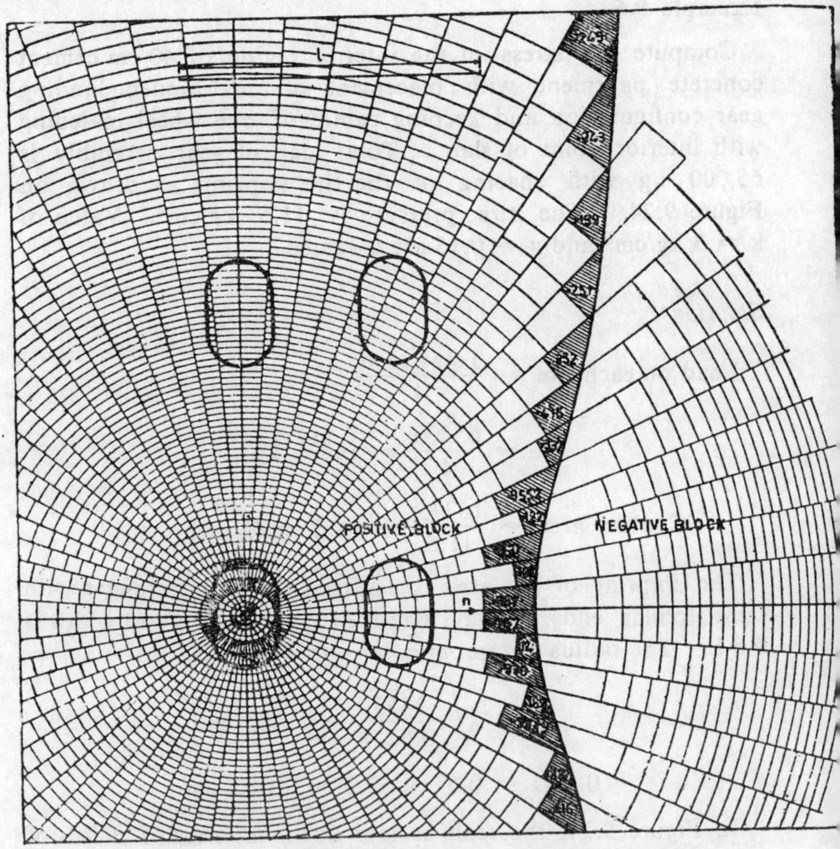

INFLUENCE CHART FOR THE MOMENT Mn IN A CONCRETE PAVEMENT DUE TO A LOAD IN THE INTERIOR OF THE SLAB

(Subgrade assumed to be a dense liquid,

(Poission's ratio for pavement assumed to be 0.15)

Figure 9.24 Influence Chart *(Pickett and Ray)*

$$\text{Tracing } L = \frac{5.75 \times 52.2}{153.5} = 1.91 \text{ cm}$$

$$\text{width} = 0.6\ L - 0.6 \times 1.91 = 1.156 \text{ cm.}$$

The prepared tracing is superimposed on Figure 9.24 as shown. The moment, as the point O is computed by the formula given below :

$$M = \frac{p\, l^2\, N}{10{,}000}$$

M = moment at 0

p = tire pressure

N = total number of blocks covered in all the imprints.

N = 248

$$M = \frac{11.5 \times (153.5)^2 \times 248}{10{,}000}$$

$$= 5870 \text{ cm kg.}$$

$$\text{Stress at interior O} = \frac{6\,M}{h^2} = \frac{6 \times 5870}{(40)^2}$$

$$= 22.1 \text{ kg/cm}^2.$$

9.5 LCN SYSTEM OF PAVEMENT DESIGN

A procedure known as *Load Classification Number* system was developed by the British Air Ministry Directorate of General Works. An extensive series of load test was conducted on existing rigid and flexible pavements with different thicknesses. Based on these load tests, a generalised relationship between failure load and contact area of loading was developed. Figure 9.25 shows load contact area curves for typical flexible and rigid pavements. Another curve with following equations is also plotted on it :

$$\frac{W_1}{W_2} = \left(\frac{A_1}{A_2}\right)^{0.44}$$

Here W_1 and W_2 are the failure loads and A_1 and A_2 are contact areas respectively.

This relationship was found to be applicable within the contact areas of 1250 cm^2 (200 in^2) and 4375 cm^2 (700 in^2).

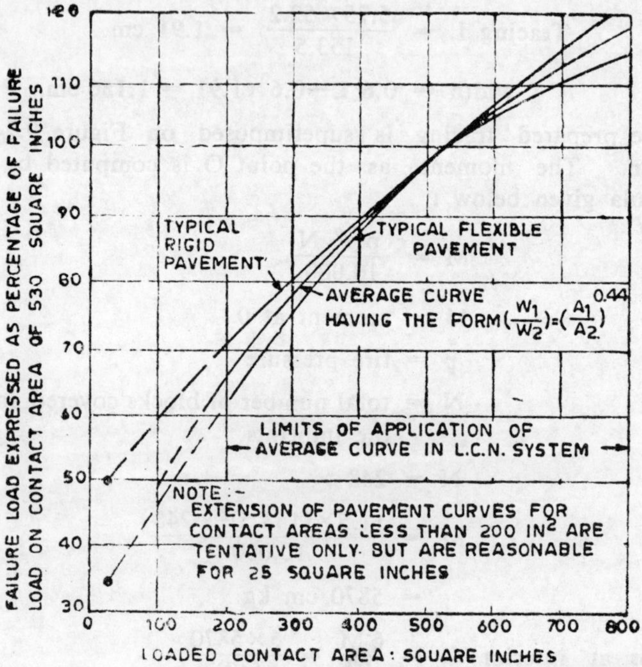

Figure 9.25 Relation Between Failure Load and Loaded Contact Area

In order to develop a system where in the capacity of a pavement to carry an aircraft could be expressed as a single number, the Standard Load Classification curve was developed. Figure 9.26 is developed by an arbitrary smooth plot on load-contact area diagram. The curve read the points as listed in the Table below.

The values listed in the Table were selected since these were typical wheel loads and contact areas of aircraft used at the time when LCN system was developed. Using the standard load classification curve as per relationship of $W_1/W_2 = (A_1/A_2)^{0.44}$, the chart as in Figure 9.27 has been prepared :

For this the following steps are observed :

(a) The lines of contact are drawn from the relationship

$$\text{Contact area} = \frac{\text{Load}}{\text{Tire pressure}}$$

LCN	Wheel Load		Tire pressure	
	kg	lb	kg/cm	psi
100	45359	100,000*	8.40	120
90	40823	90,000	8.08	115
80	36287	80,000	7.73	110
70	31751	70,000	7.38	105
60	27215	60,000	7.03	100
50	22680	50,000	6.69	95
40	18144	40 000	6.32	90
30	13608	30,000	5.97	85
20	9072	20,000	5.62	80
10	4536	10,000	5.27	75

(b) One point is taken on LCN line from standard load classification curve of Figure 9.26. The remaining points on LCN curve are plotted using the relationship of contact area and load. Figure 9.27 shows that a pavement having LCN of say 50, is one capable of bearing 22.700 kg (50,000,lbs) load on a contact area of 3120 cm^2 (500 sq. in) without failure.

LCN of flexible pavement

The LCN of a flexible pavement is obtained by carrying out repetitive plate bearing tests on the existing airport pavement. The safe load for a given pavement is calculated as that load which applied 10,000 times produces 5 mm (0.20 inch) deflection. The contact area of the plate is taken equivalent to the contact area of one main wheel of the aircraft. For civil airports 46 cm (18 inch) plate diameter giving contact area of 1652 cm^2 (256 in^2) is generally used.

LCN of rigid pavement

The plate load tests are carried out on cement concrete pavement corners. A seating load of 2267 kg (5000 lb) is applied and is then released. Subsequently, loads are applied in increments of 2267 kg (5000 lb) each until the deflection

*As LCN indicates *wheel load, in lbs/1000*, the mks *conversion of* LCN would be misleading.

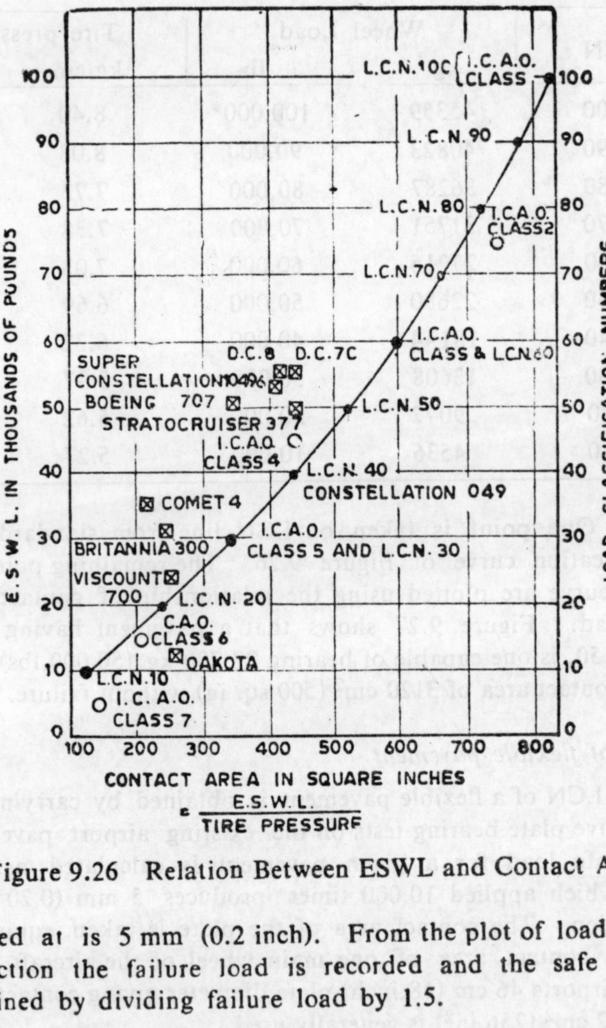

Figure 9.26 Relation Between ESWL and Contact Area

arrived at is 5 mm (0.2 inch). From the plot of load versus deflection the failure load is recorded and the safe load is obtained by dividing failure load by 1.5.

United Kingdom design criteria

For judging the suitability of the pavement for a given aircraft operation, following design criteria is adopted :

(a) If LCN of aircraft is between 1.10 to 1.25 times the LCN of pavement, then 3000 movements are allowed.

(b) If LCN of aircraft is between 1.25 to 1.50 times the LCN of pavement, then 300 movements are allowed These movements would induce minor failures.

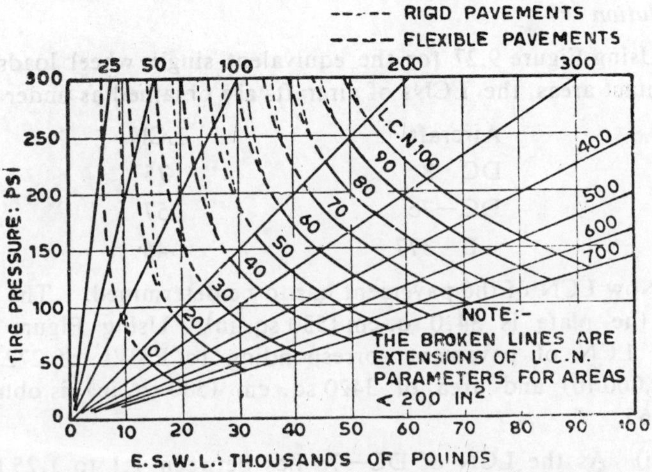

Figure 9.27 Relation between Tire Pressure and ESWL

(c) If LCN of aircraft is between 1.50 and 2.00 times the LCN of pavement, then very limited use is advised.

(d) If LCN of aircraft is greater than 2 times the LCN of pavement, then the pavement should be used in emergency only.

Example 9.7

It is required to evaluate the existing runway pavement based on U.K. criteria of LCN method for operation of the following aircrafts :

Aircraft	Mean gear load		ESWL		Tire pressure		Contact area	
	kg	lb	kg	lb	kg/cm²	psi	cm²	in²
DC-8	66224	146,000	24947	55000	11.04	157	2258	350
DC-7c	30844	68,000	21318	47000	8 86	126	2406	373
B-377	31978	70,000	19958	44000	7.03	100	2839	440

For this purpose, plate load tests were carried out at the site with 66 cm (26 inch) diameter plate and safe load was obtained as 27216 kg (60000 lb).

Solution

Using Figure 9.27 for the equivalent single wheel loads and contact areas, the LCNs of aircrafts are obtained as under :

Aircraft	LCN
DC 8	75
DC−7c	57
B−377	46

Now LCN of the pavement has to be determined. The area of the plate is 34:0 sq. cm (530 sq. in). Using Figure 9.27, the LCN of pavement corresponding to ESWL of 27216 kg (60,000 lb) and area of 3420 sq. cm (530 sq. in) is obtained as 65.

(i) As the LCN of DC—7c lies between 1.1 to 1.25 times the LCN of pavement and such 3000 movements can be allowed with confidence.

(ii) As the LCN of pavement is greater than LCNs of DC-7c and B—387, therefore there is no problem and these aircrafts can use the runway ultimately.

Because of larger number of variables involved and the practicabilities of construction, great precision in pavement design and evaluation is unjustified. Aircraft evaluation and pavement classification has been simplified by categorising aircraft and pavement LCN values into broad *load classification groups* (LCG) as given below* :

Load classification group (LGC)	Load classification number (LCN)
I	101−120
II	76−100
III	51−75
IV	31−50
V	16−30
VI	11−15
VII	10 and under

*Source-Design and evaluation of airport pavements 1971, Air Ministry U.K.

The bands have been selected to group together aircraft imposing similar stress levels on pavements in reasonable and regular increments of pavement thickness.

From experience gained over the last 30 years in the United Kingdom, it is now the practice on limit new pavement structures to the following three types as illustrated in Figure 9.28. A 100 mm base or sub-base layer of lean concrete is provided in each case.

(i) Rigid pavements of unreinforced pavement quality portland cement concrete are usually selected for runway ends, runway and taxiway junctions, apron and hardstandings, and similar areas on which aircraft will stand and where jet heat, blast and fuel attack is likely. The use of rigid pavements for other areas is a matter of economical or operational preference.

(ii) Composite pavements of continuously reinforced concrete with bituminous surfacing offer the best pump-free riding and water-free surfacing and, in particular, are favoured for those lengths of runways and taxiways along which aircrafts travel at speed.

(iii) Flexible pavements composed of bound granular materials with bituminous surfacing will not often be economical for heavy duty pavements but in conditions where they are, or for light aircrafts usage, they are an alternative to composite pavements and offer similar advantages.

The design and evaluation graphs in use are shown in Figure 9.29. They give the relationship between flexural stress in a concrete pavement, the LCN and LCG of the aircraft, the actual subgrade characteristics and the theoretical thickness of the concrete slab. These relationships were derived from the Packard programme for centre case. To this Figure Charts 1 and 2 have been added. They are empirically derived from very extensive world wide experience extending over a considerable period of time. They outline pavement construction for six types of pavements each linked to the theoretical thickness. They are based upon actual performance and therefore take into account all factors including variability from all causes, temperature stresses, dynamic loading of a frequency and intensity usually referred to as *channelised*, and an appropriate factor of safety. Chart 1 contains the types

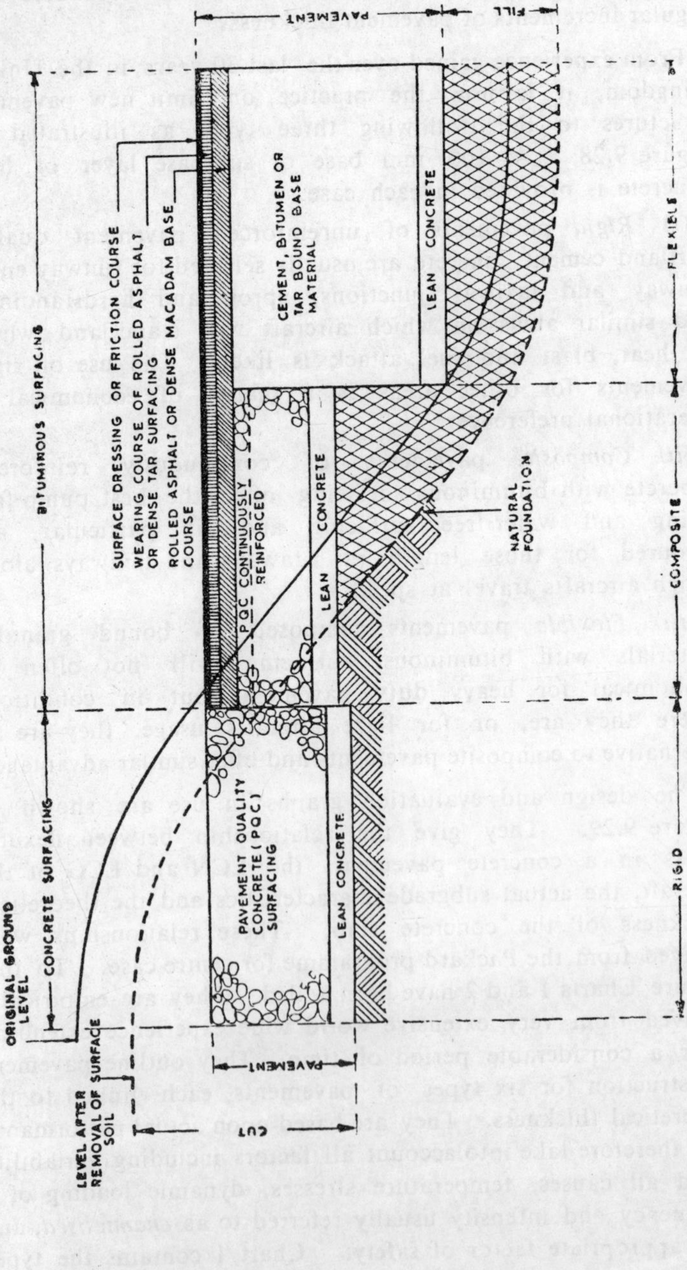

Figure 9.28 Types of Airport Pavement

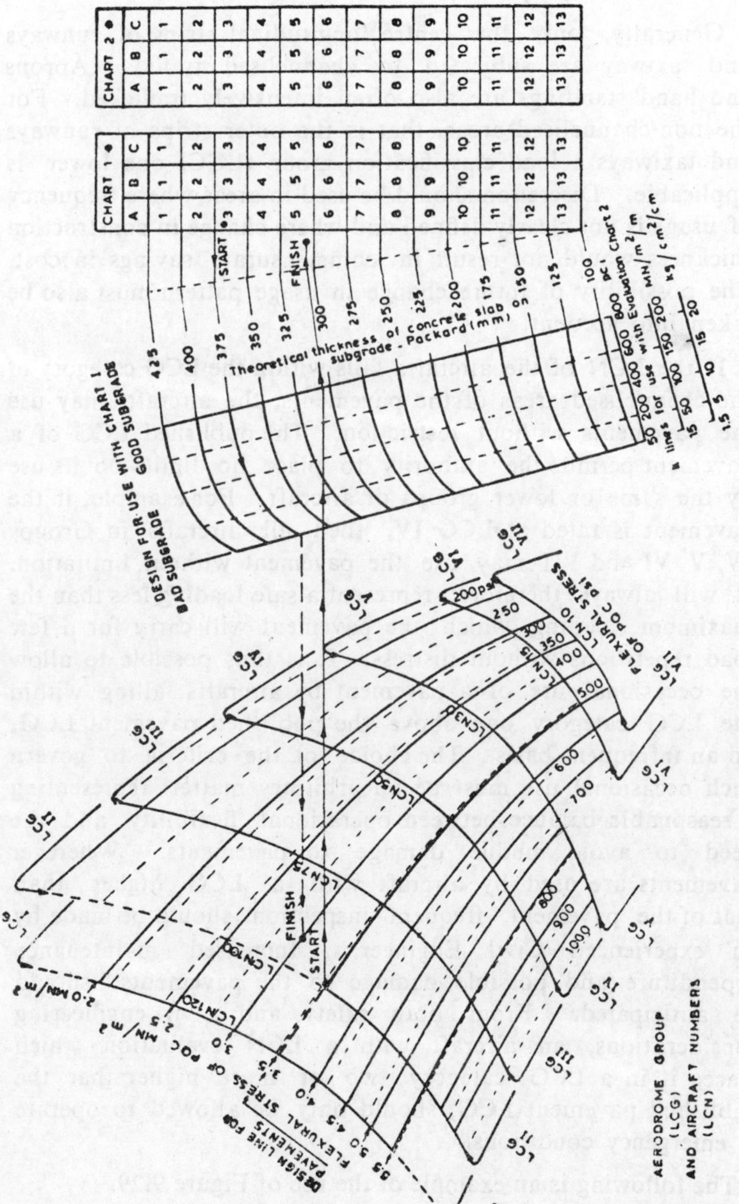

Figure 9.29 Pavement Design by LCG Method

currently recommended for new pavements. Chart 2 includes for evaluation purposes.

Generally, only the centre longitudinal strips of runways and taxiway are subjected to channelised traffic. Aprons and hand standings are also often intensively trafficked. For the non-channelised areas, that is the outer strips of runways and taxiways a load classification group (LGC) one lower is applicable. Discretion should be used in areas where frequency of usage is not clearly defined and where change in construction thickness would not result in commensurate savings in cost. The possibility of future change in usage pattern must also be taken into account.

If the LCN of the aircrafts falls within the LCG category of the channelised areas of the pavements, the aircraft may use the pavements without restriction. The published LCG of a pavement permits the authority to place no limits on its use by the same or lower groups of aircraft. For example, if the pavement is rated at LCG IV, then all aircrafts in Groups IV, V, VI and VII may use the pavement without limitation. It will always therefore, represent a safe loading less than the maximum loading which the pavement will carry for a few load repetitions without distress. It is thus possible to allow the occasional use of a pavement by aircrafts falling within the LCG category one above the published pavement LCG, on an infrequent basis. The choice of the criteria to govern such occasional use must be an arbitrary matter representing a reasonable balance between operational flexibility and the need to avoid undue damage to pavements. Wherever pavements are used by aircraft with a LCG higher than that of the pavement, frequent inspections should be made by an experienced Civil Engineer. Increased maintenance expenditure and possible damage to the pavements should be anticipated. From both safety and civil engineering considerations, an aircraft with a LCN evaluation which places it in a LCG category two or more higher than the published pavement LCG, should only be allowed to operate in emergency conditions.

The following is an example of the use of Figure 9.29.

Pavements are required for aircraft of LCN 80. This is in LCG II and the upper boundary of the group (LCN 100)

Table 9.4 LCG Method of Pavement Design

CHART 1				CHART 2			
Recommended Aircraft Pavements				For Evaluation only of Existing Pavements			
S. No.	A	B	C	S. No.	A	B	C
1	425	100	100	1	500	100	100
	100	250	700			425	1175
		100	100				
2	425	100	100	2	475	100	100
	100	240	650			400	1100
		100	100				
3	400	100	100	3	450	100	100
	100	220	600		100	375	1025
		100	100				
4	375	100	100	4	425	100	100
	100	200	550			350	950
		100	100				
5	350	100	100	5	400	100	100
	100	180	500			325	875
		100	100				
6	325	100	100	6	375	100	100
	100	160	450			300	800
		100	100				
7	325	100	100	7	350	100	100
	100	140	400			275	775
		100	100				
8	275	100	100	8	325	100	100
	100	120	350			250	650
		100	100				
9	250	100	100	9	300	100	100
	100	100	300			275	575
		100	100				
10	225	100	100	10	275	100	100
	100	100	250			200	500
		100	100				
11	200	100	100	11	250	100	100
	100	100	200			175	425
		100	100				
12	175	100	100	12	225	100	100
	100	100	150			150	350
		100	100				
13	150	100	100	13	200	100	100
	100	100	150			150	350
		100	100				

Explanatory notes for Table 9.4

(1) A, B and C denote rigid, composite and flexible pavements, respectively.

(2) In chart 1, the column A gives thicknesses of undowelled pavement quality concrete and underlying dry lean base course. The column B gives thickness of bituminous surfacing and underlying continuously reinforced PQC base course with load transfer and lean concrete sub-base course. The column C gives thicknesses of bituminous surfacing and underlying cement, bitumen or tar bound base course and dry lean concrete sub-base course.

(3) In chart 2, the column A gives thickness of PC (undowelled). The column B gives thicknesses of bituminous surfacing and underlying PQC (undowelled) base course. The column C gives thickness of bituminous surfacing and underlying unbound material base course.

(4) All thicknesses are given in mm.

---

should be taken for design purpose for the channelised areas. The subgrade has a 'k' value of 150-2000 MN/m²/m and is in the 'good' category. Taking the heavy black line for concrete with a minimum flexural stress of 3.5 MN/m², which is also used for the design of composite and flexible pavements, the point of intersection with the group boundary (LCN 100) is located.

A horizontal line is projected to the right until it intersects the 'good subgrade' line. Tracing a line from the point of intersection, parallel to the curves brings us within one of the band of Chart 1. This gives a choice of three recommended pavements designated as A (5), B (5) or C (5). The description of these pavements detailed in Table 9.4. The choices are as follows :

(i) 350 mm of PQC on 100 mm dry lean concrete

or

(ii) 100 mm of bituminous surfacing overlying 180 mm of continuously reinforced concrete and 100 mm dry lean concrete

or

(iii) 100 mm of bituminous surfacing overlying 500 mm of cement or bitumen bound base material and 100 mm of dry lean concrete.

Of these choices (i) is invariably selected for runway ends and adjoining taxiway junctions, and for aprons and hardstandings because of its resistance to heat, blast and fuel attack. Either (ii) or (iii) preferred for runways between the concrete ends and 'fast' taxiways because of the improved riding qualities and friction characteristics obtainable from bituminous surfacing.

The LCN 75 line, upper limit of the Group III boundary is used for outer strips of runways and taxiways. The intersection point of the LCN 75 line and the 3.5 MN/m² heavy black line is located, and a horizontal line is again projected to the right until it intersects the 'good subgrade' line. Tracking a line parallel to the curves until it reaches Chart 1 takes us into the band giving a choice of three recommended pavements, either

(i) 300 mm of PQC on 10 mm dry lean concrete

or

(ii) 100 mm of bituminous surfacing on 140 mm of continuously reinforced concrete on 100 mm of dry lean concrete.

or

(iii) 100 mm of bituminous surfacing on 400 mm of cement or bitumen bound base material on 100 mm of dry lean concrete.

Where pavements are founded on a formation of unfragmented rock a metre or more in depth then the total thickness of flexible pavements need only consists of the bituminous surfacing plus a minimum 100 mm regulating course of lean concrete laid directly on the rock surface after clearing any loose soil. On such a site, rigid pavements should follow the normal design procedure detailed above.

Inspite of the problems of cracking of bituminous layers laid over unreinforced concrete surfacing, it will generally be operationally and economically preferable to strengthen existing rigid, composite and flexible pavements, with additional layers of flexible construction. The thickness of this additional construction will depend upon the 'k' value of the formation below the existing pavement and will be the difference between the existing pavement thickness and the new total flexible or composite pavement thickness determined from the increased strength requirement. To reduce the incidence of cracking the thickness of bituminous surfacing over existing concrete should not in any case be less than 100 mm.

9.5 1 Evaluation for Operational Purposes

The modulus of subgrade reaction 'k', of the formation below the pavements is determined, and cores are cut to establish the pavement construction type selected from Chart 1 or 2. Figure 9.29 then allows an assessment of the LCG to be made. For regid pavement and for the composite pavement in Chart 2, the minimum flexural strength of the concrete must be determined. The upper line of the appropriate band of Chart 1 or 2 is traced to the left, parallel to the lines until it intercepts the appropriate 'bad' or 'good' subgrade line; or until it intercepts the line representing a particular 'k' value if more precise informaton is available. From this intersection point, it is projected horizontally to the left until it intersects the line representing the minimum flexural strength. The load classification group LCG in which this intersection point falls is the LCG of the pavement.

The reverse design procedure is similar for a flexible pavement, and for the composite pavement in Chart 1, except that the single heavy black line of Figure 9.29 coincident with 3.5 MN/m², is employed. No account is taken of any variation in the strength of the continuously reinforced concrete layer in the composite pavement.

From the position of the final intercept point in relation to the upper and lower boundaries of the group, a tentative assessment of the present strength of the pavement is made. Probably the most important factor however in the evaluation, of any existing pavement is a careful, thorough examination, by an experienced engineer, of its condition, its deformation, crack and failure patterns in relation to its age, and the usage it has already experienced. The final evaluation made must take into account the results of this inspection.

The following is an example of the use of Figure 9.29 for evaluation. It is required to determine the types of aircraft which may use an existing pavement. Cores taken from the 'channelised' traffic area show that its construction comprises 400 mm of PQC on '00 mm of dry lean concrete. Subgrade tests indicate a 'bad' subgrade with a 'k' of 15 MN/m²/m. Tests in the cores show that an equivalent minimum flexural strength of 3 MN/m² is appropriate. From the Table 9 4, it is observed that the construction matches the rigid specification given in the third box from the top in Chart 1 (viz. A-3). The upper line of this box is used in Figure 9.29 and traced to the left until it intersects the line representing the "bad" subgrade. A line is produced horizontally to the left until it intersects the curve representing a permissible minimum concrete stress of 3 MN/m². This intersection point falls towards the high end of LCG II. The tentative assessment of the pavement strength is therefore LCG II.

9.6 JOINTS IN CEMENT CONCRETE PAVEMENTS

The cement concrete pavements expand and contract with rise and fall of temperature and to reduce the compression, tension and flexural stresses, the slabs of concrete pavement are divided in longitudinal panels by predetermined dimensions. Each slab is tied up together with *load transfer devices* of dowel bars and tie bars at transverse and logitudial joints.

Joints are functionally divided into four basic categories :

1. Expansion
2. Contraction
3. Warping
4. Construction

Figures 9.30 to 9.33 show the types of joints in use for cement concrete pavements.

1. Expansion joint : The basic function of an expansion joint is to provide adequate space for the expansion of the pavements and thus to eliminate the compressive stresses which can otherwise damage the pavement edges. Expansion joints are provided with space of about 2 cm between two meeting slabs. This space is called in with compressible material known as filler and the top of this is sealed with material known as sealer. Typical expansion joints are shown in Figure 9 30.

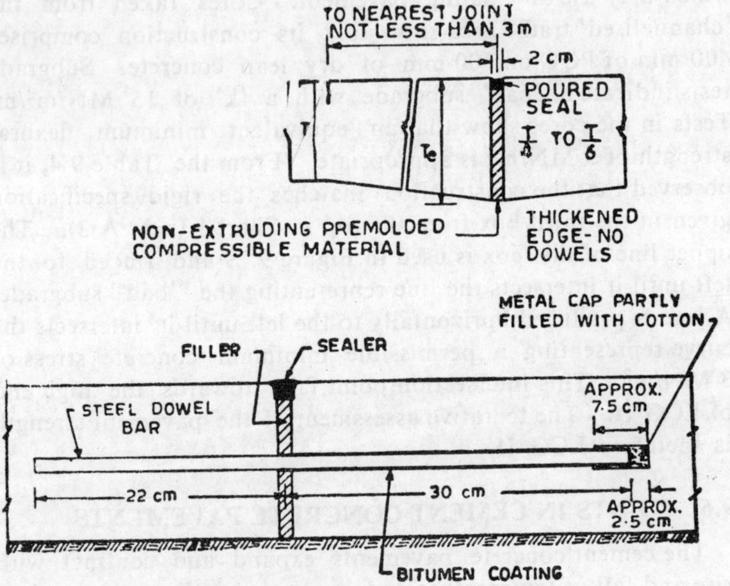

Figure 9.30 Expansion Joints

2. *Contraction joint :* Contraction joint is provided in the cement concrete pavement to limit the tensile stresses developed due to contraction of pavements within a safe value. Two types of joints i.e. 'formed groove' and 'sawed groove' are generally in use. They are shown in Figure 9.31.

3. *Warping joint :* The warping joint accounts for the possible vertical movements of edges due to curling up and down of cement concrete pavement as and when it occurs due to temperature gradient developed in the pavement depth. Such joints relieve the pavement of any additional stresses induced due to curling known as warping stresses. They are shown in Figure 9.32.

4. *Construction joint :* Joint is also provided at the end of days job during the construction of cement concrete pavement. The load transfer is thus provided in the design of such joint by using dowels or aggregate interlocking. Construction joints are shown in Figure 9.33.

9.6.1 Joint Layout at Runway Pavement Intersection

Figure 9.34 shows a typical layout of branch intersection

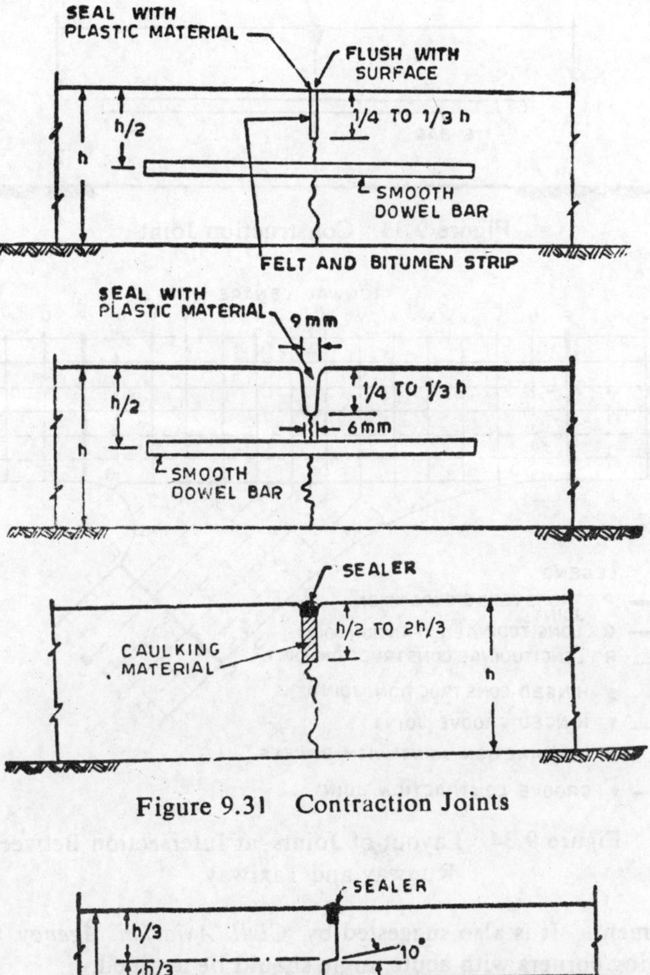

Figure 9.31 Contraction Joints

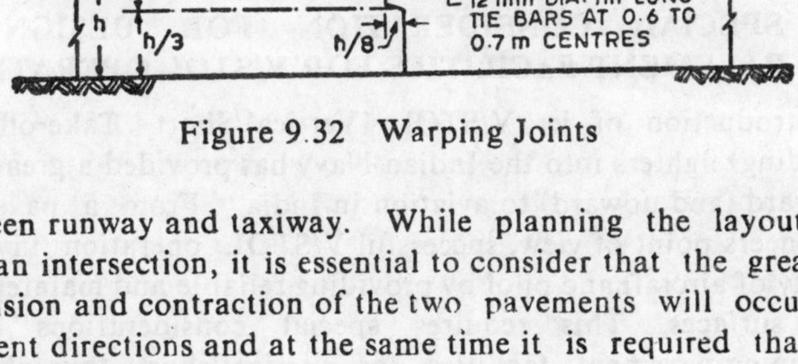

Figure 9.32 Warping Joints

between runway and taxiway. While planning the layout for such an intersection, it is essential to consider that the greatest expansion and contraction of the two pavements will occur in different directions and at the same time it is required that no pavement should restrain movement occurring in the adjacent

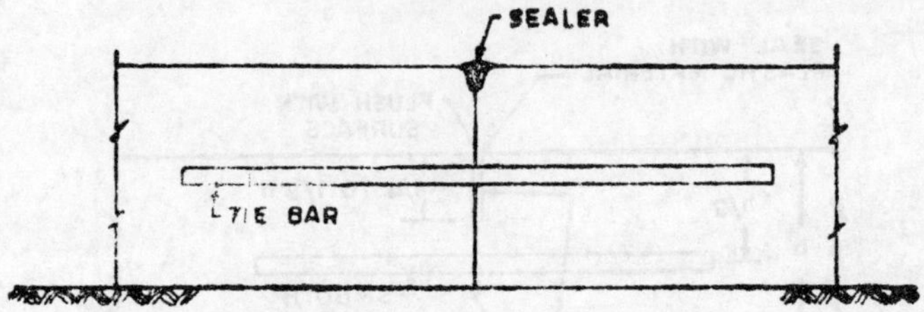

Figure 9.33 Construction Joint

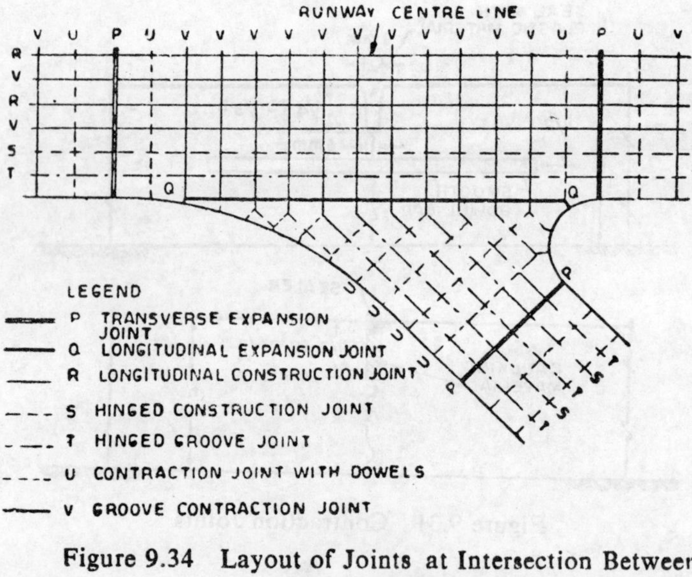

Figure 9.34 Layout of Joints at Intersection Between Runway and Taxiway

pavement. It is also suggested by *Civil Aviation Agency* that forming corners with acute angle should be avoided.

9.7 SPECIAL CONSIDERATION FOR DESIGN OF PAVEMENT FACILITIES FOR V/STOL OPERATIONS

Introduction of jet V/STOL (Vertical/Short Take-off and Landing) fighters into the Indian Navy has provided a great leap forward (and upward) to aviation in India. From a pavement engineers point of view, successful V/STOL operation involves safety of aircraft and pilot by providing reliable and maintenance free surfaces. This requires special considerations while designing pavement facilities for vertical/short take-off and landing fighters. Jet reaction control system is unique feature of V/STOL aircrafts. This system uses air which is ducted to variable-area values at nose. tail and wing tips. In hovering and V/STOL flight the air has a high energy level, and the supersonic jet which emerges from the values has a very high velocity, temperature and nozzle exist pressure. It is therefore obvious that when the aircraft is operating in close proximity to the pavement in the V/STOL modes, an energy release of this magnitude can lead to various problems.

9.7.1 Interaction Between Aircraft and Ground

9.7.1.1 Jet effects on the pavement

(i) Foreign Object Damage (FOD)

The jet flow patterns from the aircraft's nozzles can be the direct cause of debris being lifted from the pavement or adjoining unprotected areas, leading damage to the aircraft structure and engine. A further effect of the jet kinetic energy during hover operations is the tendency to blast holes in unprotected surfaces. The adjacent areas should be so engineered that when the aircraft operates with the main nozzle posture any where near vertical, no potential for FOD exists. It must be emphasised that V/STOL operations tend to disturb more surface debris than the conventional fighter operating from runways, consequently, there is greater potential to incur FOD engine. The serviceability of pavement areas for V/STOL operations is, therefore critical.

(ii) Velocity, Pressure and Temperature

In a typical hover, the front jets have a stagnation pressure of about 1.12 kg/cm^2 (16 psi), a temperature of about 105^{0}C and emerge from the nozzles at 1300 kmph (800 mph). The rear jets have a stagnation pressure of about 0.77 kg/cm^2 (11 psi) and temperature reduce with increasing distance from the nozzles. Users had indicated that life off and hover operations may last for about thirty seconds over any specified pavement area and may be repeated three to four times after every five minutes. Approximate duration of maximum exposure during take-off is 10 seconds after which the take-off would have to be abandoned.

9.7.1.2 Jet effects at joints

Joints in concrete pavements are subjected to a searching jet pressure forcing its way down and around the channel. This results in debris being dislodged and blown out violently upwards to become a concentrated FOD fountain. Expansion joints are conventionally filled with a mastic board and sealed with a bituminous compound. If the seal is not continuous along the joint length, jet pressure can penetrate and rake out entire lengths of the sealing material and associated debris. Even when the seal is unbroken and continuous, prolonged exposure to near-vertical jets would puncture the seal by softening action and progressive joint-scouring would immediately follow.

9.7 2 Design Consideration

(i) Concrete and high temperature

Based on tests conducted on a concrete airfield pavement of 36 cm thickness, it is observed that, with jet blast from a Gnat aircraft (jet engine inclination 20°), the maximum temperature reached in 15 to 20 seconds was in the range of 140 to 170°C. Stresses induced in the pavement after different periods of jet application were then calculated. For a surface temperature of 150°C, such stresses have been shown to be of the order of 20-22 kg/cm^2 flexural tension, some 4 to 10 cm below the surface, the top and bottom developing some compression at the same time. This tensile stress can cause deterioration inside the slab unless flexural strength of concrete is adequate.

(ii) Continuous reinforcement

The provision of continuous reinforcement in CRCP of the conventional type results in the formation of transverse cracks in the pavement which are held tightly closed by the steel without impairment of structural strength. The width and spacing of such cracks are dependent on the amount of steel reinforcement provided. The greater the amount of steel, the closer is the spacing of the cracks and the smaller is their openings. An optimum amount of longitudinal reinforcement is called for so that the cracks are neither too widely spaced with resulting overstressing of steel, lose in low transfer provided by aggregate interlock and accelerated corrosion of steel, nor too closely speed so as to cause distintegration of the slab.

9.7.4 Physical, Environmental and Material Parameter

(a) Physical

(i) Size

Pad size as required by users was 50 m by 45 m. This area was provided as part of a larger pavement complex.

(ii) Landing gear and aircraft loading

The main gear assembly consists of dual wheels spaced as (16 in) centres and carrying a total load of 9080 kg (20000) lbs at a tyre pressure of 6.33−7.17 kg/cm^2 (90-102 psi). ESWL was worked out to be 7510 kg (16530 lbs) for 0.870 kg/cm^3 (300 pci). This indicated an LCN of 20. In view of the vertical landing, it was considered necessary to enhance the design LCN value to cater for possible effect of impact. An LCN value of 30 was chosen.

(b) Environmental

The daily maximum and minimum temperature at the construction site varies between 28−35°C and 21−27°C respectively. The subgrade CBR was reported as 15 and the modulus of subgrade reaction was estimated as 5 kg/cm^3.

(c) Material

(i) Concrete

Slab design was based on a 28 day flexural strength of 40 kg/cm^2. Tensile strength of concrete for CRCP design, at 0.6 of the modulus of rupture, was taken as 24 kg/cm^2 (say 335 psi).

(ii) Steel

Working stress in toresteel was taken as 3080 kg/cm^2 (44000 psi). This corresponds to 75 percent of yield stress.

9.7.5 Slab, Reinforcement and Joint Design

(a) Design of slab thickness

Using design manual, a thickness of 175 mm of CRCP on 100 mm lean concrete was chosen.

(b) Reinforcement and joint design

This section present the design approach for longitudinal and transverse reinforcement, together with suggested joint design for both longitudinal and transverse construction. The procedures are based on the work done by Treybig. McCullough and Hudson.

(c) Longitudinal reinforcement

Longitudinal reinforcement should be checked by three methods to meet all of these criteria :

(i) The requirement based on the design equation for continuous reinforcement.

(ii) The requirement to resist temperature changes.

(iii) Concrete strength to steel strength ratio.

After checking the requirements by all three methods, the largest percentage evaluated was selected as the design requirement. Longitudinal steel less than 0.5 percent is not recommended. It was seen that the governing criteria is essentially concrete strength to steel strength ratio.

(d) Transverse reinforcement

Treybig et al recommended transverse steel design based on the subgrade drag theory. The concept is to enable one-half width of the slab to be held tightly to the other half by reinforcement in case of a central longitudinal crack, which requires the balancing of the separating frictional force by the counteracting force in steel. Transverse reinforcement was designed for full width and continued through the transverse joints.

(e) Reinforcement detail

Bar diameters and spacings may be so chosen in order to ensure minimum crack widths, the bond area to concrete volume ratio, for longitudinal reinforcement, and should be greater than 0.072 cm^2/cm^3. For longitudinal steel, 16 mm bars at 150 mm centres were provided. For transverse steel, 12 mm dia bars at 180 mm were provided. The longitudinal reinforcement is placed at mid depth in the slab.

(f) Joints

Typical longitudinal butt joint is provided which can be left as unsealed, however, users insist on sealing these butt joints. Consequently, sealing may be done with an urethened compound, impregnation being ensured to the extent possible, by saturation at top of the joint. The efficacy of such a treatment is not clear.

PROBLEMS

1 Explain the basic difference between airport and highway pavements ? Discuss in brief the various factors to be considered in the design of airfield pavements.

2 What is ESWL ? How can it be determined for dual and dual-in-tendem wheel assembly ?

3 Name and discuss in brief the various methods used for designing flexible airport pavements.

4 Design a runway pavement section for design gross weight of 90,000 kg. Tests were conducted on pavement and C.B.R. values so obtained are as under :

Sub-grade soil	5 percent
Sub base	20 percent
Base course	44 percent

The runway pavement is expected to sustain 20,000 coverages.

5 Plate bearing test conducted on a soil subgrade using 75 cm diameter plate, yielded 0.5 cm deflection, a pressure of 2.2 kg/cm^2 after ten repetition. Design a taxiway for capacity operation and a single wheel load of 25,000 kg with a tyre pressure of 10.5 kg/cm^2.

6 A plate bearing test using a 75 cm diameter plate yielded a subgrade support value of 45,000 kg at 1.25 cm deflection. Determine pavement thickness for a single wheel load of 36,000 kg and 14.0 kg/cm^2 tyre pressure.

7 A plate load test was carried out on a silty clay subgrade and 15 cm of base course, using, a 75 cm diameter. The pressures on the plate at 0.5 cm deflection was 0.5 kg/cm^2 and 2.1 kg/cm^2 for the subgrade and base respectively. Determine the thickness of the pavement required for a 33,750 kg dual wheel with 10.5 kg/cm^2 tyre pressure.

8 A plate bearing test using a 75 cm diameter rigid plate was made on subgrade as well as on 25 cm of gravel base course. The unit loads required to cause settlement of 0.5 cm was 0.7 kg per cm^2 and 2.8 kg per cm^2, respectively. Determine the required thickness of base course to sustain a 22,500 kg wheel load with tyre pressure of 7 kg/cm^2 and maintain a deflection of 0.5 cm.

9 Discuss in brief how the analytical method is different with the other empirical and semi-empirical methods for design of flexible airfield pavements ?

10 Discuss in brief the computer aided design application for determining the thickness of airfield pavements. What are the steps involved in the procedure for computer aided method of flexible airfield pavements ?

11 Determine the thickness of pavement required for 27,000 kg dual wheels with a tyre pressure of 5.6 kg/cm^2 modulus of subgrade reaction of 4.5 kg/cm^3 and modulus of rupture of concrete equal to 43.0 kg/cm^2 with a factor of safety of 1.5

12 Compute the thickness of a runway section for maximum use of aircraft dual wheel load of 45,000 kg and tyre pressure of 8.4 kg/cm^2. The modulus of subgrade reaction is 5 kg/cm^3. The flexural strength of concrete after 28 days is 47.5 kg/cm^2.

13 Compute the stress in the interior region of 55 cm thick cement concrete pavement with dual tandem landing gear configuration and keeping the centre one wheel matching with interior point of slab. The load of gear assembly

is 90,000 kg with dual tyre spacing as 80 cm and centre to centre spacing of tandem axle as 165 cm. The tyre pressure is 14.0 kg/cm^2. Values of $K = 5$ kg/cm^3 and $\mu = 0.15$ may be assumed.

14 Calculate the stress at the interior region of a cement concrete pavement under any one wheel of a dual in tandem assembly. Use the following data :

Load on all the four wheels = 67,500 kg

lateral spacing of the tyres = 77.5 cm

length of wheel base = 155 cm

tire pressure = 10.5 kg/cm^2,

k = 4.5 kg/cm^3 and h = 30 cm.

Assume the tire print as rectangular with circular ends such that width = 0.6 × length. Use Figure 9.24 for computation.

15 Discuss in brief, what are the critical load position in a rigid pavement ? Elaborate some of the important methods used for the design of rigid airport pavement. Discuss with sketches the various joints emlpoyed in cement concrete pavements,

16 Explain in brief the requirement of special consideration for design of pavement facilities for V/STOL operations.

10

MAINTENANCE & REHABILITATION OF AIRFIELD PAVEMENTS

10.1 NEED FOR MAINTENANCE

During the second world war, a number of airfield pavements were constructed to cater the needs of defence services. These airfield pavements were used by light aircrafts. During the last three decades, the development and advancement in civil aviation had been phenomenal and had very deep impact on the economic activity. As commerce and tourism grow, specially in a vast country like India, the requirement of services, goods and construction activities increase, thus boosting economy by creating more jobs and demand of services and goods. In the fifties only Dakotas were in operation, carrying only 30–40 passengers. In the eighties widebodied Jumbo Boeing 747–400 aircrafts carrying 450–500 passengers were added. It is expected that double decker Boeing 747 carrying 600–650 passengers and about 50 tonnes of cargo may be added in civil aviation of India very soon.

The total passenger and freight traffic in India in 1987-88 was of the order of 702 billion passenger km. and 388 billion tonne km. respectively, whereas the projected figures for 2000 A.D. are likely to be 1344 billion passenger km and 650 billion tonne km respectively. It would be seen from that within the next 12—13 years, the traffic is likely to be doubled. In order to meet the challange of such traffic growth, the investment in aviation sector upto the century is going to be very high. It is felt that for providing only functional airports, the investments on airports required by 2000 A.D. will be of the order of Rs. 2050 crores. This figure, however, does not include investments on any new airport, such as is expected to be put up at Bombay at a new site, the cost of which alone is estimated to be about Rs. 6000—8000 crores. About 30% of the investment in an airport is required in building runways, taxiways, aprons, roads, etc. The investment in airport pavements are very impressive. It is for this reason, it is essential to give importance as it deserves to airfield pavement design, evaluation and construction.

The aircraft loads in the fifties were of the order of 35,000—40,000 kg with tyre pressure in the ranges of 6 to 7 kg/cm^2. Today, the aircrafts are having weight of 380,000 kg and tyre pressures of the order of 14 to 15 kg/cm^2. In the fifties, during peak hours, the runways had 4-5 landings whereas, today during peak hours there can be 30—35 landings.

Considering the rigorous standards of safety demanded for operation of high speed jet aircraft, it is essential that the pavement surface should have an equally high standard to achieve smooth and safer operations. The functional aspects of airfield pavements therefore become a very important parameter for design. Developments in the design and manufacture of new series of jet and supersonic aircraft having different loading and speed characteristics necessitated commensurate upgradation and maintenance of existing airfield pavements.

10.1.1. Maintenance Management System

The type and extent of maintenance requirement for an airfield pavement depends on the serviceability standard, the maintenance need, funds available and the priorities for the maintenance operations.

In the recent past, airfield pavement design and management had not been handled on a systems approach. Therefore, each component of planning, design, construction, evaluation, strengthening, research and development was tackled in isolation, with the result that an effective and efficient airfield pavement system could not be developed. Considering this serious deficiency in basic approach, in India there is a need of system approach for pavement design and maintenance, with sole objective giving most efficient pavement system within the framework of given financial constraints.

Thus various factors to be included in the maintenance management system are :

(i) Minimum acceptable serviceability standards for the maintenance of different catagories of airfield pavements.

(ii) Field surveys for the evaluation of maintenance requirements.

(iii) Various factors influencing the maintenance needs such as subgrade soil, drainage, climate, traffic, environmental condition, etc.

(iv) Type and extent of maintenance requirements and various possible alternatives.

(v) Availability of funds.

(vi) Maintenance cost, availability of materials, man power and equipment.

(vii) Need based allocation for optimum utilisation of inputs and fixing maintenance priorities.

10.2 AIRFIELD PAVEMENT FAILURES

10.2.1 General

A flexible airfield pavement failure is defined by formation of pot holes, ruts, cracks, localized depressions and settlements. The localized depression normally is followed with heaving in the vicinity. The sequence develops a wavy pavement surface. The failure of any one or more components of the pavement structure develops the waves and corrugation on the pavement surface of longitudinal, ruts and shoving. Pavement unevenness may itself be considered as a failure when it is excesssive.

The subject of pavement distress and failure is considered complex as several factors contribute to the deterioration of bituminous pavements. Deterimental actions in pavements are rapidly increased when excess water is retained in the void spaces of bituminous pavement or in the cracks and joints of the cement concrete pavements.

The cement concrete pavement may develop cracks and deteriorate due to repeated loads and fatigue effects. A rigid pavement failure is observed by the development of a structural crack or break resulting in progressive subsidence of some portions of pavement. Moderate irregularities in the supporting layers beneath the cement concrete pavements are sustained due to inherent bending strength of these pavements. Rigid pavements are therefore capable of withstanding slight variations in the underlying support and they bridge the localized gaps moderately. It is the combination of many factors that induce the failure conditions in the rigid pavement. Due to the temperature effects, the newly constructed cement concrete pavement may also crack even if no vehicle moves on them. Often failure of rigid pavements starts from joints, corners and edges of slabs.

Formation of cracks in pavements is a natural phenomenon connected with its composition and type of material used and is dependent on its characteristic behaviour under various loading system and/or environment. If adequate care is not taken against their development in initial stages itself and/or treatment is neglected or delayed on their appearance, their growth takes place phenomenally leading to premature collapse of the pavement.

10.2.2 Failures in Flexible Pavements

The localized settlement of any one component layer of the flexible pavement structure could be enough to cause pavement failure. This demands that each one of the layers should be carefully designed and laid. Thus to maintain the stability of the pavement structure as a whole, each layer should be stable within itself and thereby maintain the stability of the total pavement.

Typical flexible pavement failures are :

(a) Alligator (map) cracking,

(b) Consolidation of pavement layers,

(c) Shear failure,

(d) Longitudinal cracking,

(e) Frost heaving,

(f) Lack of binding to the lower course,

(g) Reflection cracking and

(h) Formation of waves and corrugation.

(a) Alligator (map) cracking : This is the most common type of failure and occurs due to relative movement of pavement layer material. Figure 10.1 shows the general pattern of alligator or map cracking of the bituminous surfacing. This may be caused by the repeated application of heavy wheel loads resulting in fatigue failure or due to the moisture variations resulting in swelling and shrinkage of subgrade and other pavement materials. Localized weakness in the underlying base course would also cause a cracking of the surface course in this pattern.

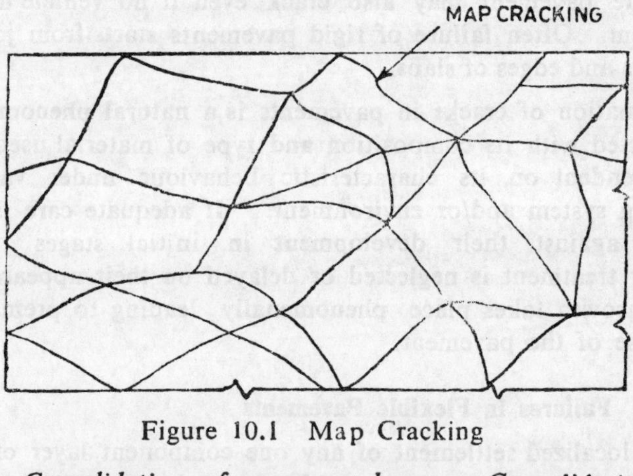

Figure 10.1 Map Cracking

(b) Consolidation of pavement layers : Consolidation of one or more layers of pavement are mainly attributed to the formation of ruts. The repeated application of loads along the same wheel path cause cumulative deformation resulting in consolidation deformation or longitudinal ruts. Figure 10.2 shows the failure due to the formation of ruts along a typical section of the pavement surface.

(c) Shear failure and cracking : Shear failures are associated with the inherent weakness of the pavement mixtures, the shearing resistance being low due to inadequate stability or excessively heavy loading. The shear failure causes upheaval of pavement materials by forming a fracture or cracking.

Figure 10.3 shows a typical section of shear failure and cracking.

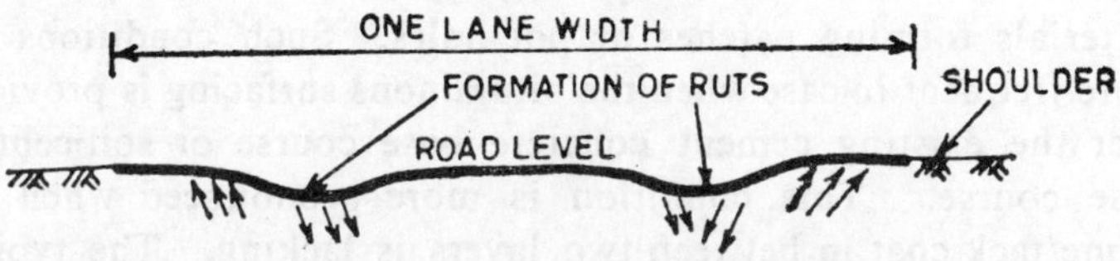

Figure 10.2 Formation of Ruts

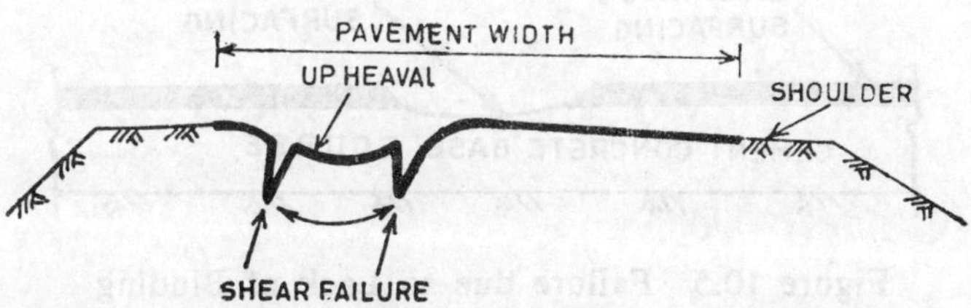

Figure 10.3 A typical Road Section showing Shear Failure Cracking

(d) Longitudinal cracking : Longitudinal cracking is caused in pavement traversing through the full pavement thickness due to frost action and differential volume change in subgrade. Settlement of fill and sliding of side slopes would also cause this type of failure.

(e) Frost heaving : Frost heaving is often misunderstood for shear or other types of failure. In shear failure, the upheaval of portion of pavement is followed with a depression. In the case of frost heaving, there is mostly a localized heaving up pavement portion depending upon the ground water and climatic conditions. Figure 10.4 shows the type of failure caused due to frost heaving.

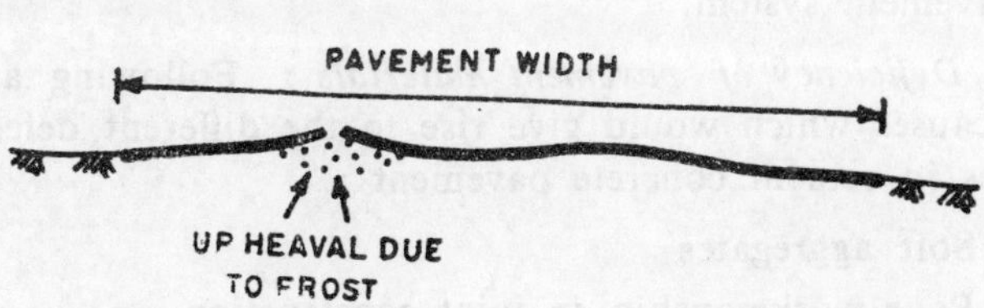

Figure 10.4 Failure due to Frost Heave

(*f*) *Lack of binding with lower layer* : When the surface course is not bound with the underlying base slipping may occur. This results in opening up and loss of pavement materials forming patches or pot holes. Such conditions are more frequent in case when the bituminous surfacing is provided over the existing cement concrete base course or soil-cement base course. This condition is more pronounced when the prime/tack coat in between two layers is lacking. The typical failure because of the above is shown in Figure 10.5.

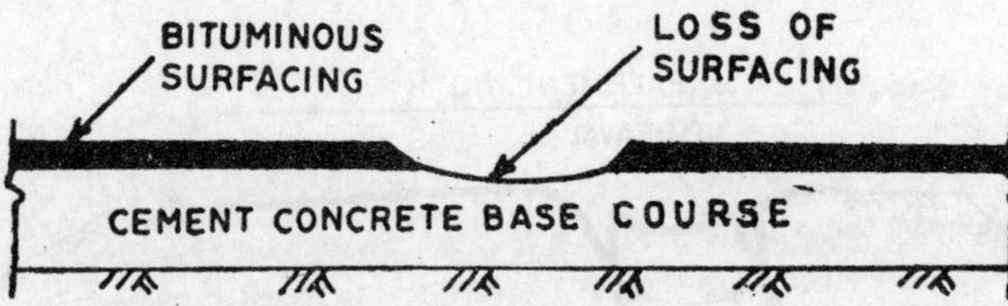

Figure 10.5 Failure due to Lack of Binding

(g) *Reflection cracking* : This type of cracking is observed in bituminous overlays provided over existing cement concrete pavements. The crack pattern as existing in cement concrete pavements is mostly reflected on bituminous surfacing in the same pattern. Structural action of the total pavement section is not much influenced by the presence of reflection cracks but since the cracks appear at the surface, these allow surface water to seep through and cause damage to the soil subgrade or result in mud pumping. Figure 10.6 shows the formation of reflection cracking.

10.2.3 Failure in Rigid Pavements

Failures in cement concrete pavements are recognized mainly by the formation of structural cracking and are occured due to deficiency of pavement materials and structural inadequacy of the pavement system.

(*a*) *Deficiency of pavement materials* : Following are the chief causes which would give rise to the different defects or failures in cement concrete pavement :

(i) Soft aggregates

(ii) Poor workmanship in joint construction

(iii) Poor joint filler and sealer material

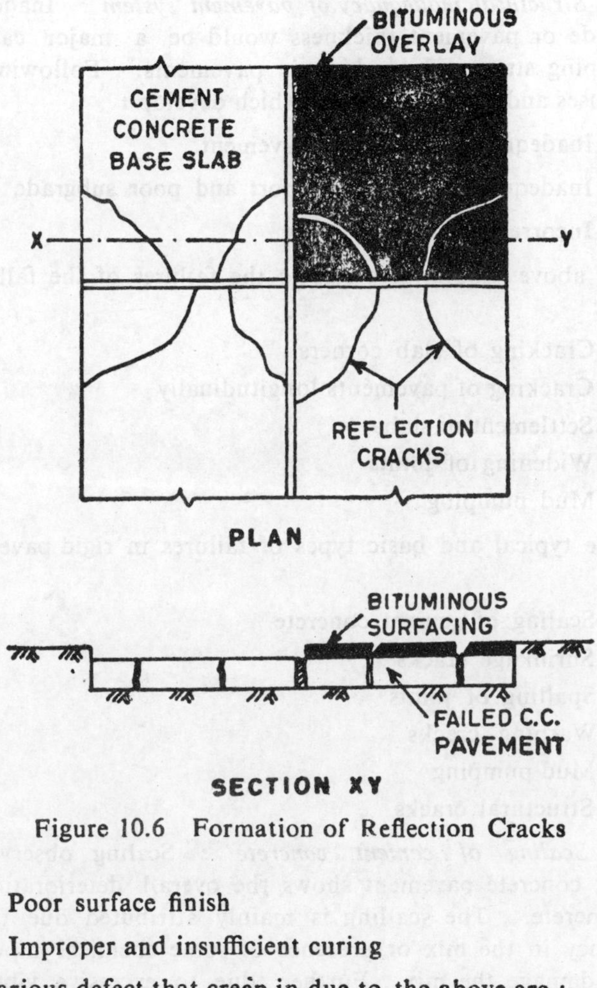

Figure 10.6 Formation of Reflection Cracks

(iv) Poor surface finish

(v) Improper and insufficient curing

The various defect that creep in due to the above are :

(i) Disintegration of cement concrete

(ii) Formation of cracking

(iii) Spalling of joints

(iv) Poor riding surface

(v) Slippery surface

(vi) Formation of shrinkage cracks

(vii) Ingress of surface water and further progressive failures.

(b) Structural inadequacy of pavement system : Inadequate subgrade or pavement thickness would be a major cause of developing structural cracking in pavements. Following are the causes and types of failures which develop :

(i) Inadequate thickness of pavement.

(ii) Inadequate subgrade support and poor subgrade soil

(iii) Incorrect spacing of joints.

The above would give rise to the failures of the fallowing types :

(i) Cracking of slab corners

(ii) Cracking of pavements longitudinally

(iii) Settlement of slabs

(iv) Widening of joints

(v) Mud pumping

Some typical and basic types of failures in rigid pavements are :

(i) Scaling of cement concrete

(ii) Shrinkage cracks

(iii) Spalling of joints

(iv) Warping cracks

(v) Mud pumping

(vi) Structural cracks

(a) Scaling of cement concrete : Scaling observed in cement concrete pavement shows the overall deterioration of the concrete. The scalling is mainly attributed due to the deficiency in the mix or presence of some chemical impurities which damage the mix. Further, due to excessive vibration given to the mix, the cement mortar comes to the top during construction and the cement mortar gets abraded exposing the aggregate of the mix.

This makes the pavement surface rough and shabby in appearance.

(b) Shrinkage cracks : The shrinkage cracks normally develop during the curing operation of cement concrete pavements immediately after construction. The placement of cracks are longitudinal as well as in transverse directions.

(*c*) *Spalling of joints :* Sometimes when preformed filler materials are placed during casting of pavement slabs, the placement is some how dislocated and filler is thus placed at an angle. The concreting is completed without noticing this faulty alignment of the filler material. Thus this forms an overhang of a concrete layer on the top side and the joint later on shows excessive cracking and subsidence.

(*d*) *Warping cracks :* Joints which are not well designed to accommodate the warping of slabs at edges result in the development of excessive stresses due to warping and the slab develops cracking at the edges in an irregular pattern. Hinge joints are generally provided for relieving the slabs of warping stresses, There is no structural defect due to the warping cracks if proper reinforcement is provided at the longitudinal and transverse joints as it takes care of the structural adequacy.

(*e*) *Mud pumping :* Mud pumping is recognised when the soil slury ejects out through the joints and cracks of cement concrete pavement caused during the downward movement of slab under the heavy wheel loads. Factors which cause the mud pumping are; extent of slab deflection, type of subgrade soil and amount of free water.

Pumping is noticed just after the rains in cement concrete pavements that are placed on clayey soil subgrade. Due to applications of repeated loads, initial spaces are developed underneath the pavement slabs and water infiltrates into these spaces through joints, cracks and edges of the pavements as shown in Figure 10.7 a. Since the soil is also of fine grained type, it holds water and forms the soil slurry or soil suspension in water or the mud.

Subsequent application of heavy wheel loads causes the pavement slab to deflect at critical locations and also forces out part of the mud each time, through the spaces in pavement joints, cracks or edge as shown in Figure 10.7 b. When more and more mud is ejected out, there is a substantial loss in fine grained soil from subgrade, resulting in considerable loss of subgrade support at these locations. With continued traffic movements, there is progressive increase in the wheel load stress in the pavement slab due to reduction in subgrade support, consequently cracks are developed and the pavement ultimately fails as illustrated in Figure 10.7 c. The pavement cracking due to mud pumping is generally a progressive type of failure in rigid pavements.

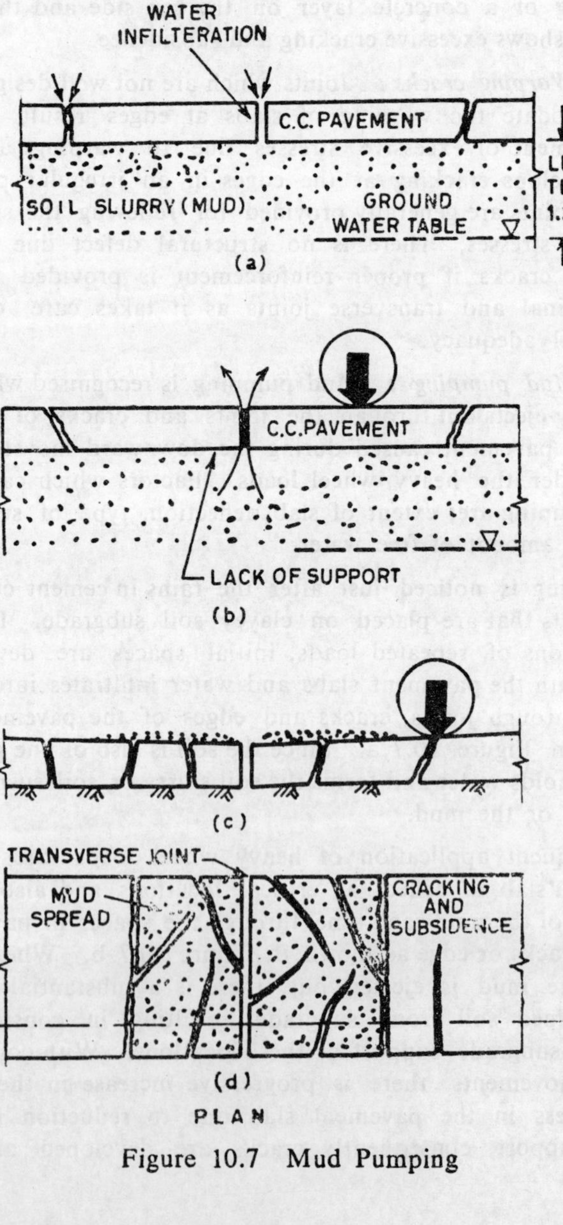

Figure 10.7 Mud Pumping

Structural cracking is formed due to the inadequate pavement thickness for the amount and type of vehicle. Largely, the pavements are found to crack at the corners and edges as shown in Figure 10.6. Longitudinal and transverse cracks are also found to exist. It becomes quite difficult to differentiate the type of cracks. Generally, if it could be decided that the crack in the vicinity of joints or corners are not due to spalling or mud pumping, then the cracks are attributed to the structural inadequacy. The cracking in the interior regions are mainly due to the temperature stresses.

10.3 MAINTENANCE AND REHABILITATION OF AIRFIELD PAVEMENTS

10.3.1 General

After knowing the various defects that may cause airfield pavement failures, it is necessary to study the different measures that one adopts to maintain and upkeep the pavement for their excellent behaviour. As a basic principle, it may be observed that an airfield pavement which is designed based on scientific standing would resist the various deterimental force and would need the minimum maintenance.

10.3.2 Flexible Airfield Pavements

The maintenance works of bituminous surfaces mainly consist of path repairs, repairs of surface treatments, resurfacing and special repairs.

(a) Patch repairs : On the damaged or improper airfield pavements surface, patch repairs are carried out. Localized depressions and pot holes may be formed in the surface layers due to defects in materials and construction. Inadequate or defective binding material causes removal of aggregates during monsoon. Patchwork may be done on affected localised areas on sections using a cold premix.

(b) Repair of pot holes : For the repairs of the pot holes, these are cut to rectangular shape and the affected material is removed until the sound materials are encountered. The excavated patches are cleaned and painted with bituminous binder. A premixed material is then placed in the sections.

Generally, cutback or emulsion is used as the binder. Bituminous emulsions can be used when the pavement surface and the aggregates are wet during monsoon. The material so placed in the pot hole, is well compacted by ramming to avoid any ravelling. The materials in pot holes are placed in layers of thickness of 6 cm or so. It is however, necessary to replace the base course materials with similar new materials if the failure has been detected in the base course layer also. The finished level of the patches is kept slightly above original level to allow for subsequent compaction under traffic.

(c) Surface treatment : The pavement becomes patchy and slippery where the surface materials bleeds due to excess of bitumin at the time of construction. Corrugations or rutting or shoving develop in such pavement surfaces. It is customary to spread blotting materials such as aggregate chips of maximum size of about 10 mm or coarse sand during summer. Necessary rolling is done to develop permanent bond between the existing surface and the new materials. The binders in the black top surfaces also get oxidized due to ageing. This develops minute cracking in the pavement surface. If the surface has been seriously damaged due to oxidization or volatilization of binder materials, it may be necessary to apply more than one layer of surface treatment.

(d) Resurfacing : When the pavement surface is totally worn out and develops a poor riding surface, it may be more economical to provide an additional surface coarse on the existing surface. In case the pavement is of inadequate thickness due to increase in traffic loads and strengthening is necessary, then an overlay of adequate thickness should be designed and constructed.

(e) Special repairs : Following are the factors which contribute to formation of waves and corrugations.

Defective rolling : If the rolling during construction stage is improper thus leaving the formation of waves then the process being progressive, the wave formation would continue indefinitely. However, the subsequent traffic operation would also cause similar effects if the rolling is inadequate during the construction stage.

Poor subgrade conditions : Subgrade consisting of poor soils including highly plastic organic soils and high water table close to subgrade surface may cause nonuniform and inadequate subgrade stability. When boulders are used as soling course in such subgrades, there is differential settement or sinking of these strones. All these would contribute to formation of corrugated pavement surface.

Poor gradation or mix : Poor gradation or mix for the surface layer is another factor which gives rise to the wave formation and pulling due to the vehicular movement and enhance the defect further more.

Compaction temperature : Viscous state of the bitmen binder greatly depends upon the temperature. High temperature during mixing and compaction of bituminous mix would make the resulting pavement surface layers with low stability and wavy surface is formed during rolling.

Unstable underlying layers : Weak underlying layers also cause the formation of waves due to repeated plying of vehicles on such road. Failure of any one of the pavement layers can cause surface deformations.

Rehabilitation measures for flexible airfield pavements : There appears to be no way to improve the surface once the pavement is found to be damaged by any reason. Usually another layer of surface course is laid after laying a levelling course. If the instability of underlying layer is due to excessive moisture conditions, suitable subsurface drainage system is warranted to remedy the defect permanently. If the failure is due to improper compaction of the lower layers this would need complete reconstruction. If the failure is due to subgrade soil which may be highly plastic expensive clay, the solution may by subgrade treatment using a modifying agent for stabilization.

The pavement would be reconstructed right from defective stage depending upon the failure of a given layer. Since the above factors would be carefully observed in replacement of layers, the pavement section so constructed may offer satisfactory riding quality.

10.3.3 Rigid Airfield Pavements

Rigid airfield pavements have certain specific advantages in case of airfield pavements, particularly for runway ends and aprons, which are exposed to jet exhaust, landing and take-off thrust and oil spillage. They need minimal of maintenance attention, but call for timely action and technology appropriate to rigid pavement for their maintenance and rehabilitation.

(a) Pre-requisites for effective maintenance & rehabilitation.

(i) Effective quality control during construction is the first essential step towards minimising M & R needs. Concrete pavements have certain inherent advantages when properly constructed-viz. stability of surface profile, long service life and minimal maintenance needs.

(ii) Timely action with regard to the identification, implementation and assurance of the requisite quality control is the basic important aspect for the requisite quality assurance of construction. This is particularly important in view of the fact that when rigid pavements, are properly constructed, these pavements have the capacity to provide good serviceability with economical rehabilitation.

(iii) Application of M & R technology appropriate to rigid pavements derive their nomenclature from the fact that they support the superimposed traffic loads by virtue of their high flexural rigidity as against the flexible pavements, which have far lower flexural strength. Any break or crack in a rigid pavement affects it flexural rigidity and hence, its structural strength, adversely. It is important that the repair techniques should be such that they fairly restore the structural rigidity of the pavement. Obviously, this cannot be achieved through the use of techniques appropriate to bituminous surfaces of flexible pavements. Resin repair technology and bounded concrete techology have been developed indigenously in the seventies and the sixties respectively, and have been used quite extensively in the country. There are some types of repairs, however, for which the techniques so far developed provide only a via media rather than a complete solution, e.g. resin repair of cracks, which helps to alleviate the problem of spalling of the crack edges, but does not restore the structural integrity of the pavement parts on either side of a structural crack. Further developments and innovations have taken place globally, which could be usefully adopted or adapted for effective and efficient M & R of rigid pavements and deserve to be duly considered.

(iv) Application of expeditious techniques are useful to obviate or minimising the closure of traffic. As repairs would normally be needed more in the disruption to traffic - and at the most, to manage with some adjustment in flight schedules only - repair techniques need to be such as can be executed and made traffic worthy very expeditiously. Bonded cement concrete, needs long curing period. Resin repair technology meets this requirement, but is very substantially costlier as compared to the cement concrete alternative and needs special precautions. Various alternative products have been developed abroad or are under development or exploration indigenously towards providing a more economical alternative. Another area, calling for high expeditious techniques, is that of emergency repairs to bomb-damaged pavements for marking the airfield operative in a minimum time.

10.3.4 Emergency Repairs of Airfield Pavements

Emergency repairs of military airfield pavements have to be carried out during war after damages caused to the pavements due to bombing: Damages due to bombing are generally in the form of craters The crater size normally 3 m to 9 m dia and 1.5 m to 3.7 m in depth. However, the maximum size of crater may be even 18 m in dia and 9 m in depth, in case of rigid pavements. The concrete slabs adjoining the craters get litted due to explosion.

The technique of emergency repairs adopted at different times by different agencies are discussed as follows :

(a) Extensive use of military airports and Air Force was made during World War II to bomb enemy targets. These targets included the enemy airfields also. This necessitated the need to evolve quick repair techniques for the damaged airfields.

The most commonly used technique adopted by Allied Forces consisted of an application of conventional civil engineering methods. This technique started with the clearance of debris and heaved pavement, followed by the placement of compact backfill and a capping layer of grouted bituminous macadam. This provided adequate structural strength to the layer of grouted bituminous macadam, and to the runway surface to sustain the loads of aircrafts, which used to be lighter those days.

The system of emergency repairs following during World War II has become unsatisfactory due to the following reasons :

(i) Longer time periods required to repair runway

(ii) Inadequate surface (both structurally and functionally) produced for modern aircrafts with higher ESWL and pressure

(iii) Dependence on bitumen as the grouting medium. This necessitates that hot bitumen would be available when required.

(b) The following factors govern the emergency repair technique to be adopted and also the effort required in terms of materials and labour to carry out the emergency repairs needed.

Craters : Total number of craters area, depth of each crater and their location with respect to stocked material for emergency repairs.

Lifted slabs : In case of rigid construction, the number and area of unheaved slabs have to be taken into account for removal and subsequent repairs of the affected area.

Time : The runway will have to be made operational as soon as possible with a realistic time frame. The repair technique should be able to meet this requirement. However, along with the limitations of time, the life serviceability criteria for the repaired portion should also be met with.

Aircraft type : The repair technique will have to be selected depending upon the the aircraft type, its gross load, ESWL and tyre pressure.

(c) Emergency repair techniques adopted and developed in India and abroad.

(i) Emergency rehabilitation technique adopted by Indian Army Corps of Engineers

Steps for repair :

— The crater is refilled with boulders upto approximately 30 cms from surface level of runway.

— 15 to 20 cms of the remaining depth is filled with aggregates of 40 to 63 mm size, 40 mm size aggregate being at top. The aggregate is filled upto approximately 8 cms below original surface. The filling is compacted in layers with mechanical tampers or frog hammers where rollers can not be employed.

— A ready made bituminous mix is then spread over the aggregates and rolled. The ready made mix can be stored near the airfield even upto a month in advance of actual requirement.

(ii) Preparation of the ready made bituminous mix.

Aggregate for the mix : Aggregate shall be of the following gradings :

— Nominal size 12.5 mm (100% passing 20 mm sieve and 100% retained on 10 mm sieve) = 15% by weight

— Crusher dust passing 2.36 mm sieve and retained on 75 micron sieve = 73% by weight

— Crusher dust passing 75 micron sieve = 5% by weight

— Fine lime stone dust or lime = 7% by weight

— Pre-heating of Aggregate : The aggregate shall be preheated in a bituminous mixing plant before the mix is made.

— Binder : Bitumen 60/70 or 80/100 flushed with 7% to 8% (by weight of bitumen) of diesel oil is heated and mixed at a rate of 7% of the aggregate mix by weight.

— It is likely that lumps may be formed during storage if the ingradients are not mixed properly or the aggregate is not preheated. In that case either the mix would be reheated before use or one half litre of diesel oil per cubic feet is mixed to give the desired workability.

— The laying temperature is approximately 120°C.

(iii) Air landing mat developed by Indian Defence R & D engineers

R & D engineers have developed Air Landing Mat (ALM) made of aluminium alloy panels joined together. Traffic simulation tests have been carried out for two fighter aircrafts with the following recommendations :

- Shelf life or panels in field = 15 years
- Can carry aircrafs upto LCN 36
- Size of panel : Full = 3.56 m × 0.419 m,
  Half = 1.82 m × 0.419 m
- Anchorage system : Hold fast anchored into the shoulder soil
- Assembly time : 90 hours for 1200 m × 45 m
- Laying System : Manual assembly. However, can be dragged over the crater with a wheel dozer.
- Time gap between laying and use of traffic : Immediate
- Subgrade strength requirement : CBR 8%
- Remarks : Any mat portion can be taken out and replaced with out disturbing others.

(iv) EBEX runway repair decking

This system has been developed in Greece. The salient features of this system are as follows

- The system consists of aluminium alloy panels joined together
- Size of units : Full 4.6 m × 0.242 m × 0.0375 m, Half 2.3 m × 0.242 m × 0 0375 m
- Ramps : Size 4.6 m × 0.184 m, Slope 7°
- System capable of carrying aircrafts upto LCN 60
- Assembly time : Assembled mat can be laid in 2 to 2.5 hours on a crater.
- Subgrade strength requirements : CBR 15 to 25%.
- Remarks Has been used by Greek Air Force for emergency crater repairs.

(v) Rapid runway repairs system developed by Laired Ltd. UK

This system consists of alluminious alloy panels of 22×16 m size to cover craters upto 16 m dia. To reduce glare and aid concealment of mats stored in the open, all components are painted to produce a grey/green finish. The area around the bomb crater is cleared of debris and fill back material removed from the crater. The crater is then filled with stones held in the stockpile within the airfield perimeter. The fill material is then filled with stones held in the stockpile within the airfield perimeter. The filled material is then compacted and levelled. The repair mat, which is stored as a roll, is towed to the site, lowered to the ground and unrolled over the filled and levelled crater. The mat is tensioned and fastened to the undamaged runway. The repair takes around one and half hours from start to finish. The mat has a strength of LCN 60 when laid and can be used immediately after laying.

(vi) Advanced Rapid Runway Repair Technique (ARRT)

This system has been developed in the Netherlands. With ARRT, craters upto 20 metre diameter and 3 metre or more in depth can be repaired in 3 hours. A crew of 12 men and predetermined sets of vehicles equipment and materials are needed. This system consists of filling the crater and on top laying prefabricated concrete slabs 2 m × 2 m.

(vii) Dallex-press System Developed in France

The repair of bomb craters by the Dallex express system entails producing in a very short time a concrete slab on a foundation, itself consisting of a certain thickness of ballast. The binder is pumped in the form of grout on a course of aggregate through which it penetrates occupying all the voids and interstics. This aggregate course, whose thickness is equals to that of the slab to be produced, is sealed at its base by a polythene film or a screen of a few centimetre (1 to 3 cm). At the end of the operation, the grout entirely covers the aggregate course. The surface produced is automatically obtained flat and even.

The binder is stored in a covered and ventilated space, it should remain protected from the sunrays and from rains. The sheld life of binder is approximately two years. The Dallexpress system can be used in all weather.

(viii) Emergency Runway Repair Compound

Denson Engineers New Delhi has claimed to have developed a special purpose runway repair compound for emergency repair of runway. The use of this compound makes the runway ready for use within 3 to 4 hours. The crater is filled with conventional methods as per availability of the materials. It is compacted using a power roller or manually to a level 5 cm from top. The special purpose runway repair compound after mixing is laid on the prepared surface of the crater ensuring 5 cm thickness.

Certain other details regarding this compound is given below :

Material : (a) Polymer concrete (Compound A),

(b) Hardner compound (Compound B),

(c) Primer for adhesion

Shelf life : 3 years (can be rejuvenated in the factory again for 3 years with 25% extra cost)

LCN achieved after repairs = 30

Flexural strength achieved after 3 hours = 40 kg/cm^2

Time between laying and use by traffic = 3 to 4 hours

Remarks : The efficacy of the compound and technique needs to be confirmed by field trials.

(ix) Quick Hardening Solution (Polyurethane Solution)

This was developed in USA for pentagon after Vietnam experience. In this method, bomb crater is first filled with debris upto 25 cms of runway surface, thereafter a layer of crushed aggregate would be laid down. Polyurethane chemicals is then mixed and poured at the prepared surface. Within minutes, the surface is ready for traffic. Certain details about the method is given below :

Materials : Isocynate, Polyhidric alcohol crushed stone aggregate

Storage : To be stored as jet fuel

Flexural strength achieved : 90 kg/cm^2

Opening to traffic : 30 minutes after laying

(x) Fibre Glass Reinforced Polyester Resin Membrane

— This system has been developed in USA. The system is prefabricated from several fibreglass matting layers of chopped fibre glass strands. These layers are chemically bonded and impregnated with polyester resin.

This method has following advantages over the Aluminium Mat Assembly

— Mats are costly

— Mat assembly system is time consuming/complex

— Surface is very rough, which may cause damage to aircrafts during landings/takeoffs.

— Maximum thickness of membrane = 1 cm

Membrane is laid over the crushed aggregate base, stretched and bottled down. US Navy is using this method.

(d) Organisation of Emergency Repair of Airfield Pavements

It is extremely important that the organisation of men and material should be such that no time is wasted to start the emergency repair work. Measured quantities of different materials should be available on site for specified number of craters. Materials should be stacked for repair of one crater at one place. Drill for repairs should be practised in advance and working parties should be available at short notice. The organisation of men and material is as important for the success of emergency repairs as the selection of correct techniques.

The need to repair a runway, which has been damaged by bombs during a war in the quickest possible time can not be overstressed. However, it is to be ensured that the runway is strong enough to sustain the aircraft loads at least for a duration of few weeks.

The shelf life of the repair compound should not be too short, the repair technique should be simple to execute and equipment should not be very heavy and cumbersome ; the men and material should also be organised that minimum time is wasted to start the emergency repair works after enemy attack. Finally, the life-serviceability criteria of the repair work being carried out has to be considered. It is to be ascertained as to how many movements (landing/take offs) of aircrafts, the repaired portion is likely to sustain. For lesser number of aircraft movements, the emergency repair may be quicker, where as for larger aircraft movements and for longer duration of anticipated runway use prior to permanent repairs, the emergency work may be time consuming. Also the life - serviceability criteria will dictate the type of emergency repair technique to be adopted.

10.4 EVALUATION OF AIRFIELD PAVEMENTS

10.4.1 General

The evaluation of an existing airfield pavements consists essentially to assess the following :

(i) Structural capacity of pavements.

(ii) Residual life of pavement at a given time.

(iii) Pavement surface characteristics frequency & intensity of present & future air traffic operations.

(iv) Climatic & environmental conditions.

(v) Drainage conditions

The above aspect involves specific quantitative measurement of relevant in situ structural and functional properties of the system. Typical parameters required to be measured are :

(i) Subgrade strength

(ii) Thickness(es) of layer(s)

(iii) Layer material response (elastic modulus)

(iv) Static and dynamic deflection and stiffness modulus

(v) Water table & rainfall data

(vi) Pavement surface unevenness

(vii) Surface texture & skidding resistance

Depending upon the type of pavement, viz, rigid, flexible or composite, the techniques of methods developed during earlier periods for measurements of various related parameters and for the analyses of data have been modified from time to time with a view to more realistic assessment. The two methods in use are destructive testing and non-destructive testing (NDT).

A number of instruments have been developed over the years for the evaluation of airfield pavements. Conventional testing requires longer testing time and even temporary closure of airports to traffic. This needs for developing a procedure which permits rapid evaluation with minimum disturbance to normal traffic. Instruments involving non-destructive testing techniques and enabling speedy evaluation have been developed world wide.

IAAI has acquired the requisite expertise in designing, constructing and evaluating runways in different types of soil and climatic conditions.

10 4.2 Functional Evaluation

Need : The surface characteristics of airfield pavements namely its riding quality, surface texture and skid resistance determines the comfort of passengers, vibrational effects in the aircraft components and safety during landing and take-off especially during flooded conditions.

Riding quality of pavements : Roughness evaluation formed two basis for the development of following criteria for runway acceptance. These two basis are :

(i) New Construction, or (ii) Reconstruction

Instrumentation techniques for roughness measurement need to be improved for developing counrries because of the non-availability of expensive equipments. In consequence, one should know about using simple and inexpensive tools for the day-to-day life.

(a) Equipments for measuring riding quality

1. Simple devices

(i) 1.5 m or 3 m long straight edge to take into account the unevenness of longer wave length which affect the aircrafts operations.

(ii) Longitudinal and transverse profiles can be measured by making rod and level measurements at suitable inervals so that unevenness of different wavelength and amplitudes can be evaluated.

Evaluation using the simple devices involves only discrete measurements and are not rigorous enough due to the slow process of measurements.

2. Advanced Equipment

(i) High speed equipment capable of continuous recording of unevennes and other geometric features of the surfaces and giving ready to use profiles/printouts and other data have been developed world wide.

The Automatic Road Unevenness Recorder (ARUR) manufactured in India is used for measurement of short wavelength bumps. Measurement is made at a speed of 30 kmph. The unevenness and the distance travelled are recorded electronically. The equipment yields Unevenness Index (UI) values in terms of mm/km.

(ii) TRRI, UK developed a High Speed Road Monitor for measurement and analysis of longitudinal profiles of new or existing pavements at speeds upto 80 kmph. Areas with amplitude unevenness exceeding a specified level and can be located and listed for closer inspection and subsequent rectification.

(iii) General Motors. USA, developed a high speed Profilometer which can be used for generating data on pavement surface profile and vehicle response to the irregularities.

3. Aircraft Response to Runway Surface Irregularities

Modern Civil Aircrafts are equipped with Aircraft Integrated Data System (AIDS) and Digital Flight Data Recording System (DFDRS) which measure and record the vertical acceleration of the aircraft.

The variables considered in this type of measurements are :

Speed of operation
Take-off and landing speed
Distribution of aircraft load
Different natural frequencies
Nature of the surface evenness
Aircraft suspension system.

(b) Suggested tentative norms

(i) 3 m straight edge : Maximum permissible size of the

deviations for surface of bituminous or concrete pavement shall not exceed 3 mm.

(ii) *Unevenness Indicator Method :* Maximum size of bumps/depressions on flexible or rigid pavements shall not exceed 3 mm.

(iii) *Rod and Level Method :*

Straight Edge length (m)	Deviation, mm	
	Avg. Deviation (Dav)	Characteristics Deviations (Dch)
1.5	7.6	19.0
3.0	12.4	26.0

Dav : Average of deviations of the longitudinal profile from the straight edge.

Dch : Characteristic deviation for 95% confidence level = Dav + 1.245

(iv) *Automatic Road Unevenness Recorder (ARUR) Method*

Bituminous Surface = 2000 mm/km

Cement Concrete = 2250 mm/km

Skid resistance characteristics of pavement :

(a) *Surface treatment method* Skid Resistance of a wet pavement surface with increase in speed demands mainly on the macro texture and how far the surface allows the water entrapped to escape. Different surface treatment methods in cement concrete runway pavements are :

(i) Grooving of fresh cement concrete. (ii) Sprinkling fresh cement concrete with chippings (iii) Stripping of fresh cement concrete. (iv) Grooving freshly and set concrete.

(b) *Restoration of skid resistance properties of existing cement concrete pavements.* Main causes of slipperness of runway surface during rains are :

(i) Waterponding due to poor drainage, (ii) Rubber accumulation at both touch down zones, and

(iii) Polishing of surface caused by the steel blade of snow removing equipment.

(c) *Runway skid resistance*. Operational safety of aircraft is the availability of adequate friction at the plane tyre runway interface during landing, especially under adverse climatic and environmental conditions (tyre pavement friction).

Tyre pavement friction components are : Adhesion or 'sticking' component, hysteresis or 'deformation' component and corrosion or wear component.

(d) Climatic conditions : Climatic conditions include the considerable influence on the availability of friction and considerable fluctuations in friction level caused by rainy season.

(e) Methods of Measurement of Tyre-Pavement Friction :

(i) Skid-Trailer : This equipment developed in U.S.A. measures the locked wheel friction between the wetted road surface and type of a standard design, size and inflation pressure at a constant speed of 64 kmph. The skid resistance is calculated as the ratio of the frictional resistance to normal load and the result is expressed as Skid Number (SN). The locked wheel test method corresponds to the emergency stopping of a vehicle. This equipment gives a high output and measurements are discontinuous. The test results are recorded electronically and printout is obtained. The test can be conducted only on straight sections.

(ii) Mu-Meter : This equipment developed in UK consists of a trailer on which two friction measuring wheels with smooth tyres inflated to 0.71 kg/cm^2 are yawed inward during measurement. Measurement is normally made at a standard speed of 64 kmph. It continuously records the Mu value (sideway force coefficient) versus the distance travelled along the pavement. The equipment gives a high output and is specially designed to suit measurements on runways.

(iii) British Pendulum Tester (BPT) : This equipment was developed by TRRL, UK and is a portable dynamic pendulum type tester. Skid resistance measurements obtained with this equipment corresponds to the performance of a patterned

tyre of a car braking with a locked wheel on a wet road at 50 kmph. It is a simple device and can be used in the field and laboratory. It has also provision for studying the polishing characteristics of aggregates. Considering the very high speed of aircraft operations, this equipment is suitable only for preliminary study on trends in skid resistance.

(iv) Stopping Distance Method : This method has been developed by CRRI. In this method, a jeep is fitted with a device for making the commencement of braking. Wet stopping distance test are conducted at a speed of 40 kmph by locking the wheels. The stopping distance number (SDN) is calculated by knowing the speed and the distance traversed by the vehicle.

Advance Techniques for Functional Evaluation :

Because of rapid advances in the computer industry, computer/microprocessor application are also being incorporated in the instrumentation used for pavement testing. Some of the latest techniques in functional evaluation in use gives faster and more realistic are given as follows :

(a) TRRL High Speed Road Monitor :

It is used for measuring rut depth profile and texture depth of pavement surfaces. It consists of a computer-based system, housed in the vehicle, that controls the measurement functions and processes the results. Laser sensors, distance measuring devices and inclinometer are fitted in the trailer. The system operates at speeds within the range of 5 to 80 kmph. A driver-operator team can record test data for a distance of upto 200 lane km per day. Measurements are stored on a floppy disc and can be processed by the vehicle itself using the system's computer facilities. Data can also be transferred to a mainframe computer for permanent storage and further processing. It has been observed that upto 26 km of profile data, 200 km of texture depth or 1000 km of rut depth data can be stored on one floppy disc. The amplitude of unevenness with a wave length of less than 3 m is measured within ± 1.5 mm unevenness, wave length of less than 20 m is measured within ± 2.5 mm and unevenness upto a wave length of 100 m within ± 40 mm. Further developments for incorporating the measurements of gradient, crossfall and curvature using this equipment, with additional transducers fitted to the trailer are needed.

(b) Laser Road Surface Tester (LRST)

It is a sophisticated, computer-based system for evaluation of functional aspect of highways and runways. It covers a total range of activities from data registration and initial evaluation to data base management system for decision makers. The first laser LRST was developed at the Swedish Road and Traffic Research Institute in 1981. The instrument essentially consists of a series of laser probes fitted on the front bumper on the measuring vehicle. The angled-out lasers on the sides of the vehicle increases the measurement range to 3.1 m. Other components of the measuring vehicle are vertical accelerometer, pulse transducer, control panel monitor, amplifier computer printer, floppy disc drives and power supply for laser electronics. The microcomputer system provides acquisition and processing facilities as well as data storage and display units.

The laser light-spot on the road and runway surface is projected on a light-sensitive displacement sensor. Electrical signals representing vertical position and light intensity of the laser spot are recorded and computer-processed. Measurements are carried out at a speed ranging from 30 to 90 kmph. All variables can be measured either simultaneously or independently. The non-contact system with the pavement provides easy calibration with high precision. LRST has been designed to measure pavement rut depth, roughness and distance traversed. Additional facilities for measurement of variables such as cracks, roughness, fine texture and surface friction (by connecting a Skidometer B VII to the vehicle) can be incorporated.

(c) Bump Integrator with Micro-processor Based Instrumentation

The microprocessor based TRRL Bump Integrator is used to measure pavement surface irregularities and comprises of control box, trailer and power supply units. The control box consists of four printed circuit boards for power supply, data-process and display. It also houses the printer, cassette and front panel controls.

The trailer consists of a single wheel with a single leaf spring on either side supporting the trailer chassis. Two dashpots provide viscous damping between the chassis and the wheel axle. A linear transducer is mounted on the chassis and coupled to the axle to measure the displacement of the wheel. A remote control unit is mounted on the chassis pointing of the nearside. A proximity switch and metal disc with slots are mounted on the wheel axle. The proximity switch is adjusted to give clearance in between 2.0 mm and 2.5 mm between the proximity switch tip and the disc.

Power supply is maintained through two 12 V batteries. Standard BI Index values R are obtained when the trailer is towed along the pavement at a measuring speed of 32 kmph. However, if the measuring speed deviates from 32 kmph by 10 kmph, the internal speed connection facility will calculate an index value which will be within ± 10% of the standard R value. Accurate index measurements are affected through a micro-processor system which records the movement of trailer wheel relative to the chassis. The index value for each sub-section length is displayed in units of cm/km.

10.4.3 Structural Evaluation

10.4.3.1 Air field pavement classification : Compatability between aircraft and pavement is necessary so that there is no excessive damage to the pavement and aircraft operations are unrestricted. So long as the aircraft having single wheel, the comparison of strength could be made by simple load tests. With the advancement of technology in aircraft design having complex wheel configurations and assemblies came in use and therefore a methodology to define the compatability between the aircraft and pavement with a common datum was felt necessary. Different methods are available in use, however, it is required that a uniform method needs to be applicable to all types of aircrafts and the most widely accepted ones are discussed here.

(i) Classification

The scientists of UK Air Ministry observed that the load carrying capacity of pavement varies with the tyre pressure (or contact radius) using the relationship $(a_1/a_2)^{\alpha}$. The aircraft is thus defined by a curve having exponent of α

passing through the point obtained by contact area and the all-upweight. A load classification number is assigned to such sets of load on single wheel and tyre pressures which are expanded to give a curve. A family of curves for various sets of load and tyre pressures is developed and such curve is assigned a number. The load classification number (LCN) defines the load effect of an aircraft. The safe load tested for pavement with reference to the area of contact plate used in the test, read on such curves gives the LCN of the pavement.

Aircraft classification number (ACN) is defined as 'the load carried by a single wheel in terms of 500 kg, at a constant tyre pressure of 1.25 MPa by the pavement required for the aircraft using standard method of design using CBR method for flexible pavement and PCA for interior loading for rigid pavement'

Pavement classification number (PCN) is the ACN of aircraft which the pavement is capable of carrying for unrestricted movement. It may be noteworthy that the ACN/PCN are the 'Constant Tyre Pressure' whereas LCN is for 'Constant Contact Area'. This makes computations of permissible load of an aircraft compatible to the pavement strength.

The study group of International Civil Airport Association (ICAA) therefore, recommended that in order to define an airport pavement, the following information is necessary to understand :

(a) PCN which is the ACN of aircraft permitted for unrestricted operations.

(b) Type of pavement classified either Flexible (F) or Rigid (R). Type of subgrade classified in four groups of A (CBR $\gt$ 15, K $\ge$ 150 MN/m^3), B (CBR 10−15, K $\ge$ 80 MN/m^3), C (CBR 6−10, K $\ge$ 40 MN/m^3) and D (CBR $\gt$ 3, K $<$ 20 MN/m^3).

(c) Limits to tyre pressure in four groups of W for unlimited, X for 1.5 MPa, Y for 1.0 MPa and Z for 0.5 MPa.

(d) Whether the evaluation is technical (T) or the experienced based (U).

This method permitted declaration of the PCN by experience of the aircraft already operating. The classification of pavement will thus be similar to :

40/F/B/X/T or 37/R/C/W/U

(ii) ACN for some of the aircraft types

ACN is determined for flexible pavement using Boussinesq method for rigid pavement by PCA method for interior loading condition are published by the aircraft manufacturers. These values are given for standard conditions of subgrade strength and tyre pressures. ACN still varies for rigid and flexible pavement and from one subgrade to another. The aircraft pavement interaction is still not defined by a single number. The ACNs are also not available for composite pavements, semi-rigid pavement or edge/corner condition of loading where nearest standard condition has to be assumed.

(iii) Determination of PCN

PCN is being defined for constant pressure and no method is available for direct measurement. This has, therefore, can be determined by combining analysis with the measurement. It provides a choice to the airport authorities to use the method of their preference. Methods available presently use the stiffness of the pavement obtained by non-destructive test method. To this stiffness, permissible deflection is applied to obtain the maximum permissible load. This load, which is for a particular contact area and pressure is modified for standard contact pressure of 1.25 MPa. The cycle is repeated for the stable values. A scheme for determination of PCN is given in Figure 10.8.

(iv) Limiting Deformation

Limiting deformation is an important input to find out PCN & ACN and are governed by total permanent deformation acceptable for smooth ride and limiting deformation of acceptable maximum stress in any of the layer.

It is assumed that the deflections increases in logarithmic proportion. For a flexible pavement, maximum permanent deformation acceptable at surface in excess of its elastic deflection is 0.2″ (5 mm). Deformation in one cycle is therefore 5.0/ (Log N+1). This deformation gives conservative estimate

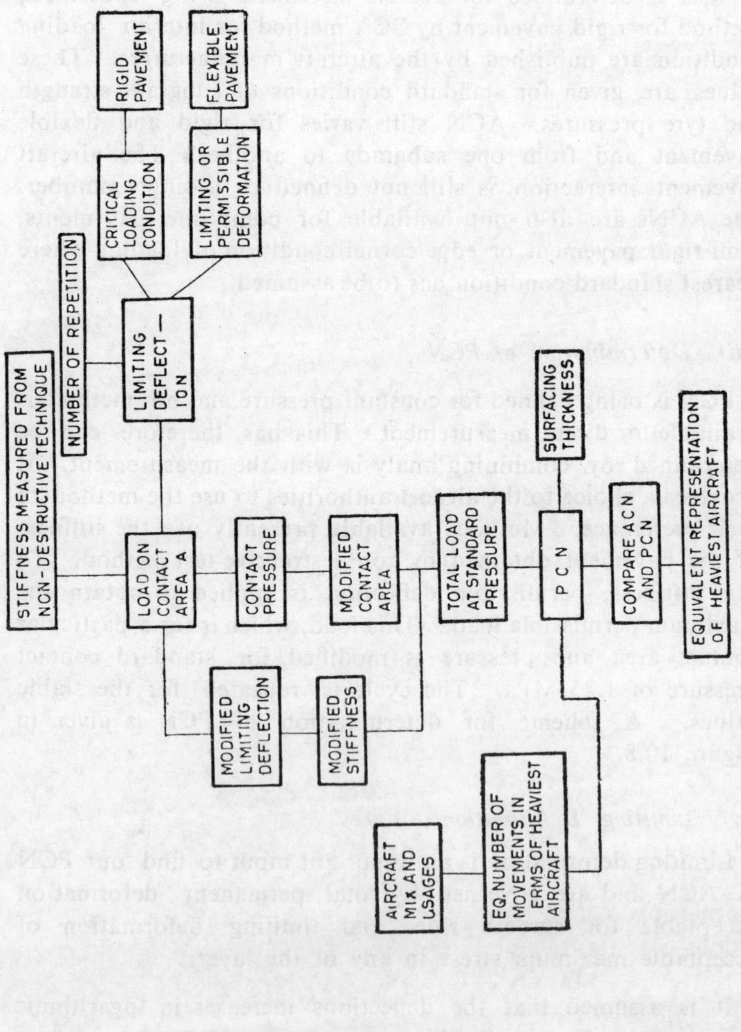

Figure 10.8 Flow Chart for Classification of Airfield Pavement

of permissible load as the permanent deformation as a ratio of total deformation and shall vary from one subgrade to another and composition of the pavement. This has to be obtained from laboratory studies.

In rigid pavement, corner or edge loadings are critical. Their limiting deflections are a function of modulus of subgrade reaction, thickness, fracture stress. Following equations may be used for determination of such limiting deformation.

Maximum permissible stress, $\sigma_{max.\ perm.}$ given by

$$\sigma_{max.\ perm.} = 0.497\,(1+\mu)\,\frac{P}{h^2}\left(4 \log_{10}\frac{L_k}{b} + 0.359\right)$$

$$\text{Edge load } W_o = \frac{1}{\sqrt{\sigma}}\,(1+0.4\mu)\,\frac{P}{kL_k^2}$$

where $L_k = 4\sqrt{D/k}$ and $a_k = a/L_k$

$$\text{Corner load} = \frac{3\,P}{h^2}\left[1-\left(\sqrt{2\,a_k}\right)^{0.6}\right]$$

determine P for $\sigma_{max.\ perm.}$

$$W_o = \frac{P}{KL_k^2}\,(1.1-0.88\,a_k\,\sqrt{2})$$

where,

$$L_k = \left[\frac{Eh^3}{12\,(1-\mu^2)k}\right]^{1/4}$$

a = radius of contact

$$b = \sqrt{1.6a^2+h^2} - 0.675\,h$$

for $a \ngtr 1.724$ h, otherwise b = a

Though for interior or edge load conditions, the subgrade stresses are low, so are the permanent deformation but for corner load condition it is significant and should be considered while deciding the limiting deformation.

(iv) Reverse Design

For airfield pavements of lesser importance and where the equipment is not available, PCN thickness charts drawn for various CBR's may be used. Fig. 10.9 gives chart for flexible

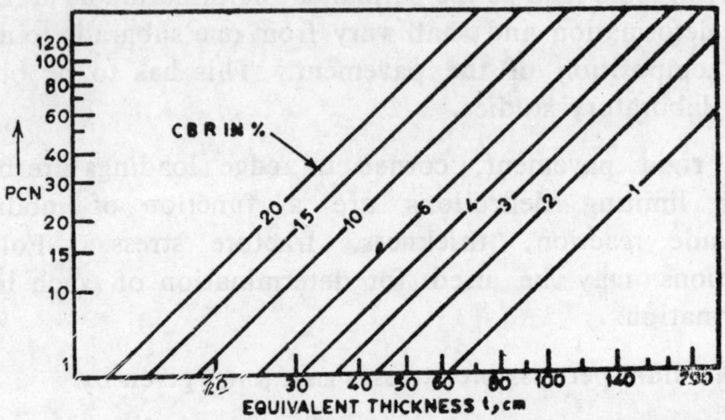

Figure 10.9 Relationship Between Equivalent Thickness, Subgrade CBR and PCN of Airfield Pavement

pavement. The layers are converted into the equivalent thickness of granular material. For appropriate CBR, the PCN value is read. Alternatively, the following equation can be used.

$$PCN = \frac{1}{500}\left[\frac{t^2}{\dfrac{1}{0.57\ CBR} - 0.525}\right]$$

here, t is in cm

(vi) Effect of Tyre Pressure

Change in ACN by modifying the tyre pressure is given by following experimental relation :

$$ACN\ mod. = ACN_{orig} = \left(\frac{P_{orig.}}{P_{mod.}}\right)^{\alpha}$$

For purely granular medium, the value of α is 0.5. For normal flexible pavements the value is recommended as 0.68 because of the stiffness provided by asphaltic layers. In case of rigid pavements, the value varies from 0.73 for very thin pavements (15 cm) to 0.885 for thick pavements;

(vii) Effect of Change in Pay Load

ACN is directly proportional to the all up weight of aircraft. Modified ACN for pay load of P is given by :

$$ACN\ mod = ACN_{min} + (ACN_{max} - ACN_{min})\ \frac{P - Mi}{M - Mi}$$

Where M is the maximum load and Mi is the Minimum load (empty).

(viii) Effect of Number of Repetitions

While determining PCN, one of the major input is the design life of pavement. This life is defined by the number of full load operations. If the aircraft of higher ACN is to be permitted, the life of pavement shall reduce hyperbolically. The relation to derive the modified life is given by :

$$N_{ops} = N_{design} \cdot e^{-9.65\left(\frac{ACN}{PCN} - 1\right)}$$

The relation is also utilised to assess the effect of the number of movement in terms of standard ACN (equal to PCN) at an airport where a mix of aircraft are operating. Thus, if there are few operations of aircraft of higher ACN, the PCN can be upgraded to match this heaviest aircraft accepting penalty in terms of damage to the pavement. In such a case, the pavement has to be frequently inspected for signs of damage and ACN reviewed.

(ix) Thickness of Surface

While deciding the PCN value, the effect of the surfacing thickness be kept in view. It is presumed that aircraft of higher ACN have higher tyre pressure too (though not necessarily). This caused excessive deformation in the unbound base. FAA recommends as a minimum asphaltic thickness of 8 cm for tyre pressure upto 9.45 kg/cm^2 (135 psi) and 10 cm for higher tyre pressure. Thickness is further increased by 25% where the traffic is channelised. Lesser thicknesses shall require consequent reduction in tyre pressure and PCN value.

10.4.3.2 Techniques and trends in structural evaluation : The various techniques available are :

(i) Dynamic Deflection Device

This device developed in USA is capable of applying a variable load upto 4500 kg with a frequency range of 0.1 Hz to 20 Hz. The dynamic loading can be sinusoidal, haversine, triangular or square wave form. This system is microprocessor-based and uses a hydraulic actuator which acts against pavement surface under operator defined (frequency, magnitude and waveform) static and dynamic loadings.

The equipment consists of two parts, namely deflection and control system. The lifts, loading system, LVDT reference beam for deflection measurements and related hydraulic form the part of deflection system and are housed in the trailer, whereas the control system along with various signal conditioners are put in the front van.

From the deflections measured at different radial distances, a number of deflection basin/profile parameters can be obtained. These are : maximum deflection, surface curvature index (SCI); base curvature index (BCI), spreadability and radius of curvature etc.

The qualitative condition of surface, base and subgrade can be obtained from these parameters. Dynamic stiffness modulus can be found by using this equipment. From the deflection basin profile parameters, layer moduli and critical strains can also be computed.

(ii) La Croix Deflectograph

La Croix Deflectograph, developed and extensively used in France is suitable for routine evaluation of large sections. Deflection obtained with dynamic measuring units (such as FWD and steady state vibration devices) are correlated to Benkelman beam deflections for overlay design purposes.

This system consists of a dual-axle, multi-wheel truck with deflection measuring beam (one for each dual wheel set) connected to a frame at the lower side, and displacement and recording devices. The frame with the two beams is lowered onto the road surface in front of the oncoming dual wheels and the deflection measurements are continued to be recorded until the wheels pass the beam tip. The system can be set up to record the deflection basins as the vehicle approaches the beams. Load on the rear axles can be varied from 5442 to 11791 kg. The vehicle can move at a speed of 2 to 4 kmph while collecting data at 3.5 to 6 m intervals. The data (operator defined) are automatically collected and analysed.

(iii) Falling Weight Deflectometer

This equipment has been procured by CRRI and Army HQ.

'irst developed in France and presently commercially available Denmark and USA, belongs to the class of light vibrators .d measures dynamic deflection. It is mounted on a small trailer which is towed by an automobile. The equipment consists of a falling mass weighing 150 kg, and develops a maximum force of 60 kN and pulse width of 28 ms when dropped from a height of 400 mm on a foot plate of diameter 300 mm, resting on the pavement. The magnitude of force and duration of impulse on the pavement can be controlled by changing the height of drop and rate of deceleration.

The deflection of the pavement is measured by velocity transducers (geophones) which have operating frequencies 1 to 300 Hz, one in the centre of the loaded area and one or two at a fixed distance from the load. The trailer accommodates the power supply: recording instruments and a remote control system, all housed in the towing vehicle.

The maximum values of deflections are digitized and stored on a tape recorder data unit or can be tabulated by a printer. The location of the points at which deflections are measured is recorded both longitudinally and transversely (in or between the wheel paths or any other position) with respect to the geometry of the road. A desk top calculator facilitates at the introduction of temperature data and is used to calculate deflection ratios, mean values, variances and other statistical data. A chart recorder is used to display the reading and calculated results.

The moduli of the pavement layers are calculated from the deflection profile/basin measured during the tests. The Method of Equivalent Thickness (MET) is used along with the Boussinesq's equations to calculate the deflections and an iterative procedure is used to determine those modulii that will result in the same deflections as measured. These modulii are adjusted for temperature, seasonal influences and pavement condition. Using the calculated modulii, it is now possible to evaluate stresses and strains in the subgrade, asphalt or concrete layers and in semi-rigid materials.

The primary criteria governing residual life and required overlay thickness have been found as :

— Vertical compressive strees or strain at the top of the subgrade

— horizontal tensile strain at the bottom of bituminous surface in addition to functional criteria (loss in Pavement Serviceability Rating)

— horizontal tensile stress or strain in cementitious base

— horizontal tensile stress in concrete layer. Strain criterion is only valid for the centre loading case, it cannot be used at joints or corners.

The procedure of evaluation and design of pavement consists basically of comparing stress or strain levels in a pavement under various traffic loads to the criteria for permissible stress or strain in the various layers. The relation between the vertical strain at the top of the subgrade and the number of strain repetitions to cause cracking under the standard design load has been obtained by analysing the data from various road tests. Similarly, the relation between the vertical strain at the bottom of the bituminous layer and the number of strain repetitions to cause cracking under the standard design load has been obtained by analysing the data from various road tests and can be based on any of various relationship recommended worldwide. The procedures are similar when dealing with rigid or semi-rigid layers. General expressions for some of these relationships are presented herein as follows.

(i) Subgrade and asphalt strain criteria

$$\epsilon = A.N^B \quad (10\ 1)$$

(ii) Subgrade stress criteria

$$\epsilon = C.N^D\,(E/E_o)^P \quad (10\ 2)$$

(iii) Concrete stress criteria

$$N = Q.\,(Z_p/Z)^R, \text{ where} \quad (10.3)$$

$$Z_p = S.\,(E/E_o)^T \quad (10.4)$$

Where, ϵ = strain

N = number of loads to cause cracking at a strain level ϵ,

E = modulus of the material considered

E_o = a reference modulus

Z_p = flexural strength for static loading

Z = dynamic stress

A, B, C, D, P, Q, R, S and T are constants.

Presentation of Results

(i) Determination of PCN Value : The programmes are run for three different ESWLs and the remaining life of the pavement is found out for each case. Since each point of the runway has different remaining life for the same load, the average value of the remaining lives of all the test points is found out. This value substracted by one standard deviation is then taken as the representative remaining life of the pavement. A graph is then plotted on a semi-log paper between the ESWLs and the corresponding remaining lives as shown in Figure 10.10. The ESWL corresponding to a design life of 10 years is read from this graph. Twice the ESWL so obtained (in kg) divided by 1000 gives the PCN of the runway.

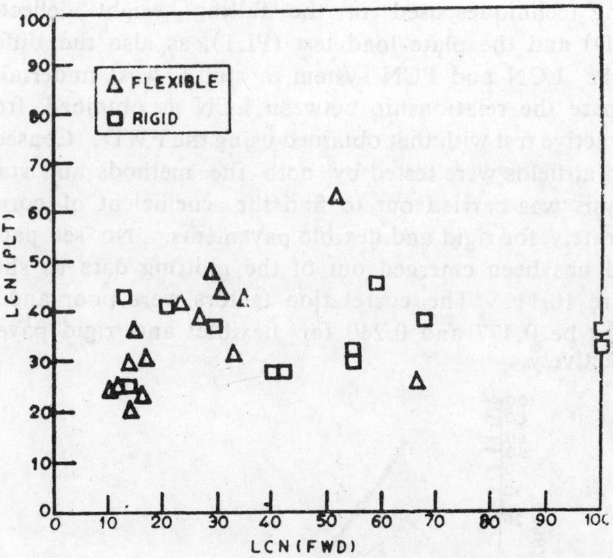

Figure 10.10 Relationship between LCN by FWD and PLT

(ii) Residual life : Once the current modulii of the distinct pavement layers are known, the residual pavement life can be calculated with the information on the traffic history of the pavement. Using a simple equivalence relationship, it is possible to convert the repetitive effect of any aircraft wheel load to that of the design aircraft wheel load.

(*iii*) *Overlay* : The programme determines the needed thickness of a given overlay material for a given design period to reduce the stresses or strains to the permissible level or to obtain the desired functional condition during the design life of the facility.

(*iv*) *Correlation between LCNs* : The FWD test system has been acquired with a view to replacing the conventional plate load system. The runways in India are generally classified by the LCN system. As discussed earlier, FWD primarily evaluates residual life and overlay thickness. PCN is ascertained through the ESWL corresponding to the design life. The same ESWL can be used approximately to estimate the LCN of the pavement assuming a standard tyre pressure of 1.25 MPa.

Without loosing sight of the fundamental difference in the testing techniques used in the falling weight deflectometer (FWD) and the plate load test (PLT), as also the differences in the LCN and PCN system, a study was undertaken to compare the relationship between LCN as obtained from the destructive test with that obtained using the FWD. Consequently seven airfields were tested by both the methods and statistical analysis was carried out to find the coefficient of correlation separately for rigid and flexible pavements. No set pattern or trend has been emerged out of the plotting data as shown in Figure 10.11. The correlation factors were poor and turned out to be 0.477 and 0.230 for flexible and rigid pavements, respectively.

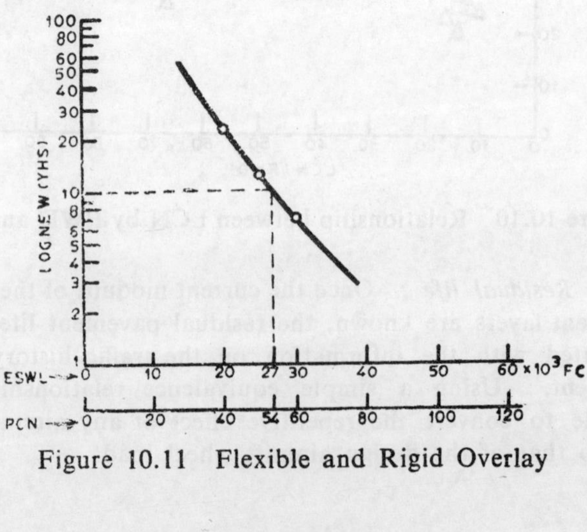

Figure 10.11 Flexible and Rigid Overlay

This however does not indicate that the FWD technique is unreliable or erratic. What it does confirm is that the LCN and PCN systems are not totally compatible and any attempt to back estimate LCN through assessment of PCN can be quite misleading. Moreover, it must be appreciated that differences in the test method, approach used for analysis, adjustments applied for environmental parameters, fatigue and failure criteria will all effect the end result. In short, PLT and the LCN system as compared to FWD and the PCN system are two different approaches altogether and any attempt to seize one against the other would not only mislead but perhaps confuse too.

Sensitivity analysis

The thickness of the pavement layers is one of the important dimensional inputs used in the analysis. This parameter may not always be known correctly at particular test point. It was therefore of interest to study the variation in residual life and overlay thickness needed with changes in layer thickness.

Table 10.1 shows the results of an analysis done for a flexible overlay on rigid pavement. The test section chosen consisted of three layers viz subgrade, rigid layer and the flexible overlay. The thickness of the overlay was varied by + 10, + 20, − 10 and − 20 percents of the original thickness. The analysis is for a constant set of deflection measurement obtained at a particular test location. Data from two test locations have been used in the analysis.

It is seen that the modulii of the overlay and the subgrade are unchanged whereas the modulus of the concrete changes in the same proportion in which thickness varied from the original thickness. For all practical purposes, remaining life is more or less constant. The trend in the overlay thickness required is more or less consistent and reasonable especially when the thickness required is significant.

Table 10.2 gives the results of analysis done for test section consisting of two layers viz. subgrade, and the flexible pavement. The thickness of the flexible layer varied by + 10, + 15, + 20, − 10, − 15, and − 20 percents of thickness. The analysis is for a constant set of deflection measurements obtained at a particular test location. Data from three test locations have been used in the analysis.

Table 10.1 Sensitivity Analysis for Rigid Pavement with Flexible Overlay

	Original		+ 10% (AC)		+ 20% (AC)		− 10% (AC)		− 20% (AC)	
Thickness (mm) AC	115		126.5		138		103.5		92	
PCC	152		152		152		152		152	
Points on runway	1	2	1	2	1	2	1	2	1	2
E1 (MPa)	3212	3212	3212	3212	3212	3212	3212	3212	3212	3212
E2 (MPa)	5695	8731	4983	7935	4475	7032	6381	9859	7215	10791
EM (MPa)	158	172	158	172	158	172	158	172	158	172
Remaining life (Yrs)	2.663	7.648	2.494	7.994	2.436	7.665	2.637	7.559	2.669	7.007
Needed overlay (mm)	86	17	91	15	94	17	85	17	83	22

AC = Asphaltic Concrete and PCC = Plain Cement Concrete

Table 10.2 Sensitivity Analysis for Flexible Pavement

Thickness	Original			+ 10% (220mm)			+ 15% (230mm)			+ 20% (540mm)			-10% (180mm)			-15% (170mm)			-20% (160mm)		
Points on	1	2	3	1	2	3	1	2	3	1	2	3	1	2	3	1	2	3	1	2	3
Modulus (of Asphat layer) EI (MPa)	3163	3812	3959	2554	3070	3084	2324	2788	2656	2130	2550	2481	3565	3917	3785	4101	3917	4398	4781	5273	5177
Modulus (of Sub. grade layer) EN (MPa)	118	101	64	118	101	64	118	101	64	118	101	64	130	120	80	130	120	80	130	120	80
Remaining Life (Yrs)	1.4	1.8	0.9	1.4	1.7	0.7	1.4	1.7	0.7	1.4	1.7	0.7	1.3	1.4	0.6	1.4	1.5	0.6	1.5	1.6	0.7
Needed Overlay (mm)	76	68	101	80	72	111	81	73	116	82	74	218	76	73	110	73	70	105	69	66	99

It is seen that the modulus of the subgrade is unchanged whereas the modulus of flexible layer generally changess in the same proportion in which thickness varied from the original thickness. For all practical purposes remaining life is more or less constant. The trend in the overlay thickness required is constant and reasonable.

General Conclusion

The analytical-empirical (or mechanistic) method is a powerful tool which is gaining widespread acceptance for pavement design and evaluation. Internationally, several countries are using the method either as a standard or on a preliminary basis. Numerous airport and highway agencies as also private consultants are using the method. It is obvious that the major reason for increased practical use of the mechanistic method is the rapid development of the FWD as also the supporting software.

There are certain difficulties and uncertainties associated with the mechanistic method. Improvement and / or verifications are, no doubt, needed for the analytical and, particularly for the empirical parts of the method. However, it is clear that predicting pavement response on the basis of a sound, fundamental approach using FWD would probably result in more reliable estimate than any other current methodology. Based on the preliminary study and initial experience gained through actual testing and analysis of a number of airfield, it appears that there is good reason to adopt the FWD system as the mechanistic method for design and evaluation of pavement structures.

(iv) Surface Wave Propagation Technique

Surface Wave Propagation technique is a low force vibrator (60 kg weight) with a very wide frequency range (5c/s to 20,000 c/s) having two sub-assemblies : one to generate vibrations and the other to monitor wave propagation. The equipment along with the power generator is fitted into a van.

Vibration imparted by the vibrator on the pavement surface lead to the generation of elastic wave which can be picked-up at increasing radial distances by a pick-up device. Phase meter is fed with two waves : One picked-up wave through a selective amplifier tuned to the working frequency and the other directly from the oscillator (feeding also to the vibrator). Phase difference between these two waves is obtained as the pick-up is moved radially away from the vibrator. From the phase curve, a plot between cumulative phase difference and radial distance wave length is obtained. At the same location, series of measurements are made with varying frequencies. High frequencies are needed for studying top layers.

The calculated phase velocities and the corresponding wavelengths plot provide phase velocities pertaining to individual layers. Dynamic modulus (Edyn.) for the material in a layer is then computed using a standard equation. This technique provides a very convenient and expeditious means for qualitative idea of variations in composition, structural state etc. of the pavement layers. It is also possible to estimate thicknesses of layers.

(v) Dynamic Loading System

The Dynamic Loading System developed by IAAI measures compactability of airport pavements and their strength to prevent pre-mature failures of airfield pavements. The mathematical model derived by IAAI helps to calculate stresses and strains in each layer of the pavement. The machine fabricated by IAAI engineers simulates the vibration and force created by B-747 type aircraft to determine in-situ properties of pavement layers.

(vi) Heavy Weight Deflectometer

(a) General

Heavy Weight Deflectometer (HWD) is a most advanced equipment for evaluation of airfield pavement where heavy and heavier planes are being introduced almost every day. Frequent take off and landing of transport plances does not permit cumburesome and time consuming practice of pavement evaluation. HWD is an upgrade version of Falling Weight Deflectometer (FWD) is used for non destructive testing of airfield pavements. In India, Rail India Technical & Economic Services (RITES) New Delhi has procured this equipment.

The Heavy Weight Deflectometer is a trailor born equipment can be operated by a single operator sitting in towing vechicle using computer. The equipment can perform 40 to 60 test per hour. Other features of the equipment are :

(i) Deflection measurements — By transducers using one at the centre and six on raise lower bar.

(ii) Load measurement — By load cell at the centre of plate.

(iii) Load — Pulse load 30 to 240 kN

(iv) Load pulse — 25 to 30 micro secs duration

Figure 10.12 shows the schematic diagram of Heavy Weight Deflectometer.

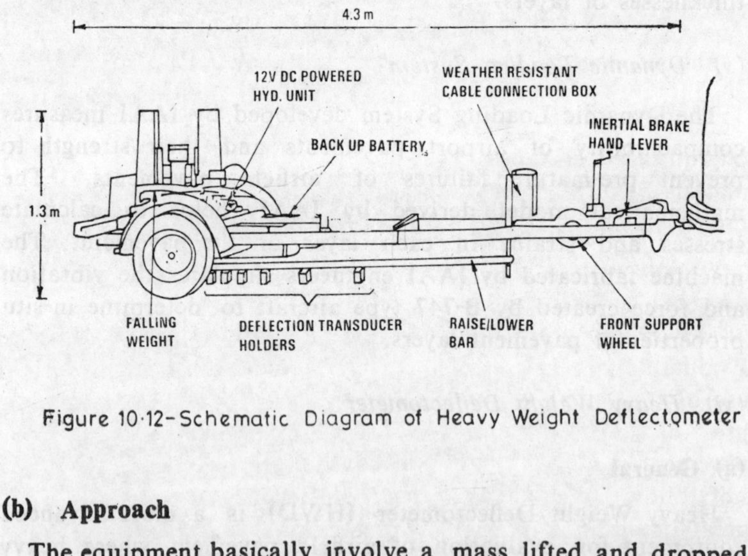

Figure 10·12–Schematic Diagram of Heavy Weight Deflectometer

(b) Approach

The equipment basically involve a mass lifted and dropped from a predetermined height and transmits an inpulsed load to the pavement surface through a spring shock system. The equipment is capable of simulating exact traffic conditions in terms of time and load. The load impulse achieved with this equipment is half sine shaped 25 to 30 micro seconds in duration which is similar to the load pulse generated by moving aircraft wheel. The magnitude of the load is adjusted in a range of 30 to 240 Kilo Newton according to the traffic condition required to be simulated by adjusting mass and drop height. The response of the pavement is noted through seven seismic deflection transducers placed at the centre of loading plate and at six respective locations from the centre of loading plate. These deflection data and deflection basin is interpreted through a microprocessor and stored in computer for further analysis.

The runway is tested along the wheel path generally followed by aircraft. Portion of runway where traffic does not pass generally and few test points of distressed area to get a fairly close picture of pavement behaviour against load weathering. The interval of test points are decided on the basis of condition of pavement. Rigid pavements are tested at slab centre, corner and edges.

(c) Pavement design model

The pavement structures are generally treated as linearly elastic three layered system in which the materials are characterised by certain basic properties such as Young's modulus of elasticity (E) and poisson's ratio (u). The materials are assumed to be homogeneous and isotropic and the layers have horizontally infinite dimensions.

Heavy Weight Deflectometer is supported with specially designed computer program called ELMOD (i.e. Evaluation of Layer Modulii and Overlay Design) and ELCON (i.e. Evaluation of Concrete Pavements). These programs make use of the above assumptions. The program also makes use of correction factors for non-linear behaviour of pavement materials are not behaved linearly elastic and does not follow Hook's law. The non-linearity of subgrade is of great importance in pavement analysis as it contributes 60 to 80 percent of overall deflection. The program is designed to take this non-linear behaviour into consideration. The deflection basin is examined by calculating surface modulus which is weighted mean modulus of half space calculated using Boussineq's equation to find out non-linearity/ abnormality in deflection basin.

$$Eo\ (o) = 2 * (1 - \mu) * 60 * a/d\ (o) \quad (10.5)$$

$$Eo\ (r) = (1 - \mu) * 60 * a/r{*}d\ (r) \quad (10.6)$$

(d) Analysis

(i) Input Data are – Deflection data (recorded in the field), climate, traffic and layer thicknesses.

(ii) Using ELMOD/ELCON Computer Programs, the modulus of plasticity is calculated making use of deflection data by reiterative process. Modulus of elasticity thus obtained are corrected for seasonal variation i.e. for temperature and moisture. The seasonal corrections can be applied upto twelve seasons. The correction factors are adopted on the basis of information collected during field investigation. Temperature changes ritically affects the asphaltic layer. The stiffness of asphalt is greately influenced by variation in temperature and affects of critical horizontal strain occred at the bottom of asphalt layer. The modulii of unbound materials are affected by moisture changes.

(iii) Calculation of stresses and strains — The Stresses and strains at every interface is calculated for corrected modulus of elasticity for each season. The program makes use of method of equivalent thickness (Odemarks assumption with Boussinesq's equation) using radius of loaded area and contact pressure.

For each season, the stresses or strains for calculated at critical position. The critical position depends on wheel configuration. The position of critical stress or strain is shown in Figure 10.13 for a dual wheel configuration.

For calculation of stresses and strains for rigid pavements, slab centre and joint conditions are analysed making use of Westergaards equation. After having calculated stresses and strains, the damage in each season is summed using Miner's law & the present condition of pavement. The residual life can be calculated using empirical relationship as follows :

Permissible stress or strain

$$= K \left(\frac{N}{10^6} \right) \left(-\frac{1}{a} \right) \left(\frac{E}{E_1} \right)^b \qquad (10.7)$$

N = Number of load repetitions

E = Moduls of elasticity of material

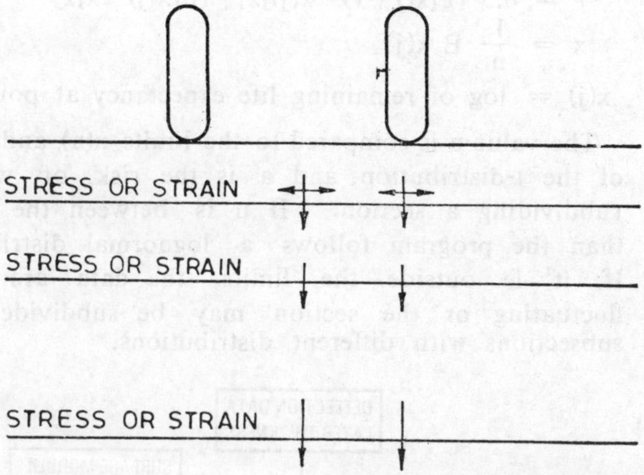

Figure 10.13 Possible Positions of Critical Stresses or Strains Under a Dual Wheel Load

E1 = Reference moduls

K. a & b are constants/functions related to environmental conditions

After the residual life is calculated, overlay can be designed by adding in layer thickness of selected specifications and repeating the whole excercise. Figure 10.14 shows the flow chart of the use of program ELMOD/ELCON. A typical computer output of program ELMOD and ELCON is given in Table 10.3 and 10.4 respectively.

A special program may be used to automoatically divide a given length of road into structurally uniform subsections, using statistical criteria. The program has a routine, that test the distribution of remaining life expectancies, and divides into subsections with log-normal distributions, with a certain confidence level. This program is especially useful in connection with a Pavement Management System.

The program uses the statistic :

$$u = (1-r)\left[\frac{(n-1)}{(n-2)}\right]^{0\cdot 5} \qquad (10.8)$$

Where,

N = number of observations

$$r = 0.5 \{E[x(j+1)-x(j)]2\} / \{E[x(j)-x]2\}$$

$$x = \frac{1}{n} E\ x(j)$$

$x(j)$ = log of remaining life expectancy at point j.

The value u is compared to the limits u(a) and u(1/a) of the t-distribution, and a is the risk of wrongly subdividing a section. If u is between the limits, than the program follows a lognormal distribution. If it is outside the limits, the data are either fluctuating or the section may be subdivided into subsections with different distributions.

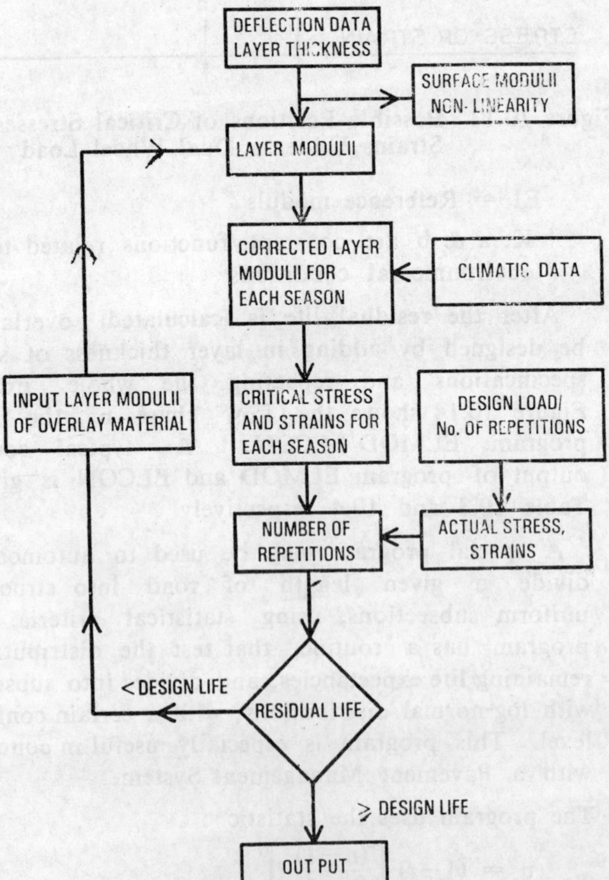

Figure 10.14 Flow Chart for Determination of Residual Life Using ELMOD / ELCON

Table 10.3 Typical ELMOD output

Station	Residual Life	Layer	Mode	Overlay (mm)
0.000	1	2	func	74.0
0.050	1	2	func	66.0
0.100	2	2	func	57.0
0.150	2	2	func	57.0
0.200	2	3	func	83.0
0.250	1	2	func	86.0
0.300	1	2	func	92.0
0.350	1	3	func	86.0
0.400	1	2	func	101.0
0.450	1	2	func	93.0
0.500	1	2	func	101.0
0.550	1	2	func	86.0
0.600	5	2	func	24.0
0.650	1	2	func	74.0
0.700	1	3	func	126.0
0.750	1	3	func	99.0
0.800	0	2	func	117.0
0.850	0	2	func	103.0
0.900	1	2	func	73.0
0.950	2	2	func	47.0
1.000	4	2	func	26.0
1.050	1	2	func	59.0

Number of calculated points : 22

Mean	1.409 yrs.	78.6 mm
Std. Deviation	1.141 yrs.	26.3 mm

Table 10.4

Typical ELCON Output

(Moduli as measured, residual life and needed overlay)

Station	E1(MPa)	E2(MPa)	CO	N	Life (yrs)	Overlay Thickness (mm)
4.100	19943	212	209	−0.10	3.2	109.0
5.100	19246	258	258	−0.02	3.7	91.0
6.100	14014	178	177	−0.11	1.3	182.0
7.100	17303	265	271	−0.18	3.2	105.0
8.100	19037	244	244	−0.02	3.4	99.0
9.100	19702	231	231	+0.00	3.4	100.0
10.024	19702	231	0	+0.00	0.3	212.0
10.100	16388	254	256	−0.06	2.7	117.0
11.100	21086	324	327	−0.07	5.8	51.0
12.100	16001	317	320	−0.02	3.4	95.0
13.100	22182	210	210	+0.00	3.8	92.0
14.100	38889	158	138	+0.00	8.0	22.0
15.100	12588	183	186	−0.27	1.1	194.0
16.100	20663	324	327	−0.02	5.6	54.0
17.100	22633	318	318	−0.01	6.4	41.0
18.100	21545	295	296	−0.09	3.4	57.0
19.100	12280	210	217	−0.18	1.3	181.0
20.100	13826	282	283	−0.03	4.0	85.0
21.100	33821	278	278	+0.00	10.8	0.0
22.100	11666	242	243	−0.01	1.4	171.0
23 100	23161	227	227	+0.00	4.5	76.0
24.100	21638	192	192	+0.00	3.3	106.0
25.100	19313	155	155	+0.00	2.1	150.0
26.100	26777	184	184	+0.00	4.7	75.0

Number of observations = 24

(i) Mean	3.78 yrs	99.79 mm
(ii) Std. Deviation	2.33 yrs	58.39 mm

The output from the ELMOD program may also be stored on a disk for automatic use in connection with a "Pavement Management System".

(e) Evaluation of Pavement Classification Number (ELPCN)

In 1977, the ICAO established a study group to develop a standard method of evaluating airfield pavements which internationally acceptable. Thus, the Aircraft Classification Number (ACN) and Pavement Classification Number (PCN) was developed and accepted internationally. The ACN and PCN are defined as

ACN — A number which expresses the relative structural effect of an aircraft on different type of pavements for specified standard subgrade strength in terms of standard single wheel load.

PCN — A number which expresses the relative load carrying capacity of a pavement in terms of a standard single wheel load.

The thickness requirement is determined by

$$t = \left[\frac{DSWL)}{C_1} CBR - \frac{DSWL}{C_2} PS \right]^{\frac{1}{2}} \qquad (10.9)$$

where,

t = Reference thickness (in cm)

DSWL = Single wheel load with a tyre pressure of 1.25 MPa

PS = 1.25 MPa

CBR = Standerd subgrade CBR (%)

C_1 = 0.5695

C_2 = 32.035

The Heavy Weight Deflectometer is supplied with a specially developed program called ELPCN which can provide PCN at each test point.

The program first calculates the modulii of each layer as in program ELMOD/ELCON considering effect of non linearity. The seasonal correction is applied to the modulii using Miner's law to add the effect of several seasons. Programme then determines a DSWL with a tyre pressure of 1.25 MPa, will rasult in permissible stresses. Thus, PCN is calculated which is twice the DSWL. Typical computer printout of of program ELPCN is given at Table 10.5.

Table 10.5

Typical ELPCN Output

(Aircraft : 0737-200, Thickness of PCC Layer = 30 cm)

Km	PCN	ACN	CODE
0.100	26	32	R/C/W/T
1.000	31	32	R/C/W/T
1.220	15	30	R/B/W/T
1.240	25	30	R/B/W/T
2.100	25	30	R/B/W/T
2.220	10	32	R/C/W/T
2.240	9	32	R/C/W/T
3.100	23	30	R/B/W/T
3.220	11	32	R/C/W/T
3.240	10	32	R/C/W/T

10.5 STRENGTHENING OF AIRFIELD PAVEMENTS

10.5.1 Objective

In India, most of the Military airfield pavements were constructed during the second world war. Since then the gross weight of the present day aircraft has increased tremendously. Possible improvements in the design characteristics of aircrafts would further increase the design wheel load. Runway and taxiway pavements thus can not be replaced with new sections as and when required, and it is essential that the existing pavements are strengthened by providing additional layers of new pavements over existing pavement sections. The overlying pavement layers are called as overlays. Overlays may also be needed under the circumstances when the existing pavements have successfully completed their useful functioning.

10.5.2 Factors for Design of Overlay

The factors which affect the design of an overlay are listed below :

(i) Supporting capacity of soil subgrade

(ii) Condition of existing pavement

(iii) Modified design wheel loading

Besides these, the type of existing construction and future overlays would also influence the determination of thickness of an overlay.

Figure 10.15 shows the possible combinations of different types of constructions while planning an overlay. Bituminous overlay consists entirely of bituminous concrete or a combination of bituminous concrete and a bituminous penetration macadam. Flexible overlay consists of a combination of high quality base course and a bituminous surface. Rigid overlay consists of a portland cement concrete slabs. The design method for each of these is explained below :

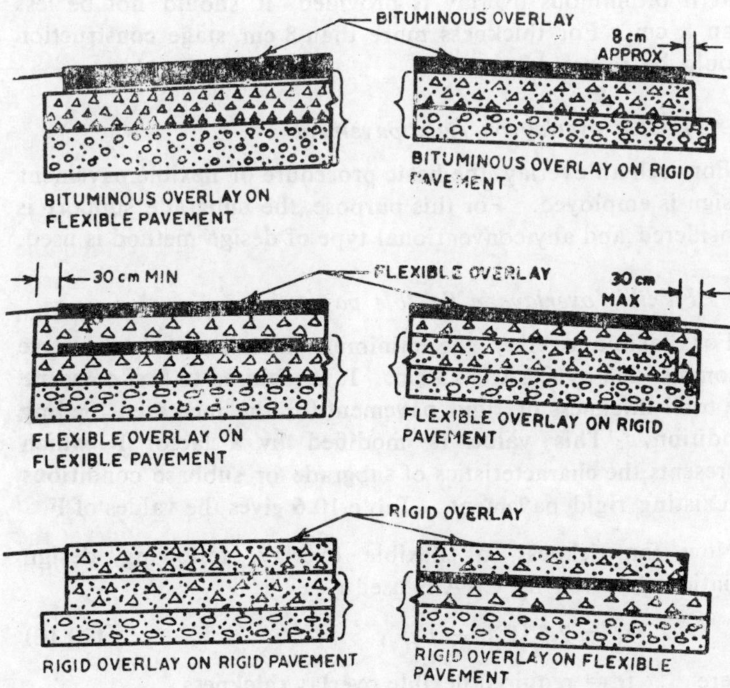

Figure 10.15 Flexible and Rigid Overlay

10.5.3 Overlay Design

For design purposes, overlays can be classified into two major groups :

(i) Flexible overlays, and

(ii) Rigid overlays.

The following determinations are made regardless of the type of overlay is selected :

(a) Soil subgrade type and strength characteristics

(b) Actual thickness of each layer in the existing pavement section.

(a) Design of flexible overlay

These overlays can be provided on any of the two types of existing pavements i.e. flexible or rigid. CAA recommends that if bituminous overlay is provided, it should not be less than 8 cm. For thickness more than 8 cm, stage construction should be resorted.

(i) Flexible overlay on rigid pavement

For such an overlay, the basic procedure of flexible pavement design is employed. For this purpose, the subgrade support is considered and any conventional type of design method is used.

(ii) Flexible overlay on flexible pavement

For flexible overlay the minimum thickness of base course recommended by CAA is 15 cm. It is required to first compute the total thickness of rigid pavement for the increased loading condition. This value is modified by a factor F which represents the characteristics of subgrade or subbase conditions of existing rigid pavement. Tab'e 10.6 gives the values of F.

Now for tickness of flexible overlay, following design equation as given by CAA is used :

$$t_f = 2.5\,(F\,h - h_e) \qquad (10.10)$$

where t_f = required flexible overlay thickness

F = factor for reduction of the thichness h

h = required rigid pavement thickness over existing subbase

h_e = thickness of existing rigid pavement

For bituminous overlay following relationship is used :

$$t_b = \frac{t_f}{1.5}$$

Table 10.6 'F' for Different Subgrade and Subbase

Existing subgrade class	Values of F when subbase is classed below				
	R_a*	R_b	R_c	R_d	R_e
R_a	0.88	—	—	—	—
R_b	0.90	0.80	—	—	—
R_c	0.94	0.90	0.80	—	—
R_d	0.98	0.94	0.90	0.80	—
R_e	1.00	0.98	0.94	0.90	0.80

Example 10.1

An existing runway and taxiway consists of 15 cm of cement concrete slab resting on subgrade. The subgrade soil is grouped as R_b type. It is necessary to strengthen the pavement for supporting ESWL of 26,300 kg. Determine an overlay thickness of bituminous concrete.

Solution

Based on the design procedure discussed earlier, it is found that the required thickness of new pavement sections of rigid type are 24 cm and 30 cm for runway and taxiway locations.

$$h_e = 15 \text{ cm}$$

$$h \text{ for runway} = 24 \text{ cm}$$

*Figures in this column apply where no subbase has been provided.

$$h \text{ for taxiway} = 30 \text{ cm}$$

$$F = 0.90$$

Therefore, t_f for runway $= 2.5\,(0.90 \times 24 - 15) = 16.5$ cm

and t_b for taxiway $= 2.5\,(0.90 \times 30 - 15) = 30$ cm

Therefore, t_h for runway $= \dfrac{16.5}{1.5} = 11$ cm

and t_h for taxiway $= \dfrac{30}{1.5} = 20$ cm

(b) Design of rigid overlay

Similar to the above considerations, rigid overlay can be provided either on existing pavement of rigid type or flexible type.

(i) Rigid Overlay on Flexible Pavement

For designing the rigid overlay over existing flexible pavement, the subgrade reaction modulus i.e. k is obtained for the existing section and is employed in determining the additional pavement thickness by the design method discussed in article 9.4.

(ii) Rigid Overlay on Rigid Pavement

For computing thickness of additional rigid pavement, the following relationship is used

$$h_0 = (h^d - C\, h_e^{\,y})^n \qquad (10.11)$$

where, h_0 = rigid overlay thickness required

h^d = computed rigid pavement thickness based on modified loading and subgrade condition

h_e = existing rigid pavement thickness

C, x, y, and n are empirical values based on the conditions of the existing slab and the overlay construction techniques. Values recommended by U S. Corps of Engineers, FAA and PCA are given in Table 10.7.

Example 10.2

Due to increased traffic, a monolithic thickness of 20 cm of cement concrete pavement is required. Compute the thickness of the rigid overlay when

Table 10.7 Coefficients for Design of Rigid Overlay

Agency	Condition	C	x	y	n
U.S. Corps of Engineers, FAA, PCA	Existing pavement, good	1.00			
	Initial cracked	0.75			
	Badly cracked	0.35			
U.S. Corps of Engineers	Placed directly on existing slab		1.40	1.4	1/1.4
	Levelling course		2.00	2.0	0.5
FAA, PCA	Placed directly on existing slab		1.87	2.0	0.5

(i) existing cement concrete pavement is 10 cm thick and is in good condition.

(ii) existing cement concrete pavement is 10 cm thick but is cracked.

Interface condition may be assumed as partially bonded, US Corps of Engineers method.

Solution

The required thickness of rigid overlays over existing rigid pavements can be determined by the equation

$$h = (h_d^x - C\, h_e^y)^n$$

Now in the present case, L_d = 20 cm, h_e = 10 cm

For U.S. Corps of Engineers method

$$x = 1.4, \quad y = 1.4, \quad n = \frac{1}{1.4}$$

(i) When existing pavement is in good condition

In this case, the coefficient, C = 1.0

The overlay thickness may be given by

$$h = [(20)^{1.4} - (10)^{1.4}]^{1/1.4}$$

$$= [66.5 - 25.0]^{1/1.4} = 14.3 \text{ cm}$$

Thus design thickness of the overlay is 15 cm

(ii) When existing pavement is badly cracked

In this case, coefficient, C = 0.35

and overlay thickness may be given by

$$h = [(20)^{1.4} - 0.35\,(10)^{1.4}]^{1/1.4}$$

$$= [66.5 - 8.75]^{0.714} = 18 \text{ cm}$$

Thus the design thickness of the overlay is 18 cm.

PROBLEMS

1. Discuss the importance for maintenance and rehabilitation of airfield pavements.
2. Discuss in detail the general causes of pavement failures.
3. Explain in brief how the repairs and resurfacing of runway and emergency repairs on airfield pavement are done ?
4. Discuss in brief the importance of maintenance management system in reference to airfield pavements.
5. Explain in brief the causes of airfield flexible and rigid pavements failures.
6. Explain in detail the rehabilitation measures which are required for flexible airfield pavements.
7. Discuss in brief the various steps to be taken for the effective maintenance and rehabilitation of rigid airfield pavements.
8. Explain the uses of various techniques developed for emergency repairs in India and abroad.
9. Discuss the importance of evaluation of airfield pavements.
10. Explain in brief the basic difference between functional and structural evaluation.
11. Explain the importance of riding quality of pavements with reference to functional evaluation of airfield pavements. Discuss in brief the various equipments needed for measuring riding quality.
12. Explain in brief the different factors which affect the tyre pavement friction.

13. List the measuring skid resistance devices. Explain in brief the merits and demerits of each.
14. How the airfield pavement is classified for the structural evaluation ? Explain the difference between LCN, PCN and ACN.
15. Discuss in brief the difference between the devices for measuring structural evaluation.
16. Explain in detail the use of Falling Weight Deflectometer for the structural evaluation of airfield pavements. How the measured deflection data are interpreted ? Explain in brief how the results are presented ?
17. Explain the importance of Heavy Weight Deflectometer for evaluation of airfield pavement. How The data is analysed to calculate stresses, strains and residual life of pavements.
18. Discuss in brief the importance of strengthening of airfield pavements. Explain the different factors required to be considered for design of overlay.
19. How the different types of overlays are classified ?
20. Explain in brief how the flexible overlay is designed for existing flexible and rigid pavements ?
21. Determine overlay thickness of bituminous concrete for an existing runway and taxiway using the following data :
    (i) Thickness of concrete slab for runway and taxiway = 18 cm
    (ii) The subgrade soil is grouped as Rc type.
    (iii) Pavement is to be strengthened for supporting ESWL of 2700 kg.
22. Discuss in brief how the rigid overlay is designed for existing flexible and rigid pavements ?
23. Due to increased traffic a monolithic thickness of 20 cm of cement concrete pavement is required. Compute the thickness of rigid overlays when
    (i) Existing C.C. pavement is 15 cm thick and is in good condition.
    (ii) existing cement concrete pavement is 15 cm thick but it is cracked.

    Interface condition may be assumed as partially bonded. Use U.S. Corps of Engineers method.

11

TERMINAL AREA AND AIRPORT LAYOUT

11.1 TERMINAL AREA

It is the portion of an airport other than the landing area. It serves as a focal point for activities on the airport. It includes terminal and operational buildings, vehicle parking area. aircraft service hangars etc. The terminal and operational buildings usually house all managerial and operational activities for the aircrafts. Vehicular circulation and parking also require careful study, if congestion and inconvenience to the airport users have to be avoided. The airport entrance or access road from a highway must be located in such a way that it will avoid conflict with airport future development. Vehicle parking facilities should also be designed with a view to accommodate future expansion. The terminal apron is the loading and unloading area for passengers and cargo. Aircraft may also be fueled and parked here. At every airport, provision of hangers for servicing and maintenance of aircrafts is planned. The size of these facilities is determined by the expected type and volume of airport activities.

11.2 BUILDING AND BUILDING AREA

The purpose of airport building is to provide shelter and

space for various surface activities related to the air transportation. As such they are planned for the maximum efficiency, convenience and economy. The extent of the building area in relation to the landing area depends upon the present and future anticipated use of airport. Location of building area with respect to runway and taxiway should provide adequate space for future expansion of all structures. Building setback distances from runways and taxiways as discussed in article 8.5, are provided for safe clearance during manoeuvring of aircrafts under the varying conditions of instrumental and visual operations.

11.2.1 Building Functions

The essential building categories for a commercial airport are : terminal and operational. The size of each category may vary depending upon the scope and type of operations.

Terminal building usually refers to a building mainly, used for passengers, airline and administration facilities. Its layout is such as to offer the enplaning passengers, the convenient and direct access from the vehicle plateform or street side of the building, through the booking and waiting rooms, to the aircraft loading positions on the apron. Deplaning passengers are also provided with a direct route from the aircraft to the baggage claim counter and then to the vehicle plateform.

The operational category includes control tower, weather bureau and other government services related to the aviation. In many cases the terminal building fulfills the function of the operational building as well. The various facilities provided in the airport buildings are as follows :

(i) Passengers and baggage handling counters for booking
(ii) Baggage claim section
(iii) Enquiry counter
(iv) Space for handling and processing mail, express and light cargo
(v) Public telephone booth
(vi) Waiting hall for passengers and visitors
(vii) Toilet facilities

(viii) Restaurants and bars
(ix) First aid room
(x) General store and gift shops
(xi) Space for magazines, news papers, advertisement display etc.
(xii) Office space for airport staff
(xiii) Weather bureau
(xiv) Post office and banking facilities
(xv) Custom control*
(xvi) Passport and health control*
(xvii) Control tower

A typical layout of terminal building with various facilities is shown in Figure 11.1 (a, b, c).

11.2.2 Site Location

The correct placement of the terminal building with respect to the runways and loading aprons result in a more rational approach for the airport development. As the planning of runway proceeds, the requirements of building sities are also kept costantly in view. The location of the runways are finalised with proper designation of adequate building area. The suitability of an area, as a site for terminal building development, is evolved in accordance with the following requirements:

(i) Sufficient area for the first stage of building development with possibility of future expansion
(ii) Sufficient area for roadways
(iii) Adequate area for car parking
(iv) Layout of above items providing functional relationship with each other
(v) Convenient access of the main highway
(vi) Central location with respect to runway
(vii) Proximity and easy installation of utilities, e.g. telephone electricity, water, sewage, etc.

---

* Only for airport providing international services

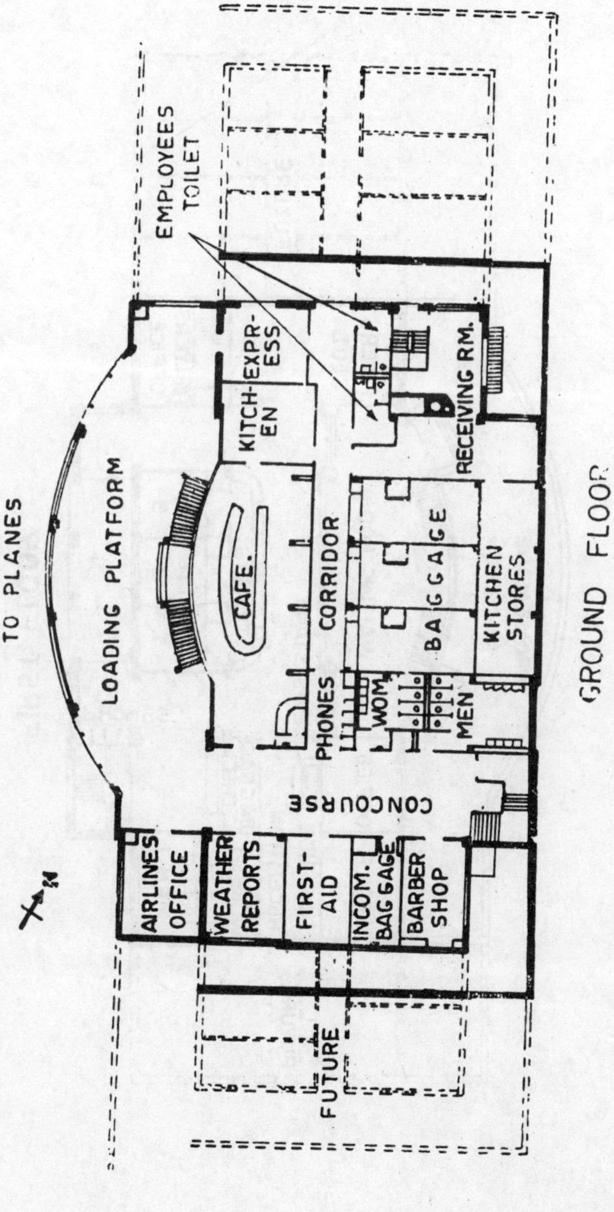

Figure 11.1 a Typical Layout of Airport Terminal Building

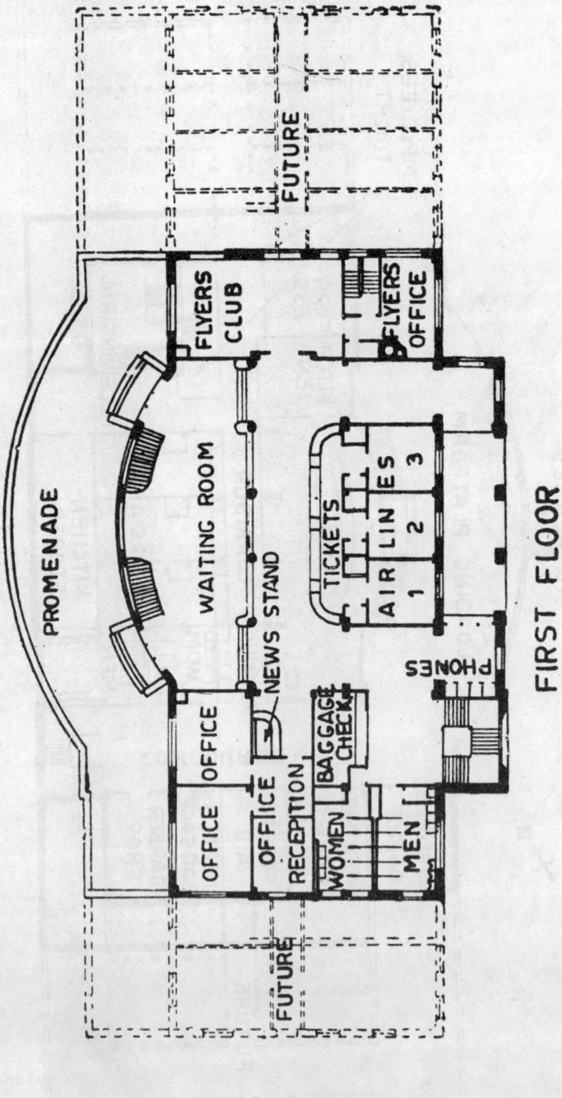

Figure 11.1 b Typical Layout of Airport Terminal Building

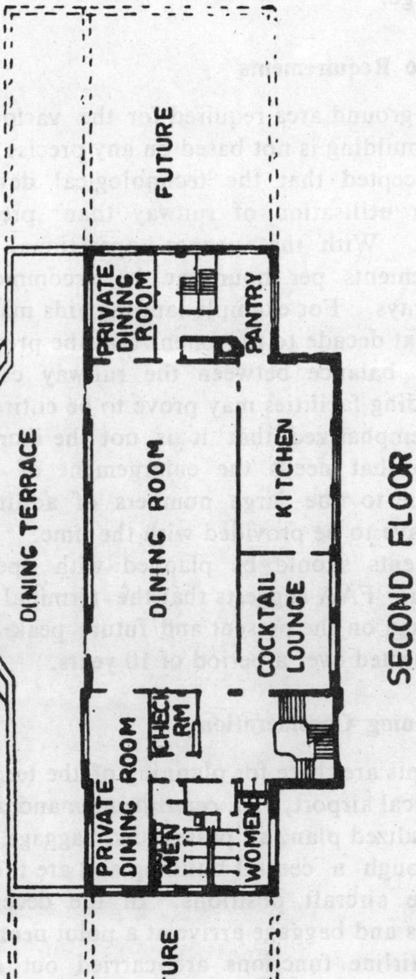

Figure 11.1c Typical Layout of Airport Terminal Building

(viii) Favourable orientation with respect to the topography and prevailing wind etc.

(ix) Good subsoil water characteristics including the natural drainage.

11 2.3 Space Requirements

The actual ground area required for the various functions in the terminal building is not based on any precise science. It is very well accepted that the technological development may allow greater utilisation of runway than predicted at the present time. With the proper operational control, more aircraft movements per hour can be accommodated on the existing runways. For example landing aids may be improved during the next decade to the extent that the present conception of a proper balance between the runway capacity and the terminal building facilities may prove to be entirely insufficient. It may be emphasized that it is not the increase in runway capacity alone that needs the enlargement of original plans. It may be due to the large numbers of additional facilities which may have to be provided with the time. Therefore, the various elements should be planned with open buffer areas between them. FAA suggests that the terminal building area should be based on the present and future peak-hour passenger activities projected over a period of 10 years.

11.2.4. Planning Considerations

Two concepts are there for planning of the terminal buildings for a commerical airport, viz., *centralization* and *decentralization.* In the centralized plan, all passengers, baggage and cargo are funneled through a central building and are then dispersed to the respective aircraft positions. In the decentralised plan, the passengers and baggage arrive at a point near the departing plane. All airline functions are carried out adjacent to the departing plane. The choice of a particular type of plan is governed by the space needed for parking of the aircrafts. When the aircraft parking area is located at an overall walking distance exceeding 180 m, a change from the centralized system becomes necessary. Further, when the number of gate positions (loading area required for each aircraft) required for the individual airliner at one airport exceeds the decentralized plan also becomes operationally uneconomical. At this situation, another shift towards the centralization of each individual airline operation becomes essential. This results in a series of centralized airline spaces, arranged in a decentralized pattern. The concept of an airport from the centralization to decentralization and finally decentralization to centralization is illustrated in Figure 11.2.

In the past, passenger terminal facilities at almost all airport in the world have been in the form of a single central terminal building containing all the required facilities and amenities. This was satisfactory when the number of aeroplanes used and the gate positions required were few; and when terminal building were relatively small and centralizing all services are the cheapest convenient way of providing them. In the last 20 years, the air traffic has increased by many folds with the result that the centralized concept has become inoperative. The decentralized-centralized concept which is also known as *Unit Terminal Principle* is now becoming popular in the design of air terminals throughout the world.

Basically it involves planning the terminal area in such a manner that facilities are provided in units of manageable size providing minimum walking distances from the kerbside to gate positions. As traffic grows and one unit becomes saturated, further units are added as required, without disrupting the use of the existing ones, until the capacity of the total number of units match with the ultimate runway capacity.

There can be a number of variations of such a concept. For example the planner may exclude all or most of the amenities. such as the waiting rooms, restaurants, shopping arcades and administrative offices etc., which are used only by a minority of passengers who have to spend some time at airport while waiting to change planes or in case of long flight delays. Most passengers wish to move quickly and over the shortest possible distance from the kerbside to the gate position and vice-versa.

The various amenities can be centralised separately in a building devoted exclusively to them. It may be located close and connected with the operating units and may serve a single unit or a group of them. The operating or handling units would be purely functional with only such essential amenities

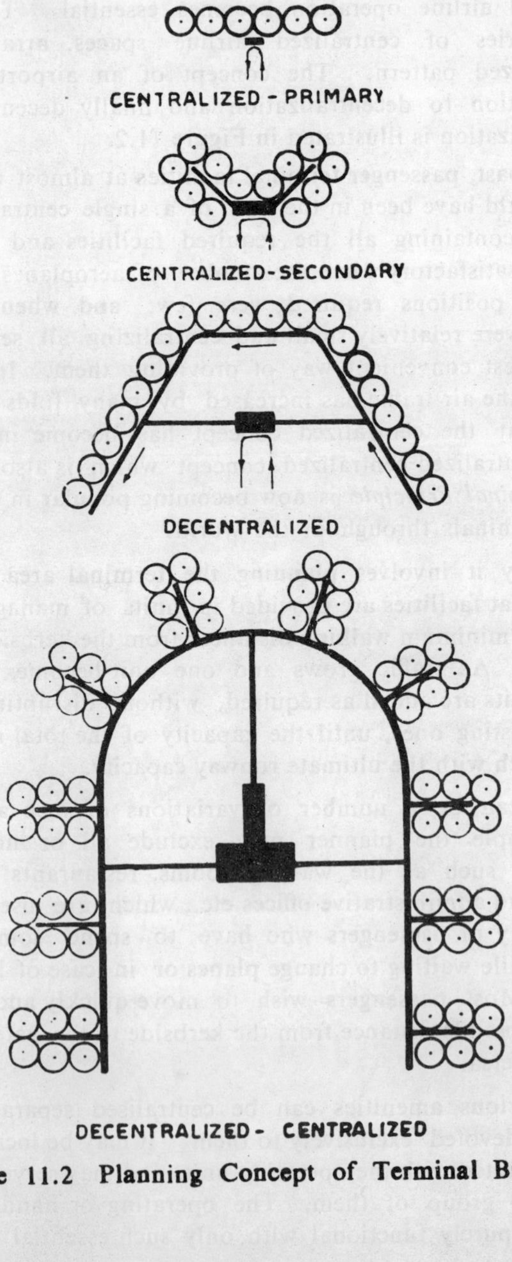

Figure 11.2 Planning Concept of Terminal Building

as book stall, money changer, flight insurance booths and toilets. This concept of a separate building for amenities would lend itself conveniently to the separation of domestic and international traffic. The principle of a separate structure connected with the handling units should be applied wherever possible, leaving space for additional units to meet later expansion needs. The unit terminal principle fits in exceptionally well with the modern concept of parallel runway patterns at large airports.

Finally, the unit terminal concept automatically minimises initial capital expenditure, while ensuring that addition can easily be made later, witout rendering any of the previous expenditure as waste. The International Airport Committee, has recommended that full consideration be given to the adoption of the unit terminal principle for the new terminal facilities to be constructed at the international airports in India.

The following broad principles with respect to the passengers flow should be kept in view while deciding the layout of the terminal building. The passengers and baggage flow are illustrated in Figure 11.3.

(i) Passengers walking distance should not be more than 180 m (600 ft) from the suface transportation to their boarding in the aircraft. All such walks should be completely protected from the weather. There should be no long corridors or stairways. The route should be direct and obvious.

(ii) The airline passengers should not have to carry the baggage or hire the carrying of the baggage by more than 22.5 m (75 ft) from the road transportation to the check-in point.

(iii) Passengers should be able to check-in without waiting.

(iv) The maximum check-in time should not exceed 3 minutes.

(v) On arrival of aircraft, the baggage delivery speed should correspond to the walking time of passengers from the aircraft to the claim or custom area. Thus the first baggage from the flight should arrive in the claim area by the time the first passengers walks in to this area.

(vi) If volume of cargo is large, a separate building for handling and storage of cargo may be required. Trucks should have adequate access to the building. As far as possible, the

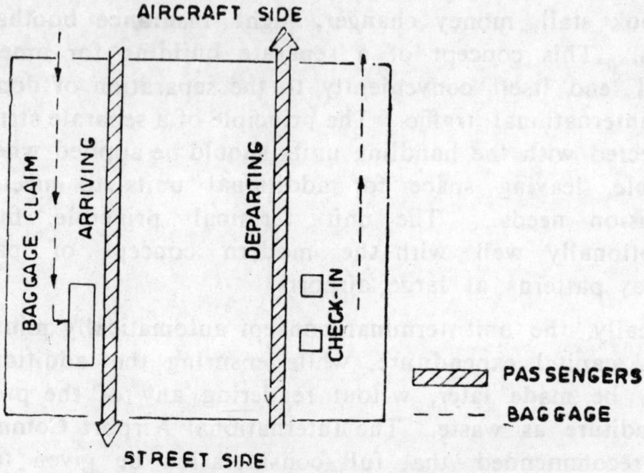

A. FOR DOMESTIC AIRPORT

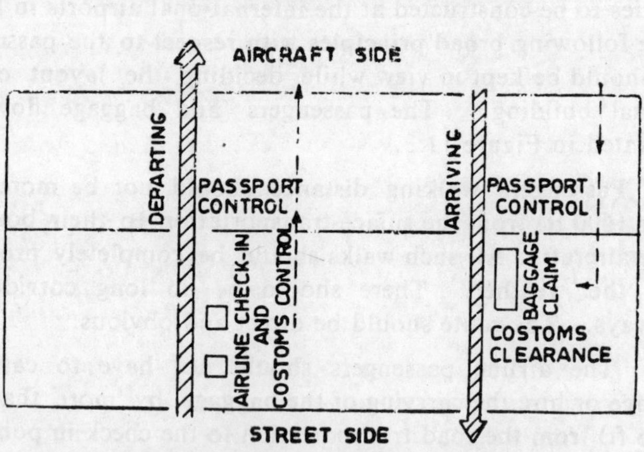

B. FOR INTERNATIONAL AIRPORT

Figure 11.3 Passenger and Baggage Flow Routes

location of the building should be such that an aircraft can be positioned along the side of the building. Further, direct access should be provided to the aircraft apron so as to load very bulky cargo.

11.2.5 Noise Control in Terminal Building

Noise nuisance is associated with air transportation. Noise control is important in those areas within the terminal building from where it is necessary to send information outside, as in the case of control tower. To solve the noise problem, the engineer should consider the noise level outside the building and assign noise criteria within the building which would allow conversation/communication in the various specialised room areas. Such room areas should be so planned and built with the materials that they would minimise the noise transmission through the walls and roofs.

11.3 VEHICULAR CIRCULATION AND PARKING AREA

Since the airport users normally arrive at the airport in automobiles, access roads and parking facilities are of vital importance in the airport design. The circulation of traffic and location of parking lots should be such that access to the terminal building is as convenient as possible.

Access roads are planned to provide fast connections between the airport and the city. One of the present disadvantages of air travel is that the time saved through air travel is lost in ground transportation. Circulation of vehicular traffic within the terminal area is also carefully planned. It is essential to categorize the vehicular traffic to provide the road network satisfying the specific needs of each traffic category. Broadly, the vehicular traffic is classified as passengers, visitors and service personnel.

The area closest to the terminal building entrance may be used for short time parking for enplanning and deplanning passengers. Sufficient space is to be provided for passenger cars, adjacent to the entrance of the terminal building for loading and unloading of passengers without any congestion and delay. Separate parking area is provided for the staff personnel.

For the most efficient airport vehicular circulation and parking system, the following points are considered :

(i) Ease of passenger unloading and loading at the terminal building

(ii) One way traffic wherever possible.

(iii) A minimum of driveway intersection.

(iv) Adequate driveway width to permit overtaking.

(v) Sufficiently and clearly defined parking and circulation routes.

(vi) Well lighted routes for pedestrians and vehicles.

For determining the size and type of parking facility necessary, a traffic survey should be conducted. FAA suggests that the size of the public parking facility should be based on 1.5 to 2 cars for each peak hour passenger. The pattern of parking is dictated by the shape and size of the parking area available. The basic parking patterns usually adopted are shown in Figure 11.4.

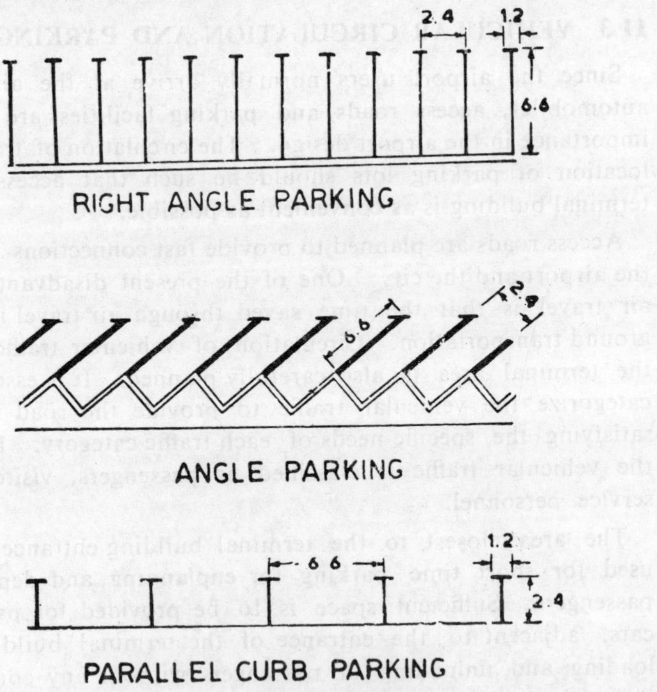

Dimensions are in metres

Figure 11.4 Basic Vehicular Parking Patterns

11.4 APRON

It is a paved area for parking of aircrafts, loading and unloading of passengers and cargo. It is usually located close to the terminal building or hangars. The size of apron depends upon :

(i) Size of loading area required for each type of aircraft. This area is also known as *gate position*.

(ii) Number of gate positions.

(iii) Aircraft parking system.

11.4.1 Size of Gate Position

This depends upon the following factors :

(i) The size of the aircraft and its minimum turning radius.

(ii) The manner in which the aircraft enters and leaves the gate position under its own power or when pushed by a tractor.

(iii) Aircraft parking configuration : Aircraft are parked causing the least interference due to heat, fumes and blast during manoeuvring into and out of the gate position. Jet engines are more critical in this respect than the piston engine aircrafts. The basic parking configurations are illustrated in Figure 11.5. The merit and demerits of each are discussed below :

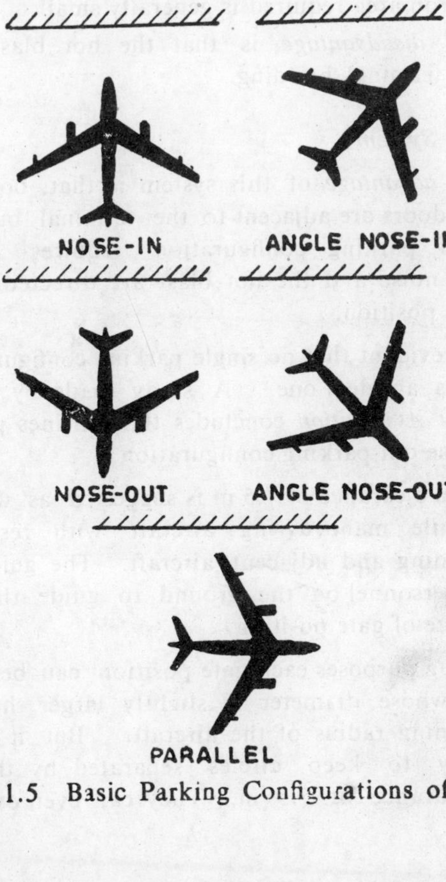

Figure 11.5 Basic Parking Configurations of Aircrafts

(a) Nose-in and angled nose-in

The *advantages* of this configuration are :

Less noise while taxing in because no turning is required.

Hot blast is not directed towards the terminal building.

The aircraft forward door is close to the terminal building.

The *disadvantages* are :

The aircraft rear loading door is far away from terminal building.

(b) Nose-in and angled nose-out

The *advantages* of this configuration are as follows :

Less power is required while manoeuvring the aircraft out of its gate position.

The rear loading door is close to the terminal building.

Overall apron area required is generally small.

The main *disadvantage* is that the hot blast is directed towards the terminal building.

(c) Parallel System

The main *advantage* of this system is that, both, the front and the rear doors are adjacent to the terminal building. But this type of parking configuration requires more space. Further, the noise and the hot blast are directed towards the adjacent gate position.

Thus, it is evident that no single parking configuration can be considered as an ideal one. A study made by *International Air Transport Association* concludes that airlines prefer to use an angled nose-out parking configuration.

A minimum clearance of 7.5 m is suggested as the desirable clearance while manoeuvring aircraft with respect to the terminal building and adjacent aircraft. The guide lines and number of personnel on the ground to guide the pilot also control the size of gate position.

For planning purposes each gate position can be represented by a circle whose diameter is slightly larger than twice the minimum turning radius of the aircraft. But it is however not necessary to keep circles separated by the suggested minimum clearance of 7.5 m. They can even overlap. The position of circles with respect to each depend upon the parking configuration of the aircrafts. One practical way of determining the required size of the gate position is to prepare a model of the aircraft and manoeuvre it in the same manner as the prototype.

11.4.2 Number of Gate Positions

This mainly depends upon the peak hourly aircraft movements and the time during which each aircraft remains in a gate position. This time in also known as the *ramp time* and it varies from few minutes for small aircraft to more than an hour depending on the size. The required number of gate positions can be obtained from relationship,

$$\text{Number of gate positions} = \frac{\text{capacity of runway}}{60 \times 2} \times \text{average gate occupancy time}$$

Here runway capacity can be taken in units of movements per hour. In the above formula, it is assumed that each aircraft occuping a gate position, represents two aircraft movements, viz. landing and take off. But this may not always be so. The aircrafts are very often brought to the gate position from a service hangar. For the design, the gate occupancy time for big aircrafts may be assumed as 60 minutes. For small aircrafts requiring no servicing, it may be assumed as 10 minutes.

11.4.3 Aircraft Parking System

Aircrafts can be grouped adjacent to terminal building in various ways ;

(i) Frontal system

(ii) Open apron system

(iii) Finger system

(iv) Satellite system

These parking systems are illustrated in Figure 11.6 and are discussed below :

(i) Frontal system : It is very simple and economical system. But its use is limited only to small airports requiring few gate positions.

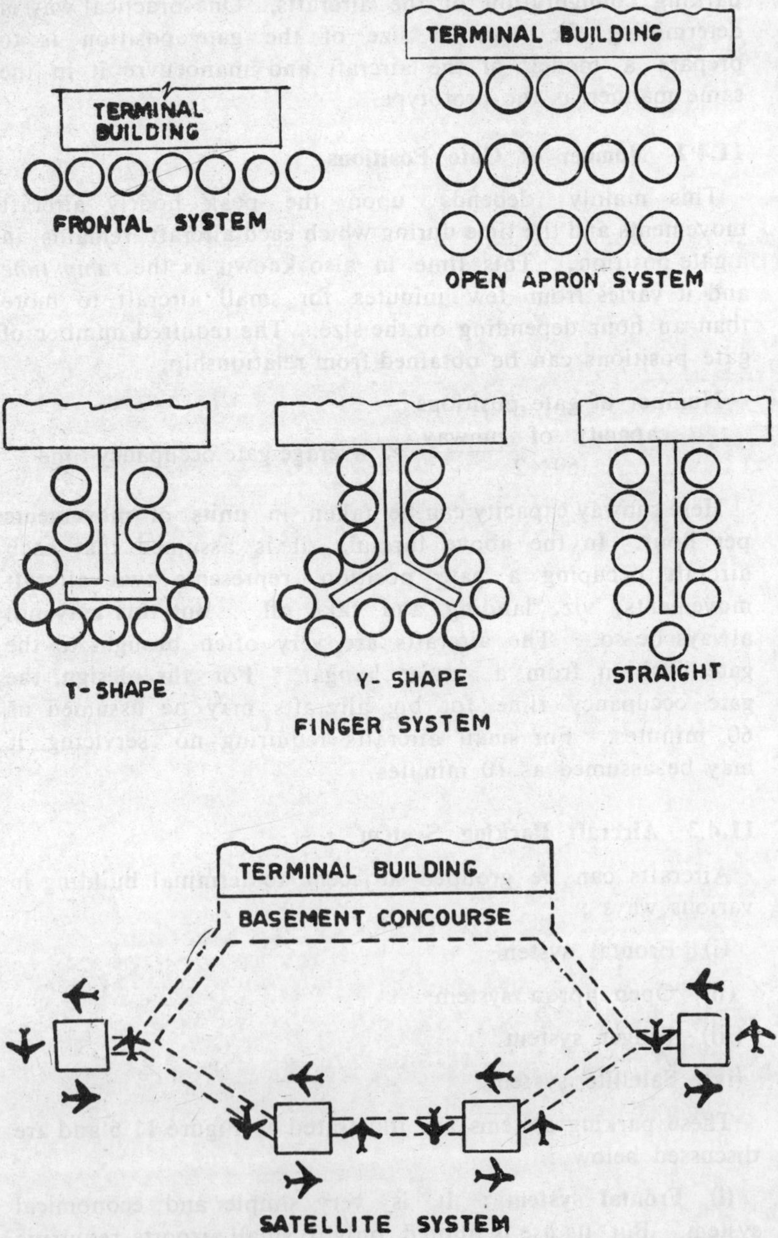

Figure 11.6 Aircraft Parking System

(ii) Open apron system : In this system the aircrafts are parked in rows. If the number of aircrafts is too large, passengers may have to walk long distances or reach the aircrafts parked in the outermost row. They are thus exposed to weather, noise and hot blast of the jet aircrafts. To protect the passengers from such nuisance, some sort of closed vehicle conveyance for the passengers may be essential. The concept of conveying passengers from terminal building to the aircrafts by buses is in use in U.K. and U.S.A. But this is contrary to the objective of apron planning where it is desired to keep the vehicular traffic away to avoid hazards.

(iii) Finger system : Processing of passengers and their baggage is mainly done within the terminal building. But the facilities for passengers, for entering and leaving the aircraft, often require extensions of the terminal building. Such extension is known as *pier finger*. A typical arrangement is shown in Figure 11.7. The pier finger can be fenced open walkway or a closed structure, single or multistoried. It can be a straight, T-shaped or Y-shaped. Its main advantages are :

(a) If enclosed, it provides adequate protection to the passengers from weather, noise, fumes etc. even when they come out of the terminal building.

(b) Future expansion is easier.

(c) All aircrafts remain close to the terminal building.

(d) It permits the installation of a short nose loading bridge or a swinging gang plank for the convenience of the passengers.

(iv) Satellite system : Satellites are small buildings located on the apron. Aircrafts are parked around the satellite buildings which are connected to the main terminal building by underground tunnel. This system is in use at the International airport of Los Angeles. It is advantageous, compared to the pier finger system only when the connections to satellite buildings are through the tunnels. In such an arrangement, the aircrafts are parked near the satellite as shown in Figure 11.6. Less turning is required to manoeuvre the aircraft in and out of the gate position. The disadvantages of this system are : (a) Large construction cost. (b) Passengers have to change the levels several times as they leave the terminal building for boarding the aircraft.

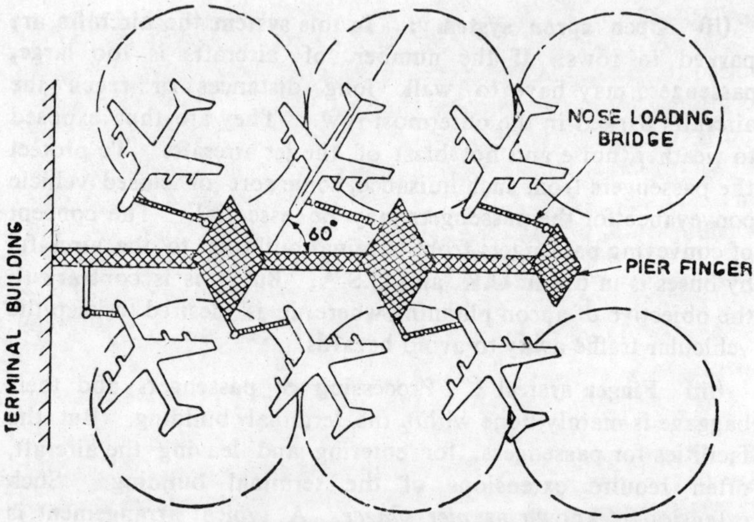

Figure 11.7 Schematic Diagram of Gate Position, Pier Finger and Nose Loading Arrangement

Figure 11.8 Aircraft Turntable used at Washington Airport

11.4.4 Apron Turntable

Apron area is an expensive space since its pavement is designed to carry the heaviest aircraft wheel load and such loads are static in nature. In order to utilise the apron area efficiently, the aircraft should be parked close to each other consistently with the freedom of movement and manoeuvring clearances. Turntables have been successfully used to expedite the parking of aircraft and save parking space. They are bolted to the apron pavement which must be reinforced at such locations. The rotating portion consists of cup shaped plate and is turned by the airplane itself. The ring plate is tapered so as to have its periphery practically flush with the apron surface. The photographs of the aircraft turntable used at Washington airport, U S A., are shown in Figure 11.8 and 11.9.

Figure 11.9 Aircraft Wheel on the Turntable

11.5 HANGAR

The primary function of a hangar is to provide an enclosure for servicing, overhauling and doing repairs of the aircrafts. They are usually constructed of steel frames and covered with galvenised iron sheets. They are also provided with machine shops and stores for spare parts. The size of hangar depends upon the size of aircraft and its turning radius. Adequate lighting inside the hangar is of prime importance. Sometime ceilings of hangar and some portions of its side walls are glazed, which work as light reflectors. Construction of single hangar to store large number of aircrafts may be undesirable both from economy and other considerations viz., difficulty in the manoeuvring of aircrafts, noise nuisance, fumes, fire hazards etc. The number of hangars depends upon the peak hour volume of aircrafts and demand of hangars on rental basis by different airline agencies.

11.5.1 Hangar Site Location

If hangar can be located close to the terminal building and loading aprons, such an arrangement offers many advantages. But is should be ascertained that this arrangement offers adequate scope for future expansion of the terminal as well as the hangar facilities, otherwise the functional efficiency of the entire airport would be impaired. The requirements of suitable hangar site are as follows :

(i) The site should be such that there is a convenient road access to it from the site to the aprons and terminal buildings.

(ii) Proximity to and easy installation of utilities, e.g., electricity, telephone, water supply and sewers etc.

(iii) Reasonable proximity to the loading apron.

(iv) The site should not be along the direction of frequent storms as this is likely to damage the hangar doors etc.

(v) Sufficient area to provide car parking facilities for working personnel.

(vi) Favourable topograph providing good natural drainage.

(vii) Adequate site area for future expansion of hangar facilities.

11.5.2 General Planning Considerations

Storage and service hangars usually occupy a considerable portion of the terminal area. Such hangars are built from designs prepared locally or they can be obtained in units from a company that fabricates stock hangars. The shape of a hangar should be such that it covers the minimum land area and yet provides adequate space for storage and comfortable manoeuvring of aircrafts. For small aircrafts, 'T' shaped hangar is the most desirable and economical design. In this design, the storage space is so arranged that the pilot can manoeuvre

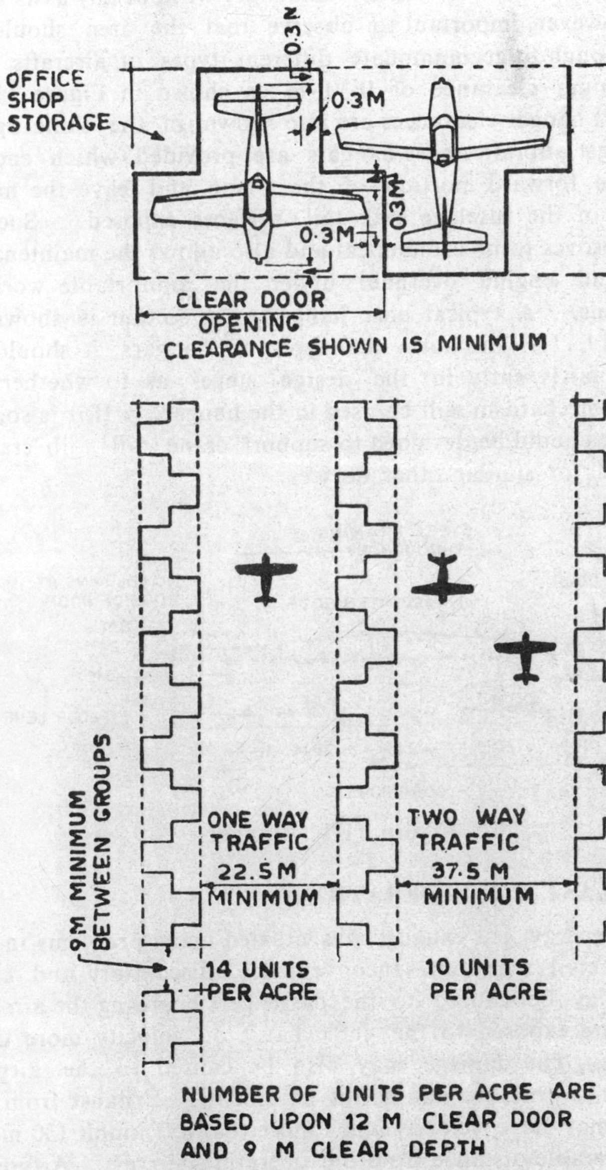

Figure 11.10 Plan Showing TEE Hangar Clearances

the aircrafts in and out of the hangar without any assistance. It is, however, important to observe that the area should be large enough to accommodate different types of aircrafts with a minimum clearance of 0.30 m as shown in Figure 11.10. Grouped hangar clearances are also shown in the same figure. For bigger aircrafts, nose hangars are provided which enclose only the forward portion of the plane and leave the major portion of the fuselage and tail surfaces exposed. Such a design proves to be economical and also allows the maintenance work and engine overhaul under the comfortable working conditions. A typical nose hangar cross-section is shown in Figure 11.11. In both the type of hangars, it should be decided fairly early in the design stages as to whether the housing mechanism will be used in the hangar. If it is so, the structure should be designed to support crane rails, jib cranes, monorails or similar other devices.

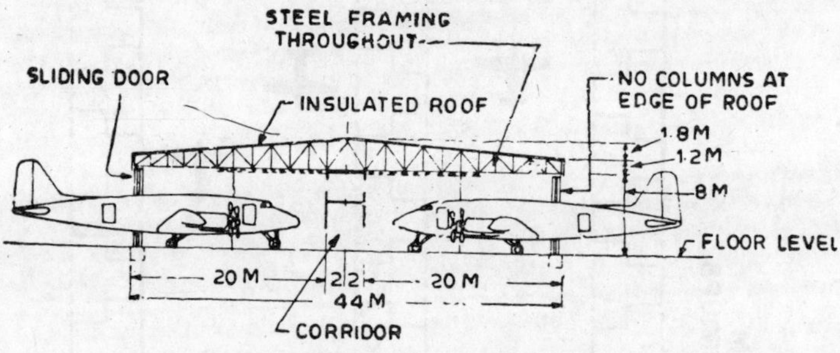

Figure 11.11 Hangar

11.6 BLAST CONSIDERATIONS

High energy jet exhaust has created many problems in the field of civil aviation. Inconvenience, discomfort and even injury may be caused to the passengers boarding the aircraft if they are exposed to the jet exhaust of velocity more than 50 kmph. The damage may also be caused to the airport equipment, structure and to the pavements. Exhaust from jet aircraft may have velocity much more than 50 kmph (30 mph) at considerable distance from the operating aircraft. A typical velocity contour as studied by FAA for jet engine aircraft under no wind condition is illustrated in Figure 11.12. The wake velocity at any distance from the exhaust end of the jet engine can be approximately obtained from the relationship :

$$V_x = \frac{4DV_o}{x} \tag{11.1}$$

where, V_x = wake velocity along the axis of the engine at a distance x from the exhaust end

D = diameter of jet exhaust pipe

V_o = velocity of wake at $x = 0$

x = distance from the engine along the axis at which the wake velocity is to be determined.

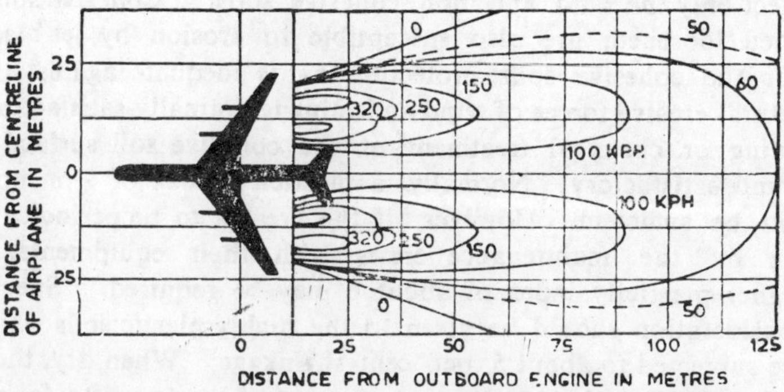

Figure 11.12 Typical Velocity Contours for Jet Engine Aircraft

Airport planning and maintenance programmes include the evaluation of the effects of jet blast in the terminal area, in the vicinity of runway ends, on the holding aprons and along the taxiways for determining the needs for their protection. Following methods are used for protection :

1 Stabilization of shoulders along the taxiways, aprons and holding aprons for the erosion control.

2 Erection of blast fences in apron areas, holding aprons, runway ends and taxiway fillets.

11.6.1 Erosion Control

Under the most taxiing conditions, blast velocities are not critical except at the intersections. With the present criterion of 22 m wide taxiways, the outboard engines of the larger jets extend outward by about 4.5 m beyond the edge of the pavement. For this reason, treatment of taxiway shoulders is recommended to prevent the erosion or blowing of debris into the tail pipe of aircraft. On the holding apron and runway ends, the jet wake approaches the maximum intensity and subjects the surrounding area to critical velocities. Drag and uplift caused by the present jet aircrafts can roll away even large size boulders. At 10 m distance from the engine nozzle, the jet exhaust can raise 0.5 m thick boulders off the ground. Flexible pavements may be severely damaged by jet exhaust. The force causing erosion, however, decreases rapidly with distance and beyond about 180 m from the jet nozzle they effect only the sand and non cohesive soils. Cohesive soils, when loosened, are also susceptible to erosion by jet blast. For the cohesive soils, protection that is adequate against the natural erosive forces of wind and rains is normally satisfactory. Oiling or chemical treatment of the cohesive soil surface is found satisfactory. Normally, a plasticity index of 2 or more will be sufficient. However, if the area is to be periodically use by the maintenance crews with their equipments, a higher plasticity index of about 6 may be required. Special consideration should be given to the highly plastic soils which are subjected to about 5 per cent shrinkage. When dry, these soils crack and become more susceptible to lift forces. Cohesionless soils erode rapidly unless they are protected. Erosion can be minimised or prevented by several methods :

(i) Bituminous surfacing

(ii) Grade stone pitching

(iii) Stabilised base with cohesive binder, e.g., sand-clay base, gravel base with cohesive fines, soil-cement etc.

(iv) Turfing

11.6.2 Blast Fences

These are used to deflect and dissipate the energy of high velocity jet exhaust. See Figure 11.13. Various possible types of blast fences are shown in Figures 11.14 and 11.15. The stability of a particular type depends upon the amount of protection desired. U.S. Corps of Engineers have conducted full scales as well as model tests on several types of blast fences. As a result of these investigations, it was found that the fences perform better than a flat plate fence or a flat louvered concrete fence. It is further observed that the performances of the single and the multiple curved fences are similar. Both

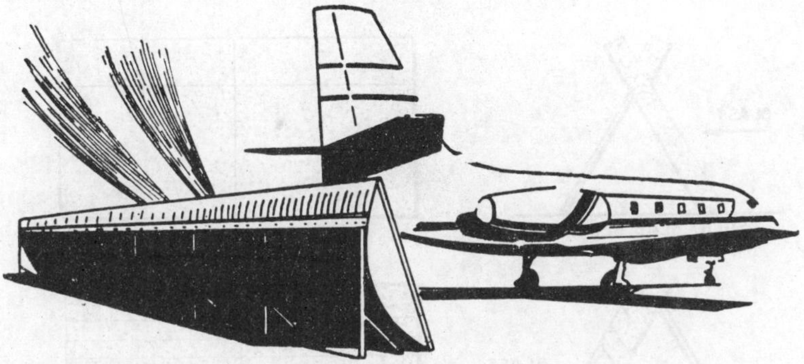

Figure 11.13 Typical Blast Fences, a Perspective View

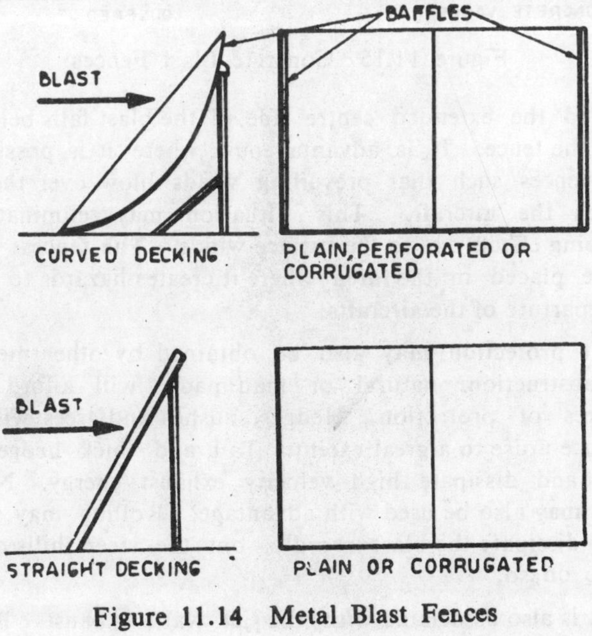

Figure 11.14 Metal Blast Fences

the types of vanes reduce the wake velocities within tolerable limits. At runway ends and at other places where full thrust is applied, fences of 2.5 m to 3 m heights have performed satisfactorily. On loading aprons, fences of smaller heights may also perform well. Location of fence has also an important bearing on its effectiveness. Generally, if the fence is closer to the source of the blast, the performance is better,

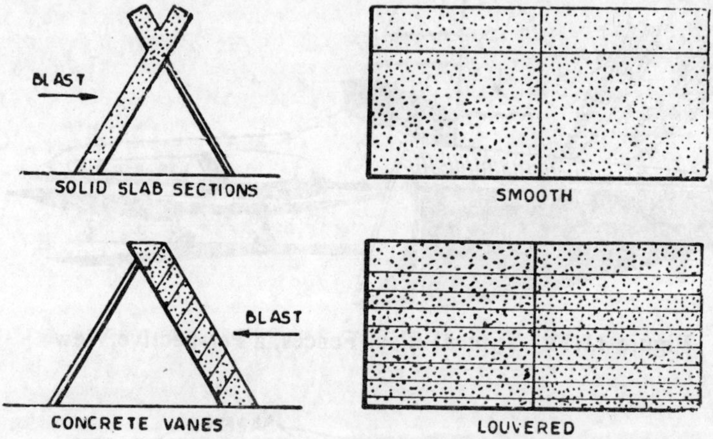

Figure 11.15 Concrete Blast Fences

provided the extended centre line of the blast falls below the top of the fence. It is advantageous, where it is possible, to place fences such that prevailing winds blow over the fence towards the aircraft. This situation may eliminate the disturbing effects due to the surface winds. The fences should not be placed in the area where it creates hazards to arrival and departure of the aircrafts.

Blast protection may also be obtained by other methods. Any obstruction, natural or man-made, will afford some measures of protection. Hedges, bushes and trees will help to reduce noise to a great extent. Tall and thick hedges may deflect and dissipate high velocity exhaust energy. Natural terrain may also be used with advantage. Rolling may not be able to dissipate the blast rapidly, but the steep hills may be able to do so.

Heat is also associated with the jet wake exhaust. But the temperature dissipates more rapidly with distance than the velocity. Further, the working personnel's equipment and structures normally do not occupy the areas where the upper limit of the heat are generated during the jet operations.

11.7 TYPICAL AIRPORT LAYOUTS

The typical airport layouts for the basic runway configurations are illustrated in Figures 11.16 to 11.22.

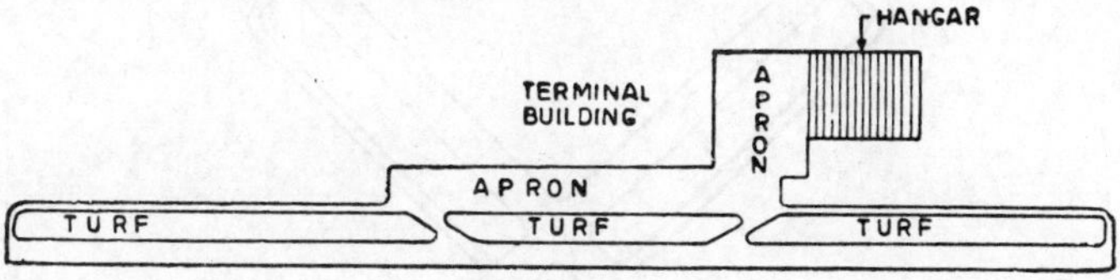

Figure 11 16 Single Runway Concept

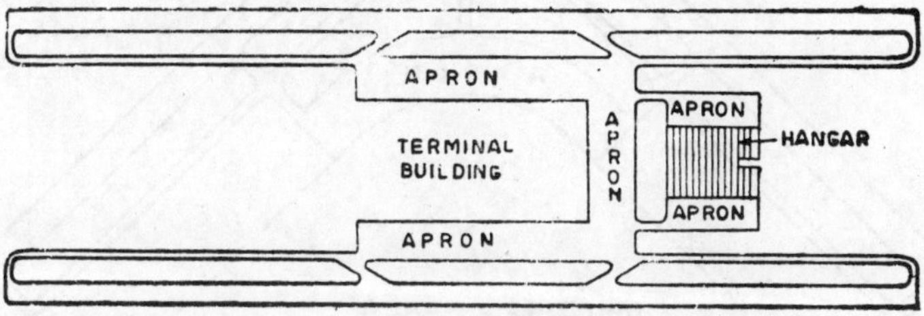

Figure 11.17 Open Parallel Concept

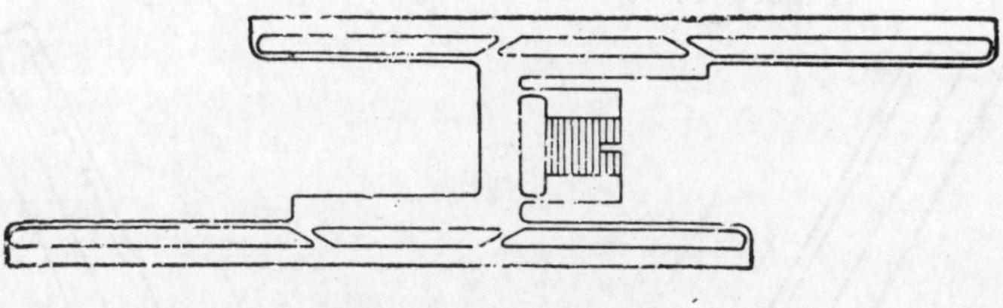

Figure 11.18 Offset Parallel Concept

The first step in the airfield design is the selection of a suitable runway configuration. The basic runway configurations have been discussed in article 7 1. There should be a good correlation between the runway and other airport elements, viz. taxiway terminal building, apron, hangar etc. The integration of all the elements of an airport provides a smooth flow of traffic, keeps the taxi distances to a minimum and provides the shortest route for passengers. A proper airport layout provides full functional efficiency with the minimum space utilization. An engineer should attempt to provide the simplest design which yields the optimum service to air passengers. A good airfield layout should possess the following characteristics :

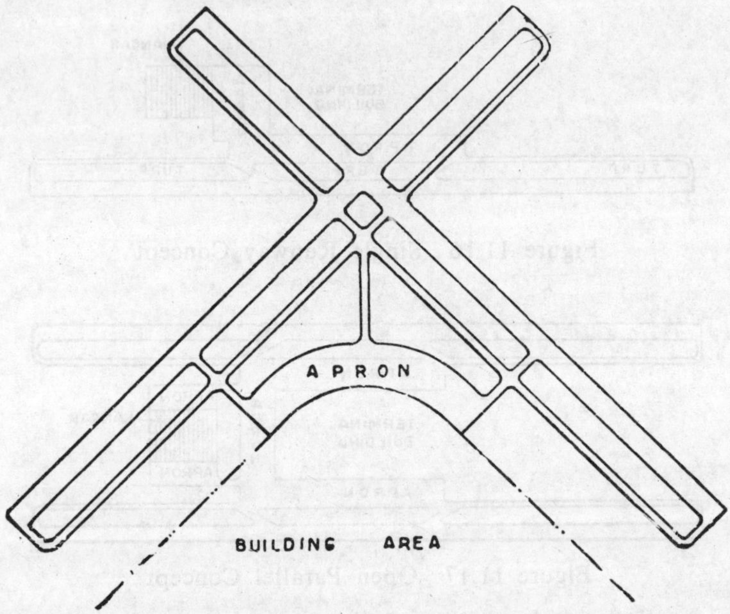

Figure 11.19 Two Intersecting Runway

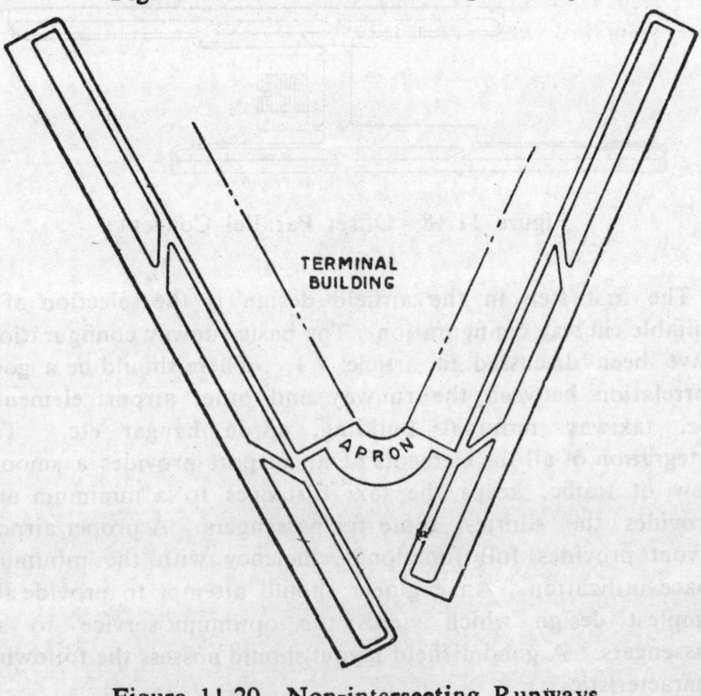

Figure 11.20 Non-intersecting Runways

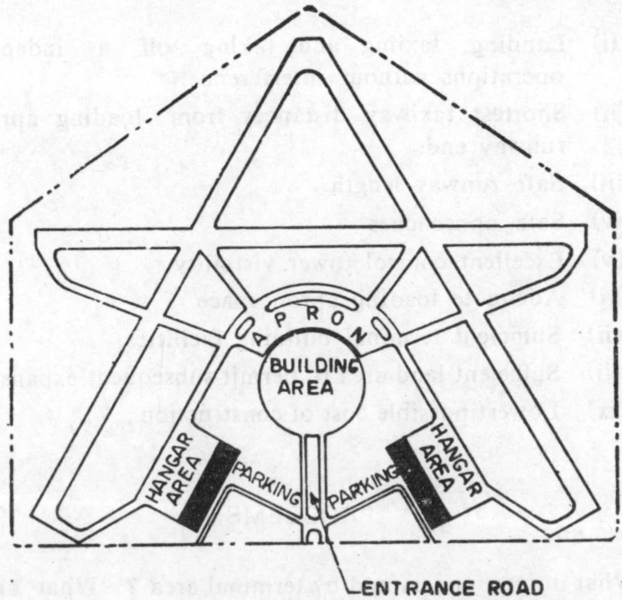

Figure 11.21 Three Intersecting Runways

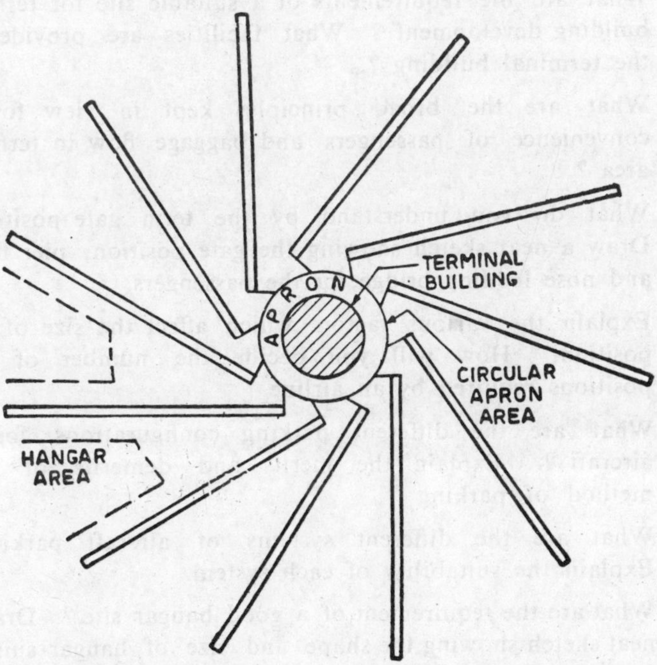

Figure 11.22 Tangential Runway Layout

(i) Landing, taxiing and taking off as independent operations without interference.

(ii) Shortest taxiway distances from loading apron to runway end.

(iii) Safe runway length

(iv) Safe approaches

(v) Excellent control tower visibility

(vi) Adequate loading apron space

(vii) Sufficient terminal building facilities

(viii) Sufficient land area to permit subsequent expansion

(ix) Lowest possible cost of construction

PROBLEMS

1 What do you understand by terminal area ? What are the facilities provided in terminal area ?

2 What are the requirements of a suitable site for terminal building development ? What facilities are provided in the terminal building ?

3 What are the broad principles kept in view for the convenience of passengers and baggage flow in terminal area ?

4 What do you understand by the term gate position ? Draw a neat sketch showing the gate position, pier finger and nose loading bridge for the passengers.

5 Explain the various factors which affect the size of gate position. How will you decide the number of gate positions required by an airline ?

6 What are the different parking configurations for an aircraft ? Explain the merits and demerits of each method of parking.

7 What are the different systems of aircraft parking ? Explain the suitability of each system.

8 What are the requirement of a good hangar site ? Draw a neat sketch showing the shape and size of hangar suitable for servicing of small aircrafts.

9 Explain in detail what measures are taken to eliminate the undesirable effect of hot exhaust gases coming out with high wake velocity from the tail pipe of jet aircraft.

10 What are the characteristics of an ideal airport layout ?

11 Sketch typical layout of an airport showing the location of taxiways, runways, apron, terminal building etc. for the following runway configurations

(a) Single runway

(b) Two open parallel runways

(c) Two offset parallel runways

(d) Two intersecting runways

(e) Two divergent runways

(f) Three intersecting runways

12

VISUAL AIDS

12.1 GENERAL

The pilot needs visual aids while landing or taking off during all weathers and at every time. The pilot usually takes help of the perspective view of the runway and other ground reference marks during the landing operations. Runway threshold, runway edges and the runway centre line are amongst the most essential items which should be clearly visible to the pilot. In order to enhance the day time visibility, runways, taxiways and other allied structures are marked with lines and numbers. Perspective view of a runway, as seen from a height of 60 m (200 ft) and distance of 1100 m (3670 ft) from the threshold is shown in Figure 12.1. All markings should be clear and should provide the maximum practicable contrast under all conditions. In the day time during poor weather conditions, or at night, the visibility reduces considerably. It is essential to provide adequate lighting in the airport which should convey the similar informations to the pilot during visibility conditions, as the markings do in day time.

12.2 AIRPORT MARKING

Airport area is marked in a simple manner so that the pilots

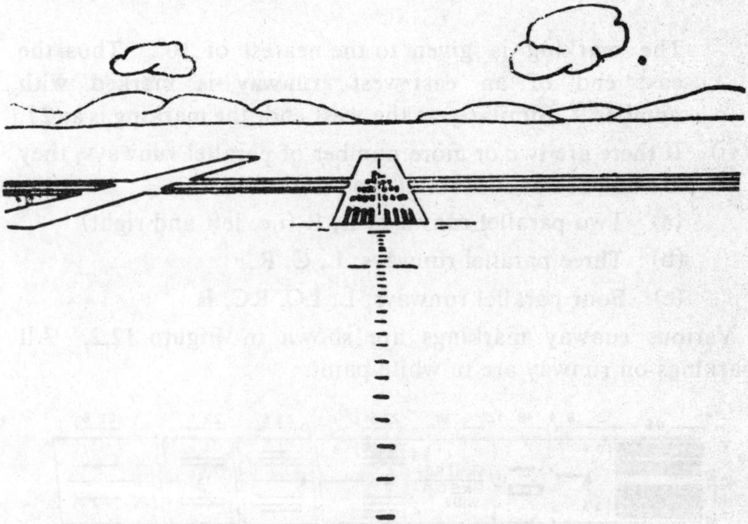

Figure 12.1 Runway Perspective View

can easily spot and recognise to the various airport elen
The pilot thus should distinctly identify the landing are:
should also know the wind direction. For this identific
marking and wind direction indicators are essential at
airport.

The airport markings are divided into the following gr

1 Runway marking
2 Taxiway marking
3 Runway and taxiway shoulder marking
4 Apron marking
5 Wind direction indicator
6 Landing direction indicator

12.2.1 Runway Marking

The markings made on the runway are of the followir

(i) Runway threshold marking
(ii) Runway touch down zone or landing zone marki
(iii) Runway edge strip marking
(iv) Runway centre line marking
(v) Runway number which indicates the magnetic a
the runway measured clockwise from North

The marking is given to the nearest of 10°. Thus the east end of an east-west runway is marked with number 9. Similarly at the west end, the marking is as 27.

(vi) If there are two or more number of parallel runways, they are marked as follows at the threshold :

(a) Two parallel runways; L, R (i.e. left and right)

(b) Three parallel runways; L, C, R

(c) Four parallel runways; L, LC, RC, R

Various runway markings are shown in Figure 12.2. All markings on runway are in white paint.

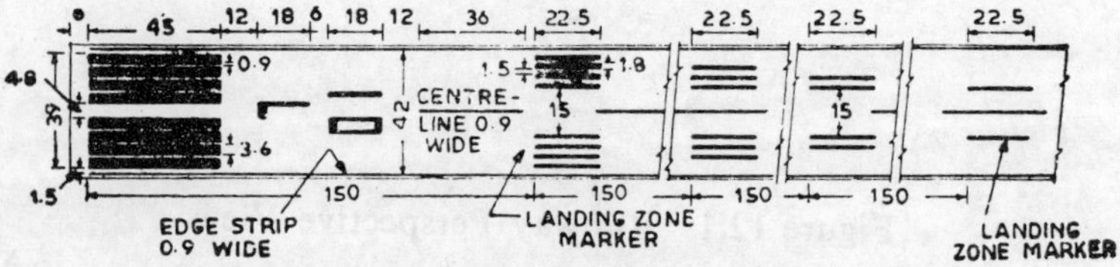

Dimensions are in metres

Figure 12.2 Runway Marking

Runway threshold is indicated by a series of parallel lines starting from a distance of 6 m (20 ft) from the runway end. In some airports, it is desirable to permanently displace the runway threshold. The displaced runway threshold is shown in Figure 12.3. The displacement may affect landing operation. There can be many reasons for displacing the threshold. Sometimes, there are small obstructions or a water course near the runway entrance in the direction of landing. Such circumstances severely damage the aircraft if it happens to

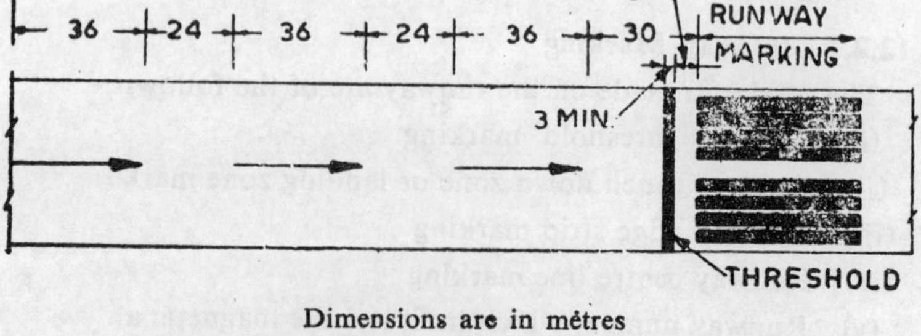

Dimensions are in metres

Figure 12.3 Displaced Threshold Markings

undershoot. The displacement of runway threshold may minimise the severity of the accident. But such displacement is possible only when the remaining runway length available for landing is adequate. Runway touch down area is indicated by series of strips marked parallel to the centre line of runway. The number of strips decreases gradually in the direction of landing. For normal landing, the pilot should be able to touch the runway within the touch down area. Runway edge strip is normally required when the runway-pavement width is 45 m (150 ft) or more. It consists of a long continuous strip 0.9 m (3 ft) wide and placed near the edges of the runway.

12 2.2 Taxiway Marking

Typical taxiway markings are illustrated in Figures 12.4 to 12.7. All these markings are in yellow colour paint. The centre line of taxiway is marked with a single strip having 15 cm width. This centre line normally terminates at the runway edge except in the case of exit taxiway where the taxiway centre line is curved into the centre line of runway, see Figures 12.4, 12.5 and 12.6. At taxiway intersection the markings of the taxiway centre lines continue through the intersection areas as shown in Figure 12.7. A holding point marker should be painted at all intersection of the paved taxiway with the runways. The holding position should be at least 30 m (100 ft) from the edge of the runway as shown

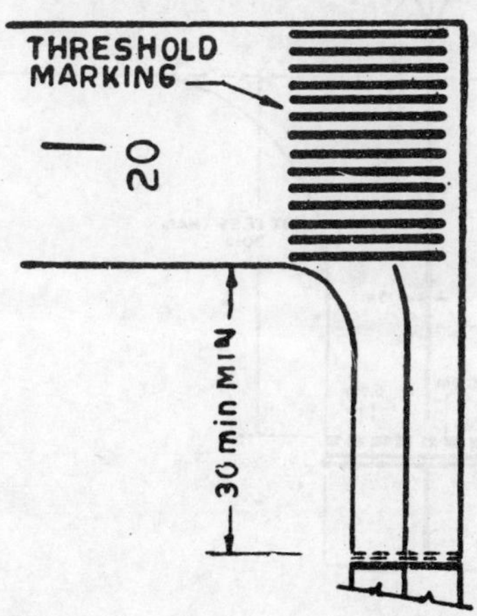

Figure 12.4 Taxiway Entrance at the End of Runway

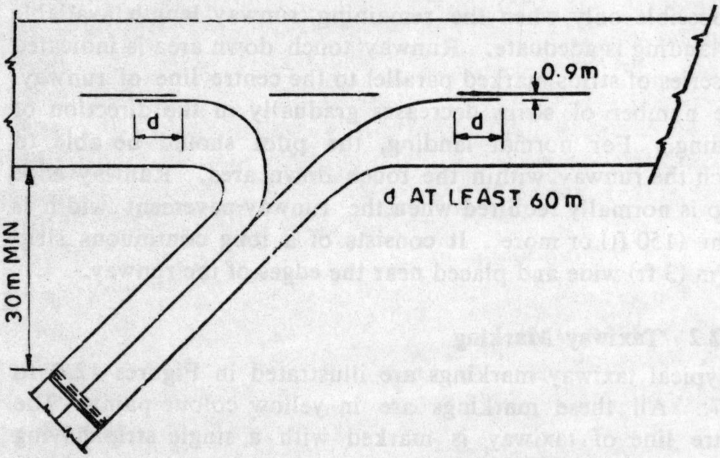

Figure 12.5 Taxiway Entrance to Runway

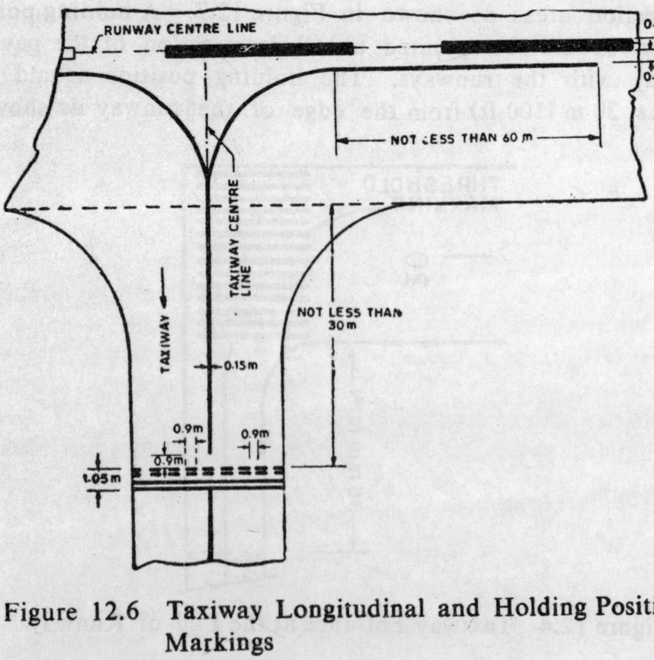

Figure 12.6 Taxiway Longitudinal and Holding Position Markings

in Figure 12.6. The distance of 30 m is minimum and the airport engineer has to decide whether this distance should be increased or not. It may be necessary for accounting the prevalent circumstances, the nature of operation and the aircraft types using the airport.

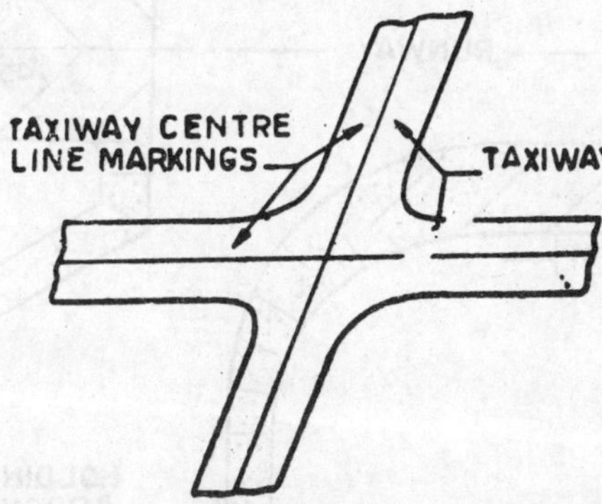

Figure 12.7 Taxiway Intersection Marking

12.2.3 Runway and Taxiway Shoulder Marking

The typical marking is illustrated in Figure 12.8. It is done with a yellow paint. Runway shoulders are marked with diagonal lines each having a width of 0.90 m (3 ft). Taxiway and holding apron shoulders are marked with lines perpendicular to the direction of travel of aircraft. Blast pad at the end of the runway is marked with a chevron pattern.

12.2.4 Apron Marking

Certain guide lines are painted on the apron to help the pilot in manoeuvring the aircraft on the apron. The marking is done with a yellow paint. Since the aprons are likely to be subjected to fuel spillage, the paint used is of a special type which is fuel resistant. Usually, the guide line is painted to indicate the path of the nose gear of the most critical aircraft. The smaller aircrafts can also use the same path and manoeuvre without difficulty.

12.2.5 Wind Direction Indicator

The wind direction indicator, which may be a wind cone, is usually placed at the centre of the segmented circle (airport)

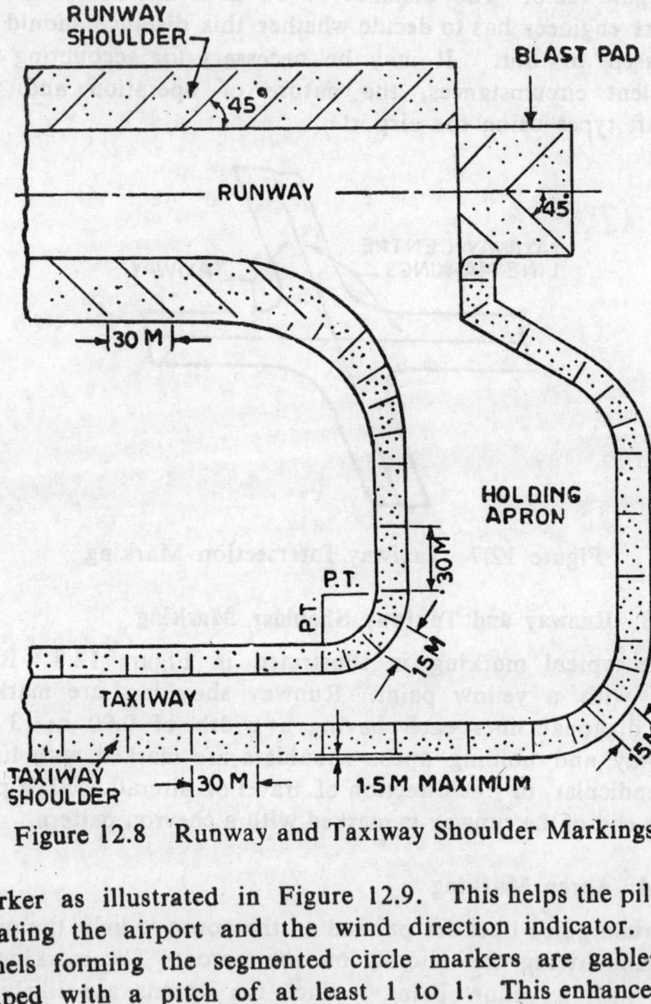

Figure 12.8 Runway and Taxiway Shoulder Markings

marker as illustrated in Figure 12.9. This helps the pilot in locating the airport and the wind direction indicator. The panels forming the segmented circle markers are gable-roof shaped with a pitch of at least 1 to 1. This enhances the visibility of the segmented circle and the pilot will be able to detect it from a considerable distance ahead. In most cases the panels are painted white so as to obtain a distinctive colour contrast between the marker and its surroundings and to protect them against weather. As per ICAO, the segmented circle should have an inside diameter of 30 m and the panel width varying from 0.90 m to 2.40 m. The wind direction indicator is generally in the form of a truncated cone made of fabric. ICAO recommends that its length should not be less than 3.6 m (12 ft) and the diameter at the larger end should

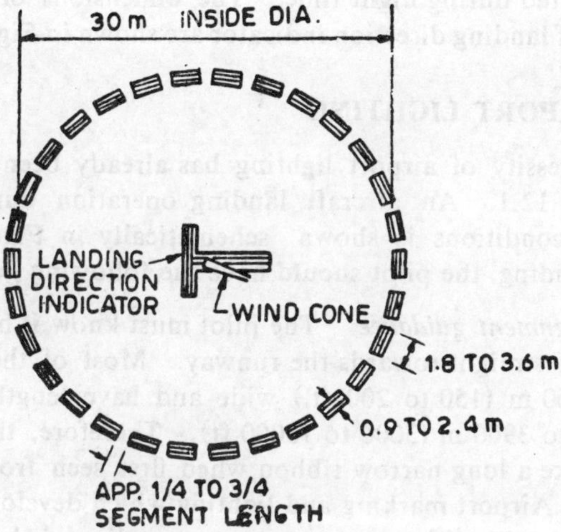

Figure 12.9 Segmented Circle Marker

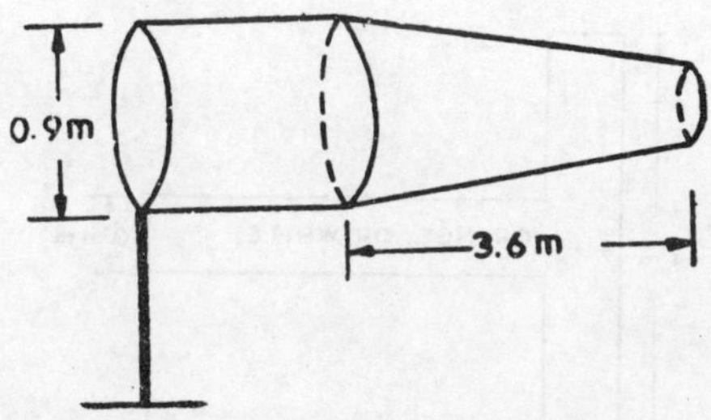

Figure 12.10 Wind Direction Indicator

not be less than 0.9 m (3 ft) as shown in Figure 12.10. It must be placed at a distinct place away from the buildings, so that it is not affected by the eddies. It should be so coloured that it is visible from a height of 300 m. To achieve a better colour contrast with respect to its background, it may be painted with bands of two different colours, viz., red and white, orange and white etc.

12.2.6 Landing Direction Indicator

This is in the form of a Tee or Tetrahedron and is placed at the centre of segmented circle as shown in Figure 12.11. The purpose of this is to indicate to the pilot the direction of active runway of the airport. It is provided at a distinct place and is lighted during night time. The dimensions of a typical Tee type of landing direction indicator are shown in Figure 12.11.

12.3 AIRPORT LIGHTING

The necessity of airport lighting has already been discussed in article 12.1. An aircraft landing operation during good visibility conditions is shown schematically in Figure 12.12. During landing, the pilot should have the following guidance.

(i) Alignment guidance. The pilot must know if his aircraft is heading straight towards the runway. Most of the runways are 45 to 60 m (150 to 200 ft.) wide and have lengths varying from 900 to 3900 m (3000 to 13000 ft). Therefore, the runway appears like a long narrow ribbon when first seen from a great distance. Airport marking and lighting which develop contrast of the pavement with respect to its surroundings help the pilot in attaining the alignment information.

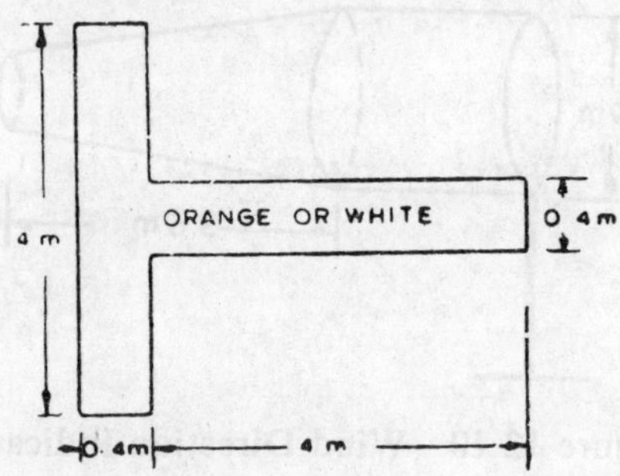

Figure 12.11 Landing Direction Indicator

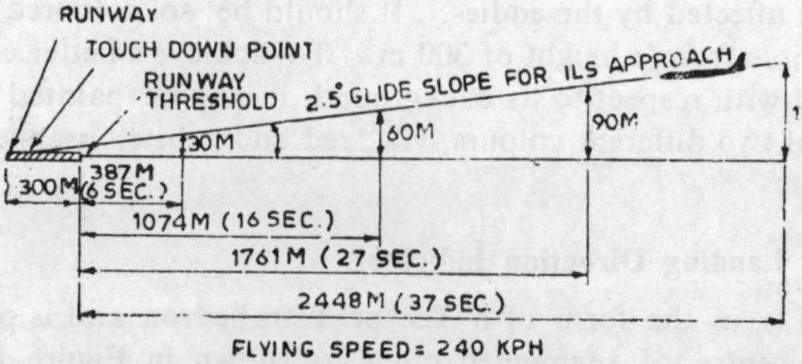

Figure 12.12 Glide, Height, Time and Distance Relationship During Landing in Good Visibility Conditions.

(ii) Height information. The pilot must know how much high the aeroplane is above the ground. When the pilot transits from the instrumental to the visual guidance, he estimates the height from the perspective view of the runway and the ground particulars e.g. buildings, trees, towers etc. A large percentage of accident, even during good visibility conditions, have been due to inadequate ground reference data which caused difficulty to the pilot in judging the height while landing. One purpose of providing lighting at the airport is to impart adequate *ground reference data* to the pilot.

(iii) Distance estimation. The pilot must know how far he is from the runway. In the daytime, when weather is cleer, the pilot uses the markings on the runway and the surrounding terrain conditions as the side for distance estimation. In the night and during bad weather, the guidance obtained from the terrain conditions is very poor. The visibility is enhanced by lighting the airfield and conveying the distance estimation by colour or intensity contrast.

(iv) Roll guidance. The pilot must know, if his aircraft is banked in relation to the ground surface. This is said to be as an aircraft *roll* or *altitude*. The roll is considered to be about the axis which coincides with the longitudinal axis of the aircraft. If such a condition is not corrected, the lower wing of the aircraft would strike the runway pavement. The view of the horizon, the natural ground terrain and the water surface etc. provide sufficient guidance for the correct angle of roll.

The colour and general pattern of lights used in airport lighting are standardized for all civil airports. The standardization of lights signals helps the pilot who is not familiar with a particular airport. There are several factors which affect the type and intensity of lighting. These factors are the amount of traffic, type of night operations planned, type of aircraft to be used, type of landing surfaces provided, airport classification, power service availability and the weather conditions. These factors are considered by the designer while preparing the airport lighting plans and specifications. The airport lighting can be divided into the following elements :

1 Rotating beacon
2 Code beacon
3 Boundary lighting

4 Approach lighting
5 Threshold lighting
6 Runway lighting
7 Taxiway lighting
8 Apron and hangar lighting
9 Lighting of wind direction indicator
10 Lighting of landing direction indicator,

A general pattern of airport lighting is shown in Figure 12.13. Specific lighting patterns for different airport elements are explained below :

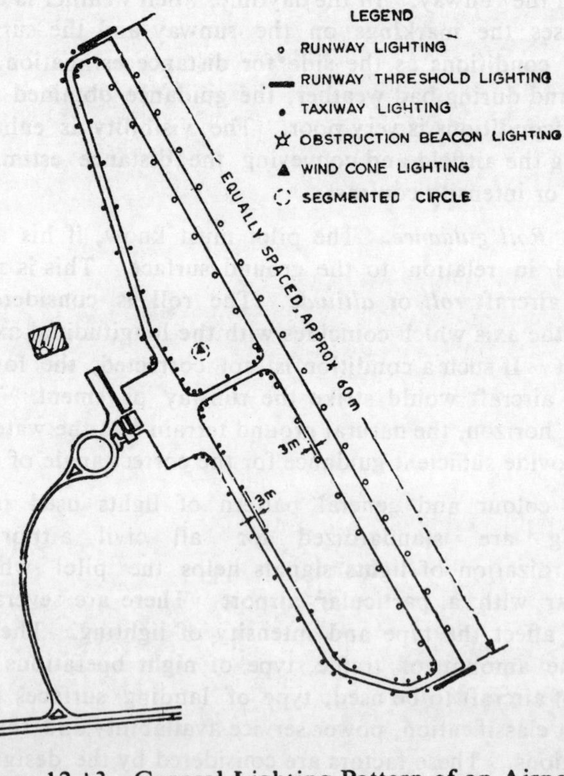

Figure 12.13 General Lighting Pattern of an Airport

12.3.1 Rotating Beacon

The beam of rotating beacon is visible to the pilot from a long distance and it indicates the approximate location of the airfield which is equipped for night operations. The beacon is mounted higher than any surrounding obstruction. The bottom edge of its beam when set horizontally, should clear all the obstructions. It is usually mounted over the top of terminal building or hangar. But if such mounting does not provide the required clearance above the obstruction, it is elevated by mounting it on a separate tower. The beacon is rotated at six revolutions per minute. It projects beams of light in horizontal directions 180° apart. One beam emits a green light and another a clear light.

12.3.2 Code Beacon

This beacon is mounted high enough so that its beam clears all obstructions. It is usually provided with two 500 watt bulbs with a green colour screen. It continuously flashes a Morse code signal designating the airport.

12.3.3 Boundary Lights

The entire landing area of the airport is outlined by the boundary lights spaced approximately *90 m (300 ft) apart.* Wherever there is fence along the boundary of the field, the lights should be placed 3 m (10 ft) inside the fence. They should be mounted approximately 0.75 m (2.5 ft) above the ground. Red marker light are used where boundary lights represent the hazardous approach.

12.3.4 Approach Lighting

While approaching the runway for landing, the approach lights are the only elements of guidance to the pilot. It has been observed through experience that, after the pilot sees a visual aid, it takes him about 3 seconds to react to it and check the response of the aircraft. For the need of a quick action by the pilot to correct the errors of alignment, roll or height and distance, the time and the visual range factors are considered, as otherwise it can result in missed approach or a crash. Assuming the speed of the aircraft as 240 kmph (150 mph), the visual range should extend 198 m (660 ft) ahead of the nearest seen ground object so that pilot may correctly respond to the ground object. The pilot generally decides, whether to land or not, when he is at a height of about 60 m (200 ft) above the runways. Assuming that the cockpit cutoff angle is 15° below the horizontal and that 180 to 210 m (600 to

700 ft) approach lights should be visible to the pilot before he transits from instrumental to visual aids, the approach lights must extend approximately 900 m (3000 ft) ahead of the runway threshold This visual requirement of approach lights to assist safe landing poor visibility conditions is illustrated in Figure 12.14.

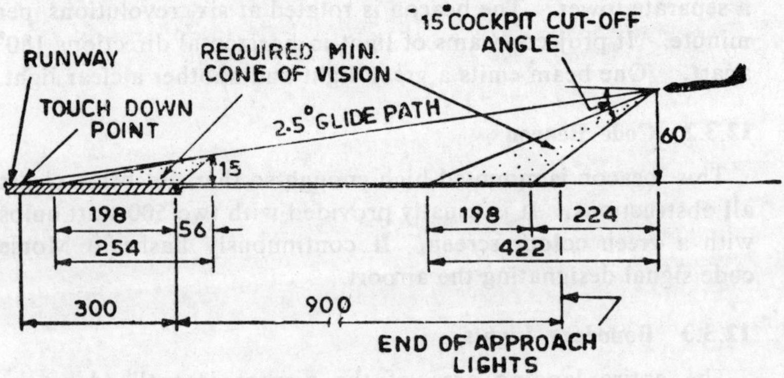

Dimensions are in metres

Figure 12.14 Visual Requirement of Approach Lighting

The approach lighting system, accepted by ICAO is illustrated in Figure 12.15. The transverse bars each 4.2 m (14 ft) wide and located at 30 m interval along the extended centre line of runway, give suitable information to the pilot of the angle of roll. The outermost 600 m (2000 ft) length of light provides some guidance to the pilot regarding the alignment, height and roll. At 300 m from the threshold, a crossbar 30 m wide is provided which serves as a distance marker and provides further horizon references. Approach light are normally mounted on pedestals of varying height. Some military airports require that the approach lights, within 300 m of the runway threshold must be nearly flush with the graded approach zone.

12.3.5 Threshold Lighting

This is shown in Figure 12.15. The identification of runway threshold has an important bearing on the pilot's decision, whether to land or not. For this reason, the area near the runway threshold is given special lighting considerations. The terminating bar of red lights, placed 60 m ahead of the runway threshold, indicates the end of approach lighting. The threshold wing bars placed 30 m ahead of the runway serve as distance marker. The threshold itself is lighted with a continuous line of green light extending across the entire width of runway. The lights may be of the elevated* or semi-flush** type.

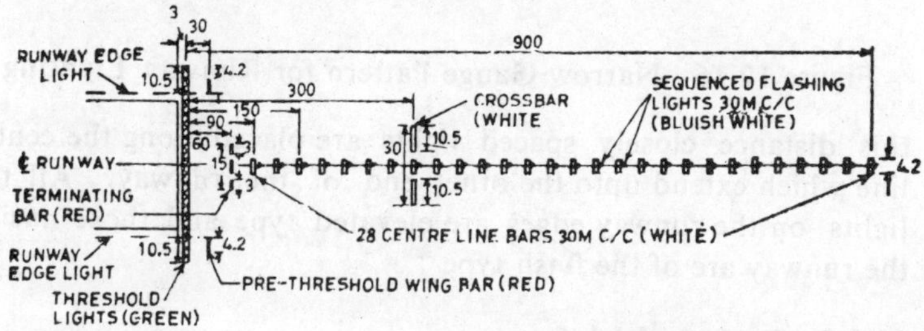

Figure 12.15 System of Approach and Threshold Lighting

12.3.6 Runway Lighting

After crossing the threshold, the pilot completes a touchdown and then rolls the aircraft on the runway. The runway lighting is so planned that it imparts to the pilot the required guidance on alignment, lateral displacement, roll and height and distance, so that he is able to correctly judge his position in the space. The old practice for night landing was to floodlight the entire landing area. But these days, flood-lighting is restricted only to indicate the preferred direction of landing. For runway lighting, a more precise design commonly known as *narrow-gauge* pattern is almost universally used at major airports. The lighting pattern is illustrated in Figure 12.16. As the pilot crosses the thershold and is about to touch the runway, he finds the central area of the runway excessively dark. To eliminate this *black hole* effect, the practice was to increase the intensity of the edge lights, but this proved to be ineffective. The narrow-gauge pattern is an attempt towards lighting up the central portion of the runway. In this system, as shown in Figure 12.16, groups of high intensity lights are placed 18 m apart and on either side of the centre line of runway. They continue upto a distance of 1140 m from the threshold. Beyond

*Elevated light is one which protrudes more than 12 cm above the surface where it is installed.

**Semi flush light is one which does not protrude more than 12 cm above the surface on which it is installed.

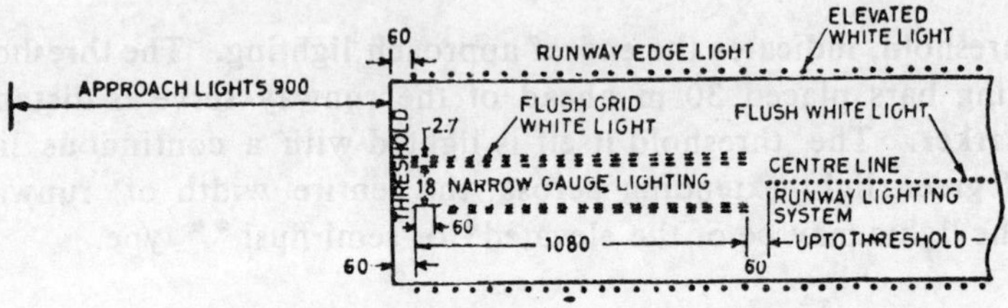

Figure 12.16 Narrow-Gauge Pattern for Runway Lighting

this distance closely spaced lights are placed along the centre line which extend upto the other end of the runway. All the lights on the runway edges are elevated type and those inside the runway are of the flush type *

12.3.7 Taxiway Lighting

The following design considerations apply to taxiway lighting:

(i) Taxiway should be clearly identified so that they cannot be confused with the runways.

(ii) Exit taxiway should be so lighted that the pilot is able to locate the exit 360 to 450 m (1200 ft to 1500 ft) ahead of the point of turn off.

(iii) There should be adequate guidance along the taxiway.

(iv) Crossing of taxiway and the runway should be clearly identified.

(v) Effective and simple presentation of guidance elements to permit rapid aircraft movement between runway and apron should be preferred.

The taxiway lighting layout is illustrated in Figure 12.17. On tangent portion, the lights are placed not more than 60 m apart, at a distance of 3 m from either edge along the taxiway. The spacing is reduced on curves and intersection to facilitate their clear identification. Spacing of light on curves is given in Table 12.1. All taxiway side lights are coloured blue and usually project not more than 0.32 m (13 in) above the pavement surface.

On exit taxiway, in order to clearly identify the point of turn off, lights are placed along the centre line of the exit

---

*Flush light is one which does not protrude more than 1 cm (0.4 in) above the pavement surface.

taxiway. With this arrangement, the taxiway centre line, at its junction with the runway centre line, forms a distinct V-shaped pattern. The centre line light is green in colour and placed at 6 to 7.5 m (20 to 25 ft) distance along the straight length and 3 to 3.6 m (10 to 12 ft) distance along the curves.

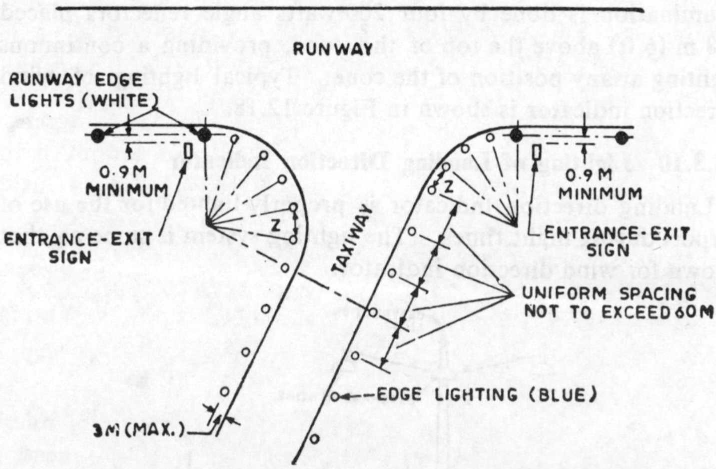

Figure 12.17 Typical Lighting Layout for a Taxiway Turn off from a Runway

Table 12.1 Spacing of Taxiway Lights on Curves

Radius ft	(R) m	Spacing ft	(Z) m	Radius ft	(R) ft	Spacing ft	(Z) m
15	4.5	20	6.0	300	90	80	24.0
25	7.5	27	8.1	400	120	95	28.5
50	15.0	35	10.5	500	150	110	33.0
75	22.5	40	12.0	600	180	130	39.0
100	30.0	50	15.0	700	210	145	43.5
150	45.0	55	16.0	800	240	165	49.5
200	60.0	60	18.0	900	270	185	55.5
250	75.0	70	21.0	1000	300	200	60.0

12.3.8 Apron and Hangar Lighting

These areas are usually flood lit. The light source is so mounted that it does not cause glare in the eyes of the pilots, the service personnel or the passengers. It is recommended that flood lights should be mounted at least 12 m (40 ft) above the pavement.

12.3.9 Lighting of Wind Direction Indicator

The wind direction indicator is illuminated for its visibility during night and during bad weather condition. The illumination is done by four 200-watts angle reflectors placed 1.8 m (6 ft) above the top of the cone, providing a continuous lighting at any position of the cone. Typical lighting of wind direction indicator is shown in Figure 12.18.

12.3.10 Lighting of Landing Direction Indicator

Landing direction indicator is properly lighted for the use of airport during night times. The lighting system is same as that shown for wind direction indicator.

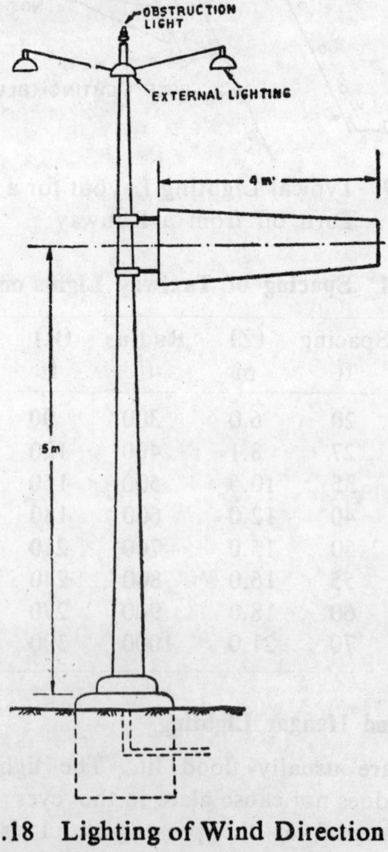

Figure 12.18 Lighting of Wind Direction Indicator

PROBLEMS

1 What do you understand by the term visual aid in connection with airport ? Name the different visual aids. What is the necessity of visual aids ?

2 Explain with neat sketches, the various markings on runways.

3 Explain with neat sketches the various markings on taxiways.

4 Write short notes on :

Runway and taxiway shoulder marking, Apron marking, Wind direction indicator and Landing director indicator.

5 Explain the necessity of airport lighting.

6 Explain the visual requirement of approach lights in terms of height, distance and speed of aircraft approaching the runway during poor visibility conditions. What is the recommended method of lighting the approaches of a runway ?

7 Draw a neat sketch to show how lighting is done on a runway ? Adopt narrow gauge pattern of lighting. What are the advantages of this pattern ?

8 What are the design considerations for a taxiway lighting ? Explain with neat sketches.

9 Write short notes on :

Beacon light.
Runway threshold lighting.
Apron hangar lighting.

10 Draw a typical sketch showing the general lighting pattern for a major airport.

13

AIR TRAFFIC CONTROL

13.1 GENERAL

The need of air traffic control is mainly for two reasons. Firstly, to safeguard life and property and secondly to expedite the traffic movements. Later inturn results in an orderly flow with no congestion and delay. The problem of controlling the ground vehicular traffic is much simpler than that of the aircrafts in space. If a motor vehicle looses its control, it can be parked on the road without much interfering the flow of traffic stream. Further, the control techniques are unchanged with weather conditions.

Two basic characteristics of aircraft make the air traffic control a complex problem. Firstly, an aircraft must continue its flight and cannot afford to stop in the air space. The helicopter is an exception to this which can hover in the air at a constant location as long as engine power is available. The second characteristic is that the aircraft lands with a gliding slope dictated by the altitude at which the trouble occurs. During bad whether conditions, when visibility is poor, certain information regarding alignment height and distance from the runway threshold are to be provided to the pilot through some instruments.

The passengers today are favouring the air travel. The aircrafts speed and air traffic density are also growing faster.

Landing and take-off operations may reach fifty millions yearly or even more in the near future. As far as aircrafts and airports are concerned, they can be designed and built to any number. Their economic and effective utilization, therefore, depends upon the air traffic control system. This system can handle large aircraft movements both safely and expeditiously. Conflicts in air traffic control signals can seriously reduce the capacity of a given airport. ICAO has certain flight rules which are necessary to be followed by all member nation for flights on international routes. Flight service stations are located along the air routes to provide contacts to the pilot during the course of his flight from one airport to another. It is essential that at all times the pilot during their flights have contacts with one of the controlling stations of two airports or with the flight service station along the air route.

13.2 NEED OF AIR TRAFFIC CONTROL

The control of air traffic deals with that phase of air transportation which ensures safe, convenient and economic movement of aircraft from one airport to another airport. The aircraft flight from one airport to another involves the following basic actions.

1. The aircraft takes off from an airport.
2. It maintains a proper altitude in air.
3. It navigates from point to point safely.
4. It lands at the desired airport.

The system of air traffic control mainly concerns with the above items. The primary functions of air traffic control devices can, therefore, be summarised as follows :

(i) Airport traffic control : This deals with the following :

(a) To guide the aircraft, desiring to land or take off.

(b) To control the taxing of arriving and departing aircraft on the airfield between the apron and the runway.

(ii) Airway traffic control : This regulates the movement of aircraft along the air routes with adequate lateral and vertical separation to avoid collision. This is particularly essential when visibility is poor.

(iii) Airway communication : This deals with conveying of airway and weather information to the pilot during the flight.

(iv) General or non-airway traffic control : This presents a serious problem when personal flying is done by a large number of people. In such cases the movement of aircraft, not flying along the airway, must be regulated to prevent interference to the main air traffic.

13.3 AIR TRAFFIC CONTROL NETWORK

The network for controlling the air traffic can be divided into three parts as follows :

1 Control within terminal area
2 Control over airways
3 Airway communication

The method of traffic control for each system depends upon the weather conditions. These are commonly known as visual flight rules *(VFR)* and instrumental flight rules *(IFR)*. If *VFR* conditions prevail, the air traffic control during the route is practically not required, since the pilots can maintain the desired separation by visual aids. The IFR conditions exist, when the visibility is lower than the limits prescribed for flight under visual flight rules. Rigid traffic control has to be exercised under IFR condition. The pilot, prior to his departure, prepares a flight plan which indicates the aircraft destination, the air route to be followed, the desired altitude and the estimated time for departure. If the flight plan is approved, no change is allowed without prior approval of the traffic control centre.

13.3.1 Control Within Terminal Area

This is done from the airport control tower which is located in the terminal area. The control tower is nerve centre of an airport. Safety of aircraft operations and the effective capacity of an airport depend upon the skill of the controller operating the system. The controller directs the movement of aircraft on the ground and in the air within the airport zone. Informations are issued to the pilot regarding airport conditions, airway traffic, visibility, speed and direction of ground winds, barometric pressure and other relevant informations for the safe operation.

The problem of controlling the incoming and departing aircraft is very complex and would probably remain so during the conditions of poor visibility until such time when instrument landings can be accomplished as quickly as landings under VFR condition. In order to control the aircraft movements efficiently the *control tower* is so located as to command a clear view of the airfield, i.e. from the parking apron to the farthest point of any runway and its approaches. The walls of the control tower room are fitted with glass panels arranged at angles to minimize the glare and reflection. They are sometime coloured to minimize the strain on the eyes. The glass panels facing towards the airfield are equipped with window wipers to keep them clean during the rains. The control tower is usually located on the top of the administration building.

The control tower which has approach control facilities directs the aircrafts to the airports through a number of specific points which are located within a radius of approximately 40 km (25 miles) from the control tower. The aircrafts are brought to these points by the air route traffic control centres, where they are taken over by the control tower. If the traffic is heavy the aircrafts are detained at this place (called a holding fix) and required to keep moving with a vertical separation of 300 m. They are released for landing, one by one, by the control tower. If the control tower does not have the approach control, the detention and clearing of aircrafts for landing is done by the air route traffic control centre and they are taken over by the control towers after the aircrafts have started their landing approach.

13.3.2 Control Over Airways

The control is provided by a number of air route traffic control centres (ARTC). Each centre controls a certain definite geographical area, thus covering the entire area of the country. These centres are usually located at major airports so as to eliminate the expenses of additional communication facilities. In India, ARTC are provided at Bombay, Madras, Calcutta, Nagpur, Ahmedabad, Allahabad, Delhi and Jodhpur. As the aircraft crosses over the boundary of one of the control areas, it is taken over by the ARTC of another area or by the control tower as the case may be. ARTC is mainly concerned with flights under IFR conditions. The pilot first gives his flight plan to ARTC who then decides the altitude at which the aircraft may fly so as to ensure a safe separation from other aircrafts operating along the same airway. Without radar coverage, aircrafts are separated by a distance equivalent to 10 minutes run when flying on the same altitude. If radar facility is available, the minimum separation is 8 km (5 miles).

13.3.3 Air Communication

This is usually done through flight service stations. These stations are located at the airports and also along the airways. Their functions are as follows :

(i) To relay air traffic control messages between the ARTC and enroute aircraft.

(ii) To give certain information to the pilots, before and during the flights, regarding the weather change navigational aids, airports that are out of use, and the procedure at a particular airports etc.

13.4 AIR TRAFFIC CONTROL AIDS

During VFR weather conditions, the flight is usually conducted by visual recognition of the objects on the ground. Instrument flight rules are used when the visibility is inadequate during night time or due to cloudy or foggy weather. During all visibility conditions, the following air traffic control aids are always available to the pilot during the flight :

1 Enroute aids or airway aids
2 Landing aids

The aids are briefly described below :

13.4.1 Enroute Aids or Airway Aid

The following aids are available to the pilot during his flight from one airport to another :

(i) Airway beacon
(ii) Low/Medium frequency (LF/MF) ratio range
(iii) Very high frequency omni-directional range (VOR)
(iv) Airground communication
(v) Tactical air navigation (TACAN)
(vi) Distance measuring equipment (DME)
(vii) Marker beacon
(viii) Direction finder
(ix) Air route surveillance radar (ARSR)

(i) Airway beacon : In the past, airway beacon lights were the only means of air navigation. They were spaced about 40 km (25 miles) apart along the air route to guide the pilot from one airport to another. These are now considered as obsolete and are replaced with more effective controls. However, few beacons still exist in key location e.g. hill peak points.

(ii) Low/Medium frequency (LF/MF) radio ranges : With the invention of LF/MF radio ranges, the air navigational aids have greatly revolutionised. The four-way LF/MF radio range emits radio beam along four directions which may or may not be at 90° to each other. Each beam is directed towards an airway. The facility may be located near the airport as shown in Figure 13.1. A pilot flying on an airway, along which a radio beam has been directed, tunes of the frequency of the radio beam. This frequency usually varies from 200 to 400 kc

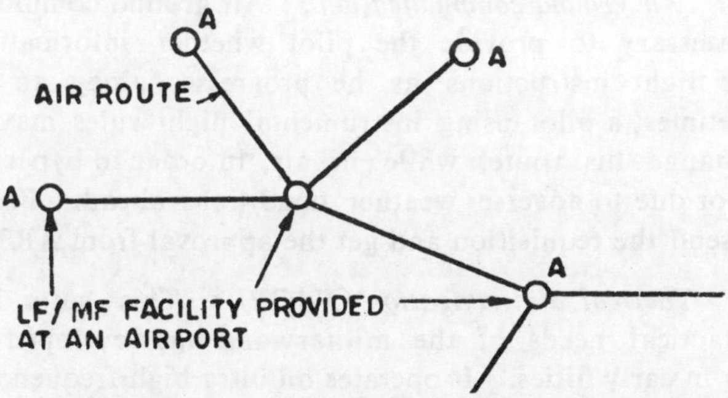

Figure 13.1 Fourway LF/MF Radio range

per second. If the pilot hears a steady tone, it indicates that he is on the right course. If; however, he hears a dot-dash or dash-dot signal which is sent in alternate quadrant, it indicates that he is not following the correct course. The pilot can easily catch the correct route provided he knows his position with respect to the station. He may have to fly over a complicated route and make repeated attempts if he is unaware of his position. Another disadvantage of this method is that it is very susceptible to static interference. Thus during bad weather e.g., during a thunderstorm, when an effective aid is very much required, the reception of LF/MF is likely to be totally absent.

(iii) Very high frequency omni-directional range (VOR) : It is commonly known as VHF omni-range or VOR. Whereas LF/MF radio range emits signals only in four directions, VOR does it along an infinite number of courses on which pilot can fly. The main advantage of this aid is that it is not susceptible to static interference and remains effective even during a thunderstorm.

The VOR receiver in the aircraft is provided with a dial for tuning the desired VOR frequency. It has also a course line indicator which indicates to the pilot whether he is to the left or right of the correct course. An indicator is also provided to show whether the pilot is leading towards or away from the VOR station. Like the LF/MF ranges, most of the VOR stations are equipped with facilities for voice transmission, so as to disseminate informations regarding the weather etc to the pilot.

(iv) Air ground communication : Air ground communication is necessary to provide the pilot whether information and other flight instructions as he progresses along an airway. Sometimes, a pilot using instrumental flight rules may require to change his route, while in air, in order to bypass certain area or due to adverse weather conditions ahead. For this he will send the requisition and get the approval from ARTC.

(v) Tactical air navigation (TACN) : This suits best for the tactical needs of the military and was developed by U.S. Navy in early fifties. It operates on ultra-high-frequency band, and measures distances and azimuth in one unit instead of two.

(vi) Distance measuring equipment (DME) : Just as in a motor car the speedometer indicates the speed of travel, similarly in an aircraft the distance measuring equipment (DME) indicates to the pilot the distance to or from a point, usually a VOR bearing station. The pilot thus gets a precise idea of his position with respect to the airway.

(vii) Marker beacons : For determining the exact positions of the radio range stations and the location on a given course marker beacons are used. Directly above the tower of the radio range station, there is a *cone of silence*. This has a limited area and is shaped like an inverted cone. Just before the aircraft enters the cone, the signals fade out abruptly.

They remain blank for a few seconds, until the aircraft leaves the opposite side of the cone when the signals again attain a high tone abruptly.

The cone of silence does not always provide a reliable information. They have been replaced Z-type markers which are more effective and precise. They are installed at almost all radio range stations. They operate on an ultra high frequency of 75 mega cycles and emit an inverted cone shaped signal directly above the range station. Owing to high frequency used, a special receiver installed for their reception at the aircraft. As the aircraft passes over the Z-marker, there is a visual indication in the cockpit which attains maximum brilliance directly over the station. Simultaneously, the pilot hears a steady high pitched signal through his earphone with the maximum intensity as the aircraft passes over the station. Like the cone of silence the duration of the Z-type marker indication increases with the increase in flight altitude.

Fan markers are used as position reporting marker on the beams of certain radio ranges. They are usually placed at a distance of 30 km (20 miles) to 40 km (25 miles) from the station. They operate on a high frequency of about 75 megacycles and send coded identification signals. When the aircraft passes over a fan marker, there comes a small light in the instrument panel in the cockpit and a steady tone is also heard by the pilot.

Inner marker and outer marker are provided in the instrument landing approach. They have been explained in article 13.4.2 under the landing aids.

(viii) Direction finder : - It is a radio direction finder (RDF) or an automatic direction finder (ADF). In RDF, the pilot rotates the radio aid installed in the aircraft till from a particular direction he receives a high pitched tone which indicates that the receiver is now pointing towards the direction of the station. A blank occurs when the RDF is directed at right angles to the direction along which the transmitter is located.

ADF is more sophisticated equipment. It keeps the antenna automatically pointing towards the source of transmission and requires no adjustment.

(ix) Air route surveillance radar (ARSR) : The word *radar* is an abbreviation to denote *radio detection and ranging*. A sharp pulse of radio frequency energy is sent out by the transmitter and repeated a number of times per second. The object to be detected receives the waves and scatters and reflects part of them. The re-radiation (echo) travels back to the site of transmission and it is detected by the radar as a signal coming from the target. The time taken for the pulse to leave the antenna and travel back as an echo indicates the distance at which the target is located. Thus the set operates as a transmitter and receiver both.

Long-range radars are installed along the airways to track the aircrafts. Each radar is effective upto a range of about 190 km (120 miles). The controller gets the picture of each aircraft in plan and thus knows the exact position of the aircraft. Prior to radar, the controller had to rely upon the pilot's accuracy in reporting his position. The long range radars permit closer spacing between the aircrafts flying at the same altitude, thereby increasing the capacity of the airways.

13.4.2 Landing Aids

The following aids are available to any aircraft while landing.

(i) Instrument landing system (ILS)

(ii) Precision approach radar (PAR) or Ground approach control (GAC)

(iii) Airport surveillance radar (ASR)

(iv) Airport surface detection equipment (ASDE)

(v) Approach lights

Each of these aids are discussed below :

(i) Instrument landing system (ILS) : It is at present the most widely used system of landing. It consists of telecommunication aids to the pilot to enable him to approach the runway and make a successful landing under condition of poor visibility even when no ground reference data is visible. ILS system provides facilities for landing even when visibility is poor. In the airfield where this facility does not exist, the landing under IFR conditions is difficult, and the aircraft is diverted to the adjoining airport where either proper visibility exists or the airport is equipped with the ILS facility. ICAO has divided the visibility into three categories for ILS approach.

Category I covers the weather conditions which provide a forward visibility of at least 800 m (1/2 mile).

Category II allows the landing upto a forward visibility of 400 m (¼ mile).

Category III permits landing under zero visibility conditions.

Figure 13.2 illustrates a typical instrument approach and the landing procedure. After passing over the Z-marker of the radio range (see-marker beacons art. 13.4.), the pilot descends at a given rate and speed for a given time. He then makes a *procedure turn* to direct the aircraft towards the runway for landing. Aircraft continues to descend till it is again intercepted by the Z-marker at a lower altitude. This altitude is usually higher than the one from which aircraft can land. Therefore further descending of the aircraft is required, till the runway comes under the plain vision of a pilot for a normal contact landing. This operation takes a minimum of 10 to 12 minutes.

The instrument landing system was developed to minimize this proc dure time and allow safe landing. But since slight delay does occur in this system as well, it may result in stacking of aircrafts during the peak hour traffic.

ILS consists of three components as follows :

(a) Localiser antenna

(b) Glide slope antenna

(c) Outer and middle markers (sometimes termed as fan marker).

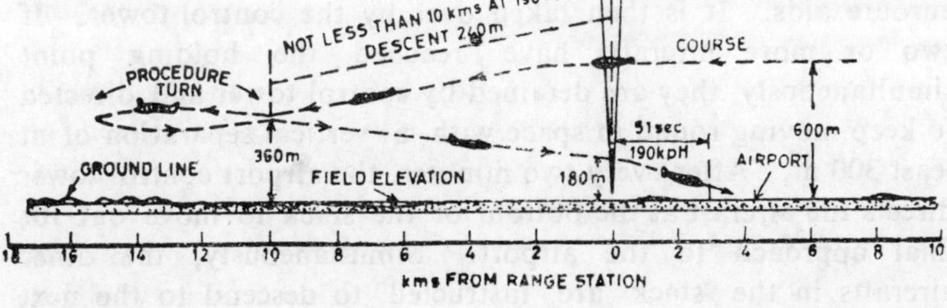

Figure 13.2 Instrument Approach and Landing Procedure

(a) Localiser antenna : It is a radio transmitter of very high frequency omni-directional range (VOR). It emits radio beam signal in vertical plane, as shown in figure 13.3 and indicates to the pilot whether he is to the left or right of the correct alignment for approach to the runway. It is located along the extended centre line of runway end as shown in Figure 13.4.

(b) Guide slope antenna : It is also a radio transmitter of very high frequency omni-directional range. It transmits radio beam signal in a horizontal plane, as shown in Figure 13.3 and indicates to the pilot, the correct angle of descent to the runway. As indicated in Figure 13.4, the glide slope antenna is located at a distance x varying from 225 to 375 m (750 to 1250 ft) down the runway from the threshold and to one side of the runway centre line at a distance y varying from 120 to 195 m.

(c) Outer and middle markers : These are small radio transmitters which serve as position reporting points. As the pilot passes over the marker, he finds a visual indication in the cockpit and receives a high pitched steady tone through his earphones.

The outer marker radio beacon gives a purple light on the instrument panel while the middle marker gives an amber light. As shown in Figure 13.4, the outer marker is located about 7 km (45 miles) and the middle marker about 1 km (0.67 mile) ahead of the runway threshold.

Figure 13.3 shows the principles of instrument landing system for a given airport. The schematic sketch of the flight procedure is shown in Figure 13.4 and is explained step by step as follows :

(i) Each aircraft is brougth to the *holding fix* by means of enroute aids. It is then taken over by the control tower. If two or more aircrafts have reached the holding point simultaneously, they are detained by control tower and directed to keep moving round in space with a vertical separation of at least 300 m. After every two minutes, the airport control tower directs the aircraft at the bottom of the stack to move out for final approach to the airport. Simultaneously, the other aircrafts in the stack are instructed to descend to the next lower level and keep moving round.

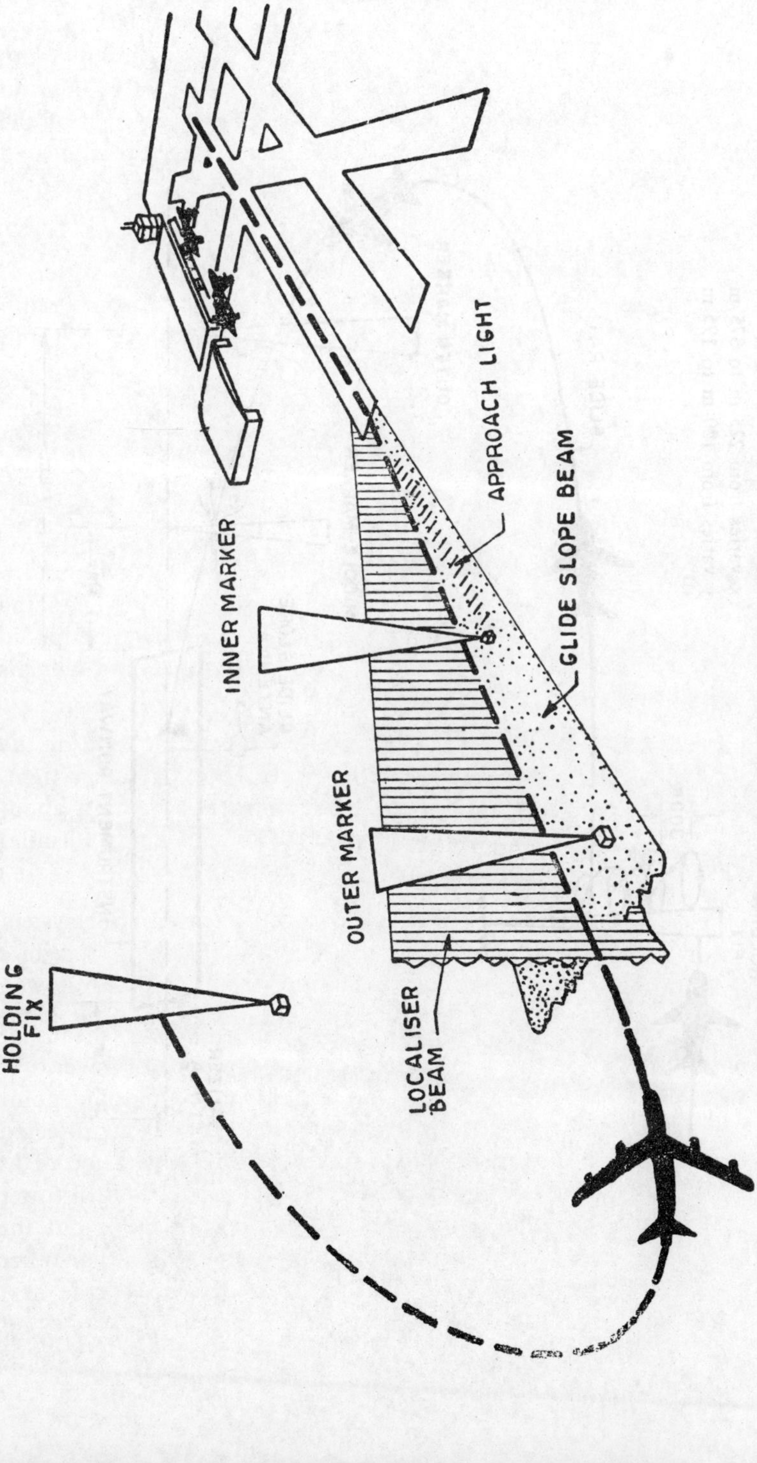

Figure 13.3 Perspective View of Instrumental Landing System

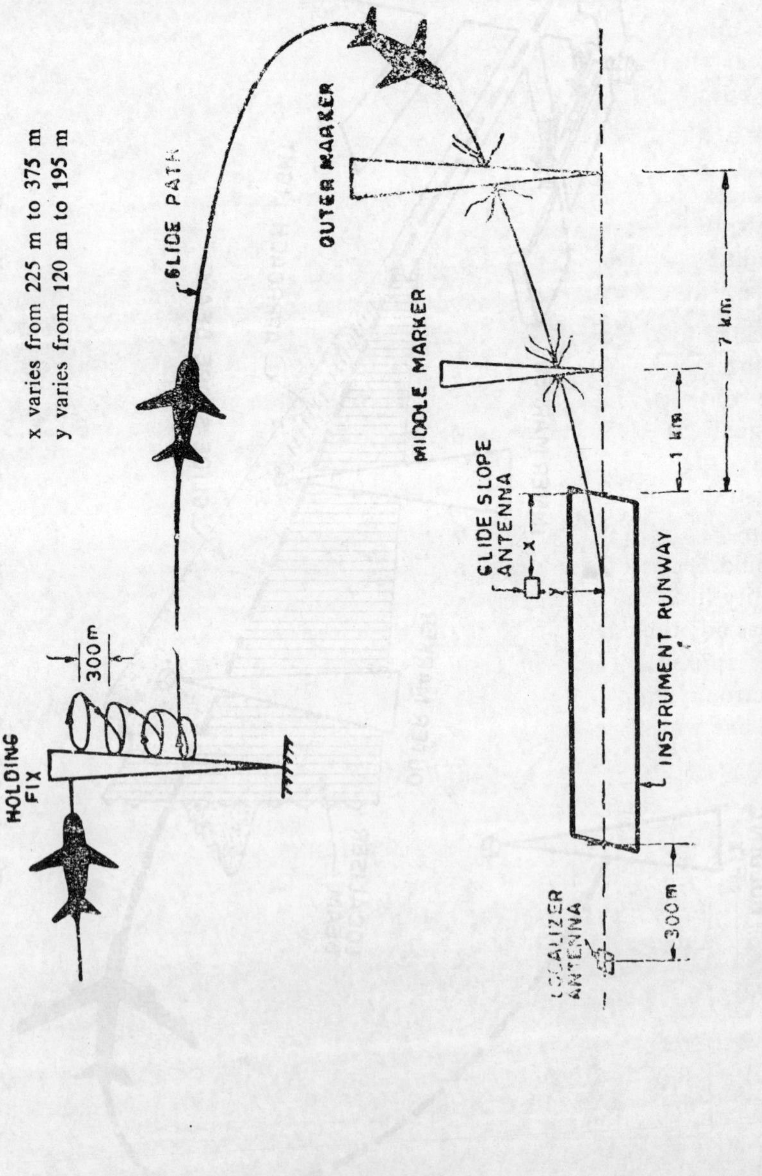

Figure 13.4 Schematic Diagram of Instrumental Landing System

(ii) As the aircraft slides out from the bottom step, it is picked up by the localiser. The localiser provides the alignment guidance along the centre line of the runway. The glide slope facility provides guidance for the angle of approach.

(iii) As the aircraft passes over the outer and middle markers, the pilot receives a high pitched steady tone and also finds a visual indication in the cockpit. These markers define the specific distances of the aircraft from the runway threshold along the localiser course.

(iv) As the aircraft crosses over the middle marker, the pilot changes over from the instrumental to visual flight system Now, the approach and runway lighting assist the pilot in visual landing.

The performance of the localiser and glide slope facility is affected by the proximity of the moving objects, e.g., vehicular traffic and aircrafts. Abrupt changes of ground slopes near the antenna may also adversely affect the transmission of singnals. Requirements for the locations of localiser antenna and the glide slope antenna, as suggested by FAA, are illustrated in Figures 13.5 to 13.7.

In Figure 13.5 for localiser antenna, the areas A and B should be free from trees, buildings, metallic fences, overhead utility lines etc. Any large objects existing or proposed in the areas adjacent to the runway, between the antenna shelter and the approach end, should be investigated by a qualified electronic engineer. The most critical area of investigation is the one which lies within a 300 m radius of the antenna shelter.

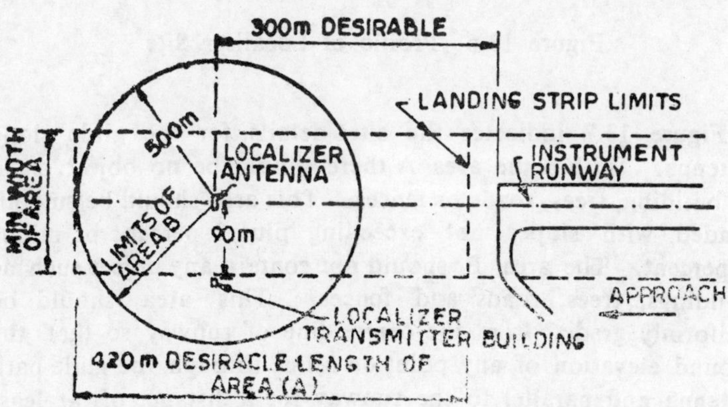

Figure 13.5 Plan of Localiser Site

In Figure 13.6, which gives the profile details of the localiser site, the transverse grades of the area A should not exceed 2 per cent. There should be a smooth transition from the transverse grades of the landing strip to the transverse grades of area A. The desired downward grade from the end of the landing strip to the localiser antenna shelter should not exceed the value which will provide a clear sight line between the top of the antenna and a point 60 m away from the approach end of the runway. The maximum upward grade should be such that the antenna array will not constitute an obstruction to the clearance line having a slope of 1 : 50. It is desirable that the longitudinal slope of area A be maintained for its full length. However, if grading to the rear of the antenna is extensive, it can be deleted unless tests indicate its necessity. In any case, the slope must be maintained for a minimum distance of 30 m from the rear of the antenna.

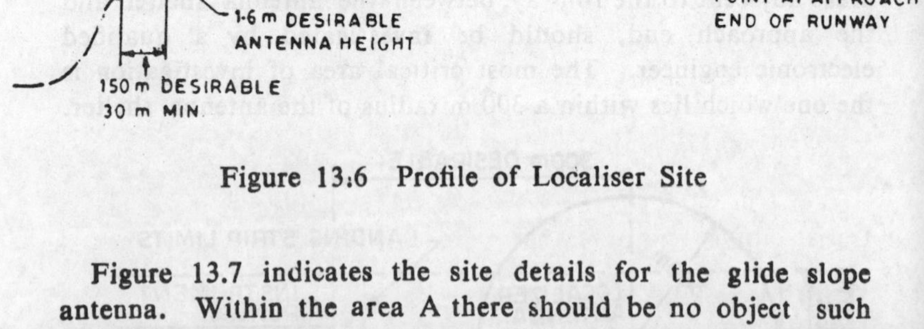

Figure 13.6 Profile of Localiser Site

Figure 13.7 indicates the site details for the glide slope antenna. Within the area A there should be no object such as building, trees, roads or fences. This area should be smooth graded with slopes not exceeding plus 2 percent or minus 3 percent. The area B should not contain any object such as buildings, trees, roads and fences. This area should be uniformly graded from the centre line of runway so that the ground elevation of any point on a line through the glide path antenna and parallel to the runway for a distance of at least 300 m in front of the glide path shall be within 2.1 m of the

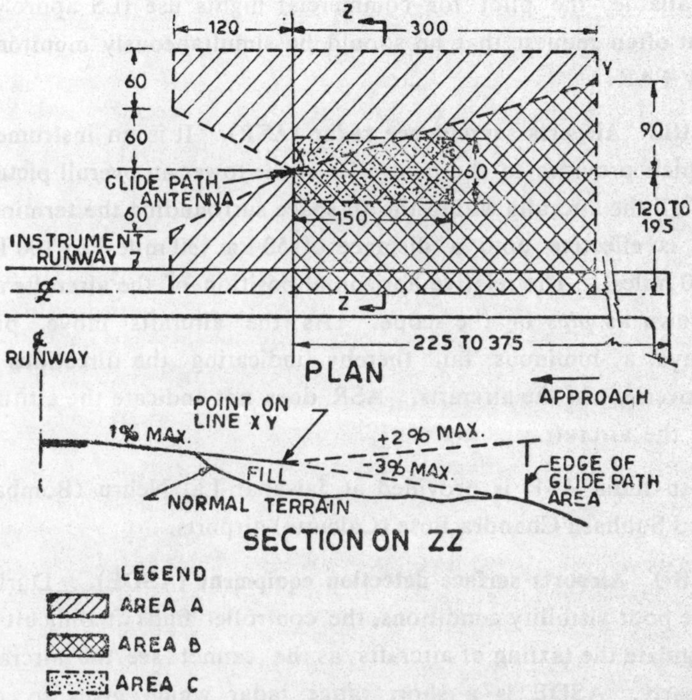

Dimensions are in metre

Figure 13.7 Site Details for Glide Slope

runway centre line elevation. Where it is not possible to keep the area A clear of taxiways or roads, at least the area C (60 m × 150 m) must be kept clear of roads and taxiways for satisfactory operation of the glide slope antenna.

(ii) Precision approach radar (PAR). It serves the same purpose as an ILS except that the guidance information reaches the pilot through his hearing aid. PAR gives to the controller the picture of descending aircraft both in plan and in elevation. The controller checks the alignment and the glide slope of the aircraft. Thus no navigational equipment is required in the aircraft. This is a definite advantage for military aircrafts since the fighter type of aircrafts have very little room for such equipment. For civilian flights, the pilot prefers to use

ILS. At airport, where both PAR and ILS facilities are available, the pilot for commercial flights use ILS approach but often request that he should be simultaneously monitored by PAR.

(iii) Airports surveillance radar (ASR). It is an instrument which provides to the controller at the tower an overall picture of all the aircrafts within the air space surrounding the terminal. It is effective upto a distance of 50 km (30 miles) to 100 km (60 miles). The relative horizontal position of the aircrafts are shown as *pips* on the scope. As the aircrafts move, pips leave a luminous tail thereby indicating the directions of movement of the aircrafts. ASR does not indicate the altitude of the aircraft.

In India ASR is provided at Jawahar Lal Nehru (Bombay) and Subhash Chandra Bose (Calcutta) airports.

(iv) Airports surface detection equipment (ASDE). During the poor visibility conditions, the controller finds it difficult to regulate the taxiing of aircrafts as he cannot see the aircrafts clearly. ASDE is a short range radar which gives to the controller a pictorial display of the runways, taxiways, terminal areas and shows the position of the aircrafts. Even during restricted visibility, this assists the controller to regulate the traffic on the airport.

(v) Approach lights : Near the runway threshold, the pilot changes over from the instrumental to visual landing. This transition is very critical as only few seconds are usually available to the pilot during which he has to complete the landing operation. To aid in the transition and to complete the landing successfully, the approaches and the runways are adequately lighted. These lighting details have been discussed in Chapter 12.

The general installation plan of the various navigational aids is shown in Figure 13.8.

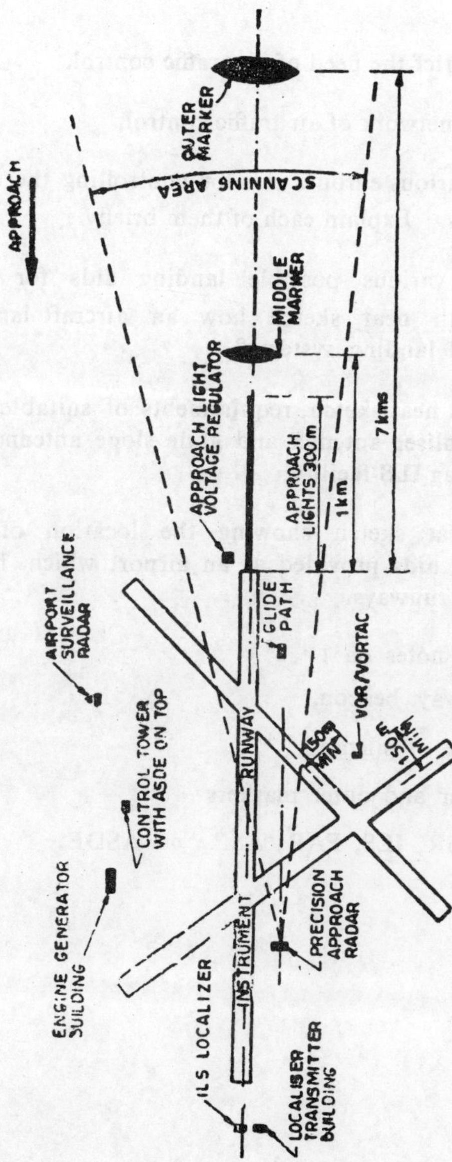

Figure 13.8 General Installation Plan of Airport Navigational Aids

PROBLEMS

1 Discuss in brief the need of air traffic control.

2 Explain the network of air traffic control.

3 Name the various enroute aids for controlling the air traffic on air routes. Explain each of them briefly.

4 Name the various possible landing aids for aircrafts. Explain with neat sketch how an aircraft lands under instrumental landing system ?

5 Explain with neat sketch, requirements of suitable sites for locating localiser antenna and glide slope antenna at the airport having ILS facility.

6 Draw a neat sketch showing the location of various navigational aids provided at an airport which has three intersecting runways.

7 Write short notes on :

Airway beacon,

Cone of silence,

Inner and outer markers

ARSR, ILS, PAR, ASR and ASDE.

14

AIRPORT GRADING & DRAINAGE

14.1 GENERAL

The site selected for airport may have undulating ground profile. The entire area is properly graded to enable the quick drainage of storm water and also to facilitate the construction of various airport elements. The grading is done with minimum cost of earthwork. Special considerations are given to the grading operations for the airports which are under stage construction. The grading for each stage construction is planned in such a way that the resulting grades conform well with the final grades.

The grading of an airport is a complex problem as it involves an additional dimension of width. For preparation of grading plan, the topographic map of the area is first prepared. This map is carefully studied so as to identify the areas that may contribute surface or sub surface flow towards the airport area. This helps to determine the overall directions of natural surface flow and to locate all the existing natural streams or depressions that may receive the discharge of the outfall flow from the airport area.

A typical topographical map is illustrated in Figure 14.1. The south-east portion of the site and the building area appears to have the highest elevation. The south-west and north-west

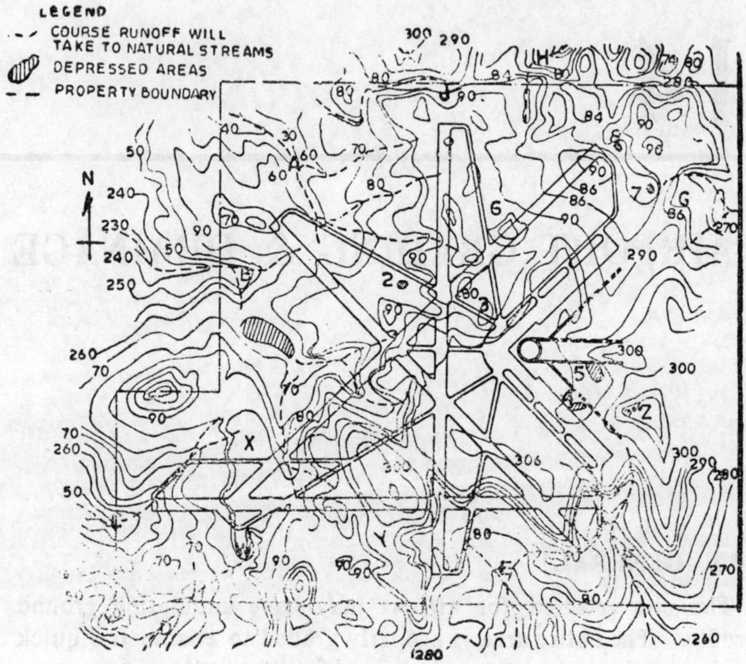

Figure 14.1 Typical Topographical Map of the Site for Airport Drainage

corners of the site have the lowest elevations. No. definite direction of surface flow can be defined here. Possible outfall points which are indicated in the figure by letters A to J should be studied in connection with the drainage system.

Few depressions are observed in the site. Soil boring when done would indicate if the water is trapped in these depression and weather subsurface drains are required to tap them. The airport master plan showing the locations of airport boundaries, runways, taxiways, aprons, and building area is surerimposed on the topographic map of the site so as to determine the earthwork. The main factors in the preparation of grading plans are the existing topography, type of soil, grades and cross-slopes to be provided, orientation of runways, taxiways, terminal buildings, aprons and hangars. As far as possible, the amount of cut and fill should balance each other and the amount of lead is kept to a minimum. If the amount of cut is more, the excess material is filled in the approaches. Sometimes the whole field area is graded. In such cases the grade lines are designed very carefully since the moving up or down of the grade lines even by a fraction of a centimetre means a substantial change in the volume of earthwork involved.

The following general points are observed in the grading :

1. The amount of cut and fill should, as far as possible balance each other. The haulage distance and the amount of earthwork to be moved should also be kept to a minimum.
2. Subgrade soils should, as far as practicable, be of a uniform character to ensure a uniform subgrade support.
3. Proper surface and subsurface drainage should be done to ensure the stability of the pavement and the embankments.
4. Grading plans should be prepared to carry the surface water away from the runways, taxiways, apron areas and building area.
5. If two or more landing strips cross each other, the intersecting runways are assigned common grade elevations at the intersection.
6. The areas at the end of the landing strips should also be graded as a precautionary measure. Thus the aircraft, which may enter these areas unintentionally due to prematured take off or due to undershooting, the strip while landing would have minimum.
7. The choice of the equipment for clearing, grading and compaction should be determined considering the nature of the material involved, job size, local practice and construction time assigned etc.

Considering the above factors, the finally proposed grading plan is prepared. The drainage working drawing is shown on the grading plan, Figure 4.2.

14.2 COMPUTATION OF EARTHWORK

The volume of earthwork can be computed by using any one of the two methods, Cross-sectional method and Mass haul curve.

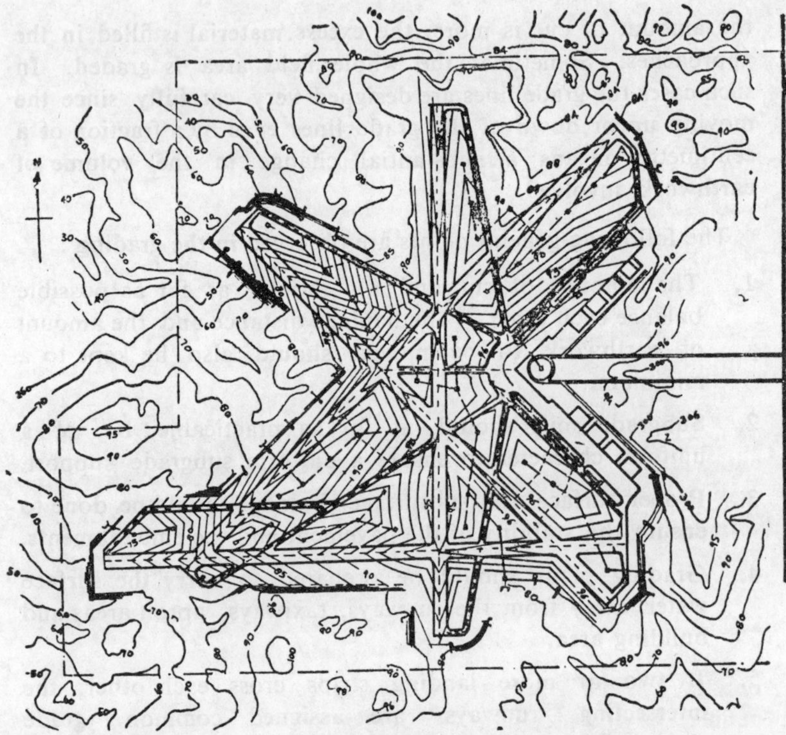

Figure 14.2 Typical Proposed Grading Plan

Cross-sectional method gives only the quantities of earthwork whereas the mass haul curve gives the direction of movement of earthwork and the haulage distances as well.

14.2.1 Cross-sectional Method

In this method, cross-sectional area is plotted at suitable intervals, say 30 m. The area of each cross-section is then determined either by graph or by planimeter. The volume of earthwork is then calculated by horizontal or by trapezoidal formula as given below. Trapezoidal formula requires odd number of cross-sections or otherwise the last cross-section is considered separately.

Trapezoidal formula :

$$V = D\left[\frac{A_0 + A_n}{2} + A_1 + A_2 + A_3 + \ldots A_{n-1}\right] \quad (14.1)$$

Prismoidal formula :

$$V = \frac{D}{3}\left[A_0+4A_1+2A_2+4A_3+2A_4+\ \ldots\ \ldots\ \ldots +2A_{n-2}+4A_{n-1}+A_n\right] \quad (14.2)$$

where, V = volume of cut or embankment

D = distance between two consecutive cross-sections,

A_0, A_1, A_2, A_n = Cross-sectional areas at zero, D, 2D ... nD distances from the beginning.

14.2.2 Mass-haul Curve

Embankments are built of material which is obtained from the excavation during grading operations or from the borrow pits. The limit of the distance up to which material is hauled without any extra cost is called *free haul distance*. If the material is to be hauled further than the limit of free haul, an extra amount is charged by the contractor. The permissible distance of free haul depends upon the means of transport, e.g. for transport by manual labour, the free haul may be upto 150 m to 300 m. There is a limiting distance beyond which it would be economical to waste excavation and to haul from a borrow pit for marking the fill. The economical haul may be defined as the maximum distance to which the excavation obtained may be utilised in filling up any depression. At the point, it will cost the same whether the excavated material is hauled up to the point, paying for the overhaul, or the cut is thrown as a waste and the earth required for filling is obtained from the borrow pit. The limit of economical haul may be determined by the formula as follows :

$$L = \frac{B}{O} + F \quad (14.3)$$

where, L = limit of economical haul in stations

B = cost of borrow per cubic metre per station

O = cost of overhaul per station metre i.e. carrying one cubic metre for one station beyond the limit of free haul.

F = free haul in stations.

The mass haul curve shows a cumulative volume of earthwork at any point. The following information is obtained from this diagram :

(i) The quantity of earthwork

(ii) The direction of movement of eartwork

(iii) Free haul earthwork

(iv) The amount of earth from borrow pits.

A typical mass haul curve is shown in Figure 14.3. It is plotted immediately below the final grade line AFLNV. The abscissas of both, the ground profile and the mass curve are in stations, each at 30 m distance. The ordinates of the ground profile are in metres. The ordinates of mass diagram indicate the net cumulative earthwork at each station. The cumulative earthwork is computed in the direction in which the stations progress.

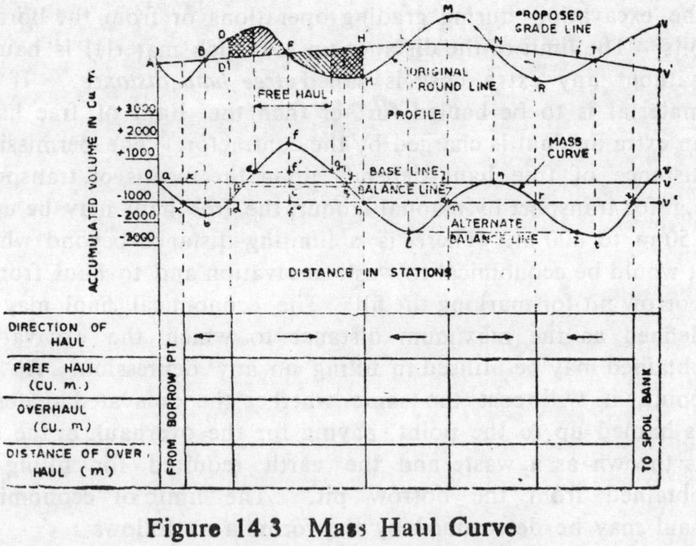

Figure 14.3 Mass Haul Curve

The mass haul curve has the following characteristics :

(i) The mass haul curve represents the algebraic summation of the quantity of earthwork from the station.

(ii) Cut is plotted upwards and fill is plotted downwards with reference to a given base line.

(iii) The lowest point of a loop that forms a sag indicates the position of a change from fill to cut. The highest point of a loop that forms a peak indicates the position of a change from cut to fill.

(iv) Between any two consecutive points where a horizontal line or balance line intersects the mass haul curve, the quantity of earthwork is balanced. For example in the loop *d e f g h* (Figure 14.3), the net cut on the mass curve from *d* to *f* is balanced by the net fill from *f* to *h*.

(v) The maximum ordinate of any loop represents the total quantity of earthwork that is to be moved from cut to fill. The quantity of earthwork to be moved in the loop *d e f g h* is represented by the ordinate *ff″*.

(vi) A balance line can be moved up or down on the diagram until the most desirable points are obtained. The balance lines need not be continuous. It can be stopped at any point where it intersects mass haul curve. The vertical separation between two balance lines indicates either borrow or waste.

(vii) If the loop mass haul curve is above the balance line, e.g. loop *d e f g h,* the excavated material is to be moved in direction in which the stations progress or from left to right in the mass haul curve. Where the loop is below the balance line, as *h l m* the material is to be moved in the opposite direction, i.e., from right to left in the curve.

(viii) The contractor obviously prefers to haul in both the directions from a cut. The balance line *x r* should be so located that the point M on the profile, which is vertically above the point of intersection *m* of the balance line with the mass haul curve is located practically in the centre of cut LMN. As a result of this, the material excavated between M and N will be hauled forward in marking the fill between N and R. Similarly, the material excavated between M and L will be hauled backward in marking the fill between L and H. By raising the balance line *x r* slightly, the point D on the cut between B and F, which is vertically above the point *d* on mass haul curve, can be brought nearer to the centre of the cut.

(ix) The direction of haul may be changed by shifting the balance line. To explain this, an alternate balance line, *l z* is drawn. Since the loop *l m n r z* is above the line, the haul is towards right. A line projected vertically from *l* intersects the profile at L and the excavated material from the entire cut between L and N must be moved to the right. Now if the part *y n* of the base line is considered as the balance line, the loop $y\ h\ l\ m\ n$ is below the balance line and this indicates that the haul is to the left. The vertical line from n intersects the profile at N and therefore the entire cut between N and L must be moved to the left. It is obvious that selected balanced line $x\ r$ is more satisfactory than any of the alternate balance lines $l\ z$ or $y\ n$.

(x) By shifting the balance lines, it may be possible to change the direction of haul from uphill to downhill and thus benefit the contractor without increasing the cost in any way.

(xi) To find out the free haul volume for any loop, say $d\ e\ f\ g\ h$, the line $e\ g$ is drawn parallel to the base line such that the distance $e\ g$ = free haul distance. The ordinate $f\ f'$ then represents the free haul volume. The ordinate $f'\ f''$ represents the pay overhaul volume. To determine the overhaul distance, the ordinate $f'\ f''$ is bisected at the point c. A line $p\ c\ q$ is drawn to intersect the mass haul curve at the points p and q respectively. The points p and q represent the centres of gravity of the crossed areas and the distance $p\ q$ minus the free haul distance represents the overhaul distance.

Example 14.1

Table 14.1 illustrates the data obtained for grading of a runway section. The profile to the proposed subgrade is levelled and is at an elevation of 97 m. The free haul distance is 100 m. Plot the existing ground profile and the mass haul curve for the section of runway under consideration.

Determine graphically the following :

(i) The division point in the cut to give the least possible total haul.

(ii) The total free haul

(iii) The total borrow

(iv) The total cost of earthwork assuming the following rates.

Cost of borrow = 80 paise per cubic meter

Cost of excavation = 90 paise per cubic meter

Cost of overhaul = 10 paise per station meter

Table 14.1 Earth Work Computations

Station	Chainage	Elevation m	Volume of cut cubic m	Volume of fill cubic m	Accumulated volume cubic m
50	1500	90			
51	1530	89		825	− 125
52	1560	91		900	−1725
53	1590	97		200	−1925
54	1620	97		0	−1925
55	1650	103	300		−1625
56	1680	105	1025		− 600
57	1710	104	1050		+ 450
58	1740	103	750		+1200
59	1770	100	600		+1800
60	1800	97	250		+2050
61	1830	89		300	+1750
62	1860	85		1200	+ 550
63	1890	85		1650	−1100
Total			3975	5075	1100

Solution

The ground profile and the mass haul diagram are plotted in Figure 14.4.

$$\text{Free haul} = 100 \text{ m}$$

$$\text{Limit of economical haul} = \frac{\text{Cost of borrow}}{\text{Cost of overhaul}} + \text{Free haul}$$

$$= \frac{80}{10} \text{ stations} + \text{Free haul}$$

$$= 8 \times 30 + 100 \text{ m}$$

$$= 340 \text{ m}$$

The balance line $x\,y$ is so drawn that the intercepts $x\,j$ and $j\,y$ in the two loops are nearly equal and each one is not greater than the economical haul distance. Lines $g\ h$ and $l\,m$ which represent the free haul distances are drawn parallel to to base line in the two loops. To determine the overhaul distance, the ordinates gg_1, hh_1, ll_1 and mm_1 are bisected at the points o_1, o_2, o_3 and o_4 respectively. From each of these points, lines are drawn parallel to the base line so as to intersect

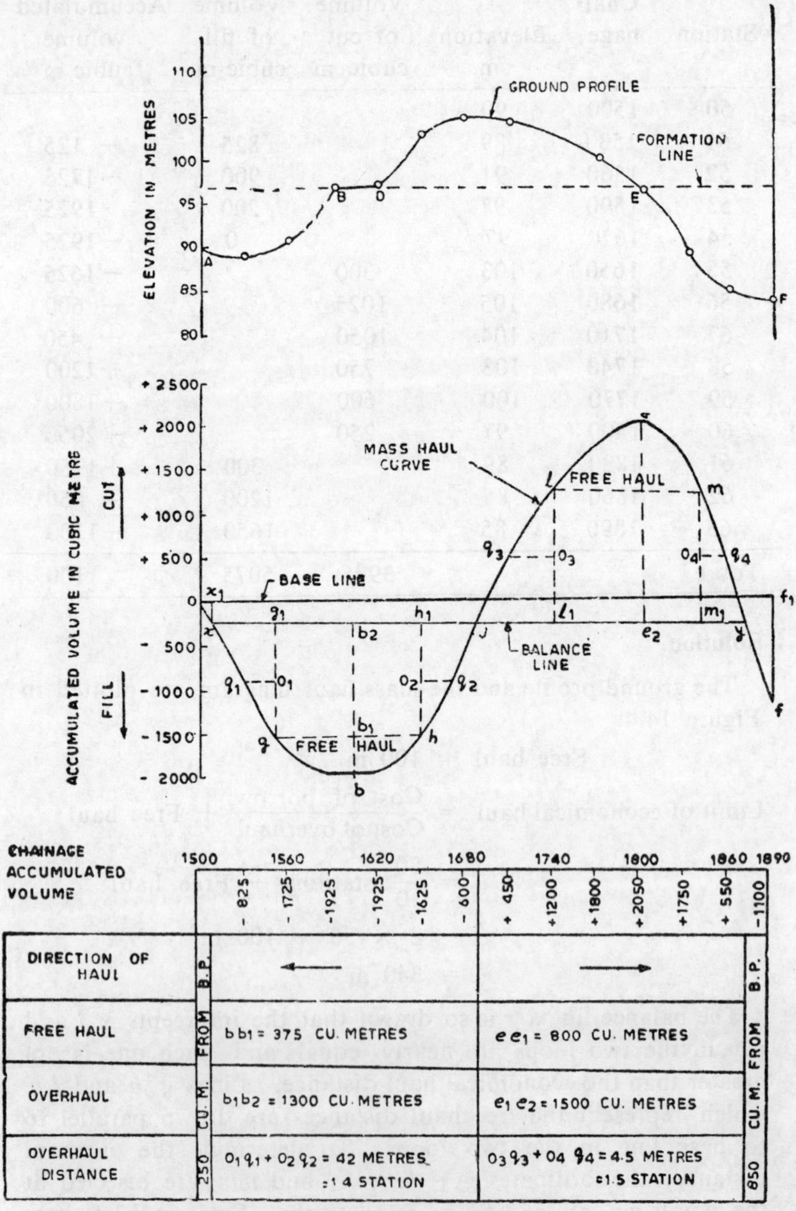

DIRECTION OF HAUL	250 CU. M. FROM B.P.	←	→	850 CU. M. FROM B.P.
FREE HAUL		bb_1 = 375 CU. METRES	ee_1 = 800 CU. METRES	
OVERHAUL		b_1b_2 = 1300 CU. METRES	e_1e_2 = 1500 CU. METRES	
OVERHAUL DISTANCE		$o_1q_1 + o_2q_2$ = 42 METRES = 1.4 STATION	$o_3q_3 + o_4q_4$ = 4.5 METRES = 1.5 STATION	

Figure 14.4 Ground Profile and Mass Haul Diagram

the mass haul curve at q_1, q_2, q_3, and q_4. The overhaul distances for loop I and II are $(o_1 q_1 + o_2 q_2)$ and $(o_3 q_3 + o_4 q_4)$ respectively. The various information desired can now be given as follows :

(i) The division point in the cut to give least possible total haul is represented by the point J having a chainage of 1692 m.

(ii) The total free haul volume is represented by the sum of the ordinates bb_1 and ee_1.

Therefore, total free haul = 375+800 = 1175 cubic m

(iii) Total borrow = $xr_1 + ff_1$

= 250+850 = 1100 cubic m

(iv) Cost of earthwork includes the following :

(a) Cost of borrow :

The volume of borrow = 1100 cubic m

Cost of borrow = 1100×0.80

= Rs. 880

(b) Cost of excavation :

Total volume of excavation = $bb_1 + ee_1$

= 1675 + 2300

= 3975 cubic m

Cost of excavation = 3975 × 0.90

= Rs. 3577.5

(c) Cost of overhaul :

Overhaul volume for loop I

= $b_1 b_2$

= 1300 cubic m

Pay overhaul distance = $o_1 q_1 + o_2 q_2$

= 42 m = 1.40 stations.

Cost of overhaul for loop I = 1300 × 1.40 × 0.10

= Rs. 182

Overhaul volume for loop II = $c_1 c_2$ = 1500 cu. m.

Pay overhaul distance = $o_3 q_4 + o_4 q_4$

= 45 m = 1.5 stations

Cost of overhaul for loop II = 1500×1.5×0.10 = Rs. 225

Total cost = 880+3577.5+182+225

= Rs. 5864.50

14.3 AIRPORT DRAINAGE

An adequate drainage system is essential for the safety of aircraft and long life of pavement. Improper drainage results in heavy ponding on the pavement surface which can be hazardous to safe landing or taking off of aircrafts. Poor drainage can also result early in failure of the pavement. The cost of replacing on airport drain, if it is found inadequate in cource of time, especially when it passes through the paved areas is exhorbitant. Thus drainage is one of the most vital item in the construction of an airport.

A drainage system for an airfield normally serves three functions.

(i) Removal of surface run off the airfield

(ii) Interception and diversion of surface and ground water flow originating from lands adjacent to the airfield area

(iii) Lowering of subsurface water level in the airfield area.

14.4 SPECIAL CHARACTERISTICS & REQUIREMENTS OF AIRPORT DRAINAGE

The airport drainage has unusual requirements. It is considered to be a complex design problem. Its special characteristics are :

(i) Extensive area under consideration

(ii) Varying soil conditions

(iii) Heavy concentrated wheel loads of aircrafts

(iv) Wide runways, taxiways and aprons

(v) Flat longitudinal and transverse grades

(vi) Shallow water courses

(vii) Absence of side ditches

(viii) Concentration of outfall flow

The drainage pipe should have sufficient capacity to carry the ground water as well as the surface water. Rapid drainage is essential for safety of the aircraft operations as well as of the pavement. This drain pipe should be sufficiently strong to withstand the heavy concentrated wheel loads of the aircrafts. The crushing of the pipe may cause interruption of the drainage which may result in the failure of the pavement or hazard to aircraft operations. Possibility of future runway extension, additional runways and taxiways should be given due consideration at the initial stages. The main drainage line should have sufficient capacity to handle run off from the future construction.

14.5 DESIGN DATA

For the design of drainage system, certain basic informations are collected. Their data consists primarily of the following :

(i) A contour map of the airport site and land adjacent to the site showing all natural water courses, the area contributing runoff on the site and possible outfalls and ditches is prepared. The countour interval should not be more than 0.6 m (2 ft.)

(ii) An additional map is prepared showing the existing layout of the runways, aprons, building area and also the future development, with tentative finished grade contours indicated therein. The contour interval should be 0.3 m (1 ft). The map should be used as the *drainage working drawing* and should also show all pipe lines, manholes, inlets, outfalls, individual drainage area subdivisions, drain pipe slopes etc. Trial computations of several different drainage layouts should be made in arriving at the most economical design. Typical drainage plan is shown in Figure 14.2 The schematic drawing showing details of drainage layouts for runways are illustrated in Figures 14.5 and 14.6.

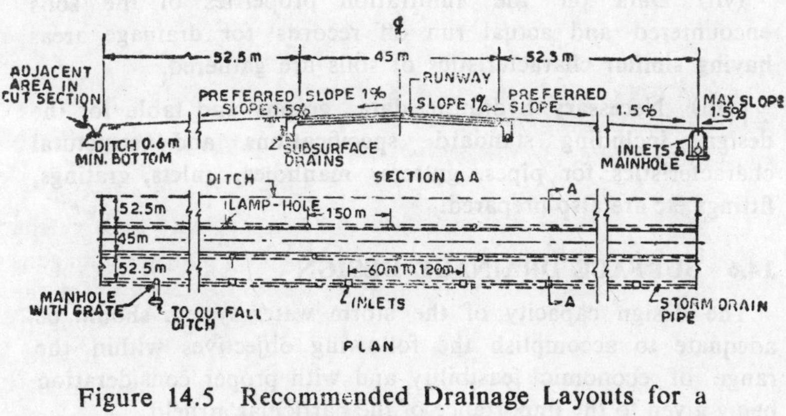

Figure 14.5 Recommended Drainage Layouts for a Runway (FAA)

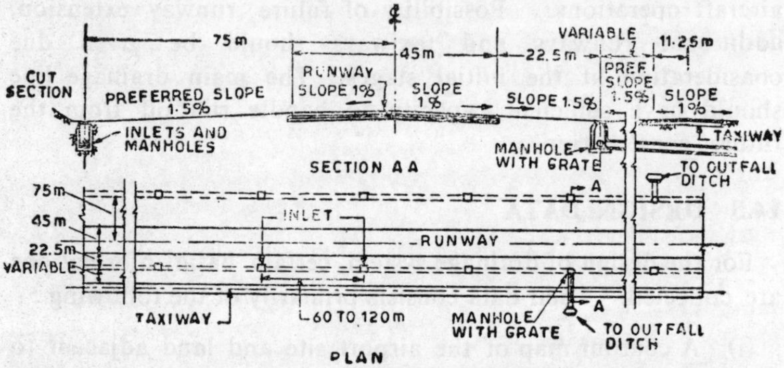

Figure 14.6 Recommended Drainage Layout for Runway and a Parallel Taxiway System (FAA)

(iii) The rainfall data such as frequency, intensity and duration of storms for a period of 5 to 10 years, is taken from the meteorological studies. The rainfall intensity-duration curve is then developed for the site.

(iv) Centre line profiles of all the runways, taxiways and apron area with necessary cross sections are prepared.

(v) Boring plans of soil strata along with ground water profile etc. are prepared.

(vi) Temperature data, especially on maximum and minimum temperatures including seasons of freezing and thawing, depths of frost penetration etc. are collected.

(vii) Data on the infiltration properties of the soils encountered and actual run off records for drainage areas having similar characteristics of soils are gathered.

(viii) Necessary hydraulic data, graphs and table for the design, including standard specifications and structural characteristics for pipes, gutters, manholes, inlets, gratings, fittings etc are also prepared.

14.6 SURFACE DRAINAGE DESIGN

The design capacity of the storm water system should be adequate to accomplish the following objectives within the range of economic feasibility and with proper consideration being given to the importance of the particular airfield.

(i) Removal of surface runoff resulting from the selected design storm without damage to the airfield facilities, undue saturation of subsoil or significant interruption of normal traffic is considered.

(ii) The possibilities of removal of surface runoff from storms greater than the *design storm* with the minimum damage to the airfield facilities and with the shortest interruption of normal traffic are considered.

(iii) Maximum reliability of the operations practicable under all climatic conditions is estimated.

(iv) Minimum maintenance and operation difficulties and expenses etc are observed.

(v) Adaptability to future expenses and interruption of normal traffic is also considered.

14.6.1 Estimation of Runoff

The amount of runoff depends upon the number of factors and is not constant for any given area even during a single period of precipitation.

The following factors may influence the rate of run off for any given area :

(i) Condition of the soil affecting infiltration.
(ii) Temperature of air, water and soil.
(iii) Extent and condition of vegetation cover.
(iv) Perviousness or imperviousness of surface.
(v) Slopes of surface.
(vi) Moisture content of the soil.

Since there are numerous factors affecting the runoff, it is difficult to cover all of them. For airport drainage, the estimation of runoff is obtained by the following expression :

$$Q = CIA \quad (14.4)$$

where, Q = runoff in cubic metres/sec, (cu. ft/sec.)

A = drainage area in 100 sq. metres (in acres).

I = intensity of rainfall in mm/sec. (inches/hr) for the time of concentration.

C = coefficient of runoff representing the ratio of runoff to rainfall

14.6.2 Time of Concentration

The time of concentration is defined as the time taken by

storm water to reach the drain inlet from the farthest point in the tributory area. It usually consists of two components, viz., *inlet time* and *time of flow*. The *inlet time* is the time taken by storm water to flow overland from the most remote point in the drainage area to the drain inlet. The time of flow is the time during which water flows through the drainage system to the point under consideration. Inlet time is obtained roughly from the empirical relationship as follows :

$$D = K\,T^2 \tag{14.5}$$

where, D = distance in metre

T = inlet time in minute and

K = a dimensional empirical factor which depends on slope, roughness of terrain, extent of vegetation cover and distance to the drain inlet.

In let time can be obtained from Figure 14.7. The time of flow can be obtained by dividing the length of drain pipe by the velocity of flow.

14.6.3 Coefficient of Runoff

The coefficient of runoff depends upon the previous storm conditions, slope of surface porosity of soil and extent of the drainage area. The values, as suggested by FAA, are given in Table 14.2.

For the entire drainage area consisting of several types of surfaces with different infiltration characteristics, the runoff coefficient is computed from the following expression :

$$C = \frac{A_1 C_1 + A_2 C_2 + A_3 C_3}{A_1 + A_2 + A_3} \tag{14.6}$$

where,

A_1, A_2, A_3 = areas of different types of surfaces

C_1, C_2, C_3 = respective coefficients of runoff

14.6.4 Intensity-Duration Curves

To allow for the worst conditions, different duration of storm is selected for each subdrainage area tributory to drain inlet. The duration of the storm is made equal to the inlet time plus the time of flow. The typical rainfall intensity-duration pattern is shown in Figure 14.8. FAA design procedure is based on 5 year frequency storm.

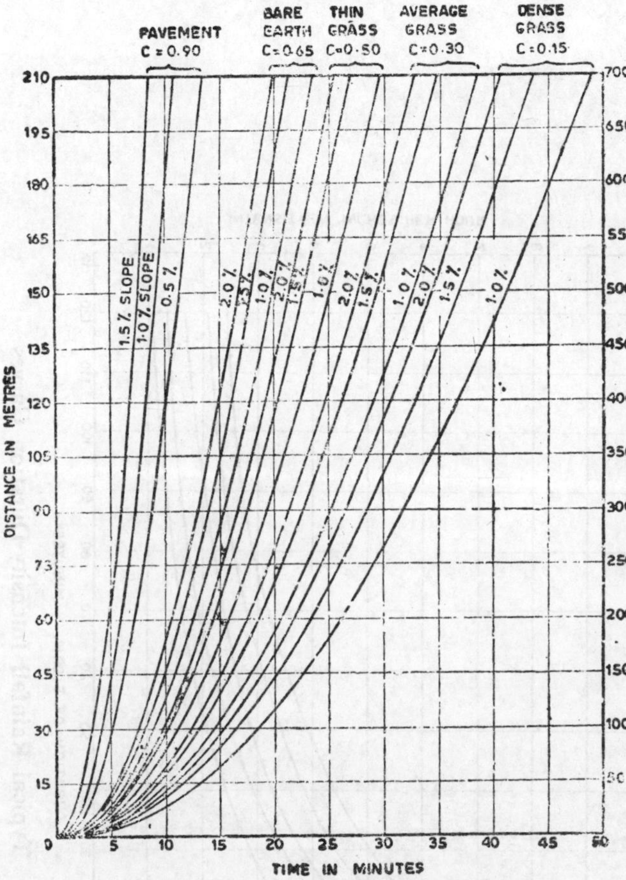

Figure 14.7 Inlet Time Curves

Table 14.2 Coefficient of Runoff, C

Type of Surface	Factor, C
Watertight roof surface	0.75—0.95
Bituminous runway pavements	0.80—0.95
Cement concrete runway pavements	0.70—0.90
Gravel or macadam pavements	0.35—0.70
Impervious soils*	0.40—0.65
Impervious soils with turf*	0.30—0.55
Slightly pervious soils with turf*	0.10—0.30
Moderately pervious soils*	0.05—0.20
Moderately pervious soils*	0.00—0.10

*For slopes of 1 or 2 per cent

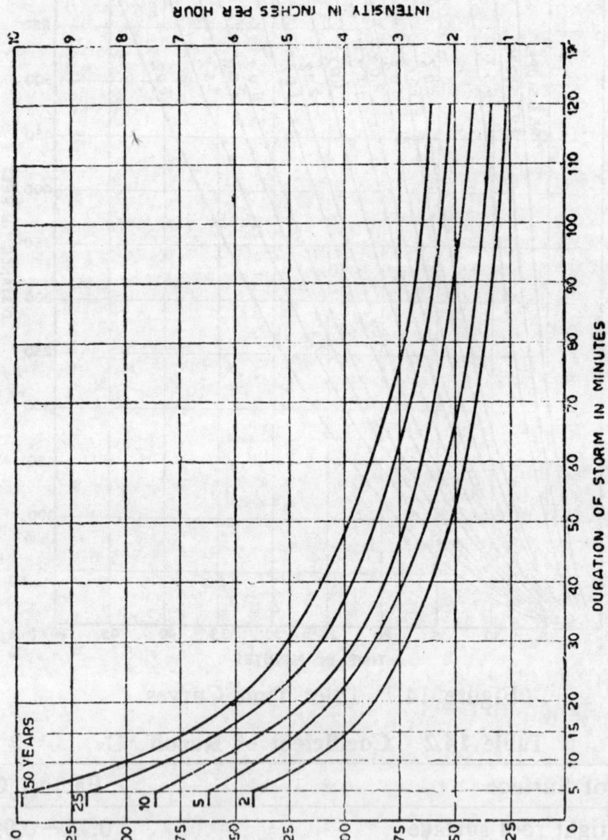

Figure 14.8 Typical Rainfall Intensity-Duration Curves

14.6.5 General Design Principles

Each pipe is designed to carry the discharge from the inlet at its upstream end plus the contribution through all preceding inlets. From economic considerations, the grade of each drainage line is fixed studying the natural topography. A minimum mean velocity of 0.75 m/sec (2.5 ft/sec) is maintained to prevent scuring action. The diameter of the storm drain is not less than 30 cm (12 in) to ensure an adequate cross section for flow at all times. The inlet is located at a distance not less than 22.5 m (75 ft) from the edges of the pavement. If there exists a taxiway parallel to the runway, the inlets are placed in a valley between the runway and the taxiway. However, on aprons the inlets are usually placed in the pavement. This is the only way by which the large area of the apron can be drained efficiently. The drain inlets are usually spaced 60 to 120 m (200 to 400 ft) apart in case of *ponding* and 52.5 m (175 ft) in case of no *ponding* condition.

The step-by step design procedure is described below :

14.4.6 Design Procedure

(i) Identify the structures and establish the length of pipe segments between the structures with sufficient accuracy.

(ii) Selected values for coefficient of run-off for all type of surfaces over which the water would flow. Table 14.2 is used as a guide in arriving at the acceptable values for this factor.

(iii) Compute weighted values of C, as explained in article 14.6.3.

(iv) Determine the distance from the inlet to the most distant point in the tributory subarea. If in flowing from such point, water traverses different types of surface, the length of flow over each type of the surface is determined.

(v) Using the distances determined as per step (iv) above and the topographical drawings, the time of flow to the inlet from the most distant point can be established. The time so determined is the *inlet time*. It may be obtained by use of Figure 14.7, keeping in mind that the total length of overland flow may consist of several sublengths, each of different surface and slope.

(vi) Determine the time of concentration for the inlet in accordance with the principles outlined in article 14.6.2.

(vii) Using Figure 14.8, find the rainfall intensity for the corresponding time of concentration.

(viii) Compute the quantity of runoff by the formula Q = CIA. This is the amount of water which the effluent pipe must accommodate.

(ix) Calculate the pipe size and slope which would carry the runoff. This can be done by using Manning's formula :

$$Q = \frac{AR^{2/3} S^{1/2}}{n} \text{ cubic m/sec} \quad (14.7)$$

where Q = quantity of water which a given size drain would carry in cubic m/sec.

A = cross-sectional area of the drain in sq-m

R = mean hydraulic radius in metre

$$= \frac{\text{area of cross-section of drain pipe}}{\text{wetted perimeter of drain pipe}}$$

n = coefficient of roughness, (as given in Table 14.3).

Table 14.3 Coefficient of Roughness, n

		Factor n
A Pipe :		
1	Clay and concrete :	
(i)	Good alignment, smooth joints and smooth transitions.	0.013
(ii)	Less favourable flow conditions ...	0.015
2	Corrugated metal :	
(i)	100 percent of periphery smoothly lined	0.013
(ii)	Paved invert, 50 percent of periphery paved	0.018
(iii)	Paved invert, 25 percent of periphery paved	0.021
(iv)	Unpaved, bituminous coated or noncoated	0.024
B Open Channels :		
1	Paved	0.015-0.020
2	Unpaved	
(i)	Bare earth, shallow flow ...	0.020-0.025
(ii)	Bare earth, depth of flow over 0.3 m (1 ft)	0.015-0.020
(iii)	Turf, shallow flow	0.060-0.080
(iv)	Turf, depth of flow over 0.3 m (1 ft)	0.040-0.060

14.6.7 Ponding

Ponding is simply a means of providing temporary storage of runoff prior to its entry into the underground system. Wherever practicable, a ponding area should be provided, whether large or small. This would protect the pavement areas from damage due to storms of intensity greater than the design value. Ponding is, however, prohibited on runway and taxiway pavements, parking aprons, runway shoulders, taxiway shoulders and on any area that might result in damage due to the saturation of pavement subgrade or base course. Ponding may be permissible on open airfield areas and graded areas where it would not saturate or damage the subgrades or base courses. To prevent the saturation of ground adjacent to the pavement, it is considered essential that all edges of ponding area be kept at least 22.5 m away from the edge of the pavements. For purposes of design computations, ponded volume is assumed to be an inverted pyramid or turncated pyramid, the height of which is equal to the depth of water above the inlet at any stage. The area of the base of pyramid is taken as the surface area of the pond.

The procedure, as outlined in article 14.6 6 is followed in case of ponding in addition to the following :

(i) Calculate the volume of possible storage by the formula

$$V = \frac{1}{3} b \left(A + B + \sqrt{AB}\right) \tag{14.8}$$

where, V = volume of pond in cubic metre

b = height of pond in metre

A = area of the upper surface of the pond in sq-m

B = area of the lower surface of the pond in sq-m

(ii) Obtain from Figure. 14.8, the rainfall intensities for duration of 5, 10, 15, 20, 30, 60, 90 and 120 minutes. Compute the volume of runoff for each case by the formula :

$$Q = CIA \times t \tag{14.9}$$

(iii) Plot the cumulative runoff versus time.

(iv) Assume suitable pipe diameter, slope of the pipe and the roughness coefficient. Determine the discharge capacity of the pipe from Manning's formula. Plot in the above graph the discharge capacity versus time curve for the selected drain pipe.

(v) Scale the largest difference between the cumulative runoff curve and discharge capacity curve. This represents the maximum amount of ponding after beginning of the storm.

(vi) For safety, this should be less than the calculated volume of the pond as per (i) above.

Example 14.2

Figure 14.9 indicates locations of the drain inlets along a portion of runway length. Design the drainage system to carry the surface runoff.

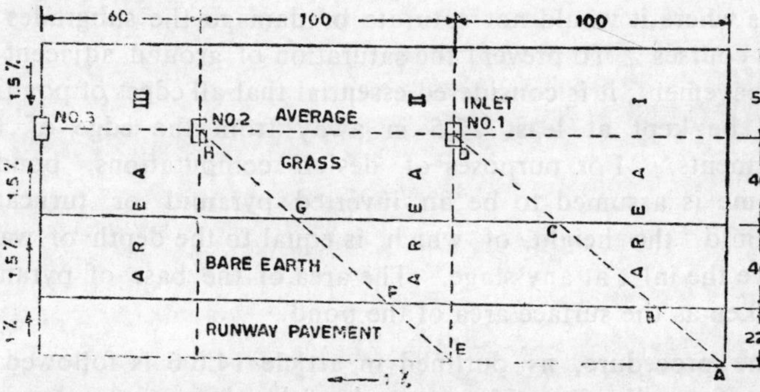

Figure 14.9 Locations of Drain Inlets along Runway

Solution

Case 1 When Ponding is not Permitted

1 Design of Inlet No. 1

(a) Determine weighted value of C

A_1 = Pavement area = 100×22.5 = 2250 sq-m

$C_1 = 0.90$

A_1 = Bare earth area = 100×40 = 4000 sq-m

$C_2 = 0.65$

A_3 = Turf area = 100×90 = 9000 sq-m

$C_3 = 0.30$

$$\text{Average } C = \frac{A_1 C_1 + A_2 C_2 + A_3 C_3}{A_1 + A_2 + A_3}$$

$$= \frac{2250 \times 0.90 + 4000 \times 0.65 + 9000 \times 0.30}{2250 + 4000 + 9000}$$

$$= 0.48$$

(b) Determine the time of concentration

The inlet time is obtained corresponding to the farthest point of the area to be drained by the inlet No. 1.

Inlet time is, therefore, calculated along the path AD.

$$\text{Distance, AD} = \sqrt{100^2 + 102.5^2} = 143.2 \text{ m}$$

$$\text{Pavement length, AB} = \frac{143.2}{102.5} \times 22.5 = 31.4 \text{ m}$$

$$\text{Bare earth distace, BC} = \frac{143.2}{102.5} \times 62.5 = 87.3$$

$$\text{Medium grass distance, CD} = \frac{143.2}{102.5} \times 102.5 - (87.3 + 31.4)$$
$$= 24.5 \text{ m}$$

$$\text{Distance } BB_1 = 100 \times \frac{22.5}{102.5} = 22 \text{ m}$$

$$\text{Distance } CC_1 = 100 \times \frac{62.5}{102.5} = 61 \text{ m}$$

$$\text{Distance } DD_1 = 100 \text{ m}$$

$$\text{Slope of AB} = \frac{0.01 \times 22.5 + 0.01 \times 22}{31.4}$$
$$= 1.415 \text{ percent}$$

$$\text{Slope of BC} = \frac{0.01 \times 40 + 0.01 \times 39}{87.3}$$
$$= 0.91 \text{ percent}$$

$$\text{Slope of CD} = \frac{0.015 \times 40 + 0.01 \times 39}{24.5}$$
$$= 4.04 \text{ percent}$$

The inlet times for different portions are calculated using Figure 14.7.

t_1 = time taken along pavement AB, having $C_1 = 0.90$,
l_1 = 31.4 m and slope = 1.415 percent is 3 min

t_2 = time taken along bare earth BC, having $C_2 = 0.65$,
l_2 = 87.3 m and slope = 0.91 percent is 15 min

t_3 = time taken on medium grass CD, having $C_3 = 0.30$,
l_3 = 24.5 m and slope = 4.04 percent is 11 min

Therefore, total inlet time $= t_1 + t_2 + t_3 = 3 + 15 + 11$
$= 29$ min

Flow time for inlet No. 1 = 0

Therefore, time of concentration for inlet No. 1 = 29 min

(c) Determine the intensity of rainfall.

From Figure 14.8, using 5 year frequency curve and duration of storm equal to time of concentration, the intensity of rainfall = 85 mm/hr which is equal to 0.0236 mm/sec.

(d) Determine the runoff

$$Q = CIA$$
$$= 0.48 \times (0.0236 \times 10^{-3}) \times 15.230$$
$$= 0.1728 \text{ cubic m/sec}$$

(e) Determine the pipe diameter

$$0.1728 = A.\ V.$$
$$\text{Assume } V = 0.75 \text{ m/second (minimum)}$$
$$A = 0.2305 \text{ square m}$$
$$= \frac{\pi}{4} d^2$$

Therefore, pipe diameter = 0.5425 m

Provide, pipe of diameter = 50 cm

Velocity of flow = 0.895 m/sec

(f) Determine the slope of the pipe

As per Manning's formula

$$V = \frac{R^{2/3} S^{1/2}}{n}$$
$$R = d/2 = 0.25 \text{ m}$$

Assume $n = 0.15$ for concrete pipe

$$0.895 = \frac{(0.25)^{2/3} S^{1/2}}{0.015}$$
$$S^{1/2} = \frac{0.895 \times 0.015}{(0.25)^{2/3}}$$
$$S = 0.18$$

II Design of Inlet No. 2 :

The inlet No. 2 is to be designed to carry the storm water contributed by the drainage Area I as well as the Area II. Two possibilities are to be considered in finding the time concentration. The first is that the water flows along the path

ABCD and then along the drainage line 1-2. The second is that the water flows along the path EFGH. Obviously, the first consideration means longer time and would, therefore decide the time of consideration.

$$\text{Time of flow along the drainage line 1-2} = \frac{100}{0.895 \times 60}$$

$$= 1.865 \text{ min}$$

Time of concentration = 31 + 1.865 = 32.865 min

From Figure 14.8, I = 83 mm/hr = 0.0231 mm/sec

Q from Area II = CIA

= 0.48 × 0.231 × 15.250 = 0.1690 cubic m/sec

Design capacity of inlet No. 2 = 0 1728 + 0.1690

= 0.3418 cubic m/sec

Assuming diameter of pipe as 50 cms

$$V = \frac{0.3418}{0.1960} = 1.744 \text{m/sec}$$

$$\text{From Manning's formula, } 1.744 = \frac{R^{2/3} S^{1/2}}{n}$$

$$\text{Here } R = \frac{0.50}{2} = 0.25 \text{ m and } n = 0.015$$

Therefore slope of drain line 2-3 = 0 257

III Design of Inlet No. 3

Time of concentration = Time of concentration for Inlet No. 2 + Flow time along drain line 2-3

$$= 32.825 + \frac{60}{1.744 \times 60}$$

Rainfall intensity from Figure 14.8,

C = 0.48

I = 81 mm/hr = 0.0225 mm/sec.

A = 60 × 152.5 = 9150.0 sq-m

Therefore, Q = CIA = $0.48 \times (0.0225 \times 10^{-3}) \times 9150$

= 0 09900 cubic m/sec.

Design capacity of inlet No. 3 = 0.3418 + 0.0990

Assuming diameter of pipe as 50 cm

$$V = \frac{0.4408}{0.1960} = 2.250 \text{ m/sec.}$$

From Manning's formula, $2.250 = \frac{R^{2/3} S^{1/2}}{n}$

Here, $R = \frac{0.50}{2}$; $n = 0.015$

Therefore slope of the drain line 3-outfall is 0.291.

Case II : When ponding is permitted

Total drainage area = $260 \times 152.5 = 39.65 \times 10^3$ sq-m.

Average C = 0.48

Rainfall intensities for durations of 5, 10, 15, 20, 30, 60, 90 and 120 minutes are obtained from Figure 14.8 and the volume of runoff are computed. The results are summarised in Table 14.4.

Table 14.4 Volume of Runoff

Time (t) min	Intensity (I) mm/sec	Runoff (Q=CIA) cubic m/sec	Volume of rainfall (V=CIA t) cubic m
5	0.0445	0.848	254.4
10	0.0378	0.720	432.0
15	0.0333	0.635	571.5
20	0.0284	0.540	648.0
30	0.0236	0.450	810.0
60	0.0150	0.286	1025.0
90	0.0105	0.200	1080.0
120	0.0091	0.174	1258.0

Assume a drainage pipe of 30 cm. diameter laid on 1.0 percent slope. From Manning's formula, the discharge capacity of pipe is obtained as 0.084 cubic m/sec.

To study the effects of ponding, comparison is made between the discharge capacity of the drain pipe and the cumulative runoff as illustrated graphically in Figure 14.10. The maximum ponding is corresponding to a storm of 60 min. duration.

The volume of ponding = 1025 − 302 = 723 cubic m. It is essential that the edges of the ponding area should be at least 22.5 m away from the edges of the pavement. In order to satisfy the above condition, if the storage capacity is found to

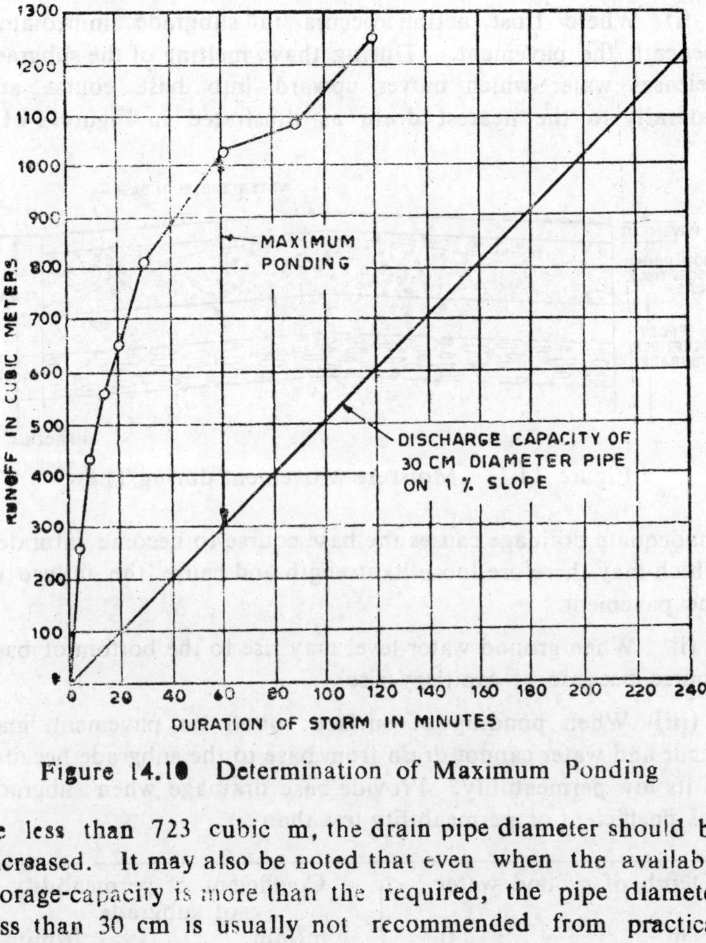

Figure 14.10 Determination of Maximum Ponding

be less than 723 cubic m, the drain pipe diameter should be increased. It may also be noted that even when the available storage-capacity is more than the required, the pipe diameter less than 30 cm is usually not recommended from practical considerations.

14.7 SUBSURFACE DRAINAGE DESIGN

The main functions of subsurface drainage are :

(i) To remove water from a base course.

(ii) To lower the ground water level in the subgrade beneath the pavement.

(iii) To intercept, collect and remove water flowing from the adjacent spring or pervious strata.

Base drainage is normally required under the following conditions :

(i) Where frost action occurs in subgrade immediately beneath the pavement. During thaw, melting of the subgrade releases water which moves upward into base course and laterally to the nearest drain as illustrated in Figure 14.11.

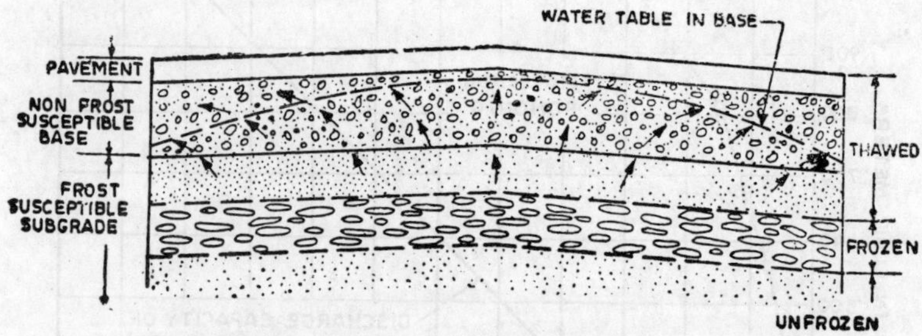

Figure 14.11 Moisture Movement during Thaw

Inadequate drainage causes the base course to become saturated which may therefore loose its strength and cause the failure of the pavement.

(ii) When ground water level may rise to the bottom of base course because of capillary rise.

(iii) When ponding of surface runoff on pavement may occur and water cannot drain from base to the subgrade because of its low permeability. Provide base drainage when subgrade has coefficient of permeability less than :

Depth of ground water		Coefficient of permeability of subgrade	
m	ft	m/min	ft/min
$\lessdot$ 2.5	$\lessdot$ 8	3×10^{-6}	1×10^{-5}
2.5 to 7.5	8 to 25	3×10^{-7}	1×10^{-6}
> 7.5	> 25	3×10^{-8}	1×10^{-7}

Subgrade drainage is required when ground water level in subgrade may rise to a depth less than 0.3 m (1 ft) below the bottom of base course. Intercepting drains are required when seeping water in subgrade raises the ground water level locally or generally to within 0.3 m from the bottom of the base course.

14.7.1 Data Required

The first step in the design of sub-surface drainage system is to carry out a survey of the pavement materials and moisture conditions of the subgrade. The following informations are collected :

(i) *Soil profile :* This includes soil type, permeability, porosity and thickness of the various stratas. For drainge purpose, soils are classified into three groups :

(a) Self draining soils : This includes gravelly sand, sandy loam and some types of sandy clay loam. These soils fall in A-1, A-2 and A-3 groups of USPRA classification.

(b) Soils drained by artificial means : These soils are loam, clay, sandy clay, sandy clay loam and certain silty loam. These soils fall in A-4, A-5 and A-7 groups of *USPRA classification.* The percentage of sand within these soils determines their ability to be drained.

(c) Soil difficult to drain : These soils contain a high percentage of clay or silty and generally are of a type like silty clay, silty clay loam, silty loam, silt and clay. These soils fall in the A-5, A-6, A-7 and A-8 groups of *USPRA classification.*

(ii) Position of the water table if this occurs reasonably close to the formation level.

(iii) Position of seepage zones if these exist.

14.7.2 Base Course Drainage

A typical base course drainage system is illustrated in Figure 14.12. The following assumptions are made in the design of this system :

(i) Base course is saturated

(ii) No inflow occurs during drainage of base course

(iii) Subgrade is impervious

(iv) Base course has free outflow into the drain trench

The design involves the following steps :

(a) Determine the coefficient of horizontal permeability of base course mateial by laboratory tests. Average values of coefficient of permeability for remoulded samples of sand and gravel type of base course materials are as mentioned below :

Percent passing No. 200 sieve by weight	Coefficient of permeability for remoulded samples m/min	ft/min
3	3×10^{-2}	1×10^{-1}
5	3×10^{-3}	1×10^{-2}
10	3×10^{-4}	1×10^{-3}
15	3×10^{-5}	1×10^{-4}
25	3×10^{-6}	1×10^{-5}

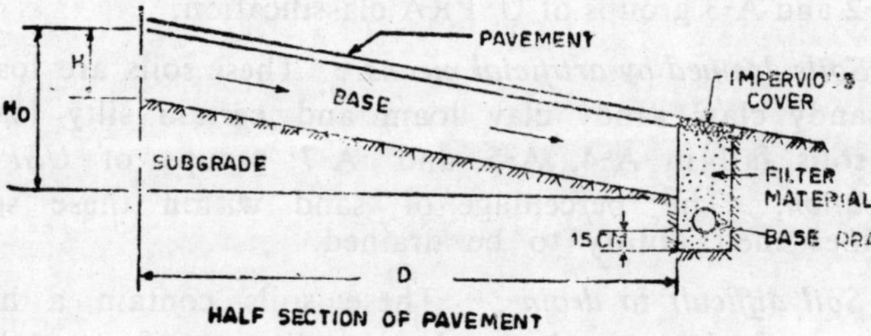

Figure 14.12 Base Course Drainage

(b) Compute the average coefficient of horizontal permeability, where more than one base course material is used by the following equation :

$$K_b = \frac{K_1 d_1 + K_2 d_2 + K_3 d_3 \ldots + K_n d_n}{d_1 + d_2 + d_3 \ldots + d_n}$$

where, K_n = average coefficient of permeability

K_1, K_2 etc = individual coefficient of permeability of different layers of base materials

d_1, d_2 etc = thickness of individual layers

(c) Compute maximum rate of seepage from base course into the base drain from the equation :

$$q = KH \frac{H_0}{60\ D}$$

where, q = maximum discharge in cubic metre per minute per metre of drain

K = coefficient of horizontal permeability of base course in metre per minute

H_0, H and D are as shown in Figure 14.12.

(d) Compute time for 50 percent drainage of base course from the following equation

$$t_{50} = \frac{n_e D_e}{2880 \, KH_0}$$

t_{50} = time in days for 50 percent drainage

n_e = effective porosity of soil

The degree of drainage is defined as the ratio expressed in percent of the volume drained in a given time to the total amount of water, that it is possible to drain from the given material.

(e) Provide drain spacing (i.e. 2D) to achieve 50 percent drainage of base course in 10 days or less. If this cannot be done with a reasonable drain spacing, use more pervious base material or thicker base course. Knowing the value of q, the diameter and slope of drain can be obtained from the Manning's formula. Usually 15 cm diameter is provided.

(f) Provide minimum thickness of filter material around the drain pipe. The type of drain pipes and gradations of filter materials have been discussed subsequently. The drain pipe should be kept at adequate depth to provide the cover required for wheel loading.

14.7.3 Subgrade Drainage

A typical subgrade drainage system is illustrated in Figure 14.13. For the design of subgrade drainage, the following assumptions are made

(i) Subgrade below ground water level is saturated

(ii) Ground water level beneath shoulder is raised by infiltration through shoulder

(iii) Subgrade is not under artesian pressure

(iv) Drains have adequate capacity

(v) Steady flow conditions exist

The above assumptions are generally satisfied when rainfall infiltration in the shoulder area has raised ground water level the the ground surface. The design procedure involves the following steps :

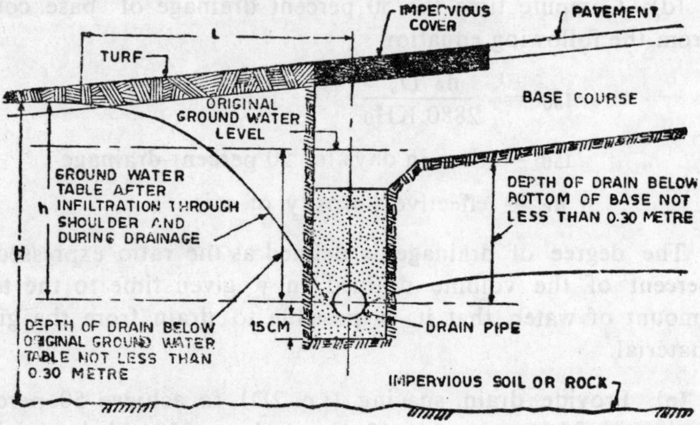

Figure 14 13 Subgrade Drainage

(a) Compute the maximum rate of discharge from the following equation :

$$q = \frac{Khc}{60}$$

where, q = maximum discharge in cubic metre per second per metre of drain

K = coefficient of permeability of soil in shoulder in metre per min

h = thickness of soil being drained in metre

c = shape factor dependents upon L and H. Values are obtained from Figure 14.14. When K is equal to or less than 3×10^{-4} m/min (1×10^{-3} ft/min) use the curve having L = 15 m

The slope and diameter of subdrain pipe can be determined by using Manning's formula. Usually 15 cm diameter pipe is adequate. The recommended minimum slope is 1 in 650.

(b) Placement of subgrade drain should satisfy the following criteria :

At depth not less than 0.3 m (1 ft) below the base course.

At depth not less than 0.3 m below the ground water table.

At sufficient depth to provide adequate cover required for stability under wheel loadings.

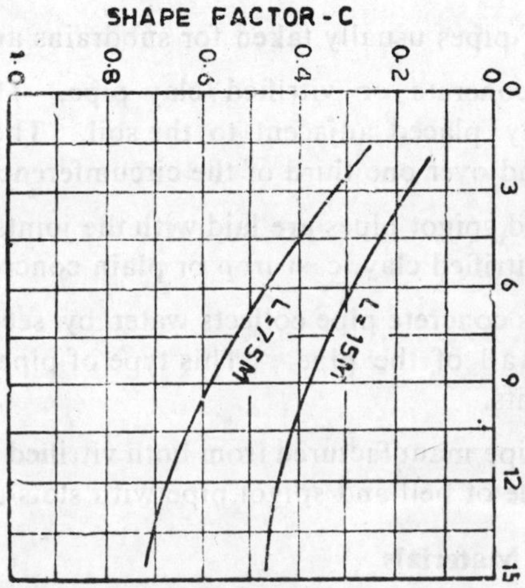

Figure 14.14 Shape Factor for Subgrade Drainage

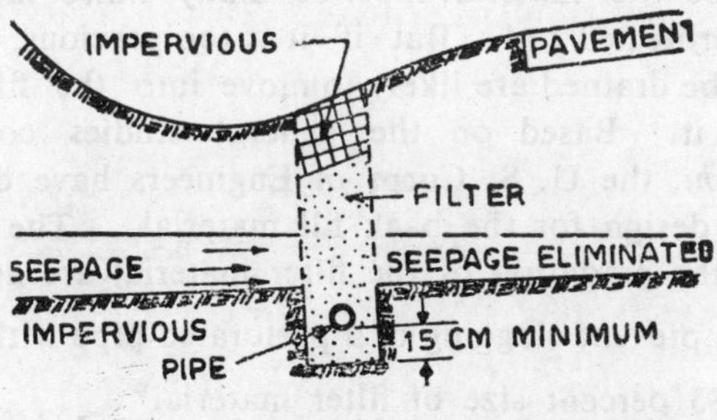

Figure 14.15 Intercepting Drain

(c) Locate drains at outer edges of paved areas except where large paved areas, such as parking aprons, require intermediate drains because of unusual ground water conditions.

14.7.4 Intercepting Drains

A typical intercepting drainage system is illustrated in Figure 14.15. It is provided at locations selected after careful investigation of the conditions necessitating the drainage. In general 15 cm diameter drain pipe, not more than 300 m in length, is quite sufficient.

14.7.5 Types of Pipes

The types of pipes usually taken for subdrains are :

(i) Metal concrete or vitrified clay pipe. The perforated area is usually placed adjacent to the soil. The perforations normally extend over one third of the circumference of pipe.

(ii) Bell and spigot pipes are laid with the joints open. These are made of vitrified clay, cast iron or plain concrete.

(iii) Porous concrete pipe collects water by seepage through the concrete wall of the pipe. This type of pipe is laid with the sealed joints.

(iv) Skip pipe manufactured from both vitrified clay and iron is a special type of bell and spigot pipe with slots at the *bells*.

14.7.6 Filter Materials

The term filter material applies to the granular material which is used as a backfill in the trenches where subdrains are placed. In order, that the free water may reach the drain quickly, the filter material must be many times more pervious than the protected soil. But if it is too pervious, the particles of soil to be drained are likely to move into the filter material and clog it. Based on the general studies conducted by *K. Terzaghi*, the U. S. Corps of Engineers have developed an empirical design for the back fill material. The criteria of selecting the gradation of the filter material are as follows.

(i) To prevent clogging of a perforated pipe with filter

$$\frac{\text{85 percent size of filter material*}}{\text{diameter of perforation}} \geqslant 1.5$$

(ii) To prevent the movement of particles from the protected soil into the filter material,

$$\frac{\text{15 percent size of filter material}}{\text{85 percent size of protected soil}} \text{ (piping ratio)} \leqslant 5$$

and

$$\frac{\text{50 percent size of filter material}}{\text{50 percent size of protected soil}} \leqslant 25$$

(iii) To permit free water to reach the pipe,

$$\frac{\text{15 percent size of filter material}}{\text{15 percent size of protected soil}} \text{ (permeability ratio)} \geqslant 5$$

*This means that 85 percent by weight is finer than the specified size.

(iv) To prevent segregation of filter material,

$$\frac{60 \text{ percent size of filter material}}{10 \text{ percent size of filter material}} \leqslant 20$$

Example 14.3

Figure 14.16 illustrates the grain size analysis of subgrade soil. Design a suitable filter material for the subgrade drainage.

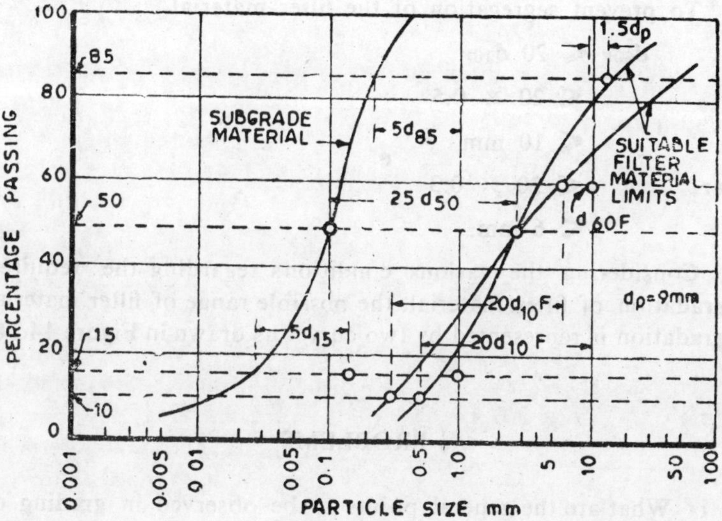

Figure 14.16

Solution

To prevent clogging of perforated pipe with filter material

$$d_{85F} \geqslant 1.5 \times \text{diameter of perforation (dp)}$$

$$\geqslant 1.5 \times 9$$

$$\geqslant 13.5 \text{ mm}$$

To prevent movement of subgrade soil into the filter material

$$d_{15F} \leqslant 5 \times d_{85}$$

$$\leqslant 5 \times 0.2$$

$$\leqslant 1.0 \text{ mm}$$

Also $d_{50F} \leqslant 25 \times d_{50}$

$\leqslant 25 \times 0.1$

$\leqslant 2.5$ mm

To permit free water to reach the pipe

$d_{15F} \geqslant 5 \times d_{15}$

$\geqslant 5 \times 0.03$

$\geqslant 0.15$ mm

To prevent segregation of the filter material

$d_{60F} \leqslant 20\ d_{10F}$

$\leqslant 20 \times 0.5$

$\leqslant 10$ mm

or $\leqslant 20 \times 0.3$

$\leqslant 6$ mm.

Considering the various conditions regarding the required gradation of filter material, the possible range of filter material gradation is represented by two curves as drawn in Figure 14.16.

PROBLEMS

1 What are the general points to be observed in grading of an airport ?

2 What do you understand by mass haul curve ? What information can be obtained from this curve ? Explain the procedure of working with this curve.

3 Explain the necessity of airport drainage. What are its special characteristics ?

4 What data is collected for design of the airport drainage ? Explain them briefly.

5 Explain step by step, the procedure of designing the drainage network to handle the airport surface runoff.

6 Plot the ground profile and mass haul curve of the section or runway described by the following data :

Station	Elevation (m)	Volume cut (cubic m)	Volume fill (cubic m)
50	90	—	—
51	92		600
52	89		650
53	90		900
54	95		100
55	95	600	
56	97	900	
57	98	1000	
58	96	800	
59	91	100	
60	90		900
61	90		1000

The profile of the proposed subgrade is levelled and is at an elevation of 83 m. Assume limit of economical haul as 200 m and of free haul as 60 m. Determine graphically the following :

(i) Division points in cut to give least possible total haul.

7 What do you understand by the term ponding ? If ponding is permitted on the airfield, how will you design the surface drainage system ?

8 What are the different types of sub surface drainage ? Explain the necessity of each type.

9 What data is collected for the design of sub surface drainage system for an airport ?

10 Draw neat sketches to explain the different methods of subsurface drainage. Explain their design principles.

11 Enumerate the various criterias for designing the filter material for sub surface drainage.

12 Draw neat sketches to explain how surface and subsurface water is drained from runway which is used for commercial air services.

13 Draw neat sketches to explain the drainage of a runway and a parallel taxiway system for a commercial airport.

(i) Total free haul in cubic metres.

(ii) Total overhaul in cubic metre stations.

(iii) Total borrow and spoil banks, if any, in cubic metres.

14 The figures below indicates the location of drain inlet along a portion of runway length. Design the drain inlet for carrying the surface runoff under the following conditions :

(i) When ponding is not permitted.

(ii) When ponding is permitted.

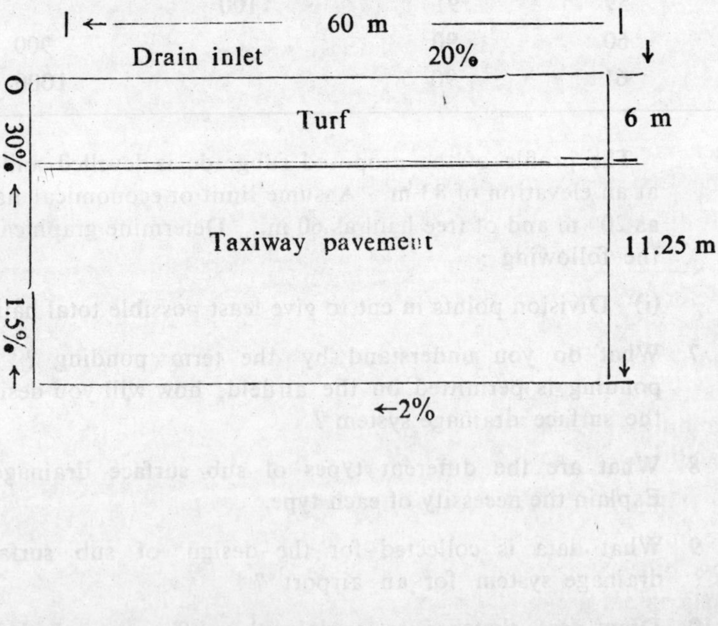

15

HELIPOTTS AND THEIR DESIGN

15.1 INTRODUCTION

A helicopter is a rotorcraft that works mainly on the lift generated by one or more power driven rotors moving about the vertical axis to impart support and motion to the machine in air.

About fifty years ago the modern helicopter was born. Before 1940, much theoretical work was done especially in the field of hovering flight performance, but no experiment survived until 1640. Helicopters can lift off the ground in a nearly vertical direction. This is referred to as vertical takeoff and landing VTOL*. Heliports are designed area where the facilities are provided for take-off and landing of the helicopters.

Helicopters are found to be most suitable for supply reconnaissance and mercy flights in areas which are inaccessible by other modes of transport. The main advantages of helicopters are briefly summarised below :

(i) The helicopter communication is of special benefit during winter weather in areas where, due to heavy snowfall,

*Sometimes the term V/STOL is used which applies to the machines which are capable of vertical and/or short take off and landing.

aeroplane flights are risky. Heavy snowfall also blocks the roads, railway tracks, coastal shipping etc.

(ii) Almost four fifths of the world's total air traffic is carried over distance of 400 km (250 miles) or less, the kind of distance which is ideal for helicopters. With the aeroplane time spent by the passenger on the ground to that in air, for these short distances, could be about 3 : 1. The helicopter, though slow, can operate from the centres of cities and eliminate much of the ground time.

(iii) The military operations need the vertical landing and take-off characteristics of a helicopter. During fighting against the Chinese in the Himalayas, Indian's best means of transport to the various places was helicopter.

(iv) For civil operations, the helicopter would become dominant type of V/STOL vehicle in future with continuous design improvements. These improvements are likely to include larger capacity, longer range, lower costs per available seat mile, the use of multiple engines and the ability to continue flight even if one engine becomes inoperative.

15.2 HELICOPTER CHARACTERISTICS

The chief point of observation in studying the characteristics is to ensure that flying is associated with the minimum danger to life and property. To ensure safety in flying, several factors are closely associated. The flying machine must be designed, made and tested to conform with an air worthiness standard. In steady flight, the behaviour of rotating wing, namely its horizontal speed and vertical rate of climb, depends on large number of controlling factors. In brief, it is said that the helicopter must be able to climb at the rate of 60 m per minute and the flight-path gradient should be 4 per cent. It must further possess some reserve of climbing capacity required only between take off level and 450 m above it. The physical and flight characteristics of helicopter are briefly summarised below :

15.2.1 Physical Characteristics

Helicopters are either single or tandem rotor, powered by one or two engines respectively. The landing gear configuration consists of two main wheels and one note wheel or tail wheel or

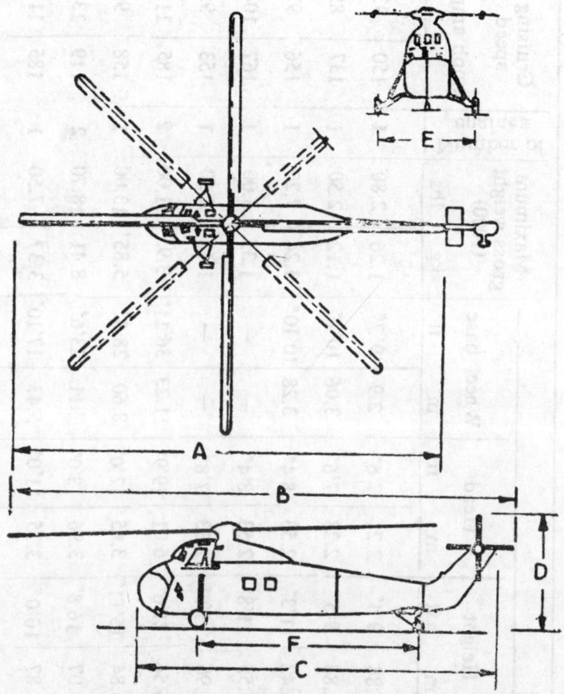

Figure 15.1 Single Rotor Helicopter

four wheels. The principal dimensions of representative helicopter, used for private and common carrier operations, are given in Table 15.1 with respect to Figure 15.1. The major division in different configurations of helicopters is between rotors driven from their extremities. Thus two groups can be considered for classification : (i) Mechanical driven and (ii) jet driven. Mechanical drive system is adopted in most of the helicopters in operations. The use of gas turbine is recent development and is advantageous as the machine becomes lighter and thus greater power is available. Figure 15.2 shows tip drive which was first used by *Issaco* in his *Helicogyro* constructed in *Great Britain*. In this machine, air screws, driven by piston engines are mounted near the extremities of the blades.

Figure 15.3 shows the mounting of turbo jet units used to drive giant lifting rotors designed in the initial stage. *Djinn*

Table 15.1 Principal Dimensions and Particulars of Helicopters

Make	Model designation	Rotor diameter m	Rotor diameter ft	Length Overall m	Length Overall ft	Length fuselage m	Length fuselage ft	Height m	Height ft	Tread m	Tread ft	Wheel base m	Wheel base ft	Maximum gross weight (1000) kg	Maximum gross weight (1000) lbs	Number of engines	Cruising speed kmph	Cruising speed amph
Bell	47-J	11.78	37'2"	13.23	43'5"	9.87	32'5"	2.84	9'4"	2.21	7'6"	2.9	9'7"	1.26	2.80	1	150	93
Bell	47G-2	11.17	35'2"	12.62	41'5"	9 27	30'5"	2.86	9'5"	2.28	7'6"	3.06	10'1"	1.12	2.50	1	137	85
Bell	204	13.41	44'0"	16.15	53'0"	13.00	42'8"	3.42	11'3"	2.53	8'4"	3.28	10'10"	3.24	7.20	1	156	97
Cessna	CH-I	10.66	35'0"	13.00	42'8"	10.01	32'11"	3.55	11'8"	2.53	8'4"	—	—	1.35	3.00	1	167	104
Killer	12-C	10.66	35'0"	12.24	40'6"	8.95	29'5'	2.96	9'9"	2.33	7'8"	—	—	1.12	2.50	1	153	95
Sikorsky	S-56	21.94	72'0"	25.24	82'10"	19.77	64'11'	6.54	21'6"	6.01	19'9"	11.23	36'11"	13.95	31.00	2	185	115
Sikorsky	S-58	17.06	56'0"	24.06	65'10"	14.82	47'2'	4.84	15'11"	3.65	12'0"	8.60	28'3"	5.85	13.00	1	158	98
Sikorsky	S-61	18.90	62.0"	22.16	72'9"	17.94	58'11"	5.07	16'8"	3.96	13'0"	7.11	23'6"	8.41	18.70	2	119	136
Sikorsky	S-62	16.15	53.0"	19.65	62.3"	13.57	44'7'	4.87	16'0"	3.35	11'0"	5.43	17'10"	3.37	7.50	1	185	115

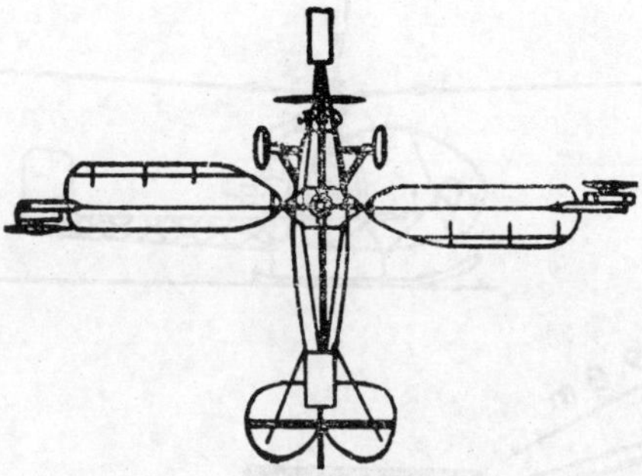

Figure 15.2 Tip Drive Helicopter

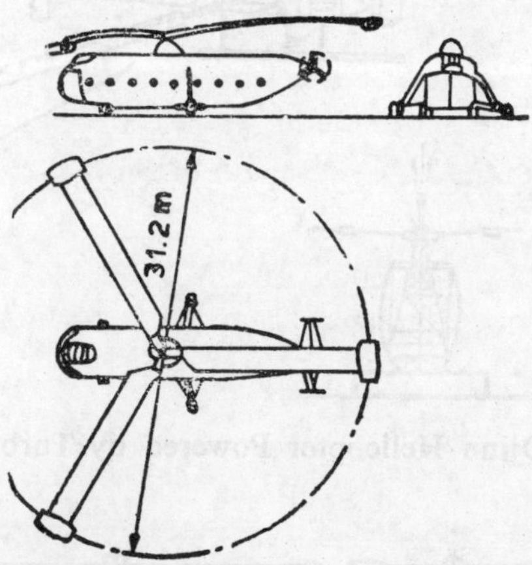

Figure 15.3 Turbo Jet Driven Rotor

is the recent representation of this system which has reached the operational stage. It is shown in Figure 15.4. Figure 15.5 shows a helicopter powered by the pulse jet propulsion.

The second important feature for classification of the helicopters is the number of rotors and their arrangements. Most of the helicopters are strictly of the single lifting rotor type. A typical such type is the helicopter *Sikorsky S-51* as shown in Figure 15.6. There are examples of helicopters fitted with twin rotor side-by-side, configuration as in Focker FA 61 and twin rotor tandem as in *Piasecki Y. H. 16*. A three rotor experimental helicopter is the *Ceria Air Horse W 11*. The single rotor machine has the advantage of fewer parts and thereby low floor space requirement. Its chief disadvantage is the control

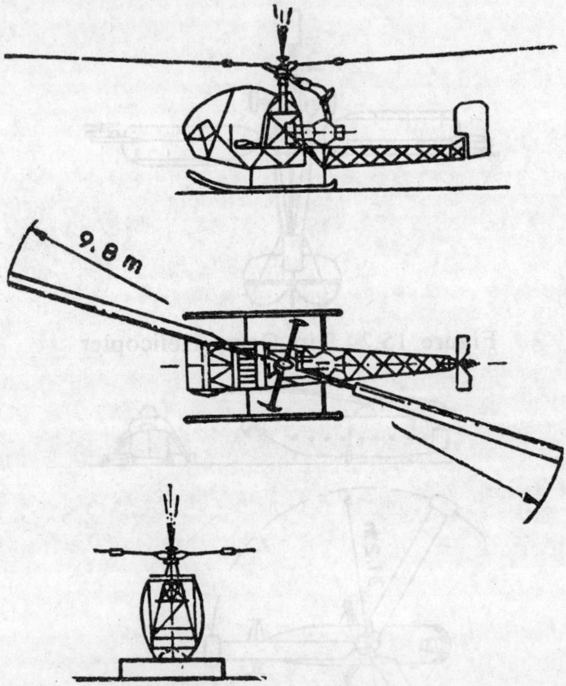

Figure 15.4 Djinn Helicopter Powered by Turbo Jet Fngine

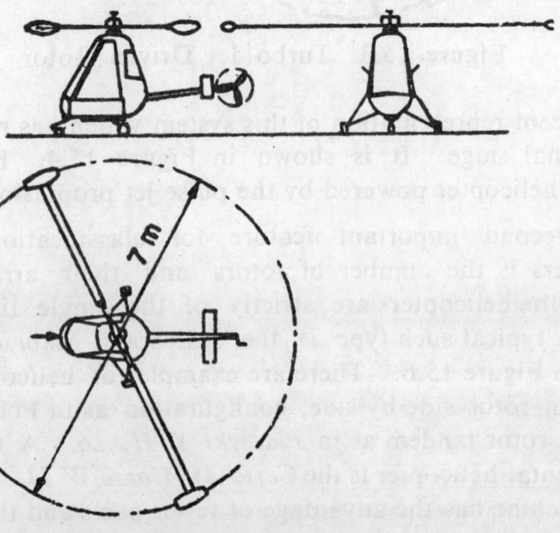

Figure 15.5 Pulse Jet Powered Helicopter

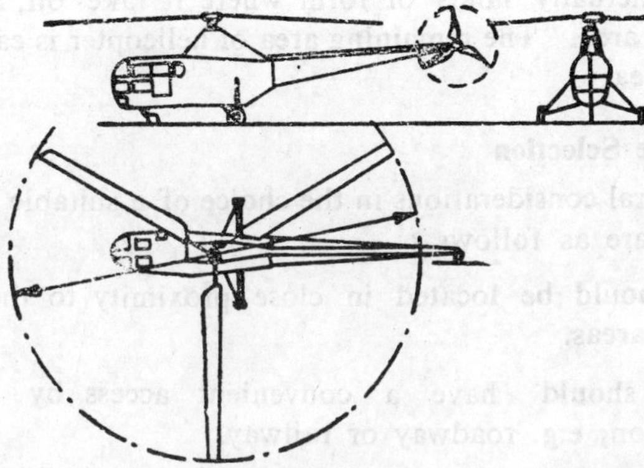

Figure 15.6 Sikorsky S-51 Single Rotor Helicopter

by lift vector inclination (i.e. some power loss due to low lift in transient stage).

15.2.2 Flight Characteristics

The chief characteristic of a helicopter is its capacity to hover through application of power to the rotating airfoils. This provides the characteristics of a much greater range of flight speed and flight altitudes than conventional aircraft. In addition, the ability to land and take-off from comparatively small areas is also achieved.

The vertical ascend is carried out to initiate the take off. The initial vertical rise to take off is helped by the ground cushion built up by the air pressure directed against the ground by revolving rotors. After about 2 m of vertical ascent, horizontal acceleration begins. Translation lift (additional lift for the forward speed) is obtained between 8 to 16 kmph (5 to 10 mph) and then the helicopter is accelerated to 65 to 80 kmph (40 to 50 mph) which is the best speed for climbing to a cruising altitude.

15.3 PLANNING OF HELIPORTS

Heliport is designed as an area of prepared ground intended to be used for landing and take off helicopters. It may provide facilities for shelter, repair and servicing of helicopters, buildings, for processing of cargo, baggage and passengers and area for vehicular parking The area, over which the helicopter actually lands or form where it takes off, is called the landing area. The remaining area of helicopter is called the terminal area.

15.3.1 Site Selection

The general considerations in the choice of a suitable site for a heliport are as follows :

(i) It should be located in close proximity to the traffic generating areas.

(ii) It should have a convenient access by ground transportation, e.g. roadway or railway.

(iii) The ambient noise level should be considered. Greater noise can be tolerated in an industrial area than in the residential area. Noise generated by the jet engine powered helicopter can exceed the tolerable limits even in the business and industrial areas. To reduce noise, it is desirable, if possible to orient the landing and take off areas in such a way that helicopters fly where noise will be least objectionable.

(iv) It is not practicable, within economic limits that helicopter can ascend and descend exactly vertically. As such the site for heliport should provide unobstructed approach-departure paths for helicopters. To establish the obstruction clearance line, certain assumptions concerning the performance of multi-engine helicopters, are made. It is assumed that during take off, the helicopter rises quickly and be able to achieve forward speed such that even if one engine becomes inoperative it continues its flight. It is further assumed that the helicopter reaches the boundary of the heliport before the engine failure, occurs. Slope of 1 in 20 is assumed as the capability of a helicopter, with remaining engines in operation. It has been observed, that with this reduction in power; the helicopter would reach a height of 105 m in a horizontal distance of 720 m from the boundary of a heliport. This means the obstruction clearance line should have a slope of 1.8 (Figure 15.7). The obstruction clearance criteria, as recommended by FAA is shown in Figure 15.7. Beyond this distance, the slope of 1 : 40 is recommended for further flight upto a horizontal distance of 225 m which is then followed by a slope of 1 : 8 upto minimum enroute altitude.

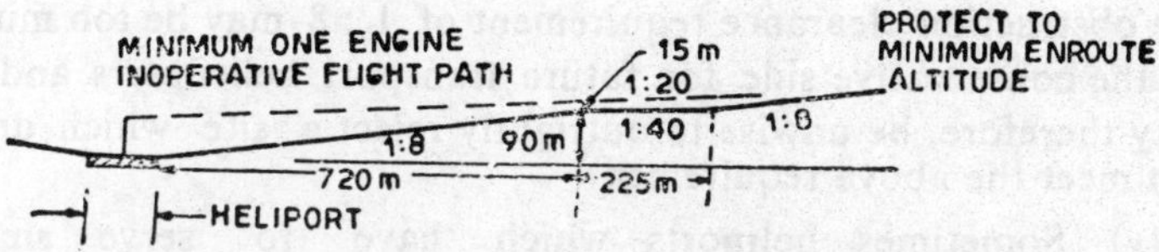

Figure 15.7 Obstructions in Approach Area

Zoning is essential to protect the approach-departure paths of helicopter from development of undesirably tall structures. The obstruction clearance requirements for helicopters have not been precisely known until more knowledge is gained about the performance of multi-engine helicopters. FAA recommendation which is illustrated in Figure 15.8, may be adopted as a tentative guide for planning. In plan, the flare of the area is 1 : 5 on either side. The recommendation of ICAO is also the same except that the obstruction gradient should extend upto 750 m from toe of the slope. In transverse direction, the slope of obstruction clearance plane is 1 : 2. As per ICAO, the transitional surface having a slope of 1 : 2 should start from a line which is at a distance of half the rotor diameter from the edge of landing area. The above dimension pertains to the heliport which serves the transport

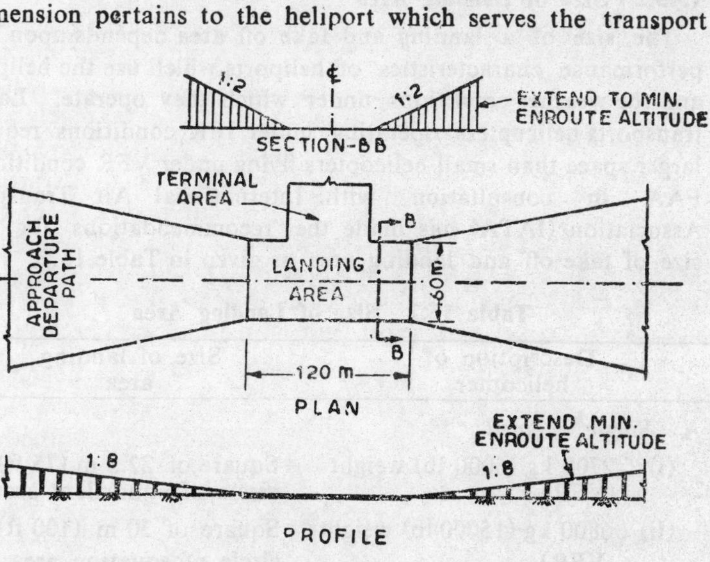

Figure 15.8 FAA Recommendations for Approach Departure Obstruction Clearance

category helicopters in all weather conditions. It is felt that the obstruction clearance requirement of 1 : 8 may be too much on the conservative side for future transport helicopters and it may therefore, be unwise to outrightly reject a site which does not meet the above requirement.

(v) Sometimes heliports which have to serve small helicopters, are located on the roofs of buildings. This may prove to be advantageous as the heliport can be located within the city and near the business centres. The effect of vibration on the building structure should be considered in its design if it has to have a heliport on its roof. Visibility is another important factor for heliports located on roof tops. Fog accumulates more at higher altitudes than near the ground. This reduces the visibility.

(vi) Where a heliport is developed on major airport, it should preferably be located where landing and take-off are made without taxiing. A roof site on the terminal building is the most satisfactory and should be considered, even though a ground site is available. The advantage of a roof site on a terminal building becomes obvious when the time factor in the handling of mail, cargo and passengers is considered.

15.3.2 Size of Landing Area

The size of a landing and take off area depends upon the performance characteristics of heliports which use the heliport and the weather conditions under which they operate. Large transport helicopters operating under IFR conditions require larger space than small helicopters flying under VFR conditions. FAA in consultation with International Air Transport Association (IATA) has made the recommendations for the size of take-off and landing area as given in Table 15.2.

Table 15.2 Size of Landing Area

Description of helicopter	Size of landing area
A *Single engined*	
(i) 2700 kg (6000 lb) weight (VFR)	Square of 22.5 m (75 ft) or circle of equivalent area.
(ii) 6800 kg (15000 lb) weight (VFR)	Square of 30 m (100 ft) or circle of equation area.
B *Multi-engined* (IFR)	60m × 120m (200 ft × 400 ft)

It is further recommended that sufficient area should be available, adjacent to the landing area, for emergency landing in case of engine failure. ICAO recommends the minimum width which is equal to twice the diameter of the main rotor of largest helicopter expected to use the heliport. Toe width of the area should, however, be not less than 30 m. The maximum slope should not exceed 2 percent. A typical layout of helipoit, capable to serve large sized helicopters is shown in Figure 15.9.

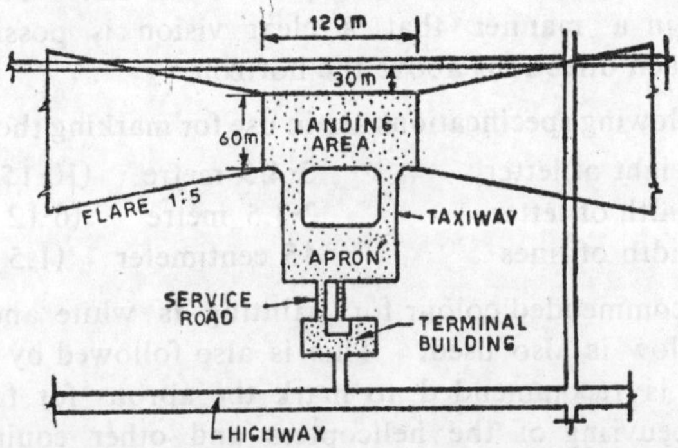

Figure 15.9 Typical Layout of Heliport for Large Size Helicopters

15.3.3 Orientation of Landing Area

The permissible cross wind component for helicopters may be much higher than that for fixed wind aircraft. The precise limit for helicopters is not yet recommended. It is preferable to orient the landing and take-off area along the direction of wind.

15.3.4. Terminal Area

If the volume of traffic to be handled by heliport is not large, the loading and unloading of passengers can be done on the loading and take-off area itself. As the traffic increases, the additional space for parking of helicopters and their loading and unloading may be necessary. As an initial guide for planning of parking space, it may be assumed that the total time taken in loading and unloading of a helicopter having a capacity of 20 to 30 passengers, its refueling and routine inspection may not exceed about 10 minutes. Thus, if a heliport has to operate 50 movements per hour, it will require four gate positions. The size of each gate position will depend upon the overall dimension of the machine to be parked. The loading and unloading area should be adjacent to the terminal building as in the case of airports. The various planning considerations for terminal area of airport are generally applicable to the heliport as well.

15.3.5 Heliport Marking

ICAO recommends that the areas of landing and take-off should be fully identified with capital letter 'H'. This should be done in a manner that a clear vision is possible from all approach directions above the horizon.

The following specifications are in use for marking the letter H :

Height of letter	3-4.5 metre	(10-15 feet)
Width of letter	2-3.5 metre	(6-12 feet)
Width of lines	45 centimeter	(1.5 feet)

The recommended colour for painting is white and in some cases yellow is also used. This is also followed by black out line. It is recommended to mark the aprons for facilitating the manoeuvring of the helicopters and other equipment.

15.3.6 Heliport Lighting

Various modes of lighting are used as aids for night operations. These are for (i) identification of helicopters (ii) wind direction (iii) landing area (iv) obstruction. It is suggested that the lighting should be of special characteristics to differentiate the heliport area from airport area distinctly. Operational experience on heliports at night is limited FAA has suggested following general guidance for lighting of heliports which may be adopted until more elaborate specifications are available.

(i) Landing and take-off area should be lighted by a flood light to provide an illumination level of 15 cm candle over the entire landing area. The design should be such that it does not cause glare to the pilot while landing or taking off from the heliport.

(ii) The periphery of landing and take-off area should be lighted by amber lights of medium intensity, spaced 7.5 m centre to centre.

(iii) Aprons may be lighted by flood lights so as to provide an illumination level of not less than 30 cm candle over the entire working area.

PROBLEMS

1 What are the main advantages of helicopter over the fixed wing aircraft ?

2 What are the chief characteristics of helicopter ?

3 What factors are considered in the selections of site for a heliport ?

4 Explain with neat sketches the observation clearance requirements for a heliport.

5 How do you decide the size of a heliport area ? Sketch the layout of a typical heliport for large size helicopters.

6 Write short notes on :

(i) Heliport lighting

(ii) Heliport marking

(iii) Orientation of heliports landing area.

16

STOLPORTS & THEIR DESIGN

16.2 INTRODUCTION

This chapter provides only the guidance material on design of stolports as no standards or recommended practices have been put forward by ICAO so far. The ICAO airworthiness committee has recognized that STOL aircraft will be the aircraft having performance capabilities which will help them to operate safely in restricted areas, i.e. from short runways and with steep approach and climb out gradients. The guidance material included here is based on the practices followed by U.K./U.S.A./Canada which have planned such ports for use.

16.2 SITE SELECTION

The advantage of the feasibility of locating stolport in close proximity to the centres where traffic is generated should be utilized as far as possible. The site should also provide adequate parking facilities and accessibility to ground transport.

Since STOL operations are different from CTOL operations, new zoning criteria are needed to define the obstruction clearance requirements. Schematic and isometric views of protection surfaces are shown in Figure 16.1 and 16.2 respectively. The recommended obstruction criterias are also summarized in Table 16.1. The surfaces have been defined on

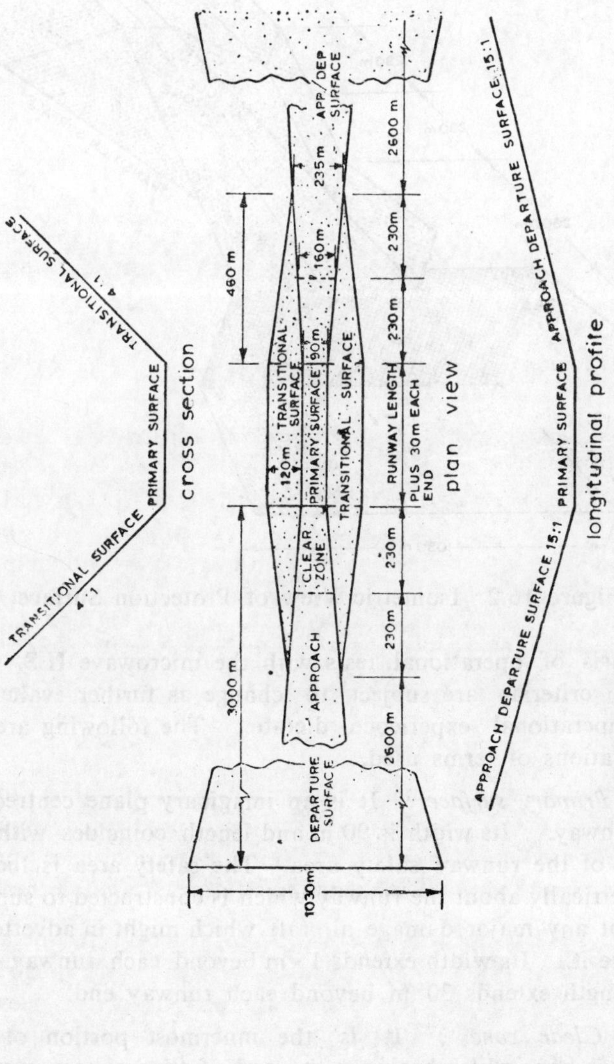

Figure 16.1 Schematic View of Protection Surface

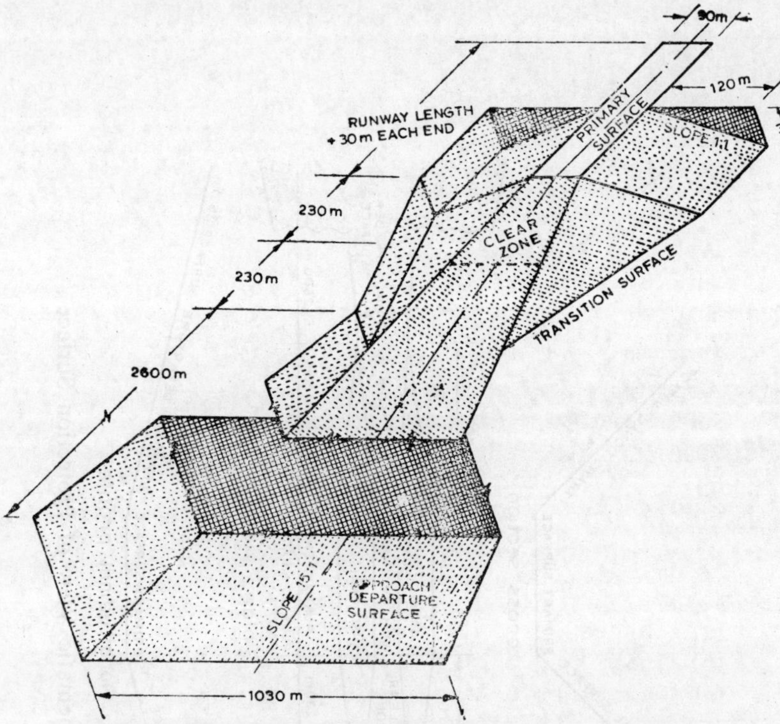

Figure 16.2 Isometric View of Protection Surface

the basis of operational tests with the microwave ILS. The design criterias are subject to change as further evaluation and operational experience dictate. The following are the explanations of terms used.

(i) Primary surface : It is an imaginary plane centred on the runway. Its width is 90 m and length coincides with the length of the runway safety area. The safety area is located symmetrically about the runway which is constructed to support without any major damage aircraft which might in advertently traverse it. Its width extends 15 m beyond each runway edge and length extends 30 m beyond each runway end.

(ii) Clear zone : It is the innermost portion of the approach zone which begins at the end of the primary surface. It extends symmetrically across the extended centre line of runway upto a length of 225 m. Its width varies from 90 m at the primary surface end to 160 m at the other end.

Table 16.1 Obstruction Criteria for Stolports

	Design Item	Recommended Criteria
1	Primary surface length	Runway length plus 30 m on each end.
2	Primary surface width	90 m
3	Approach/Departure surface length	3000 m
4	Approach/ Departure surface slope	15 : 1
5	Approach/Departure surface width at beginning	90 m
	3000 m	1020 m
6	Transitional surface slope	4 : 1
7	Transitional surface maximum height	30 m
8	Clear Zone	
	(a) Length	225 m
	(b) Inner width	90 m
	(c) Outer width	160 m

(iii) Approach-Departure surface : It is an imaginary plane extending outward and upward from ends of the primary surface at a slope of 15 m horizontally to 1 m vertically (15 : 1).

(iv) Transitional surface : An imginary surface adjacent to each side of the primary surface and a portion of the approach surfaces. It extends outward and upward at a slope of 4 : 1.

16.3 DESIGN AND PLANNING OF STOLPORTS ELEMENTS

This includes design and planning of runway, taxiway and apron to provide the capacity indicated by long term forecast. For stolport system to be fully utilized, the inflow of aircrafts should be timed to minimise possible separation in space. This however is restricted by such factors as weather, air traffic control procedure, capability of the controllers, availability of approach and landing aids, runway configuration and location of taxiways and aprons. Due to these factors, there is randomness in the flow of aircrafts which results into peaks higher than that which can be accommodated with the necessary separation standards. Although various runway configurations as described for CTOL aircrafts are also possible with stolports and the system can be designed to meet the needs of occasional peaks in the air traffic, it would necessitate considerably large land area, which may not be available in many instances particularly in the downtown area. Further, STOL concept assumes decentralization of sites which would be able to service a much larger passenger market and also provide easy access to arriving and departing passengers. Therefore it is desirable that the configuration for most of the stolports be a single runway with a parallel taxiway. A new stolport should be initiated at the time when the existing one reaches its capacity. A typical Stolport layout which is capable of accommodating aircrafts landing at intervals of 150 seconds is illustrated in Figure 16.3.

16.3.1 Runway Length

This is determined to be the longest distance required from the considerations such as (a) take-off to 10.5 m height (b) landing from 15 m height and (c) accelerate-stop activities as also applicable to CTOL airports. In order to cater for these requirements, Canadian practice is to provide 600 m runway length with 75 m stopway and 120 m clearway on either side. These recommendations are based on characteristics of STOL aircrafts in use. Characteristics of some STOL aircrafts are given in Table 16.2. The distances required by DHC-7 and those actually recommended by Canadian Air Transportation Administration (CATA) are given in Table 16.3 and shown in Figure 16.3.

FAA recommends runway length at sea level at 32°C temperature as varying from 420 m to 540 m. Corrections are to be made for elevation, temperature and gradient at the actual site.

16.3.2 Runway Width

Paved width of 30 m is recommended for runway. This width is greater than the runway width of 18 m recommended for E type of airport for CTOL aircrafts. This may be due to larger types of STOL aircrafts similar to DHC-7 which will be

Table 16.2 STOL Aircraft Characteristics

Aircraft Designation	Year in service	Take-off Gross weight kg	Overall Length m	Wing Span m	Overall Height m	Number of Passengers	Ramp Area m²	Wheel Base m	Gear Tread m
DHC-6/300 (TP)	1966	5,650	15.8	19.8	5.7	20	496	4.5	3.8
BN-2 Islander (TP)	1967	2,850	10.1	14.9	4.2	10	331	3.9	3.4
DHC-5 (Buffalo) (TP)	1972	17,200	23.6	29.3	8.7	50	952	8.5	9.3
GAC-100 (TP)	1972	12,000	21.3	21.3	7.6	36	671	5.9	6.7
DHC-7 (TP)	1974	17,430	24.5	28.3	8.0	48	956	8.7	7.2
LC-100-1070 (TP)	1974	51,650	32.6	41.6	12.0	80	1669	12.2	4.8
MDC-188 (TP)	1974	24,800	24.6	23.9	10.1	67	830	7.2	6.1
Canadian CL-246 (TP)	1975	24,100	27.1	23.5	7.3	70	889		3.8
Grumman 487 C (TP)	1995	43,100	35.7	35.1	12.2	90	1594		6.1
STOL BLC (TF)	1978	45,650	31.1	37.0	11.6	90	1483		
B-751 (TF)	1978	63,950	40.2	33.8	12.2	150	1720	13.7	
CL 1147 (TF)	1978	68,000	37.9	36.7	14.1	136	1703		
LGX 192 B-1 (TF)	1978	49,900	31.7	24.6	9.4	104	1058	14.0	6.3
Augmentor wing STOL (TF)	1978	42,600	31.1	31.5	8.3	100	1287		
NR 260 C (TF)	1978	63,500	35.9	38.5	13.4	150	1748	13.2	5.3

Table 16.3 Distance Required by DHC-7

Item	Calculated	Recommended
(a) Take-of distance to 10.5 m height	666 m	720 m
(b) Landing distance from 15 m height	567 m	600 m
(c) Accelerate-stop distance	497 m	675 m

using the runway in near future and also due to larger variability in the operating characteristics of STOL aircrafts.

16.3.3 Taxiway Width

For first generation STOL aircrafts such as DHC-6, taxiway width of 6.75 m is adequate to ensure that when the cockpit of the aircraft remains over the taxiway centreline marking, the lateral separation between the outer wheel of the aircraft and the edge of the taxiway pavement is not less than 1.5 m. For second generation aircraft such as DHC-7 a taxiway width of 18 m is recommended both by FAA as well as the Canadian Air Transportation Administration.

16.3.4 Safety Area

The limits of this area along with other necessary dimensions such as distances from building line etc. as recommended by FAA are shown in Figure 16.4.

16 4 VISUAL AIDS

This deals with specifications for marking and lighting of stolports. Typical markings on runway and taxiway are explained by Figures 16.5 to 16.8. They are based on various practices in existence at U K., U.S.A. and Canada. Figures 16.9 to 16.11 indicate the practices for stolport lighting.

16 4.1 Stolport Marking

There are four elements of runway marking viz. (a) threshold marking (b) touchdown zone marking (c) centreline marking and (d) runway edge marking.

As per U.K. practice, the threshold mixing is shown by a series of white strips of dimensions and types shown in Figure 16.5. This type of marking provides a high contrast to define

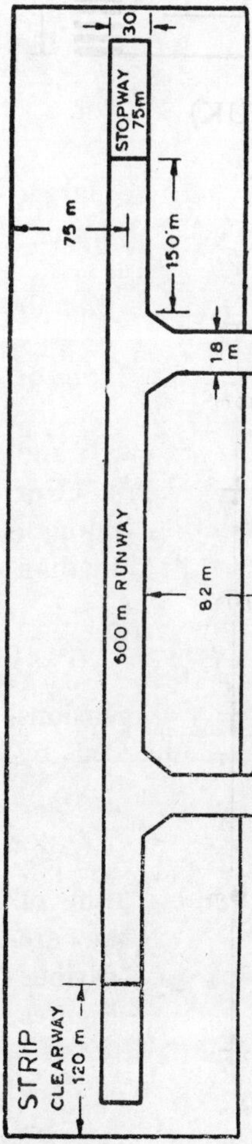

Figure 16.4 Stolport Dimensions (FAA)

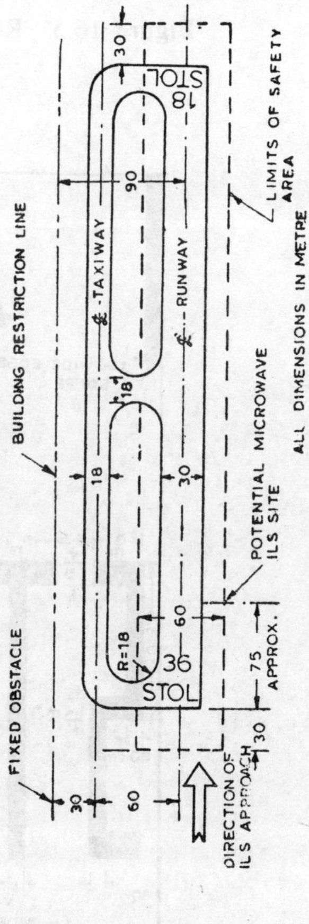

Figure 16.4 Stolport Dimensions (FAA)

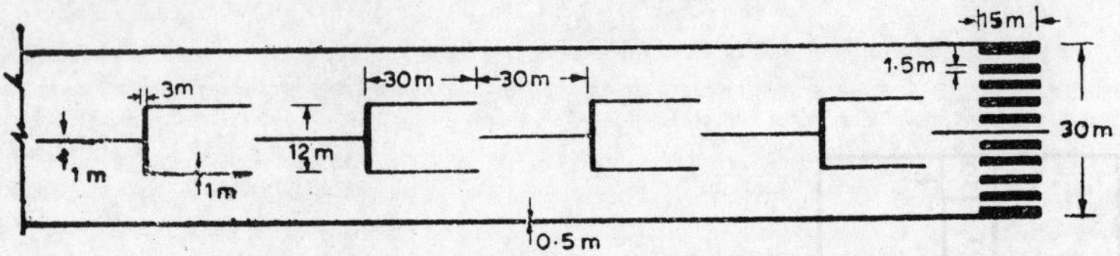

Figure 16.5 Runway Marking (UK)

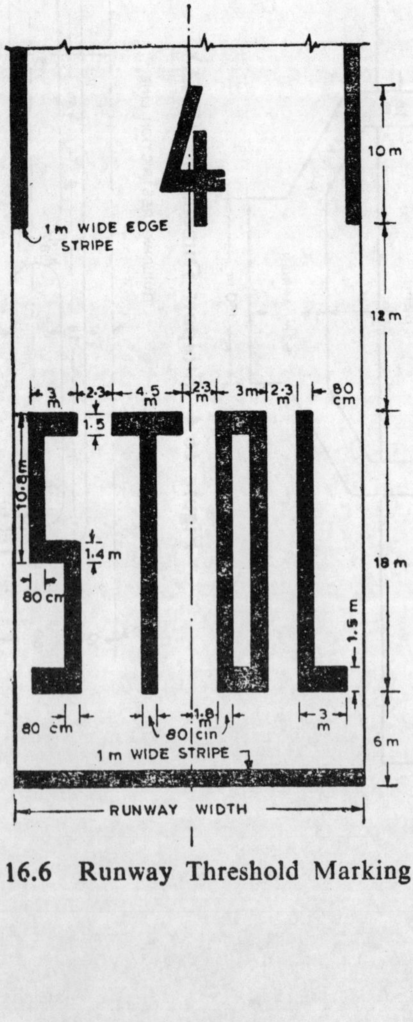

Figure 16.6 Runway Threshold Marking (FAA)

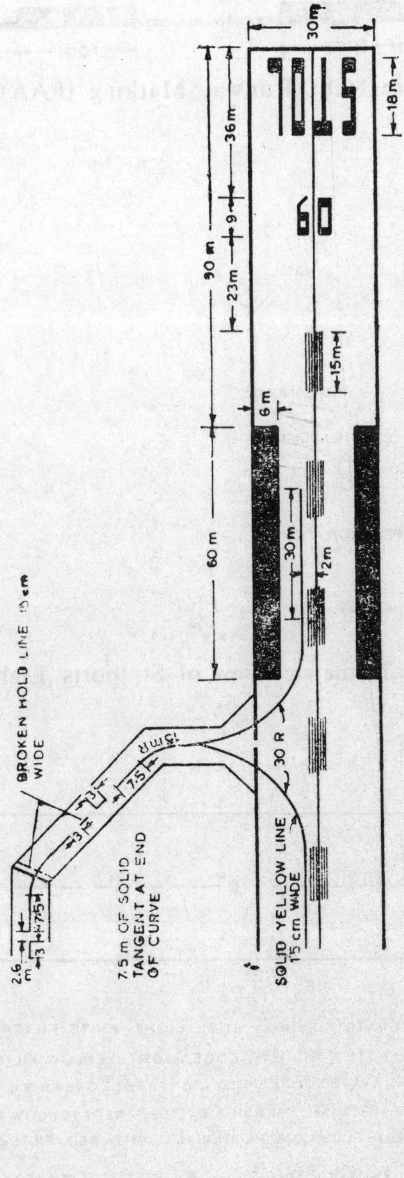

Figure 16.7 Runway and Taxiway Marking (Canadian)

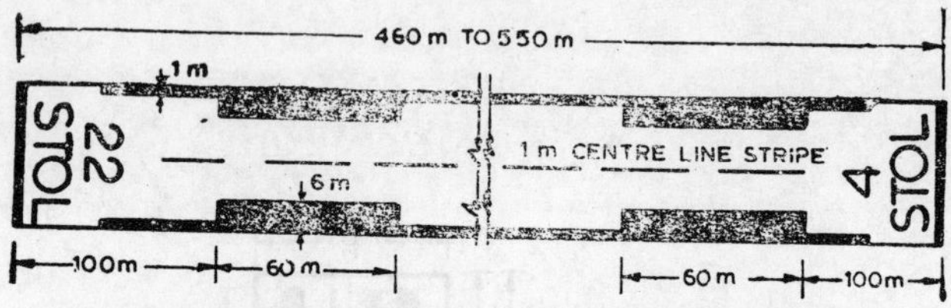

Figure 16.8 Runway Marking (FAA)

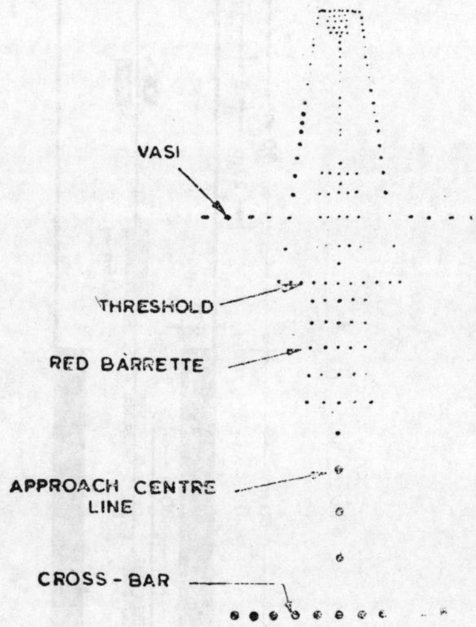

Figure 16.9 Isometric View of Stolports Lighting

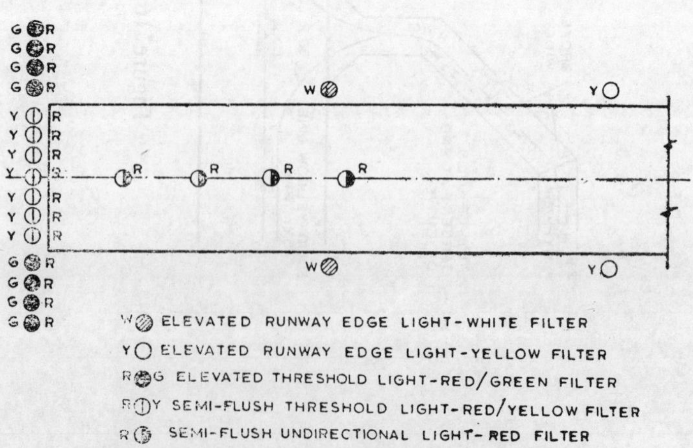

Figure 16.10 Runway Lighting (FAA)

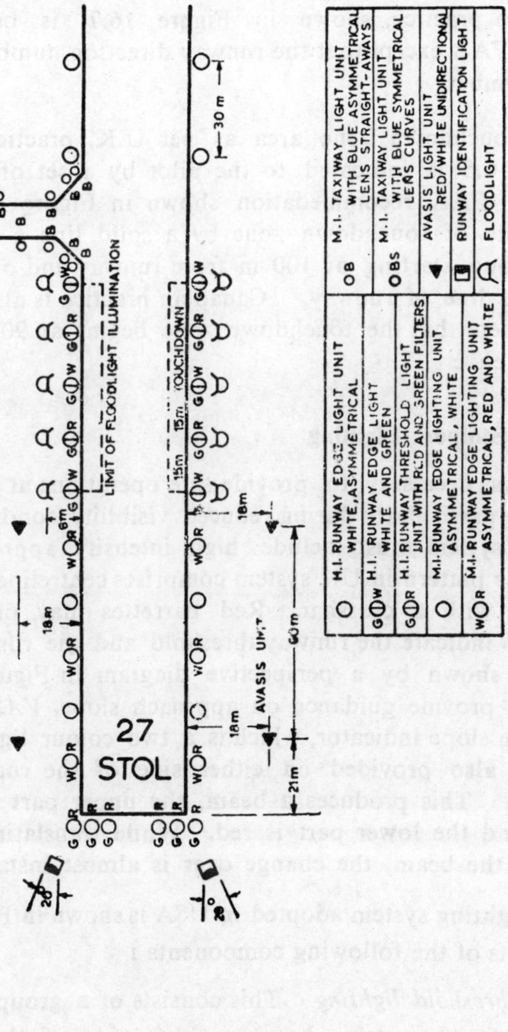

Figure 16.11 Runway Lighting (Canadian)

the runway end and to enable the pilot to adjust his final alignment prior to landing. FAA recommends threshold marking in the form of letter STOL and a wide transverse strip at the beginning of the runway as shown in Figure 16.6. Runway direction number is above the threshold marking which gives the bearing expressed to the nearest of 10°. The Canadian practice, shown in Figure 16.7, is basically the same at FAA except that the runway direction number is a two digit number.

The touchdown zone area as per U.K. practice shown in Figure 16.5 is indicated to the pilot by a set of inverted U shapes. FAA recommedation shown in Figure 16.8 reveals the limits of touchdown zone by a soild line 6 m wide and 60 m long starting at 100 m from runway and on either side of centre line of runway. Canadian practice is also similar to FAA except that the touchdown zone begins at 90 m from the runway end.

16.4.2 Stolport Lighting

This is necessary to provide safe operations at night and at day time particularly during reduced visibility conditions. The lighting system must include high intensity approach lights. The basic pattern in UK system comprises centreline 300 m long together with a crossbar. Red barrettes may preferably be added to indicate the runway threshold and the runway length. This is shown by a perspective diagram in Figure 16.9. In order to provide guidance on approach slope, *VASI* i.e. visual approach slope indicator, which is a two colour light projector unit, is also provided on either side of the runway at 6 m interval. This produces a beam, the upper part of which is white and the lower part is red. While translating vertically through the beam, the change over is almost instantaneous.

The lighting system adopted in USA is shown in Figure 16.10. It consists of the following components :

(i) Threshold lighting This consists of a group of 4 light fixtures forming wing bar on either side of the centreline of runway. The lights do not exceed 0.36 m above the runway edge.

(ii) Edge lighting. This consists of alternate yellow and white light fixtures spaced at interval of 30 to 60 m. The lights are not more than 0.36 m in height and 3 m from runway edge.

(iii) Runway end lights. These are on line with runway threshold lights and are spaced 1.5 m apart. The centre light is on extended runway centre line.

(iv) Distance indicator lights. These consist of four lights beginning at 15 m from runway threshold and spaced at 15 m interval along the direction of roll-out.

Canadian practice of stolport lighting is shown in Figure 16.11. It also comprises threshold light, runway edge light, runway end light and the touchdown zone light. Touchdown zone lights from the portion of runway edge lighting. The area is further illuminated by a series of 5 flood lights on each side of the runway.

PROBLEMS

1. Explain briefly the importance of STOL aircrafts.
2. Discuss in brief the various factors to be considered for the site selection of stolports.
3. Discuss in brief the various elements need to be considered for design and planning of stolports.
4. Explain in brief the various specifications for marking and lighting at stolports.

17

ENVIRONMENTAL GUIDELINES FOR AIRPORT PROJECTS

17.1 INTRODUCTION

The purpose of this chapter is to assist the project authorities in planning and carrying out Environmental Impact Assessment (EIA) and evolving Environmental Management Plan (EMP) for Airport Projects. The guidelines as presented in this chapter have been prepared with the basic assumption that the EIA is to be used as planning tool and the environmental considerations should be incorporated in the initial stage of planning of airport projects. The cost of environmental protection measures should be treated as integral component of the total project cost. These are applicable to all new projects as well as the projects involving significant changes in existing facilities: However, if no environmental impact assessment was carried out at the time of creation of existing facilities, all modifications should be subjected to the EIA process.

17.2 ENVIRONMENTAL IMPACT ASSESSMENT

Environmental Impact Assessment (EIA) is a procedure for bringing out potential effects of human activities on environmental system. It helps in inter-comparison of various options and the screening of alternate sites for locating the airport projects.

To identify the impact, the parameters relevant to the type of projects under consideration are listed. Some typical environmental parameters associated with transportation projects are given in Table 17.1. These are classified as : natural physical resources, natural ecological (or biological) resources, human/economic development resources and quality of life values including aesthetic and cultural values.

Table 17.1 Some Environmental Parameters Associated with Transportation Projects

Developmental Projects	Environmental Parameters
Highway	Surface Water Quality
Airport	Air Quality
Port and Harbours	Siesmological/Geology
Railway/Rapid Transit	Erosion
	Land Quality
	Fisheries
	Forests
	Terrestrial Wildlife
	Noise
	Land Use
	Aesthetics
	Industries
	Resettlement
	Archaeological/Historic Significance
	Public Health
	Socio-Economic

17.3 ENVIRONMENTAL IMPACT STATEMENT

Environmental Impact Assessment (EIA) is to be followed by preparation of Environmental Impact Statement (EIS). An EIS is a final analysis to an Environmental Impact Assessment and covers the following aspects :

(a) A brief description of the project

(b) Description of the existing environment : namely,

(i) Identification of the project's area of influence.

(ii) Pertinent environmental resources within the area of influence.

(c) Likely impact of the proposed project : namely,

(i) Adverse and beneficial.

(ii) Reversible and irreversible, and

(iii) Where the impacts are likely to be short and/or long term.

(d) Mitigation, protection and enhancement measures including the following :

(i) The possible means for adopting environmental safeguards.

(ii) Minimising deterimental impact.

(iii) Enhancing beneficial aspects of the project and

(iv) Effective management of environmental resources affected by the project.

(e) Consideration of alternatives which would include recommendations :

(i) Ranking the proposed development alternatives including the preferred plans for the most to the least acceptable, in terms of the impact of each alternative on environment;

(ii) Net effects to be assessed on the basis of ability to mitigate overall significant impacts.

(f) Consideration of 'No Change Alternative' : Future status of environmental parameters to be determined for a "No Change/No Build" case. This provides a clear measure of impacts resulting purely due to a certain project.

(g) Summary and Conclusions giving

(i) A review of gains versus losses in environmental resources and values.

(ii) Overall net gains which justify the need for the project.

(iii) Explanation of how unavoidable adverse impacts have been minimised or off-set and composited for;

(iv) Explanation of use of any irreplaceable resources, and

(v) Provision for follow up surveillance and mointoring.

17.4 ENVIRONMENTAL MANAGEMENT PLAN

An Environmental Management Plan (EMP) is an implementation plan for mitigation, protection and/or enhancement measures which are recommended in the EIS. The EMP presents in details the operational plan including the required resources and implementation schedule. In EMP, the implementation of protection measures is elevated to a level suitable for incorporation in design phase of the proposed project. The protection measures which require formulation of detailed implementation plans and, therefore, inclusion in the EMP are selected on the basis of EIS review by the concerned agencies.

The EMP document should contain an implementation plan for each of the selected mitigative, protection and enhancement measures. EMP may therefore, consist of one or several implementation plans. Each plan should include the following :

(i)	*Objective* :	Description of the protection measures and impacts it is expected to mitigate.
(ii)	*Work plan or Design criteria* :	Work plan and the design criteria needed to implement the protection measures.
(iii)	*Implementation schedule* :	Timing of the work plan as to when the protection measures are to be installed and/or be operational.
(iv)	*Man power requirement* :	Management, technical and supporting staff and any resources required to implement the protection measures.
(v)	*Monitoring* :	Continuous monitoring including field observation/sampling/analyses must be carried out in order to assess the effect.

The EMP report should include consideration of a monitoring programme including discussion of applicable parameters, field/sampling stations, measurements/analyses, frequency of measurements/sampling, transportation, collation and interpretation of data, format for preparation of monitoring reports and suggested description of the reports. It should also project the estimate of costs involved and suggestions for assignment of responsibility for carrying out and financing the monitoring work.

17.5 IDENTIFICATION OF IMPACTS

Noise, vibrations, air pollution, pollution due to solid and sanitary wastes and pollution caused due to surface runoff are the environmental effects commonly associated with airport projects.

Noise, out of all these factors is the most difficult environmental hazard associated with airport operations In many cases, residences, buildings etc. in the affected zones require either resettlement or compensation for serious loss in property value. Aesthetic degradation can be a problem in airport development. Proper landscaping can help in minimization of noise.

Airports are often located in swamp lands and estuarine zones and can significantly affect ecological resources in these areas and as such sufficient care must be paid to effects of wildlife especially birds on airport operations. Special measures are needed to safegurad airoplanes from potentially disastrous birdstrikes, which include covering/removing garbage tips or use of scare-guns.

The effect on traffic is the final consideration and many airports fail to design adequate access/exit points and parking leading to traffic congestion.

17.5.1 Physical Resources

(a) Soil and Geological Impacts : The primary and irreversible long term impacts on soil and geology result from site, formation, the application of soil improvement schemes, design and construction of earth structures such as embankments, dykes and other infrastructure such as building foundation and basement walls.

(i) Impacts of Site Formation : The major impact would be on excavated areas and the areas which need to be filled up to the proposed site formation level.

(ii) Impacts of Soil Pre-consolidation Scheme : The untreated areas without the sand drain will be subjected to continuous ground subsidence.

(iii) Impacts of Trench Excavation : The impacts associated with excavation of trenches disturb the stability of excavated areas and increase the soil erosion.

(iv) Impacts of Basement Wall : During excavation for preparation of basement wall, the ground water level in adjacent areas may sometimes be affected. Lowering of water table will cause settlement of the adjacent ground which may affect existing buildings/structures.

(b) Impact on Water Demand & Waste Water Discharge : The development of an airport results in increased water demand. This places additional stress on existing surface or ground water sources, water treatment systems, and water distribution systems.

Another impact would be the increased waste water load. Dust and chemicals deposited on land surface, runways and roads will be transported by stormwater run off and add a significant pollution load to receiving water and decrease the water quality.

(c) Air Quality Impacts : The Airport projects lead to increase in emissions of certain air pollutants such as Carbon Monoxide (CO), Hydrocarbons (HC), Nitrogen Oxides (NOx), Suspended Particulate Matter (SPM), lead (Pb) etc., in the area. The incremental changes to the existing ambient air quality may produce detrimental effects on some sensitive receptors. Air quality assessment may be carried out as follows :

(i) Background pollutant level should be found out by actual sampling for CO, HC, NOx, SPM and Pb.

(ii) The background level sampling should be carried out for 1 hr., 8 hr and 24 hourly levels of the pollutants.

(iii) The resultant pollutant levels should be estimated by using appropriate model after taking into account :

(a) Emissions due to activity of aircrafts.

(b) Emissions from ground service vehicles.

(c) Emissions resulting from traffic generated on access roads.

(d) Emissions from any other activity at the airport.

(iv) Emission rates for each type of aircraft, vehicle/source for all the pollutants should be clearly outlined.

(v) Resultant air-quality should not be in violation of ambient air quality standards in effect at the time of study. However, additional standards may be formulated in due course for airport air quality.

(vi) All procedures, models etc. used in air quality impact estimation should be clearly described in detail.

(d) Noise Impacts : A detailed noise impact assessment should be carried out as per the following guidelines :

(i) Hourly noise contours be prepared for the area surrounding by the airport.

(ii) For day time operations, i e. 8 a m. to 9 p.m the equivalent noise level, (hourly) i.e. Leq (h) should not exceed 60 dBA. This limit will apply if any type of human activity falls within the limit of 60 dBA contour. Additionally, operations at the airport should not result in any substantial increases (⩾ 10 dBA) over existing background levels.

(iii) For the purpose of computation of Leq (h), maximum hourly traffic design should be used. However, conversely Leq (h) criteria could determine number of flights which can safely be operated from a given airport.

(iv) For night time operations (9 p.m. to 6 a.m.) two levels of criteria shall apply :

(a) Leq (9 p.m to 6 a.m.) or L_N (Night) may not exceed 30 dBA; L_N - average noise level from 9 p.m. to 6 a.m.).

(b) Leq (h) during 9 p.m. to 6 a.m. may not exceed 35 dBA. However, as opposed to day time criteria these night time criteria should apply to residential areas only.

(v) In keeping with the requirements stated in (iv), two sets of contours will need to be developed for night time, namely : L_N and Leq (h).

(vi) Noise emission levels for each type of aircraft and source should be clearly outlined.

(vii) The noise contour maps should be drawn in such a scale as to clearly show the different types of land usage and noise impacts involved.

(viii) All results should be clearly tabulated and diagrammed.

(ix) All noise impacts should be identified and tabulated individually.

(x) In case, noise criteria are exceeded, mitigation measures as outlined under mitigation section should be considered.

(xi) Effect of each mitigation measure should be quantified in terms of reduction in noise level as well as in terms of number of impacts reduced.

(xii) Cost involved in each of the mitigation measures should be estimated and outlined clearly.

17.5.2 Ecological Impacts

The general ecological impacts arising from the development of an airport can be described in two categories viz. site development and facilities operation.

(a) Impacts Associated with Site Development

(i) Direct and indirect impacts on ecology of plants and animals in the area, due to clearing of trees and strips of land.

(ii) Turbidity increases in down stream area causes less light penetration, is aesthetically unpleasant and reduces primary productivity.

(iii) Noise and dust generation due to construction of access roads will frighten away animals.

(b) Impacts Related to Facilities Operations

Population of birds in the vicinity of the airport is hazardous as far as operational safety is concerned. As stated earlier, prevention measures includes removal of garbage tips and use of scare guns.

17.5.3 Socio-Economic Impacts

Location of airport in a particular site may result in profound impacts of socio-economic nature. On the positive side, it is helpful to the local economy by increasing its access to tourists, businessmen etc. Area near airport also becomes important after location for hotels and other related development.

However, on the negative side, it may result in uprooting of people such as residential dwellers, farmers and businesses. This may lead to large scale resettlement and associated problems.

17.6 MEASURES FOR OFFSETTING ADVERSE IMPACTS

17.6.1 Soil and Geology

(a) Before commencement of the fill work, any organic matter existing at the ground, such as trees, vegetation, etc. should be cleared. The filling work should be carried out in layers in order to achieve uniformity of the fill.

(b) The use of heavy machinery which could affect the stress condition of the underlying soil should be avoided in initial earthwork stage, if possible.

(c) Trench and canals should not be excavated too deep below the existing ground level. The construction activities involved in excavation and filling of earth materials should be carried out during dry period of the year.

(d) Soil erosion as a consequence of vegetation clearing preceding construction can be minimised by replanting and turfing. However, in arid areas, it may be necessary to incorporate artificial erosion protection measures such as facing of escarpments, paving of taxiway flanks and lining of drains.

17.6.2 Hydrology and Water

(a) Embankments need to be constructed in approach road area for road bridges and a continuous dyke must be build around the airport perimeter for flood protection.

(b) Temporary sanitation facilities be installed at the construction site. Sedimentation basin providing appropriate detention time should be provided to intercept surface water runoff from the construction site.

(e) The airport should install a wastewater treatment facility for treatment and safe disposal of the wastewater generated.

(d) The quality of water in the vicinity should be monitored after development and during operation of the airport.

17.6.3 Air Quality Impact Mitigation

(a) In the engineering design stage, runways for landing and take-off should be designed for maximum dispersion of air pollutants.

(b) During construction dust and particulates can be minimised by water spraying.

(c) Continuous monitoring of air quality in the airport vicinity is recommended. In case air quality deteriorates beyond recommended standards and severe impacts result, consideration should be given to control emissions within the airport area. Mitigation measures may include shutting off one engine while taxying etc.

(d) A long term measure required is to improve aircraft engine designs so as to minimise emissions. It will be mandatory, if quality is a persistent problem.

17.6.4 Noise Impact Mitigation

Some of the possible mitigation measures are :

(a) Buy the land around airport to avoid exposing people to aircraft noise.

(b) Requiring design and manufacture of quieter planes.

(c) Adjusting flight paths in a way which minimises the effect of noise.

(d) Orienting runway so as to avoid noise exposure.

(e) Introduction and maintenance of operational and Air Traffic Control (ATC) procedures which contribute minimum noise.

(f) Adequate provisions at the airport to allow aircrafts to avoid running on auxiliary power units during turn around time.

(g) Relocating residences and other noise sensitive receptors.

(h) Hotels, an inevitable and necessary development near airports should always be required to incorport sound insulation and other noise control features at the design stage.

(i) Providing sound insulation etc., to receptors adversely affected (e.g. hospitals, schools etc.).

17.6.5 Ecological Resources

(a) If there is wildlife in the area, enough space should be reserved for it. The area should be kept free from urbanisation and promoted as feeding grounds for animal species.

(b) To minimise flocking of birds, land use pattern within and around the airport must be carefully planned.

(c) Large areas of orchards should be avoided. Bird scaring devices may be employed for safety of aircrafts.

17.6.6 Socio-Economic Impacts

(a) The measures to relocate private house holds should be taken by providing them incentives to move away from the airport site.

In this connection, following measures are proposed :

(i) Environmental clearance be obtained sufficiently in advance of the actual commencement of construction.

(ii) Provision of options for accommodation through government institutions.

(iii) Provision of low interest loans through the Government for those who wish to find non-government accommodation. In special cases, the government may provide a direct cash grant for rehousing.

(b) Farmers may be most adversely affected by relocation since they lose the land from which they drive their livelihood. The compensation paid out at the time of the land appropriation may not be adequate to allow them to obtain new land at higher prices. The measures must be proposed to assist the relocated population in maintaining their income levels.

17.7 ENVIRONMENTAL MONITORING PROGRAMME

Environmental management and monitoring programmes must be recommended to support normal control systems and/or give emergency warning or provide control over accident proneness. Brief summary of environmental management and monitoring programme for future could include the following

(a) Monitoring of water quality should be carried out at sufficient frequency.

(b) Monitoring sites for air quality should be decided after the operational mode of the airport has been scheduled. There should be one monitoring station at the control tower to provide hourly, 8 hourly and 24 hourly samples every day.

(c) There should be permanent noise monitoring stations as well as mobile units.

(d) A post project analysis after a few years should be carried out to assess the ecological environment.

(e) Following four programmes should be recommended for monitoring socio-economic impact after the airport is in operation :

(i) Maintenance of accurate registration data on population and economic activities.

(ii) Occupational training programme for the affected population.

(iii) Periodic surveys to monitor health status due to pollution.

(iv) Monitoring of industrial development and activities.

PROBLEMS

1. Discuss in brief why there is a need for environmental considerations for airport projects ?
2. What do you mean by environmental impact assessment (EIA) ? How, EIA is useful for finalizing transportation projects ?
3. Discuss in brief the various aspects defining the environmental impacts statement (EIS).
4. What do you mean by environmental management plan (EMP) ? What information is needed to prepare the EMP document ?
5. How will you identify the environmental impacts commonly associated with airport projects ?
6. Explain in brief the measures for offsetting adverse impacts caused due to airport projects.
7. Discuss in brief the various aspects of environmental management and monitoring programme needed after the airport is in operation.

LEXICON OF TERMS

Aerodrome A defined area of land or water which is intended to be used for the arrival, departure and movements of aircrafts. It may be provided with the facilities for shelter and repair of aircraft and for processing of passengers, baggage, mail and cargo. Unlike airport it may not necessarily be used for all scheduled air flights. Sometimes the term aerodrome is used in place of airport.

Aerofoil A wing like structure which may be flat or curved and is designed to obtain reactions upon its surface from the air through which it moves.

Aeroplane A power driven heavier-than-air aircraft which derives its lift in atmosphere chiefly from aerodynamic reactions on its surface which remain fixed under given conditions of light.

Aileron A movable surface whose main purpose is to serve as a lateral control in the flight of an aeroplane. It produces rolling moment about the longitudinal axis of the aeroplane.

Air harbour A landing facility for sea planes on a quiet body of water adjacent to a community.

Aircraft Any machine which can derive support in the atmosphere from the reactions of the air and is intended for aerial navigation. It may be heavier or lighter than air. It may or may not be power driven. Balloon, kite, aeroplane etc are its examples.

Aircraft Classification Number (ACN) It is defined as the load carried by a single wheel in terms of 500 kg at a constant tyre pressure of 1.25 MPa.

Airfield An area of land or water which is used for landing and take off of aircrafts. It may or may not be provided with the facilities for convenience of passengers and for shelter, repair and servicing of aircrafts.

Airpark A community landing facility for personal aircraft and is provided within the residential areas or business districts.

Airplane *Same as aeroplane.*

Airport It is an area of land or water which is to be *regularly* used for landing and take off of aircrafts. It is provided with facilities for shelter and repair of aircrafts in addition to the other normal facilities for passengers and cargo.

Airport capacity It indicates the number of movements of aircrafts which an airport can handle safely within a unit time, usually an hour. A landing or take off operation is taken as one movement. Airport capacity during IFR conditions is usually less than during VFR conditions.

Airport configurations Airport configuration is the most important factor and is defined as the general arrangement of the various parts or components of the airport system.

Airport control radio station A station providing radio communication between an airport control tower and an aircraft.

Airport control tower A unit which is established within the airport to provide air traffic control services to airport traffic.

Airport established elevation The elevation of the highest point of the landing.

Airport identification sign A sign which is placed adjacent to an airport to aid in identifying the airport from the air.

Airport pavement It is a prepared surface which is laid on natural ground or on compacted earth. It is designed to carry aircraft wheel loads without exceeding the bearing capacity of ground beneath it.

Airport reference point The point representing the designated geographical location of an airport.

Air route *See airway*

Air Route Surveillance Radar (ARSR) ARSR are installed along the airways to track the aircrafts. The long range radars permit closer spacing between the aircrafts flying at the same altitude, there by increasing the capacity of the airways.

Airship A power driven lighter-than-air aircraft.

Air strip A long and comparatively narrow strip suitable for landing and take off of aircrafts. It is generally used for emergency landing and located at certain intervals along the air routes.

Airport Surface Detection Equipment (ASDE) ASDE is a short range radar which gives to the controller a pictorial display of the runways, taxiways, terminal areas and shows the position of the aircrafts.

Airports Surveillance Radar (ASR) It is an instrument which provides to the controller at the tower an overall picture of all the aircrafts within the air space surrounding the terminal.

Airway An air route along which aids to air navigation such as radio beams, beacon lights etc are maintained.

Amphibian An aeroplane which is designed to take off and land on water as well as on ground.

Approach areas These are wide clearance areas of ground located beyond both the ends of a runway. They fall under the approach flight path of an aircraft. They are trapezoidal in shape and are centrally placed about the extended centre line of a runway. These areas should be kept clear of obstructions.

Approach surface The imaginary inclined plane representing the obstruction clearance line and located directly above the approach area.

Approach zone *Same as approach area.*

Apron A defined area which is used to accommodate aircrafts for loading and unloading of passengers and cargo, parking, refueling etc. It is usually paved and planned adjacent to terminal building.

Aspect ratio The ratio of span to chord of an aerofoil.

Authorised aerodrome A custom or other aerodrome specially designated as such by the competent authorities and on which aircraft may make their first landing on entering a territory or from which they may depart on leaving a territory.

Baggage Personal properties of passengers or crew carried on an aircraft with the permission of the competent authorities.

Balloon A non-power-driven and lighter-than-air aircraft.

Beaufort scale It is a code adopted by International Meteorological Committee for wind velocities.

Beaufort Number	Description	Velocity at a standard height of 10 metres above flat open ground (Knots)
0	Calm	⩽ 1
1	Light air	1 — 3
2	Light breeze	4 — 6
3	Gentle breeze	7 — 10
4	Moderate breeze	11 — 16
5	Fresh breeze	17 — 21
6	Strong breeze	22 — 27
7	Moderate gale	28 — 33
8	Fresh gale	34 — 40
9	Strong gale	41 — 47
10	Whole gale	48 — 55
11	Storm	56 — 63
12	Hurricane	64 — 71

Blast Pads Specially designed shoulders provided at the take off ends of the runway and along taxiway to protect them from erosion due to high velocity of the jet exhaust.

Boundary lights Aeronautical ground light delineating the boundary of a landing area.

Boundary marker Markers used to indicate the boundary of a landing area.

Biplane A form of aeroplane in which the main supporting surface is divided into two parts, one above the other.

Calm period The period of the absence of appreciable wind, generally considered as 6 kmph (4 mph) or less.

Capacity *See airport capacity.*

Cargo Freight, other than passengers, baggage and mail, which is carried by a transport aircraft.

Clearway Defined area at the end of the landing strip in the direction of take off over which aircraft may make its initial climb.

Conical surface An imaginary surface which extends upwards and outwards from the periphery of the horizontal surface with a slope of 1 : 20 measured in a vertical plane.

Control area An airspace of defined dimension within which air traffic control is exercised.

Control zone An airspace of defined dimension within which, rules, additional to those governing flight in control area apply for the protection of air traffic.

Controlled aerodrome An airspace of defined dimensions within which air-traffic control service is provided to IFR flights.

Control tower It controls the air traffic within the airport control area by supervising and directing the arriving and departing aircrafts. It is usually situated at the top of terminal building.

Critical height The height below which the minimum prescribed vertical clearance cannot be maintained either on normal approach or in the event of a missed approach.

Critical point A point at which the failure of engine is assumed to occur. It is used to determine the accelerate-stop distance.

Cross wind component It is the component at right angles to the direction of travel when wind is inclined to the direction of landing and take off of aircraft.

Cruising speed It is the speed of aircraft with respect to the ground when the aircraft is flying in air at its maximum speed. This is also known as ground speed.

CTOL It means conventional take-off and landing.

Design landing weight The maximum aeroplane weight used in runway design for landing conditions at the maximum velocity of descent.

Design take off weight The maximum aeroplane weight for flight load conditions which is used in the structural design of pavements.

Distance Measuring Equipment (DME) DME indicates to the pilot, the distance to or from a point, usually a VOR bearing station. The pilot thus gets a precise idea of his position with respect to the airway.

Elevator The movable part of the tail whose only purpose is to ensure longitudinal control and contributes to the longitudinal stability.

Empennage *See tail*

Environmental Impact Assessment (EIA) It is a procedure for bringing out the potential effects of human activities on environmental system. It helps in inter-comparison of various options and the screening of alternate sites for locating the airport projects.

Environmental Impact Statement (EIS) EIS is a final analysis to an EIA and covers the various aspects like description of the project, description of the existing environment, likely impacts of the proposed project, mitigation, protection and enhance measures, consideration of alternatives, consideration of 'No change alternative' and summary conclusions.

Environmental Management Plan (EMP) EMP is an implementation plan for mitigation, protection and/or enhancement measures which are recommended in the EIS.

Exit Taxiways These are provided at busy airports and are located at various points along the runway so that the landing aircraft leaves the runway as early as possible and keeps it clear for use by other aircraft.

Expected approach time The time at which it is expected that an arriving aircraft will be cleared to commence for landing.

Fan marker beacon A. type of radio beacon, the emission from which is radiated in a vertical fan shaped pattern.

Fillet Additional portion of pavement provided at the junction or intersection of any trafficways to facilitate the turning movement of aircraft and to prevent it from going off the pavement on shoulders.

Fin The fixed part of the tail unit whose purpose is to contribute to the transverse and directional stability.

Falling Weight Deflectometer (FWD) This equipment is used for measuring the dynamic deflection and belongs to the class of light vibrators. The equipment consists of a falling mass of 150 kg and develops a maximum force of 60 KN and pulse width of 28 m when dropped from a height of 40 cm on a foot plate of 30 cm dia. resting on the pavement. This is used for structural evaluation of pavements and design of overlays.

Flaps These are some what similar to ailerons and are used for increasing the lift on aerofoils.

Flight time The total time from the moment an aircraft first moves under its own power for the purpose of taking off until the moment it comes to rest at the end of the flight.

Flight visibility The average range of visibility in forward direction from the cockpit of an aircraft in flight.

Frequency

Frequeney subdivision	Nomenclature	Range
Very low frequency	VLF	30 kc/s
Low frequency	LF	30-300 kc/s
Medium frequency	MF	300-3000 kc/s
High frequency	HF	3000-30000 kc/s
Very high frequency	VHF	30-300 mc/s
Ultra high frequency	UHF	300-3000 mc/s
Super high frequency	SHF	3000-30000 mc/s
Extremely high frequency	EHF	30000-300000 mc/s

Fuselage The part of an aircraft which forms the main body and to which the wing structure, tail unit and under carriage are attached.

Gate It is defined by an aircraft parking space, adjacent to a terminal building and used by a single aircraft for the loading, unloading of passengers, baggage and mail.

Gate capacity It is defined as the ability of a specified number of gates to accommodate aircraft loading and unloading operations under conditions of continuous demand.

Gate Position The space allotted to an aircraft parking at a loading apron.

Hangar Large shed erected at the airport for the purpose of servicing and repairing of aircrafts.

Heavier-than-air aircraft Any machine which is heavier than air and which derives its lift chiefly from aerodynamic forces.

Helicopter A heavier-than-air aircraft-which is supported in atmosphere by the reactions of the air on one or more power-driven rotors rotating about an approximately vertical axis. Helicopters are suitable for special uses, e.g. the oil industry, electrification projects, air ambulance and emergency service etc.

Heliport Area for landing and take off of helicopter.

Holding apron The designated portion placed adjacent to the ends of runways to allow check of aircraft instruments and engine operation prior to take-off and to enable the aircrafts to wait for take off clearance.

Horizontal surface It is the imaginary horizontal surface, circular in plan and located at a level of 45 m above the airport established elevation.

IFR flight The flight in accordance with the Instrument Flight Rules. Such rules are observed when visibility is poor.

IFR weather conditions Weather conditions during which the visibility is below the minimum prescribed for flights under Visual Flight Rules.

Inner Horizontal Surface (IHS) It is the surface located in a horizontal plane above an aerodrome and its surrounding.

The radius or outer limits of IHS shall be measured from airport reference point (ARP) or points established for such purposes.

Institute of Air Transport (IAT) An association of individuals and organisations with interest in civil aviation.

Instrumental landing system (ILS) A radio aid navigation which is intended to facilitate aircraft in landing. It provides lateral and vertical guidance to the aircraft and indicates the distance of the aircraft from the runway threshold.

Instrument runway The runway of an airport which is equipped with devices permitting the landing of an aircraft under conditions of poor visibility.

International air service Such service which passes through the airspace over the territory or more than one country.

International airport Any airport designed by the country in whose territory it is situated, as an airport, of arrival and departure where the formalities related to customs immigration and similar procedures are carried out.

International Airports Authority of India (IAAI) It was set up in April 1972 to plan, develop, construct and maintain the four international airports in India.

International Airport Transport Association (IATA) Its role is to foster the interests of civil aviation to provide a forum for industry views and to establish industry practices.

International Civil Airports Association (ICAA) An association of civil airport authorities to serve as a forum and focus for the views and interests of civil airport operators.

International Civil Aviation Organisation (ICAO) ICAO provides the machinery for the achievement of international corporation in the air. It also provides the international link between civil and military flying activities.

Landing area The portion of airport which is used for landing and take off of aircrafts. It does not include the terminal area.

Landing strip A long and narrow area, forming part of an airport, which is suitable for the landing and take-off of aircrafts. It consists of a runway plus shoulders on either side of the runway.

Load Classification Group (LCG) Aircraft evaluation and pavement classification has been simplified by categorising aircraft and pavement LCN values into broad LCG's. The published LCG of a pavement permits the authority to place no limits on its use by the same or lower groups of aircraft. LCG are varying from LCG I to LCG VII.

Load Classification Number (LCN) LCN system was developed by by the British Air Ministry Directorate of General Works. LCN of a flexible pavement is obtained by carrying out repetitive plate bearing tests on the existing airport pavement.

Class A messages Message essential to countries and to airline operating agencies or the safety and regularity of international air services. The messages comprise of :

(i) Distress message

(ii) Messages for the safety of human life and urgency message

(iii) Flight safety message

(iv) Meteorological message

(v) Flight regularity message
(vi) Notices to airmen
(vii) Service message

Class B messages Message essential to airline operating agencies for the economic operation of international air services. The messages comprise of :

(i) Reservation message
(ii) General airline operating agency message

Mach Number This indicates the speed of any body relative to the speed of sound. Mach 1 means the speed is equal to that of sound.

Meteorological information All classes of meteorological report, analyses, forecasts, warnings and advices originating from or available through meteorological authorities.

Missed approach When landing is not effective after an instrument approach.

Monoplane A form of an aeroplane whose main supporting surface is a single wing extending equally on each side of the body.

National Airports Authority (NAA) NAA was established by Govt. of India on June 1, 1986. Responsibilities of NAA consist of the managment of air routes and airspace in the country for domestic and international airports.

Outer Horizontal Surface (OHS) OHS is circular in plan with centre located at ARP, where the longest runway lies between 900 to 1500 m, OHS shall extend to 9900 m from the ARP. For longest runway lies between 1500 m and more, the OHS shall extend to 15000 m from the ARP. Height of OHS is 150 m above the ARP elevation. The constructions protruding above this surface shall not permitted.

Pavement Classification Number (PCN) PCN is the ACN of aircraft which the pavement is capable of carrying for unrestricted movement.

Pawan Hans Pawan Hans was formed in 1985. Its primary goal is to reduce the foreign chartering of helicopters for use by the oil industry. They provide services in regions where road transportation is extremely difficult and time consuming.

Precision Approach Radar (PAR) It serves the same purpose as an ILS, except that the guidance information reaches the pilot through his hearing aid. PAR gives to controller the picture of descending aircraft both in plan and in elevation.

Rudder A control which helps the pilot to turn the nose of the aeroplane in any particular direction. It can move to and fro about a vertical axis through about 33°. It is usually hinged to the fin at the tail.

Runway A long and comparatively narrow strip which is paved except for small aerodromes.

Runway Capacity It is defined as the ability of a runway system to accommodate aircraft landings and take-offs. It is expressed in operations per hour or operations per year. The factors affecting runway capacity are air traffic control, characteristics of demand, environmental factors and layout and design of the runway system.

Seaplane An aeroplane designed to take off and land on water.

Standard atmosphere An imaginary atmosphere having the following conditions :

(i) The air is a perfectly dry gas

(ii) The temperature at sea level is 15°C

(iii) The pressure at sea level is 760 mm of mercury

(iv) The temperature gradient from sea level to the altitude at which the temperature becomes −15.5°C is −0.0065°C per metre and zero at the elevation above the altitude when temp. is 15.5°C

STOL It means short take off and landing.

Stolport It is an area used for landing and take off of STOL aircrafts.

Stream line To give a body such a shape that its head resistance to motion through the air is lessened.

Stopway Rectangular area at the end of the runway in the direction of take off, in which an aircraft can be stopped after an interrupted take-off. Its width is equal to the width of runway and thickness sufficient to bear the weight of the aircraft.

Subsonic aircraft Aircraft which travels at speed less than the speed of sound.

Supersonic aircraft Aircraft which travels at speed greater than the speed of sound.

Surveillance radar It provides an overall picture of the surrounding atmosphere. The information about any aircraft within of range is received on its scope.

Tactical Air Navigation (TACN) This is used for the tactical needs of the military and operates on ultra high frequency band and measures distances and azimuth in one unit instead of two.

Tail The rear portion of an aircraft to which rudder, elevator and fin are usually attached.

Taxiway A defined path on land aerodrome over which an aeroplane may taxi to and fro the runway and loading apron.

Taxiway Capacity Capacity of a taxiway system generally far exceeds the capacities of either the runways or the gates. Taxiway capacity depends on the runway operations, rate, the aircraft mix and the location of the taxiway relative to the departure end of the runway.

Terminal area Portion of the airport other than the landing area. It includes the following :

(i) Terminal building for processing of passengers
(ii) Facilities for loading and unloading of passengers, baggage and cargo.
(iii) Apron for parking of aircrafts
(iv) Vehicular parking areas
(v) Cargo storage buildings
(vi) Hangers for maintenance of aircrafts

Terminal building A focal point in the terminal area. It provides space for air line operations, facilities for convenience of passengers, office for the airport management and other non aeronautical functions.

Transition surface Imaginary inclined plane with a slope of 1 : 7 measured upward and outward in a vertical plane at right angles to the centre line of runway.

Vayudoot Vayudoot is a jointly owned company of IA and AI incorporated to provide low cost connections to the inaccessible areas such as North East region. However, its use has been extended to other areas where the passenger demand is low.

V/STOL Operations From airport pavement engineers point of view, successful vertical/short take-off and landing (V/STOL) operation involves safety of aircraft and pilot by providing reliable and maintenance free surfaces. Jet reaction control system is the unique feature of V/STOL aircrafts.

Very High Frequency Omni Directional Range (VOR) It is commonly known as VHF omni-range or VOR. The main advantage of this aid is that, it is not susceptible to static interference and remains effective even during a thunder storm.

VFR flight A flight in accordance with the Visual Flight Rules.

Visibility The greatest distance at which conspicuous points can be seen and identified.

Wind rose The diagram showing direction, duration and intensity of wind over a certain period.

Zoning It pertains to restrict the development of the area surrounding the airport as that no structure protrudes above the obstruction clearance line, as otherwise it may cause hazards in air navigation. It generally applies to the approach and turning zones.

REFERENCES

1 A.S. Niles and J.S. Newell. Airplane Structures, Vol. II John Wiley and Sons, New York.

2 A.W. Judge, Elementary Handbook of Aircraft Engines, Chapman and Hall Ltd., London, 1965.

3 Arnold Field Obe, International Air Traffic Control, Management of the World's Air Space. Pergamon Press.

4 Benjamine Everett Beauin, Zoning Maps for Airports, American Society of Civil Engineers (ASCE) Proceeding Vol. 79, 1953.

5 Charles Foresch, Airport Planning.

6 D.M. Finch Recent Developments in Airport Lighting, Journal of Air Transport Division ASCE, No. 2698, AT-2, 1961.

7 D.M. Burmister, The Theory of Stresses & Displacements in Layered Systems and Applications to Design of Airport Runways, Proceedings of Highway Research Board, Vol. 23, 1943.

8 Design and Evaluation of Airfield Pavements, Directorate of Civil Engineering Development, Department of the Environment, United Kingdom, 1971.

9 Development of CBR Flexible Pavement Design Methods for Airfiled, A Symposium, Transactions ASCE, Vol. 115, 1950.

10 Environmental Guidelines for Airport Projects, (Report Prepared by a Working Group) Ministry of Environment

and Forests. Department of Environment, Forests and Wildlife, Government of India, New Delhi, 1989.

11 G. Edward Walter and Wincent J. Roggeveen, Airport Approach, Runway and Taxiway Lighting Systems. Journal of Air Transport Division ASCE, Vol. 84 No. 1669, 1958.

12 G. Pickett and G.K. Ray, Influence Charts for Concrete Pavement, Proc, ASCE, Vol. 76, 1950.

13 Gal Ahlborn and Robert Horonjeff. Effect of Gradient on Jet Transport Runway Lengths. Journal Air Transport Division ASCE, Vol. 89, No A1 : 1, 1963.

14 George DeMent, Determining Airport Needs for the Future, Journal Air Transport Division ASCE, Vol-87, No. AT-2, 1961.

15 H.E. Morgan, Turbojet Fundamentals, McGraw Hill Book Company, New York, 1950.

16 H.M. Westergard, New Formulas for Stresses in Concrete Air Field Pavement, Proceeding of American Society of Civil Engineers, 1947.

17 ICAO-Report of the Third Air Navigation Conference, DOC 7730-AN CONF/3, Part IV, 1956.

18 ICAO-Aerodrome Manual Part IV, Air Routes and Ground Aids Division, Document 7920, AN/865.

19 ICAO-Terrain Clearance & Vertical Separation of Aircraft Circular 26-AN/23, 1956.

20 ICAO-Lexicon of Terms used in Connection with International Civil Aviation, DOC-7200, 1952.

21 ICAO-Stolport Manual, 1976.

22 ICAO-Procedures for Air Navigation Services and Aircraft Operations, DOC 8168-OPS/1961.

23 Isral Gilbaa, Parking and Circulation of Vehicular Traffic at Airports, Journal Air Transport Division ASCE, Vol. 87, No. At-2, 1961.

24 IRC : 15—1981, Standard Specifications and Codes of Practice for Construction of Concrete Roads (Second Revision).

25 IRC : 27—1967 Tentative Specifications for Bituminous (Base and Binder Course).

26 IRC : 76—1979, Tentative Guidelines for Structural Strength Evaluation of Rigid Airfield Pavements.

27 IRC : 77-1979, Tentative Guidelines for Repair of Concrete Pavements using Synthetics Resin.

28 IRC : 85-1983, Code of Practice for Accelerated Strength Testing and Evaluation of Concrete for Road and Air field Constructions.

29 IRC : 91-1985, Tentative Guide lines for Construction of Cement Concrete Pavements in Cold Weather.

30 IRC : 95—1987 Specification for Semi Dense Bituminous Concrete.

31 IRC : 105-1928, Tentative Specifications for Bituminous Concrete (Asphaltic Concrete) for Airfield Pavements.

32 IRC : SP : 17-1977 Recommendation about Overlays on Cement Concrete Pavements.

33 J.L. Nayler, Aviation : Its Technical Development, Peter Owen Ltd. London, 1965.

34 J V. Casamassa, Jet Aircraft Power System, McGraw Hill Book Company, New York, 1950.

35 Kinneth K. Wilde, Helicopter Performance and Heliport Design, Journal Air Transport Division ASCE, No. 3213, Vol. 88, 1962.

36 Krishna Srivastava, Air Transportation.

37 Legant, Airport Design for Highway Engineers.

38 MacDonald The Aircraft of the World, Macdonald and Co. Ltd., London.

39 NASAP—Proc. National Seminar on Airfield Pavements, Vol. I, CRRI, New Delhi, Feb. 22-23, 1990.

40 Norman Ashford and Paul H. Wright, Airport Engg., John Wiley & Sons; 1979.

41 Norman W. Mcleod, Flexible Pavement Thickness Requirement, Proceedings of the Association of Asphalt Paving Technologists, 1956.

42 Paul H. Stafford and D. Lany Stafford, Space Criteria for Aircraft Aprons, Transportation Engineering, ASCE, Vol. 95, TF-2, 1961.

43 Ralph. T. Glasson and Weldon F. Rhoades, Trends in the Aircrafts Design Affecting the Airport, Journal of Transport Division ASCE, Vol. 85, No. AT-2, 1961.

44 Randall K. Kirle, Experience in Air Terminal Operations with Jet Aircrafts. Journal Air Transport Division, ASCE, 2115, At-3, 1959.

45 Ray O. Kuscha, Importance of Regional Airport System Planning, Journal Air Transport Division, ASCE, Vol. 87, 1961.

46 Richard H Jordan, Airport Location in Relation to Urban Transport, Air Tran port Division ASCE, Vol. 89, 1963.

47 Robert Hororjeff. The Planning and Design of Airports, McGraw Hill Book Co.

48 Robert G. Hennes and Martin Eske Fundamentals of Transportation Engineering, McGraw-Hill Book Company.

49 Robert Horonjeff and Richard Coykendall, Runway Lengths for Jet Transport, Journal Air Transport Division, ASCE, Vol. 87, To AT-1, 1961.

50 Robert Horonjeff, Runways and Taxiways for Supersonic Transports, Journal Air Transport Division ASCE, No. 3236.

51 Report of Steering Committee, Perspective Planning for Transport Development (Civil Aviation), Planning Commission Govt. of India, New Delhi, 1988.

52 Reports of Planning Group on Civil Aviation (PGCA), Planning Commission, Govt. of India, New Delhi, 1986.

53 S.K. Khanna & C.E.G. Justo, Highway Engg., Nem Chand & Bros; Roorkee, 6th edn. 1990.

54 Temple A. Tucker; Meeting USAF Blast Fence Requirements Journal Air Transport Division, ASCE, Vol 85, At-I, 1959.

55 The Design of Airfield Overlay Pavements. Proc. ASCE, Paper 777, 1955.

56 The Times of India Press, The Times of India Directory and Year Book.

57 U.S. Federal Aviation Agency-Aviation Forecasts, Fiscal Year 1961-66.

58 U.S. Civil Aeronautic Administration, Air Traffic Rules Guide Book, 1948.

59 U.S. Federal Aviation Agency, Airport Drainage 1960.

60 U.N. Sinha, Evaluation of Load Classification Number of an Airfield Pavement by Plate Load Method, Proc. Int. Conf on Road & Road Transport Problems (ICORT-88), New Delhi, Dec, 12-15, 1988.

INDEX

R

S